George Moore, 1852–1933

George Moore, 1852–1933

Adrian Frazier

Yale University Press
New Haven and London

to Edwin Gilcher

Set in Ehrhardt by Best-set Typesetter Ltd, Hong Kong
Printed in Great Britain by St Edmundsbury Press

Library of Congress Cataloging-in-Publication Data

Frazier, Adrian Woods.
    George Moore, 1852–1933/Adrian Frazier.
    Includes bibliographical references and index.
    ISBN 0-300-08245-2 (cloth : alk. paper)
    1. Moore, George, 1852–1933.   2. Authors, Irish – 19th century –
  Biography.   3. Authors, Irish – 20th century – Biography.   4. Art critics
  – Ireland – Biography.   5. Landowners – Ireland – Biography.   I. Title.
PR5043.F57   2000
823'.8 – dc21   99–88360

A catalogue record for this book is available from the British Library.

10 9 8 7 6 5 4 3 2 1

Contents

Illustrations

Acknowledgements

This book is dedicated to Edwin Gilcher, of Cherry Plain, New York. He is the author of *A Bibliography of George Moore* (1970), a work he keeps up to date in a continuously revised manuscript for its ultimate edition. In the early 1930s, he was an actor in New York (he went to the American Academy of Dramatic Arts in 1927), and one evening, picking up a book by Moore in a friend's apartment, he noticed that it differed from his own copy of the same title. Ever since, he has collected editions of George Moore and catalogued their differences in text, bindings, size, edge trimmings – everything down to the last detail. While employed later in life as a journalist (he ended his career recently with *Hemmings Motor News* in Bennington, Vermont), he continued to pursue his private passion for the bibliography of George Moore. His life as an independent scholar brought about working friendships with great bookmen like Allan Wade, Sir Rupert Hart-Davis, and the late Clinton Krause. One of Gilcher's complete collections of Moore material is at Arizona State University, and he is now well on his way to assembling another. Not long after I first began to work on the life of George Moore in 1990, I found my way, as many another Moore scholar has done, to the door of Edwin Gilcher, and his door has been opened to me ever since. He lent me scrapbooks of articles about Moore and editions of his works; he provided detailed answers to dozens of letters of inquiry; he alerted me when new letters of Moore appeared for auction; he put me in touch with other Moore scholars; he read drafts with the strictest care for accuracy; and he constantly cheered me on. It has been very difficult not to fall obviously short by his measure. He is a great bookman – indeed, a wonderful man, pure and simple.

My colleague William M. Murphy, Thomas Lamont Professor Emeritus, has played the part of mentor since I came to Union College in 1982; my affection and respect are no secret to him. His biography of John Butler Yeats, *Prodigal Father*, is a model of thorough research and classic prose. He showed continuing interest in this project, gave sage counsel, and supplied me with choice quotations from his transcriptions of the voluminous correspondence of the Yeats family. To wrap it all up, he took on the considerable job of reading page proofs over the Thanksgiving holidays of 1999.

It was at a dinner in Professor Murphy's house in 1990 that I decided to write a biography of Moore, upon the suggestion of Roy Foster, who was then doing research on the life of W. B. Yeats (the first stage was brought to a triumphant conclusion with *The Apprentice Mage* in 1997). Throughout this Moore project, Roy Foster has shown a friendly confidence that it would be successful; he advised me to cut no corners, to leave no stones unturned; he proposed Yale University Press as the best publisher for the book; and in his own wide trawl through the archives of North America, Ireland, and Britain, he kept an eye open for unpublished material that might be useful to me.

Lucy McDiarmid also has to be specially acknowledged for the help she has rendered over the course of this project. She was herself at work on a book about Irish controversies, some of them during the period of Moore's Dublin residence, and in her scouring of the archives, she kept an eye out for what might be useful to me. She welcomed the first papers I wrote about Moore, and, in her own work, set an example for how to make detail enlivening rather than burdensome. Her taste for delicious irony has been instructive.

Robert Becker I do not know personally (though he has responded generously to letters of inquiry). It is his remarkable 1980 dissertation for which I have to be grateful. In this edition of Moore's letters from 1863 to 1901, Becker not only tracked down and transcribed nearly 1,500 pages of letters, he also supplied in the notes an immense amount of information about Moore's life and the lives of his family and friends. Without Becker's dissertation – regularly cited in the notes – this long project would have taken much longer.

One cannot do justice to all those to whom one owes thanks by the time one has completed a long biography, but I must at least list the following names.

A publisher of George Moore, the agent for the heirs of his literary estate, and owner of a valuable archive of Irish photographs, Colin Smythe; amid multifarious projects, he made time for my many requests.

Scholars who have worked on George Moore, and helped another follow in their footsteps: the late Malcolm Brown, Richard Cave, Elizabeth Grubgeld, Robert Langenfeld, Hilary Laurie, and Jack Weaver.

Journal editors who welcomed the first fruits of research on Moore's life: Tony Bradley (*ACIS Annual*, 1997), Robert Langenfeld (*English Literature in Transition*), Thomas Staley (*James Joyce Annual*, 1992), Thomas Dillon Redshaw (*New Hibernia Review*), John Maynard and Abigail Bloom (*Victorian Literature and Culture*, 1996).

Director of the Synge Summer School (Wicklow, 1996), Nicholas Grene, and Director of the Yeats International Summer School (Sligo, 1998), George Watson.

Administrators and Selection Committees for the Union College Humanities Development Fund, the National Endowment for Humanities, and the

Irish American Cultural Institute, who partially funded research for this project.

Authors of works on related subjects, who lent a helping hand: Bruce Arnold, Terence Brown, Brendan Fleming, Warwick Gould, Sir Rupert Hart-Davis, Dillon Johnston, John Kelly, Peter Kuch, Ben Levitas, Richard and Janis Londraville, Janet Montefiore, J. C. Nolan, Séan O Lúing, Michael O'Sullivan, James Pethica, John Ryan, Julie Speedie, Deirdre Toomey, Karen Vandevelde, and Robert Welch.

Colleagues at Union College, for reading drafts, offering fruits of their own expertise, or happily helping out in many other ways: Thora Girke, Peter Heinegg, Hugh Jenkins, Harry Marten, Jim McCord, Hyungji Park, Scott Scullion, Jordan Smith, Christie Sorum, Ann Thomas, William Thomas, and Brenda Wineapple.

Colleagues at the National University of Ireland, Galway, whose suggestions find a place in the final text: Kevin Barry, Dan Carey, Cliodhna Carney, Tadhg Foley, Sue Jones (now at St Hilda's College, Oxford), Donna Monroe, Riana O'Dwyer, William O'Reilly, Gearóid O Tuathaigh, Lionel Pilkington, and Pat Sheeran.

Readers of Moore or friends, with the patience to hear about his life, and offer suggestions about the telling of it: Gareth Browne, Martin Carney, Richard Howard, the late Clinton Krause, Derek Mahon, John Minahan, John Montague, Patsy Murphy, the late Darcy O'Brien, Elizabeth Wassell, and Guy Williams.

Research librarians, curators, and keepers of private collections, who helped to locate manuscripts and illustrations, or arranged for permission to publish them: Mrs M. G. Anderson; Anthony Bliss, Bancroft Collection, University of California Library; Lydia Cresswell-Jones and Julie Nobel, Cecil Beaton Archive; Lucy St Giles, Beerbohm estate; Philip Milito and Rodney Phillips, Berg Collection, New York Public Library; Chris Sheppard, Brotherton Collection, Leeds University Library; Doris Dysinger, Bucknell University Library; Cathleen Cann, Cambridge University Library; Judi Churchman, Fitzwilliam Museum; Thomas Staley, Cathy Henderson, Leslie Wearb Hirsch, and Tara Wenger, Harry Ransom Humanities Research Center, University of Texas at Austin; the staff of Houghton Library, Harvard University; Sue Hodson, Huntington Library; William Crowe, University of Kansas; Caroline Wykes, Museum of London; Ruth Greenbaum, City Gallery, Manchester; Sandra Fritz, Metropolitan Museum of Art; Musée de Montmartre; Jane MacAvock and Marie McFeely, National Gallery of Ireland; Gerald Long, Noel Kissane, Colette O'Daly, Dónall Ó Luanaigh, the staff, and Trustees of the National Library of Ireland; the staff of the National Photographic Archive, Dublin; James Kilvington and Jill Springall, National Portrait Gallery; Marie Boran, Library of the National University of Ireland at Galway; Justine Egan, Rosensteil's Fine Art Publishers; Guido Martini and Jonathan Thristan, Tate Gallery; the staff of the Trinity College Library, Dublin University; Pat McClean, the Ulster Museum; Chris Petter, McPherson Library, University of

Victoria; the staff of the University of Virginia Library; Karyl Winn, University of Washington Library; the Musée Zola.

The staff of Schaffer Library, Union College, who made an undergraduate library do the work of a research library, including Mary Cahill, Bruce Connolly, Donna Cook, Ellen Fladger, Dave Gerhan, Christine Glover, and Maribeth Krupczak.

Families and heirs of artists and authors: Marcia Geraldine Anderson; V. Bevis; Anthony Hobson and the heirs of Nancy Cunard; Viscount Norwich; Patricia and Paul Medley; Hazel Radcliffe-Dolling, and Susanna Seguit, the heirs of William Orpen, and Michael Butler Yeats.

Residents of County Mayo, who passed on stories about George Moore and Moore Hall: Sean Murphy, James O'Reilly of Castlebar, James O'Reilly of Carnacun, and Art O'Sullivan; and Dr Patricia Noone of Claremorris.

Dr Frances Knott, whose medical authority cured a crux in the text.

My indexer, Helen Litton.

Editors at Yale University Press, especially Robert Baldock for commissioning the book, and Candida Brazil for seeing that it emerged from many of the flaws in the manuscript.

Finally, it is a pleasure to name those who had to put up with most from the author: Marge Davis, Alison Knowles Frazier, Rufus and Helen Frazier, baby Clea Carney Frazier, and Cliodhna Carney.

Introduction

Moore Hall, the birthplace of George Moore, was burnt out by the IRA in February 1923, in the course of the Irish Civil War, along with two hundred other country houses belonging to the landed gentry. The demesne in County Mayo later came into the hands of the Irish government, and Coillte, the state forestry board, planted it in rows of Sitka spruce. The bed of the mature forest is now padded in fallen fronds, and one may walk through the shadows of tall trees in near silence up to the crest of the hill. There the walls of the three-story Georgian house still stand. From the portico, saplings can be seen growing up from the deep rubble in the basement. Some small pieces of plasterwork, all that is left of an Adam ceiling, cling at an upper corner. Outside, graffiti are scratched into the pillars and walls: evidently the ruined house of the Moores has become a spot for boys and girls to do what their parents will not let them do at home. A plaque was raised in 1964 by the Ballyglass regiment of the "Old IRA." It belatedly honors the patriots who had lived in the house – John Moore, crowned "King of Connaught" by General Humbert in the Rebellion of 1798, and George Henry Moore, Member of Parliament for Mayo in the mid-nineteenth century. The novelist George Moore, however, goes unmentioned and unhonored. A priest from Ballintubber visiting the house with a resident of the nearby village of Carnacun supplied a possible reason. Seeing the family motto engraved on a slab above the hall door – *Fortis cadere cedere non potest* – the priest reportedly remarked, "That is not true of all the Moores. Not all of them were strong. George fell." The novelist died as neither an Irish patriot nor a Roman Catholic.

On 14 December 1998, an article in the *Irish Times* announced that a scheme had been approved by the Mayo County Council for the restoration of Moore Hall. The £4 million plan to clear the forest and reconstruct the house is the brainchild of Art Ó Suilleabháin, a former teacher at the junior school at Carnacun, who hopes to bring investment, tourism, and local pride back into the community. He also makes use of Moore's books about the area to "read back in the land he lives in," to adapt a line from the nineteenth-century poet

Samuel Ferguson. The *Irish Times* article notes that the plan for reconstruction has the support of the George Moore Society in Claremorris, which operates a summer school and sponsors arts projects. Summer schools and cultural tourism have proliferated in Ireland. The Yeats Summer School in Sligo was followed by schools for readers of James Joyce, J. M. Synge, Gerard Manley Hopkins, John Hewitt, Augusta Gregory, William Carleton, and Brian Merriman. So George Moore too is coming to be counted as part of a rich literary heritage.

With George Bernard Shaw, Oscar Wilde, Bram Stoker, and W. B. Yeats, Moore was one of the writers of Irish birth who remade English literature at the end of the nineteenth century. While living in London in the 1880s and 1890s, Moore introduced French naturalism and the Flaubertian art-novel to English fiction with *A Mummer's Wife* (1885) and *A Drama in Muslin* (1886); he scripted a bible of hell for young aesthetes in *Confessions of a Young Man* (1888); he wrote a generally accepted classic of the English novel in *Esther Waters* (1894). A friend of Manet and Degas in the Paris of the late 1870s, he became one of the first among the London press to espouse Impressionism during the 1880s and 1890s, and to find equivalents for its values in literature. He was one of those who started the Independent Theatre Society in London in 1890 and the Irish Literary Theatre in Dublin in 1899. Upon taking up residence in Dublin for a decade after the turn of the century, George Moore furnished Irish writers with an example of the European short story set in their own land, *The Untilled Field* (1903), a lesson not lost on the young James Joyce. Upon his departure from Dublin in 1911, Moore left the best (and most scandalous) literary memoir of the Irish Revival, *Hail and Farewell* (1911–14). Settled in Ebury Street, London, for his last two decades, Moore did not lose his talent for the perfectly produced scandal. His retelling of the Gospels in *The Brook Kerith* (1916) was greeted by an attempt to suppress its publication, yet into it he put his better self and greatest skills as a storyteller. In his seventies he brought out ten further books, including *Celibate Lives* (1927) – a polished treatment of a theme that had drawn his attention again and again over the previous forty years: men and women without a match in the world, and in whom desire is not a desire for procreation. In his old age, Moore was recognised as having been eminent among the prose artists of a great literary era. George Moore came into property by birth; as a result of his own labors, at his death he left a 20-volume edition of his collected works, a shelf in that library of books written with distinction.

George Moore was somewhat forgotten in the years after his death in 1933, forgotten even as some lesser figures returned to public attention. Scholars recorded his impact on English literature – that he introduced the Zolaesque novel into English fiction, that he was a bellwether of the aesthetic movement, that he became an enemy of Yeats and an influence on Joyce, that Henry James personally detested him only slightly less than Thomas Hardy did, and that Max Beerbohm feasted upon his face and shape in dozens of cartoons. Moore was often treated as an influence, a predecessor, or a character in the story of another, not as a central figure in his own right, whose best works would never grow old.

There are several reasons, reasons quite external to the quality of his writing, for the decline in Moore's reputation. He had no clear affiliation during his life with any single national tradition; no country has wished to claim him after his death as part of its tradition. Over the years, he had an elective affinity with several countries and, even more so, with several cities – chiefly Paris, London, and Dublin. Manet certainly spoke the truth when he remarked to Moore, "There is no Englishman that occupies the place you do in Paris," but it was not the place of a Frenchman. "In England," Moore discovered after his first publications, "I am an Ishmael, almost a Cain: everybody's hand against me and mine against everybody." Moore's plan to become a French writer after the banning of his first three novels by the London circulating libraries was never going to succeed. He soon returned to trying to make his name as a London writer, but he was never to occupy a place there as an Englishman, even after the success of *Esther Waters* in 1894. By turns, he was treated as too sexy and French, or too rebellious and Irish. In the late 1890s, Yeats convinced him he would be welcomed as a famous Irish writer in Dublin, but Moore arrived under a cloud of suspicion (too French, too English), a cloud that only darkened during his decade of residence there. Moore certainly has a European sensibility, yet he insistently transgressed national boundaries and made sport of patriotic shibboleths. Since literature tends to be organised for the purposes of education into national traditions, this quality of Moore has not done his reputation any good thus far, though it may yet stand him in good stead in a post-nationalist era.

A further cause of the lapse of Moore's reputation is that he created so many styles of narrative that he lost, or repeatedly abandoned, his "name-identification." One knew what one was going to get when buying a Hardy novel; buying one by Moore, one could get French naturalism, English social comedy, stream-of-consciousness, an historical art-novel (à la *Salammbô*), or a Russian tale in the manner of Turgenev. The quality was uneven too, as Moore's powers appeared to wax and wane according to the harmonies between his subjects and his sensibility. Speaking of having done his best with a recent book, GM (as he was called) said to a friend that he had tried to beat Balzac, but still "you can't fart higher than your arse." A reader could be sure of only two things when opening the covers of a new volume by George Moore: that the book would be forcefully crafted and that it would disrupt expectations.

Alarm was an object of Moore's aggressive art – an art that was by turns polemical, confessional, and invasive of the private lives of his living subjects. He was drawn again and again to the investigation of sex and religion, non-normative and extra-matrimonial sex, and unorthodox views on religion. Neither subject was within the sanctioned scope of the traditional English novel; both excited automatic reproaches from the guardians at the gate – the reviewers, clerics, and librarians. By his death, the critical world was populated with Moore's enemies, just as it had been at the time of his first publications. Some of them, like W. B. Yeats, would do their best to turn Moore into a clown. They had considerable success. The facts that he was a man of extraordinary intellect and an artist who enlarged the house of fiction were forgotten in an effort to settle scores, or to condemn lastingly one who, as the Ballintubber priest said, "fell."

There is yet another good reason for the decline of Moore's reputation as a great novelist: his greatest works are not novels. In 1905, he came to believe that what he did best was write autobiographically. He had then written *Confessions of a Young Man* (1888), parts of *Avowals* (1919), and *Memoirs of My Dead Life* (1906), and was just about to start his trilogy about the Irish Renaissance, *Hail and Farewell* (1911–14). While the Victorian period is an age of autobiography in English literature, writers in England generally avoided the example of Rousseau in his *Confessions*. "That I, or any man, should tell everything of himself, I hold to be impossible," Trollope wrote at the start of his *Autobiography*, for "Who can endure to own the doing of a mean thing?" Moore could endure it, and, though Rousseau predicted his confessional enterprise would "have no imitator," GM incautiously followed in the footsteps of his "Saint Jean Jacques." It became Moore's specialty to be beyond embarrassment. To Rousseau's shamelessness, speculative freedom, and self-fascination, Moore added his own heightened devotion to literary experiment. The question for reviewers in his time was often not how his memoirs were written, but whether they ought to have been written at all, or even whether he ought to have been the man he described himself as being – an attitude of censorious reserve that is beginning to be overcome in books like Elizabeth Grubgeld's *The Autogenous Art of George Moore* (1994).

Finally, Moore's life and work have not been available to the public; he has disappeared from bookstores, classrooms, and local libraries. *A Mummer's Wife*, *Confessions of a Young Man*, *Esther Waters*, and *Memoirs of My Dead Life* have now and then been published in an edition by Penguin, Everyman, or Modern Library, and some of the books about Ireland are kept in stock by Colin Smythe, but Moore's works are not generally available. It is also not easy to come by reliable information about Moore. A fine biography was published three years after his death, Joseph Hone's *The Life of George Moore*. Hone was an Irish scholar-author, and he knew Moore slightly; what is more, he had the help of Moore's friends and his brother Maurice. As a result, Hone's biography has a wonderful style of social knowingness. Yet the chronology is neither complete nor always accurate; the story is heavily weighted towards the latter decades of Moore's life, which were within the living memory of Hone's informants; the treatment of Moore's sex life is cautious and winking; most important, Hone was forced to leave out of his account both Lady Cunard and her daughter Nancy, in Moore's own opinion the crucial figures in the story of his life. Jean Noel's *George Moore: L'Homme et l'oeuvre (1852–1933)*, published in 1966, is excellent on Moore's French years (1873–80), his subsequent reappearances in Parisian cultural life, his allusions, borrowings, and stylistic shifts; for the facts about the rest of Moore's life, Noel generally relied on Hone. While valuable to another biographer, *L'Homme et l'oeuvre* leaves room for a full, documentary life in English.

That is what this book aims to provide: a new narrative of the life of George Moore, built up from the thousands of private letters and many manuscripts that have come to light since his death. His letters of advice to potential biographers (there were at least half a dozen of them) shed light on his self-conception. The letters Moore's friends supplied to Hone contain valuable pointers. It is now possible to investigate the factual basis for Moore's fictions about the women in his life. His relationships with the chief writers and painters of his period – Manet, Degas, and Zola; Pater, James, Archer, and Hardy; Yeats, Augusta Gregory, and Joyce – can be more fully understood because of the scholarship recently published about such contemporaries. In the 1880s and 1890s, Moore published over 250 articles and stories in weeklies and monthlies; he took an independent line on the reform of English theater, painting, and fiction; and this material, mostly unexplored by Hone, is central to a picture of his life during those decades. At the heart of the latter half of this book is Moore's relationship to Lady Cunard. GM came to believe himself the father of her only daughter, Nancy. Though constrained and fractured by secrecy, a secrecy sharply policed by Lady Cunard, his relationships with mother and daughter were for the bachelor author his experience of family life.

Moore's autobiographies are, because of their richness and unreliability, a problem for any biographer. Like all autobiographies, they have a double reference – both to the events they purport to recall, and to the moment of recollection itself. They may have their sleights in their portrayals of an earlier "George Moore," but they are absolutely true of – because identical with – the George Moore writing them; they are the works of his hand in that hour, that day, that year of their invention, the trace of his passing being, the goal of all his gathered energy. Here the version of the past the autobiographies offer is compared, where possible, with contemporary documents; and each autobiography receives direct treatment in light of GM's purposes at the time of its composition. More than most memoirs, those by George Moore are deliberately literary and experimental; indeed, the chapters of *Confessions of a Young Man* are an anthology of contemporary Parisian literary styles, and one of his last essays in the genre, *A Story-Teller's Holiday*, is not recollection at all, but an extravaganza of fabulation by the literary persona Moore had publicly evolved over decades of authorship. Nonetheless, *A Story-Teller's Holiday* is a distillation of an intimate side of its author's temperament. Although Moore happily would write both parts of a supposedly real dialogue, or, in supposedly reporting his own words in a scene from his life, he might engage in quotation from a favorite novel, his autobiographies are fundamentally not falsifications of experience, but bold and writerly uses of it. Selection, detachment, design, rearrangement, and all the other skills of a successful novelist went into their fabrication; so did an extraordinary memory. Moore's motive was literature, not deception; his goal was never good opinion, but fame. His stories about himself are regulated by a principle of anti-reticence – they stage the telling of improper truths. Finally, while Moore's life shows up in his autobiographies, much of his life was that of an autobiographer. His writing of the volumes, and his friends' responses to them, were major events in Moore's extra-autobiographical life.

Moore is sometimes represented as a peculiar, contradictory, or even incoherent man. The description of himself in his ironic *Confessions of a Young Man* as a "man of wax" has been read as uninflected by irony, a mistake akin to taking *A Portrait of the Artist as a Young Man* as Joyce's straightforward autobiography. Yet the non-categorical aspects of Moore's identity cause problems for those who would classify him. Is he French, English, or Irish? He is neither a married heterosexual nor an active homosexual. Neither Protestant nor Catholic, he is devoted to inquiry into Christianity, speculatively exploring the experience of faith from the position of faithlessness. As a novelist, he inaugurates, then leaves behind, literary styles – literary naturalism, realism, aestheticism, and other trends – before creating out of suggestions from Turgenev, Pater, Sterne, and Landor a narrative voice utterly his own, an idiomatic style without precedent, storytelling that is pictorial, lucid, sinuous, and subtle.

So what is one to say Moore finally *is*? The solution to the problem of Moore's identity is not to throw in one's lot with a single-factor analysis, concluding, for instance, that he was essentially one of the last of the Irish landlords, though he was that and saw himself as such. One might say that he embodied a highly fluent phase in the history of European masculinity, as he wrote a trilogy in the late 1880s on the condition of the young male in his era, and continued to explore the margins of gender definition in later works. That would be true, but not all the truth. He saw himself as an Oedipal son, rebelling against his father, the conscientious Catholic and Member of Parliament, but in this way GM was like many other sons, for whom, as Zola told him, it is a law of life to devour the father. Nor is it any solution simply to call him a contradictory man, as if a person were, or ought to be, a logical proposition. The best answer to the question of who George Moore was is the story of how he came to be himself.

Biography itself may be an epistemological tool, a way of knowing. Ultimate truths or secure foundations may no longer be found, but one can recover the documentary traces of a life; one can strive for accuracy; one can adjust one's conclusions by means of practical reason, choosing the better over the worse explanation, and leaving unanswerable questions with their mystery intact. A story that integrates many kinds of concern – that is, a biographical way of knowing – may take steps toward bringing some hidden things to light, things that matter to readers. As a genre, biography is open to many aspects of literature that naturally interest people – why beauty might matter to a particular author, relations between representations and realities, the quarrel of the man with the world as found, the origins of the world as imagined, and the ways a particular life overstrides norms. A biographer may remain keenly aware of the illusions of narrative, the trickiness of authorial intentions, the variety of readers' responses, the disunities of a text, and the presuppositions of any critical practice, while still aiming to give a relatively accurate account of a life.

Moore, however, was not simply a consequence of all the material factors that uniquely configured themselves, like the constellations, at the hour of his birth. A man of the Age of Wilde, Moore was an artist in self-invention. He lived his life in such a way as to make it worthy of his autobiographies. He took himself on errands to witness what was dramatic, sowed the seeds of conflict among friends and took notes on the result, turned literary collaborations into romantic affairs and romantic affairs into literary collaborations, abstracted himself from himself and made observations upon the comedy of his own behavior, and subsequently retold the story that he had composed of the events in his life. His profound urge to recreate himself, to write books of such a quality that they would be read long after his death, beautiful proofs of his having been, drove him to the desk week in and week out for the last fifty-five years of his life. For the intensity of that fundamental urge, there is no final explanation; one falls back on words like *genius*.

This is not a literary or critical biography. It does not devote the largest portion of its space to interpretations of Moore's books, assessments of his importance, descriptions of his literary style, or full accounts of many other subjects, such as the impact of his exploitation of two new forms of publication, the cheap one-volume novel in the mid-1880s, and the deluxe, signed, limited edition in the 1920s. My main aim was to write a well-documented, chronological narrative that would be an interesting story and a basis for further engagement with Moore and his works. In general, my practice was in favor of understatement: to say nothing where there was no evidence; to be cautious in the ascription of motive, to pay attention to chronological sequence and the gradual emergence of ideas, to stay clear of exclusive theoretical commitments, to leave mostly alone questions (such as modernism) that arose for critics at a later date, to treat matters of reputation or success in the terms in which Moore and his reviewers raised them at the time, and to create interest by specifically narrative means, bringing the story into focus episode by episode, rather than through summary or digest. Moore lived so long – eighty-one years – and wrote so many articles, stories, plays, and books, that a premium was placed on concision. There is no subject in this biography that could not be amplified, but this is only one book on Moore, and not the last.

Some paths for further exploration are signposted in this biography. No one has written 'The Collaborative Arts of George Moore', 'George Moore and Female Authors', or 'The Painterly Craft: George Moore and Literary Landscape'. The social history of satire in nineteenth-century newspapers – those nearly libelous "personalities" – is worth a wider look. Denis Donoghue has made a place for Moore in the school of Walter Pater; the "School of Moore," however, awaits its historian, who could trace Moore's occasional influence upon Arnold Bennett, Ford Madox Ford, James Joyce, D. H. Lawrence, Austin Clarke, and others. James Hepburn's *The Author's Empty Purse* (1968) showed Moore to be a canny, belligerent character in dealing with publishers; there is more still to be said about his agility in a changing book market – he kept his creative freedom and earned a good income. Patrick Bridgwater's *George Moore and German Pessimism* (1988) is entertaining on Moore's piecemeal readings in philosophy; a different sort of study could be done on Moore's visceral skepticism and his lifelong swim in the abyss of significations. Brendan Fleming, an Oxford graduate student, is working on Moore's relationship to the Home Rule movement. Another might some day examine the late prose as the true style of an old Tory, privately issued for a subscription list of aesthetic aristocrats and aristocratic aesthetes. *The Field Day Anthology* (1991) grouped Shaw and Wilde as "London Exiles" from colonial Ireland; there were non-Catholic "exiles" from the Irish Free State as well – W. K. Magee, George Russell, Gerald O'Donovan, Ernest Longworth, and others – with whom Moore felt at home in the 1920s. They await revisionary attention. Moore's letters to the editor would make an entertaining collection, as they carry the favorite genre of cranks to high comic perfection, and disport themselves over a range of subjects: traffic noise, the tastiness of the grey mullet, machine printing, dogs in the city, the death of art, the loss of the horse-drawn carriage, overpopulation, art after the age of fossil fuels, the evil cancer of Franglais, popular literature as a cause of deforestation, and the vulgar claptrap of George Bernard Shaw. Critics who like controversy will have a field day with the works of George Moore.

What nettled some early readers of Moore was the question of his apostasy. Can a man like him really live a good life, brazenly by his wits in an earthly world, with no settled faith in God at all? In 1911, Moore received a letter from a Carmelite nun in France, his twenty-three-year-old cousin Germaine. She lamented that he had turned his back on Roman Catholicism, so would surely go to hell. It would be best if he burned all his books. She had found, she wrote, perfect happiness with God and the sacraments; religion filled her life from top to bottom. In a sweet but unpersuaded reply (in French), Moore wrote that he was glad that she had found peace with God. As for himself, he too could say that he had found perfect happiness – with Art. It filled his life from top to bottom. They were dreamers in a family a little bit dreamy. In the place of vain and fatiguing efforts to live, they two were content to meditate. What matter the dream, so long as it is a dream! With that, he gave his dear cousin his sympathy in her life of sacrifice, so like his own, and so different. In an age when many have had to fashion for themselves an uncredal life it may be easier to forgive him his doubts and errant ways, for the sake of the happiness he was able to create for himself and for many readers.

1. Moore Hall, Co. Mayo, seat of George Moore, Esq.; lithograph; from a copy belonging to novelist Maria Edgeworth.

Chapter 1
His Father's Funeral and the Birth of George Moore

I

On 15 April 1870, George Henry Moore, Member of Parliament for County Mayo, and father of the novelist, suddenly left his family in London and took the mail train from London to Holyhead, the steamer to Kingstown, and another train west as far as Athenry, where, because the service on the northern line to Claremorris was closed for Good Friday, he took a post-chaise thirty-five miles north and west, across the bog below the Partry Mountains, and around the upper end of Lough Carra, on the far shore of which stood Moore Hall, atop a wooded hill in the Barony of Carra, the south side of the parish of Ballyhean.[1] Exhausted, he reentered the house in which he had been born, and he never saw his wife and five children again. Within five days of leaving them, he was dead in his own bed. It was not sickness from overwork that brought him home, or the need to consult local leaders before he introduced a Home Rule bill, as papers reported at the time.[2] Forty years later, the real story behind his return was revealed by his son Maurice in *George Henry Moore: An Irish Gentleman*.

A few months before his journey west, Moore had been forwarded a communication circulated by a Ribbon society to the tenants of an outlying Ballintubber estate of his 12,481-acre property, a little note in red ink:[3]

IMPORTANT

Notice is hereby given that any person who pays rents to landlords, agents, or bailiffs above that of the ordinance valuation will at his peril mark the consequences.

By order,
Rory

Ribbonmen were local agrarian societies in Ireland, bound by secret oath, linked into lodges from one locale to another, and often anti-Protestant.

Sometimes, they used the tactics of crop-burning, cattle-maiming, and assassination to resist evictions, tithes, high rents, and other sorrows of the tenant's life. George Henry Moore, however, had a record as a model landlord. He played a role in Parliament in ending the privileged position of the tithing Protestant Church in largely Catholic Ireland; he had never evicted tenants in order to turn his property over to graziers as his cousin Lord Sligo had done; and indeed he had recently been reelected to Parliament as the candidate of the tenants.[4] By rights, he ought to have been the last man to have been targeted by Ribbonmen. When he received the note from the Ballintubber Ribbonmen, he concluded that they were simply out to blackmail him, making use of his awkward position as a landlord against landlordism, and as a rich Catholic living on the rents of poor Catholics.

Moore's first step, and a well-calculated one, was to write to Father Patrick Lavelle on 4 February 1870, sending him a copy of the note with a request that he intercede. Father Lavelle was the parish priest at Cong, sixteen miles south of Ballintubber.[5] He was a perfect go-between for the Catholic nationalist landlord and the Ribbonmen in many ways. Father Lavelle published a volume in 1870 attacking landlordism, and he supported the Irish Republican Brotherhood, originally the armed wing of the Fenians. Moore had worked with Lavelle earlier in political causes, as both were protégés of Archbishop John MacHale, the most nationalist of prelates, and enemies of Cardinal Paul Cullen, who had tried to keep the priests out of independent opposition politics and to bring the Irish Church under the control of Rome.[6] To Father Lavelle, Moore wrote that just because as an MP he was in favor of tenants' rights did not mean he was going to surrender his rights as a landlord. He would not be intimidated; without flinching, he would evict every tenant who did not pay rent. He would quit Parliament right away if necessary, and live again at Moore Hall in order to keep his estate together. So the Ballintubber cottiers were caught between the threats of their landlord and those of the Ribbonmen. It would be an act of charity to the poor, Moore wrote, if Father Lavelle would intervene.[7]

That was in early February 1870; during March, George Henry Moore paradoxically spoke up in Parliament in support of tenant relief, just as he had pledged to do in the 1868 election. In the debate over the second reading of Gladstone's Landlord and Tenant Act, Moore explained that he would vote for the bill because it included the Three Fs (Fair rent, Fixity of tenure, and Free sale), but he regretted that the bill did not go farther: it should also have protected tenants against eviction by means of remorseless increases in rent, and he went on to attack landlords who clear their properties of tenants by driving out the old and the sick.[8] It could have been mistakenly concluded from this speech upbraiding bad landlords that G. H. Moore was against landlordism as a whole.

But he wasn't. Nor did threatening the hooded gangs of Ribbonmen who moved through his estate in the night mean that he was altogether against secret societies. It was apparently before the 1867 Fenian Rising that Moore had

2. George Henry Moore, the novelist's father; carte de visite.

himself taken the Fenian oath from its chief, James Stephens, a risky step for any man, and especially for a landlord and politician. The Fenians were an armed revolutionary organisation that grew up among the Irish immigrant communities of the United States following the collapse of the Young Ireland movement in the 1840s. Membership in this outlawed society could have put Moore out of Parliament and into prison.[9] In the week of 26 March Moore again rose in Parliament to give a defiant speech against Gladstone's new Coercion Bill, intended to suppress resurgent Fenianism. Moore had spoken on earlier occasions in defense of the rights of Fenian political prisoners, like O'Donovan Rossa and John O'Leary; he spoke of these men as patriotic heroes acting in a noble cause against unjust domination.[10] How is it that he could at the same moment privately fight one secret organisation, the Ribbonmen, while standing up in Westminister to defend another, the Fenians? Perhaps he believed the local sense of outrage that fed the Ribbonmen, as well as the desire for political recognition of the new Catholic professional class, could both be channeled into a national, patriotic, and interdenominational organisation for an independent Irish parliament – his own vision of the Fenian organisation.

His speech on the Coercion Bill therefore could reasonably both blame and taunt the British executive in Ireland: blame them for not stamping out Ribbonmen, and taunt them for failing to discover the Fenians. After the 1867 Fenian Rising, the British had filled the country with soldiers, he complained, and still assassins went about terrifying the people, while the Queen's regiments marched everywhere to no purpose except the annoyance of law-abiding Irishmen: "Thus far with victory their arms are crowned," his quotation began, and to the laughter of the opposition it ended, "For though they have not fought, yet have they found/ No enemy to fight." In response, the Solicitor General quoted to Moore a letter the government had in its possession that was written by John Mitchell, "the leader of the Fenians"; it proposed that landlords should be shot. Moore, sidestepping the subject of landlord assassination, objected that Mitchell was not the leader of the Fenians.[11] Well, his honorable friend knew better than he did, the Solicitor General retorted, gaining a laugh at Moore's expense.[12] It was a laugh that exposed the untenable situation in which Moore found himself, a Member of Parliament and yet a Fenian himself. Worse yet, though a Fenian, he was being attacked by another secret society.

In Mayo, the Ribbonmen agitation continued. In the week of 19 March at the Mayo assizes, 189 outrages against persons and property were reported. From one to two hundred men were roaming the county visiting farmers and administering oaths. The County Inspector had discovered thirty-five cases of such intimidation in recent months.[13]

As soon as the Easter recess began, Moore made his last return to Ireland, arriving on Good Friday. On Saturday he arranged for a Monday trip with his agent, S. Nolan, to the Ballintubber estates and a Tuesday return visit by Father Lavelle to Moore Hall.[14] Then he wrote his wife Mary Blake Moore that if she did not receive a telegram from him on Monday, she should prepare to come over to Ireland, as there would be a great deal to be done at Moore Hall. Apparently, he contemplated acting on his threat to leave Parliament and defend his rights as a landlord. On Sunday, he attended Easter Mass at the local church in Carnacun. But on Monday, he retired early to his bed, leaving a note for a visitor due that afternoon that he was too ill to see him. On Tuesday, 19 April, his servant failed to rouse him on the first call, and coming a second time with Moore's agent, found him unconscious. A doctor, G. E. Barron, MB, was fetched from down the hill. Finding Moore breathing hoarsely and unable to speak, the doctor said, "Mr. Moore has an attack of apoplexy, such as statesmen very often get," and sent a rider for Dr. James Dillon Kelly from Ballinrobe.[15] A little before two o'clock on Tuesday afternoon, the doctor pronounced G. H. Moore dead of apoplexy – that is, of a stroke. The Last Sacrament was administered by Father Lavelle.[16]

2

Mary Blake Moore and George, the oldest son and heir, came from London for the funeral, scheduled for Saturday, 23 April. As they passed through Ballinrobe, many of the businesses were closed out of respect for the dead Member of Parliament. At Moore Hall, there were two priests in the house to comfort them, Father Lavelle and another activist priest, Father Peter Conway. The grief of the son, the *Freeman's Journal* wrote, was "excessive in the extreme"; however, GM himself later recalled, again and again, that when he heard his uncle Joe Blake say that all was over, his father was dead, he tried to be sad, and wondered at the sorrow of his mother, but his soul said, *I am glad.*[17] As she wailed, he sobbed, but inwardly he was shocked at the wickedness of his relief that his father would not return.

Inside the house, the steward Joseph Apply led mother and son to the second-floor bedroom at the front of the house, in which George Henry Moore was laid out in the same bed in which his son had been born eighteen years earlier.[18] When Apply was questioned by the anxious mother and son – had Moore shown signs of despair? met with strange men? taken any unusual medicines? made a last confession? – the steward could affirm nothing, but told over and over the mysterious details of the last days.[19] Nothing seemed to explain why the master of the house now lay stretched out, his face under a white handkerchief. Mary Blake Moore, as GM reinvented the scene forty years later, had to have one last look, and snatched the handkerchief off, giving her son a final image to remain in his memory of his father's face, now terribly changed.[20]

By ten o'clock on Saturday, on the lawn reaching down to Lough Carra below Moore Hall, 400 tenants had assembled. They came from all over the 12,000 acres of the estate to mourn a landlord who, according to their folklore, saw to it during the Famine that no one on his estate died of starvation, though the Famine was nowhere worse than in County Mayo.[21] The avenues were filled with vehicles of all sorts, from donkey-carts to carriages drawn by a team of horses. At eleven o'clock the door was opened, and the coffin of polished Irish oak was carried out to the hearse on the shoulders of eight of the tenantry, followed by the mourners. George Moore, as heir, came first as the chief mourner, leaning on the arm of Father Peter Conway.[22] He was followed by Mary Blake Moore, two of her Blake brothers, Llewelyn and Joseph, and her brother-in-law George Browne of Brownestown, who were joined in the procession by

Fathers Lavelle and Conway. Behind this party, in the march down the long serpentine drive through the wood below the garden, and out of the Grand Gate, up the road, then to the Carnacun chapel, came Archbishop MacHale, twelve parish priests, another dozen justices of the peace, Phillip Callan, MP, and Richard Pigott, the forger who twenty years later would attempt to destroy Parnell.[23] Once in the chapel, George sat by his mother while a choir of priests sang dirges, and Reverend James Browne, PP, a high-shouldered man with a large hooked nose, told them that the dear departed had always gone to Mass, and death had no sting, the grave no victory.[24] Then the coffin was carried back out of the chapel, along the road past the Grand Gate to the edge of Lough Carra, around the shoreline below Moore Hall, past the boathouse and pier, to the gateway of Kiltoom, less than a mile short of the racecourse where G. H. Moore's famous horses had trained. Once the party had arrived at the family burial ground, and the coffin had been lodged in the vault, Father Lavelle, though Father Browne pleaded with him not to do so, mounted the tomb to deliver a terrific panegyric to the multitude, beginning, "God Save Ireland! Woe, woe is Ireland to-day! O my country, now mayest thou weep – weep scalding tears from your million eyes!" The full address was written up in several columns in the *Freeman's Journal*.[25]

3

There was indeed a lot to be said of the life of G. H. Moore, as wonderful, the novelist reflected, as any in Balzac or Turgenev, and Father Lavelle was not the only one memorialising the sixty years of Moore of Moore Hall.[26] In Dublin a great meeting was held the next day, which culminated in an oration by Isaac Butt on G. H. Moore as the most eloquent voice of Irish nationality. Papers in Liverpool, Manchester, and London also carried obituaries of a great intransigent enemy of the English, a man one paper wishfully called the last of the Irish Nationalists.[27]

In the family vault, George Henry Moore (1811–70) was laid next to his father George Moore the historian (1770–1840) and his grandfather George Moore of Alicante (1729–99); only a few places were left, one of them reserved for, but never to be occupied by, the fourth George Moore, the novelist (1852–1933).

The Moores had originally been an English Protestant settler family, but turned Catholic when George Moore of Alicante's own father John Moore married Jane Lynch Athy from one of the principal Catholic families in Galway.[28] Using her connections among the "Wild Geese," Irish Jacobite exiles in Spain, she helped her son get established in the wine import business in Alicante.[29] There he changed his religion, and married in 1765 Katherine de Kilikelly, an Irish Catholic raised in Spain. He made his fortune, returned to erect Moore Hall in 1792 above the shore of Lough Carra, and thus solidified the shift of the family from being New English settlers of Protestant faith to their nineteenth-century identity as Irish Catholic landlords who had never been humbled by the "Penal Laws" – that set of regulations aimed at limiting the property and power of Irish Catholics, and put in force after William of Orange routed James II at the Battle of the Boyne in 1688. The change in the confessional identity of the Moore family, like the circumstances of G. H. Moore's death, is important to the story of George Moore. These matters would one day be the occasion of a quarrel about family history that broke up the surviving Moore brothers, saw Moore Hall become vacant, and scattered the last generation of Moores abroad.

Of the four sons of George Moore of Alicante, the oldest was John Moore (1767–98), a scapegrace trained in Paris and London for the law, and for a few days in 1798 the first President of the Republic of Connaught. Aided by French invaders at Killala, John Moore participated in the surprise victory of General Humbert over a British garrison at Castlebar on 27 August 1798, assumed nominal leadership of the rebels, then got captured after the rout of the small Irish forces. President Moore died while under house arrest in a Waterford tavern.[30] The second son of Moore of Alicante was a mild-tempered man, also named George Moore. A gentleman scholar rarely out of his library, he wrote histories of the English and French revolutions, something in the manner of Gibbon.[31] Moore the historian had three sons by Louisa Browne, the first being George Henry Moore, the only one of the three not to die by a fall from a horse.

Following a brilliant career in school – he published Byronic poems in the *London and Dublin Magazine* when he was sixteen years old – G. H. Moore went to Cambridge University. There he played billiards and bet on horses. His watchful mother withdrew him from university; he then took to women. She was worried he would marry a Protestant, and he was worried he would have to marry a woman who was Catholic but poor; Catholic but dirty, or ignorant, or ugly. Mrs Moore was advised on her son's future by her friend, the aging novelist Maria Edgeworth, who conspired with her to turn him again to the path of science and letters. Eventually the two women succeeded in getting G. H. Moore to agree to travel abroad, and the boy after some shifts and dodges finally tore himself away from his mistress, a married woman he met at Bath, and headed for Russia in 1834. It was three years before he was back in England. In the meantime he had been to Russia, Syria, and Palestine, where he mounted an expedition to explore the Dead Sea, only the third British traveler to do so.

When G. H. Moore got back to England, he spirited his brother Augustus from Cambridge and a promising career as a mathematician. The two developed a passion for horses, and within a few years had, against the wishes of their mother (her youngest son had already been killed by a fall from a horse), set up a racing stable at Moore Hall. They became known as two of the most daring riders of the West of Ireland, with George Henry gaining the name of

"Wolfdog" Moore after one of his horses. The brothers had begun to run with bucks in the fast aristocratic crowd, such as Lord Waterford, who on a wager set up a gate inside Curraghmore House, and, mounted on his hunter, leapt it by candlelight.[32] The two Moore brothers were bold even by this measure of hard-riding country gentlemen. They would, for instance, on a bet take their horses over a six-foot iron-spiked gate, or engage in "pounding contests" – that is, matches between two horses, taken to ever more difficult places, rock walls on a hill, walls falling away toward a stream, etc., until one horse either fell or its rider resigned the challenge. In racing, the brothers astonished other jockeys by riding fast right up to the big fences, without pausing to let the horse gather itself before the jump. In 1843 and 1845, George Henry Moore won the Irish Gold Whip by his hard riding; in 1846, he won the English Whip. However, Augustus Moore was killed in a fall while riding Micky Free in the Liverpool in March 1845. George Henry Moore continued to race, and in May 1846 his horse Corranna won the Chester Cup and £17,000. However, his own nearly fatal falls and his brother's death caused him thereafter to turn away from the track.

He was by this time moved by the terrible spectacle of the Famine as it swept across County Mayo. The potato crop first failed in September 1845, and famine did not relent until 1849. G. H. Moore rejoiced that the victory in the Chester Cup had given him the means to be useful to the poor in the first year of suffering.[33] He set aside £1,000 of his winnings – £500 for work projects, £500 for direct charity. He also entered a by-election at this time on the side of the landlord interest and in opposition to Joe MacDonnell, an epic drinker known as "the Twenty Tumbler Man." MacDonnell was an O'Connellite candidate in favor of repeal of the Act of Union between Great Britain and Ireland.[34] "Wolfdog" Moore was well known as a jockey, but as little else. His speeches revealed his landlord hostility to the popular cause of Repeal, and he lost. Instead, in late 1846 he became chairman of two relief committees to dispense aid to famine victims, and the experience radicalised Moore. By January 1847, not yet himself an MP, he was one of the proposers of an Irish convention at which Irish MPs of all parties were sworn to a pledge to end party strife and work together in the interests of Ireland. This independent parliamentary opposition – called "The Irish Brigade" – saw its ranks reduced rapidly by the co-optation of leaders like John Sadleir into government appointments. Nonetheless, in the course of the short unhappy life of the Irish Brigade, G. H. Moore emerged as a unique figure on the political scene, a radical, patriotic, Catholic landlord. When an election was called in 1847, Moore garnered the votes of many in the popular party (nominally in favor of repeal of the Act of Union), without losing the support of the landlords, and he won by a large margin over three Repealers.[35]

Moore spent the next five years in Parliament, and he made a name for himself quickly as an orator good for column inches in the daily papers. He developed his style of address from the highly formalised habits of addressing a challenge to a gentleman with whom you wish to have a duel, a form of correspondence in which the Moore brothers excelled. Between the track, the mortgages, the Church of Rome, and Mother Ireland, there were plenty of opportunities for an Irish Catholic gentleman to feel his honor had been insulted, and to demand satisfaction. The form involves addressing the friend whom the man you wish to challenge has chosen for his second, making reference to previous correspondence, to the rules of affairs of honor, to the facts of the case under dispute (all this part politely legalistic), and then proceeding to calling your enemy a liar, a cheat, and a thief, before signing off in the most courteous of manners. Shots were never fired, with the exception of verbal shots: the letters were always published subsequently, so one's style had to be rapier, pistol, and club. By invective, however, Moore kept up the family reputation passed down through a local Mayo saying, "Scratch a Moore and your own blood will flow."[36]

The other influence on Moore's oratory was his background as a poet; he could quote brilliantly, and with a kind of cruel aptitude. In the election of 1868, when he ran against the landlord interest and without the support of an English party, he told the electors a story of an old ballad about the dragon of Wantley, which devoured the people and knocked down their houses, until "Moore of Moore Hall/ With nothing at all/ Slew the dragon of Wantley." He went out to duel with the dragon without a sword or shield, just covered all over in spikes, but he knew that the dragon was vulnerable in one spot, and "it was not before." So when the dragon jumped him, the bristling champion gave him a kick in the behind with the spike on his boot, and that is how "Moore of Moore Hall/ With nothing at all/ Slew the dragon of Wantley." Moore's point, of course, was that the dragon of old legend was now landlordism, and he was the champion without the sword of class or party interest.[37] But one can also note that he chose a fitting image for himself, going out in a duel of honor, armed all over with spikes of witty invective and a specialised knowledge of insult. In an era in which public speaking was a main spectator sport and the chief art of power, Moore was a champion gladiator, not someone with whom any politician would want to get into the ring: he would tear your character to pieces while the crowd laughed at the joy, and the sheer brilliance of belligerence, with which he went about his work. It was lamented after his death that, while he did have a terrific tongue, he did not use it only on the English; if his own cohorts strayed from the path of honor, he was quick to become the most terrible of enemies. His pugnacity and inability to trust his friends, as Joseph Hone remarks, were qualities inherited in some degree by his eldest son; so were his powers of invective.[38]

In terms of the political positions he took, his biographer and son, Maurice Moore, would like to claim that George Henry Moore was a Parnell before Parnell, certainly an Isaac Butt before Isaac Butt. And it is true that, like these men, he worked early, brilliantly, and for a short time successfully to create a disciplined independent Irish party in Westminster that would hold the balance of power between Tories, Whigs, and Liberals, and shift its influence from one to the other in order to gain advances for Ireland. It gave a lasting twist to his political character that his cohorts in organising the Irish Brigade were corrupted by offers of ministerial positions by the party in power, and that Cardinal Cullen accepted this result with prelatical satisfaction, and simply tried to funnel the patronage to Catholics.[39] Moore was also one of the first Irish MPs to support the Tenant League, organised to secure fair rents and fixity of tenure for tenants after the Famine. However, both these stands hurt him at the polls. By defending Catholics, he lost the Protestant vote; by defending tenants, he alienated his fellow landlords. In the 1857 election, though he had on his side Archbishop MacHale, a raft of enthusiastic priests, and the majority of votes, Moore was turned out of office on a charge of vote corruption, and he left bitterly, if courteously.[40] Nothing good, he felt, could be done in Parliament: the Irish members were there just to shop their integrity about for a price.

In 1851, George Henry Moore made the sort of match that his mother had feared he would never make. He married Mary Blake, the twenty-three-year-old daughter of Maurice Blake of Ballinafad, Balla, County Mayo. Her mother, Anne Lynch Blake, was the daughter and heir of Marcus Lynch and Maria Blake, eldest daughter of Isidore Blake of Towerhill.[41] The Blakes of Ballinafad and the Blakes of Towerhill (two miles from Moore Hall) were the two most successful junior branches of one of the "Twelve Tribes of Galway," the great merchant families of the city who from the fourteenth century traded with ports in Spain and France. The senior branch, that of Sir Valentine Blake of Menlough Castle, Galway, declined from its eminence in the sixteenth century, while the Towerhill and Ballinafad branches increased their wealth by inter-marriage with other members of the "Tribes" (such as the Lynches and the Brownes), as well as between the different branches of the Blake tribe itself (as in the case of Mary Blake Moore's mother and father).[42] The Blakes of Ballinafad were a Catholic family, but they conformed strategically to the Protestant Church of Ireland during key periods of the Penal Laws, and also entered into marriages with Protestant families. In these ways, they managed both to preserve and enlarge their estates through the period in the eighteenth century when there were severe obstacles in the way of Catholics owning land. By the mid-nineteenth century, Maurice Blake of Ballinafad was a wealthy man of large estates. He had ten children; Mary was the eldest of the five girls. For her marriage to George Henry Moore, Catholic neighbor of the Blakes of Towerhill, Maurice Blake of Ballinafad provided his daughter Mary with a dowry of £4,000.[43] Other daughters married into other landed families in the West of Ireland: in 1854, Catherine married Arthur O'Connor of the Palace, Elphin, Roscommon; in 1858, Julia married G. E. Browne of Brownestown; in 1859, Victoria married Thomas ffrench.[44] By his marriage to a Blake, George Henry Moore affiliated himself to a powerful network of tribes in the West of Ireland. His children would be related by marriage to the Brownes, Martyns,

3. Mary Blake Moore,
the novelist's mother.

Lynches, ffrenches, O'Connors, and, of course, to the numerous branches of Blakes.

As first George (1852), then Maurice (1854), Augustus (1856), Nina (1858), and Julian (1867) were born, G. H. Moore turned his attentions again to Moore Hall and to horse-breeding. By 1861, he had a horse that could win any race, Croaghpatrick, and along with his wife and eldest son, he took the racehorse over to England for the season, leaving the boy at Cliff's racing stables at the time of the Goodwood races, won by Croaghpatrick, and the Chesterfield Cup, also won by his champion. Having restored his fortunes by the track, G. H. Moore then frittered them away on the track, and he was no longer a comfortably rich landlord when he saw a new political opportunity in Ireland after the 1867 Fenian Rising.

In the 1868 election, working again in close federation with Archbishop MacHale, he drew the priest into politics in a new way. Formerly, landlords drove their tenants to the polls in herds, and made them take the consequences if they did not vote according to the landlord's wishes; now the priests were taking an equally strong hand with their parishioners. Moore was running with the support of the nationalist clergy, but also against the dragon of landlordism. On the hustings, he spoke of a landlord who evicted one of his own tenants for going against him at the poll: "The only difference . . . between Mr. H. de Burgh and the greater part of the landlords in Mayo is, that he has the imbecile manliness to acknowledge what they have the wise cowardice to conceal."[45] The flamboyance of candidate Moore's mob oratory against his own class led even his closest friend, Lord Sligo, to break with him. But he was back in Parliament, to fight for the Tenant League and the Fenian prisoners until the month of his death.

4

When Father Lavelle had finished his panegyric, and the mallet blows of Michael Melia, the estate mason, closed the vault, young George (as he later constructed the scene) felt the eyes of the multitude upon him, before they dispersed to their cottages in Derrynanny, Ballyhoolly, and Ballintubber. He conjectured, using a steeplechase image for the national struggle, that they were all wondering "how much of my father's talent I had inherited, and if I would take up the running at the point he had dropped out of the race."[46] He was not ashamed to admit that he felt no kinship with the tenants, nor were they to feel any with him. There was no denying that "in those days we looked on our tenants as animals, and they looked on us as kings." They lived in hovels, and came twice a year to pay their rent, taking out of their tall hats banknotes dirty with sweat and soil.[47] Most of them could not speak English, and when he was a child, George recalled always having been afraid of them: he used to run into the woods when he saw the women coming up from Derrynanny with the men's dinners.[48] On Sundays at the Carnacun chapel the family in its carriage would pass by the men in knee breeches, frieze coats, and stovepipe hats; inside the church, the men sat on one side, the women hiding their faces behind shawls on the other, while from the family pew the boy stared down on a grinning dwarf, a blind girl, and other people strange in the young master's eyes. During the sermon Father James Browne threatened them all in Irish with hellfire, making the women fall to knees and beat their breasts. GM claimed to have wondered what would happen should they meet their tenants in heaven: would the men doff their hats, and say, "Long life to yer honor"? Would the women curtsey?[49] In the days after the funeral, they paid the heir all respects; indeed, he mischievously boasted that a woman came to the door with a donkey, laden with two creels of chickens, and her daughter, shyly hiding behind a shawl. Both the girl and the birds were an offering to the new master of Moore Hall, but he had seen, Moore later wrote, the women of London with their kits off, as painted by his uncle Jim Browne, and would have none of the shy girl.[50] In contrast to his father's remarkable identification with his Catholic tenants, George Moore confessed that he felt for them only bewilderment, fear, and repulsion.

While the tenants wondered in what way the new master would plead their cause, George Moore was becoming conscious of the fact that he had just become owner of the one of the 300 largest estates in Ireland, heir to £3,596 a year; for him, that meant that he was now free to enjoy life as he pleased.[51] In *Confessions of a Young Man*, GM wrote that while he followed the hearse, the feeling of strange and horrible pleasure came back to him, and it dawned on him that his father's death "gave me the power to create myself" – that is to say, to create a complete and powerful self out of the partial self which was all that the restraint of home had permitted: "This future self, this idea George Moore, beckoned me, lured like a ghost; and as I followed the funeral the question, 'Would I sacrifice this ghostly self, if by so doing I should bring my father back?' presented itself without intermission, and I shrank horrified at the answer."[52]

5

George Moore's inability to achieve a condition of mourning at the death of his most admirable father was more than an instance of the shocking inability of humans at all times to grieve as they should like to grieve. He could not believe that he was really the boy who had grown up as this father's son, one who from the start never measured up. Later in life he tried to understand how it was that he could never fully believe in himself, and, while truculent and bombastic to others, was himself inwardly trembling, "shy as a wren in the hedgerow or a mouse along the wainscotting." He wondered whether he was born that way, or made that way, and he traced his self-doubt back to how his parents treated him in childhood.[53] One of his earliest memories was of Honor King, an old woman who periodically came begging at the door of Moore Hall; his parents used to joke that he would certainly end up marrying Honor King, and then they would all laugh. This became a family joke, to be repeated again and again to his confusion and their delight. He realised why they thought it was funny: "the joke rested on the assumption that I was such an ugly little boy nobody else would marry me." It is not wise of parents, the grown man reflected on the life of the growing boy, to make a youngster feel himself to be an inferior person.

But he was not only made to see himself as a slope-shouldered, droopy-eyed, silly-looking child (taking after his mother, as a matter of fact), he also was made to feel stupid. Back from Parliament in 1857 and deep into Moore Hall and its stables again, GM's father employed a woman as a governess whom Moore calls "Miss Westby" in his memoirs. It was her job to teach young George to read. Two years later, when the boy was seven, his father picked up an early edition of Burke's speeches, and asked George to read a few pages out loud, but he had not got very far when he ran up against double *s*'s printed like long *f*'s, and faltered, to the alarm of his father, who marched in Miss Westby and his mother for a conference about his backward heir – why, he himself could read *The Times* by the time he was four. This trial was such an ordeal that his son recalled it in three different books of recollections. After George Moore grew up, he often asked his mother if he really had been so stupid as a child, but he could never get a straight answer out of her.[54]

After the trauma of failing the reading examination, the boy was evidently left largely alone again to play with his spinning top on the gray and blue tiles of the entrance hall to the big house;[55] to steal grapes from the greenhouse; to hunt the laundry cat as if it were a hare or squirrel, knocking it from a tree and beheading it with boyish savagery, using his jackknife; to shoot the seagulls on the lake (such lust to kill as astonished him later); or to climb the beech by the stable-yard to watch Fright, the stallion, cover a mare.[56] Sometimes his father would tell George stories of the Far East while he shaved, or row out with the family to Castle Carra for a picnic, where father would recite Walter Scott's *Marmion* to mother, but mostly the boys seem to have been left alone, like wild young beasts, the pups of Wolfdog Moore, set among a flock of deferential sheep.[57]

In July 1861, when George was nine years old, he went over with his mother, father, and the racehorse Croaghpatrick to Cliff's racing stable, where – as noted earlier in this chapter – they left him behind and followed Croaghpatrick to his Goodwood and Chester victories.[58] The winnings enabled George Henry Moore to begin to look after his firstborn's education, or to employ another to do so. He took him from Cliff's stables to his alma mater, St Mary's College, Oscott, a Catholic boarding school outside Birmingham, and left him there, the youngest of 150 boys.[59] Master George was accustomed to large liberties and to having to do a lot to capture the attention of rather negligent adults. In an early incident in Dublin, he had thrown his clothes in the hawthorns of a park, and danced naked up the avenue out of reach of his nursemaid.[60] This was not the way to get on in school. The first day, told to be quiet on the march to the rectory, he turned to his neighbor and asked in a loud voice why the priest told him he wasn't to talk. After lunch, he offered to fight the smallest boy he could find ("it seemed to me a fine thing"), and got pummeled.[61] By 1864, a few winters, many floggings, iridescent beef, and cheese like soap or decayed cork had all conspired to break down his health. Apparently he could read, because he recalls lying in the sickroom with his companions in whooping cough, trying to read Lord Lytton's *The Last of the Barons*. He failed to make anything of the plot, until he discovered that his schoolmates advanced his marker twenty pages every time he left the room.[62] But he certainly could not spell, to judge from his lonely letters home, asking for food packages, new clothes, and news of the racehorses. He remained at Oscott, hungry and unhappy, until a lung infection sent him home for all of 1864, setting back the course of an education that had not yet gone anywhere.[63]

Back at Moore Hall, he was tutored by the Carnacun parish priest, Father James Browne, a tall gaunt man with tufted nostrils, who was able to appreci-

4. George Moore, aged 9; tinted daguerreotype.

ate the distinctions between the *Iliad* in Greek and in Irish (Archbishop MacHale's translation), and between the virtues of Caesar for a landlord's son, and the dangers of Propertius (GM was eager, he says, to read the latter). One morning Father Browne told the boy that he would some day give up all his sports for the classics, and GM rode home in elation. When he told his mother this priestly oracle, she treated it like a joke, so he did the same.[64]

It may also have been during his Moore Hall sojourn of 1864 that another augury in his life occurred, recalled in *Confessions of a Young Man*, when he stole away from the schoolroom to the library and found a pocket edition of Shelley, which opened, with the magic of sortilege, at "The Sensitive Plant." For months afterwards he read the little book, comprehending little, yet loving a great deal.[65] Knowledge for GM was something better stolen by the student than administered to him. He often also recalled an earlier theft, the one that had ultimately led him to Shelley. He had been riding in the great family coach along a narrow Mayo road; opposite him and his sleepy little brother in their smart clothes, his parents were talking about a novel, *Lady Audley's Secret* (published in 1862 by William Tinsley, who was to publish GM's first novel *A Modern Lover* in 1883): did Lady Audley murder her husband, or did he escape alive? Once they returned to Moore Hall, young George lost no time in steal-ing M. E. Braddon's hugely popular sensation novel about a woman with a past. When abandoned by her first husband, Lady Audley had been forced to foster out their child and turn to bigamy to support herself. By and by, her first husband returns, and she schemes to dump him down a well, but he crawls out with a broken arm, years later to return from foreign travels once more. GM's own fascination may have been with Lady Audley's nephew Robert, an idle *flâneur* living in the Temple near London's Fleet Street, not much attracted to women, but very much a friend of her first husband. It is he who traces the crimes of Lady Audley. GM buried himself in whatever novels of M. E. Braddon he could lay his hands on, until he found in *The Doctor's Wife* a heroine who loved Shelley and Byron, and through their names as through magical portals, he says that the romance of unintelligible poetry came over him.

In January 1865, a month before his thirteenth birthday, he was sent back to Oscott, this time with his younger brother Maurice, and he came armored with Shelley against the priests.[66] He continued his education by caprice, reading novels and poems, and refused to study by rule. After a year's tuition there, J. Spencer Northcote, the principal, wrote to G. H. Moore on 22 December after the boys had returned to Moore Hall for Christmas. He reported that Maurice, with greater application, might do well, but he hardly knew what to say about George. There was one other case in the school almost as bad, but that boy was improving.[67]

There were ructions between George and his father through the holidays. When George returned in January to Oscott, he was under orders to write his father three-page letters every day in order to prove his progress in spelling and composition. Within weeks, he earned a paternal reprimand for not writing on schedule. GM answered it in a battling spirit on 25 January (the misspellings are George's at fourteen years of age): "I did not willfully disobey your com-mands . . . I could not as it was quite impossible for me to do it every day if you will only try it for a week or two you will find it more difficult that you expect just you write me thee pages every dad you will soon get puzzled about you could say to fill up the three pages keep my poket money if you will but cant keep me here during the vay [vacation][*sic*]." Anyway, he ended, he was making rapid progress and would soon know how to "spill" perfectly.[68] The letter, two pages long, not three, brought further scolding from G. H. Moore, but Master George was still bucking under the saddle. It was no good being cross, he lectured his father. Why didn't his father just correct his mistakes, and return the letter, so GM could learn? George could then write less fre-quently, and at shorter stretches than three whole pages. "I am sure that we will do much good," he concluded the letter to G. H. Moore, "if you will only follow the advice in this letter."[69]

The high-spirited child so ready to advise his father sagely was reduced to a frightened, blubbering coward within six months.[70] The long vacation had begun at Oscott on 4 July, and all the other students had packed up and gone, but George was left behind for further lessons; he hated the laughter of his departing schoolmates. He begged his father on 5 July, "If you will only take me home for this vacation I will try to improve myself If you only knew what I will suffer by stopping here for goodness sake take me home."[71] Later in life, he had nightmares about being sent back to Oscott for spelling lessons. In another letter of that summer, he hoped that his father would allow him to come home if he wrote one correctly spelled letter, and in its second (unpunctuated) sentence, he bewailed his condition as "the onely boy left here."[72]

It is unknown if GM had to spend the whole lonely summer at Oscott, but he was back there by 20 September, when Northcote again wrote G. H. Moore, and pondered the singular backwardness of the future Parnassian stylist. He just would not pay attention. As an old man, GM printed a conversation with Edmund Gosse about the novels of the mid-century he had read as a boy, and Moore recalled a number of them with affection and in detail: those by the Brontës, for instance, four or five by Lord Lytton, and a few by Disraeli (whom he found unendurable). It appears that the inattention so much regretted by Northcote involved GM setting up his Latin grammar between himself and his teacher, putting his head between his hands, and then dreaming of the romantic novels he would return to reading when classes were over.[73] The priests could do nothing with the dreamy, stubborn son of an Irish landlord. If he did not make progress by Christmas, Northcote wanted to throw in the towel. The family could hire a private tutor at home.[74]

This leaves the impression that George Moore was expelled from Oscott as ineducable, and that he was. But in his many reminiscences on the strangeness of his beginnings as a man of letters, and a man of letters who wrote a good hand, usually spelled correctly, and labored for a perfect correctness of form, George Moore suggested that in some ways he managed his own departure from Oscott for the more pleasant environs of Lough Carra; in short, that his efforts to be expelled were ultimately crowned with success. One of his stories was that he brought his copy of Shelley to the prefect, and said, hoping to be expelled, that he had been reading the book constantly, and wondered if that could be right, for Shelley denied the existence of God. The result was that the priest took away GM's favorite book.[75] Then Moore set himself up as the college odds-maker, taking bets on the horse races of the season, in correspondence with a London turf accountant; his letters were intercepted, and his little business shut down. Next he set up a prize fight, and again got caught – "always in a row of some kind," his brother Maurice confirmed. One of George's finer pieces of devilry occurred after he was asked by the Latin teacher to stay after classes for private tuition, while the other boys played cricket. The priest put his arm around George when he recited his lines, and finally had his hand nearly into the boy's trouser pocket. To be avenged for the loss of his recreation on the cricket ground, George mentioned the incident in the confession. After 1907 when GM was arguing against a Catholic boarding-school education for his nephews, against everything Catholic in fact, he liked to crow that the secrecy of the confessional was not kept, because the tall, bald-headed Latin teacher with a love of boys disappeared soon after Moore's confession.[76]

In *Confessions of a Young Man*, he provided this account of the *coup de grâce*: Shelley led him to atheism, and after refusing to go to confession at Oscott, he was sent home. It is true that no memorial exists of any period in which George Moore believed in God. When Moore writes of churchgoing, he depicts himself as a spectator of religious conduct, watching others worship – such as the four girls in the Clogher pew, just behind the Moores – and not worshipping himself. He can give a fine description of the blind girl who lifts herself to receive on her tongue the wafer, and then sinks back, overcome, overawed, to wait for the next Sunday; however, he never describes the experience of taking Communion himself. His amazement is that it could have meant so much to somebody else.[77] He did not so much lose his faith, as wake up to the fact that he never had any. Maurice Moore recalled a moment for Joseph Hone, when GM, standing on the staircase of Moore Hall, declared himself an unbeliever; his mother startled him by merely saying she was sorry, then passed on. Perhaps, Hone suggests, she thought silence and indifference the best policy. Since her strange son evidently wanted to shock, she would attach no importance to his opinions.[78] Certainly, GM sometimes did things just to astonish, but in the case of religion, he had taken a stand on his own sense of the world, and never backed away from it. Living by his instincts was to be his law in life, and it had already taken him from killing the laundry cat at age twelve to twisting a tiger's tail when he was just fifteen. After all, he supposed, it wasn't a real tiger anyway.

By the time Moore wrote *Salve* (1912), he elaborated a scene in which his father was called to Oscott – this would have been in April 1867 – because George had been caught giving a bouquet to an Oscott maidservant, a low-sized girl named Agnes. The girl was threatened with dismissal, and GM wrote to his father that if she were sent away, he would follow her and marry her. When G. H. Moore arrived for an interview with George and the great-bellied, hairy-knuckled headmaster Northcote, the matter was raised of GM's refusal to go to confession, even on penalty of flogging. GM claims to have got the better of Northcote by saying he had doubts, and Northcote as a former Oxford Anglican led by Cardinal Newman to convert to Catholicism (widowed and still with a son in the school) ought himself to be able to sympathise with youthful uncertainties, since there was a time in the headmaster's own life when Northcote could not have believed in the sacrament of confession. Northcote was thus triumphantly discomfited, and G. H. Moore, as his son pictured the scene, had to turn away to hide his laughter.[79] Maurice Moore could recall very little of the Agnes incident, and the whole episode may just have been the famous storyteller's revenge on one who thought him a hopeless case.[80] In the story "Hugh Monfert" (1922), the Northcote-figure (a convert and school principal) has a son who is the homosexual love-object of the hero (patterned on GM's friend Edward Martyn).[81] Whatever the cause, whether it was idleness, worthlessness, or incorrigibility; girls, betting, atheism, or fagging, it was agreed by principal, father, and son alike that George's days at Oscott should end that summer in 1867.

6

For the next six months, GM again had the run of Moore Hall, and he made the racing stables his schoolyard. He rode to hounds weekly, and exercised the horses on the race-ground daily. The racing calendar and the stud book had a charm the Gallic Wars lacked, and the butler Joe Apply, an ex-jockey with a 56-acre plot of Moore Hall land, proved a better teacher than anyone on Northcote's staff. His highly specialised erudition was an object of admiration at Moore Hall, at least among the house servants. Like the furtive and clandestine Mr Leopold in *Esther Waters*, Joe Apply liked to sit in the pantry smoking his long clay pipe while he discussed the weights of the next handicap, and when questioned could go to his press and extract back issues of *Bell's Life* or the *Sportsman* to prove a point about a race run thirty years ago.[82] He filled the boy with dreams of one day riding the winner of the Liverpool,[83] and GM, like Ginger, the gentleman jockey in the same novel, was evidently teased by Apply with stories of how G. H. Moore had a way of using the whip at the finish not to be seen among the gentleman jockeys of this day. By encouraging reckless riding and making the occasional loan to young George, Apply effectively was playing a part like that of Thady Quirk, the wealthy steward in Maria Edgeworth's *Castle Rackrent*, who sees off one generation after another of his employers, done down by drink, litigation, duels, and politics, until the estate comes into the possession of his own son. Moore Hall, however, was not Castle Rackrent, and Apply died many years later, an old man still in his pantry.

In the November 1868 elections, G. H. Moore was returned for the last time to Parliament, and he decided to take a residence in London. Before finding a suitable house to lease, the family rented rooms in Thurloe Square, Brompton, not far from where the Victoria and Albert Museum now stands (the South Kensington Museum then). The landlady introduced the idle boy to Dick and William Maitland, sons of a retired magistrate from Athlone, Ireland. The Maitlands were caught up in the writing, rehearsing, and staging of French musicals, versions of Offenbach and Hervé, with a chorus of pretty girls. GM caught the operetta fever: he loved listening to Mrs Maitland play the piano; even more he loved "bouquets, stalls, rings . . . scent and toilette knick-knacks"; most of all he wanted to meet an actress.[84]

Soon the family found a house at 39 Alfred Place, across the way from the South Kensington underground station. In London, GM was introduced to his uncle on his mother's side, Jim Browne, a great blond man, who talked incessantly about beautiful women, and painted them sometimes larger than life, in somnolent attitudes, recumbent amid elaborate mythological settings, like those of Doré.[85] GM was impressed. He asked his father over and again why Jim Browne was not the greatest painter in the world if he could paint a picture like the one at Moore Hall – a whole tribe of Indians reining in their horses at the edge of a cliff. Why wouldn't the Academy hang Jim Browne's pictures?[86] Though he was discovering new excitements in music and painting, GM kept up with the life of the track through a correspondence with Joe Apply back at Moore Hall. By July 1869, when Moore was seventeen, he was bragging to Apply that he had backed Starter in the Goodwood (a racecourse near Chichester), and Restitution in another race, for a double event at 48 to 1, and won, even though Apply himself said Restitution could not win carrying a nine-stone handicap. He offered his services, too, in placing a bet for Joe on "the Cassearwitch and Cambrishire races" [sic].[87]

His father became impatient with a son who divided his time between loitering in a small tobacconist's shop, his ear out for tips dropped by someone who knew Lord So-and-so's footman, hanging about the music halls with the Maitland boys, and dreaming of Jim Browne's women. He was not satisfied with George's expectation in life – that he would ride the winner at Liverpool – and demanded that he choose an occupation. Law was out of the question; you had to spell to do that. Would he be a country gentleman and learn farming? Join the priesthood? Or become a colonel and serve in the colonies? George recalls that he "said Yes to the Army, only because the courage to say No was lacking." Anyway, he reasoned, the purchase of military commissions had been abolished, and "the chance of my passing any examination was, indeed, remote."[88]

His father counted on the reputation of an army tutor named Jurles, famed for success with the stupidest boys: he had, GM recalled, gotten 1,753 into the Army. Now he could try his luck with George and his brother Maurice, back from Oscott in June 1869.[89] Taking his seat in a row of desks at the military training academy, GM resumed his dreaming, sometimes of the thirty-year-old wife of old Jurles, sometimes of what kind of death each one of his fellow-pupils would one day meet on the battlefield. In a revealing invention in *Vale*, GM recalls worrying that it might be his lot to die for his country too, or worse, to be wounded for it, when "It seemed to me that myself was my country."[90] To save himself from a glorious fate, he found a simple expedient: he read the *Sporting Life* under the table in place of his textbooks, and gave himself the afternoons off to go to betting clubs.

In an 11 August 1869 letter to Joe Apply, GM offered to send along the bi-weekly *Sporting Life*, and told Joe that he has joined two private betting shops. He continued to keep Apply abreast of turf matters through the summer and early fall, getting ever more savvy in his stable idiom: "A friend of mine told me that Cannon the Jockey told him that he did not know anything about Vacuum for the long race but told him to back him for the short one . . ." But he had dipped deeply into his allowance for wagers, and then could not cover all his bets: "I am afraid I am in a mess." He wanted to get into the Victoria Club, a betting shop on Wellington Street in the Strand, "only it is rather dear 5 quids." He kept on through September, however, bragging about picking Pero, winner of the St Leger on 15 September, and fancying Mary Ann for an upcoming race, "a slashing fine mare and has never tried yet."[91]

At Jurles's academy, Moore met two boys who also liked the ponies but were more enthusiastic about the British Army than George: Colville and Belfort Bridger, from Shoreham in Sussex. Colville had a military mustache, £500 a year, thirty-six pairs of trousers, and a mistress in St John's Wood.[92] After winning £50 on a race, GM at least briefly could keep up the running with the Bridgers, and they contrived to gain the acquaintance of some of the ladies with private houses in Mayfair, in *Vale* named "Kitty Carew," "Margaret Gilray," and "Sally Giles," who permitted the boys to spend money on them. GM claims he took lessons in coach-driving, once the only means of transportation, now in the age of the railroad becoming the sport of gentlemen; he then drove a coach transporting Margaret Gilray and Sally Giles out into the night, and nearly got lost on Wandsworth Common. He also claims the ladies sent a groom to Jurles's with a note for GM and the Bridgers, and Jurles, intercepting the note, told GM he was a bad student, often absent, inattentive when present, and would never get into the Army. So things were going according to plan.

He had been seeing more of Jim Browne, who lived in one of the large Victorian mansions in Prince's Gardens. Browne was becoming for the boy something between a father-figure and an ego-ideal, a man of the sort he wished to become, a man of some sort, at any rate, and one who led a life of pleasure. GM studied Jim Browne's taste in women, asking which ones were the most beautiful, and why, and hoping not to make a mistake himself. There is nothing unusual, perhaps, about a boy finding the study of the opposite sex more intriguing, more deserving of both field research and library study, than spelling or Latin grammar, but GM seems to have had from the beginning an unusually sharp consciousness of the arbitrariness of human sexual styles. His father, while shaving, had once given his son some early lessons in the women who were worth admiring. G. H. Moore showed young George photographs of pictures by Sèvres, and told him the slender nymph was a beautiful woman (a mild betrayal of his stout wife), but GM preferred, he says in the1889 *Confessions of a Young Man*, the corpulent Venus, with a Cupid behind her knees who shot arrows at the doves in the trees.[93] Both in the motherliness of the admired female image and the misdirection of the little boy's arrows, GM was signaling the sexual confusion of his early years. He would remain fascinated by the world of sexual beauty, but he stood outside it, with its customs as strange to him as those of religion, patriotism, or class. He formed a solution to this problem: he would become a painter. To be a painter was to be a professor of beauty, a lifelong student, with sufficient excuse to look thoughtfully upon the female form – the perfect professional cover for an amateur voyeur.

He went out and bought himself easel, palette, brushes, and paints.[94] For a stylish smock, he got a teagown, such as the one he had admired on Sally Giles, as she sat on his lap, making a joke of trying to get a rise out of him.[95] His father permitted him to take drawing lessons at the South Kensington Museum but sent young Maurice along as well, which irritated George, who thought he had found his own peculiar vocation; moreover, he noticed that Maurice's drawings were as good as his own, or better.[96] In spite of GM's head-over-heels infatuation with Jim Browne and his extravagant arts, Jim appears to have thought his young nephew and devotee a little fool in his teagown, with his worries about his yellow hair. Jim would not stop to introduce George to friends encountered on the sidewalk as the boy tagged along, but GM claims his uncle was impressed later on when Kitty Carew stopped one day in Hyde Park to talk with George.

In January 1870, GM came back to 39 Alfred Place to find his father and mother looking very troubled; they had mysterious, quiet conversations with one another. GM feared that old Jurles had let them know that he had failed at school and gotten into trouble with horses and women. GM gives no sign of having known, then or later, anything of the "Three Fs," the Ecclesiastical Titles Bill, or the Ribbon Societies of Ballintubber. Then one day after dinner, George Henry Moore announced that he was going to Ireland by the mail train.[97]

7

In the days after the funeral of G. H. Moore, Mary Blake Moore lingered about the place, taking flowers to her husband's grave in Kiltoom. Her life had begun its decline, but George Moore felt that his own life was just beginning, and his decline had come to an end. He was afraid he would be stuck in Mayo for months, and only with difficulty was he able to get his mother on a train for London. GM tells the story this way himself in *Vale*, the story of an atrocious boy, but one with an engaging manner; in *Confessions of a Young Man* (1889) he even admits to feeling like a murderer when he turned to leave the place he had just inherited, but still he went, and began his long career as Moore Hall's absentee landlord.[98]

On the train he told his mother that he would not be going back to Jurles's academy. He was going to become an artist, and all along the journey by rail and steamboat back to London, to borrow the heroic language of the 1889 *Confessions*, his brain was made of this one desire. Near the end of his life, when he advised Charles Morgan about how to write his biography, GM went back to this time when he first conceived of his own identity as George Moore: "the story you have to tell is not of a man who wrote this book or that . . . Your story is of a man who made himself because he imagined himself . . . The man you will tell of imagined himself as an artist . . . and it was not until he threw away his brushes that his imagination paired with his nature."[99]

It is difficult to bring into focus the serious and the comic in George Moore at any time in his life, but especially in his youth. It is difficult, that is, to reconcile the artistry with the humor with which the old George Moore regarded the young George Moore imagining becoming George Moore, the author. He himself pondered this peculiarity of his nature when talking of a time after the death of his father when he wore ladies' boots to a county hunt, carried his father's old breech-loader, and admitted to the English gentry that, yes, he was in love, he was always in love, gaining the name of "Mr. Perpetual." "To be ridiculous," old George Moore concluded, "has always been *ma petite lux*," his own little folly, "but can any one be said to be ridiculous if he knows that he is ridiculous? . . . It is the pompous who are truly ridiculous."[100] The old George Moore clung to the silly young George Moore, constantly recreating him and never outliving him, so that he won, as his friend Robert Ross remarked, "a sort of perpetual youth with which it is impossible to be indignant [and which] has been one of his extenuating circumstances and one of his passports to the good opinion of a younger generation."[101]

He was not, however, the blank, unlettered idiot he represents himself as having been. It was probably in the spring after his father's funeral (he says he had recently turned eighteen) that he went down to Sussex to stay with the Bridgers in Shoreham. He carried with him an edition of Kant's *Critique of Pure Reason*, because he was deeply interested in religious problems and ways of thinking about the world without recourse to God. Mrs Bridger was a lovely woman, GM was always spooning with her, and he tried to interest her in a theological discussion, pursuing her into her greenhouse to explain, as best he could, "The Deduction of the Categories." She just laughed and declared she would from that day call him "Kant Moore," and she did.[102] In this anecdote, he again sees himself, and is seen by others, in a joking light, but in it one can also see a young boy whose mind has outrun the sporting weeklies, one who was inflamed by Shelley and then Darwin, Spinoza, Godwin, and Mill, yearning to ponder the questions of life, and keeping, all the while, a great charm for women, who smiled at him like a son still not yet sure how to be a man.[103]

8

Back in London, GM continued his drawing lessons. In *Vale* he recalls that it was after his father's funeral that he joined the atelier of a French amateur artist, Monsieur Victor Barthe, on Limerston Street in Chelsea. James McNeill

Whistler, having left Paris for London, was advertised to be the visiting master, and in the summer of 1868 Whistler showed up with the Greaves brothers. Whistler drew from the nude, while the Greaveses practiced drawing from Whistler's drawing of the nude.[104] Another student in the life-class was the Pre-Raphaelite boy genius, Oliver Madox Brown, who began work there when he was just sixteen, in 1871, and stayed two more years.[105] GM recalls being drawn to Oliver Madox Brown, whose long fat body was an even stranger envelope of sensibility than his own, perhaps no more likely to win a woman's love. Eventually, he got up the courage to speak with Brown and was invited back to the large family home in Fitzroy Square. At the door, he met the boy's father, Ford Madox Brown, a notable Pre-Raphaelite painter, who as he took GM up the stone staircase to Oliver's room, told him all about his adored son, how he had written a book of poems and a long prose romance.[106] Here was GM, brought up to believe himself stupid; there was Oliver Madox Brown, showered with love by his father, William Michael Rossetti, Dante Gabriel Rossetti, and a host of others. Oliver Madox Brown had been brought up to be the Leonardo of the age (and might have won great fame, but died in 1874, three years later). Listening to Ford Madox Brown sing his son's praises, GM was too overwhelmed both by what the boy had done, and by the father's love, to give any answer.

Whistler invited Barthe's students to call on Sundays at 96 Cheyne Walk, and GM took up Whistler's offer not long after *The Artist's Mother* had been completed (the fall of 1871).[107] GM attempted to express his enthusiasm for the Pre-Raphaelite pictures he had seen at the home of Ford Madox Brown, and Whistler capped GM's boyish praise with a cutting anecdote about the Pre-Raphaelites.[108] The little incident is prophetic of what would be a lengthy and grating history between Whistler and Moore.

One day when Whistler was working in Barthe's studio, GM asked Oliver Madox Brown to read his manuscript romance during one of the model's rests. The sitter was, he says, "Mary Lewis," a lovely woman Whistler liked to draw. While the boy read, the other students were drawn into the inveigling mysteries of the story, and Mary Lewis herself sat entranced, her shawl slipping down by inches, until at last she sat quite naked to the waist, oblivious to all but the charm of narrative.[109] Meanwhile, Whistler sat in the corner neglected. As a piece of the symbolic history of an artful voyeur, this is rich: by the power of literature, one can (even with a long fat body) win love in the end, and in Oliver Madox Brown's storytelling GM found a possible future life for himself, one that included victory over painting, parents, and self-confident geniuses like Whistler.

9

During the years after the death of his father, George Moore continued to loiter about the studio of Jim Browne. Browne one day showed him one of his smaller pictures, four feet by six, of a brown satyr overtaking a nymph. "My eyes dilated and I licked my lips: The best thing you ever painted in your life, Jim. Why do you turn it away to the wall?" Jim explained that his sisters sometimes visited.[110] How could GM learn to paint the like of that? "If you want to learn painting, you must go to France – France is the only school of art," Jim answered, and became the unconscious messenger of another of Moore's "echo-auguries," life-changing moments, like the moment years earlier when he read M. E. Braddon's novel about the character who loved *Shelley*, a name that produced vibrations in the young boy.[111] Now it was Paris that meant volumes to him, beckoning him toward the self that he would become. He was not, however, of age, so he dissipated the hours until he could go to Paris to become an artist.

GM spent a lot of money, but he thought he had much money to spend. Although he wasted a lot of time at theaters, music halls, and the Cremorne Gardens, he had little to do with the time before his twenty-first birthday except to waste it. GM was truly a Moore in that he never drank to a state of drunkenness, and he was more particularly himself in that he was not self-destructively improvident. He spent his money, he says, on scent, toiletries, rings, clothes, theater tickets, and women – models, opera singers, and the ladies of the Argyle Rooms and the Cremorne Gardens. In *Vale*, he reflected that a young man who went to these places with sovereigns in his pocket could only procure "a gratification hardly on a higher level than that which schoolboys practice"; he wouldn't be loved for himself until he left at home all but cab fare for two.[112] As of yet, he had not himself made the leap from prostitution to scheming male promiscuity.

Once he nearly did get into trouble. He was induced by his Thurloe Square neighbor Richard Maitland to invest in a theatrical production. Perhaps it was the English version of Offenbach's *Les Brigands* which opened on 18 November 1872 at the St James's Theatre, or else the naughty quadrille with dancers from Paris Maitland had scheduled for 26 December 1872.[113] On this St Stephen's Day, the orchestra, perhaps unpaid, did not show up, and the theater had to close its doors and pay its debts. Maurice Moore recalled that GM got out of being answerable to creditors because he was under age. GM's hopes for a stage-door romance apparently went unfulfilled. He did succeed, he says, in getting a promise of love from "Alice Harford," an actress and the mistress of Jim Browne. Before the rendezvous occurred, he bragged about it to Jim Browne, with the result – Moore recalled in *Vale* – that Alice did not keep her appointment. Throughout his life, when writing of women, GM tended to tell not of successes, but of the shadows he had embraced.

Finally, his mother induced Lord Sligo, G. H. Moore's old friend, to say something to Jim Browne about restraining GM in his pursuit of women of no reputation. Browne subsequently talked of the dangers rather than the delights of womanly beauty. He suggested GM should have a project – Browne did not propose the discovery of the depth of the Dead Sea (G. H. Moore's former goal in life) but, even worse, the discovery of the origins of the Nile.[114] GM, however, already had a project, and only waited for his twenty-first birthday to commence it.

George Moore was born on 24 February 1852. Only a few weeks more than twenty-one years later, his mother could no longer keep him back, and on 13 March 1873, when his sister Nina had a ring she wished to present to him, he was already *en route*, with a fancy writ of passage in his valise, headed for the Hôtel Quai Voltaire alongside the Seine, and attended by a little bit of Mayo in the person of his valet, William Molony.[115]

Chapter 2
Paris, His Oxford and Cambridge

I

On 30 June 1873, George Moore's manservant William Molony wrote from the Hôtel de Russie to Joseph Apply, the butler of Moore Hall:

> Mr George Moore is as happy as a prince here and not a foolish hare [*sic*] on his body but so good natured a person never lived. He will be a great artist he can lick Jim Browne into saddlebags but he works very hard from 8 o'c in the morning till 5 in the evening. He is the devil to please. There is nothing right when he is out of humour.

The valet from Mayo was not as happy as a prince: Molony was being "broil to death both day and night" by the Paris summer. Still, the best brandy was "two franks a bottle and claret for a song peaches and grapes enough for two pence and *Women* for *asking*."[1] And Molony had a bet on the Grand Prix at Longchamps. Taking it all together, he would rather be in London, where he could at least speak the language. There is no mention by Molony of missing County Mayo, in spite of its cool summers and the wife he had living in a village near Moore Hall.[2]

When the two travelers had arrived at the Gare du Nord in mid-March, three months earlier, GM read his French dictionary on the way to the Hôtel Quai Voltaire, but he did not have enough French to ask for a room, hot water, and a fire.[3] Within three weeks, according to *Confessions of a Young Man*, he was able to hold a kind of conversation in French, although his language was "like nothing heard under God's sky before."[4] He made his way to the studio of Alexandre Cabanel (1823–89), intending to purchase a place there as a special student. Once the favorite painter of Napoleon III, Cabanel was now, along with Jean-Léon Gérôme and Henri Lehmann, one of the painters with separate teaching studios at the Académie des Beaux-Arts.[5] GM liked Cabanel's decorative nudes in mythological settings, like his famous *Birth of Venus*, a

Venus not standing wind-blown and covering her breast with an arm like the Venus in Botticelli's famous picture, but writhing prone in a white excitation of foam upon the vast blue bed of the sea – a virtuoso piece of high academic eroticism, which may give a hint of GM's ambitions at this stage. Cabanel looked over GM's sketches before telling him that he did not take private pupils. As GM prepared to withdraw, Cabanel (known to be a sympathetic man) stopped him and ultimately succeeded in communicating the message that GM might gain entrance to the Beaux-Arts if he used the influence of the English Ambassador, Lord Lyons.[6]

On 25 April 1873 Moore in fact obtained admission to Cabanel's class at the Beaux-Arts.[7] In the summer, classes began at seven o'clock in the morning, and only an hour later in the winter. With Molony there to wake him and see after his clothes, GM managed the discipline for a time, got himself to the great buildings on the rue Bonaparte, at the heart of the Left Bank, and entered the courtyard with its huge sculptured heads staring down from pillars. In the studios, however, he found that newcomers were expected to submit to a regime of ragging. In the traditions of the Beaux-Arts, one *nouveau* might be required to square off with another for a duel in the nude with paintbrushes.[8] Nothing delighted the students as much as for a *nouveau* to lose his temper: then they might tie him to a ladder and set him up against a wall on the street outside.[9] There was also fierce competition among the students for honors in the monthly competitions, judged by the visiting masters and open to outside students. In such competitions, the young Irish visitor, with so little French and not much artistic training, had little chance of hiding the oddity of his great aspirations.

One was supposed to remain a *nouveau* at the Beaux-Arts for a whole year; GM remained for a few weeks. The "many turbulent fellows," with their rough life in the studio, made the young landlord artist conclude he needed different facilities for carrying on his education.[10] He made his way to the studio of another of the most popular teachers in Paris, Jules Lefebvre (1836–1911), who, like Cabanel, said he did not take private pupils, but sent Moore off to the public studio of Rodolphe Julian in the Passage des Panoramas. At length, GM was able to understand that it was in the Académie Julian that Lefebvre himself did his teaching, calling there every other week.[11]

Life at Julian's studio proved to be more to GM's taste. While Julian had been teaching for years, he was just beginning to establish the Académie Julian in 1873. The idea was to provide, for a fee, training to students who wished to become good enough to compete successfully for entrance into the Beaux-Arts. Julian would hire models, set the positions, arrange for weekly visits by successful painters like William Bouguereau (1825–1905) and Jules Lefebvre, hold little competitions, and in many other ways provide a training like that of the Beaux-Arts. One way in which the Académie Julian differed, however, was in the treatment of newcomers.[12] At Julian's, they were the customers of a new business, to be cosseted and coaxed to remain.[13] Julian held out to his customers the appealing belief that one person had as much talent as another, and with a small fee and much work before a naked model, they could all paint the female figure as well as Cabanel did.[14] Julian was glad of GM's monthly subscription of 40 francs, "nor were [Moore's] invitations to dinner and to the theatre to be disdained."[15] At last, GM had found a place in which his money and class could do their work.

Rodolphe Julian himself was a "stout man of about thirty" with short legs, slightly bowed, a big trunk, and enormous shoulders. The son of a school-teacher, he had come up to Paris from Marseilles with only Balzac for a guide, hoping to be a Rastignac.[16] In May 1863, Julian exhibited at the Salon des Refusés along with many painters who later made a name for themselves – Whistler, Manet, Cézanne, and Pissarro had works among the 780 exhibits – and after 1865 he exhibited at the Salon itself, but still he fell upon hard times. One year he got by only through setting up a little circus in Paris, and bringing twenty-five wrestlers up from Provence, one of whom, *l'homme masqué*, was advertised to be invincible; and indeed, for the championship bout, he overthrew the wearied victor of the earlier rounds.[17] In later years Julian would take his students on painting expeditions to the countryside, and he would sometimes give the young artists tips on tricky falls, until the moonlight was "filled with straining and prostrate forms."[18]

Julian's atelier in the Passage des Panoramas off the Boulevard Montmartre was a large room, some 35 feet by 20, on the second floor; Julian lived on the first floor.[19] There was a small wooden partition at the studio's entrance, behind which Julian kept his accounts and the visitor was screened from the sight of the model. In 1876, Julian exhibited *An Academy of Painting*, presumably as a sort of shop advertisement for the growing business. A slim, nude woman, with a most innocent face, sits on a three-foot-tall platform, her legs crossed and her hands loosely clasped over her knee; beside her on the floor rests a coffee service. She is posed in the foreground; in the background and facing the viewer are ranged eighteen student artists on short stools, peering over small easels at the nude model. The few students who are women have their hair up, and long-sleeved dresses buttoned to the neck. The male students, several bald and bearded, look to be in their thirties (one has been said to be Moore and another, Moore's friend Lewis Welldon Hawkins).[20] Julian's representation of his studio advertises a mood of alert, studious concentration, a facsimile of the intensity in a theater of surgery.[21]

On the day that GM entered the door of the studio represented in this advertisement, he found himself one of about twenty students. There were a few retired solicitors, some fashionable young men (one of them, Sir Arthur Temple Clay, was to become Sir William Gregory's brother-in-law),[22] and about ten women: four were American (including, it seems, Elizabeth Gardner, who later married William Bouguereau),[23] three English, one Chilean, and the rest, GM recalls, were retired actresses hoping to find, like Sarah Bernhardt, a second talent in art.[24] A male and female model sat on alternate weeks. On Mondays models would come, be asked to strip, take a turn, strike a position, and then the students would vote on whether they should be hired for the week.

In a later polemic on women and education, GM pretended to be indignant that a young lady, fresh from Bayswater, should be asked to settle her eye-glasses and participate in such an election. That polemic was written sixteen years later, by which time Julian had made himself a fortune in art education, with eighteen studios in Paris, and been awarded the Légion d'honneur in 1881 for services to art. GM was then aghast at the profiteering on false promises of immortality for everyone, irrespective of natural talent: "Humanity asks for eternal life; Christianity supplies it . . . Humanity wants to be artistic; Julian says why not?"[25] In other recollections of Julian's Academy, Moore shows every sign of having found the whole scene delightful, and with nothing at all like the advertised aura of a theater of surgery. The fatherly friendliness of Julian, the girls suffering the boys in their singing of dirty songs and smoking of cigars, the life of artists' cafés – it was a charming existence for a young man from Mayo.[26]

Through the lessons of the visiting masters, the students learned to count heads, eight ovals to a body length; then to note the "swing of the figure" by the use of a plumb-line, as it dropped through the ear, right breast, hipbone, and heel. The next step was to draw the spaces that took the light and those that kept their shadows; they had to learn to "draw by the masses," to paint *au premier coup* (at one sitting), and to tell a story clearly by a pose.[27] According to the doctrine of the Academy, the nude was the basis of all art, and the students applied themselves to its geometries from eight in the morning to five in the afternoon.

By 30 June 1873, when William Molony was writing his letter to Joseph Apply, GM had moved from the Hôtel Quai Voltaire to the Hôtel de Russie, which offered cheaper accommodation, and at 1 Boulevard des Italiens was just a block away from Julian's Academy in the Passage des Panoramas.[28] Molony judged Master George to be fast on his way to "lick[ing] Jim Browne into saddlebags," and other Parnassian achievements. After describing to Julian *Cain Shielding his Wife from the Wild Beasts* by Jim Browne, Moore gathered that Julian did not think much of what George had learned "on his native bogs."[29] With French tuition, GM could look forward to being as good as his uncle, and better, if he just followed the rules of composition and studied hard. In *Confessions of a Young Man*, Moore admits that he found the long days difficult; the mind would wander. "The sense of sex" communicated by the young female students, with their hair lifted, their sleeves open to the elbow, was an intoxication. But GM did not, he swears, fall in love with one of them; it was for Lewis Welldon Hawkins that he fell.

2

When GM wrote up the scene of his first meeting with Hawkins in *Confessions of a Young Man* (1888), he did it using all the conventions of love-at-first-sight episodes and the maiden-seduced; when he retold the story in *Vale* (1914), he simply enhanced this effect. One day, he says, he was watching the women students in the front row, when into Julian's Academy walked a newcomer, fashionably dressed. He sat down to sketch; GM followed this personage with his eyes, and noticed that this *nouveau* could already draw very well indeed; he astonished the other students by sketching not only the model, but the stove, the screen behind which the model dressed, and the back curtain.[30] He had shoulders, GM continued to observe, "beautiful and broad; a long neck, a tiny head, a narrow, thin face, and large eyes, full of intelligence and fascination"; in *Vale*, GM recalls his long legs, strong arms, and "soft violet eyes."[31] At the end of the day, Lewis Welldon Hawkins introduced himself, and asked GM if they had not met before . . . in London, it had been, at Jim Browne's studio. Hawkins (1849–1910), though born in Esslingen (Württemberg), came of British parents, and was distantly related to Browne.[32] GM hired a cab, and rode off with Hawkins, at each moment noting in him "new superiorities": Hawkins knew actresses, what restaurants were fashionable, and how to have your hair properly curled. Back at his apartment, Lewis played a waltz on the piano – just a little something he had composed – while GM took in the accoutrements of a true, number-one ponce: a Japanese screen, oak chairs covered in red velvet, brass harem lamps, and a Turkish rug.[33] His wonder grew when Hawkins next took a violin from the wall, and began to play Stradella's "Chant d'église." Did GM know it? A beautiful girl then burst into the room, breathless; she had come to take Lewis for dinner. GM was allowed to make up a third to Lewis and "Alice Howard." As they paraded along the street, Lewis went across to order some coal, skipping from stone to stone: "What a toff he is!" Alice said.[34] GM joined in her admiration.

Julian wanted to show his new pupil a good time, so he took Lewis, Alice, and GM with a few other students for a Sunday outing to Meudon, a village of 6,000 south of Paris, with a steamboat station beside the Seine.[35] They sketched the scenes along the river, and when the sketches were compared, GM lavished all his admiration on the one by Lewis. After dinner, the students ran races, and GM lost by a little to Hawkins. At the end of the evening, he tried to tell Lewis that this would one day be a very happy memory, but the depth of his emotion made him ashamed, and anyway, Lewis "had not heard, he was talking to Alice."[36] When they parted, GM headed for the Hôtel de Russie and William Molony, and Alice went home to bed with Lewis.

Later in the summer, the three friends traveled slightly further south of Meudon, and took rooms in the same inn. It was hot, so they hired a boatman to row them out to an island for a swim. Lewis was a glorious swimmer, and Alice was not, so GM remained in the shallows with her, admiring Lewis "disporting himself in midstream."[37] George, setting himself up as a swimming instructor, then nearly drowned Alice – just meant to be a friendly ducking, he pleaded afterwards.[38] That day was spoiled, and for his next outing to paint in the open air, Lewis decided to leave GM behind in the inn with Alice, and he spent the mornings gossiping with Alice in her bed. The young English girl, only seventeen or eighteen, was kind enough, or cruel enough perhaps, to permit her Irish chum to chat with her about her lovers while she made her morning toilette. She told him fascinating stories of her life as a paid cocotte, ambitious of becoming a famous *demi-mondaine*, with a coach and men in livery. Lewis she loved for his own sweet sake, of course; and GM she had no idea of loving at all.[39]

At Julian's Academy, GM found it harder and harder to carry on with his studies.[40] It just seemed too hopeless to compete with Lewis, for whom everything was easy. So much could be taught to Lewis, so quickly and easily; with GM the reverse was the case, and he had not yet come to believe that education is a curse, not a blessing – that it is not what can be put into a person that makes an artist, but what can be drawn out of the depths.[41] So he idled his days away, often with Alice, observing like a cat before a mousehole her little mannerisms.[42]

In the autumn, according to the chronology of *Vale*, Hawkins suggested that the three of them should visit a medieval village beloved by painters. GM says the village was Cernay, 50 or 60 kilometers outside of Paris, but Cernay is near Strasbourg, much farther from Paris than that. The description in *Vale* suggests one of three famous artists' inns near Barbizon: the Ganne Inn, decorated by Rousseau, Corot, and Diaz in the 1850s; the White Horse Inn at Chailly-en-Bière, where Monet, Renoir, and Sisley stayed in the 1860s, or Mother Anthony's Inn in Marlotte, frequented by Sisley, Renoir, and Zola in the 1870s.[43] On their visit to such an inn, George, Lewis, and Alice ended up sharing a single room. When Lewis had gone to sleep, George posed a curious question to Alice. Would it make any difference whether she had to swallow "something incredibly nasty" from the body of Lewis or swallow it from the body of George? A great deal, she said, and woke Lewis up to see if he would not feel the same way about her effluvia versus that of George. No, snapped the sleepy Lewis, "crap was the same all the world over, and he would prefer to swallow a pinch rather than a pound."[44]

The combination of poignancy and sober-faced hilarity in GM's tales of his enthrallment to Lewis and Alice could not be achieved until some forty years after the event. Certainly, the circulation of desire in this *ménage à trois* must, for the twenty-one-year-old boy, have been painful in its inescapability: George loves Alice because he wishes he were Lewis loving her, and he loves Lewis because he wishes he were Alice loving him. Neither Lewis nor Alice, however, treats George as anything but a most devoted friend, on a good allowance from his agent, Joe Blake. The gender-bending, transsexualising situation is like that of one of Moore's sacred books from his French years, Gautier's *Mademoiselle de Maupin*. Rodolphe finds a man – who underneath a disguise is actually Mademoiselle de Maupin – to be dangerously beautiful, until he sees this "man" dressed as a woman in a private performance of *As You Like It*. Then Rodolphe almost forgets her manly attractions in his admiration of her female loveliness.[45] Gautier could resolve the agonies of undecided sexuality by a more complete eroticism, an aesthetic forgiveness of the flesh, but Moore leaves no doubt that in the early years of his relationship to Hawkins, he was simply in pain.

By the following spring, around March 1874, GM had found a way to break out of his psychological entanglement. He was still staying at the Hôtel de Russie when he wrote to his mother, saying he was sorry she had been lonely in London, but he himself had enjoyed a gay time during the Paris winter carnival.[46] At a masked ball before Lent, with the orchestra level of the Opéra-Comique cleared to become a dance floor, he had gone with a whole party dressed as the characters in Gounod's *Faust* – himself in the military costume of "Valentine," Hawkins as "Faust," Alice as "Margaret," and other friends as "Mephisto" and "Sybil." From Manet's painting of such a ball, one can see that gentlemen usually dispensed with masks; costumes were normally worn only by those women wishing to engage in sexual commerce.[47] The masquerade of Moore and his friends made enough of a sensation, GM boasts to his mother, to get into the papers the next day. In his edition of Moore's letters up to 1901, Robert Becker plausibly suggests that this was the same ball described in *Vale* at which GM, then a good dancer,[48] summoned the courage to ask a dance of one of the famous cocottes, *La Belle Hollandaise*, and was accepted as a partner. At the end of the night, with GM still fearing things would once again for him turn out platonically, the revelers returned for a grand bivouac in Alice's apartment. There George was paired off with *La Belle Hollandaise*. She coiled beside him, he recalled, like a serpent of the Old Nile, and, caught in the strange interlacings of her limbs, he "often called out in terror" during the night, awakening Alice and Lewis.[49] Something was apparently being done to George that had not been done before, and it gave him a lasting fright.[50] It did not free him from Lewis Welldon Hawkins, but it was at least a step into a further enthrallment.

3

In the months since George Moore met Lewis Hawkins, he had lapsed in his dedication to the study of painting, though he would take it up again later. In the meantime, he tried his hand at writing. At the Hôtel de Russie, he encountered a person who would have a lasting influence on his life as an author. Meals at this hotel were served *en famille*. Every Monday, a certain visitor took a seat at the common table, a short, fat man with a bald head, "his chin descending step by step into a voluminous bosom, a sort of human guinea pig."[51] This was Bernard Lopez (1817–96), a French playwright of English parentage. GM was in awe when he learned that Lopez had written 160 plays and collaborated with a long list of famous French authors, including Alexandre Dumas *fils*, Eugène Scribe, and Théophile Gautier; his pieces had been played on the stages of the Variétés, Opéra-Comique, Odéon, Palais Royal, Théâtre-Français, and others.[52] He began to sit beside Lopez every Monday, and then to take him out to dinners, buying him cigars and glasses of Chartreuse, while anecdotes of the author's trade poured out of that voluminous affable bosom. Lopez described the literary life as a professional and very social business. An author did not get into an attic and go mad. Instead, one made an appointment with a fellow worker at ten o'clock to consider Act I of a vaudeville; after breakfast, there would be a *séance de collaboration* at the other end of Paris over a plot for a drama; at a café in the afternoon, one might talk about an opera, before spending most of the night writing. If GM cared to write poetry, Lopez advised, he should buy a copy of Baudelaire's *Fleurs du Mal*, and copy it into English. Readers across the Channel had not got wind of such perversities, so the style would shock them, and thus make a name for George Moore.[53] This whole picture of the writer's life – the society of the famous, the busy workday, the long hours of the night, the design to size up a literary state of affairs before contriving a scandalous novelty – all appealed to the young GM as the best of worldly wisdom.[54]

Under the inspiration of Lopez, GM got the idea that his own experience with Lewis and Alice might lend itself to dramatic treatment, something in the manner of a Restoration comedy, still popular in the late nineteenth century on the London stage. He had seen such plays there, but had no idea what a play looked like on paper until he bought Leigh Hunt's 1840 edition of Restoration drama.[55] It was possibly during the spring of 1874 that GM worked on his modern version of Wycherley and Congreve's cynical plays about literary rakes and ladies of every quality, all of them out for sex and money. Moore's three-act was called *Worldliness*; in the 1917 edition of *Confessions*, he recollected that it concerned Lewis's attempt "to marry his mistress to one of his friends."[56]

In *Vale*, Moore gave what looks like a rendition of the play's plot in the form of an autobiographical vignette. Lewis and Alice were, Moore wrote, tiring of one another, so Lewis offered Alice to GM. Her face "wore an odd smile," making GM think it might be her idea. Afterwards, he came to ask her to dine, and she said she would be a while, inviting him into her bathroom while she bathed. On stepping out of the bath, she struck many "picturesque attitudes," and GM, always the willing voyeur, discussed with her the various beauties of her body. He did not, however, make any move to take her in his arms, because he suspected that Lewis might have hidden himself somewhere behind a curtain. The scene is redolent of Restoration comedy, and of many a subsequent sex-farce.[57] It is the story of a young man from the country learning of the worldliness of beauty and desire, by standing between masculine and feminine, watching and afraid of being watched, unable to act.

Lopez did not think much of *Worldliness*,[58] but Moore's manservant appeared to be impressed by the play, though he may only have seen in it his ticket for a return to London. Once Moore had completed the last act, according to *Confessions*, Master George and William Molony gave up their rooms in the Hôtel de Russie and set off to find a London producer.[59]

4

When did George Moore leave Paris and his pursuit of *la bonne peinture* in order to return to London? From 1873 to 1880, there are not two dozen rock-solid dates concerning Moore's life. He wrote letters to his mother and uncle, but ordinarily he did not date them. Throughout his life, Moore kept none of the letters he received, except certain precious correspondences of an amatory nature; nearly all of the letters from the many famous authors and painters with whom he would one day correspond went into the wastepaper basket as soon as he had read them.[60] During his early life, Moore goes unmentioned in the extant correspondence of persons of note, not yet being himself a person of note. Contacted by Barrett Clark in the 1920s and Joseph Hone in the 1930s, both of them looking for biographical data on Moore in his Paris years, Léon Hennique (1851–1935), a naturalist author, vaguely recalled meeting Moore in the late 1870s at Manet's house, and again at Zola's, maybe once at Goncourt's. Another naturalist, GM's friend Paul Alexis (1847–1901), mentioned encountering Moore at Manet's studio. So toward the end of the decade Moore was at the center of French cultural life, but even then the French artists and writers were not watching him with the alertness of the cat before the mousehole, and they cannot tell us of him so well as he tells us of them.[61] It was during the Paris years that Moore gathered the experience of life out of which he would create his self as an author, but he is not independently traceable in any very thorough way within those years.[62] We must in large part find him where he is offered to us, in his many volumes of autobiography. That youthful being emerges as a figment of the ironic relationship between the unactualised self of the boy in the process of becoming, and the ever more assured incarnations of the endlessly reminiscent fictionaliser "George Moore." "Myself was the goal I was making for," as he himself states the paradox of identity, and the Self on show is all mirrors on mirrors.[63]

The very work under discussion, *Worldliness*, is recorded by I. A. Williams in a bibliography of 1921 as Moore's first publication "*Circa* 1874"; however, no single copy of this volume has come to light in all the decades during which avid collectors traded in old editions of George Moore's works.[64] Edwin Gilcher, Moore's superb bibliographer, reports that the offer of £100 in the October 1921 *London Mercury* failed to turn up a copy.[65] This complete absence of evidence does not, however, compel us to discredit GM's several accounts of the play or of his return to London to arrange for its publication in 1874.

5

Maurice Moore, after a spell with a military tutor, took his examinations to enter the Army Officer Corps in the spring of 1874, then paid an early June visit to George at the Hôtel de Russie.[66] Maurice recalled that the two brothers returned to England together by 15 June 1874, when George wrote from the family residence, 39 Alfred Place, Kensington, to his uncle and agent, Joe Blake in County Mayo, in order to say that he was desperately in need of money. He had to have £50 to pay at least some of what he owed. Staying in a Paris hotel for a year, treating Lopez and the Hawkins *ménage* to dinners and weekends in country inns, he had outrun his allowance.[67]

Moore recalls that he took his play to the Olympic Theatre but had a hard time getting past the stage door. He was told he would have to have his manuscript copied, with stage directions in red, before it could be considered, and this copy is possibly the only publication *Worldliness* received.[68]

It would have been reasonable for GM also to try the play on his old friend from Thurloe Square, Richard Maitland. Since early May 1874, Maitland had been involved in a production of Offenbach's *Vert-Vert* at St James's Theatre. This production, however, severely curtailed Maitland's future as a producer. The operetta concerned a romp of two hussars through a girls' school. Maitland danced the part of a hussar, and the chorus of thirty female students, advertised as specially imported from Naples, Paris, and London, were scantily attired. The Lord Chamberlain was called in to measure the skirts, and he required another inch in length, so Maitland advertised the "brilliant new bacchanalian finale, the *Piff Paff*," as being danced in costumes "designed by the Lord Chamberlain." By the time GM arrived in London, *Vert-Vert* had become a "successful riot," and Maitland had quietly been blackballed from any further appearances on the London stage by an embarrassed Lord Chamberlain.[69] *Worldliness* thus could not have been produced by Maitland in the West End even had he thought it worthy of production. Moore himself soon judged his first comedy as, in fact, a good subject spoiled by bad writing.[70]

Settled back into his mother's house, GM took a private studio, decorated it with tapestry hired from another artist, and brought in a few models. Next, he worked at the studio of Charles Lutyens, father of Sir Edwin, the famous architect.[71] According to Wilfrid Meynell's contemporary survey of English artists, Charles Lutyens was a fine draughtsman where a horse was concerned, having the masterful ability to "differentiate this year's Derby winner from last year's."[72] Moore did not last long at Lutyens's studio: he recalled gathering with the students of Victor Barthe to speak of the sudden death of the boy genius Oliver Madox Brown, who died on 5 November 1874. Without Brown's presence, this studio too lost its charm for GM.[73] It is surprising that there is no evidence that Moore had by this time met Arthur O'Shaughnessy, John Payne, Edmund Gosse, or William Michael Rossetti.[74] These London poets were all part of the Oliver Madox Brown circle in the early 1870s, and later in the decade they definitely came within Moore's own circle of literary acquaintance, but on this first return visit from Paris to London, GM evidently moved in another ambit.

Possibly, GM had not yet begun to think of himself as a writer and to search out the acquaintance of other writers. Maurice Moore told Hone that at this stage all GM's talk was of the stars of the music hall stage, not of literary composition or *la bonne peinture*.[75] Evidently, GM was playing the part of a "masher" with a French curl, a young man of fortune in smart clothes, who after some hours of sketching from the nude, would resort with his old friends the Maitlands to the music halls and the haunts of his adolescence, the Cremorne Gardens, with their fireworks over the Thames, hanging lanterns, polka band, and shady women. It is hard to see him with a walking stick and a toothpick, singing choruses of risqué songs with the other Champagne Charlies, but he was evidently not a serious character during this period in London.[76] The painter Dampier May once reminded Moore of a night passed in the Cremorne Gardens, and how Moore would encourage his companions to revelry, "pointing out that it was proper for men and women to make merry, and on occasion to occupy the same bed." At last, GM broke in on this tale, saying to Dampier May, "Don't you ever forget anything?"[77] He himself made a practice of forgetting most of his lengthy stay in London, which lasted from June 1874 to sometime in the summer of 1875 but carried him no closer to the goal of becoming himself, "George Moore," an artist of a distinctly personal stamp.

6

In an undated letter, probably of summer 1875, George wrote to his uncle and agent Joe Blake to explain his intention to make a second try at becoming a painter in Paris. His mother planned to give up her London house (and did so in 1876). GM claimed he could live by himself more cheaply in Paris than in London, and as he promised not to "buy a rig of any kind," far more cheaply than during his first French sojourn. Even as the new Moore of Moore Hall, he now knew he had to economise; he had not had a quid in his pocket for a month, he complained. Now wouldn't Joe be a good man and send him £35 a month, and he would be off for Paris before Christmas?[78]

Maurice Moore recalled visiting his brother in the Hôtel de Russie in August 1875. GM was again back at Julian's studio, working from eight to five, and by night talking of Balzac, a favorite of Rodolphe Julian's.[79] On this visit, Maurice met Lewis Welldon Hawkins, then "in low water"; Hawkins had taken a job painting on porcelain at a factory on the outskirts of Paris. For the atelier, this departure was a sad turn of affairs. According to *Vale*, GM soon returned to his old Paris haunts, now dressed to the nines as a "sort of minor Lewis."[80] Without William Molony, he felt liberated from conformity to all the conventions represented by his Irish valet, who would have resented brushing French trousers and hats.[81] Moore left the Hôtel de Russie and rented rooms at 61 rue Condorcet, a seven-story building constructed around a central courtyard, located only a few blocks east of Place Pigalle.

Fitted out with a new rig, Moore looked up Alice and Lewis. She had a lush apartment, paid for by an admirer. Lewis complained of not being able to pay fees for the Academy, or even the price of a train fare so that he might finish a landscape painting. So GM escorted him on trips to the Barbizon woods. They would be out all day, and return at night to talk of art, until Alice complained, "Where do I come in?" She headed off to the Bois de Boulogne to parade with the famous courtesans of Paris. Alice was struggling to move into the front rank. The two men assisted by escorting her to the *Folies Bergère* of an evening, then off to restaurants – all part of her career. Playing the part of pander and gigolo, Lewis confessed, embarrassed him, and this embarrassment shocked George: he thought that if he were lucky enough to be a true ponce, an *amant de coeur*, he would enjoy being treated frankly as one, swaggering unashamed as a man who never had to pay for it. At present, GM's role seemed to be that of the escort who picks up the bills but never becomes the object of desire.

It was in this pass, according to *Vale*, that Julian made a suggestion Moore at least later regarded as humiliating: GM should become the patron of Lewis Hawkins, who was already shamefacedly living off loans now from George, now from Alice.[82] Too embarrassed to say no, GM made an offer to Hawkins, who wasted no time finding a studio at 27 Galerie Feydeau, Passage des Panoramas, the same building that housed the Académie Julian. The studio was above an umbrella shop; it had no windows, but at least it had a glass ceiling.[83] Hawkins took up residence in the studio, and Moore went there to paint alongside his friend. It was from the studio that he wrote to his mother, telling her he could not return for Christmas; he was working too hard at his painting.[84]

The agreement was that Hawkins and Moore would both work hard at their art and make a general reformation. Presenting the resolution to Joe Blake in the fall of 1875, Moore wrote that he meant "to make up for the folly and foolishness of my life." If Blake would punctually send him £40 on the first of each month, GM thought he had a "good chance of succeeding in painting."[85] In the previous letter to Blake, written before his departure for Paris, Moore had asked for only £35, but if Lewis was costing him only an additional £5 a month, that was remarkable.

On 26 April 1876, GM reported to his mother on the progress of his art education. For three months he had been really working hard: "it was Hawkins who got me to do so." Now he knew that Uncle Jim Browne's work was "below contempt"; Charles Lutyens didn't know anything either. Her son was at last surely on the verge of achievement.[86] Yet apparently within a matter of weeks of writing his mother that success was within reach, Moore looked at the drawing he had been worrying over all day and was heart-stricken at "the black thing."[87] He put down his pencils in despair and left the studio. In *Conversations in Ebury Street*, Moore evoked the sense of loss at this moment: "Think, reader, what a shock it is for a man to leave one self without knowing that he can acquire another self. I shed tears, and the bitterest."[88]

7

In *Flowers of Passion* (1877), George Moore published "To a Lost Art," a sonnet about the collapse of his hopes to be a painter.[89] He addresses painting as the child of his heart, but also a mistress, one "Wooed long, – but never won," and still beloved, though he has "wed thy sister," Poetry. He promises to be faithful in his fashion to his first unfulfilled love:

> My dreams and secret thoughts will ever pour,
> Not gifts of tribute shells around thy feet,
> But love's sad offering of my impotence,
> A fruitless wave that can but kiss thy shore.

Moore appears in his sonnet as a perverse new kind of lover, not just unre-quited in his desires, but impotent, incestuous, and perhaps cunnilingual. This alarming self-presentation is not altogether the result of ineptitude running riot: it reflects both his real distress and a practiced artifice. Upon his return to Paris, he had not just wooed painting, Alice, and Lewis Welldon Hawkins. He had also sent himself back to school with Bernard Lopez, who directed him in a further course of reading in Baudelaire, Gautier, Catulle Mendès, and the French satanic aesthetes.

In a sequence of letters brilliantly concocted by Moore as a preface to his second play, *Martin Luther* (1879), he provides a prehistory for the play's invention. The style is, as Noel says, reminiscent and fantastic, authoritative if unscholarly, the sudden prefiguration of Moore's late manner of *mémoire fantaisie*.[90] Beneath the sports of GM's literary personality, there may be some biographical truth. According to GM's dating in *Martin Luther*, it was in November 1875, not many months after his return to Paris, that he took Lopez out for a dinner of oysters, Sauterne, and "the poularde financière."[91] Over cigars, Lopez spoke of how some subjects could be safely treated on stage in England and not in France, and vice versa. The lines of outrage were drawn differently in the two countries. It occurred to GM that one subject that would engage highly charged national taboos was the life of Martin Luther – impossible to stage in Catholic France, but quite the thing for Protestant England.

In a letter dated May 1876 by the *Martin Luther* preface, Moore proposes a collaboration with Lopez on an historical drama, though it is only in August 1876, after six letters of arch-playfulness, that the younger man confides that his subject is Martin Luther. Lopez, however, raises an obstacle. That subject might anger French priests and consequently upset the plans a nephew of

Lopez had to make a marriage of fortune into a Catholic family. GM claims that no sophisticated Catholic would now defend the persecution of the Albigensians; the plans of Lopez's nephew are safe.[92]

Lopez then raises a second objection in a letter dated January 1877 in the preface: the age of tragedy is long gone. Anyway, how could a "*romantique enragé*" like GM incite Lopez to the crime of a modern tragedy? GM retorts that surely, after reading his poems, "Sappho," "Hermaphroditus," and "The Metamorphoses of the Vampire," Lopez cannot think him a person to write something antique in style. He has read the pseudo-archaic verse plays of the English poets – Coleridge's *Remorse*, Wordsworth's *Borderers*, those by Scott, Byron, Browning, Tennyson, and Shelley. (A whole baccalaureate of study lies between the twenty-one-year-old George Moore entering the Académie Julian and the twenty-five-year-old George Moore under the tuition of Lopez.)[93] With the help of Lopez, Moore would return English poetry to the stage in a truly actable play. Lopez agrees to assist, and GM makes him promise to cast aside his religion and his fears about his nephew's marriage. He must speak as Luther would speak, and Luther "must be in the right . . . To art ecclesiasticism is as deadly as arsenic to the body."[94]

In a letter dated April 1877, Lopez reports that the marriage question has been resolved. His nephew gave up the Catholic heiress and married "Agatha," a Jewess, a really pretty girl . . . Lopez would like to offer Agatha his own love, but there are four problems: marriage is serious, she might not agree, he might not agree, and the husband might not agree. With marriage out of the way, Lopez is ready to meet his young Irish friend over breakfast for a *séance de collaboration*.[95]

8

The episode from the preface of *Martin Luther* concerning marriage schemes may not reflect the life of Bernard Lopez's nephew at all; instead, it may allude to events in Moore's own life during the same period – that is, after the defeat of his hopes as a painter in May or June 1876, and before the discovery of the true start of his life as a writer in early 1877. In the vaguely defined, undecided space between these two moments, Moore made a stumbling try at becoming a husband.

Moore's hunt for the hand of Mary de Ross Rose, an heiress from County Limerick, with cousins living on the Avenue Marcei, belongs to the Paris spring and summer in Boulogne, most likely during 1876.[96] In an undated letter to his mother, Moore asked her to get Joe Blake to send him money right away; he was in a fix, and his check had bounced. He was seeing the Roses constantly. In a second letter, written from the address of the Académie Julian, Moore declared that the chase was on: he needed all his mother's help. What could she find out about Miss Rose? "You have often spoken to me about marrying – well, now is the time . . . I have as we used to say in racing run up to the leaders. If I go to the front I will compromise myself. I really do not know how to proceed what am I to do if my family do not do something I am at a loss."[97] He had that evening escorted the Rose family to the Bois de Boulogne for a promenade; they let him walk ahead with Miss Rose, and she "evidently PERCEIVED MY GAME." What was to be done if he were accepted?

Mary de Ross Rose was not the first or only woman in Moore's life at the time. GM had climbed his way into high Parisian society, "the haut monde of the last empire . . . the most vicious and splendid in Paris," he boasted to his mother.[98] He was a guest at the mansion of Princess Rattazzi for her masked ball, a 60,000-franc fête. Princess Rattazzi, born Marie Wyse (1833–1902), was on her father's side a Waterford girl; her mother was the daughter of Lucien Bonaparte. Princess Rattazzi married three times: a rich Alsatian followed by an Italian politician, Urbain Rattazzi, and finally Louis de Rute, a complaisant Spaniard. She made a name for herself by writing novels that reminded Zola of those by Paul de Kock (in *Ulysses*, Molly Bloom's favorite writer), and had celebrated affairs with several minor French authors.[99] After the ball thrown by the Princess, Moore was astonished to find himself lucky enough to be loved. Assuming his mother would doubt it, GM assured Mrs Moore that he had been granted, in spite of his looks, "the most certain of all proofs" that a woman could love him. The woman in question cannot be identified, but she may have been Iza, Madame de Coëtlogon, known as Georgette. She lived in the Place des Vosges near the Marquise d'Osmond, another sophisticated woman to whose entertainments GM got himself invited, when he ascended from the level of Lewis Hawkins into the proper sphere of an Irish landlord. Madame de Coëtlogon, American by birth but utterly French in her manners, held GM's interest from this time until the mid-1880s by writing him witty, affectionate letters after his departure from Paris.[100]

But just because a lady of fashion had slept with him did not mean the Irish Catholic debutante would marry him – he realised this, he assured his mother. He also admitted his regret that he might be obliged to give up his mistress for a wife: "Heigh ho it makes one sad . . . I will marry for seven hundred thousand francs not a halfpenny less."[101] What he didn't yet know is whether Miss Rose had the equivalent of £28,000, or if she would think him a husband worth such a dowry.

The Rose family planned to vacation that summer in Boulogne. GM got himself invited to join the party of Princess Rattazzi headed for the same popular seaside town. Still, he could not quite find his way in such a courtship – "with all my experience . . . I am travelling over new ground" – and asked his "dear mama" to send his aunt to join him in Boulogne and grease the wheels of matrimony. At least, he begged, Mrs Moore could send a check.

Moore set off to spend the summer in the Imperial Hotel in Boulogne and left Hawkins behind in the Galerie Feydeau apartment, hoping he would have the grace to quit it when the quarter's lease was up.[102] Once Boulogne became "the seat of war" in his march for the hand of Miss Rose, he withdrew his forces before the end of the summer, having found out that the Irish heiress had only £800 a year: "I do not think that enough," he told Joe Blake.[103] The Rose family may not have thought enough of him either. They were reportedly worried when George's companions hailed him by the name of "Lucifer" Moore.[104] Furthermore, instead of his aunt being sent over from London to aid in his matrimonial campaign, help came in the form of his scampish younger brother Augustus, who assisted GM in running through his resources, so that the two had no money to pay for their rooms. Their baggage was impounded by the hotel manager until the Moore brothers succeeded in borrowing two sovereigns from another guest.[105] To judge from the sonnet "Summer on the Coast of Normandy," GM wrote verses in the intervals of his courtship. Some lines dote on the wind that blows through the fair fragrant hair of a woman who does not sound like Mary de Ross Rose. Later evidence points to Georgette Coëtlogon as the subject of the sonnet. Incidental verses inscribed to "G. C." in a copy of the 1881 *Pagan Poems* regret that she and GM may never "waltz again together/ Or bask in sun in brisk Boulogne/ In the pretty sunny weather."[106] The ultimate reason for the failure of Moore's marriage plans – silly as they were, his most determined attempts at matrimony for another twenty years – cannot be fully known. There were, as Lopez said of Agatha, four problems. Whether it was because he would not agree, because she would not agree, because her parents would not agree, or because marriage is a serious thing, GM returned to Paris unwed in the fall of 1876, and took up the pursuit of poetry and his verse drama.

9

According to *Vale*, GM, on his return from Boulogne, found Hawkins still in possession at the Galerie Feydeau studio. Moore took a tongue-lashing from the penniless artist for leaving him in an empty flat with no money for food. By rights, of course, it should have been Moore who was outraged. He owed Hawkins neither room nor board. In writing his memoirs, GM depicted the subsequent events as if they were an ordinary lovers' quarrel: GM moved out, broke off communication, then sought a reconciliation, and being the weaker of the two, asked forgiveness from the one who had wronged him. It was a sore test of Moore's aesthetic of shamelessness to have to tell this story. The man who always made GM realise that he was not handsome, not graceful, and not talented in painting, was invited to share the apartment at 61 rue Condorcet.[107]

Hawkins undertook its redecoration. When Moore came to describe the interior for the 1888 *Confessions of a Young Man*, he clearly added to its appointments some elements that he derived from Huysmans's *A Rebours* (1884). A truly bohemian bachelor suite, its drawing room was said to have been hung in a cloth of cardinal red, suspended from the ceiling like a tent, with Turkish couches and lamps for furniture. Another room was reportedly done up by Hawkins as a decadent shrine, with a Buddhist temple, a statue of Apollo, and a bust of Shelley on the altar. GM claims to have kept three pets: a parrot, a white Angora cat and a python; elsewhere, it is two cats, one called Blanchette, the other Blancblanc.[108] Exotically decorated apartments were in style among French painters, and they were regularly written up in newspapers by visiting reporters. The description of the habitation in *Confessions* is a literary fantasy, but that is not to say the two men did not dwell in a comparably fantastic apartment.

After Hawkins decorated the apartment, he turned to its owner, and gave GM some tips about how to make a more attractive impression. Since GM's chin "deflected," as Moore later preferred to say, Hawkins thought a beard would strengthen his profile.[109] Moore was told that he needed to practice being more nonchalant; women were said by Hawkins to like that. Moore did his best, grew a rather faint beard, and thereafter attempted to attract women by pretending to be unattracted to them. Finally, the two men settled their respective roles: Moore was henceforth the poet, and Hawkins remained the painter.

10

Nearly all Moore's acquaintances from the early 1870s in Paris were of English-speaking parentage: Lewis Hawkins, Alice Howard, Bernard Lopez, John O'Leary, Madame de Coëtlogon, Princess Rattazzi, and Elizabeth Gardner (American wife of William-Adolphe Bouguereau, and now and then, GM stated, his own mistress).[110] How did Moore finally acquaint himself sufficiently with Paris, the French language, and the society of intellectuals, to become a witness, an echo, and to some degree a participant in one of the great creative moments of European art? In one of his accounts of his success, he makes it appear as if he had finally touched a single button which opened a secret panel into the hidden passages of a *palais* in the heart of Paris.

One evening during Moore's collaboration with Bernard Lopez on *Martin Luther*, the story goes, the two were dining at the Rat Mort at 7 Place Pigalle. It was here that in 1872 Rimbaud had sliced the wrist of Verlaine, and a female habituée still bragged of having once slept with Baudelaire.[111] At dinner, Lopez introduced Moore to Villiers de l'Isle Adam (1838–89), one of the most exotic personalities in bohemian Paris. Villiers claimed to be by birth a prince of the Holy Roman Empire, a grandee of Spain, a count twenty-two times over, and a Knight of Malta.[112] At present, however, he lived from hand to mouth, while seeking to arrange a dynastic marriage, or perhaps a marriage with an American "afflicted with a dowry of several millions."[113] Villiers, hearing that Moore was an English poet, suggested that he get to know Stéphane Mallarmé, also a poet. Mallarmé was interested in things English: he taught English in school, and wrote monthly notes on Paris literary news for the London *Athenaeum*. GM recounted how he followed up Villiers's sugges- tion, and came to Mallarmé's apartment in rue de Rome for a Tuesday "At Home." Offering his host the gift of *Flowers of Passion*, Moore received in return Mallarmé's *L'Après-midi d'un faune*, illustrated by Manet – hardly a fair trade for the Frenchman.[114] Thereafter, Moore says he was a faithful visitor each Tuesday, and soon knew not only Villiers and Mallarmé, but José-Maria Heredia, the Comte de Montesquiou (des Esseintes in Huysmans's *A Rebours*), Catulle Mendès, and Augusta Holmes, an Irish composer and the mistress of Mendès. Before GM had time to realise it, he was "launched on Parisian literary and artistic society." Within six months, he concludes, Manet would be talking with him, and saying, "There is no Englishman who occupies the posi- tion you do in Paris."[115]

Such was the story as Moore told it in his memoirs. Did this rapid-fire sequence of events occur, and if so when did it occur? If the first time Moore met Mallarmé, he brought him *Flowers of Passion*, it would have had to be after November 1877, and that would confine GM's period of being in the swim of Parisian intelligentsia to the last two years of his French sojourn. However, other evidence suggests that Moore's story of the trade of *Flowers of Passion* for *L'Après-midi d'un faune* is an ironic fiction. Jean Noël, Moore's French biog- rapher, detected in GM's many recollections of Mallarmé certain clues that can be corroborated by other documents, and these clues bracket the meeting between December 1875 and March 1876.[116]

A key piece of evidence for a date in these months is to be found in a letter GM wrote to Gosse on 2 December 1912 for inclusion as an appendix to his *Life of Algernon Swinburne*. Moore describes a correspondence between Mallarmé and Swinburne. Setting the scene, GM writes that he had begun to attend Mallarmé's weekly "At Home" at his 87 rue de Rome address (where Mallarmé moved in the fall of 1875). Mallarmé not yet being a celebrity, the French schoolteacher-poet and the Irish landlord-artist sometimes spent the evening alone together. One night Mallarmé showed GM a French poem in manuscript which Swinburne had submitted for publication in Mallarmé and Catulle Mendès's new journal *La République des lettres* (launched in December 1875).[117] These verses were amended by Mallarmé at Swinburne's invitation, but Moore recalled that the emendation "drew from Swinburne at least three voluminous epistles," written out in a shaky hand on blue foolscap paper, partly concerning Mallarmé's query about the term "l'orme" (the elm). Swinburne also poured out a torrent of commentary on a compliment a Frenchman had offered to his verses, as "les efforts géants d'un barbare." Swinburne did not believe that his French verses were those of a barbarian.[118]

That letter exists: it was written by Swinburne from Holmwood, Henley- on-Thames, on 5 February 1876. In it Swinburne pens an excitable paragraph in schoolboy French (but the French of a brilliant schoolboy) about the "unhappy word . . . *l'orme.*" In place of the confusing verses about the elm, Swinburne supplies three different variants all ending in *l'amour*, which translated would read:

> Where the naked foot of love set itself down . . .
> The fiery trace of the naked foot of love . . .
> The lost (or bloody) feet of fugitive love . . .[119]

It was to these naked, fiery, and fugitive feet that GM was asked by Mallarmé to apply his native intuitions of what Swinburne may possibly have had in mind, while the young Irish landlord sat in the apartment on the rue de Rome, on an evening after 5 February 1876, an evening he recalled with amazing precision thirty-six years later for Edmund Gosse. It was memorable as the day of his entry to the councils of his gods. "I was ignorant, of course," he admitted, "but I was already George Moore with something to say for myself though I did not know how to say it."[120]

Upon meeting Mallarmé, GM came into the acquaintance of the co-editor of *La République des lettres*, Catulle Mendès (1842–1909), formerly the son-in-law of Théophile Gautier, and now the lover of the composer Augusta Holmes (1847–1903).[121] In *Vale* Moore says Mendès invited him to the apartment he shared with Holmes in the rue Mansard: "he takes you by the arm . . . he leans towards you, his words are caresses, his fervour is delightful, and listening to him is as sweet as drinking a fair perfumed wine. All he says is false – the book he has just read, the play he is writing, the woman who loves him . . ."[122] Moore admired the personal style of Mendès sufficiently to make a literal translation of the French poet's "La Sérénade," without mentioning the name of the author when he published it.[123] Mendès was the epitome of the Parisian man of letters, a man with a mistress, a journal, and entrée into every fashionable salon. GM followed the deceitful, elegant indecencies of Mendès in the hope that this path might lead to a similar status in life.

Through Villiers, Mallarmé, Holmes, and Mendès, GM learned about the celebrated soirées at the house of Nina de Villiard (1843–84).[124] She was a poet, painter, and actress (an amateur at all these arts), and an accomplished pianist. Nina was a republican at the time of the Commune, a hostess of considerable income, and a great friend of Manet (who painted her portrait, *La Dame aux éventails*, in 1873). GM remarked that her passion was particularly excited by failures, but this was a piece of sarcastic literary and artistic criticism. Her lovers were accomplished men: poet Charles Cros, novelist Anatole France, Impressionist painter Franc-Lamy, and possibly Villiers de l'Isle Adam.[125] In the 1870s and early 1880s, she had a small *hôtel* with a garden in the rue de Moines, hidden away behind the Boulevard de Clichy, where she lived surrounded by artists and pets, including a monkey, parrots, dogs, squirrels, many cats, and according to GM, even an alligator, a brood of badgers, and a sleeping bear. Edmond Goncourt described her parties as beginning around dinnertime when a coterie of hungry young men of rebellious mind turned up, maddened with all the debaucheries of thought, twitching with paradoxes and aesthetics even more subversive, overexcited by Nina, the muse of flippant dementia.[126]

Moore says he came only once to Nina's. The particular party Moore attended resembles one described by Paul Alexis for Zola in a letter of 25 July 1877.[127] Moore's developing and continuously revised memory of "Ninon's Table d'Hôte," as published first in an 1890 issue of the *Hawk*, and expanded by 1906 in *Memoirs of My Dead Life* (revised in 1907, 1915, 1920, and 1928), seems partly to have been constructed in imitation of and competition with the many prior literary accounts of Nina's parties, including ones by Goncourt, Georges Duval, Catulle Mendès, Paul Alexis, and especially Villiers de l'Isle Adam.[128]

The account of Nina's party Moore first gave in an 1890 issue of his brother's weekly, the *Hawk*, may partly originate as a counterattack on Villiers for publishing in *Gil Blas* his own memoir, "Une Soirée chez Nina," with its sardonic mockery of a certain Englishman at the party.[129] No one wants the intruder there, and Mallarmé and Mendès make sport of "this brilliant individual" by means of mystifying paradoxes. The "Englishman" asks if they rhyme for the eye or for the ear, and is told, "for the odor." Eventually, he begs of Leconte de Lisle, "Are they serious?" Realising at last that he is being insulted, he takes his leave with British stiffness. Did GM see himself as the unwelcome British guest in Villiers's story? It is possible, because while Moore's own account of Nina's party shares a few details with that of Villiers, it also includes sentences offensive to the honor of the poet who claimed to be a count twenty-two times over and a grandee of Spain. For instance, after describing Nina's mansion, her person, her garden, and her animals, GM arrives at Villiers, and gossips that Villiers, having once been the lover of Nina, now took advantage of her hospitality. Charged with being a free-loader, Villiers snaps, "All that fuss for a few cutlets!" In the first 1890 *Hawk* version of the party, GM makes Villiers turn up in the middle of dinner, his collar buttonless, and say proudly that he has already dined: "Fortunately for him the statement was not believed," GM quips.[130] In the later *Memoirs of My Dead Life* editions of the story (1906 and after), young Moore tries to pick up the wife of a businessman by retelling a tale Villiers had never published ("every year he gets less and less of himself onto paper"), and thus in effect Moore presents himself as a successful inheritor of the spirit of Villiers.[131] The animosities about Villiers may originate in the older George Moore's recollections of the pain of the young George Moore's first awkward entries into *la vie bohème*, and the restoration of his pride through the ability he has at last acquired (with every year getting more and more of himself onto paper) to rise with narrative ease in mockery of both himself and his mockers.

I I

It would be a mistake to accept GM's account of his magically sudden entrance into relations of artistic sympathy and equal esteem with the Parnassian poets, realist novelists, and Impressionist painters of Paris. There was a series of doors, one after another, with a longer chain of introductions, staggered over the last three years of his time in Paris. After meeting Mallarmé prior to February 1876, he followed Lopez's curriculum for writing outrageous Baudelairean verse, took his weekly tutorial from Mallarmé, and apparently aped the mannerisms of Catulle Mendès, doing his best to be a satanic, super-aesthetic, and sophisticated poet.[132] His sympathies at this stage were incoherent and in transition: Parnassian in verse, Balzacian and anti-naturalist in fiction, and still Beaux-Arts academic in painting, though he was having his first encounters with the new fiction and painting. Mallarmé was an old friend of Zola, and in late 1875 he was trying to arrange for English publicity for Zola's *Son Excellence Eugène Rougon* through his contact at the *Athenaeum* (Arthur O'Shaughnessy). Mallarmé would have talked about Zola to Moore, especially after *La République des lettres* assumed serialisation of *L'Assommoir* from July 1876 to January 1877.[133] GM read a few installments, but the scales did not fall from his eyes. He at first thought Zola's naturalist fiction "ridiculous, abominable," "only because it is characteristic of me to instantly form an opinion and assume at once a violent attitude."[134] In early 1877 he certainly was not of the party of naturalist writers – J. K. Huysmans, Paul Alexis, Henri Céard, Léon Hennique, and Guy de Maupassant – who used to dine together regularly at Chez Joseph in the rue Condorcet, just down the street from Moore's apartment.[135]

In early 1877 Moore had not yet acquired that taste in modern French painting for which he later became famous. Even while composing his epistolary preface for *Martin Luther*, he lets stand a February 1877 letter claiming that Cabanel and Bouguereau have painted better pictures of the Virgin than Raphael, and these high academic French painters were abusive of, and hated by, the Impressionists.[136] In April 1877 he accompanied Hawkins to the Third Impressionist Exhibition held at 6 rue Peletier, the best and most coherent of all eight Impressionist shows. There were 16 Cézannes, 25 paintings by Degas, 30 by Monet, 21 by Renoir – 241 works in all by the leading artists of the new school.[137] Moore and Hawkins stood in front of Monet's *The Turkeys*, and laughed: "Just look at the house! Why, the turkeys couldn't walk in at the door. The perspective is all wrong."[138] Moore and Hawkins, like many others who came to scoff, had an academic knowledge of perspective, composition, and anatomy that kept them from understanding, or forgiving, painters who were eager to sacrifice the art of schools for new effects of light, new arrangements of tradition, and new openness to modern urban experience.

By the summer of 1877, "Poet" Moore had finished a sufficient number of verses to go to London to find a publisher.[139] He carried a letter from Mallarmé introducing him to Arthur O'Shaughnessy (1844–81), poet, illegitimate son of the novelist Lord Lytton, and British Museum expert on reptiles. Mallarmé himself had been welcomed in London by a number of young English poets in August 1875.[140] As an English teacher, and the most hospitable of men, Mallarmé was sensible of his role as a conductor of influences between French and English aestheticisms, a cross-Channel traffic in aesthetic trends that was to become GM's own stock-in-trade.[141] Mallarmé's article on "The Impressionists and Edouard Manet" was published in the 30 September 1876 issue of the *Art Monthly*. O'Shaughnessy served as Mallarmé's connection with George Robinson, editor of *Art Monthly*, in arranging for the English publication of this important early statement of the new movement.[142] Now in the summer of 1877, on Mallarmé's recommendation, O'Shaughnessy befriended Moore, helped him find a publisher, and introduced him around.

Evidently, O'Shaughnessy put Moore in touch with the lawyer and poet John Payne and the animal artist J. T. Nettleship (all three men had been the lover of the unfortunate Mrs Snee, literary wife of a commercial traveler).[143] Moore also met Edmund Gosse, another young London poet of French taste, in the circle of Ford Madox Brown and the Rossettis. All of these young London poets worshiped Swinburne, and behind Swinburne, Baudelaire. O'Shaughnessy's introductions included one to the household of the editor George Robinson. Moore was impressed by the scholarly daughters of the editor, Mary and Mabel, then nineteen and eighteen years old. They recall him as a young man of twenty-four with a "pretty blond beard" and a black velvet coat that set off his hair, the color of which called to mind the wild jonquil, "pale yellow without the least tint of red," falling over an absolutely white, high, and bulging forehead. His "first follies" seemed to have passed, and he was seriously in pursuit of Art and Beauty.[144] These observant sisters were to be among his lifelong friends.

A final piece of London business may also have originated with Mallarmé. GM sought out the popular publisher William Tinsley to propose an English translation of Zola's *La Curée*. At the end of his life, GM recalled meeting the bibulous editor in the bar of the Gaiety Theatre, and following him across Catherine Street to the offices of Tinsley Brothers, Publishers. There Moore explained to Tinsley that in Paris the novelist with the biggest trade subscription was Emile Zola. Tinsley in his turn explained to Moore that in London things were a bit different from Paris: the circulating libraries controlled the market in fiction, usually published in three volumes at high prices, and by subscription. The 600 or so copies were stocked in reading shops, where ordinary middle-class readers borrowed novels from Mudie's Select Library for a fee. And the circulating libraries, Tinsley feared, would take objection to Zola's book, "especially if there were a divorce, or a woman living apart from her husband, or a husband living apart from his wife." The "Select" in the title of Mudie's Select Library was meant to guarantee readers with a yearly subscription that they would be supplied only with novels chosen for their morality.[145] GM supposed that as a businessman, Tinsley would like this censorship to be smashed, but Tinsley doubted there were many novelists with the strength to do that. Certainly, no London publisher would risk publishing Zola and thereby offending the *pudibonderie nationale*.[146] So Moore returned to Paris without a contract for a Zola translation, but with ideas about the English fiction market and an agreement to have his first collection of poems published.[147]

12

That autumn Provost & Co. of Covent Garden brought out *Flowers of Passion* in black cloth with a cover design of skull and crossbones, laid over a lyre with broken strings.[148] It is not unfair to judge the book by its cover, or to assume that the title is taken from the more famous *Fleurs du mal*. The poems are confections of morbid, exotic, French decadence. Jean Noël has traced with impressive patience the various thefts from Baudelaire, Gautier, and especially Catulle Mendès. Sometimes the ineptitude is so rich that one suspects that GM was up to a game, as if going to a masquerade ball dressed as "Lucifer Moore." There are sonnets in the voice of a suicide, a prostitute, and a pair of half-believing lovers in a church. An unacknowledged translation of Catulle Mendès's "Succube" appears in Pre-Raphaelite diction ("List well," it begins), as well as a plain pastiche of Baudelaire in "Ode to a Dead Body," with the rhyme:

> Poor shameful lips! That never knew a kiss
> Of innocence, I wis.

One cannot find fault with Noël's assessment: in seeking to follow Gautier's ambition to celebrate love in words that would scorch the page, Moore spoke only with a juvenile and ridiculous violence of expression.[149] GM did not really have the weary, desiccated sensations appropriate to such poetry. His own force of nature and love of lively tomfoolery turned the whole project into a carnival.

Still, it is tempting to see the agony of Moore's Paris period of undecided sexuality finding expression in the imitations of Swinburne, such as "The Hermaphrodite," "Laus Veneris," and "The Triumph of Time."[150] The book is enthusiastically and polymorphously perverse. There are straightforward references to incest, necrophilia, cunnilingus, lesbianism, and the drowning of a woman-lover. In "Hendecasyllables," for example, Carmen and Eliane in the "absolute love time" say: it is that time of day, let us go into the garden together and get away from men; they are false anyway; we will find some place where there's a bed and lots of flowers; then let's have sex.[151] It is no wonder that Edmund Yates warned readers of the 28 November 1877 *World* not to leave the book lying around the house; he recommended it be "burnt by the common hangman, while its writer was being whipped by the cart's tail."[152] While androgyny and homosexuality were fashionable in Paris, and in a prosodically sophisticated Swinburnean form could pass as tolerable in London, GM's more gauche projections, his cheerfully enthusiastic imitation perversities, were assailed as "dirty, emasculate, loathsome." The reviewer in *Truth*, finding GM's collection among volumes of Christmas garlands like *Our Little Sunbeam's Picture Book*, would only say that its publication was "an insult to society."[153] The *Examiner* almost caught the spirit of the volume when it concluded that the author tried his best to be disgusting, but only succeeded in being ridiculous. This reviewer, however, had not reckoned on the possible value of one who was good at being ridiculous.[154]

Moore's reaction to the reception of his first publication evolved over the weeks. A visitor to 61 rue Condorcet found that Moore had "taken to his bed in protest," with the sheets pulled over his head.[155] Moore sought advice from Alice Meynell, the Catholic poet: should he challenge Edmund Yates to a duel? Come over to London to horsewhip him? That might lead to damages in court. By the way, he concluded, could Alice find a magazine that would publish the enclosed poem? He got an answer not from Alice, but from her husband Wilfrid, saying that GM should have burned that poem.[156] Moore read "A une Poitrinaire" to friends – the story of a poet-lover who falls in love with a tubercular beloved, watches the flesh fall from her emaciated body, buries her, digs her up, and then, in the climax, eats the worms that eat her. At this last detail his friends got up and threw him down the stairs.[157] Understandably, he was temporarily discouraged at the reception of his first book. Around the end of January 1878, when all the reviews were in, he laid them before his mentor, Bernard Lopez. Sitting in the Café Madrid, Lopez, though accustomed to violent reviews, was impressed by the force and unanimity of these denunciations. He concluded there really must be something to his young acolyte. Only then was Lopez prepared to get down to business on the long-mulled-over *Martin Luther*.[158]

13

Writing Joe Blake in February 1878 for help with a debt warrant, Moore had recovered his spirits sufficiently to describe his "little volume of poems" as having "made quite a little success. I was terribly abused for immorality but not for bad writing."[159] He happily inscribed a dedication copy of the book to "Fluffie" on 11 February 1878; another copy was laid "Aux pieds de Jenny"; and a third he offered to "Miss Fox" as a souvenir.[160] GM already had forty or fifty pages of verse toward a second volume of poetry, with the provisional title, "Roses of Midnight." His main task, however, was to turn Lopez's plot outline for *Martin Luther* into his own English blank verse.

As he occupied himself through 1878 with *Martin Luther*, the *demi-monde* of Jennies and Fluffies, and what he called the "three-quarter world" of Madame Rattazzi and Madame de Coëtlogon,[161] he may also at this time have first entered into the acquaintance of Paul Alexis, a chubby, good-humored Paris journalist, and one of the "Soirée of Medan" who made up the school of Zola. In August 1878, Alexis wrote Zola, then at his new home in Medan, the news from Paris. Alexis was writing an article about the parties of Nina de Villiard, dining at the home of Madame Rattazzi, meeting other naturalists for Sunday lunches at Chez Joseph on the rue Condorcet, and spending some evenings at the Café Nouvelle Athènes in Place Pigalle, where he listened to Edouard Manet, Camille Pissarro, and Edmond Duranty debate the politics of Parisian art.[162] Alexis's particular social round intersected with that of Moore. GM was also acquainted with Madame Rattazzi and Nina de Villiard, and, while he was not yet one of the clique of naturalist novelists, Moore probably had by now found his way to the Café Nouvelle Athènes, immediately across the street from the Café Rat Mort (where, with Bernard Lopez, he had met Villiers) and only a few blocks west of his apartment building in rue Condorcet.[163] Over the years Alexis was to become Moore's *bon ami*, his new *collaborateur*, and his continuing contact with French writers.

In December 1878 GM was in London staying at Morley's Hotel, seeking a publisher for *Martin Luther*, and working on the French stanzas of the "Ode Dédicace" to Swinburne, whom Moore addressed as "Pindar britannique," "moderne Sophocle," and "Shelley resuscité." The play itself is wooden, awkward, and, in spite of Moore's declared intention, undramatic. It covers Luther's life from his visit to Rome as a youthful priest, through his debate at the Diet of Worms, his love for Catherine Bora, the struggle with the peasant revolt, then a struggle with a daughter in revolt (she wishes to join a nunnery), to his death, through five acts and seventeen scenes, involving a cast of miners, Anabaptists, the population of Eisleben, flocks of monks and nuns, etc. The cast and scenes would require an enormous investment from a producer. If *Martin Luther* is an even worse play than the *Flowers of Passion* is a book of poetry, its preface is sometimes evocative of the particular talent for which Moore would one day be known.

In his December letter to Lopez from Morley's Hotel (printed in the preface), Moore gives a vaudevillean account of his journey from Paris to London by way of Calais. On the train, he is glad to find a lady and her maid coming into his cabin, which he also shares with a Scotchman. After playing with "Fanny," the lady's cat, Moore recollects that this is a woman to whom he once made love during a visit to Marlow.

> And the worst and the most of this is
> That neither is most to blame
> For you have forgotten my kisses
> And I have forgotten your name.

In the ensuing conversation, Moore makes an observation regarding the lady which causes the Scotchman to jump up in defense of her honor. The

Scotchman leaves the train during a rest stop, and GM takes the opportunity to make a more directly indecent proposal to the woman, who, just before shouting for the guard, suddenly recalls his face: "Marlow! . . . Can it be? Is it possible?" – and she is in his arms. Once on the Calais/Dover steamer, she proposes spending the voyage on deck. George Moore was always a poor sailor. Still, he follows her above. Things seem to be going all right. She asks him to tell her once more how much he loves her. As he opens his mouth, he loses his dinner over the rail. Thus, at the curtain of this little romance, "Love is dead. Love is dead." The letter then shifts gear to recount a dream in which Shakespeare and then Richard Brinsley Sheridan appear to Moore, asleep in Morley's Hotel. The two great English playwrights lament the current state of English literature: the lyric and the novel have improved, but the drama is in poor condition. In rhyming couplets, Sheridan asks why there are no English comedies any more:

> Society, has it no tender horns
> To walk upon? Do husbands carry horns
> No more? I heard, indeed, a vague report
> That something called Divorce has cut them short.
> Is vice stamped out, and do you go to church,
> And flog your sinning bodies with the birch?
> Are drunkenness and prostitution dead
> And human nature now quite perfected?
> If such be not the case, why, why then not
> Write comedies as I did? Where are thought
> And wit?

The letter mixes genres, aims to shock, and exploits the oddities of Moore's personality in a way the drama itself could not. He is literate and vulgar by turns, juvenile and philosophical, conscious that "the serious is always . . . inextricably mixed with the comic," and a satirist who finds his best butt in himself.[164] But it would be years before GM realised that the matter of the preface really ought to be the subject of a book by which he should be judged as an artist, and the matter of the play (highly schooled, ambitious of respect) was merely prefatory to his real career as a writer.

While in London, GM was invited to the home of William Michael Rossetti (brother of the poets Christina and Dante Gabriel Rossetti) for a dinner with "my friends, the lyric poets" – presumably O'Shaughnessy, Gosse, Payne, and perhaps the blind Philip Bourke Marston (1850–87).[165] He read them a scene from *Martin Luther*; they falsely assured him he "would find but little difficulty in getting the play produced."[166]

Once GM had finished his "Ode Dédicace," he tried to present his respects to his hero Swinburne, who was living in London during the winter of 1879, his last before Theodore Watts kept him under permanent homecare in the Pines, Putney. At this stage, if Swinburne's friends did not prevent him, he would seize tumblers of spirits off the dinner table and "suck . . . in the liquid with a sort of fiery gluttony . . . violently opening and shutting his eyelids"; he might also pursue a mad crush on a young boy of the streets.[167] It was William Michael Rossetti who gave Moore the address in Great James Street. In his supplement to Gosse's Swinburne biography, Moore describes how thirty-four years earlier he had walked up to the first floor of the old house:

> and . . . began to wonder on which floor Swinburne lived; thinking to see a clerk engaged in copying entries into a ledger I opened a door and found myself in a large room in which there was no furniture except a truckle bed. Outside the sheets lay a naked man, a strange little impish body it was, and about the head, too large for the body, was a great growth of red hair. The fright this naked man caused me is as vivid in me today as if it had occurred yesterday, possibly more vivid. I had gone to see Swinburne, expecting to find a man seated in an arm-chair reading a book, one who would probably ask me if I smoked cigarettes or cigars, and who would talk to me about Shelley. I had no idea what Swinburne's appearance was like, but there was no doubt in my mind that the naked man was Swinburne. How I knew it to be Swinburne I cannot tell. I felt that there could be nobody but Swinburne who would look like that, and he looked to me like a dreadful caricature of myself. The likeness was remarkable, at first sight; if you looked twice I am sure it disappeared. We were both very thin, our hair was the same colour, flaming red; Swinburne had a very high forehead and I had a very high forehead, and we both had long noses, and though I have a little more chin than Swinburne, mine is not a prominent chin. It seemed to me that at the end of a ball, coming downstairs at four o'clock in the morning, I had often looked like the man on the bed, and the idea of sitting next to that naked man, so very like myself, and explaining to him that I had come from William Michael Rossetti, frightened me nearly out of my wits. I just managed to babble out, "Does Mr. Jones live here?" The red head shook on a long thin neck like a tulip, and I heard, "Will you ask downstairs?" I fled and jumped into a hansom, and never heard of Swinburne again until he wrote to Philip Bourke Marston a letter about *A Mummer's Wife*.[168]

This is *Moorisme* in its final phase of development, the period of his greatest memoir, *Hail and Farewell*.[169] In the outing of Swinburne, Moore figures as in a mirror his own self-exposure. The presence of the homosexual body evokes from within his own body his secret homosexuality and his utter panic at its presence, but the whole recognition scene is viewed by an older, more worldly Moore who has come to terms with the beauty of all that is odd in nature, and expects other men, similarly sophisticated and worldly, to be able to laugh along with him at George Moore, Algernon Charles Swinburne, and themselves.

After a closet in Great James Street was opened and quickly closed, Moore turned his attention to finding an actor-manager to put on *Martin Luther*. Henry Irving had already achieved fame, and Moore had him in mind for the lead.[170] Irving was on tour in the provinces, but GM tracked him to a hotel in Liverpool, approaching the great actor at his breakfast table. Irving tended to regard authors of modern plays as ranking somewhat above stagehands and equal to scene painters in the general staff hierarchy of a West End playhouse; receiving an unknown and uninvited author at breakfast time, "peddling his wares," was a gross breach of etiquette. Irving rejected the play out of hand.[171] This was an insult Moore would remember – he may have been a fledgling playwright, but he was an Irish landlord too, not to be snubbed by some middle-class mummer.

14

Back in Paris, Moore provided another progress report to his mother, still at Moore Hall. Paris now seemed to him "so like my own home that I am startled when something or someone reminds me I am a stranger":

> I go into the frenchest of french society – houses where an Englishman is never heard of. I dine twice a week generally at the Princesse de la Temoille and at her most select dinners, dinners of eight ten or twelve. The other day I was very pleased for a lady told me the princesse said that my manners were absolute perfect. I was both pleased and astonished for it is astonishing that it should be so; I can scarcely credit the low society that I have so much cultivated has not soiled me. Sometimes if I get away early I go to a low artists cafe, where, with my two elbows on the beer stained table I scream the beastliest and slangiest french to groups of bohemians. There is such an abysme between the two that I often think "If the princesse saw me now she would never believe me to be the same man who three hours before was talking across her dinner table." I have studied the art of conversation a great deal lately; it is extraordinary what there is to learn and how much all that has to be cultivated . . . life [in the time of Louis XVI] was really worth living, how charming it must have been never to meet anybody but ladies and gentlemen. It is a terrible fast society but people are fast as the Pompadour's were fast vice in silk and with good manners is better than virtue in common dress and ill-bread . . . I am playing my cards now to be the lover of the marquise d'Osmond, she is very swell but not very young but I don't mind (I mean the latter). The first thing a young man who wants to get on in Paris must do is to get under the wings of some lady with a good name and in a high position. That done with tact he can wriggle himself anywhere.[172]

GM added in this letter that he had called on his father's old friend (and his own former guardian) Lord Sligo, leaving a copy of *Martin Luther*; but that there were two other Irishmen with whom he did not aim to keep company: his country cousin Arthur Blake O'Conor (1855–?) and Reverend John Burke, Professor of Moral Theology at the Irish College in Paris ("a kind old man, but . . . it was too

5. Café Nouvelle Athènes, rue Pigalle; postcard.

absurd"). On the whole, he preferred to cultivate either the French nobility or the crowd at that "low artists cafe," the Café Nouvelle Athènes.

Everyone has seen the Café Nouvelle Athènes: it turns up again and again in the paintings of Manet and Degas. In Manet's *The Artist* (1875) the model in the slouch hat with a loose white tie, Marcellin Desboutin, has just stepped from this café – he was a regular at a sidewalk table.[173] Ellen Andrée, the student posed by Degas with a louche Desboutin sitting at a table in *Absinthe*, was another habituée. She was described by a contemporary paper in artists' slang as a "cocodette" with plenty of "chien," an air of urban sass she didn't have to put on but wore naturally, the perfect Parisienne in the eyes of Montmartre. She also appears on the canvases of Henri Gervex, Renoir, Alfred Stevens, and Manet, who once posed her, like Degas, in front of the Café Nouvelle Athènes (*The Plum*).[174] To this café, Manet came daily, as did Degas, Renoir less frequently, Pissarro when in town, and Monet now and then.[175]

This café became George Moore's "academy of fine arts": "I did not go to Oxford or Cambridge, I went to the Café Nouvelle Athènes." He remembered it with the intensity of an old boy's love for his alma mater nearly ten years later when he wrote *Confessions of a Young Man*:[176]

> With what strange, almost unnatural clearness do I see and hear, – see the white face of that cafe, the white nose of that block of houses, stretching up to the Place, between two streets. I can see down the incline of those two streets, and

I know what shops are there; I can hear the glass-door of the cafe grate on the sand as I open it. I can recall the smell of every hour. In the morning that of eggs frizzling in butter, the pungent cigarette, coffee and bad cognac; at five o'clock the fragrant odour of absinthe; and soon after the steaming soup ascends from the kitchen; and as evening advances, the mingled smells of cigarettes, coffee, and weak beer. A partition, rising a few feet or more over the hats, separates the glass front from the main body of the cafe. The usual marble tables are there, and it is there we sat and aestheticized until two o'clock in the morning.

Moore goes on, both here and in other collections of memoirs written later in life, to recall the fascinating characters he encountered at the Café Nouvelle Athènes – Ernest Cabaner (1833–81), for instance, "child of the pavement, of strange sonnets, and stranger music," who believed that in order to render the effect of silence three military bands would be required. When GM showed him the poetry he had been writing, Cabaner sadly commented, "My dear Moore, you always write about love, the subject is nauseating." Cabaner would aestheticise until the café closed. And day by day, Moore learned also to *aestheticise*, a form of enjoyment for which there is no common English word. One did not just talk about art; one speculated. One invented the idea of works of art that did not yet exist; one sought for a description of all existing works of art that showed their limits, and proved that the existent was not everything; there were other worlds to make. In aestheticising, paradox and aphorism were the preferred elements of composition. For example, Cabaner's bland witticism – "Mon père était un homme dans le genre de Napoléon 1er, mais plus fort, plus fort" – illustrates his own personal style of aphorism. As a person belonging to no known social group, living on the streets, to say that his father was a man the like of Napoleon, only more so, more so, is not just a comic exaggeration, but an elegant and utterly French joke upon himself.[177] Such an aphorism is a model for the *Moorisme*, that "violent rhetoric of mingled self-assurance and self-mockery peculiar to [GM's] vision."[178]

Sitting in the Café Nouvelle Athènes one evening in early April 1879, GM pretended to be absorbed by his study of the proofs of *Martin Luther*, but he was longing on this as on many other nights to be invited to the two tables in the corner that were reserved for the elite circle of Manet and Degas. Moore, mindful of his own comical face, broad hips, and narrow shoulders, would watch Manet, "that face, the beard and nose, satyr-like, shall I say? . . . the square shoulders that swaggered as he went across the room and the thin waist."[179] GM leaves no doubt that he found Manet personally beautiful. Then the great painter approached him and said, "Does not our conversation interrupt you . . . ?" "Not in the least," GM recalls answering; or, in another version, "No, but you do, so like are you to your painting."[180] Degas then called Manet back to the two reserved tables, but Manet, in parting, asked GM to call the following day at his studio, 77 rue d'Amsterdam. Moore left the café and returned up the Boulevard de Clichy like one enchanted.[181] This was the moment toward which all his Paris years were heading, the introduction of all his introductions, the one that finally led him into his proper idea of art. Of all GM's ego-ideals – Jim Browne, Rodolphe Julian, Lewis Hawkins, Bernard Lopez, Villiers de l'Isle Adam, and Catulle Mendès – Edouard Manet was to become the last model of what GM wished to become, the one character important to his life whom he would never treat with irony.

As instructed, Moore came the next day to 77 rue Amsterdam, a new studio into which Manet moved on 1 April 1879. In the late afternoons, it was becoming the resort of those who loved art, wit, and beauty. Fashionable beauties like Méry Laurent could be seen there, avant-garde writers like Mallarmé and Paul Alexis, statesmen like Antonin Proust. It was not a bohemian workshop; it was the salon of a gentleman genius. Manet, like Degas, was a man of wealth and class. "I do not pride myself on being more democratic than others," Manet would say. "In fact, I am very aristocratic." Manet loved the company of writers, and he had a taste for literature – the poetry of Baudelaire, the fiction of Zola, and the memoirs of that most natural of men, Rousseau, all favorites of Moore as well.[182] By the critics of Paris, Manet was regarded in the late 1870s as a violent, extravagant artist who was bent on outraging public taste, but who lacked the qualities of a true master. Nonetheless, Manet gathered about him, Théodore Duret recalled, "a select circle of writers, artists, connoisseurs, and distinguished women, with a small band of disciples . . . [who all] displayed every mark of the warmest friendship for him."[183]

What did he find attractive in the company of George Moore? Duret (who was close to both Manet and Moore) recalled that GM was then, for the French artists and connoisseurs, just "a golden-haired fop . . . but he was very welcome wherever he went, for his manners were amusing and his French very funny. He tried to shock and astonish people; but he was always the gentleman, and would never associate with those whom he thought to be below his rank as an Irish landlord. Degas himself, never an easy critic, thought Moore was 'very intelligent'."[184] Moore himself was not sure why Manet enjoyed his company, "for there was nothing in my verses nor in my drawings to entreat Manet's consideration, and I dare not allow my memory to recall the crude opinions I used to pick up and express in those years." On Moore's first visit to the studio, Manet immediately began to paint his portrait, and continued to paint him in different poses thereafter, so Moore subsequently guessed that his attraction may just have been that he was "a fresh-complexioned, fair-haired young man, the type most suitable to Manet's palette." "The colour of my hair never gave me a thought until Manet began to paint it. Then the blonde gold that came up under the brush filled me with admiration."[185] It astonished Moore when Manet scraped away hours of work on the portrait, and then, still using the same canvas, painted ochre on ochre, without muddying the color, and bringing back the unique jonquil-colored shade of GM's hair. As a painter of modern life, Manet at once wished to document the new urban types (the Artist, the

Cocodette, the Frenchified English Aesthete), and to show the curious formal beauty of the new social configurations. GM was perhaps one such new character, a strange new effect.

For the first of his three extant portraits of Moore, Manet procured a table like the ones at the Nouvelle Athènes and a tall glass, because he wanted to sketch GM in the circumstances in which they first met. In *George Moore au café* (early April 1879), GM wears a bowler hat tipped back off his brow, a *lavallière* cravat, and long starched sleeves coming out from the cuffs of his jacket – as bohemian as a tailor could make him.[186] His chin still sports the Capoul beard designed by Hawkins. With his left elbow on the tabletop, and his head leaning against his fist, he has a dreamy, hyper-aesthetic nonchalance in his gaze off to one side. The representation of the face captures the "amazed and speculative pair of eyes" and their look of "startled curiosity about everything that life was to unfold before his gaze," that the friend of GM's old age, W. K. Magee, called Moore's "original endowment from Nature."[187] The whole image is captured by Manet in less than a hundred masterful strokes of the brush.

GM became a regular at Manet's studio, one of the crowd that showed up around five o'clock when a waiter would move about the room taking orders for drinks. Those in attendance smoked, cracked jokes, and drove one another to paradoxical extremes. If the Café Nouvelle Athènes was the university, this was the graduate seminar in aestheticism. The notorious *Olympia* (1863) hung on a large wall, the Goyaesque *Balcony* (1869) beside it. The colossal *Execution of Maximilian* (1867) was over a doorway.[188] When the young Jacques-Emile Blanche came to 77 rue d'Amsterdam, he noticed around the studio props that had been used for famous pictures: the table where the lovers sat for *At Père Lathuille's Restaurant* (1879), the cheval-glass from *Nana* (1877) and the zinc tub in which Méry Laurent had stood. On the easels Blanche saw pastels of George Moore and Méry Laurent.[189]

Moore may possibly be telling the truth when he says he aspired to a flirtation with Méry Laurent (1849–?), who was a "daily visitor to Manet's studio when friends came to chat and laugh."[190] Manet had painted her in the nude, standing half bent over in the tub, the water dripping from her sponge, as she looks sweetly back at the spectator, the viewed viewing the viewer (*In the Tub*, 1878). She was for a long time the mistress of Dr Thomas Evans, an American dentist with a fine practice in Paris, whom she met while playing Venus in a flesh-colored suit for an Offenbach opera. With his astonishing curiosity, and rudeness, GM asked her why she did not leave Dr Evans, especially as he had settled money on her. She won his admiration by replying, "Why should I descend to a meanness when I could find content and perhaps happiness in being unfaithful to him?" In the late 1880s, after the death of Manet, she added another string to her lyre, to use GM's phrase, and became the lover of Mallarmé. For the young Moore, Méry Laurent was the epitome of the witty, charming woman of fashion, an embodiment of the spirit of liberation from hypocrisy.

6. *George Moore au café*, Edouard Manet (April 1879).

GM might dream of being the lover of the woman with whom the man he most admired slept, but he was not yet in her league. He turned his attention to another studio visitor, Countess Albazzi, née Iza Kwiatowski, "a splendid creature in a carriage drawn by Russian horses from the Steppes, so she said." She had come to call off a sitting with Manet, but as she left she took with her two of the young crowd at the studio, GM and another. This time, GM recalls, he was the lucky one. He made love to the Countess Albazzi "'not with conviction . . . but successfully in the end.'"[191] Some days later, Manet did a pastel sketch of the lady, and "with that grace of mind that never left him," flattered his young friend by giving him the picture with the comment, "Now I think this comes to you by right."[192]

To judge from "A Love Letter" in *Pagan Poems* (1881), GM and Iza, Countess Albazzi, spent "the July heats" together. The poet asks his lover if she can remember when "your sweet/White body was surrendered to my tears?/Do you remember when I kissed your feet – /Your dove-like feet, and then your shell-like ears?" True, the poem explains, she left him soon enough, but while they were together she "never thwarted any febrile wish,"[193] and his misdirected kisses found their targets. "The Portrait" also reflects his affair with Iza. It is divided into three parts, "The Triumph of the Flesh," "The Triumph of the Soul," and "The Triumph of Time." In the first triumph, the poet feeds like a tiger on her flesh as on "delicate fruit" (a vegetarian tiger); in the second, he is alone, but still in "the odour" of her presence; in the final triumph of art over time, he recalls twenty years later that the writers he once admired in Paris are now dead, the woman withered and faded, but still beside him is the portrait "signed by my dear friend Edward Manet."

> Yes, yes, I now remember well the story:
> He gave me that sweet pastel as a present,
> Because he always said I was her lover.
>
> It is the portrait of a Polish lady, –
> I wonder if she is now dead or living, –
> I loved her once, but love is soon forgotten.
>
> Love is not soon forgot, but there is nothing
> That time doth write out not with firm erasure;
> Sooner or later all must pass and perish.

The theme of remembered pleasures surpassing pleasures in the moment of experience would stay with George Moore. What is most intriguing, however, is that the enduring affection expressed in the poem is for his "dear friend Edward Manet." The woman and her beauty furnish an occasion by which that affection is experienced, recalled, made into literature, and still embodied in a picture on a wall. The desires of George Moore were those that had as their highest destiny an aesthetic moment.

It was momentous for Moore that Manet showed every sign of taking a fond interest in him, that he took pleasure in GM's companionship, and, with Degas, seemed to find him well worth talking to about art, literature, and women. Manet was the epitome of the attractive, manly, cultured Parisian gentleman. He was especially at ease where other French men of art and government were stiff – in the company of women. Most men in such company, Alexis judged, were like bears doing a polka; they were too bitter, distraught, and hobby-horsical.[194]

> Now let us examine [Manet] through our lorgnettes in his element, among a bouquet of lovely women, at a grand soirée; let us sketch him there in a silhouette in his evening clothes as the perfect man of the world. To be in the vicinity of lovely women gives his eyes light and depth, the flame of youth. His lips, mobile and mocking, strike certain attitudes as he takes the confessions of the women of Paris . . . Amiability, spirit, politeness, all seasoned with the one originality, born of the air of freedom . . . A woman who is a great friend of his

described him for me the other evening in three words: "Un grand enfant!" Yes, a big baby sometimes, with a candor and a courage that declares itself at each instant in his work and attracts to him many other men of genius.

To be befriended by such a man gave Moore an altogether new sense of himself and of his possibilities. His father may have thought him a booby; Lewis Hawkins may have treated him as a good pal who sadly could neither paint nor find a lover, but could always provide a loan; but here was Manet treating him like a friend, even an equal. It would be an enterprise well worth his pursuit to become whatever it was that Manet had seen in him. He would also aspire to become like Manet – an artist of candor and courage, one who would make each work of art a new beginning, disdainful of the outcry of critics.

15

On 29 April 1878, the crowd around Manet's studio and the Café Nouvelle Athènes went to a costume ball at the Elysée Montmartre, given in honor of the cast of the Théâtre Ambigu after the one hundredth performance of the play adapted from Zola's novel, *L'Assommoir*.[195] Manet prodded Moore to go as a Paris workman, "for he enjoyed incongruities." Four thousand citizens of the world of theater, letters, and the arts went to the event, all posing as characters in the novel, or costumed as members of the criminal class. It was, Alexis says, a naturalist ball, unheard of, faerylike; the throats of the high-cultured were wetted with 5,000 francs' worth of champagne, all getting drunk in honor of a play about the vice of drunkenness.[196] As Moore followed Manet through this carnival, the painter remarked somewhat ambiguously that "There is no Frenchman living in London who occupies the same position as you do in Paris," words GM later repeated as a mark of special distinction.

At the Bal d'Assommoir, Manet made a passing introduction that would later assume significance in Moore's life:

"But I must introduce you to Zola. There he is," he said pointing to a thickly built, massive man in evening clothes for, as Manet said, a serious writer cannot be expected to put on fancy dress.

Zola bowed and passed on, chilling us a little.

GM was disappointed, but Manet assured Moore he could call on the writer any time he liked at Zola's house in Médan.[197] So GM danced away with a woman dressed as "Gervaise," the alcoholic laundress in *L'Assommoir*.

At this ball, Moore was in the company of two of the great influences on his life as a writer, Manet and Zola. George Moore had already met the other of his three artistic heroes at a similar event a few years earlier. In December 1876 as *L'Assommoir* was being serialised in *La République des lettres*, Moore encountered for the only time Ivan Turgenev, an immense man "walking as if through a crowd of pigmies" at the students' ball.[198] Moore was introduced as an English poet, so the Russian novelist talked of Rossetti and Swinburne, or was about to talk, when the young Moore caught sight of a lady he had on his card for a dance, and broke away, bringing a smile to the author of *Virgin Soil*. When the dance ended, they resumed conversation. Turgenev admired Zola's *L'Assommoir* because "for the first time Zola has created a human being; Gervaise is a woman . . . Still, the same vicious method pervades the book – the desire to tell us what she felt rather than what she thought." Not everything can be related by the novelist, Turgenev complained: "I ask myself, what difference does it make to me whether she sweats down the middle of her back or under her arms?"

In May 1879, just after the Bal d'Assommoir, Moore was ripe just for that revelation about which Turgenev had been skeptical a few years earlier. In *Le Voltaire* Moore read Zola's article on "Le Roman expérimental." Naturalism was defined by Zola as a scientific method of observation and experiment that demonstrated truths about human nature and society. GM was astonished "at the vastness of the conception, and the towering height of the ambition" – a whole new art, based on scientific principles. In *Confessions of a Young Man*, Moore listed his reading of the article in *Le Voltaire* as the third of his "echo-auguries," words from an unexpected quarter, but like a divination solving the particular difficulty of the moment. First, in the days of Oscott, it was Shelley leading to atheism and away from priests; second, when he was in London, it was Jim Browne's remark, "You must go to Paris," leading Moore from family to art; and now it was Zola beckoning him from poetry to the novel. GM says he began to regard the poems he had been writing as "sterile eccentricities," and went out to buy the novels of Zola he once had dismissed.[199]

As Moore was plunging into naturalist fiction, he became caught between Manet and Zola. For more than a decade, the painter and the novelist had stood together as leaders of modern art.[200] They admired and inspired each other. Manet took the name of his painting *Nana* (1877) from a minor character in *L'Assommoir* (1876); Zola then used Manet's picture as the storyboard for a novel about the career of a high-class Parisian prostitute (*Nana*, 1879). But in June 1879, only a month after the start of Moore's new enthusiasm for naturalism, Zola attacked Manet in a "Paris Letter" to a Russian newspaper. This piece of exasperated pontificating was republished, to Zola's embarrassment, in the *Revue politique et littéraire*.[201] In it, Zola said that while Manet had a sound perception of tones, he did not successfully execute his conceptions; he was easily satisfied with hasty painting; he had no method; when a painting succeeded, it would be outstanding, yet the next could just as easily be a failure. As a result, while Impressionism was a further advance of Courbet's realist movement, it had no great painter, not Monet, and not even Manet. Those who were truly successful, Zola concluded, were Henri Gervex and Jules Bastien-Lepage, who "owed their success to the application of the naturalist method to painting." The day after the publication of this article, a headline in the *Figaro* announced that Manet and Zola had severed relations. Zola protested to Manet that he had been misquoted and that he still admired Manet's work unreservedly. On 28 July 1879 Manet asked Zola to print his retraction in the *Figaro*.[202]

In July 1879, Moore was seeing a lot of Manet and saying a lot about Zola. Alexis recalls meeting Moore at Manet's studio at a time when GM feverishly desired to contribute to the naturalist cause. But that cause had been thought to be the same cause as Impressionism: "Everything goes in a common direction – painting with the novel . . . All go toward nature and science . . . the scientific method has put its imprint on all the arts."[203] Now it was beginning to appear that for Zola not all the modern painters identified with the movement were sufficiently scientific or naturalistic. Manet had never claimed to be a doctrinaire "naturalist," or "Impressionist" for that matter; and under attack from Zola, he reasserted his view that the essence of art is the personality of the artist.

In July, Manet continued to do portraits of Moore. There is a summertime portrait of a wide-eyed Moore sitting sassily with his legs apart on either side of the back of a folding chair, his elbows on the backrest.[204] In the evenings they would go to the Café Nouvelle Athènes and argue about Zola: "We discussed things endlessly," Degas told Daniel Halévy. "Zola's idea of art, cramming everything about a subject into a book, then going on to another subject, seemed to me puerile."[205] The things GM remembers Manet saying about art and the artist are part of Manet's argument against naturalism, represented by convert Moore in place of its prophet, Zola. For instance, "Art is not mathematics," Moore recalls the painter saying, "it is individuality. It does not matter how badly you paint, so long as you don't paint badly like other people."[206] GM also long afterwards cherished Manet's statement about the autobiographical element in art: "It is often said the personality of the artist concerns us not, and in the case of bad Art it is certainly true, for bad Art reveals no personality, bad Art is bad because it is anonymous. The work of the great artist is himself . . . Manet's Art was all Manet."[207] But Zola's art did not claim to be Zola; it was offered as the truth of society and nature.

When Moore matured as a writer, Manet came to represent for him the defiant rejection of all doctrines about art, naturalist or symbolist, moral or aesthetic: "The artist must arrive at a new estimate of things; all must go into the melting-pot in the hope that out of the pot may emerge a new consummation of himself. For this end he must keep himself free from all creed, from all dogma, from all opinion, remembering that as he accepts the opinions of others he loses his talent, all his feelings and ideas must be his own, for Art is a personal rethinking of life from end to end, and for this reason the artist is always eccentric. He is almost unaware of your moral codes, he laughs at them when he thinks of them, which is rarely, and he is as unashamed as a little child. The word unashamed explains Manet's art better than any other."[208] In 1879, however, GM was ashamed of his clumsiness and bad education, and he was

7. *Portrait of George Moore*,
Edouard Manet (1879).

comforted by the notion that the truth of art could be discovered in the naturalist doctrine.

Still, the lesson of Manet – *Be ashamed of nothing but to be ashamed* – made a lasting impression on Moore, ultimately to be developed by readings in Rousseau (especially Book 1 of *Confessions*) and Nietzsche. The message may initially have been borne in upon GM by a particular scolding he received from the painter. Manet recalled that after he finished a portrait of Moore, the young Irishman came back to ask for some retouching:

As far as I was concerned, it was finished in a single sitting, but [Moore] didn't see it that way. He came back and annoyed me by asking for a change here, something different there. I won't change a thing in his portrait. Is it my fault if Moore looks like a squashed egg yolk and if his face is all lopsided? Anyway, the same applies to everybody's face and this passion for symmetry is the plague of our time. There's no symmetry in nature.[209]

This was a reprimand based on a deep truth, one that would later become the heart of Nietzsche's eternal return: if you wish to become yourself, and your self is the goal you have been making for, then you must want to become what you have indeed become, and not want anything about yourself to be different – only then can one be no longer ashamed of oneself.[210] Indeed, the artist, like Rousseau, should delight in the reflection that he is not like anyone he has ever seen, and venture to think he is not even like anyone who has ever existed. There was a wide difference, Moore would come to realise, between being natural and being a naturalist.

16

One day in Moore's post, there arrived a letter from Joe Blake. It explained that the tenants were not paying their rents; worse yet, they were taking shots at local landlords. If GM wanted to get his rents, he had better come and collect them himself; Joe Blake would not risk his life as Moore's agent.[211] The National Land League was founded on 16 August 1879 at Daly's Hotel, Castlebar, less than twenty miles from Moore Hall; the tenants throughout the area were organising resistance to landlordism. In *Confessions of a Young Man*, Moore parodied his indignation that "some wretched miners and farmers should refuse to starve that I may not be deprived of my demi-tasse at Tortoni's," and that he should "interrupt the austere laws of nature which ordain that the weak shall be trampled upon, shall be ground into death and dust, that the strong shall be really strong." In *Communication to My Friends* (1933), Moore represents himself as having been less indignant than depressed and terrified – he considers ignoring Joe Blake's letter, or lying to him that he has an advance for a novel. A contemporary letter to Blake shows that Moore was, in fact, frightened, and also that he was putting pressure on his uncle to continue to oversee not just his own estate at Tower Hill, but also the estates of Moore Hall:

> This question of the tenants refusing to pay rent is horrible! What does it mean – communism? If you dont get the rents what is to be done? If I have never looked into my business at all events I have never committed any follies. I never spent more than 500 a year, and I was told when I came into the property that I had ever so much. Enfin, I suppose you will do your best. I will try to meet you in Dublin if you like and have some understanding, about Christmas.[212]

His time in Paris was coming to an end. The Ribbonmen who worried his father had given place to a far more organised political movement, the Land League, led by Michael Davitt. The significance of that movement is captured by the title of Davitt's book: *The Fall of Feudalism in Ireland*. GM could no longer bankroll his quest for George Moore on the rents of cottiers on the 12,000 starve-acres of his County Mayo estate. Joe Blake evidently would not wait until Christmas in Dublin; he met GM in London that fall of 1879. Blake would not back down; GM was given no way out other than to take charge of the estate himself. A phase of his life was over, and on his return to Paris he knew it:

> And catching sight of Manet's portrait of my Polish mistress, I began to ask myself: In whose shop will she hang and what manner of man will buy her? I will run away, leaving everything to be sold, and if I answer no letters Paris will dissolve like a dream; I shall never know how much my tables and chairs and pictures fetched at the sale. Let them go, let them go – I belong to Paris no longer.[213]

GM took a last look around his apartment at 61 rue Condorcet – at the armchairs, couch, and chaise-longue, the ebony bureau and armoire, his white draperies, the candelabras, iron torches, lantern, hanging porcelain lamp, at the 200 volumes of literature and history in the ebony bookcase with which he had fed his fantasies about the author's life. He had a final dinner with Lewis Welldon Hawkins. Then without saying farewell to his landlord or friends – by September Manet, slowly dying of syphilis, was convalescing in the suburbs – George Moore slipped out of Paris and the life he had found there of balls, studios, bohemian cafés, and *séances de collaboration*.

Chapter 3
The Novelist as Absentee Landlord

I

In December of 1880, the year after George Moore received his fateful letter from Joe Blake, he was living again at his birthplace, Moore Hall, Ballyglass, County Mayo. One morning, his sister Nina came down the staircase to find George jubilant. He had in his hands the *Spectator* for 11 December, just arrived by the post from London. It contained a poem by himself – "The Love of the Past" – which he read out to his sister:

> As sailors watch from their prison
>   For the long, grey line of the coasts,
> I look to the past rearisen,
>   And joys come over in hosts
>   Like the white sea-birds from their roosts.
>
> I love not th' indelicate present,
>   The future's unknown to our quest,
> To-day is the life of the peasant,
>   But the past is a haven of rest, –
> The joy of the past is best.
>
> The rose of the past is better
>   Than the rose which we ravish to-day;
> 'Tis holier, purer, and fitter
>   To place on the shrine where we pray, –
> For the secret thoughts we obey.
>
> There, are no deceptions or changes,
>   There, all is placid and still;
> No grief, nor fate that estranges,
>   Nor hope that no life can fulfil;
> But ethereal shelter from ill.

> The coarser delights of the hour
>   Tempt, and debauch and deprave;
> And we joy in a poisonous flower,
>   Knowing that nothing can save
> Our flesh from the fate of the grave.
>
> But surely we leave them, returning
>   In grief to the well-loved nest,
> Filled with an infinite yearning,
>   Knowing the past to be rest, –
> That the things of the past are best.

Having a poem featured in "a first-class London newspaper" would open doors for him, so that he might get paid to write reviews, paragraphs, and more poems; in short, he could launch himself in London as a young man of letters.[1] By December 1880 Moore had been in Ireland for half a year, and for the last several months he had been shut up in Moore Hall with his younger sister. His mother was in Dublin, Maurice Moore – back from fighting in the colonies – was barracked with the Connaught Rangers at the army depot in Galway, and Augustus Moore was scraping together a life as a society journalist in Fleet Street.[2]

For George himself, these were not the best months in the history of Ireland to be a landlord in a big house on an estate; it was reasonable to identify with sailors in their ships at sea, watching for "the long, grey line of the coasts." GM was surrounded by hostile, hungry, and penniless tenants. Crops had failed in 1880 for the third year in a row, and the tenant farmers, short of food, had few pigs or potatoes to sell for money; as a result, they could not pay either their rent to the landlords or their loans from the local shopkeepers; so landlords could not pay installments on mortgages, and town shopkeepers could not manage their own borrowing and lending. With bad weather, bad soil, bad agricultural management, bad land-ownership arrangements, a bad position in competition with cheap agricultural products from North America, and a bad system of banking, the whole rickety system of life in the West of Ireland was crashing. Agrarian crime in Ireland for the last quarter of 1880 was twenty-five times what it had been for that period two years earlier, and assassinations, while still not numerous, had tripled.[3] In Moore's own parish of Carra, the surveyor could not identify the boundaries of small holdings without the protection of police, and no one would dare to serve notices of rent due.[4] A few pages before coming to "Love of the Past" in the 11 December 1880 *Spectator*, George and Nina Moore could read that Charles Stewart Parnell, the new Chairman of the Irish Parliamentary Party, and now working hand in glove with the Land League, was openly agitating in Waterford for "a great measure of territorial confiscation" – that is, confiscation of the property of landlords, property like the estate and grounds of Moore Hall. Parnell referred to landlords as "the enemy," "an isolated garrison." In his Waterford speech, he sounded a warning: the landlord garrison had better take the chance to depart, while the "people of Ireland" were still in a mood to let them depart in peace and with compensation.

GM would have been only too happy to depart in peace and with compensation. After living outside Ireland for twelve years, returning only once briefly for his father's funeral in 1870, he had the luck to come back just in time for the Land War (1879–82), and to the one county in Ireland, County Mayo, where it had begun and where it would be most fiercely fought. R. H. Hutton, editor of the *Spectator*, must have been quite happy with a topical submission sent him from a Mayo landlord, the son of a famous tenant-relief Member of Parliament. How fitting that the son should repeatedly bemoan the past as best, and "love not th' indelicate present"! The defeatism of much of the landlord class in Ireland was perfectly captured for the *Spectator*'s readers by the poet's direct concession: "To-day is the life of the peasant." What indeed was there now for the country gentlemen but "the coarser delights of the hour"? Debauchery, depravity, and death awaited them, Moore's poem foretold, with interludes of nostalgia. That Nina Moore nonetheless found George jubilant, reading his poem to her again and again, is a sign of how completely his own happiness rested in December 1880 upon recognition as a literary artist, and not on the future of his estate.

2

Upon his departure from Paris a year earlier, George Moore had not returned directly to Ireland. In 1879, he stopped by 19 Delamere Terrace in London to present Edmund Gosse with a copy of *Martin Luther*. He also resumed his friendship with Arthur O'Shaughnessy and his circle, which now included another aspiring, Swinburnean Irish poet, Thomas Pakenham Beatty.[5] The self-advertised cosmopolitan Heinrich Felbermann, new editor of the London *Examiner*, recalls giving Moore the job of "second secretary." GM had no experience of employment, very little education in English grammar, and small acquaintance with current affairs in London. Felbermann found his second secretary to be "rather dear at two guineas a week."[6] In late spring 1880, GM left the *Examiner*, gave O'Shaughnessy the manuscript of a new book of poems to see through the press, and set off for Ireland.

He was going to meet his family for the Horse and Ram Show, a chief event in the social calendar of the Irish Ascendancy, then held from 31 August to 3 September at the Royal Dublin Society premises in Kildare Street (now the site of the National Library and Museum). According to Maurice Moore, recalling the events many years later, the family were reunited for the first time in many years by May 1880, all of them lodged in the house of Mrs Moore's sister, Catherine Blake O'Connor, at 22 Merrion Square.[7] In the intervals between the tennis parties, dances, and parades, Augustus Moore was sending "society para-graphs" to Edmund Yates's *World* (which once proposed that the author of *Flowers of Passion* be "whipped by the cart's tail"), while George prevailed upon Maurice to write an analysis of the political crisis in Ireland, and Nina to trans-late it, so that GM could send the result to a Paris newspaper.[8]

Eventually, GM had to have a showdown with his mother's brother Joe Blake. GM was sharing accommodation at 22 Merrion Square with his age-mate and cousin, Arthur O'Connor, whose own father had also died a decade earlier. Arthur was in the same fix as George: Llewelyn Blake, Joe's brother, was acting as land agent and manager of the O'Connor family estate at Elphin, Ros-common, and, in the face of tenant resistance, Blake was not collecting rents. Arthur's course of action was to sue Llewelyn Blake for the right to manage the family estate himself.[9] Would GM also take Joe Blake to court?

Blake and Moore met in the newly landscaped St Stephen's Green, opened to the public on 27 July 1880 by its owner, Lord Ardilaun.[10] In his final piece of writing before death, *A Communication to My Friends*, Moore depicted himself as a dreamy Parisian poet, but still a canny and dignified Moore not to be diddled by a low-minded horsy fellow like Joe Blake. In spite of his affecta-tion of dreaminess, GM got the picture: the tenants had turned angry and violent, and Joe himself had been forced to run into the high-walled garden of Moore Hall to save his skin. Now there was little to be done, Joe explained, but to offer them a big reduction in rent, and hope to get that, rather than nothing at all. If the Tenant League accepted their offer, then George himself could try to collect the arrears he was owed for the previous three years of bad harvests. Once he had these monies in hand, he could see about paying Joe Blake back the £2,000 he was owed for sundry improvements of the property and advances to George in Paris.

GM says he then proposed that the two walk to Joe Blake's hotel, where GM could collect the account books for delivery to his solicitor, who would have them examined by a chartered accountant; GM knew nothing about accounts himself. When they arrived at the hotel, and Moore began to lift the books, Joe Blake warned GM that an accountant would charge a heavy fee, and after all, what difference would it make? "'Well, that is part of the game, Joe, accounts can't be signed unless they are examined,'" GM has himself replying in *A Com-munication to My Friends*.[11]

Maurice Moore's memory and a contemporary letter confirm that there was trouble over the accounts. Weeks were consumed in wrangling. Mrs Moore was horrified at the prospect that George would start a lawsuit against her brother. Joe Blake was afraid of the same thing; he had been preoccupied with his racing stable, and, the gentle and discreet Maurice Moore admitted, while an "hon-ourable man," Joe was "not up to date in the matter of accounts and agency."[12] This was the judgement of the accountant too: he reported that the books were altogether improper, so the solicitor advised GM not to sign them; that in turn might force Blake to renegotiate the amount of the supposed loan. But George recalls that the literary instinct was "so inveterate" in him, that he could not bring himself to care sufficiently about being robbed to fight the thief. Rather than following Arthur O'Connor's legal course against Llewelyn Blake, George Moore signed Joe Blake's fraudulent books, though when he wrote Joe a year later, Moore was still disgruntled about the obscure loan and the "impossible" rate of interest Joe had charged him.[13]

GM, however, was not blind to the truth of Blake's report on the state of the country; indeed, Moore envisioned civil war breaking out by November and famine settling again on the country by winter. In a letter published by the *Freeman's Journal* on 14 August 1880, Moore addressed his fellow-landlords, then jubilant over the defeat of Gladstone's Relief Bill in the House of Lords:[14]

> Landlords and tenants may now become friends as before. The golden opportunity has arrived. The Lords have rejected the bill, and the tenant-farmers are in despair. Let the landlords coalesce with their arch-enemy, the Land League, and offer to the people of Ireland a better, not a stronger, Land Bill than the one which failed to find acceptance with the Lords. Let old differences of opinion be put aside; let landlords give way a good deal on their side, and the League a little on theirs; and let them draw up together an efficient Land Bill, one that popular opinion will enforce as strongly as any law coming from England is enforced by the bayonet, and so by its acceptance forever divide the good landlords from the bad; and moreover establish the basis for a great principle for which we are all striving – "Home Rule."

No Home Rule landlords eager to settle the land war on the tenants' terms wrote to the paper in support of Moore's proposal, but the letter is important contemporary evidence of Moore's liberal politics in Irish matters.

From Dublin George Moore made his way west with his sister Nina, with the prospect ahead of him of becoming his own agent at Moore Hall, during a period of the assassination of bailiffs and agents. On 9 August 1880, a few weeks before he set out, there was a report in the *Freeman's Journal* about a massive demonstration at Ballintubber Abbey, just a few miles down the road from Moore Hall, in which tenants carried signs reading: "Land For the People" and "Let Tyrants Remember the Grave."[15] On the journey west, the Moores stopped first at the Palace, the O'Connors' country house in Elphin, County Roscommon. Getting back into the swim of county society, the Moore brothers attended the Holliford ball. Maurice remembers hearing a rumor that one of the prominent guests, Viscount Montmorres, was a marked man in the Land War and would not live a month.[16] Some time later GM joined Robert Ruttledge, Tom Ruttledge's brother, in a hunting party at Castlemagarett, County Mayo, the seat of Lord Oranmore and Browne, an aggressive advocate of landlord rights.[17] The hunters on their return from the shoot crossed a wooden bridge, and they, their horse and trap suddenly all went down with the collapsing bridge into the river. Hostile tenants had engineered the accident by sawing the bridge timbers almost all the way through. No one in the carriage was badly hurt, but they all got a drenching and a fright.[18]

Viscount Montmorres was not so lucky. On 25 September 1880 he had been prosecuting one of his fifteen tenants in a Galway court, and on his return to his 400-acre estate in Clonbur, he was shot once in the head, three times in the neck, and twice in the body.[19] His murder sent a shock through the Connaught landlords. Just a day before, on the 24th, Captain Charles Cunningham Boycott, Lord Erne's land agent for Lough Mask House, County Mayo, was ostracised by the Land League. All the Captain's servants left, no one would deliver goods, no one would have anything to do with anyone who had anything to do with Captain Boycott. Boycott was "a friend and neighbour" of the Moores, residing just south along the string of lakes, down Lough Carra and across Lough Mask, not far north from the head of Lough Corrib where Montmorres was murdered.[20] GM at first measured Captain Boycott by the standards one country gentleman uses for another – "He is as fine a sportsman as I ever knew, a fearless rider and an excellent shot" – but he came to realise that the old measures of man's worth had vanished into thin air, and a new era of morality had appeared. The rapidity with which Captain Boycott's name became a word for a new form of political intimidation GM judged to be a sign "of the rapid advance of the Irish struggle and the inevitableness of [the] Irish idea in the future."[21] Home Rule may have been a good thing or a bad thing, but it was certainly, Moore thought, a sure thing.

In a letter to the *Mayo Examiner* of 4 September 1880, GM again asserted his eagerness to see a popular land bill agreed between landlords and tenants, without the management of Parliament, in order to establish the first principle of Home Rule: "that the Irish are capable of governing themselves." He tried to make the case that the Land League policy as he understood it – don't pay rent, and shoot the landlords – was not a good policy. "Landlords do exist, will exist, and must exist, until the world again returns to a primitive state," he wrote; there were landlords in many prosperous countries – France, America, even Belgium – there just were not enough of them in Ireland. His solutions were to break the law of entail (which tended to keep property in a small number of hands), to aid a peasant proprietorship, and to offer seven-year leases with free sale of the rental by the tenant. In the meantime, however, he argued that if a tenant did not pay rent, the landlord had to evict him, or go bankrupt and give way to a new landlord. It was exciting business being a leader like his father, but no one was yet following.

While ready to be a liberal landlord, Moore shrank from the idea of being his own agent and the peasants' target. He wrote a cringing, pleading letter to Joe Blake from the Palace. He had lain awake thinking about the matter, he explained, and at last concluded he could not manage the estate himself. A "Mr. Powell" had been recommended to him as an agent; what did Joe think?

You must understand that we are differently constituted. You would find your-self hopelessly at sea between the four themes of a sonnet. You would probably not succeed in writing one: – I would, without difficulty. In the same way in regard to this business, I lie awake all night thinking about it. I fancy that if I went with Mr. Powell it would be much better . . . I dread a failure. Give me a word of encouragement and advice.[22]

In this letter is to be heard the voice of the silly young man lately returned from the Café Nouvelle Athènes to his estate, an image of himself GM created in his penetrating, satirical letters to the Paris *Figaro* in the summer of 1886, later published in English as *Parnell and His Island*. There Moore describes himself in a "long green coat," wearing "a tiny hat" over his long hair, with Parisian-cut clothes and a Capoul beard, volumes of Baudelaire and Verlaine in his pocket, the whole turnout giving him an "anomalous air" in the West of Ireland during the Land War. "Of all the latest tricks that had been played with French verse he was thoroughly the master; of the size, situation, and condition of his property he knew [nothing]. Indeed, he hated all allusion to be made to it, and he looked forward with positive horror to meeting his tenants."

After leaving his aunt's Roscommon country house, George Moore recalled in his last book, he continued his hesitant progress west with his sister. They stopped next at Cornfield, the house of their Mayo cousins, the Ruttledges, also a racing family.[23] He took quickly to the young son, Tom Ruttledge, whom GM's rather less impressed mother described as "that fellow with the long legs and round head who smokes cigars in the drawing-room and rides steeplechases and is a disappointment to his mother."[24] From GM's point of view, Tom Ruttledge was just what was needed: Tom knew the area, the people, and the political situation; best of all, he wanted to get married, and so needed a job and would be glad to be GM's land agent. As Moore tells the story in *A Communication*, there was thus a method in Moore's hesitant progress westward; he went so slow that he never arrived as his own agent. By 25 September 1880, a sarcastic leader in the *Connaught Telegraph* announced that Moore, "the degenerate son of a worthy father," had appointed a new agent.

The sarcasm of the *Connaught Telegraph* was the result of incidents on Monday, 20 September, in the hamlets around Gallen on the Moore estate. Whether with or without Ruttledge's advice, GM followed the line he laid out in his 4 September *Mayo Examiner* article: "The landlord asks for the rent, and the tenant pays it; if not, he is evicted." At Moore's request, twenty side-cars arrived loaded with police carrying firearms, later joined by a contingent of the Royal Irish Constabulary from Balla, and a process-server. In the village of Coolfox, this force met the determined resistance of a dozen women, and with-drew after serving four writs of ejectment for non-payment of rent. The *Connaught Telegraph* excoriated GM as a rackrenting landlord, and begged him to stop "writing slimy productions to the newspapers."[25]

Seeing Moore Hall for the first time in over ten years, Moore found the stables that once housed thirty to forty racehorses were now a ruin. The race-course that had been laid out down the hill weaving in and out of the great wood was overgrown. Few peacocks remained (Moore says just one, thinking of himself) of generations that had strutted on the terraces reaching down to the "pale, mild, merelike lake . . . surrounded by amphitheatrical mountains."[26] Inside the house, his recently acquired sense of architectural style made him see its furnishings as hardly worthy of "a retired soap-boiler," in the description from *Parnell and His Island*. In the library, he found that no book had been added since the death of his grandfather fifty years earlier. Indeed, "The things of the past [were] best."

In *Parnell and His Island*, the agent of the young Parisian-Irish landlord suggests a visit to the tenants on an outlying estate, some thirty miles to the north. The agent was Tom Ruttledge; the outlying estate was Ashbrook, the original home of the Moores near Strade Abbey, Bellavary, County Mayo; and the aesthetic landlord was, of course, young George Moore as satirically depicted by a slightly older George Moore. The Parisian Irishman is even surprised by the condition of Carnacun, the village just down the hill from Moore Hall, noticing as if for the first time the dwellings of those who worked in his family's smithy, laundry, sawmill, stable, byres, and garden.

> About each doorway is a dung-heap in which a pig wallows in the wettest and the children play in the driest part . . . [Inside] the floor is broken in places and the rain collects in the hollows. A large pig, covered with lice, feeds out of a trough placed in the middle of the floor, and the beast from time to time approaches and sniffs at the child sleeping in a cot by the fireside . . . as we have seen the pig, let us see the family at dinner . . .

And the horrible, fascinated description continues in *Parnell and His Island*, etching a humanity utterly degraded, without "the beautiful sentiments that flourish in the soul only when wealth begins to gild the furniture," in Balzac's epigram quoted by Moore.[27]

From the village, the journey north of the landlord and his agent takes them through a town – that would be Castlebar – where they stop to listen to Land League speeches. Indeed, the priest they hear giving an oration in which he draws Jesuitical distinctions between two kinds of murder (behind-the-wall murder and eviction murder) may have been modelled on the still active Father Lavelle, who gave the funeral panegyric for G. H. Moore in 1870.[28] Landlord and agent continue their journey north past the mountains and into a great bog, where they meet, of all miserable families, the most miserable, a family of seven, living up against a turf cutting under a sod roof – tenants evicted from the poet's lands. Arrived at the outlying estate (that is, Ashbrook), his agent takes the young landlord with him to the ruined chapel where his ancestor (John

Moore, b. 1706) was buried. The coffin has been despoiled of its lead by peasants scavenging for anything of value:

> and the bones of him who created all that has been wasted – by one generation
> in terraces, by another in race-horses, and by another in dissipation in Paris, lie
> scattered about the ground trodden by . . . the passing feet of the peasant.
> Notwithstanding his cynicism, the poet was touched to the heart. Three days
> afterwards he began a poem on the subject, the chief merit of which lay in the
> ingenuity of rhyming Lilith with lit.[29]

The extraordinarily icy justice of Moore's irony about himself in *Parnell and
His Island* does not, however, reflect either his mood or his style in the fall
of 1880.

A leading article in the 9 October 1880 *Mayo Examiner* reported that
GM and Thomas Ruttledge had been visiting his estate and "gaining by personal view an amount of information which it is right and proper he should
possess." It was announced that after reflection, and upon the advice of
Ruttledge, Moore had stayed the ejectment proceedings on his Gallen property. In addition, he offered to forgo all arrears of rent for those tenants who
would pay the year's rent of May 1879 to May 1880, a potential forgiveness of
£5,000 in total rent due. For those tenants owing only a year's rent, Moore
offered a 25 percent reduction. The article ended with a panegyric to G. H.
Moore, "devoted and fearless champion of [Ireland's] Bishops and Priests – the
great Catholic."[30] The *Examiner* could not mention what it did not know: that
just before he died G. H. Moore demanded that tenants pay their rent or suffer
eviction.

After GM's effort to be (like his father) both a liberal patriot and a firm landlord had met with resistance, he clearly changed course. His nerves were shaken
by scenes of destitution, reports of murders, and Land League threats; how
deeply shaken can be measured by a contemporary message he wrote to Wilfrid
Meynell, enclosing a letter for Meynell to convey to the editor of the London
Times. Moore was afraid to send such a letter directly to the address of the
Times through the Ballyglass post office:

> The country is an awful state. Don't mention that I asked you to do this. Things
> go back and a life is worth from the sum of five to twenty shillings. I know lots
> of men who would do a job for me at the price. Regards to Mrs. Meynell.[31]

Moore was well and truly terrified. On 12 November Protestant Orangemen
from County Monaghan (many from the estate of Lord "Derry" Rossmore)
marched into County Mayo to save the crops of Captain Boycott. The
seventeenth-century Plantation of Ireland was originally a military operation,
and the nineteenth-century harvest in County Mayo had become one as well.

As a lifeline, GM kept in touch with the London poets. On 22 November 1880, Arthur O'Shaughnessy wrote him about the printing of *Pagan Poems*, the volume GM was subsidising Newman and Co. to publish. Newman was delaying publication, supposedly on account of the need for fresh advertising, but O'Shaughnessy urged Moore to demand immediate publication. On 13 December 1880, Thomas Pakenham Beatty wrote GM at Moore Hall about his own problems getting someone to publish *Three Women of the People*, his "fiery . . . Swinburnese." Beatty congratulated Moore on the appearance of "Love of the Past" in the *Spectator*; Moore had succeeded in his aim, Beatty judged, of erasing all signs of Swinburne and O'Shaughnessy from his work. Significantly, Beatty assumed that GM, now a "Zola-zealot," scorned Swinburnean verse as just "the hobble-gobble of the day."[32] GM imagined that in *Pagan Poems* he had invented a Zolaesque verse: highly formalised French stanzas, with naturalistic subject matter and philosophy, as GM understood these – that is, philosophically fatalistic and immoralist treatment of the human animal, trapped and shaped by its environment and instincts.

On 15 December 1880 Moore learned that there was further trouble afoot in London. Newman was getting cold feet about this new lyrical naturalism coming out under his imprint, even if he did not have to bear the costs. O'Shaughnessy advised GM to demand that Newman immediately send all the printed stock of *Pagan Poems* to Beatty's apartment in Earls Court, or else remit GM's subsidy of £25. If Newman failed to do one or the other, Moore should, O'Shaughnessy concluded, put the matter into the hands of a solicitor.[33]

Moore was not sorry, one supposes, to conclude that his presence was required by important literary business on the other side of the Irish Channel. He entrusted Moore Hall and its affairs to the hands of Tom Ruttledge, who had located a timber merchant who would give £500 to thin the great wood around the house.[34] On that sum, Moore figured he could live a pared-down existence in London for years, no matter what happened to his rents. He set off then for his brother Augustus Moore's apartment at 17 Fleet Street, hoping to make his way, and his name, as a writer in London. His aim was to slough "the skin that I grew in Paris" and find an "affinity with my original self."[35]

3

In London, Moore discovered that O'Shaughnessy had come down with pneumonia. After leaving a theater in early January with the Salaman brothers, Malcolm the lyricist and Charles the composer of light operas, O'Shaughnessy found himself in a snowstorm, with no closed cabs to be found. He was forced to ride home on the top of an omnibus. The next day, the small poet-herpetologist got through his work at the British Museum, but thereafter could not leave his bed. GM came daily to his apartment to read to him, along with

John Payne, Philip Bourke Marston, the Salaman brothers, and other friends; apparently, no one called a doctor. On 26 January another great snowfall covered London, and, in a cold room, O'Shaughnessy died on 30 January 1881, not yet thirty-seven years old.[36]

Moore, settled at 17 Fleet Street in Augustus Moore's room above a tavern, went to work finding out what had become of *Pagan Poems*. With O'Shaughnessy dead, he turned for help to William Michael Rossetti, explaining to him that in France the custom was for a younger author to ask an older one for advice, and a preface. Rossetti was initially kind enough to promise an article about Moore's book, but on 19 March GM was forced to report to Rossetti that the volume had been decisively withdrawn.[37] A reviewer had threatened Newman with a "two-column [article] in a leading journal attacking my book bitterly" unless publication was stopped.[38] Moore was eager to make this censorship public and fight for the freedom of the press, but what did Rossetti think? Rossetti privately judged that the book although "wild" was "certainly not deficient in poetical feeling"; still, he thought it best to advise GM not to protest about the suppression of his poems, and not to reissue them.[39] GM persisted: wouldn't there be a few poems that could be retained for publication, as not "offensively immoral," or at least a little better than the rest? So on 6 May Rossetti went through the pages of *Pagan Poems* (rescued by GM from Newman's office), and proposed cancelling "Sappho" (lesbianism), "A Parisian Idyll" (adultery, French style), and "The Portrait" (pure lust), some of which GM admitted were "stupidly dirty" or "Swinburne more or less."[40]

Eventually, Moore gave up hope of a critical success. He passed around dedication copies to friends and notable people. One inscribed to Alfred, Lord Tennyson had to be reinscribed to Henry "Pot" Stephens, one of the *Sporting Times* staff, possibly after Queen Victoria's Laureate declined the gift.[41] Moore rediscovered his old friend Richard Mansell (formerly Maitland), and gave him a copy signed by the new London personality, "the author, George Moore." Another went to Oscar Wilde, a boyhood friend of the Moore brothers; in 1881 the "Poet Wilde" had not yet published a play, a novel, or an essay, but he had already invented a self to startle London. GM would have been happy with an equal notoriety. Other copies of *Pagan Poems* went to friends in Paris, such as Iza Georgette de Coëtlogon, with whom he waltzed in Boulogne.[42] All told, he distributed a sufficient number to be spoken of by June 1881 in the social notes of the *Sporting Times* as "Pagan" Moore, one of the minor celebrities at the Gaiety Theatre production of *La Dame aux camélias* starring Sarah Bernhardt.

At the Gaiety Theatre, GM was reportedly name-dropping for all he was worth, pointing out a man in the audience as "My old friend, Swinburne." The man was not Swinburne, Swinburne was not his old friend, and Swinburne would never come to be his friend if the poet, then confined at the Pines, Putney, ever learned that Moore was the author of the 5 March 1881

Spectator review of his *Studies in Song*. The review concedes that Swinburne is a great writer – at least he has "certain tricks of alliteration and antithesis" – but he has no "curious or profound thoughts," he knows nothing of the world, his emotions are "abstract sentiments," there is no "character drawing"; indeed, in his poems, "there is nothing exact, nothing complete, nothing true."[43] GM was seeking a naturalistic painting of modern life, with elements of character and narrative, not just lyrical effusions. Swinburne was yesterday; Zola was today; tomorrow, GM was hoping, would be George Moore, the author.

On 17 May 1881 the *Spectator* published another review by Moore, this time of Alexander Knox's travel guide to Algeria, *The New Playground*. Moore ridicules Knox as "a middle-aged man who went with his wife to seek sunshine,"[44] as if he expected him to be Rimbaud among the Arabs. Moore tried to learn the house style of the *Spectator*, but he tended to confuse surliness with judiciousness, and his attempts at the old Corinthian style of abuse had too much of simple meanness about them. His next review did not appear in the *Spectator* until 24 December, and it was to be his last. He examined a translation of Villon's complete poetical works by John Payne, O'Shaughnessy's bedside nurse. Concerning Payne's version of "Where are the Snows of Yesteryear," Moore writes: "Were Villon's poem like, or anything like, this, we venture to say that it would not have lived an hour in anyone's memory. We do not think, even as an original poem, any magazine would print it, so wretched is the verse, if it be verse at all."[45] Reviewing was often a blood sport in the 1880s, but Moore did not make a very pretty toreador, and later admitted that "my articles were draggle-tailed."[46]

4

Amid the wild obscenities of *Pagan Poems*, one can find franker statements of Moore's own thought than could be discovered in the pastiches of *Flowers of Passion* of four years earlier. "Ambition," for instance, may have been written to shock, but it is the shock of his personal truth:

> Yea, I would change my lot with any one,
> A king, a scavenger, a courtezan,
> A priest, a murderer, an artizan,
> For nothing worth the doing have I done.
>
> Just once before I sleep beneath the stone,
> I want to act and not to dream, I can;
> And leave within the future world of man
> Some seed to blossom when I shall be gone.
>
> If I am bad or good I little heed,
> For are not all things vile or virtuous
> According to the standard of our need?

> A soldier burnt the temple of Ephesus, –
> It was, perhaps, a very dreadful deed, –
> But it preserved his name, Erostratus.

Things are missing here that were too often found in the earlier volume – archaicisms like *methinks*, *meward*, *hark*, *plenilune*. In the place of outmoded Pre-Raphaelite diction, GM owns up to outlandish sentiments. Moore was sincerely afraid that he would amount to nothing by the time of his death, in spite of having been given every advantage by birth.

Another sonnet tries to picture in verse what Manet had shown of the prostitute in *Olympia*, Degas in *A Woman Leaving her Bath*, and Zola in *Nana* – the same clinical, professionally aesthetic attention to form. The strange *aubade* implies on the part of its female objectified subject an echoing professional unconcern – You want to look, go ahead and look; you paid for it:

> Idly she yawned, and threw her heavy hair
> Across her flesh-filled shoulders, called the maid,
> And slipped her sweet blond body out of bed,
> Searching her slippers in the wintry air.
>
> The fire shed over all a sudden glare, –
> Then in her bath she sponged from foot to head,
> Her body, arms, breasts, thighs, and things unsaid,
> Powdered and dried herself with delicate care.
>
> Then Zoe entered with the *Figaro*,
> The chocolate, the letters, and the cat,
> And drew the blinds to show the falling snow.
>
> Upon the sofa still her mistress sat
> Drawing along her legs, as white as milk,
> Her long stockings of finely-knitted silk.

It has been customary to laugh at Moore's poetry, or the very idea of it, but ten years later Ernest Dowson, Richard Le Gallienne, and Arthur Symons would be writing decadent verse not much different from, or better than, this sonnet.

Of course, there are embarrassments in the volume. In a sonnet describing his apartment at 61 rue Condorcet, "Chez Moi," GM, as self-satisfied as a cat with a bowl of cream, fantasises about the women he has loved, "Alice and Lizzy, Iza and Juliette," then concludes:

> Heigh-ho! The world spins in a circle yet . . .
> My life has been a very pleasant one.

Some poems lead away from concern with the French-polishing of a stanza and toward the qualities of a novel. "The Beggar Girl" gives a Zolaesque description of its subject both before and after her suicide in the Seine. Two poems are narrative in form: "A Modern Poem" is effectively a short story in verse, with a diminuendo ending, about a woman's choice during the intervals of a tennis party of a wealthy over an attractive suitor; "La Maitresse Mater-nelle" is a verse drama with two speakers, elaborating much of the plot used later in Moore's first novel, *A Modern Lover. Pagan Poems* is the verse labora-tory of a writer, born to be a prose artist, experimenting with his subject-position, his philosophy, and his material. It is also his last book of poetry, though he would occasionally later make use of verse for purposes of flirtation, or to state his credo, as in the following noteworthy summation of the aesthetic atheism for which "Pagan" Moore wished to be known:

> God is not more than man divine
>   And immortality exists
> Nowhere but in the Muses nine;
>   He lives who to the great truth lists
> That perfect good is perfect form.[47]

5

By April 1880, George Moore had moved out of his brother's lodgings in Fleet Street. Augustus was leading a wild life with the merry pranksters of the *Sporting Times* (*The Pink 'Un*), a society and racing weekly. Gambling, betting, drink-ing, whoring, and punning largely preoccupied this crowd – mostly made up of journalists, young lords, and scholars sent down from Oxford. Their mer-riment made it difficult, GM says, to get on with his novel, though he some-times accompanied them on their outings to music halls, aquariums, zoos, and theaters. More importantly, GM established contact with William Tinsley, whose publishing firm was operating a monthly magazine for which GM hoped to write. One day while passing through the swinging doors of the Gaiety Bar on the way to Tinsley's offices on Catherine Street, GM recalls he finally found the shape for his first novel: "to which delightful surprise was added the con-viction, not less delightful, that I had found at last my real business in life: I was a tale-teller."[48]

To gain time to learn his craft, Moore found a room of his own at 17 Cecil Street, a road that then ran between the Strand and Cleopatra's Needle on the Thames, just west of the Savoy Hotel.[49] In the neighborhood, one could eat at chophouses, fish-and-sauce shops, oyster shops, a German beer garden called the Tivoli, or at Romano's with the *Pink 'Un* crowd. The area was rough, cheap, and not very respectable – "the channel of all that is unloveliest in London," according to Max Beerbohm.[50] Moore found little beauty in his own rooms, as described in *Confessions of a Young Man*:

The sitting-room was a good deal longer than it was wide; it was panelled with deal, and the deal was painted a light brown; behind it there was a bedroom: the floor was covered with a ragged carpet, and a big bed stood in the middle of the floor. But next to the sitting room was a small bedroom which was let for 10 shillings a week; and the partition wall was so thin that I could hear every movement the occupant made. This proximity was intolerable, and eventually I decided on adding ten shillings to my rent, and I became the possessor of the entire flat.

According to *Confessions*, the landlady, Priscilla Harding, was fat, lascivious, and snoopy, with seven children.[51] Above him lived an actress with whom GM liked to chat in the stairwell. Moore also recalls his conversations with the servant, Emma, who worked seventeen hours a day, "scouring, washing, cooking, dressing those infamous children . . . at the beck and call of landlady, lodgers, and quarrelling children." When he posed as the cruel, aristocratic aesthete in *Confessions*, Moore addressed Emma as "very nearly, oh, very nearly an animal; your temperament and intelligence was just that of a dog that has picked up a master . . . Dickens would sentimentalize or laugh over you; I do neither."[52] Yet, dropping this pose when he came to write *Esther Waters*, Moore would profoundly humanise the maidservant heroine, whose original worked in his Cecil Street lodging-house. GM moved into his drab apartment just about the time of the 26 March 1881 auction of all the personal belongings he had left behind at 61 rue Condorcet, a change of circumstances often the subject of bitter reflections in *Confessions of a Young Man*.[53] Yet Moore was lucky to have landed at the right time in the very interior of a Zola novel.

On 1 April 1881, George Moore got up the nerve to write to Emile Zola from 17 Cecil Street. He sent the French novelist "Zola at Work," an article he had written for the April number of the *Burlington Magazine*. It was a well-informed piece of advocacy, explaining the grand plan of the Rougon–Macquart series of novels, defining the technique of literary realism, and asserting that truth was the only morality. In his cover letter to Zola, GM says his next step would be a twenty-page essay on Zola's work, that is, if Zola would accept GM as his publicist in London. Perhaps Zola would remember him from the *L'Assommoir* ball? He had been introduced by "my great friend, M. Manet." Should Zola have forgotten the Irishman then dressed in the costume of a Paris workman, maybe he had since heard of Moore from "my great and intimate friend, Alexis"? Or maybe his friend Léon Hennique has mentioned his name? With all of his calling cards on the table, Moore then suggests that a "great London publisher" would like a translation of *L'Assommoir*. Would Zola accept Moore as translator as well as publicity agent?[54] GM's first letter to his "cher maître" Zola decidedly makes a pitch for a sub-office in London, run by himself, on behalf of the larger firm of French naturalism.

No answer came back from Médan. On 12 April Moore wrote a second time, repeating his request to be accepted as Zola's translator for *L'Assommoir*; he had an editor lined up, who was seeking someone to "reconstitute" Zola's style in English.[55] Zola then invited his new recruit to Médan, and GM wasted no time in crossing to France for the visit. By 26 May 1881, he had returned with a precious new acquaintance. He did not keep it a secret. In the *St. James's Gazette* GM gave an account of "A Visit to M. Zola."[56]

Moore describes Zola's overbuilt country house in Médan, with its towers, multitude of staircases, and winding hallways, through which he was led to an upstairs room like a painter's studio, with an immense window in front of a heavy medieval writing desk. Zola, now grown rather stout, rose from a couch to greet him. The first impression of Zola as a "cold and distant man" wore off while he talked warmly of the novel he was reading, *Adam Bede*. The French novelist considered George Eliot to be "the English Flaubert" because of her "perfection of phrase and wonderful sense of reality," quite better than Dickens, "your magical storyteller . . . but nothing more." According to GM, Zola "greatly deprecates our circulating library system. The English novel, he says, is dying under the yoke. It forbids the complete and exact analysis of man, and confines the novelist to telling stories fit for family reading." GM may have been putting words in the mouth of the master, since these are objections to Mudie's Select Library that Moore himself had made in his 1879 letter to *Le Voltaire*. The interview ended with Zola plugging his new novel, *Pot-Bouille*, and reading to GM a scene from the play he was constructing out of *La Curée*, sure to be "one of the greatest literary triumphs of modern days," GM puffed.[57]

While holed up at 17 Cecil Street, Moore toiled over the works of Zola, translating parts of *L'Assommoir*, but evidently not finishing the job.[58] He also began his education in the English novel. In *Confessions of a Young Man*, he found a sassy, sarcastic, and insightful way of writing about the novels of the period, and it is clear from that critical survey that he had read widely in his English contemporaries. His landlady Priscilla Harding, he says, gave him a copy of George Meredith's *Tragic Comedians* (1880). He was disturbed when he realised after reading fifty pages that he could understand nothing of it; surely he "should be more literary than [his] landlady." He grilled her about her knowledge of Meredith, and found she had not heard of his poetry. Not even "Make the bed for Attila"? Moore pressed, "forgetful for the moment that she sometimes made my bed."[59] In addition to Meredith, Moore read the novels of James (all of those available; GM was impressed), W. D. Howells, Walter Besant, David Christie Murray, John Hill, Robert Buchanan, Rider Haggard, Ann Ritchie Thackeray, Ouida, Rhoda Broughton, Margaret Veley, Thomas Hardy, Richard Blackmore, Robert Louis Stevenson, and others publishing in the mid-1880s (with all of these, he was not very impressed). He gave himself the full course in the late nineteenth-century English novel, before deciding how to introduce into the fiction market a work of English naturalism.

In October 1881, Moore left his studies to go to Dublin for a meeting with Maurice Moore and Tom Ruttledge. Some weeks earlier, on 22 August,

Gladstone had won passage in Parliament for his second Land Act, paving the way for settlements between landlords and tenants. Of the three years' rent owed him, Moore agreed to wipe out one altogether, take one from the government under the new scheme provided under the Land Act, and receive the third from the tenants. Henceforth, things would be back on a sound footing. Within a year, the total rentals for the Moore estate were back up to £1,780, nearly £2,000 less than in the mid-1870s, but far better than the stoppage of recent years.[60] After the meeting, Maurice Moore wrote his mother that George would not be coming out to Mayo: "George insists on returning to London almost immediately; he says he must continue his writing."[61]

This writing may have included the paragraphs for society papers Moore admits doing when the *Spectator* stopped sending him books for review. But it is difficult to identify among the thousands of unsigned paragraphs in the *World, Pan, Cuckoo, Sporting Times,* and *Truth,* the as yet unfound personal style of George Moore. On 11 November the "Sporting Notes" of the *Sporting Times* reported an anecdote presumably provided by GM, an "Irish poet" lodged in "Cecil Street, Strand." The previous summer, the poet had suffered from somnabulism. At three one morning, he found himself, dressed only in his nightshirt, taking a walk down Fleet Street. By luck, a hansom passed; the poet hailed it, and gave his address. "You're a literary gent by the looks of yer," the driver said, and demanded prior payment. The poet showed he had no pockets in his nightshirt. "Yah!" yelled the driver, whipping his horse, "I knows yer. You've put on that costoom as an egscoose for not carrying a purse." So the Irish poet was forced to run down Fleet Street toward home, "as though all his creditors, editors, and evicted tenants were after him *en masse.*"[62] Most of the "good things" in this paper seem to modern sensibilities not much better than this anecdote. For their effect, jokes depend upon the release of tension, and the tensions released by anti-Irish, anti-Semitic, anti-matrimonial, anti-Liberal, anti-creditor, and anti-sobriety jokes have been replaced by other tensions and other jokes. For the sake of its Irish gentry readership, the *Sporting Times* was especially laced with shrill humor about poets, peasants, and Parnellites, a category into which the Cecil Street poet anecdote partly fits.

How Moore's own politics at the time harmonised with those of the *Sporting Times* is unclear. The story of his duel with Lord Rossmore suggests that GM remained sympathetic to the Liberals and Parnellites. Lord "Derry" Rossmore (b. 1853) owned a great estate in Monaghan, with a 10,000-acre grouse moor; in 1883 he became a master of the Grand Lodge of Monaghan Orangemen.[63] GM and Rossmore both attended a wild party at James Davis's Curzon Street house.[64] For some reason, perhaps because Moore came from a Catholic family, or because he had settled with his tenants, Rossmore was "attempting to make a butt" of him. Proposing a toast to the downfall of Gladstone, Rossmore made a speech "plainly intended to turn [Moore] into ridicule." Finally, Moore broke in:

"I don't agree with you; the Land Act of '81 was a necessity."

"Anyone who thinks so must be a fool."

"Very possibly, but I don't allow people to address such language to me, and you must be aware that to call anyone a fool, sitting with you at table at the house of a friend, is the act of a cad." . . .

"I only meant politically."

"And I only meant socially."

Rossmore slapped GM with his fingertips; GM "took up a champagne bottle, and struck him across the head and shoulders."[65]

In *Confessions of a Young Man* Moore claims that in the days following this fracas he wished to seize the opportunity for publicity by forcing a duel with pistols. English friends refused to act as his second, so Moore sent for Lewis Welldon Hawkins. Hawkins reasoned that GM had already avenged the insult by means of the champagne bottle, but Moore "sincerely wanted to shoot this young man." He had the courage to kill Rossmore or be killed by him, but Moore confesses he lacked the courage to tell Hawkins "that I looked upon the duel as a way to notoriety."[66] According to Rossmore, three weeks after the Saturday night at Curzon Street, a tall, offensive, dictatorial individual was announced by his servant. Moore's second demanded an apology, or else the names of Rossmore's *témoins*. Rossmore told Hawkins to be damned, but after further parley, and subsequent negotiations through Rossmore's brother-in-law, the terms of a mutual apology were agreed. In Moore's own manner of retelling this story, he is driven by his desire to shock and to make himself appear worse than he is – frivolous, vain, and scattershot. One suspects that, in truth, he was serious in his support of the Land Act of 1881. The whole force of history, as he saw it, was on the side of a better deal for peasants, and if the Land Act had the additional benefit of restoring the flow of his own income, he was one landlord who was satisfied to agree to its terms.

6

Even if George Moore was rather bleakly supportive of Gladstone and Parnell, he cannot have sorted very well with the patriotically Irish staff of *Tinsley's Magazine*. William Tinsley himself had no sympathy for the Irish cause; indeed, he ordered his sub-editor, Edmund Downey, not to wear shamrock on St Patrick's Day, and to keep clear of Irish stories – there was no money in the subject, Tinsley thought.[67] But the elderly editor left the magazine in Downey's hands, and Downey gave space in the monthly to many Irish writers newly arrived in London – Richard Dowling, Tighe Hopkins, John Augustus O'Shea, J. Fitzgerald Molloy, Lady Wilde, John F. Keane, John Hill, and Katharine Tynan. They often wrote about Irish subjects, usually in a romantic, humorous, or nostalgic vein. GM realised that in this office quality did not matter; if one wanted to be published, one had to go through the ritual of straddling the counter, petting the cat, idling the days away.[68]

In February 1882 Moore got his turn, and *Tinsley's Magazine* paid him for his first published story, "Under the Fan."[69] It is his first essay as well in the naturalistic (even cynical) style; there is nothing humorous, nostalgic, or romantic about it, much less Irish. He drew on his adventures with Dick Maitland ("Dick Lendsell" in the story), his chats with the actress upstairs at 17 Cecil Street, and his associations with the *Sporting Times* mashers, for a tale about two women and one eligible bachelor, "Lord Wedmore." Mrs White is thirty and divorced; Miss Vincent is twenty and an actress in light opera. At the theater with Mrs White, Lord Wedmore has eyes only for Miss Vincent. Because he is bankrolling Dick Lendsell, Lord Wedmore is privileged to go backstage and pay his respects to the actress; then he has Dick set up a champagne and oysters late-night supper. In the cab home, Lord Wedmore, quite drunk, proposes. Miss Vincent, however, is in love with a young actor, so she visits Mrs White the next day, and for a promissory note of £20,000 on Wedmore's fortune, agrees to jilt him, so Mrs White can catch the lord on the rebound. Things go like clockwork, and the two intelligent, practical women remain fast friends after their successful marriages, Miss Vincent to her actor, Mrs White to the Lord.

In the array of magazine fiction of the era, "Under the Fan" is noteworthy for being unmoralistic. The two women are explicitly said to be as moral as anyone, because they find reasons that satisfy themselves for their actions, and who could do more? The narrative is competent, but the writing is littered with obvious blunders, as when "diamonds flashed around necks turned pensively to listen," or when the reader learns that Mrs White's waist "had not lost its symmetry." It would have been difficult for the editor to tell from such prose that of all the contributors to *Tinsley's Magazine*, Moore would be the only one to amount to something as a novelist. Downey published no further stories by GM. Instead, he transferred his admiration to John Hill, a tall Irish graduate of Oxford and Heidelberg who looked like Henry Irving and wrote in a humorous, capable style. Hill moved into Cecil Street lodgings near GM, and GM hated everything about him: his education, his looks, his ease, his success. He seemed like Lewis Hawkins all over again. Moore could do nothing but silently scream at his own limitations, when "in the office which I had marked down for my own I saw [John Hill] installed as a genius."[70]

7

In May 1882, Moore was "working incessantly" at a novel; he reacted angrily after being scolded by his mother for not answering her letters:

> I have absolutely nothing to say to you. I am working incessantly at my novel and hope to finish it soon. It takes a great deal of time to write nine hundred

pages, particularly in my minute way of writing. I am so glad about Nina [married on 21 February 1882 to John Kilkelly] . . . I must go back to my novel, so good-bye. You are all right, quite well, n'est pas?[71]

If the 900-page manuscript was of *A Modern Lover*, and not the scrapped project for a novel entitled "An Aristocracy of Vice," Moore was overly optimistic about how soon he would finish the book; he had nearly a year's work to do on it.[72]

In James Davis's fanciful, sarcastic column, "Playhouses Without Plays" in the *Sporting Times*, Moore makes an appearance in the 2 September 1882 issue. At a Covent Garden promenade concert, Davis came upon George Moore near a stand with the motif of a Spanish market ("girls from Seville imported by Messrs Jones and Barber"). Moore was "in earnest conversation" with Henry "Pot" Stephens and Dr Gustave L. M. "Toxicologist" Strauss, a regular contributor to *Tinsley's Magazine*.[73] "The Pagan" Moore, "having read in the *Telegraph* that 'London is in want of a writer like Emile Zola, but without his offensive and unnecessary grossness,' is endeavouring to prove he is that man. 'You would do, Pagan,' says the Toxicologist, 'if the offensive and unnecessary grossness were required with the other qualifications of the French Johnnie.'"[74] The 24 September issue of the *Sporting Times* mentions that Augustus Moore ("Burgess," "The Poet") was now also reading the novels of Zola, in the intervals of working at his new job as literary agent to Augustus Harris at the Drury Lane Theatre.[75] And in the 18 November issue, "The Pagan" refuses to go along with James Davis to the Gus Harris production of *Macbeth* because he is "sick of these played-out pieces" (Shakespeare, that is), and wants to save himself for Tennyson's new play at the Globe Theatre, opening that night. At the intermission of *Macbeth*, Augustus Moore takes James Davis and Reginald Shirley "Blobbs" Brooks around to the Albion tavern for a drink. There they find George Moore once again "in a discussion on the same old subject, Zola's novels."[76]

All the experience of years spent in Parisian Bohemia is being slowly dropped into the ear of a bland-looking gentleman in spectacles. The Pagan . . . makes point after point in the one-sided argument, and looks around occasionally for applause from us. The following conversation ensues:

The Stranger: I cannot agree with you. I think we have had some excellent English novelists.

Pagan: I should like to know who they were. Except Frenchmen, who has written a novel worth reading?

The Stranger: My father, I would suggest, wrote –

Pagan (interrupting): Your father wrote novels, did he?

The Stranger: Yes, have you never read them?

Pagan (turning to Blobbs and winking): Not that I am aware of. What were they, the "Bloodthirsty Thunderer" or the "Pirate's Revenge"? And you think them as good as Zola's, do you?

The Stranger: They are generally admitted to be pretty good.

Pagan: I will most certainly read one of them if you will kindly tell me what novels were written by your father, or, in fact, by any member of your family. (The Pagan feels sure he has scored, and looks to us to applaud his sarcasm.)

The Stranger: He wrote a good many, amongst others –

Pagan: Any that were published?

The Stranger: Yes, certainly. Have you ever heard of –

Pagan (once more interrupting): I never heard of you or your father either. Tell me the name of one of his novels.

The Stranger: *David Copperfield*.

The Pagan collapses on discovering that the bland Stranger in spectacles is none other than Mr. Charles Dickens, junior.

The wind is taken out of Moore a second time that evening when Tennyson's play, which he swore would be magnificent, is judged by his friends to be "insipid, senseless stuff," not nearly as good as the stagey production of *Macbeth* at the home of late nineteenth-century pantomime, Gus Harris's Drury Lane.

At the end of 1882, GM contributed two items to Augustus Moore's "Christmas Annual," *Walnuts and Wine* – "A Russian Husband," a short story apparently worked up from anecdotes he heard from his Polish friend, Countess Kwiatowski,[77] and a translation of "Dolorida," a love poem Swinburne had written in French for Ada Menken. Swinburne destroyed the privately printed 1867 edition, but Augustus Moore retrieved a copy of the poem from Menken's keepsake book. Swinburne was furious, but the prank publicised *Walnuts and Wine*, and serves as a good example of Augustus's practices as one of the first literary agents.[78]

In the new year, GM moved to a better apartment at 3 Dane's Inn, again in the Strand, and right next door to his old friend Dick Mansell (or Maitland).[79] He then followed Augustus and Mansell into various theatrical preoccupations. First, GM evidently fancied himself a scout for undiscovered musical talent destined for success in light opera. His wish to be a new "Barnum" provokes a long *Pink 'Un* parody on an odyssey into the sidestreets of the suburbs in which GM leads the merry pranksters to the home of first one, and then another, already celebrated music-hall star ("He'll next discover St. Paul's Cathedral").[80]

In the hope of big royalties, the Moore brothers collaborated on an English translation of the popular French light opera, *Les Cloches de Corneville*.[81] Dick Mansell and F. C. Fairlie (alias F. C. Phillips) paid the Moores £30 for new lyrics, arguing that an existing English version had a faulty copyright.[82] The complicated plot, set in seventeenth-century Normandy, involves several young female wards, a dishonest agent, a haunted castle, the son of a rebel marquis who returns from American exile, lost letters rediscovered, and true identities revealed at the curtain's close. Working through the night, George and Augustus collaborated with the conductor Jimmy Glover while trying to match their lyrics to the music Glover hammered out on a piano at 3 Dane's Inn. The Moore brothers came up with airy, silly, lyric naughtiness like the following, to be sung by a female chorus:

> First look up here, and then down there,
> And criticize us everywhere.
>   You'll find us sweet
>   From head to feet
> And quite perfect and complete.

The three collaborators would then sleep through the day, and resume their *séance de collaboration* the following evening at Gatti's or the Tivoli restaurant.[83] The 31 March 1883 production was not a success in London, and closed after six nights, but Moore, who rarely writes a word about his part in this collaboration, gathered theatrical anecdotes from Glover that he would soon use in *A Mummer's Wife*.[84]

Moore's literary sidelights – the story, the poem, the light opera – did not get in the way of composition of *A Modern Lover*; he finished the manuscript, it seems, in the late fall. Richard Bentley and Son, to whom the manuscript was first offered, rejected it for publication; Moore next tried it on William Tinsley.[85] According to *Communication to My Friends*, Tinsley, asking first what title Moore had in mind for his novel, thought it a good one for publicity, but possibly also a red flag to the circulating library censors. Hearing next a synopsis of the plot, Tinsley judged it a "risky story," though still perhaps passable. If GM would allow Tinsley's trusted reader to mark passages it would be necessary to suppress, Tinsley would consider publication. The reader was the novelist Byron Webber. He was the first to see a dash of genius in George Moore's writing, and on his advocacy the book was accepted, on condition that GM guarantee any losses Tinsley suffered up to £40.[86] When the manuscript had gone to the printer, GM wrote to his mother taking his own audit of his first novel and his promise as a writer:

> It is the best thing I have done and the only thing I have done. People may like it or dislike it but I do not think that anyone will take it for anything except the work of a person who has endeavoured to think for himself. That it is peculiar goes without saying. I was born, I live, and I shall die a peculiar man – I could not be commonplace were I to try. The bitterest thing is what I think myself: – it is not a work of genius, not of great talent. It is the work of a man affected with that most terrible of all maladies, a dash of genius. We are unfortunate who lead the way, who perish unknown in the fight, and upon whose bodies others ascend the peaks of fame.
>
> My novel is a new method. It is not a warming up of Dickens or Thackeray. It is a method that will certainly be adopted by other writers but will the first effort meet with recognition? I scarcely think so.[87]

Much of the essential Moore speaks in this letter: his characteristic wonder at his own identity, his unmoralistic affirmation of his quirks, his modernist commitment to the avant-garde, his acknowledgement that he carries the disease of artistic ambition, that indeed he is defined by his yearning for greatness, not by greatness itself. Yet his very willingness to acknowledge his partial self could paradoxically create the fullness of a literary self that would gain him the lasting attention of readers that he so painfully desired.

On 30 April 1883, the artist whose lesson to Moore was to "be ashamed of nothing but to be ashamed" died in Paris. There is no evidence that Moore was among the 500 present for Manet's funeral on 3 May, but he arranged to buy from Manet's widow two paintings ahead of the official auction of Manet's works held in Paris on 4–5 February 1884.[88] GM acquired *Le Clairon*, the bugle boy, and, a strange choice, *Buste de la femme*, one of Manet's very few nudes, a wide-eyed woman in a chair, nude to the waist, arms across her stomach and under her full breasts, which have enormous pink aureoles.

8

A Modern Lover was published in June 1883. It is the story of "Lewis Seymour and Some Women," to give it the phrase Moore used as a title for his 1917 revision of the novel. It has the formal simplicity of a fable, the topicality of a leading article in a monthly, and the bleak cynicism of a new generation raised on Schopenhauer. Lewis Seymour, a young painter, has come down to his last sovereign. He goes to his dealer, Mr Bendish, a large investor in the canvases of a group called "the Moderns." The leader of the Moderns, Thompson, is a clever fellow, but he does no classical, picturesque, or currently fashionable subjects; instead, he paints pictures of acrobats in flesh-stockings, or bar-girls serving beer to clerks (like Degas and Manet, respectively). Lewis once saw himself as a Modern, but he has deserted their cause for what he hopes are more saleable and conventional products. Yet on this day, Mr Bendish refuses to buy Lewis's watercolors.

So Lewis returns to his lodgings thinking of suicide, or maybe a loan from his lodging-house neighbor, Gwynnie Lloyd, a kind Methodist girl who would not refuse to save his life by sharing her wages. Back at his apartment, the dealer Mr Jacobs arrives with a request for a decorative panel of Venus rising from the sea, accompanied by Cupids – some inexpensive substitute for Cabanel's famous picture. Lewis takes the order (the first of what Jacobs tells him will be many, if his work is satisfactory). He coaxes the modest but lovesick Gwynnie Lloyd into posing nude for him. His life, he says, depends on it; after he succeeds, he'll marry her. She runs away when she sees that he has accurately painted not only her body but her face as well.

Bringing the finished picture back to the dealer, Lewis has the luck to arrive when another customer, Mrs Bentham, comes in seeking a decorator for her ballroom. The dealer supplies her with Lewis Seymour. Mrs Bentham, neither young nor pretty, has for some time been separated from her violent husband. She "longs for a large sweet affection wherein she could plunge her whole soul, as a trout on the warm grass longs for the cool stream that ripples in sight."[89] After months of romancing her in her country house, Lewis thinks of asking her to seek a divorce, so she could "bestow on him her heart, and her wealth."[90] Then at a tennis party hosted by Mrs Bentham, Lewis catches the eye of a third woman, the beautiful, wealthy, and young Lady Helen. She has no desire for the "traffic in maternity," but loves love for its own sake; she finds something of herself to love in Lewis, "for self-love being the basis of life, we love best a wavering image of ourselves."[91] Jealous of Lady Helen, Mrs Bentham grants Lewis a kiss, but rejects his request that she divorce and marry him. The rejection ends their sexual relations for a time, but not Mrs Bentham's financial support of Lewis.

When the decorations are completed, Lewis goes to Paris to work at the Beaux Arts on an allowance from Mrs Bentham. She comes to visit him and he is pleased that people will mistakenly think that she is his mistress; it consoles him that nobody knows the truth. The suspicion "haunted him that many people fancied that he was the screen used to shelter an unknown and more favoured lover. This false shame was of all things essentially a part of his nature."[92] He tries to get her to kiss him again, but she refuses, even after he threatens to throw himself in the Seine, which must puzzle Lewis, as Gwynnie yielded when he threatened to do the same in the Thames. But returning from the opera, "they were possessed by desires from which they could not fly, and at last, like the fisher conducting the tired fish to the bank, love led them to the carriage, and maliciously cried 'à l'hôtel' to the coachman."[93] After this event, Mrs Bentham gives herself up to the life of a Paris woman of fashion, and starts an international salon, until she is tracked by Mr Bentham, who is outraged at her indiscretion. He blackmails her for £1,000. Lewis, demoralised by Paris, now seems so utterly foolish and trivial to Mrs Bentham that he is not worth the trouble of a divorce.

Mrs Bentham decides to set Lewis up with a studio in London, in the hope that English society will have an improving effect on him. There he meets, in the company of the Modern painter Thompson, a novelist named Harding. Harding studies Lewis "as a chemist might a combination of gases."[94] In the company of the Moderns, Lewis begins to suffer the malady of the love of art for art's sake; he has a desire for greatness, but cannot fulfill it; he has the pains of childbearing without the happiness of delivery. He is, however, saved by his bad qualities, and goes after pleasure and comfort, not greatness and misery.

With sales secretly subsidised by Mrs Bentham, and introduced by her to society, his career thrives. At a ball thrown by Mrs Bentham, Lewis once again meets Lady Helen, courts her, and, interrogated by her, protests that he could not possibly be having an affair with Mrs Bentham, because she is old enough to be his mother. Mrs Bentham overhears this crushing statement. She breaks with Lewis, who becomes engaged to Lady Helen. The parents of Lady Helen oppose a marriage to Lewis: he is a man of low birth, rumored to be a scandalous gigolo, but the strong-willed Lady Helen prevails. She then goes about proving her family wrong by working for the public success of Lewis.

In the conflict of the "Moderns" (Impressionists) with the "Medievals" (Pre-Raphaelites), Lewis positions himself in the art market as a classicist, doing motifs like "Salomé," "Clytemnestra," and "Sappho." His specialty is the nude laid in a marble setting, with antique furnishings. Lewis uses Lady Helen's body in one such mythological picture, of "Sappho" among her attendants, the *frisson* of which brings him still more attention. Lewis makes big commissions, but the arch–Modern Thompson has a triumph too. With a large canvas, Thompson finally wins widespread acknowledgement as a master, even though (like Manet) he had only worked "for his own heart's praise, and for that of the little band of artists that surrounded him."[95]

Lady Helen grows more jealous as Lewis gets more successful, because she knows for a fact he is unfaithful both with his models and his portrait subjects. Lewis defends himself by saying that he has to flirt to get commissions; if she would learn to do it too, she could bring him portrait commissions from men. She does learn to flirt, and does secure the commissions. Finally, she schemes to get him elected to the Royal Academy in place of Thompson. Late in the novel, Gwynnie, disfigured by smallpox, reappears as a maid in Lady Helen's house. All three women are reunited and regard the artist whose success they have created. Each has sacrificed: Gwynnie her innocence, Mrs Bentham her money and respectability, Lady Helen her social position and her natural pride. They have been to him, respectively, as sister, mother, and wife, but, by the power of his sexual attraction, he has been able to treat each of them in an insensitive, faithless, and exploitative manner.[96] How the weakness of his character becomes a form of power over women is the novel's subject, its enigma, and its moral.

It is not difficult to identify the biographical bases for many characters and incidents in Moore's first novel. Thompson is largely drawn from Manet; the penetrating theoretical wit of Harding is that of Degas, though Harding also emerges as a projection of the sort of novelist Moore would like to be. The role of the art dealer Bendish in buying up "the Moderns," later to profit from their success, is adapted from Durand-Ruel's relationship to the Impressionists. Mrs Bentham in her Paris phase as queen of a salon is presumably built up from Moore's observations in the drawing rooms of the Marquis d'Osmond and Madame de Coëtlogon. Augustus Moore may have been irritated by the contemptuous portrait of Ripple, a paragraphist for a society paper.[97] And a great deal of the character of Lewis Seymour is a study of Lewis Welldon Hawkins:

both were attractive and stylish, both exploited women, both were facile artists without genius who admired Impressionism without being able to commit themselves to its uncommercial principles, both were eager for social success, both won recognition by the art establishment for their work.[98] The long period in which Moore suffered under his enchantment to Lewis created the spite that is expressed in this deadly novel about male mendacity, in addition to a considerable amount of envy on the part of a man of little sex appeal for another with a great deal (the mysteries of sexual attractiveness are the sign under which Fate manifests itself in the novel). It is true that in the creation of the novel's hero Moore drew upon his own self-contempt as well as his contempt for Lewis Hawkins. The passage quoted above in which Lewis fears being thought by others to be a "blind" used by a woman to hide an affair with a second man may have been taken from GM's own experience with Georgette de Coëtlogon.[99]

While the character flaws of the hero seem to be drawn from Lewis Welldon Hawkins and GM himself, the painter's London career and the type of painting he does strongly suggest another model: Lawrence Alma-Tadema, the fashionable expert in fur, flesh, marble, and Roman antiquities. Alma-Tadema (born 1836) was a Dutch painter who lost his first wife to smallpox in 1869, then came to London, married the wealthy and lovely nineteen-year-old Laura Epps in 1871 (sister of Edmund Gosse's wife Ellen), used her as a model for classical pictures like *Sappho and Alcaeus* (1881), and succeeded in becoming a Royal Academician in 1879.[100] Moore could have known from Gosse about Alma-Tadema's life.[101] The adaptation of generalised aspects of Alma-Tadema's career succeeds in giving the novel an English rather than a French setting. Moore's transfer of the Impressionists and naturalists (the "Moderns") to London, on the other hand, does not reflect reality; instead, he means to stimulate a change in the way things are. He wanted to start a debate about art and literature based on the many pages of aesthetic discussion interleaved with the plot.

Reviewers do not always notice talent at first sight, and they would often treat Moore brutally in later years, but in July 1883 they recognized in *A Modern Lover* the arrival of a talent, though one with dangerous tendencies. The *Athenaeum* gathered that Moore had "an inclination towards naturalist literature and impressionist art," but he was "not at all shocking." If he would just clear his mind of cant, "he might do something." Moore was mildly chastised for poor chronology, a weak grasp of English society, and bad spelling of French names, but his book, it was conceded, had merit.[102] *St. James's Gazette* agreed that the novel was not so "startlingly improper" as it might at first appear; Moore's characterisation of Lewis Seymour was "worthy of much praise," and Gwynnie Lloyd's struggles of conscience before posing were singled out for approval. Though he was credited with "plenty of talent," Moore was warned to "leave off studying Zola" and "divest himself of the notion that he was born to found a new school of impressionist writers of fiction."[103] Zola was a red flag for the *Academy* as well: "It is Zola in evening dress and with a clean face, but Zola all the same."[104] The *Spectator* judged Moore to be a better novelist than Zola, or "the hogs of his sty," because Moore was a Christian and a gentleman; otherwise, how could he have written the tender and moving scene of Gwynnie's self-sacrifice to the penniless artist? In spite of Moore's solecisms and Franglais, this reviewer found him always intelligent and interesting.[105]

Moore was elated with reviews like these from the major monthlies. He had guaranteed Tinsley against losses up to £40 if the edition did not sell; with the balance of reviews approving his morality and taste, he was happy to think the book would be well subscribed by the circulating libraries. Moore recalled that when the *Spectator* review came out (18 August 1883), he went to Tinsley's office to read it to him. Tinsley waved it away as of no consequence. Mudie's Select Library had taken only fifty copies and W. H. Smith only twenty-five. Without a larger subscription from the two circulating libraries, Moore's novel would never sell its print run at 31s. 6d. for each three-volume set. Moore suggested that Tinsley might have broken the stranglehold of the circulating libraries by publishing the novel in a new form – one volume for six shillings, so anyone could afford it. "'I could not have sold your novel at six shillings,' Tinsley replied, 'nor at three-and-sixpence, nor at any other price, for Smith owns all the bookstalls, and what he will not circulate, he will not sell.'" Then Moore realised the gravity of his difficulty in fighting the libraries.[106]

Furious, he then marched up from the Strand to New Oxford Street, near the British Museum, and into Mudie's central office. The proprietor turned out to be "a dull, almost lifeless, thick-set, middle-aged man," perhaps the son Arthur Mudie, rather than sixty-five-year-old Charles Edward Mudie. Moore blurted out all he could remember of Zola's *Le Roman expéri- mental*. Mudie suggested that Moore would find a better model than Zola in Trollope.

If Moore was only a first-time novelist, he was also a Mayo landlord, and as angry as such a person could be with a middle-class English tradesman standing directly in the path of his success. He threatened to destroy Mudie's business. He would publish in a cheap, one-volume format, and end the monopoly of overpriced, unaffordable novels. Moore says he also confronted the reader for W. H. Smith's bookstalls, William Faux, whom GM knew as a close friend of Tinsley's who liked to tell smutty jokes. Faux informed Moore that W. H. Smith had banned the book after the protest of two ladies in the country, who were scandalised by Gwynnie's posing in the nude. But the tact of that passage was singled out for praise in the reviews, GM complained, and, with a cunning twist, added: "You surely don't want to find fault with the morals of the *Spectator*"![107] And what moral standard would Faux use? "I have no standard to set up; I shall take the advice of my customers." "Two ladies in the country"?

The fury ran deep in George Moore. He had campaigned diligently for himself and for naturalism ever since coming to London. He had put all his hopes into making a name, and a living, as a novelist. Now, just as he was about to enjoy as complete a triumph as he might have wished for for his first novel, he was silenced by men he regarded as pious, hypocritical shopkeepers, each one "a tradesman who considers himself qualified to decide the most delicate artistic questions that may be raised."[108] Moore's long war with the circulating libraries had begun.

Chapter 4
A Ricochet of Zola in London

I

In 1930 Charles Morgan, working on a biography of George Moore, asked George Bernard Shaw for his early memories of his fellow Irishman. Shaw said he knew Moore when he lived in Cecil Street, before he had made a name as a novelist. He knew Augustus Moore too, but seldom if ever saw the two brothers together. "There was always a certain delicacy about George and he knew how to be a gentleman when he wanted to." However, he was "always telling stories about himself and women"; the stories usually ended up with the woman throwing a lamp at George. "If you said," Shaw recalled, "'But George, don't talk such nonsense, you are making it all up,' he was not in the least put out . . . but just said, 'Don't interrupt me,' and went on as before."[1] Shaw lost sight of Moore. Then one day William Archer said he had been reading a wonderful naturalist novel by a new author. Shaw asked who it was. "Well," Archer replied, "his name is George Moore." "'Nonsense,' Shaw replied, 'But I *know* George Moore. He couldn't possibly write a real book. He couldn't possibly do anything.' But there it was. He had written it, and then I began to understand the incredible industry of the man."

There was a self-consciously comical side to George Moore, the funny incompetent little boy his father and mother had laughed at, and later the laughing-stock of the *Sporting Times*. Yet there was another George Moore too, one very like his father, G. H. Moore. The son also had the desire for greatness, the capacity for lasting anger, and the family gift for creating a disturbance, all caught in the Mayo saying: "Scratch a Moore and your own blood will flow." In George Moore, these qualities were to make him a superior "enemy of the people," to use Ibsen's title for those intellectual aristocrats who stand outside the good, hypocritical, bourgeois majority. In his autobiographical preface to the Carra edition of his works (1922), GM staged the comical George Moore melodramatically crying out his threat in the offices of the circulating libraries magnate –

I will wreck this big house of yours, Mr. Mudie . . . I will appeal to the public!

– while looking about the room, as if measuring the strength of the architecture.[2] If this scene occurred at all, and if it occurred after the *Spectator*'s 18 August 1883 review of *A Modern Lover*, the real George Moore had already seriously set to work on his second book. In *A Mummer's Wife*, he had already conceived the very sort of novel that would most defiantly challenge the censorship of English fiction, an unmoralistic narrative of adultery, in which the seducer was a fundamentally good man.[3] Furthermore, he had already made, or was on the point of making, arrangements with a firm that would introduce a type of publication new to the English fiction market, the cheap single-volume novel, which ultimately would supplant the triple-decker circulated for rental through Mudie's Select Library. The story, the style, the packaging, and the marketing campaign of *A Mummer's Wife* were all designed as a free-market, free-speech attack on the immorality of monopoly and censorship. Moore would deploy the English tradition of liberty against English Low Church monopoly capitalism.

When *A Modern Lover* was in press, Moore gathered material about theatrical life for *A Mummer's Wife*. His collaboration with Augustus Moore and Jimmy Glover on the new translation of *Les Cloches de Corneville* in March 1883 gave him contacts in the world of light opera and anecdotes about its folkways. During their work together, for instance, Glover told him a story about how he and his friends from a theater company touring the provinces cheated a railway restaurant by telegraphing down the line for a lunch for forty during the next short stopover. The telegraph was signed "Mr. Simpson," a generous and wholly imaginary personage. All the lunching actors claimed to know "Mr. Simpson" when questioned by the waiters during the stopover, but he was not to be found when the train departed. This anecdote formed the basis for Chapter 12 of Moore's novel.[4] Years later, Glover claimed to have been the "true author" of the then classic novel, and Moore only his biographer, so GM coolly and snidely credited him with the experience of pilfering "buns and sandwiches from the refreshment bars," so that the music conductor was nicknamed by the press "'Sandwiches' Glover."[5]

Moore also worked with Glover on a light opera, *A Fashionable Beauty*.[6] This operetta provides lyrics for a leg show, built around a satirical plotlet making fun of American millionaires, English aristocrats, Lily Langtry ("Miss Pears Soap"), Professional Beauties in general, and poets like Wilde who celebrate their celebrity. One lyric attains the ordinary level of music-hall burlesque (if not the high standard of Gilbert and Sullivan) and may give an impression of the rest; it is sung by the Lily Langtry character:

> I was a lovely spouse
> Three years, and then at Cowes
> A Marquis thought me fair

And Jenkins wrote a par
And a poet said a star
Was shining in the air.

Next season in the row
They crowded to and fro
My Lily face to see

And on my dainty shape
I wore the yellow cape
And they called it after me

My fame went East and West
They knew how I was dressed
Both in China and Japan

And the King of Hottentot
Bought a photo on the spot
I was loved in Isphahan

The Lords and Dukes and Earls
Went mad about my curls
But my husband was a dear

Though he wondered how I dressed
Like a queen among the rest
Upon fifty pounds a year.[7]

Why did Moore commit his energies to the production of such mean little frivolities? In *A Mummer's Wife*, a novelist, Harding, is asked by the stage-manager hero, Dick Lennox, to "do the book" for some music his lanky friend Montgomery (i.e. Jimmy Glover) has written. Although "Harding was going in for writing novels, and didn't seem to care much for theatrical work," Dick Lennox knew you could "get at authors when you had a bit of coin to show beforehand."[8] Moore like Harding may have done lyrics for music by Glover as a favor to Mansell or for ready money, yet Moore unlike Harding was also gathering notes for his next novel. He acquired still more material by going along with Mansell and the "second company" of *Les Cloches de Corneville* on a provincial tour, until he was brimming with theater lore and backstage slang.[9]

Moore credited Byron Webber, the reader for William Tinsley, with helping him on his second novel in two important ways. First, Webber introduced Moore to Herman de Lange, a small actor who seemed born to play comic parts. De Lange assembled Glover and half a dozen actors in the Gaiety Bar, and Moore briefly laid out for them the plan of his book: the manager of a travel-ing opera company runs off with the wife of his landlord, and her life goes to pieces outside the moralities of a settled home. De Lange and company drank whiskeys and obligingly told stories of romances with landladies, while GM, never much of a drinker, took notes. De Lange also suggested, GM says, that the novel be set in Hanley, one of the "Five Towns," and "a town, ugly and dull, that would not excite the imagination even of George Borrow . . . a pottery town" that manufactured chamberpots, wash bowls, dishware, and cheap decorative vases.[10] GM liked the idea of comic actors in an industrial town, and he thought of going to Hanley with his notebook.[11]

Even more importantly, Byron Webber introduced Moore to Henry Vizetelly (?1812–89), who Webber believed might publish *A Mummer's Wife*. Moore's partnership with Vizetelly became the key to making a real challenge to the monopoly of the circulating libraries. Immigrants from Italy many generations earlier, the Vizetellys were glassworkers in seventeenth-century London, and printers in the eighteenth century. Herman Vizetelly helped start the *Illustrated London News* in 1842, the first paper of its kind. Later he worked as its Paris correspondent (1865–72). In 1880 he started a publishing company with his sons; it specialised in literature with a French interest.[12] On Webber's advice, Moore went off to meet Vizetelly and found a "truly gaunt and grey" man of sixty or seventy, thin as a rake, and too small for his clothes, "yet with a strange vitality in his eyes."[13] Moore sketched out the story of his new book. Vizetelly asked him questions about Zola and Maupassant; presumably, the publisher also explained his line in "fine French novels" – Daudet, George Sand, Mérimée, etc.

It is not clear whether it was GM or Vizetelly who subsequently proposed bringing out the complete series of Zola's novels in one-volume editions. According to Vizetelly's son Ernest, his father and GM worked together closely as pioneers in the publication of one-volume novels and the popularisation of realistic fiction, and Ernest says that his father deserves principal credit for setting the price at 6 shillings a volume; 4s. 6d. wholesale – still too high a price, in Moore's own opinion.[14] The first Zola novel in a Vizetelly edition, *L'Assommoir*, came out in 1884; the anonymous translation, begun by Moore, was completed by Vizetelly's son Ernest.[15] Concerning Moore's own novel, Vizetelly encouraged him to carry out his plan to visit Hanley and "search out everything."[16] Moore was impressed by the old man: Vizetelly was himself an author, had read Gautier (always GM's measure of perfect aestheticism), and possessed entrepreneurial courage.

In September, Moore set out for Tillyra Castle in the West of Ireland, where as Edward Martyn's guest, he meant to begin writing *A Mummer's Wife*. In a 17 September 1883 letter to Zola from Tillyra, Moore informed the master of the latest news about the progress of the movement in England. His first novel, he explained, was published and it had been a success ("I owe everything to you"), in spite of the frightful temporising dodges he had been forced to make. But what would Zola wish? "It had to be done; it was done." Now that GM had created some taste for naturalist fiction in England, his next step would be to translate *Thérèse Raquin*, if Zola would permit it.[17] Moore says that he has located a new publisher (Vizetelly is not named) who would certainly accept GM's offer to translate the book. Moore promises Zola that he will give an exact idea in English of Zola's style, unlike the American translators who "massacre" the original author. Indeed, GM and this publisher mean to bring out not just *Thérèse Raquin*, but Zola's complete works, those already written, and those yet to be published. Unfortunately, GM admits, the editor is not in a position to actually pay Zola, yet a trial of naturalism in England could not but interest the French master. Meanwhile, GM had drafted a version of a little comedy by W. S. Gilbert, "Sweethearts," which he and Paul Alexis were hoping to bring to the French stage. In the spring, Moore would be coming to Paris, and naturally would call upon Zola in Médan.[18] Thus, Zola's English agent completes his progress report on the transplantation of a French style to the English novel.

2

Tillyra Castle was the home of Edward Martyn (1859–1921), whose friendship with Moore was to last nearly forty years. Like Moore, Martyn was a Catholic Irish landlord of literary ambitions. The Martyns and the Moores had a long association, though they were related by marriage and not, as is sometimes reported, by blood.[19] Edward Martyn had been a classmate of Augustus Moore at Beaumont School in England from 1870; indeed, he and Augustus tried, quite ineffectually, to burn the school down as a protest against its system.[20] Mrs Annie Smyth Martyn (widowed in 1860) moved with her two sons to 8 Onslow Square in 1875, not far from the Moores' London residence of the time, 39 Alfred Place. As Irish Catholic widows in London, trying to cope with growing boys, Mrs Moore and Mrs Martyn became good friends. It was in London that GM, staying with his mother at Alfred Place from the summer of 1874 through the summer of 1875, met the young Martyn. In later decades, as the only Irish friend who knew him from his youth, Martyn used to tease Moore by saying that he had evolved out of nothing, "developing from the mere sponge to the vertebrate and upward," a simile whose authority GM had to accept, though he preferred to say that he was both the artist and the block of marble in the shaping of his self, "George Moore."[21]

From 1877, Martyn was at Christ Church, Oxford, where he performed unsatisfactorily in one subject after another, and was finally sent down at the end of Michaelmas Term, 1879.[22] Although morbidly awkward and unhappy at Oxford, he made some interesting friends there among the followers of Walter Pater's High Church, Hellenistic aestheticism, including Count Stanislaus Edward Stenbock, an eccentric Estonian homosexual, who kept a toad for a pet, carried a golden vial of perfume, and published love poems to boys as early as 1881:

> And if some maiden beautiful
>   Become thy love and joy,
> Think on that passionate male heart
>   That loved thee when a boy.[23]

Many undergraduates were then under the spell of Pater. They admired with Pater the beauty of the Catholic ritual; they followed Pater in believing that the wisest spend their life in art and song. But what most caught Martyn's ear in the Paterian moment at Oxford was the celebration of Greek ideals of male beauty and Greek relations among men. John Addington Symonds could have been speaking about Martyn when he complained to Benjamin Jowett of the "dangers" of an education in Greats at Oxford: the boys "discover that what they had been blindly groping after was once an admitted possibility – not in a mean hole or corner – but that the race whose literature forms the basis of their higher culture, lived in that way . . . derived courage, drew intellectual illumination, took their first step in the paths which led to great achievements and the arduous pursuit of virtue"; in short, that homosexuality in the greatest of Western cultures was not a crime but a cultural ideal.[24] Edward took a tour to Greece, collected replicas of Greek statues, came to believe Greek the most beautiful of all languages (including Irish), and began a poem with a Greek setting.

After Edward failed at Oxford, his mother appears to have desired to place him under the manly wing of George Moore, the oldest son of her best friend Mary Blake Moore. In the fall of 1880 when Moore was in Ireland, it is possible that he was induced to spend some unrecorded time at Tillyra, as suggested by Moore's account in *Ave*. There, not far from Sir William Gregory's estate at Coole, he would have found the slightly fat, slightly balding, and large-booted Edward, at twenty-one the master of a 4,932-acre unencumbered estate, with a twelfth-century tower, and a £20,000 annex still underway, erected at Mrs Martyn's insistence to suit Edward's hypothetical wife. It was a neo-Gothic building designed by George Ashlin with hexagonal corner turrets, mullioned windows on three of the sides of each corner; on the ground floor, the ceilings were coffered and ornamentally painted; each room had a different style of marble fireplace – all this, as bait for a bride.

Edward would be Annie Smyth Martyn's only hope for an heir to Tillyra after the death of her quite different son, John Martyn, on 5 March 1883. But Edward was a "woman-hater," the contemporary phrase for a man who loved men, though for all that Edward was a misogynist as well. Mrs Annie Smyth Martyn could not admit to herself, as Moore puts it, "any more than you can, reader, or myself, that we come into the world made as it were to order."[25] As the heiress of the pious, wealthy Smyths of Masonbrook, Mrs Martyn had made an alliance with Edward's father in order to save a great Catholic Ascendancy family of the West; the idea that the Martyn line would die out one generation later was dreadful to her. Yet Edward "was averse to women from the time he was born. It was not her fault; it was not his. Education could do nothing. His will to be different was helpless."[26] When Edward confided that he could not, being what he was, marry, and asked what he would do with this huge annex under construction, GM told him to leave it unbuilt and follow his instinct. Edward was "startled by the idea."[27] He continued to be despondent about his future: "I am too different from other people, he used to say, ever to be a success."[28] Moore encouraged Martyn to pursue, at least, his poetry.

On his September 1883 visit to Tillyra, GM found that Edward had retired from the annex completed at his mother's insistence, in order to take up residence in the ancient tower, which he had fitted out according to his own tastes. Up the steep stair of the tower, on the first stage Martyn had set up his private place of worship, with a seven-foot-tall candlestick, and a wooden chair copied from a picture by Dürer; on the next stage was the study, lit by Pre-Raphaelite stained-glass windows just completed in 1883 in London by Edward Frampton: the saints depicted are Chaucer, Milton, Dante, Shakespeare, and Plato. The bedroom at the top had a flagstone floor, a slightly cramped oak four-poster (hardly big enough for two) made in 1616. Beside it was Edward's prie-dieu, kneeler, and prayer rail. Cloistered and encastled, Martyn had built his aesthetic stronghold against his mother's matrimonial plans.[29]

The Land Law under which GM had settled with his tenants in October 1881 was no inducement to Edward. Relations between landlords and tenants in his area were as bad as in Mayo, and worse than at Moore Hall. Lord Clanricarde ("Lord Clan Rackrent" to his tenants) was an infamously unsympathetic local landlord and the owner of the town of Loughrea. Clanricarde received in London the £80,000 collected by his land agents each year and visited Ireland only for the funerals of his parents.[30] In Loughrea, in the summer of 1881, a constable was shot, agents were threatened, and graves were dug for those tempting the anger of the League. By the turn of the century, Edward became a Nationalist (first President of Sinn Fein in 1907); however, in the 1880s he was no friend to the land movement. He was "severe, strict, and hard on the popular class."[31] The plain people of Ireland, he thought, needed both the Roman Catholic Church and the Ascendancy class as safeguards; otherwise, they would all become communists. He was sufficiently frightened of the moral character of the Land League to put into his early will a clause about the measures to be taken should he be "murdered, maimed, or injured in his person."[32]

While at Tillyra, GM apparently not only set to work on his novel, but also showed a benevolent interest in the poems Edward was then writing. These may have been the poems with Greek settings that Edward, after a terrible crisis, burned in late 1885. He then told his friends that poems like "Pheidas" and "Pericles," harmless though they might seem, were dangerous to faith and morals; at least they did not "conduce to the glory of God."[33] In 1883, Edward was not yet so fanatical about his Catholicism; culture was his form of worship, as illustrated in the stained-glass windows of his study. Seeking help for Martyn's poetry, Moore contacted George Barlow (1847–1913) – along with John Payne, Mary Robinson, and the Rossettis, a friend of the tall blind poet, Philip Bourke Marston.[34] GM had written Barlow for a "Greek and Christian poem" – just Martyn's sort of thing – to publish in a magazine GM hoped to edit. Barlow apologised that he had mislaid that particular poem; the rest of his current work, he lamented, was at a standstill, though he was satisfied with his "curious" essay, "Polygamy and Monogamy, from an Artistic Point of View."[35] In addition to providing Edward with an introduction to Barlow and the Marston circle, Moore tried to get William Michael Rossetti to read Edward's verse ("totally different from other people's poetry").[36] If Edward wished to be a writer, Moore advised, he should leave Tillyra and come to live in the Strand with other writers. In a few years, Edward would come to be GM's neighbor in the Temple, and the two Irish landlord aesthetes, one desperate for the love of women, the other afraid of them, would continue their strange boon companionship.

From Tillyra, GM went north to spend three months with his mother at Moore Hall, some of the happiest months of his working life.[37] He was still on his estate on 28 November 1883 when he received a letter from Georgette de Coëtlogon, the Parisian-American with a house on the Avenue Bois de Boulogne. In *Memoirs of My Dead Life*, Moore told how he was reading on the balcony with Georgette one day, and while her husband was walking about within the apartment she had raised her eyes to Moore and said, "Well, you can kiss me now." "But her husband was in front, and he was a thick-set man."[38] GM suspected she never forgave him for his cowardice. Now, in Paris, Georgette found herself disheartened by another romance; "Have you," she asked, "ever been utterly disillusioned about some one for whom you cared very much & in whom you believed certainly?" And so she unfolded to GM, patient listener and note-taker, the tale of a man who treated her badly when she wouldn't give him all that he wanted of her. (He made good use of this and other letters from Georgette in *Confessions of a Young Man*; she is his model for the "woman of thirty.") He really must come to visit her, as he promised, the following spring. He would find her "a little naughtier and more Parisienne"; she would find him, she surmised, without his "*cote Parisienne*" but hopefully not "an uncompromising John Bull." Yet perhaps GM was going to turn a page in his life, and leave Paris and the women of Paris behind? He had spoken to Georgette of marriage plans:

> And now you are going to marry some square-backed, big-footed British virgin and have a dozen children *après la manière de votre pays*, and become a respectable *père de famille* and think of us all here in Paris as pagans – it is all wrong, it is not your vocation!

During the fall of 1883, Mrs Moore, like Mrs Martyn, tried to get her son to form an Irish marriage.

An aging cousin of the Moores told Joseph Hone that GM neither rode nor hunted during his autumn 1883 residence at Moore Hall, but worked from breakfast till teatime at *A Mummer's Wife*, and then joined the company still attired in his white dressing-gown. This conduct belongs more to a writer on holiday than to an Irish landlord looking for a bride. Nonetheless Moore evidently paid social calls on the Ruttledges at Cornfield and the Brownes at Browne's Grove, thirty miles south near Tuam. In subsequent correspondence he mentions the daughters of both families. It was Maud Browne who most caught his attention. Thomas Browne, her father, was a Crimean War veteran with one arm.[39] He had an estate of 2,259 acres with a valuation of £1,013 a year in 1876 – though actual rentals were probably less than that in post-Land-War 1883.[40] That Maud Browne was the daughter of his mother's sister did not seem to deter either George or his mother.[41] The Blakes, Brownes, and other "Tribes of Galway" made a practical policy of intermarriage. A marriage between Moore of Moore Hall and Maud Browne of Browne's Grove would have been a sensible marriage of the very sort GM's father made when he chose Mary Blake of Ballinafad.

Throughout his ensuing courtship of Maud Browne GM remained as much the observant novelist as the earnest suitor. In February, he had traveled from Moore Hall to Dublin in order to attend the Castle Ball with Maud and other eligible Irish débutantes and bachelors. GM's arrival at the elite Shelbourne Hotel was noted in the 2 February 1884 *Irish Times*. He went shopping for a suit of velvet for the levee, and was shocked to find it would cost £40; he "only got the coat, waistcoat, and trousers, and borrowed the rest, [and] economised 25 pounds."[42] Albeit with prudence, he was willing to outfit himself for a determined Irish Ascendancy courtship.

At the same time as he was entering the lists for the hand of Maud Browne of Browne's Grove, Moore was doing research for his next novel, *A Drama in Muslin*, a study of the marriage market in Ireland. GM closed a letter from Dublin to his mother by swearing her to silence on what he meant to do with the State Ball held in Dublin Castle – that is, paint its secrets from an unfriendly, naturalist point of view. Years later, Moore recalled with amusement the ridiculous appearance he had himself made in the mirrors of the Castle as he tripped down its staircases one early morning after a ball: "his lank yellow hair (often standing on end), his sloping shoulders, and female hands – a strange appearance which a certain vivacity of mind sometimes rendered engaging."[43]

In the course of the courtship of Maud Browne, she proved willing, but her family finally did not. Maud became, in GM's view, the helpless object of argument over the suitability of the match by the female family experts in dynastic matrimony. Maud "always loved George," but she was not allowed the final say in the matter; her aunt (an "ogress," according to GM) did not care for cousin George Moore.[44] On 17 February 1883, he wrote in a resigned, indignant tone to his mother that the match was off: "I consider everything now over between Maud and me but I shall never forget the horrible system of terrorism to which she has been subjected. The poor girls life is one of those unknown tragedies which the historian must pass without noticing but in which the history of nations is written as much as in chronicles of battles and conquests."[45] Here in the space of a sentence, one can see life turning into literature, a proposal for marriage into a book proposal, and love into an aesthetic impulse. However qualified GM's devotion to Maud Browne may have been, to be found unworthy was unpleasant. The clan of Blakes and Brownes might reject the novelist as a husband fit for one of their own daughters, but he would have his say about them too, sometimes under fictional names, and sometimes not, in *A Drama in Muslin, Parnell and His Island*, and *Hail and Farewell*.

While at the Shelbourne Hotel, Moore – very much the author, not at all the country gentleman ready to settle down and marry – dispatched a progress report to Zola on *A Mummer's Wife*. GM had "renounced the pleasure" of translating *Thérèse Raquin*, but he promised to write an article about, or a preface to, the English edition. His own second novel was, he estimated cautiously, a more solid piece of work than *A Modern Lover*; indeed, it would, he declared, plant a dagger in the heart of the sentimental novel and bring about a change in the literature of his country. It was his hope to be *"un ricochet de Zola en Angleterre"* – a ricochet of Zola in England.[46] Moore's writing had been going well, and this letter shows fits of grandiose confidence and a dawning prescience about the role he would play in the history of the late Victorian novel.

3

After the Dublin "Season" of 1884, GM went straight on to London in late February, and from there, by the end of March, to Paris. On 30 March 1884, Paul Alexis, GM's collaborator in a French adaptation of *Sweethearts*, wrote to Zola proposing that the two visit their master at Médan; a luncheon date was set by Zola for 6 April.[47] On that visit (written up soon afterwards by Moore), Zola's two admirers were treated to an account of his preparations for *Germinal* (its serialisation in *Gil Blas* began in November 1884).[48] Turning from his own to English fiction, Zola joined Moore in holding that the great tradition was in decline, owing to "the monopoly the circulating library holds, and its tendency to cater exclusively to young girls, to the detriment of other classes of readers": "Any story is good enough provided it be sentimental enough." There was more than a trace of masculine, scientific, research-oriented contempt for naturally prolific female scribblers in Zola's attitude: "The work is done chiefly by women who produce their two or three books a year," he observed with lordly irony. "Ah! How I do admire their facility. Here am I, just come back from Azin, where I have been for the last two months compiling notes . . ." – and he was off on a long plug for *Germinal*, and a calm prediction of revolution by coal-miners exploited by the market in manual labor. Zola concluded by laying down a lesson about the dignity of artistic labor, which was not lost on George Moore: Zola said his 500 pages of notes for *Germinal*, "if they do no more, will at least prove I lived to work, and to work sincerely."

During his stay in Paris, Moore also attended a breakfast at the home of novelist and diarist Edmond Goncourt. Afterwards, GM requested permission to publish an account of this high-society literary event, along with a preface to Goncourt's novel *Chérie*. Goncourt may have accepted the offer of English publicity ("A Breakfast with Edmond de Goncourt" was published on 13 May in *St. James's Gazette*), but subsequently, following Moore's ridicule of his precious apartment in the 1888 *Confessions of a Young Man*, the aristocratic French diarist complained that Moore, while dining at Goncourt's table, "took notes on his cuff."[49]

On the same visit to France, the English exponent of naturalism met another of the *Soirée de Médan*, the group of early followers of Zola. Moore says he encountered Guy de Maupassant only three times – at Zola's house, at Maupassant's rooms, and at a masked ball.[50] The second of these meetings occurred on this April visit to Paris, after the publication in 1883 of *Une Vie*, Maupassant's first novel, and before the French writer began *Bel Ami* in the summer of 1884. On 19 March 1883, an ophthalmic surgeon diagnosed Maupassant's eye problem as a symptom of syphilis, a fact unknown to Moore (possibly unknown to him even in 1892 when he published his recollections of the recently deceased author).[51] Moore describes himself as having been surprised that the French writer did not seem devoted to literature; even on the threshold of his first big success, Maupassant appeared to be tired, and complained all the time of eye trouble. "He spoke of literature almost with disdain, and seemed to incline to the belief that yachting in the Mediterranean was more sensible . . . I was conscious that some evil must await one who so evilly denied – and, no doubt, for some strange reason hidden deep down in his nature – . . . the very *raison d'être* of his existence."[52] Maupassant roused himself to tell Moore the plan for his next novel, *Bel Ami*. Moore was shocked: it was the plot of *A Modern Lover*. "But I have written that book, and I published it last year in London." "That does not matter," the Frenchman replied. "My book will be much different from yours." It was, in fact, but not different enough to prevent people ignorant of the relevant dates from accusing Moore of plagiarising Maupassant's novel.

Moore was not a member of the party of French naturalists in the late 1870s, but he became their recognised English affiliate during his April 1884 return to Paris. On this trip, GM solidified his working friendship with Paul Alexis, entered into an almost apostolic relation to Zola, became an accepted guest of Goncourt, and sat down for serious conversation in the home of Maupassant. This was a significant improvement in Moore's position, and when he returned to London, he took advantage of his insider status by writing articles about his visits to French writers in the May issues of the *Pall Mall Gazette* and the *St. James's Gazette*. The articles are unsigned, but editors were notified that he was a man in the know.

4

Moore's excited self-absorption shows in his 15 May letter to his mother, written from 3 Dane's Inn. No, he protested, he had not forgotten her; he was just caught up in his novel, and answering requests for articles: "I am asked to write everywhere." He was also pursuing his connection to Mrs Moore's sister, Anna Blake Murphy, a witty woman with "pretty, graceful" daughters – perfect subjects for his "girl book," if not for matrimony. He was shocked by Mrs Moore's news that his sister Nina, married to John Kilkelly on 21 February 1882, was already expecting her second child: "how careless she is . . . she will produce quite a brood I suppose." Moore generally tended to regard pregnancies as mistakes. He was also worried about his youngest brother Julian: "he thinks of nothing but theatres and similar folly. I have very little hope – no hope that he will pass any examination," for the military, the police, the law, or the civil service.[53] As a substitute father, George Moore neglected his sister and youngest brother. When he did express an opinion, it was often in the caustic mode of G. H. Moore. Julian must have been trying to emulate George and Augustus (the following month, for instance, Julian published a story in *Tinsley's Magazine*, just as GM had done),[54] yet GM treated him to the bleak skepticism with which their father had regarded George's earliest efforts.

The chief concerns of George Moore were to finish his book and to look after his French connections. On 16 May he met Manet's friend, Théodore Duret, who was in the wine-trading business in London,[55] and on the 19th, just after Duret's departure, he sent Zola a letter enclosing a copy of the *St. James's Gazette* article, "A Breakfast with Edmond de Goncourt," with the wish that Goncourt would excuse Moore for inviting the world into his home; a similar apology would cover GM's other enclosure, the *Pall Mall Gazette* article, "My New Novel by Emile Zola," with its description of Zola's rooms. Regarding *A Mummer's Wife*, then two-thirds complete, Moore wondered if he was fit to "engage in battle now" – the battle for naturalism and against the circulating libraries.[56] GM showed more swagger in a letter to his mother written on the same day: "I am working hard for fame, and I think I shall succeed. I feel that I must conquer. I am conscious that I am a force, rather that I am becoming a force."[57]

The militant, heroic style in which GM now tried to conceive of himself – "I am a force," "I must conquer," "I am ready for the battle" – was partly borrowed from Zola, the Napoleon of French literature. As an avid, emulative student of the French novelist, Moore had picked up a number of lessons about how to turn a novel into a polemical intervention. One should, first, design a novel as a development of new fictional territory (coal-miners in Zola's current case, traveling actors in GM's), never being peaceable, never staying within the boundaries of the already mapped. Second, one should "mark up" or highlight the points of interest in one's novel by means of articles in periodicals, keeping the public abreast of one's progress, and teaching them how to receive the shock of the new book. Third, when crossing into debatable moral ground, always seize the still higher ground, connecting your work to something like truth, sincerity, artistic freedom, or the dignity of labor. Finally, take up an aggressive, audacious attitude with respect to majority opinion and the common run of novels, regarded as philistine or oppressive; instead, appeal directly to hypothetically discerning readers, and by means of that appeal call into existence a class of purchasers who may hitherto not have been a self-conscious part of the population of consumers. These naturalist methods of campaign – invasive, provocative, high-toned, and abusive – endured for Moore long after he gave up his practice of the naturalist methods of fiction-writing.

By August 1884 Moore had completed *A Mummer's Wife*. At a literary soirée hosted by Mabel and Mary Robinson, he met an editor upon whom he tried to impose a note announcing the novel as due out in September, and dealing with "the lowest strata of the theatrical profession."[58] He made several more interesting acquaintances at the Robinsons' apartment on Gower Street near University College, London. One was Violet Paget (1856–1935), who wrote under the name "Vernon Lee." She had recently proposed to dedicate her satirical *roman-à-clef*, *Miss Brown* (1884), to Henry James, an offer he strove courteously to decline on 31 July 1884, just before the Robinsons' party.[59] *Miss Brown* mixed the sinful atmosphere of Ouida's novels – harlots, mistresses, drugs, effeminate males, and spiritualism – with pen portraits of Arthur O'Shaughnessy, the Robinson sisters, Rossetti, and Burne-Jones. James wrote to a friend, "it is to be hoped" that *Miss Brown*, Miss Paget's first novel, "may be her last."[60]

Violet Paget, brilliant and learned but slightly hunchbacked, was devoted to Mary Robinson, whom she visited in London in 1880, 1882, and now again in 1884; she also entertained Mary intermittently in Venice. GM used his acquaintance with the Robinsons to make a study of Violet Paget that bore fruit in his third novel, *A Drama in Muslin*, where the hunchbacked Cecilia is passionately attached to the novel's heroine, Alice Barton. Violet Paget thought GM a "cad," but, after *Miss Brown*, in the matter of embarrassing fictional portraits of real people, she was the last one who could complain of impropriety.[61]

At the Robinsons' party, GM was impressed by Henry James, "the first English novelist [he] knew whom [he] could look upon as an artist."[62] As the two novelists left the house together for the underground station, the Irish beginner told the American veteran the story of his current novel. James's reply was to urge GM to look out for his own essay, "The Art of Fiction," published in *Longman's Magazine* in September.[63] What message James circuitously aimed to deliver to Moore by means of this critique of both the French and the English novel was left to be guessed. Perhaps James meant to warn GM away from discipleship to Zola, or he may have thought Moore would appreciate the essay's criticism of the Victorian English novel for its "moral timidity," due to its being addressed "in a large degree to young people."

James gave an informed judgement of Moore's novel a few months later, after receiving a copy of *A Mummer's Wife*. He wrote Moore a long letter, now lost, in which he stated (truly, GM thought) that the novel seemed "to have been thought in French and inadequately translated." James added, according to Moore's recollection in *Avowals*, that the length of the book was disproportionate to the importance of the matter related, James possibly thinking that a dressmaker's destiny did not count for much. Why was *Portrait of a Lady* (1881) not too long? Moore says he asked in a return letter. Nothing finally happened in it. James continued the exchange by admitting his own novel was not so short as it might be, but that the intelligent Isabel Archer lived an "intenser life" than unintelligent Kate Ede, so *A Portrait* could afford more scope for the realisation of her life than it was sensible of Moore to spend on that of Kate. This reply just made things worse for GM: he thought Kate's instincts and emotions sufficed to supply interest to her life. What was so intense about the life of "idle, passionless Americans wandering over Europe"? Furthermore, at the end of James's novel, the kiss Caspar Goodwood gives Isabel Archer seemed to Moore one of the "worst [kisses] in literature." Old George Moore has young George Moore concluding, with some satisfaction, that "Henry James knows very little about kissing, and . . . it does not interest him."[64] It certainly interested Moore, and he would make his speciality just what he took to be James's inadequacy.

5

While awaiting the publication of *A Mummer's Wife*, Moore read a novel by one of the *Soirée de Médan*, Joris-Karl Huysmans (1848–1907). To judge from Moore's review of *A Rebours* in *St. James's Gazette*, he was at first puzzled by Huysmans's book; however, coming together with the snub from James, it began the disturbance of Moore's commitment to naturalism. Moore was fascinated by the calibre of Huysmans's prose, his devotion to art for art's sake, his ironic celebration of the character of the wealthy aesthete in pursuit of new sensations, and Huysmans's neo-Schopenhauerian theory that modern humanity should remain uncivilised, for with civilisation comes self-consciousness, and self-consciousness is the beginning of pain. The absence of progressive politics in *A Rebours* (compared with Zola's books) also appealed to Moore. Social pessimism made sense to the Irish landlord, and the deliberate care Huysmans took in the writing of the text appealed to GM's notions (shared with Flaubert and James) that novel-writing should be a high art, not a trade or a form of humanitarian propaganda. Huysmans introduced into the novel erudition – art, history, and philosophy – and made prose narrative more than a romance in which the desires of the middle classes are fulfilled (like the English novel), or an epic in which the sorrows of the masses are detailed (like a novel by Zola). A full spectrum of response fans out in Moore's review of *A Rebours*, but his enthusiasm was hesitant.[65] "What about the story?" Moore asked skeptically; there hardly was one. *A Rebours* did not seem to be a great novel, perhaps not even a novel, but still it was "A Curious Book."[66]

Moore was not yet ready to break from Zola; far from it. On 22 September 1884, while he was correcting proofs for *A Mummer's Wife*, in his letter to "*Mon cher maître*" he continued to sign himself "Your devoted student." He would dedicate the novel to Zola, he said, but to do so would just tip off reviewers to call the book a pastiche of Zola's novels. Perhaps Zola would accept, Moore hoped, the dedication of his next book, a novel about young girls. Some sign of gratitude was in order, because what Zola recommended, and GM had not thought possible, had come to pass – GM was delighted to announce that *A Mummer's Wife* would indeed be published in one volume, and sold directly to the public. Moore enclosed his review of *A Rebours*, and suggested that Zola might pass it on to Huysmans. Nothing ominous was intended by the enclosure; among the naturalist foot-soldiers, GM was for the present still marching in step.

In early October, Paul Alexis paid a five-day visit to London, and Moore was his guide to the town for half a day, a tour Alexis wrote up in *Le Cri du peuple*.[67] Alexis repaid the favor by giving GM a plug in *Le Matin*, describing Moore's first novel as a success, his second as impending, and his third as an attack on the education of middle-class girls for nothing but marriage – a signal of Moore's early intentions for *A Drama in Muslin*.[68] Alexis reported to Zola that his chief aim in England had been to fetch back his mistress, the sweet-natured Marie (1865–1900), from her job in a London department store. He found Moore occupied on Zola's behalf, trying to place *Germinal* in the *Daily Telegraph*.[69] Over the next three weeks, Moore had no luck in selling Zola's book to an English paper, though after the *Telegraph* refused *Germinal*, GM tried both the *Pall Mall Gazette* and *Pictorial World*;[70] Zola eventually made arrangements himself on 20 November for the serialisation of *Germinal* in the *People*, a populist progressive paper.[71]

Moore confessed his failure as a literary agent to Zola in a letter of late October. Duret, he gossiped, had recently been in London again, and the two amused themselves by planning projects for a visit of Zola to England. That night he was going to dine with Duret again, and hoped to hear what Duret thought of *A Mummer's Wife*. On 29 October, Duret himself wrote to Zola to announce that George Moore had really turned out to be something. His novel was a very remarkable work: a powerful story, with a realistically created milieu, truth in the expression of human types, and "strong painting," using the sort of phrase with which Duret wrote about the work of Manet. The novel, Duret continued, was without a touch of pastiche, and the color of phrasing was very English, making one think of Dickens or George Eliot. There was no doubt that their friend George Moore had arrived.[72] Duret's amazement is obvious: back in the 1870s at the Nouvelle Athènes, he had thought GM no more than an Irish landlord with amusing manners and very funny French.[73] It was Moore's most shocking stunt to date that he turned out a really impressive English novel.

6

A Mummer's Wife begins with twenty-seven-year-old Kate Ede trying to cope
with her irritable husband, Ralph, who is suffering from an attack of asthma,
described with all the unappetising biological details of a medical textbook.
Ralph Ede is a linen-draper in Hanley, a pottery town, and, as he is half-
disabled, his business is not doing well. To earn more money for the family,
Kate runs a dressmaking business, while her mother-in-law, a good-hearted but
narrow-minded Wesleyan, looks after the house. Before marriage, Kate loved
to read poems and stories in the *Family Herald*, an amusement scorned as sinful
by her mother earlier and her mother-in-law now. Between cheap fiction and
the Christian pulpit, Kate's "soul is made up of two thirds of sentiment, one
third of superstition."[74] Her favorite novel was M. E. Braddon's *A Doctor's
Wife*, a sort of bowdlerised *Madame Bovary*.[75] Now Kate's form of self-
indulgence is gossip with her assistant Hender, the girlfriend of a backstage
employee of the Queen's Theatre.

In need of money, Ralph Ede lets a spare bedroom to an actor with a traveling company, and actors are, by his mother's book, no good. The tenant is Dick
Lennox, manager of the Morton and Cox Opera Company. The large, fat, and
friendly actor looks to Kate very much like a hero in a *Family Herald* romance.
He likes the look of the landlord's wife too. On his second day in Hanley, Dick
meets Kate by chance in the street, and gets her to accompany him on a tour
of the pottery works where her mother once worked (Kate "looked around the
old brickyard with tenderness").[76] Managing to ditch the guide and three
clergymen in their party, Dick forces himself on Kate, stumbles over her, and,
in a crash of pottery, cuts himself. She feels sorry for him for having been
wounded in pursuit of her. Kate thinks his offer of theater tickets is gallant;
however, her mother-in-law would never allow her to go. Kate then plots with
her assistant Hender to make a secret visit to the play, but on the appointed
night, Kate happens to run into the mother-in-law on Market Street, frustrat-
ing her plan. At the end of the week's run, Dick leaves the Ede house but
promises to return in three months. During his absence, Kate sends Dick a sentimental poem cut from the *Family Herald* and placidly resumes sexual relations with Ralph Ede (indicated by the convention of a line of asterisks,
followed by "Next morning . . ." at the end of Chapter 8).

On Dick's return, he is again given the spare room. Kate methodically compares the progress of her passing conversations with Dick (when, for instance,
she takes him his hot water in the morning) with what she had read in cheap
novels about the course of true love.[77] Ralph Ede, now quite impressed with
his lodger, agrees to send Kate to the theater chaperoned by Hender. "Demoralised by hundreds of sentimental and romantic stories," she has no resistance
at all to the illusions of the stage. The sight of Dick waltzing on stage in the
red coat of a Captain of the Guard powerfully affects her. He walks her home
that night, and elated, she sings from memory a song from the opera; Dick is
struck by her perfect pitch and recall. That night, husband Ralph has another

asthma attack and Kate is the one who must go down to let Dick into the house after his late night on the town:

> Although she could not see his face she felt his breath on her neck. Strong arms were wound about her, she was carried forward, and the door was shut behind her.
>
> Only the faintest gleam of starlight touched the wall next the window; the darkness slept profoundly on landing and staircase, and when the silence was again broken, a voice was heard saying, "Oh, you shouldn't have done this! What shall I tell my husband if he asks me where I've been?"
>
> "Say you've been talking to me about my bill, dear. I'll see you in the morning."[78]

The next evening, she can bear it no longer at home with her husband, and slips off without an alibi to see Dick at the theater. She now feels as if she belongs to the actor, and he complacently accepts her: it is lonely on the road, she is a sweet thing, and she does have a promising voice. She leaves town in the morning with the Morton and Cox Opera Company.

For a year, Kate enjoys the sweet domestic happiness of a newly-wed in a Victorian novel.[79] Dick's placid, amiable, kindly, animal being gives her the sort of love she has been missing. It is hard for her, however, to become accustomed to the irregular life of the actors, especially to their utter absence of moral rectitude about love and property. She is especially shocked when they conspire to eat a railway lunch for forty without paying their bill. Lonely from spending her days in rented rooms, she decides to join the chorus herself, and Dick asks the lanky music conductor Montgomery to give her some voice lessons. She progresses rapidly, and Montgomery just as rapidly falls in love with her. Montgomery is too ugly to hope for her love in return, but he does aspire to hear her love stories and bask in her feminine presence.[80] She first joins the chorus, then becomes the understudy for the star, Leslie, and finally, when Leslie sprains an ankle, débuts as a star herself in *Les Cloches des Corneville*, coquettishly lifting her skirt as she sings to the roar of the whole house,

> Look at me here, look at me there,
> Criticise me everywhere.
> I am most sweet from head to feet,
> And most perfect and complete.
>   [from the George and Augustus Moore translation]

In spite of her success, once Kate is divorced by Ralph Ede, she becomes nostalgic for the stability of marriage and the linen-draper shop. She takes a nip of brandy now and then, hoping to settle her nerves, but when she drinks, she becomes more irritable still, and worries whether Dick will stand by her. She doesn't think he can "respect" a woman who left her husband, but Dick is a "poor good-natured creature, who neither respected nor disrespected any living thing, but lived only for the enjoyment of the moment."[81] Kate's uneasiness worsens when she finds herself pregnant, but Dick is good enough to marry her.

After the wedding, a financial depression in England cuts the receipts of the opera company. The backer, Mr Cox, pulls the plug, and Kate, Dick, Montgomery, and advance-man Williams go on the road as the Constellation Company, doing vaudeville through the mining country of Lancashire. Finally, Kate's time comes round, and the tour breaks up. Running out of money, and with Kate nearly confined, the couple have to sneak out of an apartment without paying the rent, with money only for one train fare to Manchester; Dick himself walks. There in a shabby apartment, Kate gives birth to a baby girl. After the birth, she resumes her old habit of reading stories about heroes and heroines "who lived unsullied by any too dark stain of humanity in a sweetly regulated world of convention."[82] She also resumes drinking gin to "sustain her strength." Dreaming away half-drunk, she ignores the baby, and it falls ill; as the baby gets sicker, she gets drunker, until it dies in convulsions as she passes out from intoxication. Just to make ends meet, Kate and Dick immediately have to go back on stage at different theaters. Kate's drinking, and the attendant jealousy, get worse.

Dick discovers a backer in an eccentric lady, Mrs Forrest, who sets him up in the Novelty Theatre, London. He parks Kate in a room behind the Cattle Market, Islington, to be free of her drunkenness and jealousy, especially while he milks the vanity of wealthy Mrs Forrest. Kate finds out anyway and takes a cab to the theater. Wearing her vomit-bespattered dress, she makes a hideous scene, beating Dick on the street and attracting the unfavorable notice of a policeman. Dick's attitude passes from kindness through indulgence to indifference. Finally, he leaves her, but with an allowance of £2 a week.

Kate goes downhill fast. Her companions are streetwalkers; she recalls one morning having herself spent the night with a strange man. When she falls ill, a doctor is called, and diagnoses liver failure. Dick refuses to go to her bedside, but Mrs Forrest does. Kate sings verses of Wesleyan hymns mixed up with a lyric from an *opéra bouffe*:

> Look at me here, look at me there,
> Criticise me everywhere.
> I am most sweet from head to feet,
> And most perfect and complete.

Like her baby, she dies in convulsions, alone.

7

As a colorful character on the Strand in the area of Fleet Street, George Moore was well known to English book reviewers as a writer who aspired to be the

English Zola. For most of the reviewers, Zola had satanic status; his name had the sort of power to inspire panic among the English that the name Karl Marx had among Americans in the 1950s.[83] So it is no surprise that *A Mummer's Wife* was at first abused in the press. William Wallace in the *Academy* (who hunted GM remorselessly in reviews of subsequent novels) snidely began his report by saying that Moore, as a disciple of Zola, presumably intended to disgust readers; he succeeded, for, Wallace said, "a more repulsive story was probably never written" than *A Mummer's Wife*.[84] The *Graphic* review also identified the novel as the first English attempt to carry out "the principles of realism to their final . . . result." That result was tedium. Still, *A Mummer's Wife* did not appear to the *Graphic* reviewer to be an evil book, because sin was exposed in all its "loathsome deformity."[85] The reviewer for the *Pall Mall Gazette* summed up the supposedly well-known qualities of Zola's novels – they were tedious, revolting, and obsessed with "the darker facts of life" – and was therefore surprised that Zola had found an English disciple. *A Mummer's Wife*, the reviewer judged, was indeed tedious, but also interesting; and it was revolting, but fascinating too. How could it achieve this paradoxical effect? Because GM "observes closely and accurately, describes vividly and unflinchingly." The book deserved recognition, this reviewer concluded, for attempting something better than the ordinary fictional "frivolities of the day."[86]

It was fair enough to say that *A Mummer's Wife* was an imitation of Zola. Indeed, it became a pattern for the way in which to imitate Zola for a host of English naturalists after Moore: Arnold Bennett, Hubert Crackanthorpe, Cunninghame Graham, Arthur Morrison, and James Joyce.[87] Like Zola, Moore gave his heroine carefully plotted phases of life; he described a low-down environment in a fashion heightened by a supersensitive horror of ugliness (a suburb of Hanley "slept like a scaly reptile just crawled out from its bed of slime"). Like Zola, Moore maintained a coldly distanced narrative tone; he even exceeded the pseudo-medical excesses of Zola in diagnostic descriptions of Ralph Ede's asthma and Kate Ede's cirrhosis. Environment is treated as a strongly deterministic force in her life: when Kate changes her dwelling from the shop in Hanley to the lodging-houses and hotels on tour, her character changes, her body changes both physiologically (cheeks fuller, face softer, eyes more colorful, etc.) and psychologically (tastes more complex, desires more febrile).[88] A major plot element also is transplanted from Zola: the way in which alcoholism works like Fate to bring about the denouement is lifted from *L'Assommoir*. Milton Chaikin may be overdoing it when he says that GM stole Kate's revolt from the dullness of life from Hélène in *Une Page d'amour* (1878) and the theatrical milieu from *Nana* (1880), but Moore doubtless did wish to give English readers a bargain: all of Zola for a cheap price in one volume.[89]

Zola, and more: a major theme of *A Mummer's Wife* is "bovarisme." Moore took from *Madame Bovary* Flaubert's concept that the disease of bourgeois life is the ability to believe oneself other than what one is, and so to become blind to sordid reality; he took as well the cause of this disease (romantic fiction), and its cure (realistic, impersonal fiction).[90] Kate Ede's problems begin with the *Family Herald* and the sort of novels M. E. Braddon wrote and Mudie circulated. The fantasies they inspire cause her to leave Ralph, to submit to the illusions of the Morton and Cox Company, to go on the road with Dick, to suffer dissatisfaction with the reality of her actual romance, and to sustain her illusions with drink. Sentimental fiction is the villain of the piece, ably abetted by Low Church puritanism; all the other characters are innocents. By his handling of this particular borrowing from Flaubert, Moore showed his originality as a controversialist: it turned his novel not only into a provocation of Mudie's, courting censorship, but also into an indictment of Mudie himself as the real author of immorality.

GM did not wait long to see if reviewers would get the point. He published an article in the *Pall Mall Gazette* timed for the release of the novel, deliberately intending to whip up a controversy that would "mark the whole affair up."[91] With "A New Censorship of Literature," Moore inserted an attack on the circulating libraries into an ongoing debate about the condition of the English novel, which had been initiated by Walter Besant in a 25 April 1884 lecture on the "Art of Fiction" to the Royal Institution and continued by Henry James with the article he recommended to GM, published in *Longman's Magazine* in September 1884. Moore began his own article by saying he agreed with both Besant and James that a novel should be a fresh imitation of life, but what was the use of saying to writers, Go and study nature, when they were not permitted to circulate works dealing with religion, politics, or morals?

> The subtraction of these important elements of life throws the reading of fiction into the hands of young girls and widows of sedentary habits; for them political questions have no interest, and it is by this final amputation that humanity becomes headless, trunkless, limbless, and is converted into the pulseless, nonvertebrate, jellyfish sort of thing which, securely packed in tin-cornered boxes, is sent from the London depot and scattered through the drawing-rooms of the United Kingdom.[92]

The circulator of the tin-boxed, jellyfish novels, Charles Mudie fixed prices and intimidated publishers; they in turn, Moore explained, intimidated or starved out original novelists. Moore recounted his own conversations about *A Modern Lover* with Tinsley and with "Mr. B——" and "Mr X——" of the circulating libraries. Who, GM asked, should decide the merit of a novel: the men of high literary culture writing in great journals like the *Spectator*, the *Athenaeum*, and the *Academy*, or the "tradesmen" of the circulating libraries, as advised by "two ladies in the country"? There was more than a hint of landlord paternalism in GM's contempt for both ladies and tradesmen.

Moore strung through his long letter an advertisement for *A Mummer's Wife*, Vizetelly and Sons, and his new method of publication, along with an appeal for fair consideration based on the fundamental values of the Liberal Party: free trade, free speech, and tolerance. Just so that readers would not miss this political affiliation, he concluded by calling himself an unworthy champion of Liberalism: "My only regret is that a higher name than mine has not undertaken to wave the flag of Liberalism and to denounce and to break with a commercial arrangement that makes of the English novel a kind of advanced school-book, a sort of guide to marriage and the drawing-room."[93] G. H. Moore, duelist and mob orator *par excellence*, would have been proud of his son.

Letters poured into the *Pall Mall Gazette*, at least four of them from male authors who had suffered at the hands of their publishers or the librarians: Max O'Rell, Marion Crawford (both 12 December), Robert Lanstaff (13 December), and George Gissing (15 December). In December the *Gazette* also published "The Case for Publishers," an opinion from an "authoress of strictly moral books," and a testimonial from a mother who was quite satisfied with Mudie's fare and detested "morbid-minded men" like Moore.

Mudie's Select Library and W. H. Smith, in the midst of this controversy, banned *A Mummer's Wife*. Subsequent reviews of the novel in the press, like the one in the *Athenaeum*, took pains to state that there was "no uncleanness" in Moore's novel. Indeed, its omnibus review (also covering a collection of tales by Henry James and two novels by authors described as "lady novelists") accorded *A Mummer's Wife* the fullest and most respectful treatment of the bunch.[94] So Moore's strategy of opposing two segments of the book trade – Liberal male-oriented weekly reviews versus conservative, female-oriented publishing houses and libraries – was remarkably successful. Moore told Duret he had received sixty or seventy clippings of articles in response to "A New Censorship."[95] The first edition of *A Mummer's Wife* was sold out within six weeks, and it went through six further "editions" (more accurately, impressions) in the next four years. George Moore's account of his success to Zola demonstrates that Zola was behind Moore's polemical strategy from the start: "*According to your advice*, I had attacked the library system immediately after my book had been published, publishing a ferocious article in the *Pall Mall Gazette*. A hundred articles followed, long articles, in different English journals."[96] Moore promised Zola to write a strong preface to Vizetelly's edition of *Pot-Bouille*.

In that preface, Moore said that, as one who had seen the French master in the company of Daudet and Goncourt, he could say that Zola stood out as "grander, greater, nobler" than them all. Daudet could only hide from Zola behind an epigram, and the aristocratic Goncourt "bitterly admits . . . there is a colossus whose strength he is unable to oppose." Even in the midst of this hero worship, Moore redefined the character of Zola's genius in a way that reflects GM's recent admiration of the work of James and Huysmans, and forecasts his ultimate disenchantment with the reputation he had created for himself, as "Zola's ricochet in England." Zola, he says, is not a realist, but an artist and epic poet. What gave distinction to his novels was Zola's discovery of the *mot juste*, his "perfect construction," and his "firm, logical comprehension" of the wholeness of the subject – Zola, in short, is the true successor to Flaubert. Realism is only "the most obvious, not the most dominant quality of his work."

After a summary of the Rougon–Macquart saga, GM took up the question debated by Henry James and Walter Besant: why was English fiction so bad? Because, GM declared, it is controlled by the circulating libraries, and Mudie and W. H. Smith are "the true authors of our fiction." The "wheezing, drivelling lot of bairns" in the lap of Rhoda Broughton, "not a virtue among them, and their pinafore pages sticky with childish sensualities," were fathered on the "lady novelist" by Mudie and W. H. Smith. They permitted an author to write anything, so long as the author followed certain rules. One could have an unmarried woman get seduced, but only according to the formula used by George Eliot for Hetty Sorrel's pregnancy in *Adam Bede*. She and her lover go walking in the woods together, the curtain falls, and we next hear that after three months Hetty found herself with child. It was deliberately to break this formula, Moore claimed, that "I was daring enough in my *Mummer's Wife* to write that Dick dragged Kate into the room and that the door was slammed behind her. And it is on this passage that the circulating libraries base a refusal to take the book . . . it is for this reason and no other that the writers of the present day have ceased even to try to produce good work." If you are going to have good novels, true novels like Zola's, instead of the soft lies circulated by Mudie, you had to grant the author freedom of speech and the right to address readers other "than sentimental young girls."[97] In this polemical introduction to Zola's novel, Moore not only verbally horsewhips Mudie one more time, he also very cannily redefines the sort of fiction GM meant to defend: not socialist, progressive, documentary realism, but realism of the Flaubert lineage – a high literary art, anti-moralist, and international in its standards of achievement.

By the end of 1884 Moore was well launched as a personage, and on 22 December he was at Tillyra (where he had gone to continue work on *A Drama in Muslin*), providing biographical information to an American correspondent wishing to write an article on the new man of note in London literary culture. Moore mentioned *Flowers of Passion* and *Pagan Poems*, but hoped the journalist wouldn't. They were not parts of the self he was now creating – a serious character, and an international modernist author.[98]

Chapter 5
Two Farewells to Ireland

I

With the controversy over *A Mummer's Wife* well underway, George Moore left London to spend the Christmas holiday season of 1884–85 with Edward Martyn at Tillyra Castle. The liberty, servants, and solitude of Tillyra and Moore Hall provided ideal circumstances for the writing of novels, while the editorial offices, crowded restaurants, and theaters of the Strand were best for creating a public identity as an author. At Tillyra, Moore was still gathering material for his third novel. Edward unwittingly assisted him by inviting Father Thomas B. Considine, the parish priest of Ardrahan, to dinner. The Martyns had donated money for the construction of a bell-tower and an elaborate roofed altar of Sicilian marble for the Ardrahan village church, so the priest was a frequent caller at Tillyra.[1] According to *Ave* (1911), Edward was embarrassed by Father Considine's custom of spitting on the carpets. Would George be able to have a word with the priest? When Moore drew attention to the spittoon, the cleric said, "such things were only a botheration."[2] GM took the measure of this priest again on a Sunday, when he accompanied Edward to the Ardrahan chapel.

In Chapter 4 of *A Drama in Muslin*, Sunday services at Ardrahan are seen through the eyes of Moore's heroine Alice Barton, an atheist like himself. A "large fat" priest ascends the altar, his "new, thick-soled boots creak[ing] terribly." "The mumbled Latin, the by-play with the wine and water" seem to Alice "appallingly trivial." That a wafer blessed by this big-booted peasant should be thought to incarnate the "Creator of the twenty million suns in the Milky Way" is depicted as absurd. The real reasons the people met there on that Sunday, Alice observes, were, in the case of the gentry to plan a Spinsters' Ball, and in the case of the tenants to arrange a land meeting.[3] After the publication of *A Drama in Muslin*, Father Considine warned Edward that if George Moore came to Mass in Ardrahan again, he would personally throw dirty water on him.

At Tillyra, Moore received back from an editor an article (now lost) that he had submitted on the position of women. *A Drama in Muslin* had originally been conceived as his "girl book" about the Irish marriage market, the genre from Jane Austen, the treatment from Emile Zola, and the theme partly from current discussions of the "Woman Question." Pages in the novel show signs of reading in Wollstonecraft, Mill, and Charlotte Brontë, the syllabus GM used in his re-education into a feminist.[4] Moore's lost article on the "Woman Question" was both homework for the novel and advance publicity for it. In reply to the letter of rejection, Moore explained that the intention of the article had been to "strike between the two influences" of those in favor of female emancipation (university education and professions for women) and those who were stuck in the old grooves (the home is the only place for women).[5] Moore's notion of a golden mean was to grant to young women the freedom both to labor and to love. Why should women, of all created beings, be denied the right to fulfill at their wish "the one universal instinct"?[6] It had been his hope to spark a "glorious polemic," in which the old guard cried out against the new. Moore could then insert *A Drama in Muslin* into the revived debate about the "Woman Question," just as Meredith and Olive Schreiner had done with their novels, *The Egoist* (1879) and *Story of an African Farm* (1883). In the judgement of the editor, however, GM's daring advocacy of free love, poorly masked as compromise, "overshot the mark."[7]

That winter in Ireland, Moore trailed his coat before the officials of Dublin Castle in order to create a defining controversy of a different kind from feminism. He sent a request for an invitation to a State Dinner to Colonel Gerald Dease, a stiff, urbane Catholic courtier in Dublin Castle. Moore explained he had already attended, two years running, the Levee, the Drawing Rooms, the Castle Balls, and other highlights of the débutante season, but he had not yet been a guest at the Viceroy's table. In the novel he was currently writing, he would like to give as true and vivid a picture as possible of "the social and political power of the Castle in Modern Ireland," and he could not do this without seeing everything with his own eyes, those of "the passionless observer, who, unbiased by any political creed, comments impartially on the matter submitted to him for analysis." The Castle officials did not wish to abet Moore's plan to expose the private ceremonies of the Viceroy's dinner-table, and Colonel Dease and Lord Fingall, the State Steward, tried to put him off, saying first it was too early for invitations, and then it was too late – no chair left at all for one solitary, observant novelist, even if he was a landowning Irish bachelor.[8] When the rejection by Colonel Dease became final and explicit, Moore went up to Dublin to give the whole correspondence to the *Freeman's Journal*, the organ of parliamentary nationalism, which at the height of the Castle Season delightedly plastered it across the pages of the 9 February issue.

Moore enjoyed his part in the published correspondence: he flaps unflappable British officialdom and with tortuous patience inspects what will not bear inspection. On 18 February, Justin Huntly McCarthy (1861–1936), an Irish

Member of Parliament and fellow London author, congratulated GM as the nationalists' "best ally in our crusade against that stronghold of shame," Dublin Castle.[9] On the other hand, the *Freeman's Journal* correspondence may have had something to do with the fact that the Marquess of Clanricarde, the famously rich and malodorous absentee landlord, decided to write GM a personal letter of rebuke for neglecting to contribute to an Ascendancy charity appeal for the daughters of the late Thomas Mackevin.[10] It was no more easy in GM's time, than in his father's, to be both a nationalist and a member in good standing of the landlord class.

What played well to nationalists in Dublin was panned by imperialists in London. W. T. Stead picked up the *Freeman's Journal* story, and retold it in the *Pall Mall Gazette* to Moore's discredit. Stead applauded the Lord Chamberlain's "infinite politeness" in dealing with this worshiper of "the great god Realism."[11] This sort of British resentment did not stop Moore from giving the Castle officials a cameo appearance in the middle of *A Drama in Muslin*. There he staged the promenade of débutante carriages through dark, wet Dublin streets lined with "vagrants, patriots, waifs, idlers of all sorts and kinds . . . Poor little things in battered bonnets and draggled skirts, who would dream upon ten shillings a week; a drunken mother striving to hush a child that dies beneath a dripping shawl," and so on, as poverty and wealth are brought together in plainest proximity.[12] After the débutantes arrive at the Castle, they are greeted by a formal parade of state officials:

> The first to appear were the A.D.C.s. They were followed by the Medical Department, by the Private Secretary, the Military Private Secretary . . . the Gentleman Usher, the Comptroller, the State Steward, walking with a wand, like a doge in an opera bouffe; then came another secretary, and another band of the underlings who swarm about this mock court like flies about a choice pile of excrement.[13]

Nationalist in politics, Moore was still an Ascendancy duelist in manners, and he took a kind of pleasure in settling scores, careless of the resentment he inspired.

Even if kept on the perimeters, Moore made a last tour of inspection of the Dublin "Season" in February 1885, then went west with Willie Wilde (Oscar's brother, and a London society journalist).[14] Moore himself stayed at Moore Hall from the latter part of February until 16 April. Scholars have sometimes named Moore as one of those present at Whistler's "Ten O'Clock," a lecture given on 20 February in London. This lecture was a famous statement of aestheticism, wrapped up in a highly arch satire on Oscar Wilde, who was perfectly equal to the challenge. The following day Wilde reviewed the lecture, and said that in his opinion, Whistler was one of the greatest masters – "And I may add that in this opinion Mr. Whistler himself entirely concurs."[15] Though Moore appears in the "Seating Plan" prepared by Whistler, in fact he did not attend.[16] On 7 March GM wrote to Jacques-Emile Blanche with some disdain that "needless to say" he did not go to "Whistler's soirée"; Whistler had better stick to painting, Moore added, and leave the jokes to Oscar Wilde.

From his Moore Hall outpost, Moore continued his enthusiastic generalship of his personal publicity campaign by incautiously manufacturing a literary news event. Ever since the controversial success of *A Mummer's Wife*, he had been boasting about the book to his French friends and trying to persuade Alexis, Zola, and Duret to help him get a contract for a French edition of the novel, so that he might be recognised not just as the leading English naturalist, but as a naturalist pure and simple, of the true Paris strain. Madame Judith Bernard Derosne, a secretary of the Comédie Française and translator of M. E. Braddon's fiction, had offered to translate GM's novel into French, and in January Moore had asked first Duret, and then Zola, to check her out; Zola gave him a sign to go ahead on 25 January.[17] GM took this advice, but he took more than that, and told *Le Voltaire*, in order to interest the paper in serialising the translation, that the book version would include a preface by Zola himself. The cheeky man then used the pseudo-revolutionary ethics of the struggle in order to justify having taken this liberty. Zola must know, he wrote, that the struggle was difficult for Moore, and that every measure had to be taken if he were to succeed. "Then, my dear Master, am I forgiven?"[18] Zola agreed to write "*la petite lettre d'introduction*" to the translation, and, furthermore, to speak to the publisher Charpentier about publishing "La Femme du Cabotin," the French *Mummer's Wife*.[19]

In Moore's defense, it may be said that Zola had a way of turning other naturalist novelists into his servants. He would ask Huysmans and Céard to gather notes for his novels-in-progress,[20] running "Naturalism, Inc." like a corporation or a private army. For a long time Zola had leaned on Moore too, who was finding him translators and publishers in London. Such one-sided treatment could incite in grown men, especially in novelists with their own ambitions, a resentful spirit of independence. GM was not the only one to get tired of being the servant of Zola; he meant to get some service out of the master too – though that little letter of introduction would in fact never be written by Emile Zola.

2

George Moore has left several accounts of his first reading of Pater's *Marius the Epicurean*, "the book to which I owe the last temple of my soul."[21] After coming up to Moore Hall from the Dublin Season of 1885, he had promised his mother to stay with her until the buds came to the beech trees in the spring.[22] While she knitted and he read reviews of *A Mummer's Wife*, GM came across a notice for Pater's book, and having heard of Pater as a writer of beautiful books, and seeing himself despised in London as a writer of ugly Zolaistic ones, he sent off for it. Its first lesson for him, he says, was that "by helping one's mother with her white and purple wools . . . it was possible to win . . . an urbane and feminine refinement."[23] He was so excited by the possibilities it opened of a truly artistic temperament that he wanted to write to Pater or, short of that, to get back to London and hear what was said of the book in the little salon held every Tuesday afternoon by Mary and Mabel Robinson.

As Vizetelly's literary advisor, Moore had lately given a helping hand to Mabel Robinson by placing the manuscript of her first novel, *Mr. Butler's Ward*, in Vizetelly's line (initiated by *A Mummer's Wife*) of naturalistic one-volume novels. Mabel was uncertain about just what a "naturalistic novel" was.[24] Could the phrase fit her tale of the ward of a cruel Irish bailiff, a beautiful girl who ultimately falls in love with the son of a farmer who had righteously murdered the bailiff? Her novel was, at any rate, good Home Rule propaganda.[25] Mabel thanked Moore for the "sympathy and encouragement" he offered after receiving an early copy of the novel in March.[26]

On 1 April, James Davis (to whom *A Mummer's Wife* had been dedicated) asked Moore to return to London right away. Davis had got backing from John Corlett, editor of the *Sporting Times*, to start his own weekly, the *Bat*,[27] and he wanted Moore to be a contributing editor. Davis's chief gift as a journalist was for libel; five times he would be brought to court for his blood-curdling portraits of statesmen and celebrities, which he called "Plain Speaking to Public Men"; five times in court, and five guilty verdicts. Davis's plans for the *Bat* promised regular features on "Letters to Eminent Actresses," "Actresses' Husbands," "Horse Racing," and "Things We Ought Not To Have Done, By Those Who Did Them."[28] But Davis assured Moore that his magazine would indeed review books too, so long as the reviewer made his articles "amusing to the people who are not very interested in the subject."[29]

Moore was quick to contribute to the *Bat*. He is the author of the 14 April review of Andrew Lang's *Rhymes à la Mode*. The sarcasm about the "poemlets" redolent of the "ineffable complacency of the lettered Scotchman" sounds like Moore; so does the heavy irony in his compliment that Lang's book is not entirely bad, "for some of the ballades are more than milk and water, they are milk and soda water." Lang was both a don and a journalist, and he used his Oxford/London axis of power in favor of those who wrote boys' adventure stories (like Rider Haggard and Robert Louis Stevenson) and against those who wrote "serious" art-novels about real men and women (such as Moore and James) – cause enough for a sniping review from Moore. In the same omnibus article, Moore wrote a puff for Mabel Robinson's *Mr. Butler's Ward*. He identified her as a naturalist, not a melodramatic novelist, and predicted for her a career "of the very highest order and value."[30]

"The Fashionable Beauty" (GM's operetta, revised by Harry Paulton) ran at the Avenue Theatre from 6 to 16 April. Prior to its opening, Davis did his best to hype the play in the *Bat*, saying that if it was anything like *A Mummer's Wife*, either the police or thousands of customers were likely to flow into the theater. After seeing it, however, Davis discovered that the stage manager, Violet Melnotte, a prominent London "hostess," had recruited the chorus from the ranks of women who meet paying customers at private balls; these she either dressed in short skirts, or cross-dressed as men in hose. Davis's taste for vulgarity was broad, but not this broad. Along with his sarcastic review, he offered on Moore's behalf the excuse that the "great novelist" had written "The Fashionable Beauty" many years earlier, and now regretted that it had been dragged out on stage.[31]

GM did not, however, turn his back on music-hall burlesque as a whole. On 28 April 1885 the *Bat* published his article, "Can the Nineteenth Century Produce a Dramatic Literature?". The essay is influenced by Matthew Arnold's *The Function of Criticism at the Present Time* (1865), a seminal work on how to create the conditions for a literary renaissance. According to GM, the "current of dramatic thought" in England (compare Arnold's vague and famous phrase for what England lacked: a "current of fresh thought") was now "dammed up" for one major reason: long runs. These tied up the theaters in just a few productions, led to the expectation of expensive, elaborate sets, and thus limited the number of active playwrights to the few with past experience of success. Playwrights could not write "unrestrainedly, naturally, personally"; they had to focus on giving each star a "turn," and setting up the action in places susceptible to romantically painted backdrops. What was the solution to the death of drama in England? The government should, Moore argued, permit music halls to stage scenes in spoken dialogue; that would give more authors the chance to learn the playwright's trade in the boisterous, experimental environment of the halls. Moore stuck by this analysis of the question for some years – it is essentially repeated in "The Stage as Seen by a Novelist" in the 5–6 December 1887 *Evening News*. Only after seeing Ibsen's *Ghosts* in Antoine's Theatre did GM really change his sense of the possibilities of the drama.

3

Before seeking out Walter Pater at the Robinsons', Moore took Edward Martyn on a tour of Paris. At a dinner with Jacques-Emile Blanche on 26 April 1885, Moore began to interest his Irish friend in contemporary French painting. Blanche (1861–1942), pet child of the Impressionists, had studied under Henri Gervex; Degas was a family friend; and Manet had once given him a painting lesson. GM next brought Martyn to Durand-Ruel's gallery, and convinced him to buy an autumn river scene by Monet and two pictures by Degas. One represents a pair of harlequins, and the other two female ballet dancers offstage, the face of each blunt and stupid. The positions of the two dancers are physically awkward and strained: one is tying a bow behind her back, the other is doing a stretching exercise, bending over with her forearms on the backrest of a chair and straightening her legs. Degas's pictures of ballet dancers were initially understood by many (Moore and Huysmans, for instance) to be expressions of misogyny, with "an inventive cruelty, a patient hatred" of women, and in that spirit the painting may have appealed to Martyn.[32]

On "varnishing day" before the 4 May opening of the Salon, Moore brought Martyn to the Palace of Industry with the other elite guests, but when Zola appeared, GM did not introduce his country cousin, and left Edward to his own devices while he himself "walked round the gallery with the great man."[33] Edward may again have been left behind when GM went to a dinner with Zola, Duret, Alexis, Céard, and Léon Hennique, at which Zola told his cohorts about all his preparations for writing *L'Oeuvre*.[34] Using Edward Martyn as a yardstick – where he should be taken in Paris, and where he couldn't be – Moore could measure how far he himself had come from simply being a Catholic landlord from the West of Ireland.

On their return to London, GM recalls obligingly introducing Edward to his friends the Robinsons at 10 Earls Terrace, where GM had gone in search of Pater. Not until they were seated in the drawing room did GM notice, according to the recollection in *Salve*, that Edward's boots were more suitable to Galway than Kensington, but even after purchasing patent leather shoes Edward was never to feel at home in a drawing room, the domain of ladies. GM felt it was just the spot for himself.[35] Mary Robinson's recollection of this day implies that GM overdid his own possession of urbane effeminate refinements. She describes him walking into the little salon with its French doors opening onto a large terrace that dominated the gardens of Edwardes Square. Dressed with "nonchalant elegance," he saluted Mrs Robinson, but paid no attention to the other guest, Mrs Stillman, an aging beauty who had often been painted by the Pre-Raphaelites. Then he exclaimed, "I love this salon . . . Its walls are of a blue that sets off my yellow hair." Mrs Stillman stared at him "with the regard of an angry Minerva."[36]

At the Robinsons', he again met Vernon Lee and Henry James. GM steered the conversation around to *Marius*, one of the greatest books ever written, he blustered.[37] What most excited Moore in the ensuing discussion was not James's assessment that the center of consciousness was wrongly placed in that novel, but the news that Pater himself had recently become a neighbor of the Robinsons, just a few doors down at 12 Earls Terrace; indeed, he often called for tea. Tuesday after Tuesday GM returned, but it was probably not until late June that he finally met the author of the book he so adored.[38]

Lawrence Evans is surely correct in saying Pater met Moore's "assaults on his acquaintance with studied reserve": it was characteristic of the man.[39] Pater had an "unhappy and even furtive timidity (so excessive that he could never look another man in the eye)."[40] But GM was not easy to escape, and Pater permitted, if he did not seek, the courtship of young aesthetes like Moore and Arthur Symons.[41] In the second week of July, GM met Pater again in the fitting circumstances of a party at Marc-André Raffalovich's house, where the two were the honored guests.[42] The wealthy Russian expatriate Raffalovich was a close friend of Wilde, and later the long-time companion of John Gray. At the time of this party, Raffalovich was the author of two cosy aesthetic quires of poems, *Cyril and Lionel* (1884) and *Tuberose and Meadowsweet* (1885): the *uranisme* of these books is adequately indicated by their titles. By the company he was keeping, Moore was effectively posing as homosexual. He managed to get himself invited to Pater's home, and on the third visit, Pater took him for a walk in Kensington Gardens. In *Avowals* (1919), GM said he had been "spying on Pater," trying to get him to drop his mask. But despite his "genius for intimacy," GM could not get the "Vicarage Verlaine" to share his "real self," except for a moment in the street, after Moore had told Pater that his "Prince of Court Painters" was "the most beautiful thing ever written." Pater then sighed with pleasure, "'My dear Moore!' He put his hand upon my shoulder and the mask dropped a little."[43]

What was behind the mask of the beautiful stylist? A man who had conceived as a most beautiful moment the last night in the life of Flavian, when, to keep the dying man warm, Marius slept in his bed – in other words, a man with desires not to be safely satisfied except in death, or in intimacies of understanding between men, exchanged through the perfection of phrases and sensations refined from grosser forms of fulfillment.[44] After the interception in 1874 of his letter to an Oxford student, William Money Hardinge, signed "Yours Lovingly," Pater conducted himself in life with caution. In his work, however, he continued to make beautiful certain forms of masculinity and types of affection which were a great stimulus to his readers. They found that what they had done, or wished to do, was not ugly, but aesthetic, antique, refined, the very mark of an artist. Moore was one of those inspired by Pater to believe that a boy more comfortable helping his mother with her needlework than following after his father in dueling, Arabian caravaning, and electioneering might have the true makings of the highest culture. Moore was grooming himself to become like the man addressed in Tennyson's poem "On One Who Affected an Effeminate Manner."

4

While courting the confidence of Walter Pater, GM may have been trying out a new style of masculinity, but he was not changing his sexual orientation, at least in so far as his compass needle ever pointed fixedly toward a true north. In the summer of 1885, he was enjoying a new status as a literary lion, not on the scale of James or Pater, much less Wilde, but of the same tribe. He was invited everywhere, he reported with some giddiness to his mother.[45] A further reward of fame was that interesting women were becoming interested in George Moore. One of these was Olive Schreiner.

Schreiner (1855–1920) was born in South Africa, the daughter of working-class German-English missionaries. She rebelled early against her parents' teaching, left home to become a governess, and began writing fiction that examined, in a South African setting, issues taken up by nineteenth-century European free-thinkers. She carried the manuscript of her first novel, *The Story of an African Farm*, to London where George Meredith helped her revise and then publish it in 1883. It was a huge and controversial success. The choice of the heroine to have her love-child out of wedlock in spite of offers of marriage excited concern; so did the plot development in which a conventionally British and patriarchal character puts on women's clothes and secretly follows his beloved, pregnant by another man, so that he can play in drag the part of her nurse attendant. The novel brought Schreiner into contact with socialist and free-thinking intellectuals such as Eleanor Marx, Havelock Ellis, and Karl Pearson (founder of the Men's and Women's Club for open, earnest discussion of sex).

By 1884 Schreiner had entered into an intimate but difficult relationship with Ellis, not yet the graphomaniac and renowned sexologist he was to become in the 1890s, but just a mildly socialistic man-of-letters who was devoted to the memory of James Hinton, a now-forgotten sex guru. The interests that ultimately led Ellis to tabulate the varieties of human sexuality were, however, already present; at his request, Schreiner reported the frequency with which she masturbated. Her own approach to sex was more spiritual than scientific: she compared Ellis's nude body to that of Christ in the carpenter's shop in Holman Hunt's *Shadow of the Cross*.[46]

On 25 March 1885, Ellis sent Schreiner a gift that had consequences troublesome to him – *A Mummer's Wife*.[47] After a reading of the novel, Olive Schreiner wanted to meet its author. She asked Frank Harris, lady-killer and editor of the *Evening News*, if he could tell her about Moore. Harris was sorely put out. "No one could be really important to me," Harris wrote later, "who admired Moore so intensely."[48] On 11 May 1885 Philip Bourke Marston was asked to host a party at which Schreiner could be introduced to Moore.[49] Eleanor Marx showed up at Marston's party in early June, but Moore didn't. He had gone to Brighton to see his old friends the Bridgers, having run into Colville Bridger on Regent's Street.[50] By late June Moore was back in London, and a meeting between Schreiner and GM was finally effected at about the time Moore was making his first acquaintance with Walter Pater.

Schreiner assured Havelock Ellis that she was not going to be taken in by Moore: "I enjoyed my walk with Moore pretty well. As his character grows clearer to me I see that his virtues are all intellectual, not moral. He is very selfish, I think. I told him so."[51] On 23 June, Moore visited Schreiner in her rooms at 41 Upper Baker Street after Philip Bourke Marston and her other guests for the day had departed. Would she allow him, he asked, to speak of *The Story of an African Farm* in the pamphlet he was writing against the circulating libraries, *Literature at Nurse*? By 30 June, she was bristling at Ellis that he (presumably, unlike Moore) would not take her seriously as an intellectual – whatever topic she raised, Ellis said he already knew everything about it. Were she to give herself over to Ellis sexually, she would, she feared, soon be living a "Hintonian life," on the model of Ellis's hero, James Hinton, the self-proclaimed sexual messiah, who was attended by a harem of self-sacrificing Marys and Marthas.[52]

Moore continued his suit on Monday, 13 July. Miserable, Schreiner wrote Ellis that Moore had come to her rooms and told her he loved her: "I don't believe it," she wrote Ellis; "he only wants to make me love him." Still, she advised her "darling comrade" Ellis that he could come on either Tuesday or Thursday, but Wednesday was to be kept for another tête-à-tête with GM: "Moore does fascinate me & yet I know he's so bad."[53] In August, Moore continued to draw Schreiner into his own intellectual life by asking her if she would translate for him some of the fiction by the Dutch naturalist, Frans Netscher.[54] In September, Schreiner brought the two men in her life together. Ellis and Moore met at Schreiner's new flat, 16 Portsea Place, Connaught Square; she'd been thrown out of her previous rooming house on Baker Street because she had too many male visitors. On 17 September, she admitted to Ellis that GM had made yet another evening call the previous day.[55] On 11 October 1885, Schreiner protested to Karl Pearson that she could never be converted to his philosophical belief in "free love," and even "worldly men like George Moore" had to admit that she would only accept the society of those whose notion of love was "pure and high"; indeed, it was her mission to "call out the higher and more ideal nature that does slumber in *every* man."[56] In late October Moore nearly disappears from Schreiner's correspondence, and Schreiner from Moore's.[57]

One of Moore's French habits was to talk freely of the women he had loved, or hoped to love, yet in all his amorous recollections he says nothing of his relationship to the remarkable Olive Schreiner, though it is obvious she was quite gone on him, and he hunted her persistently, as persistently as he hunted Pater, from July through October 1885. The omission is still more surprising since it is possible that her work and range of interests influenced *A Drama in Muslin*. Elizabeth Grubgeld suggests, for instance, that Alice Barton's ideal of marriage as a partnership in labor was borrowed from Schreiner's own feminism. It is certainly possible that Schreiner and those to whom she introduced Moore solidified and extended the ideas GM had worked out in his January 1885 draft article on "The Woman Question."[58] Furthermore, Schreiner put Moore in touch with her friend Eleanor Marx (a devout Fenian) and other young socialists, Havelock Ellis and G. B. Shaw, for instance, both members of the New Democratic Federation. In Moore's novel, the analysis of property relations is sharp-eyed and demystified, with a Marxian edge of lampoon about it; *Parnell and His Island* (1887) is even more sharply focused on the cash nexus in Irish social relations.

To her sister, Eleanor Marx described Moore as "a thoroughly kindly and good fellow, though after the manner of his kind he poses as being 'awfully bad.'"[59] In 1886, Marx had reason to be grateful to Moore, because he got her a contract from Vizetelly to translate *Madame Bovary*. When she was bringing the translation to a conclusion on 23 April, she sought Moore's help with some difficult points of French idiom.[60] Moore largely influenced her introduction to the volume: it rails against the circulating libraries and against censorship in general, compares Flaubert with Zola to Flaubert's advantage, and says that Moore himself is one of only two living novelists who belong to the school of Flaubert, rather than the naturalist school of Zola.[61] That is just how Moore wished to be seen in April 1886.

Earlier in the year, on 15 January, Eleanor Marx had invited GM to a reading of "Nora" (her translation of *A Doll's House*) at her rooms in Great Russell Street, with Edward Aveling as Helmer, G. B. Shaw as Krogstadt, and Eleanor Marx herself as Nora.[62] Schreiner, Marx, and Aveling all regarded Ibsen's play as a manifesto for revolution in the relations of men and women.[63] Moore was astonished by the play. He had "a hatred as lively as Ibsen's of the social conventions that drive women into the marriage market," but he was too deeply committed to his own story, told from a different point of view, to really judge the play fairly. He thought it absurd that Nora should leave her husband and children for schoolbooks. Why not for a lover? Later he realised that Nora had been for too long a sensual toy, and Ibsen was trying to make the point that "a woman is more than a domestic animal." Still, the feminist rejection of sex did not sit well with him.[64] In *A Drama in Muslin*, just beginning its serialisation at the time of the play-reading in Great Russell Street, Moore excoriates a woman-centered attitude to life, along with feminist hatred of sex with men, through his bitter characterisation of Cecilia, the hunchbacked Irish lesbian who changes her religion in order to join a nunnery.

The association of Aveling, Eleanor Marx, and Ibsen stuck with Moore, and when he came to write his own realist drama, *The Strike at Arlingford* (1893), developed on what he took to be Ibsen's lines, he built the plot around principal characters who resemble Edward Aveling and Eleanor Marx. Aveling was a charismatic, philandering underachiever, whether in poetry, the stage, or politics, his three spheres of failure; Marx was his brilliant, but self-destructively devoted lover, who deserved better than the handsome cad Aveling. Moore's play concerns a poetical labor leader with no backbone, who betrays the devoted love of his proletarian fiancée and sells out to the charming, cunning, and attractive daughter of a factory owner.

5

In the summer of 1885, when Moore was involving himself in the separate spheres of Schreiner and Pater, his main literary sideline was his battle with the circulating libraries. In the flush of what he took to be his great victory with *A Mummer's Wife*, he imagined he could finish off the opposition with a pamphlet. He worked on *Literature at Nurse, or Circulating Morals* through June and July, and it was published in early August by Vizetelly. Arguments are repeated from his 10 December 1884 article in the *Pall Mall Gazette* ("A New Censorship of Literature"), but with many illustrations. Mudie and W. H. Smith had condemned his whole novel by picking out one or two lurid passages (for instance, the scene of Gwynnie's nude modeling); Moore treats the fashionable novels Mudie circulates in the same fashion. He summarises their plots, quotes the lurid scenes, then raises a shocked eyebrow. Mrs Campbell Praed, W. H. Mallock, and Robert Buchanan cannot have been pleased to have been selected as his chief illustrations, nor did the seventeen other authors like being briefly highlighted (Violet Paget hated Moore for including her in his pantheon of panders).

Most of Moore's wrath was reserved for the great circulating librarian, treated in the pamphlet as a Sporus-like creature of amphibious sexuality. How did people come to the strange belief that Mudie himself is the "British Matron"? GM can't really say . . .

[N]or will I undertake to say if it be your personal appearance, or the constant communication you seem to be in with this mysterious female ["the British Matron"], or the singularly obtrusive way you have of forcing both your moral and religious beliefs upon the public that has led to this vexatious confusion of sex. It is, however, certain that you are popularly believed to be an old woman. But although I am willing to laugh at you, Mr. Mudie, to speak candidly, I hate you; and I love and am proud of my hate of you. It is the best thing about me. I hate you because you dare question the sacred right of the artist to obey the principles of his temperament; I hate you because you are the great purveyor of the worthless, the false, and the commonplace; I hate you because you are a fetter on the ankles of those who would press forward to the light of truth; I hate you because you feel not the spirit of scientific inquiry that is bearing our age along; I hate you because you pander to the intellectual sloth of to-day; I hate you because you would mould all ideas to the narrow limits in which your own turn; I hate you because you impede the free development of our literature. And now that I have told you what I think of you, I will resume my examination of the ware you have in stock.[65]

Moore's vituperation is also a declaration of faith, faith first of all in the impulses of the artist's personality. Later in the pamphlet Moore stated a second key belief: literature should be allowed to include a serious examination of the lives of adult men and women. Authors should "write as grown-up men and women talk of life's passions and duties," not titter over dirty stories, or turn squeamishly away from the subject of vice.[66] There is something noble about Moore's commitment to literature as an art and to freedom of expression, a nobility undiminished by his grandiose rhetoric or the big-headed sense that he would single-handedly liberate England from moral restraints on the market in ideas.

In July and August of 1885, while Moore was imagining himself to be putting paid to the moral opposition, there were forces gathering that would eventually do him serious damage. Most of these forces were controlled by W. T. Stead (1847–1912), editor of the *Pall Mall Gazette* from 1883 to 1889, and thus, paradoxically, the publisher of GM's "A New Censorship." In the spring of 1885, Stead had been campaigning, along with General Booth of the Salvation Army and Josephine Butler of the Ladies' National Association, for changes in the Criminal Law Amendment Bill. Their main interest was in the control of "white slave traffic," specifically the sale of virgins to London gentlemen, though this parliamentary bill became notorious because of the provision introduced by Henry Labouchère specifically naming and prohibiting homosexuality.[67]

In June and July, Stead dramatised the problem of white slave traffic by going undercover as a man seeking to buy a night with a young virgin, and then, in lurid detail, describing his arrangements with the madam, his trip to the place of assignation, the arrival of the girl, everything up to the very moment at which sexual relations would commence. The drama in which the pornographic wolf comes dressed in the sheep's clothing of puritanism reaches its climax after her interview with the journalist when doctors are brought into the rented room in order to certify that the young girl is still a virgin. The *Pall Mall* articles, sensationally entitled "The Maiden Tribute of Modern Babylon," sold 100,000 copies. Originally unsigned, the articles were rumored to be by Moore himself, so cleverly had the "new journalist" Stead mimicked the appurtenances of fictional realism.[68] When his authorship became known, Stead was widely accused, as Moore had been, of writing for prurient reasons, and with indifference to the potential of his own articles to corrupt young girls in the country.[69] The *Bat* teased GM by saying that he was disconsolate at Whistler's Sunday afternoon "At Home" on 12 July, because the *Pall Mall Gazette* had "out-Zolaed Zola in the matter of dirty realism."[70] Certainly, it was difficult for Moore to decide if "Maiden Tribute" was good for his cause or bad for it. In his 16 August report to Zola on the English literary situation, he judged that the sensational interest aroused by the articles indicated that there was a public in London for a more truthful depiction of contemporary reality.[71]

He could not have been more wrong about the character of the forces in the public that Stead released and directed. In late August, after the *Pall Mall Gazette* articles and the passage of the Criminal Law Amendment Bill, Stead, Josephine Butler, and Mrs Booth organised three meetings to consider how to bring about prosecutions under the terms of the bill. At these meetings, it was unanimously agreed to form local committees of vigilantes, under the umbrella organisation of the National Vigilance Association (NVA). The ten principles of the Association mingle feminism with puritanism: they include a principle binding men as well as women to "the law of chastity"; another denounces the cruelty of momentary male pleasure, which dooms women to a lifetime of shame; yet another stresses the need for new economic conditions to contribute to the preservation of chastity (that is, education or emigration for women, and jobs for women besides prostitution); and crucially, "the importance of personal purity of all good citizens" – which appears to make strictly observed heterosexual monogamy a condition of British citizenship.[72] On 28 August 1885 the NVA ominously set up a "Literature Subcommittee."

Stead selected W. A. Coote to be the secretary/manager of the National Vigilance Association, and put him on his personal payroll. This man became a shadowy anti-self of Moore's, equally driven and ambitious, active in the same sphere, but utterly antipathetic in principles and temperament. Coote, of Irish descent, grew up in the Strand among "thieves and women of the unfortunate class," as he recalled. After the death of his father, when the young Coote was just three, his mother subsided into a worse class of slum than the one into which he was born, but still in the Strand. Coote says that he was ambitious of going to Trinity College Dublin, though his circumstances left him with no further schooling after the age of twelve. His widowed mother was forced into prostitution. At twelve, Coote was apprenticed to a printer in the Haymarket, where the public houses were open all night, and some featured prize fights – Coote himself learned to box. At sixteen, he was converted by the reading of a religious tract, which made him suddenly aware of the hideousness of his habits of masturbation. From then on, his life was changed. As Secretary of the NVA, Coote was eager to take up the prosecution of "indecent literature and exhibitions," because such enticements to bad thoughts were the "crying evil" of London, "thrust before" young men, "and to an appalling extent were part of the stock-in-trade of disorderly houses." He was angry that the government would only prosecute "grossly and obviously indecent" publications; more subtle forms of literary indecency were ignored, though these too "were obviously subversive of the best interests of the growing generation, and opposed to the ideals of a true citizenship."[73] Moore did not yet know about W. A. Coote, but this man was the instrument by which an outraged public would have its revenge on Moore and Vizetelly.

Another development in the summer of 1885, not then known to Moore, was also to have complex, tangential consequences for him. In July, Sir Charles Dilke, projected as the future leader of the Liberal Party, was named in the divorce case that his colleague in the Liberal administration, Donald Crawford, brought against his young wife, Virginia Smith Crawford. Dilke was horrified, because, even if he had not slept with Virginia Crawford, he had to admit he had slept with her mother, while his brother Ashton had been married to her sister May; furthermore, Dilke was just at that time himself engaged to be married to the widow of Mark Pattison, a famous Oxford intellectual.[74] The possibilities for sexual/political scandal looked like a gold mine for newspapers, and at the time of the trial, which opened on 12 February 1886, and long after it, W. T. Stead worked the vein for all it was worth. It was the steadfast purpose of this journalist to hound Dilke out of public life, and he succeeded. In the first trial, Dilke did not take the stand, Mrs Crawford confessed, and divorce was granted without prejudice to Dilke. Stead raised an outcry, and Dilke was forced to try to clear his name in a second trial, concerning whether Mrs Crawford's confession of adultery, or Dilke's public denial, was true.

On the stand, the beautiful young woman proved to be a brilliant witness, unshakeable by hundreds of questions from lawyers. She described how in the autumn of 1881 Dilke met her, then just nineteen years old, in Bailey's Hotel and kissed her; in February 1883, she met him at a house of assignation in Warren Street for deeper intimacies; she met him again in May 1883, then caught a late train to join her husband as a guest of Mark Pattison in Oxford. Later, Dilke insisted that she allow Fanny, the sister of one of his servants, to join them in bed, and this wish he ultimately succeeded in getting her to fulfill in his own house. In bed together, Dilke said Virginia reminded him of her mother in earlier years. Virginia Crawford explained that she was forced to come out with the truth because someone who knew about the affair was writing her husband anonymous letters of accusation, and it had become useless to deny it.

Dilke, during his own time on the stand, unchivalrously accused Virginia of making the whole thing up to fix on him the blame for her own adulteries with both a medical attendant and a young officer. Her testimony, he said, was all part of a still-undiscovered conspiracy aimed at destroying his political power. Dilke labored with difficulty to explain his whereabouts on the days in earlier years when he was accused of being in bed with Virginia. Questioned as to whether he had been the lover of her mother, he at first refused to answer, next admitted it was so, but many years earlier. The following day, he corrected his statement to read that he had had a protracted affair with Mrs Smith that continued up to 1880.[75] At the conclusion of testimony, Judge Hannen instructed the jury that they were to decide, "from what you know of human nature, which of the two things you think it most probable, that a man should do such a thing, or that a woman should invent it if it were not done." Thus instructed, the jury took only fifteen minutes to decide in favor of Virginia Crawford, but in a hundred years of subsequent legal and scholarly inquiry, no one has authoritatively laid the question to rest.[76]

The initial significance of the famous *Crawford* v. *Crawford* divorce case to novelists like Moore appeared to be that the public had a hunger for inquiring into the woe that is in marriage, and a great tolerance for a press that printed details about French letters, venereal disease, houses of assignation, and three-way sex. In short, if courts could interrogate the sex lives of people, and news-papermen could print their testimony, why couldn't novelists more sensitively meditate on the same details? But the long-range effect of the case was not in fact liberalising. The press excitement over the trial was a sign of the hungry vindictiveness of the middle class against the private pleasures of the great, and the public did not want a sensitive meditation on a real-life love triangle; it wanted the dirt and then a fifteen-minute judgement with damages.

A decade later, Moore was to seek out and befriend Virginia Crawford; she would advise him on his novel of illicit love, *Evelyn Innes* (1898), and afterwards remain his lifelong friend.

6

Moore did not comprehend these forces at work in English society in October 1885; he was caught up in the toils of composition. When Jacques-Emile Blanche offered to visit Moore early in that month, and paint his portrait, Moore explained that he could only give his friend a little time to walk about together in the afternoons; he was working through the mornings and evenings to bring *A Drama in Muslin* to a conclusion. He expected to sell it for seriali-sation by the end of the month.[77] By the following week, his chance of imme-diate serialisation, and £300 for the rights, fell through. Disappointed, Moore explained to his mother the difficulty of supporting himself as a novelist. At six shillings a copy, his novels had to sell at least 5,000 copies for him to have a good annual income, especially as he was getting little from his rents, aside from the support they provided for his mother and the minimum upkeep of Moore Hall.[78] The previous May he had received £65 for the first three months of *A Mummer's Wife*, and Vizetelly then told him he could expect about £150 in total from the novel.[79]

For the new revised eighth edition of the novel, issued in early November 1885, Moore tried to whip up additional sales, not by correcting scores of in-felicities of phrasing (though he did so), but by printing a preface in which he claimed that his book had been attacked by "Philistines," and for a moment "squeaked the squeak of death." He had saved it at the last minute by "vigorous advertising," and "the Philistine was routed."[80] It did not dawn on him that the philistines had recently organised themselves into an army of vigi-lantes, the NVA.

In early November, Moore broke from his work on *A Drama in Muslin* to write a preface for the Vizetelly translation of Zola's *La Curée*, issued under the title *The Rush for Spoil*.[81] In the preface, Moore makes an effort to recon-cile Walter Pater and Gustave Flaubert with Emile Zola. As he had done in his preface to *Piping-Hot!* (*Pot-Bouille*), Moore proclaims that Zola is at heart an epic poet, the furthest thing from a journalist; the novel is "a gorgeous, a golden poem." He picks out a passage to praise for its "precision and delicacy of touch," equal to anything except "that supreme success, that final vindication of the supreme power of words – Flaubert's *L'Education sentimentale*." The impression left by Zola's novel is of "intense artistic beauty" – he did not have to say, like that of a "hard gemlike flame," Pater's ideal in life and art.[82] Moore had tried to remake *A Mummer's Wife* through the scrupulous toil of revision into something more like Flaubert in its finish than like Zola, and now he was trying to remake Zola too.

The defensive attitude of the preface to *The Rush for Spoil* was continued in Moore's article on Zola's forthcoming *L'Oeuvre*, "the history of the art struggle of the illustrious author himself," as Moore called it. "M. Zola's New Book," published in the 10 November 1885 *Bat*, admits that a "rational attack" on Zola's work is that he describes "physical rather than psychical phenomena," and that the naturalist novel is not a psychological novel. That, in fact, was Henry James's judgement on Zola in "The Art of Fiction." But *L'Oeuvre*, Moore promises on Zola's behalf, will be "a complete refutation of these superficially conceived judgements": it will be a picture of "the martyrdom of the human mind," the mind "fevered with the love of art." The modern French painters had been Zola's personal friends, GM explained, and therefore in this novel Zola would not have to rely on external documentation.[83] Although Moore accurately summarises the plot and themes of *L'Oeuvre*, in fact he had not yet read it; he was relying on Zola's descriptions of the book. Much would later hang on Moore's judgement of Zola's success in fulfilling the promises made in this advance publicity. In his late December update to Zola, Moore expressed his eagerness to see a copy of the novel; he felt sure it would be Zola's best book. His own news to Zola was that he had managed to sell the serial rights of *A Drama in Muslin* to the *Court and Society Review* for 4,000 francs (£158).[84]

7

The *Court and Society Review* was a weekly journal offering the "Best and latest Court News, Best Club and Society Gossip, Articles written in brightest and most vigorous style on social subjects." Its politics were professedly "from the point of view of the national good," in other words, highly conservative, and morally speaking, it promised to exclude "contributions likely to render it unfit for family reading." The editor, Henry Barnett, was a friend of Edward Martyn, who was a backer of the paper. When the magazine made arrangements to publish Moore's novel, Martyn threatened to cancel his subscription if the book contained anything "contrary to faith and morals."[85] The serial version left out a degree of sexual exuberance in the man-crazy May Gould and the woman-loving Cecilia Cullen, but Martyn may have been equally concerned about the depiction of his parish priest as loathsome, and the atheist heroine as admirable, both of whom appear in the serial version as they do in the book.[86]

The pre-publication gossip in the *Court and Society Review* suggests that the editor hoped the novel would discredit the Liberal government's Lord Lieutenant of Ireland. Moore's japes with the Castle over its refusal to issue him a dinner invitation were rehearsed in detail a few weeks before publication began on 14 January 1886. Yet Moore's politics was not that of the Tory *Court and Society Review*. Over against the editor's publicity for the serial, Moore himself sent in a letter setting the novel against the background of the general election concluded on 19 December 1885, in which Parnell's Irish party gained the balance of power in Parliament.

> For the next six months Mr. Parnell will hold his demand for Home Rule like a red-hot poker at the throat of England; Mr. Gladstone and Lord Salisbury

already stand bracing up their nerves, a huge crowd will assemble to see, or to prevent, the swallowing, and here and there through the groups you will insinuate yourself, a bundle of papers under your arm, crying – "buy, buy, who will buy a picture of Ireland, all complete, castle, landlords, and landleaguers, and painted by an Irishman."

The last phrase was crucial, Moore continued, for, "although a landlord by birth," he was a "nationalist at heart." He was giving a picture of an Ireland that throbbed in that heart:

Landlords overpowered with debts, whining their lives away in intellectual and physical atrophy; peasants in dull ignorance and poverty sighing for freedom and national individuality.

The book contrasts these two classes – "there are no middle classes in Ireland" – by focusing on "the shrill wail of virgins heard through the thunder of a people marching to nationhood."

This description of his novel is both powerful and opportunistic. *A Drama in Muslin* had been projected as a book on rational atheism; it had been a book on the "Woman Question"; and it had been a book providing serious discussion of relationships between men and women. Indeed, it could be read as any or all of these. The plot of this "girl book" certainly features women's destinies, treating in an original way the conflict between the sexual desires of the débutantes and the social ambitions of their mothers.[87] It neatly evaluates the alternative destinies of the female characters – Violet gets a lord, May gets pregnant, Alice gets a job and a dispensary doctor, and the beautiful, brainless, and ambitious Olive gets nothing. The simplicity of the "This Little Piggy" plot enables GM to examine the moral worth of his heroines, and to show that the rational, independent, atheistic, considerate, and sexually honest Alice deserves the reader's admiration.[88] But just before publication, Moore changed course, taking advantage of news bulletins about Parnell's new power, and Gladstone's conversion to Home Rule ("the Hawarden kite"), and defined his novel as a book on Irish national liberation.

In fact, *A Drama in Muslin is* a political – even a Home Rule – novel too, indicting with a sort of merciless, inward sympathy "an entire race, a whole caste, [who] saw themselves driven from their soft, warm couches of idleness, and forced into the struggle for life . . . What could they do with their empty brains? What could they do with their feeble hands?"[89] The "Woman Question" and the "Irish Question" were related in that Irish landlords and European bourgeois women both had idle hands and empty brains, and both would now have to join "the struggle for life." Comparisons of class with gender and the personal with the political are implied by the form of the narrative. The novel's most distinctive and famous feature is the fugal treatment of Mr Barton negotiating with tenants on the gravel drive, while inside the house Mrs Barton negotiates with an unsuitable suitor. The montage effect is repeated with variations frequently in the novel, by moving the focus from dialogue among named gentry characters in the foreground, seeking profitable alliances, to description of unnamed peasant characters in the background, seething with grievance. The parallelism of the personal and the political is kept up throughout, as the novel tracks the progress of Mrs Barton's marriage schemes for her two daughters, the beautiful Olive and the plain Alice, against the major Irish political events of 1881 and '82: assassinations, intimidation, and evictions, the Phoenix Park murders, the 1882 bill for the prevention of crime, the No-Rent manifesto of the imprisoned leaders of the Land League, and the Land Act judicially fixing the rents, which led "the lurid phantom of the League" to vanish "suddenly as a card up the sleeve of a skilful conjurer."[90]

In a crucial moment near the end of the story, foreground and background, plot and subplot, marriage and politics, all come together when Alice, departing with her husband, notices – usually the poor are either unsightly or completely invisible to the gentry – a family of peasants just evicted from their cottage, and asks, "Is it not terrible that human creatures should endure such misery?"[91] Her husband offers to do something for them: he pays their rent and talks with them. This is no "solution" to the Irish question. As sardonic land agents immediately point out to the couple, there are plenty more peasants over the hill if they wish to give away their money, and Alice and Dr Reed then leave Ireland, resolving, somewhat fatuously, that they can best serve humanity "by learning to love each other." However, the incident does shatter the glass walls of isolation around the Irish classes with a short-lived act of awareness.

It is possible to take a strong view of the irony in this passage, as showing Moore's own fatalism about reform in Ireland,[92] yet Moore's pessimism at this stage was not all-consuming. The novel makes clear what he thought ought to be done: clear out Dublin Castle, educate women, put the landed aristocracy to work, gradually enable the peasants to come into ownership of the land, and begin to create a degree of civilisation in Ireland. These are the views that entitled him to say he was a nationalist, quite in the spirit of his father, G. H. Moore.

As soon as the novel began its serialisation in January 1886, Moore allowed himself to be drawn aside into a dispute with one signing himself "An Amazed Parent" of a child at the Convent of the Holy Child, the scene of the opening chapter of the novel. Moore revelled in the publicity, as his letters and those of the "amazed" Catholic parent, Catholic Attorney General Charles Russell, Canon Wenham, and a Mother Superior, all defending the confidences of the nuns and the purity of their students, appeared in the *Tablet*, the *Weekly Register*, the *Bat*, and, at Moore's urging, alongside his novel in the *Court and Society Review*.[93] GM was always good at settling scores, but it did not leave a good impression to win a ringing victory in a battle with nuns.

In early February 1886, Moore refocused the theme of his novel for the public; it now became chiefly a defense of atheism. He sent the novel, or parts of it, to an editor, along with a covering letter meant to instruct a reviewer:

> I have attempted to paint the portrait of a virtuous woman, – I have attempted the supremely difficult task of using the realistic method as a means not of imposing vice but exposing the mechanism of the virtuous mind. My heroine is an atheist: she is an atheist on the first page, she is an atheist on the last; she is neither prude nor prostitute but a woman endowed with much common sense and a deep rooted belief in the practical rectitudes of life.

With all of his marketing instructions, Moore confused his readership. Victorian readers on the whole would not have been quick to approve of any one of his subjects – not feminism, nor Irish nationalism, nor ethical atheism. Readers of the novel would discover more unpleasant subjects than just these three. The heroine's Catholic mother is engaged in adultery with Protestant Lord Dungory, apparently for money, while her husband turns a blind eye. The heroine's best friend, the Protestant Cecilia, is a lesbian, who converts to Catholicism and becomes a nun. Her next best friend, May, gets pregnant by a young cad, has the baby out of wedlock, sees with little sorrow the baby die, returns to have sex with a worn-out gallant, and throughout it all remains the heroine's dear friend. Such things are not supposed to happen in Victorian fiction. William Wallace, the *Academy* reviewer, ignoring all Moore's urgings about how to read the novel, said that *A Drama in Muslin* was "daringly and disgustingly suggestive, and descriptive of what ordinary writers of fiction leave undescribed"; he hoped such stuff did not have a market.[94]

In early February, with his novel only through its first few weeks of serialisation, GM told his mother that he would not dare go to Moore Hall that winter: "I hear my book has given so much offence that it would be better for me to keep away . . . Of course, I regret nothing." He had to confess he no longer was on visiting terms with Mrs Moore's sister, Anna Blake Murphy, "nor indeed [with] any of the Irish lot."[95] Mrs Martyn had banned him from Tillyra for his depiction of the parish priest of Ardrahan. There was no sign that even the Irish nationalists liked Moore's harsh, brilliant, experimental tale. Quarreling with the nuns at the Convent of the Holy Child was bad; worse still was the fact that in Moore's novel, Irish women like sex, even good women. Not only does May Gould happily give in to the desires of Fred, but in the next room of the hotel the heroine Alice Barton, thinking of the novelist Harding, feels "a distinct desire possessing for her an intrinsic value" and envies May for at least knowing "what the rest of [the débutantes] might never know."[96] Irish patriots have not been kind to authors who attack Catholicism and sexualise their womenfolk. In the 11 August 1887 issue of *Truth*, Charles Russell called the author of *A Drama in Muslin* a "night-soil novelist"; as late as March 1901, Russell remained angry enough to blackball Moore from the Irish Literary Society.[97]

8

In March 1886, Duret brought GM along to the banquet in Paris at which the Impressionists planned a spring exhibition, their eighth and final collective exhibition. The guests included Camille Pissarro, Monet, Mallarmé, Huysmans, and the critic Philippe Burty. There was much talk about Zola's *L'Oeuvre*, just completing its serial in *Gil Blas*; mostly, the talk was against it. The novel's hero Claude Lantier is a combination of Cézanne and Manet. After early promise, Lantier becomes powerless to fully express his ideas, and the once promising *plein-air* movement he heralded turns into a commercially successful form of decoration. The admirable character in the book is the journalist/novelist Sandoz, a wise hardworking family man of great integrity who is writing a series of interconnected novels on a multi-generational family. Sandoz is clearly meant to be taken for Zola. So in the novel Zola inflated himself and naturalism, and deflated Manet, Cézanne, and Impressionism as a whole.[98] The significance of the evening's conversation for GM lies in the fact that he had, like the others, long assumed an identity of basic goals between naturalism and Impressionism, between Zola and Manet. The social break of the French author from the painters he had once supported added to the growing pressure on Moore to separate himself from Zola.

By mid-April, Moore had read *L'Oeuvre*. To Zola's Dutch acolyte, Frans Netscher, Moore admitted that he did not care for the novel at all.[99] The review he had promised Zola to write remained unwritten, but in the introduction to Eleanor Marx's *Madame Bovary*, composed that same April, he allowed the condemnation of Zola in favor of Flaubert to pass, even in a publication by Vizetelly & Co., which had built its name and fortune on Zola's works.

In early May, GM was back in Paris to review the Salon and the Impressionist Exhibition for the *Court and Society Review* and the *Bat*, respectively. On varnishing day of the Salon, he had the honor of walking through the crowd arm in arm with Daudet, Goncourt, and Zola.[100] Moore's review of the Salon focuses attention on a vast, dreamy allegorical landscape with female figures by Puvis de Chavannes, and on the work of his friend Jacques-Emile Blanche, whose picture of a girl in red was praised for its "personal impression of life," GM's new Manet-inspired touchstone.[101] At the Impressionist exhibition, held above the Restaurant Doré on the rue Laffitte, Moore saw fifteen new pastels of women bathing by Degas, and Seurat's huge picture, *La Grande Jatte*, along with paintings hung in the same room and painted in the same pointillist manner by Camille Pissarro. Moore later confessed to complete amazement upon walking into this gallery – the brightly-flecked canvases were "something entirely new" and "not without merit," but he could not tell the difference between a Pissarro in the pointillist style and a Seurat, except by getting down on his knees to examine the signatures.[102]

In "Half a Dozen Enthusiasts," published in the 25 May issue of the *Bat*, Moore reaffirmed his commitment to the Impressionists at a time when Zola was making them out to be failures. They were for him heroes of the artistic life, who rejected the patronage of the Salon to hire "a little house of their own, where they can exhibit . . . their personal dreams of men and things." They are "young men who feel that life is nothing if it is not personal." Gradually, they have won respect, yet people still do not realise, GM complains, that Degas is "one of the greatest artists the world has ever known." In his new sketches of women bathing, drying, rubbing down, and combing out their hair, Degas had done, Moore argued, what Baudelaire had done before: he had created a "*nouveau frisson.*" "The short, coarse, thick thighs of the poor working woman, deformed by the toil of modern days, have never been seen on canvas before."[103] Corrupted by the weak obscenities at the Salon, the nude had become impossible for a serious artist, but "with cynicism Degas has rendered the nude again an artistic possibility."[104] Moore also had praise for Guillemet, Pissarro, and Seurat, whose great picture of Paris on a Sunday afternoon GM described as a modernised version of an Egyptian frieze. Moore's years spent failing to become a painter were now making for a new kind of success: his art criticism as much as anyone's was to show the English how to understand the new French painting. Yet it had another value for Moore's own craft – it enabled him to articulate values of personality and perspectivalism that were to become the keynotes of his literature.

9

After his return from Paris, Moore went to visit the Bridgers at Shoreham, on the Sussex coast just west of Brighton. The Bridgers owned a manor, Buckingham House, and 4,000 acres of farmland stretching from the sea up into the Downs along the Adur river. Colville Bridger, retired from the Army, was considering a life as a gentleman farmer. He remained unmarried, but had formed a lasting attachment to his mistress, whom he kept in a Brighton apartment. Colville had two sisters, Florence (b. 1856) and Dulcibella (b. 1859). A cousin of the Bridgers, William Bridger, passed on to Joseph Hone a letter from GM, written in old age, in which he says of the girls: "I used to go to balls with the two young women (who are now old women). I used to have one of them & could have had the other . . . They had long fair hair down to their waists." William Bridger told Hone that GM was not lying about having been the lover of one of the sisters, but, prior to Hone's interview with the two old ladies, would not tell him which was the lucky one: "Your problem will be to guess."[105] (The sister in question was evidently Dulcibella.) The sisters gave Moore two nicknames: "Mr Perpetual" because he was always in love, and "Kent" because, like Lear's advisor, he was so often sententious.

Their mother, Eliza Ann Bridger (1829–89), continued to call him "Kant" because of his boyhood interest in the German philosopher. Mrs Bridger was his favorite in the family. In "A Remembrance," written shortly after her death,

Moore recalls that even in her mid-fifties she kept a "girl-like figure." GM flattered her by telling her of all her frocks which ones he liked best. Catching her in the potting shed (she loved to garden), he was scolded for coming upon her when she was in an old bonnet, but, in an odd "love-passage," he confessed she looked charming to him. She regarded him "with that love in her face which an old woman feels for a young man who is something less and something more than her son. As the flush of summer lingers in autumn's face, so does a sensation of sex float in such an affection."[106] The tenderness he felt for her went deep in him.

Moore so much enjoyed his late June visit to the Bridgers that he decided, after a month's return to London, to take a room for the summer in the nearby village of Southwick. He was lodged there by 26 July, when he wrote Frans Netscher about the reception of *A Drama in Muslin*. The *Bat* and *Court and Society* had praised the novel written by their staff writer,[107] but as the reviews poured in from the major weeklies, GM had to conclude that the book had been "badly misunderstood."[108] He tried to be pleased with a somewhat censorious review in the *Athenaeum* (GM was competent, but nasty), and he was thankful to William Archer for a serious treatment of his work in the *Pall Mall Gazette*,[109] but the *Saturday Review* and *Academy* were snide and extensively hostile about the novel's "coarseness," "pseudo-philosophy," "portentous length," and "disgusting suggestiveness."[110] By 27 July, the novel had been banned by the circulating libraries. In "Our Daily Dirt," the *Bat* complained that the "flood of filth" printed by newspapers about the Dilke trial was far worse than anything in the books of Zola and Moore, but the "British pharisee" exulted in his own virtue.[111]

Moore hoped he had written a novel that was far more artistic and individual than *A Mummer's Wife*, and in fact he had, but he was shaken by its reception. He asked Netscher, Duret, and the critic Harry Quilter for their honest opinions: was there any "falling off" from his previous standard?[112] All three friends said that the book was very good, but Moore's confidence remained rattled. In a fury, he wrote a letter to the *Times* on 12 August 1886 bidding goodbye to the English novel-reading public. He was indignant at the way his "literary conduct" had been "grievously impugned," and his practical existence as a professional writer undermined by the ban on circulation of his books. Henceforth, he declared, he would write in French.[113] His petulant defiance was an easy target for sneers in the daily press, as far away as New York.[114]

GM believed he could change the language in which he published his literature because *La Femme du cabotin* had begun its serialisation in *Le Voltaire* on 7 July 1886, and he had got a commission from *Figaro* to write a series of articles about Ireland, explaining the Irish to the French just as Max O'Rell (the pseudonym of Paul Blouet) had explained the English to the French in *John Bull et son île: moeurs anglaises contemporaines*.[115] By early August Moore was negotiating a deal with Charpentier for the publication of these *Figaro* articles as a book.[116] Published in Paris as soon as he could finish them in his room above Mrs Feist's grocery on the Southwick Green, Moore's letters on Ireland were proving a big success, and Zola congratulated his supposed apprentice on them, urging him to "audacity, audacity, and audacity again!"[117] The advice was unnecessary, GM was audacious enough already. He had just been mocking Zola himself in a letter to his Dutch pupil Netscher. Did Netscher "believe in these ridiculous theories which my great friend Emile Zola has written so much about"?

> You surely do not believe in the naturalistic school? You surely do not believe in scientific art – I love art because it is not nature . . . The great thing to do, it seems to me, is to create men and women as Shakespeare and Balzac did and this Zola cannot do, but of his numerous books all that remains to me is Gervaise Coupeau . . .

By naturalist standards, Netscher had found *A Drama in Muslin* to be "too lyrical," but Moore declared he did not believe in the naturalist or any other school: "I want each book to be different from the last, slightly different, and I want to be personal."[118] Instead of being Zola's ricochet in England, GM was now set on being George Moore in Paris, but he had not yet told the master that his student had come of age.

10

Lettres sur l'Irlande (the English title is *Parnell and His Island*) was meant to be Moore's hello to Paris and goodbye to England, but it kissed off Ireland even more emphatically. GM's anger at the treatment of *A Drama in Muslin* by Irish friends and English reviewers was unleashed in a savage reorganisation of the materials he had fictionalised in the novel. Like Harding in that novel, Moore "desired to astonish"; and like Harding's book-in-progress, GM worked from a plan for "a series of descriptive sketches" of "representative characters – the landlord, the grazier, the tenant farmer, the moonlighter, the parson, the priest," in which he would "tell their history, their manner of life, and their aims and ambitions."[119]

Parnell and His Island opens with a depth-charge of ironic allegory. The aesthetic narrator takes in the Turneresque view of Dublin harbor from Dalkey, and sees the mountains as "the mailed arms of a knight leaning to a floating siren whose flight he would detain and of whom he asks still an hour of love." Out of the Norman rape of Ireland, Moore makes beauty.[120] The book is mined throughout with explosives of this sort. Ireland itself he compares to an "old clothes shop": nothing seems to belong to the people themselves; "language, dress and manners at one time or another" belonged to other people, a deadly image of the colonial condition. All the Dublin society people worship the Castle officials: "Every man wears the red ribbon of the Castle in his buttonhole; and more than one woman wears it instead of a garter." The members of the Ascendancy Kildare Street Club are people "gifted with an oyster-like capacity for understanding this one thing: that they should continue to get fat in the bed in which they were born."

The satire doesn't stop with Dublin society and the landlord class. About the peasants, among other things just as harsh, he says he cannot judge whether Home Rule will civilise them, but "At present [the peasant] is a savage, eminently fitted for cattle-lifting, but ill-suited to ply the industry of farming which the law forces upon him as the alternative of starvation." Nine marriages out of ten, he claims in "The Tenant Farmer," are shotgun marriages, forced by the Land League and the priest. The only way a man can escape such a forced marriage is to be a member of the League, in which case the pregnant girl's own family will send her to the workhouse. In "The Landlord," he described the domestic arrangements of his uncle Joe Blake, using Blake's own name. Landlord Blake had taken his peasant housekeeper as a bedmate; she was the mother of his children. When Hone asked if this story had any basis in fact, Maurice Moore replied that it was indeed true, and true of other local gentry and their tenants, but was never mentioned, and ought not to be mentioned by Hone. The violation of the taboo against landlord–tenant miscegenation was one of the secrets of Irish life. Yet, having sketched the character of the Blake household, Moore suavely generalises:

> About every landlord's house traces are to be found of immorality with peasant women, and it is curious to note the proportion of tenants that bear the land-lords' names, and often at a petty sessions the magistrate will not convict the prisoner because he knows Blake to be his half-brother or his son . . . I know of no novelist who has touched on this subject, and yet how full it is of poor human nature: vice, degradation, pity, hard-heartedness, grow on its every branch like blackberries on an autumn hedge.[121]

There were going to be no more annual trips to Ireland after writing in this manner, however true and curiously poignant the subject might appear to be in Moore's eyes.

However influential the book may have been in Paris – for instance, on Huysmans's *En rade* and Zola's *La Terre* – it was unforgivable in Ireland. [122] That Moore had satirised himself as the affected young landlord-poet just back from Paris, ignorant of, and indifferent to, the needs of his tenants, did not at all suffice to make up for the offense given by his satire of every other class of person in Ireland, as well as certain families – the Blakes, the Ruttledges, and the Martyns among them – which had been his closest connections in the country. The book severed his ties to Ireland for the next twelve years. Even as late as 1916, when Susan Mitchell published a vengeful book on Moore, she declaimed against *Parnell and His Island*: "It is indecent . . . What shall we say of Mr. Moore who exhibits his country's sores for the coppers of the Paris press . . . There is no art in 'Parnell and His Island,' and there is sufficient truth in it to make it a horrible exhibition of Mr. Moore's soul."[123] By patriotic standards, Moore's crime was to exhibit Ireland to the eyes of Paris; from Moore's own standpoint, it was his achievement to be able to see Ireland through Parisian eyes.

I I

During the summer Moore spent in Sussex, he may have courted not just Dulcibella and Florence Bridger, but also Julia Davis Frankau (1864–1916), the sister of *Bat* editor James Davis. While the course of his relationship to her is undocumented by letters between the two, in a 31 August 1886 letter to Netscher, Moore mentions Davis and the novel he was helping her write, *Dr. Phillips*: "Her hero is a Jew doctor. I do not think a woman ever painted a man so cunningly before."[124] The Davises were tennis enthusiasts and spent summer weeks at Eastbourne, just down the coast from Moore's room on the Shoreham village green. GM had known Julia and her sister Eliza Davis Aria since around 1881 when he began to frequent the house of her brother James. In 1883, Julia married a cigar merchant, Arthur Frankau.[125] After April 1885, GM would have been likely to run into Julia again at her brother's house; the *Bat* was composed at Davis's dining room table. That Moore urged her to write *Dr. Phillips* was characteristic of him: his main, if not sole, mode of approach to women was through co-authorship. Like Zola, he wanted a school, but in his case he aimed to propagate his form of literature through female students.

In *A Babe in Bohemia* (1889), a vindictive *roman-à-clef* Julia Davis Frankau published after falling out with Moore, she satirised George and Augustus Moore under the names Sinclair and Tom Furley. Sinclair, author of a volume of suppressed French poems and some notorious realistic novels, has "fishlike eyes" with which he "gloats" over the exotic if undeveloped beauty of the young Lucilla.[126] Meeting Sinclair at a play, Lucilla gets the creeps when contemplating his "narrow chest and sloping shoulders," "light, curiously expressionless" eyes, and "boneless, fat, soft, and white hands" – a hateful but recognisable portrait of GM.[127] The "poisonous suggestiveness" of his conversation and manner alarms her, as his "thick lips almost touching her ear" whisper his comments on the play. At a dinner in Savile Row, he pursues Lucilla into a corner and praises her cleverness, the beauty of her figure, and her lips, then asks her to confess to him her past sexual experiences. Seeing him press his suit on the young girl, one male guest becomes protective, but Sinclair's brother Tom says not to worry: Sinclair likes to make people think he is a devil among women, but "in reality he is frightened to death of them, and never has had a genuine affair in his life." He was always, the story went on, flattering women by trying to get them to dance, sing, or write under his direction, but really he was only interested in them as ways to incite his own sensations, so that he could study these and use them in his books.

Eventually, Lucilla is quite taken in, and agrees to a *séance de collaboration*. She is ready to drop into his hands, but he brings a large pile of manuscript, his own, and, preaching Zolaism, "He forgot to make love to Lucilla while he talked of himself." Afterwards, he accepts the chaffing of male friends about Lucilla, and allows them to believe that he is having his way with her. At one stage of the story, he does indeed get her to submit "to his kisses – to his mucilaginous, soft-skinned personality."[128] She is rescued by her brother from the clutches of Sinclair Furley, but she is not sorry to have known him. Sinclair Furley had "added to the development of her nature," with his wide reading, great ambitions, and worship of notoriety. She finds another man, Mordaunt, who loves her with a love that brings her peace. Yet Sinclair comes one day when Mordaunt is out, and after one of his soft wet kisses, she cuts her own throat.

This novel is clearly an act of revenge, but for what crimes is undocumented. Evidently Moore pursued her, objectified her, indulged his vanity with her, collaborated with her, talked with her very much, and made very little love to her. The sensations of lust and loathing he excited would be described by more than one woman, though others felt simply loathing, or lust, or nothing at all. After the spell was broken, Julia called him "the white slug."[129]

In the summer of 1886, however, Julia was still under Moore's sway. The novel she was then writing, *Dr. Phillips*, is an extraordinarily powerful book. It is the story of an anti-Semite Semite, Dr Phillips, who keeps a Christian mistress and their child in one house, while he lives in another with his kindly, dumpy, and aging Jewish wife. The mistress detests the diamonded, "dirty" Jewish women she must meet; privately she hates Phillips too, and has a young Gentile admirer on the side. The novel includes a convincing analysis of the erotics of male jealousy and male infidelity in the divided character of the doctor. Phillips is brilliant, scientific, atheistic, and contemptuous of the Maida Vale Jewish society on which his practice depends. Perhaps on Moore's counsel, Julia Davis Frankau kept out of the book explicit moral judgements, and there are no characters who are not both vile and sympathetic.[130] Moore arranged for publication by Vizetelly in the "One-volume Realistic Novels" series, as he had done with Mabel Robinson's novel.[131] Since *Dr. Phillips* did for London Jews what *Parnell and His Island* did for Irish Catholics, it was greeted with rage as the work of "a savage and vindictive Jew-hater" even in her brother's own weekly, the *Bat*.[132] *Punch* said "it should never have been written; having been written, it should never have been published; having been published, it should not be read."[133] It was Julia Davis Frankau's first book of many, and decidedly her best.

12

At the beginning of October, GM made light of the trouble his *Figaro* letters were causing in Ireland, where his agent, Tom Ruttledge, suspected that his family had been described in the book. Moore denied it. Anyway, he was done with Ireland; and he described his new home in "a real English village around a green; a horse pond at one end and the long undulating line of the Downs at the other." He had had a "summer of tennis and girls and literature."[134] During the day, the villagers played "never-ending cricket on the green," and by moonlight he had "watched a score of boys playing football in the moonlight." "A nation brought up so must be great," he wrote Duret.[135] Half an outlying suburb of Brighton, a part of the little town of Southwick, old Shoreham, fascinated the novelist, and he wrote lovingly about its village green in *Spring Days* (1888):

> In the summer months, the green seems a living thing. It is there the children talk and tumble when school is over. They are told to go to the green, they are forbidden to go to the green, and it is from the green the eldest girl leads the naughty boy howling. When they are a little older, they avoid the green, it is too public then. Only lovers love not the green. It is to the green that the elevens come from far and near to play their matches. All the summer the green is a fête of cricket. It is to the green the brass bands come on Saturday . . . The green is public; horses and cows are turned out there. All profit by the green. It is on the edge of the green housewives come to talk in the limpid moonlight. It is on the green the fathers smoke when the little cottages are unbearable with summer heat. It is on the green Mrs. Horlock walks with her pugs and the chemist's wife, to the enormous scandal of the neighborhood. There are no houses at the end of the green, it is open to the Downs. To the right, facing the embankment, and overlooking the fields, is the famous Southdown wood, and parallel with the green is Mr. Brookes [Bridger's] property – a solid five acres, with all modern improvements and embellishments, and surrounded by a brick wall over six feet high . . . The inhabitants forget they live by the sea, and when the breeze fills their gardens with a smell of boats and nets they think of the sea with surprise.[136]

George Moore was falling in love with what he thought to be the pleasant communalism of rural England. Like Frank Escott, the hero of *Spring Days*, when he thought of his Sussex friends, "his life appeared to be theirs, and theirs his, and he wished it might flow on forever in this quiet place. He seemed to unde stand it all so well, and to love it so dearly. He accepted it all, even in its vulgarest aspects."[137] "How nice and clean everything looked; how unlike Ireland."[138] Turned away by his Irish friends and family, Moore was ready to embrace a new identity as an Englishman in the counties, one who wrote French novels.

The news from France concerned a new journal, *La Revue indépendante*. During October, Mallarmé and Blanche were gathering subscriptions for its young editor, Edouard Dujardin (1863–1949). Moore agreed to become a backer of the journal, which, like *Décadent: le symboliste*, was a sign of change in the literary movements of Paris.[139] The naturalist Paul Alexis was worried about the development, especially since the leader of the new movement was the powerful Mallarmé: "The naturalists now pass into the state of being reactionaries. Melancholy! The [symbolists] claim to write for the aristocracy of the soul; naturalists, they say, write for the masses and the body."[140] Zola was still keeping in touch with GM, and complaining that Moore had not negotiated a high enough price for the rights to *La Terre*. Maybe 3,000 francs was not much to Zola, GM rejoined, but it was paid promptly by Vizetelly, without chicanery, and no one else was offering more money.[141]

Even while a little testily doing this work for the master, GM was entering into a treaty with the opposition at *La Revue indépendante*. On 10 November, back in London at 3 Dane's Inn, he thanked Dujardin for the invitation to join up – "Nearly all the writers are my personal friends, and their art is the art which excites and delights me."[142] The prospectus listed Mallarmé as drama critic, Huysmans as art critic, and Villiers de l'Isle Adam as music critic, and Paul Bourget, Goncourt, and Alexis were named as future contributors. In early December, Moore began to do research on a story for the *Revue*, "Le Sinstre de Tonbridge," getting permission to ride in an engine as the train went through a tunnel. The climax of his story is a crash in such circumstances.[143] Why he thought such a naturalist piece of sensationalism would be right for this new journal is difficult to guess, but *La Revue indépendante* published the story in March 1887.

As 1886 ended, with snow all over London, GM wrote to Dulcibella Bridger that he hoped she would like the description of Buckingham House – her family home – that he had just written for his next novel, *A Mere Accident*. He asked about the lodge on top of the Downs that Colville was building. Was that finished? As a gentleman farmer, Colville had decided that rabbits would be his specialty, so, along with a house, he had under construction large rabbit pens high atop the Downs overlooking the sea. Colville asked GM if he would like to live in his new lodge and go into partnership in the rabbit business.[144] A few weeks after his letter to Dulcibella, GM accepted Colville's strange offer. The air of London was bitter with his rejection – the cold welcome offered *A Drama in Muslin* was galling – and he was coming to love the quiet, dull, warm-hearted people of Sussex.

At the New Year, Moore provided the *Bat* with a seasonal poem. "A Farewell to 1886" gathers into its rhymes Moore's disgust with the moralistic salaciousness of the "Maiden Tribute" articles, with Stead's grotesque use of doctors to certify that his fourteen-year-old interview subject had an intact hymen, with the reports of the Armstrong, Campbell, and Crawford divorce cases where nothing was clear except that everybody was having sex and lying about it, with the jeering public curiosity about the sister of Dilke's maid, Fanny, and her appetite for a *ménage à trois* with an MP and another MP's wife, with the hectoring reviews of *A Drama in Muslin*, indeed, with the whole stench of the city:

> O year of filth, O year of mighty bawd!
> Armstrongs and Campbells bear thy banner, Dilke

Thy crown, and Fanny of ambiguous ilk
Thy leaflets sibylline. The idle gaud,
The tumbled hair, the keyholes, May and Maud,
Heard of when waking, their mouths pressed for milk:
Of rapes in rags, of adulteries in silk
They learn the tale, and parents smile unawed.
The bookstalls groan beneath great quires of lust,
Of perjury, of virgins certified,
Until it seems as if the Pig had thrust
Its snout through all and tossed the world aside.
O year of filth! The filthiest that may be –
Be it my fame that I was scorned of thee.

Chapter 6
Devouring the Father

I

At the beginning of 1887, Moore completed the short novel he had been working on through the fall of 1886, *A Mere Accident*. Its publication by Vizetelly the following July would bring to a very early termination GM's counter-boycott of English libraries. Set in the Sussex landscape of the Bridgers' house, and based on the character of Edward Martyn, the novel is stylistically caught up in the trends finding expression in the anti-naturalist *Revue indépendante*, which serialised the novel as *Un Simple Accident* (May–July 1887).

In particular, the Paris vogue for Schopenhauer captured Moore's attention at the time he was writing this novel. Edouard Dujardin, the editor, and Teodor de Wyzewa, the assistant editor of the *Revue indépendante*, made much of Schopenhauer's concepts of the world as will and idea in their theories of symbolism. The notion that the world of each person was differently conceived from that of other people appealed to those wishing to give priority in art to mental states, symbolically suggested. Furthermore, Schopenhauer's conception of the world as will – that an instinct of self-preservation powered the ego, the thoughts, and the pseudo-moralities of the herd – made the unconscious a new area for investigation by artists, as in Dujardin's 1886 volume, *Les Hantises*. This collection of tales consists of first-person narratives of obsessed people – the successful merchant, for instance, who fears that every girl he meets may be his abandoned illegitimate daughter, or the distinguished scholar who lives in fear of going to bed because he imagines that an unknown thing under the sheets will tug at his leg.[1] Even before Dujardin's *Les Hantises* was published, Huysmans's *A Rebours* made fashionable Schopenhauer's ideas as the basis for an experiment in living. Moore read *Les Hantises* and reread *A Rebours* while writing *A Mere Accident*. He also took the trouble to add to his parlor knowledge of Schopenhauer by reading at least Book 4 of *The World as Will and Idea* in English translation, and, probably, Schopenhauer's last collection of aphorisms, *Parerga and Paralimpomena*.[2]

Schopenhauer's writing, especially in the late aphorisms and essays, is literature: he uses no school terms or difficult dialectics, and his ideas are shot through with his melancholy temperament. Christianity for Schopenhauer is simply a confession that life is worthless – a conclusion that may have appealed to Moore's natural pessimism. Moore, however, did not share the haunted sarcasm behind Schopenhauer's description of women: "Only a male intellect clouded by the sexual drive could call the stunted, narrow-shouldered, broad-hipped, and short-legged sex the fair sex . . . More fittingly . . . women should be called the unaesthetic sex."[3] Yet such misogyny is characteristic of Edward Martyn and the hero of *A Mere Accident*, John Norton.

Moore's understanding of philosophy has been disparaged,[4] but he had a pragmatic grasp of the German philosopher's basic premises, and understood that for Schopenhauer the will to live is primary, the intellect secondary, so that the intellect is normally just a tool of the unconscious will. Since every individual's desire to live overrides the desire to live of others, life is universal conflict and suffering the normal condition of humans. The only way out of suffering offered by Schopenhauer is for individuals to draw upon the special human powers of consciousness in order to deny their own will, to reject the universal conflict, not to have any children, and to get out of life happily when the hour comes round.[5] Yet only with the complete extinction of humanity will all suffering end, and a beautiful dream be realised: the world as idea, the world without will. At first GM seems not to have been sure if such a portrait of life were funny, insane, or even correct, but it haunted him through the period in which he wrote his next four novels, and fragments of Schopenhauer's philosophy – the imperative power of instinctual will and the inferiority of procreation as a goal of life – stayed with him forever.

Moore's enchantment with Schopenhauer came up for notice in the *Bat* of 11 January 1887 in "Pessimism à la Mode." In spite of the smart-aleck sarcasm meted out to Schopenhauer, French aesthetes, and GM himself, the article may actually have been made up from a recipe by Moore subsequently seasoned by James Davis and the wiseacre staff of the *Bat*.[6] It explains that Schopenhauerism is the latest boutonnière worn by French aesthetes (a metaphor repeated by Moore in *Confessions*);[7] Comteism is *passé;* socialism is tediously optimistic. Anyway, all great novelists have been pessimists – Dostoevsky, Tolstoy, Zola. This new fad is superior to aestheticism as well, in that, the article points out, it does not require you to grow long hair or to lie about languidly. What is more, the Schopenhauerian question – why precipitate another unfortunate into the abyss of being? – may work effectively as a pick-up line,[8] causing many a young woman to prove to you that platonic love is not the only option. The *Bat* article dates the rise of Moore's interest in Schopenhauer, but its caddish irony does not signal the seriousness of the challenge that the German philosopher's ideas posed to Moore's view of life. The naturalist drive in him to go beneath illusions found it hard to cope with the philosophy of pessimism. His enmity for unreality could find here no false happiness to expose.

A Mere Accident explored the problem of a man who refuses life, and the principal way in which life is refused is, as in Schopenhauer, by the rejection of women and sexual procreation. Moore's John Norton is remarkably like Des Esseintes, the hero of Huysmans's *A Rebours*. Both love Schopenhauer, but they are also alike in many details: they have a taste for absinthe, pursue arcane knowledge, sleep in an iron bedstead, kneel at a private prie-dieu, weary of human stupidity, bear the marks of a Jesuit education, and invent an individualised version of Catholicism. The detailed similarity of the heroes was intended to be noticed by readers of the *Revue indépendante*. Moore told Wyzewa, the assistant editor, that he aimed to rescue fiction from the dead end into which Huysmans had led it, evidently by starting from the same Schopenhauerian premises, but arriving elsewhere.[9] In Huysmans's fiction, the aesthetic sensibility of Des Esseintes infiltrates every aspect of the text; in Moore's novel, Norton is one of several distinct characters, and the narration is not always in harmony with Norton's sensibility. The experiment was to include a symbolist character within a realist frame.

In addition to its effort to go Huysmans one better, *A Mere Accident* is an offering to Walter Pater. John Norton has among his books at college Walter Pater's studies of the Renaissance, though *Marius* had been banned by the school authorities for its "realistic suggestion."[10] John Norton later reads it anyway, and recommends it to a clergyman, William Hare, for the depiction of beautiful altar boys. Through reading *Marius*, Norton explains, "I was made known to myself . . . the rapture of knowledge came upon me that our temporal life might be beautiful; that, in a word, it was possible somehow to come to terms with life."[11] It was inconceivable to him that anything could be more beautiful than the death of Flavian. While Norton adores altar boys and dying adolescents, he finds women hateful. There is "something very degrading, something very gross" to him in the idea of sexual relations with women;[12] besides that, they are "cunning and mean."[13] But his mother takes very seriously her duty to get John married, and his duty to sire an heir. It is not good enough for her that John makes a will leaving something to all the tenants. Out of dread of his mother's plans, John considers entering the priesthood, except that he would then have to listen to women in the confessional, "a kind of marriage bureau";[14] instead, he contemplates becoming a Carmelite monk – he likes the dress, the dangling rope belt, and the tonsure. Anything but marriage.

For Martyn, Norton, and, indeed, Moore, marriage meant that life had no other meaning than the perpetuation of life. In Schopenhauer's terms, it was surrender to the world as will, loss of the world as idea. In Pater's terms, it was an unbeautiful, merely natural life; the aesthetic life was against nature, above nature. Creation was set against procreation, art against nature, and perversity against normality. To be an artist, it was perhaps necessary to explore other ways of being male.

However, Norton is really no artist; he has no "spiritual procreancy," to use a Pateresque term.[15] He has scholarly, architectural, and literary projects, but, like Martyn's poems, they "always met with failure, with disapproval."[16] As a result Mrs Norton is able, in the course of the plot, to so contrive matters that Kitty Hare, the daughter of John's closest male friend and confidant, is placed constantly in propinquity to her son, until at last, and quite implausibly, Norton finds her almost sexless innocence attractive, and proposes. Anyway, there is nothing in life for him to do, he concludes, but marry. Now the crisis antici-pated by readers is, What will a homosexual man actually do in a heterosexual marriage? This eventuality is astonishingly prevented when Kitty Hare is raped by a tramp on the road. After hallucinations painted in many pages of purple prose, she throws herself out of a window upon fantasising a return of the rapist at the sight of John Norton entering her room. Norton, thus rescued from marriage by a mere accident, resolves that he shall become a secular celi-bate: "the world shall be my monastery."[17]

The climactic incident of the rape, which gives the novel its title, is not fore-shadowed on the literal level: the rapist appears and disappears from the cast of characters and from the plot with the rape. On a non-literal, symbolic level, it may be that the rape is foreshadowed by Norton's feeling that sexual inter-course is "something very degrading, something very gross," that it is, in other words, a brutal manifestation of the world as will.[18] Following the incident of the rape, the center of consciousness shifts from the hero to the violated heroine. We enter her nightmarish hallucinations; we depart from Norton's high-principled, dogmatic, but will-driven mind.

In spite of its interesting premise, the novel has so many tedious and inept passages, in addition to the awkward surprises in the plot, that there could be no argument for its success, but in a 31 December 1887 letter GM still objected after George Bernard Shaw wrote in a *Pall Mall Gazette* review that GM invented the psychology of John Norton. No, Moore complained, he had known the original of Norton since he was a boy, Martyn/Norton had confided to GM "his most secret thoughts." Yes, the rape was improbable, but GM chose it because it was "the most violent blow to [Norton's] character that could be imagined" (one might ordinarily have thought the violent blow was to Kitty).[19] Yet the ending of the novel remained a problem for all the reviewers. Moore would make two more tries at recasting the narrative in later years (in "John Norton" [1895] and "Hugh Monfert" [1922]). There had to be some way to get the problem of homosexuality, and the character of Edward Martyn, into a story.

One of the most disappointing aspects of *A Mere Accident*, only a few months earlier believed by GM to be his "best book – I shall never do better,"[20] was that as homage to Pater, it was a complete failure. Upon its publication in July 1887, he sent it to Pater, with a request for a review in the *Guardian*. The "vicarage Verlaine" was not about to associate himself with such a thing, neither discreet nor beautiful. In a letter of August 1887 he made GM understand that "descriptions of violent incidents and abnormal states of mind do not serve the purpose of art."[21] After reading this letter, GM held out no further hope for the book in its present form: it had failed both as a gift and as a novel. Pater had revealed by means of *Marius* his desire for intimacy with men. GM had tried to show through his own answering novel that he was sympathetic – in fact, enthusiastic for confidences – and Pater basically acted as if he was shocked at the thought that GM might approach that unmentionable subject in print. Pater would identify himself aesthetically *as* a homosexual, without identifying publicly *with* homosexuals. GM countered by identifying with homosexuals, but stopped short of identifying himself as a homosexual. It was a wretchedly embarrassing impasse on both sides: two men lodged in a doorway, unable to come out, or go back in.

2

After finishing *A Mere Accident*, Moore crossed to Paris, where he attended a fête at Alphonse Daudet's home on 10 February, held to celebrate the opening of a play based on Daudet's *Numa Roumestan*. Zola agreed to come to the party in order to renew his friendship with Daudet and Goncourt; the two older novelists had recently been severe about the arch-naturalist's army of scribblers and his monstrous popularity.[22] The guests included a number of writers who were becoming followers of Daudet as opposed to Zola, such as Paul Margueritte, Paul Bonnetain, and Lucien Descaves, all of whom later signed "The Manifesto of the Five," a bitter repudiation of Zola. The faithful Alexis was there, and so was the old guard – Goncourt, Leconte de Lisle, François Coppée, Heredia, and Hennique. According to GM's report on "An Evening at Alphonse Daudet's," to be invited you had to be, if a man, famous; and if a woman, beautiful. The evening involved a supper, then theatricals, and finally a dance into the early morning.

The pantomime conceived by Daudet and acted by Paul Margueritte filled GM with wonder. It was a story of Pierrot in despair about having killed his wife, mimed to an accompaniment of piano music. In white-face, with a long white dress spotted with large buttons and wide sleeves, Pierrot enters with a large doll in his arms – Mrs Pierrot, dead. In front of a woman's portrait, he relives his crime: how, wanting to go on a spree, he decided to kill his wife for her money, and rejected shooting (too loud), stabbing (too messy), strangling (too detectable), finally settling on tickling to death as the ideal form of murder. Moore was in ecstasies over Pierrot, which he saw as the great symbol of French civilisation. Pierrot embodied a perception of the animal nature of humans, seen in its comical fatality. It was a symbol he picked up for his own strange self in *Confessions of a Young Man*.

While in Paris, GM had a lot of literary business to conduct: on behalf of Vizetelly, he finalised a contract with Zola for *La Terre* (sight unseen by either GM or Vizetelly);[23] made some changes in his railway story before its printing in the *Revue indépendante*;[24] and forged a lasting friendship with the editor of the *Revue*, Edouard Dujardin, then a "perfervid youth . . . long-limbed, small-headed, broad-shouldered, whose temper alternates between fierceness and affection." Dujardin had, Moore recalls in *Conversations in Ebury Street*, a "large and loose mouth, a coarse tongue [that] licks at the lips, and when we catch sight of his tongue, we think of a man so greedy for life that he would lap it all up, almost an animal, without power to stay his desires."[25] His new French friend, attired in waistcoats with Wagnerian motifs and sporting a monocle and gardenia boutonnière,[26] had the makings of the perfect "boon companion" for GM: aesthetic, good-looking, conversational, cigar-smoking, and appreciative of women. Indeed, both Dujardin and his sub-editor Wyzewa were in love with the dancer famously painted by Toulouse-Lautrec, Jane Avril: she sometimes slept with Dujardin, but lived with Wyzewa.[27]

GM and Dujardin quickly struck up a fast friendship that was to last for forty years. It may have been on this visit to Paris that Dujardin took Moore to meet Verlaine, then unknown in England.[28] Verlaine had promised a sonnet to Dujardin, and, with the review going to press, it had not arrived. The editor went to fetch it, taking GM along – from an omnibus, to a tram, into a cab, then another tram, until GM asked, "Are we going to take a boat?" Past many courtyards, they went up a slippery stair and found, in 6 Hôtel du Midi, Verlaine – ill, his bad leg up on a chair, with his great domed forehead under a nightcap. He was dosing himself with cheap wine. Verlaine told them about the gross abominations he was putting into his splendid sonnet, which would, he promised, certainly be written on the following day. Finally, he explained how he wished he had raised his son to be a waiter, the best of all professions.

While in Paris, GM saw *Francillon* by Dumas *fils* and Daudet's *Numa Roumestan*. As usual with his Paris junkets, Moore made literary capital out of all his experiences, writing a review of *Francillon* for the *Hour Glass*[29] and making use of Daudet's play when he came to write the preface to the 1889 edition of *Confessions of a Young Man*. On Moore's return to London, he was delighted to find that the "Paris Day by Day" column of the *Daily Telegraph* had given a lot of space to *Terre d'Irlande*, the French edition of *Parnell and His Island*, comparing GM's writing with that of Flaubert – a great relief to one sick to the gills of being regarded as Zola's ricochet in England.[30] Moore felt himself to be a power, shaped it is true by all his Paris experiences, yet not a London retail outlet for Zola's manufacture of French obscenity, which is the kind of product-identification he had won for his own fiction thus far.

That reputation was reinforced by an article published when Moore was still in Paris. Rider Haggard, flushed with the success of his African adventure stories, *King Solomon's Mines* and *She*, published an article "About Fiction" in the *Contemporary Review*. He described French realism as an "accursed thing" that "thrust before readers' eyes" "whatever there is that is carnal and filthy."[31] Moore was taken to be the exponent of realism, and Robert Louis Stevenson, along with Haggard himself, of romance, the only sort of prose fiction, according to Haggard's article, that satisfies and improves readers. Moore had two quick responses to Haggard's "About Fiction": the first was to defend himself without defending French naturalism, the second was to attack Haggard. And then he had a third response: to get his brother Augustus to attack Haggard.

Moore used *Time*, a weekly run by Swan Sonnenschein, to publish "Defensio pro scriptis meis." He had contracted with Sonnenschein to publish his next novel. By this move he hoped to escape the circulating library ban that had fallen like a blanket on Vizetelly publications. With "Defensio" Moore tried to clear his name before he made a début with his new publisher. It announced his abandonment of naturalism; henceforth, he declared, he would focus on the psychology of his characters rather than their physiology. Moving from defense to offense in the *Court and Society Review*, Moore brought up the charge that Haggard lifted his plots from Thomas Moore's *The Epicurean*. Mrs Haggard had denied that her husband had even read *The Epicurean*. That was easy to believe, Moore said; indeed, "there is no book that could be readily named that I would have the slightest difficulty in believing that [Rider Haggard] had not read."[32] There were indeed two schools of fiction, as Haggard had claimed, but they were not realism and romance; they were "the literary and the illiterate school," and GM belonged to the first, Haggard to the second. GM's "school" included Tennyson, Ruskin, Zola, Daudet, Pater, and the supposed romancer Stevenson; Haggard's was made up of himself, Hugh Conway, and "Florence Warden." GM predicts that Haggard, like General Booth of the Salvation Army, would have a brilliant future; his adventure stories would continue to sell like Holloway's Pills or Pear's Soap. "He may be made a knight or a lord; but there is one thing he will never do – he will never obtain our literary esteem." This was prescient: Haggard was knighted in 1912, but he remains outside the canon of fine writers. Augustus Moore's follow-up article in *Time*, "Rider Haggard and the 'New School of Romance,'" was a point-by-point, tale-by-tale indictment of Haggard's originality, taste, and grammar.[33] But that was still not enough: while GM was writing *Confessions of a Young Man* that spring and summer, he continued to kick Haggard. His books, Moore wrote, were simply furniture for the club, like a cigar, a leather chair, and a glass of port; finally, "his literary atrocities are more atrocious than his accounts of slaughter."[34] In the course of defending himself and attacking Rider Haggard, Moore made a decided effort to realign himself with contemporary writers of fiction. He was indeed an experimental, aesthetic, and intellectual prose writer, but he would with great difficulty escape the reputation of being George Moore, author of *A Mummer's Wife*, and Zola's ricochet in England.

3

Settled back at the Green, Southwick, in April, Moore negotiated with Herbert Wigram of Swan Sonnenschein over the text of *Parnell and His Island*. William Swan Sonnenschein was a man of wide culture, who especially liked to publish works of philosophy and advanced socialism (he was the publisher of Marx's *Capital*), but the specialty of one partner Hubert Wigram was a series of High Church books of devotion, and the other partner, Walter Sichel (editor of the Sonnenschein monthly, *Time*), was a Tory, educated at Harrow and Balliol, who would later seek the post of Lord Chamberlain, the stage censor.[35] The partners of the firm were not equally keen to launch George Moore as their flagship novelist. Before signing a contract with him, they obtained his promise that he would allow the firm to propose changes in his manuscripts if "for commercial and other reasons" they found certain passages unacceptable for publication.

In April 1887, Messrs Spottiswood, the printers used by the firm, declined to print *Parnell* out of fear of obscenity charges. GM permitted Wigram, the High Church Anglican, to "revise the whole book," but asked for the right to pass the proofs for publication. On 14 April Wigram admitted that he had "emasculated" the text, but he wanted to "make the book such as Messrs. Mudie and Co. will have no valid reason for repressing" – and told GM there was no reason for him to see the proofs.[36] Moore swallowed his pride: the point of going from Vizetelly to Swan Sonnenschein was to escape the total censorship of the circulating libraries, and the price was a degree of censorship by his own publisher.

On 28 April, however, the buyer for W. H. Smith told Wigram the circulating library would ban *Parnell and His Island* in spite of the efforts at compliance and the good relations that the publisher had hitherto enjoyed with the libraries. W. H. Smith's investigation of the book apparently went no farther than the cover. The stated complaint was that the title was inflammatory because it implied that Ireland was an independent country. GM sent Swan Sonnenschein a blistering attack (now lost) on the circulating libraries: "I shall make Smith *sit up* and you will sell a lot of *Parnell*. This will be the biggest [advertisement] ever known."[37] But the editors of Swan Sonnenschein had no stomach for a fight. Their more conventional notion of an advertisement was a half-page taken out in a weekly for blurbs from favorable reviews, not a public denunciation and a name-calling fracas on the editorial page. It had been their plan from the start to make Moore into an author of respectable books. What they did not realise is that it was not the books the circulating libraries were boycotting, but the author. Moore had been blackballed.

With *Parnell and His Island* and *A Mere Accident* in the hands of the printers, GM set to work in May on another book for Swan Sonnenschein, *Confessions of a Young Man*, scheduled for serialisation in the publishers' weekly *Time* for July through November. As Moore began writing, he was reading

Dujardin's *Les Lauriers sont coupés* in the May through August numbers of the *Revue indépendante*. A complete record of a day in the life of an indecisive young lawyer's clerk from the country, haunted by hopeless love of a Parisian actress, this work is generally credited with being the first essay in the stream-of-consciousness technique. James Joyce named Dujardin as his source for the method in *Ulysses*. Along with Mallarmé, Moore was one of the few to praise the experiment when it was first made.[38] He thought it unveiled "the daily life of the soul . . . for the first time: a kind of symphony in full stops and commas. All I am afraid of is monotony."[39] In *Confessions*, he began to explore the possibilities of the method in the chapter "Thoughts in a Strand Lodging" and elsewhere in the movement of the narrative backward and forward in time, as the world in GM's autobiographical novel is simply the idea in the mind of the hero. Moore would continue to look for other ways to catch the drift of consciousness within the net of syntax, especially in *The Lake* (1905), though, out of fear of monotony, he never gave a record of the daily consciousness of a character with the minuteness or totality of Dujardin's book, much less Joyce's.

Except for running up to London to meet Dujardin on 14 June,[40] Moore evidently stayed on the Green in Southwick through the summer, working on *Confessions*, while first *Parnell* in June, then *A Mere Accident* in July were made available for sale to those who could find them; neither book was stocked by the circulating libraries. Still hopeful for his novel on 5 July, he sent *A Mere Accident* to Swinburne with a letter explaining that this was a "more mature" and "more original" book than *A Mummer's Wife*. Swinburne had written about that novel with elaborate condescension: "When I attacked the Philistine, it was not with a chamber pot for a buckler and a dung fork for a spear."[41] GM claimed he got a laugh out of this laborious quip. Anyway, he told the poet, he was not a member of the naturalist school. Yet Moore could not make an elaborate effort with every reader to persuade him or her to see *A Mere Accident* as he himself saw it; they saw it in their own way, and they did not like it. After George Bernard Shaw's review of the novel in the *Pall Mall Gazette*, another dismissal in the *Athenaeum*, a cold shoulder even from the *Bat*, and finally Pater's "grave and timid" reproof in early August, Moore knew the novel was not what he had hoped.[42]

Within a week of writing Moore about *A Mere Accident* in August 1887, Pater was reading an article by Arthur Symons in *Time* on his own volume of *Imaginary Portraits*, and noticed in the pages of that journal some chapters of *Confessions of a Young Man*.[43] These were chapters about the young "Edwin Dayne" in Paris, how he loves his fellow-student in Julien's atelier, Lewis Marshall, of ample shoulders and soft violet eyes, who lives off the earnings of Alice Howard, a young English prostitute. Unable to bear his failure to compete with Alice for the love of Lewis, or with Lewis for prizes in painting, Dayne retreats for a time to London, then comes back to Paris months later turned out like a "minor Lewis." With Dayne planning to become a poet, they move into an apartment together, Dayne paying the rent. But Dayne's impotent defeat as an artist leaves him in despair. Having read these chapters, Pater wrote a second time to Moore, and admired his account of himself.[44] After the book was published, Pater wrote "My dear audacious Moore" a third time, praising GM's "Aristophanic joy" but wondering at the "questionable shape" in which GM presented himself, "'shape' – morally I mean.'"[45] Once again Pater was trying to put a little distance between himself and his followers, and GM was not only trying to follow Pater but to come out in front of him.

4

The portrait Moore presents of himself in this remarkably influential book is as one who came into the world "bearing no impress, like a smooth sheet of wax."[46] Is he alluding to the uncertainty of his sexual identity, which he later confessed to his brother? That seems to have been part of the story. Indeed, in an addition made to the text for its French serialisation, never completely adapted in later English editions, Moore explicitly offered this self-diagnosis. Under examination by his conscience, he says that for years he had thought it impossible that women, creatures so beautiful and desirable, could love men, who are "so ugly, almost revolting." While fascinated by women, "I loved women too much to give myself wholly to one." Certainly, he would never marry: overpopulation of the planet is such a terrible threat that "The crime of bringing a being into the world exceeds by a thousand, a millionfold that of putting one out of it." This much may be parlor Schopenhauerism, but Moore, taking Manet's courage to heart, ashamed of nothing but to be ashamed, goes on in the French text:

> Never before me has the soul of a man been so embroiled with that of a woman, and to explain the abnormality of my sexual sympathy for women, I can only imagine that before my birth there was some hesitation in the womb about the sex. Nevertheless, I was a happy boy and excellent sportsman: once I had a horse between my legs or a gun in my hands, I left behind all these morbid imaginations, all strange desires to travesty women, to wear their little boots and peignoirs.[47]

That horse and gun are good: there were plenty of conscious jokes about "phallic symbols" before Freud. Moore continues that even if he were otherwise than he is, he supposes marriage would be stifling:

> Such a promiscuity of body and spirit is not reasonable. I have never spent one whole night with a woman: in that sense, at least, I am a virgin. The idea of never being alone, of losing that intimacy of self, which like a wild bird flies out of sight during the day but is with you, oh with what intensity in the morning, at

the hour of clear languor! To lose the camaraderie of the body – for like your spirit, your body is most intensely yours at the hour of waking . . . To lose all that, for marriage!

This was a side of himself he had reined in upon his return to England in 1880, at least until after reading a novel by the fellow of Brasenose College. Then he could approach the subject with an ironically tender sympathy for the troubles of his own youth, now safely past.

One of the formal features of *Confessions* that GM may have picked up from Pater is its mode of address, its attempt to call into being a new community of men through what has recently been called an "aesthetic minoritizing discourse," a system of sub-codes by which male beauty is "preferred and validated," and thus a readership within the general readership is "presupposed and invoked at the same time [as] it is being constructed in the discourse itself."[48] This double-voiced rhetoric – art criticism for the masses, homoerotic self-affirmation for the minority – proved rather too emphatically audible in the famous conclusion to the first edition of Pater's *Studies in the History of the Renaissance* (1873), with its urgent message to be sure to spend life in passionate moments, "for those moments' sake." In the 1877 edition, Pater was pressured into deleting it, "because it might possibly mislead some of those young men into whose hands it might fall."[49] GM was much more explicit still: he deliberately addressed himself, as a former young man, to other young men. He divides his readers into two groups: the hypocrites (clubbable, married men, who never acknowledged instinctual desires) and "young men."[50] To the latter he recommends the pleasures of the "woman of thirty" as a great teacher in life: it was such a woman – probably Georgette de Coëtlogon – who taught him how to be a man. And once he knew, he discovered that the later nineteenth century in England was a paradise for the single young man of means: he is "fêted, flattered, and adored," women drop at his feet.[51]

One may continue to contemplate the slim-hipped perfections of the male ephebe, whom GM calls "Lovelace" – not GM's subjective self-presentation, as some have thought, but the male sex object of GM's dreams: "clean about the hips and his movements must be naturally caressing."[52] In 1886, a year before the composition of *Confessions*, Marc-André Raffalovich, at the time Oscar Wilde's young friend, published a plausibly homoerotic poem called "Lovelace": Lovelace once said "No" but now has come to love all things dangerous.[53] GM, while also using the name of the Cavalier poet as a symbol for the male love-object, himself was less in love with danger. He preached the *risqué*, not the risky, life.

GM's formation of his own masculinity was, by his own reckoning, more or less complete, and the despondencies of the artless, unlovable youth are gone. He was still fighting to be something other than a husband, a worker, and a dutiful subject, but his chosen form of perversity would be to see women as objects of pleasure, the intellectual always leading to the bodily pleasure, and men as associates in intimacy, the bodily desire always leading to the intellectual pleasure. Far from being ashamed of where he had come from, or the place at which he had arrived, GM was (like Pater at least in this) setting himself up as a teacher in the aesthetics of passionate masculinity. And the text he chose most to explicate was one liberating motto of Manet: "To be ashamed of nothing but to be ashamed."[54]

5

GM had no idea that his serial in *Time* was a good book and *A Mere Accident* a bad one until Pater praised the early chapters of *Confessions*; then Moore knew he had something. He soon thanked Blanche for having said that "nothing could be more interesting" than a book of Moore's memories of Paris personalities; Duret had told Moore, on the other hand, that he had better not do it. But Blanche turned out to be right: everyone liked the serial. "What a curious and mysterious thing art is," GM sighed. "We do well when we least expect it; I thought nothing of the *Confessions*."[55] Now he thought enough of it to write Swan Sonnenschein and renegotiate the terms of his contract: rather than sell the book outright, he took £40 for the serial, £100 for the first 3,000 copies, and retained the rights to further editions. It was a smart move. The book was to emerge as a classic of its era, going through five variant English editions, followed by Modern Library and Penguin popular editions.

Duret suspected that GM would write on their behalf other people's confessions as well as his own. He might even unleash his tongue on Zola; Moore had been sharing with Duret his reservations about the master's work. In a letter of 23 August, Moore began to sound off to Zola himself. He did not like Zola's new play, *Renée*; he was impatient about delays in the publication of *A Mummer's Wife* in France; and he wondered if Zola would send him "The Manifesto of the Five" along with his own reply.[56] This manifesto had been published just five days earlier in the *Figaro* by five younger novelists – Paul Bonnetain, J. H. Rosny, Lucien Descaves, Paul Margueritte, and Gustave Guiches – who said that though once Zola's followers, now after the publication of *La Terre*, they had become his enemies. Zola was lazy, they claimed; he used documentation gathered by others, rehashed old plots, relied on personal clichés, because of a renal disorder and the too-late loss of his virginity worried too much about sexual functions, and pretended to a knowledge of science, while credulously counting on "the hereditary line" and, in spite of its "childishness," "the famous genealogical tree."[57]

Whether or not Zola sent the manifesto, Moore got his hands on a copy, and then transfused its spirit of rebellious ridicule directly into the chapter of *Confessions* he was writing.[58] The gibes at Zola appeared in the October 1877 issue of *Time*, in a chapter entitled "The Synthesis of the Nouvelle Athènes." It takes the form of a free-floating stream of internally contradictory conversations about art, with no speakers identified, supposedly aired around the tables of the Paris café that had been GM's Oxford and Cambridge. The elusive point of view in this chapter – to what degree did Moore stand behind the jabs at Goncourt, Zola, and others? – would give GM just the sort of trouble about which Duret had warned him.[59]

But for the present, London was astonished, and laughing. In Shoreham, GM was surprised to see *Confessions* remarked in the Sussex *Daily News*, and on 10 September *Vanity Fair* spoke of the serial in the following manner:

> In *Time* there is a queer, clever, and hateful autobiography running . . . Mr. George Moore, the author, has invented a style which is without parallel in English. There are many better styles, but none so personal, so attractive – and so provoking. As we read this brilliant piece of rottenness, we hate the author, though we have never seen him.

GM was especially pleased by this review and sent it to his publisher.[60] Indeed, it may have given him an idea for the new chapter he wrote in October as a conclusion to the serial version of the book, the story of his duel with Lord Rossmore. Was he hateful? Oh, yes, very hateful: he wanted to kill a man just for an advertisement. This chapter would be, he boasted to the editor beforehand, "the confession of his baseness."[61] GM had learned from Rousseau that if you are going to write confessions, you have to betray yourself, and profoundly; by this betrayal you will unmask the criminal character of humanity as a whole. Moore's own trick was the cool cheekiness with which he did himself dishonor, while openly jeering that the readers were no better; indeed, they were worse, because they were the Baudelairean *hypocrites lecteurs*.[62]

GM's confessions soon proved to be more than Messrs Wigram and Sichel dared to print unexpurgated in *Time*. Wigram allowed GM to tell stories about not succeeding with women, even with those of low character, and other inverted indecencies, but he called a halt at blasphemies: the public would not stand for these, he wrote GM. Moore bridled: after Wigram's "Irish victories" with *Parnell and His Island*, Wigram ought to be satisfied. GM's supposedly guileless defense of his outspokenness was that William Faux, W. H. Smith's reader, had told him that the circulating library "had no prejudices [about religion], that an author could say what he pleased." Wigram should have another look at Swinburne's *Songs before Sunrise*, Moore barked, where in one poem the rhymes are *ram*, *cram*, and *lamb* then *foul spume* and *womb*, "yet Chatto and Windus . . . continue to publish this book." Wigram had been the judge of the final text for *Parnell and His Island*; "pray, allow me to be the judge in this matter."[63] And Moore was a good judge in such matters, but what he judged so delicately was where the invisible trip-wires lay in the moral sensitivities of his readership, how they might be triggered, and what a splendid sequence of aesthetic explosions might then be detonated.

6

By 19 October, Freshcombe Lodge, Colville Bridger's new house, was at last ready for occupancy by Colville and his rabbit-farming partner, George Moore. GM left Mrs Feist's apartment and his beloved Southwick Green for the top of the Downs, 720 feet above the sea, three miles from the highway, four miles from the railway station. The rabbits were taken from the grounds of the Bridgers' Buckingham House in several vans, while GM and Colville followed on foot, "talking as we went by Thunders Barrow Barn, of the great fortune that always lay about waiting to be picked up by the adventurous." Colville had hired a keeper to chase off stoats that might kill the rabbits, and bought a bloodhound, ten couples of blue-haired beagles, and a huge mastiff to chase the rabbits and the poachers. It was the plan that GM and Colville would shoot the full-grown rabbits running loose across the Downs, and then convey their bag to the markets; this was before they learned that there was "not much market for shot rabbits." Colville later had new ideas for planting furze on the Downs, cut into strips so as to make it possible to net the rabbits; then he had a plan for an orchard of fruit trees.[64] GM admits that he gave his business partner "tactless advice," and was told to go to his own quarters.[65] As early as the end of October, Moore admitted in a letter to William Archer that "all is not plain sailing at Freshcombe Lodge."[66]

In December 1887, GM's brother Maurice sent him a polo pony to ride over the Downs in Sussex. Maurice had been ordered back to India, and thus had to make arrangements for his stable of horses. Thanking Maurice for the pony, GM explained that he had sold a new novel to the *Evening News*, at which Augustus Moore worked.[67] *Spring Days* would be published in daily supplements from April through May 1888, so now GM was "slaving at it like a galley slave at the oar." Planned to be "light and gay and different in tone from [his] other works,"[68] the novel was a portrait of the Bridger family – father, sisters, and brother Colville with his mistress – in their struggles to find happy love in West Sussex.

After finishing *Confessions* and before starting *Spring Days*, the furiously productive author also wrote a major article on Turgenev commissioned by Frank Harris for the *Fortnightly Review*, a series on "The Stage as Seen by a Novelist" for the 3–6 December *Evening News*, and a story first entitled "Grandmother's Wedding Gown" for the Christmas number of the *Lady's Pictorial*. Revised as "The Wedding Gown" for the June 1902 *English Illustrated Magazine*, then put into Irish as "An Gúna-Posta" in the January 1902 *New Ireland Review*, and back into English for *The Untilled Field* (1903), this well-traveled short story would become one of Moore's most popular, yet – "how mysterious a thing art is" – he seems to have thought little of it at the time.[69] Perhaps this was because he had not thought it was his line to write tender, mysterious tales about a young girl's relationship with a forbidding old female relative, and her discovery of a woman's rites of passage, but in fiction Moore often did best what was furthest from his own experience.

Correctly aware that *Confessions* would be an important book, Moore was now taking a greater interest in its appearance than he had with his earlier novels, where the emphasis had been on a cheap sale price, in order to under-sell the triple-deckers popular with circulating libraries. For *Confessions*, Moore wanted fine bindings, rich cloth covers, a portrait of the author inside, and a cover design by Blanche – a *Symboliste objet d'art*. Things did not go perfectly according to plan because Blanche, given a free hand, sent him a picture of a *jeune fille symbolique* for the cover. Moore was forced to reject the design on 2 December, and his reply was misinterpreted by Blanche: "If I were to put a young woman on the cover," Moore explained, "it would announce exactly what I wish to conceal . . . My confessions are purely literary."[70] In his memoirs, Blanche took this letter to be an admission that GM had had no sexual relations with women; he just invented his stories for the sake of books. Joseph Hone then followed Blanche's interpretation in his *Life of George Moore*. What this letter in fact means is that *Confessions* is an intellectual autobiography, immoral in spirit, yes; but not a tale of fleshly conquests like *Mémoires de Jacques Casanova de Seingalt* – or worse yet, a purely physical treatment of life, like Zola's *La Terre*.[71] GM had finally read that novel, and he hated it; he told Blanche he would never read a novel by Zola again because "he does not address the *scholarly instincts* in readers."[72] Part of the whole joke of *Confessions of a Young Man* was supposed to be that readers, having heard of the author as a Zolaesque pornographer, would be hungry for lubricity, and then would find something else indeed – a surprisingly scholarly statement of aesthetic controversies among the avant-garde, along with ironic philosophising about the condition of the late nineteenth-century male. J. M. Northcote's hopeless student at Oscott was becoming a Don Juan of the mind. He was living extravagantly through ceaseless self-invention, discovering and indulging all that made him himself. Moore was coming into a purely elective form of identity. He was not to be defined by where he was born, by schooling, by religious training, or even by the customs of his family.

Before Christmas, Moore wrote his mother one of his shockingly frank letters. This time, he tells her he has renounced his country, his religion, and, effectively, his family:

> I have now taken up my abode I hope for good in Sussex . . . I am very fond of my friends and have entirely adopted their life – have said, in fact, thy people shall be my people, thy god shall be my god. I put on a high hat, take my umbrella, and march to church every Sunday. I do not believe but I love Protestantism; if it is not the faith of my brain, it is the faith of my heart . . . you will agree with me that it is better to acquiesce in outward forms than to protest and give scandal and offence. I have had some chances of marrying but I do not think I shall ever marry.[73]

Moore had not seen his mother since writing in *Parnell* that her brother Joe Blake bred bastards by his cook; now he writes that he's made himself part of another family. Certainly, some of the Blakes if not the Moores would have been glad if he had been from the beginning part of another family. Only a few months before, in the October number of *Time*, Moore had published the following statement:

> Two dominant notes in my character – an original hatred of my native country, and a brutal loathing of the religion I was brought up in. All aspects of my native country are violently disagreeable to me, and I cannot think of the place I was born without a sensation akin to nausea . . . with Frenchmen I am conscious of a sense of nearness . . . when I am with them I am alive with a keen and penetrating sense of nearness . . . The English I love, and with a love that is foolish – mad, limitless . . . England is Protestantism, Protestantism is England. Protestantism is strong, clean, and westernly; Catholicism is eunuch-like, dirty, and Oriental.

The passage is breathtakingly indifferent to the embarrassment he brought upon his mother, family, and Irish friends. To an extreme degree, Moore had what Nietzsche calls "the terrible egotism of the artist, which is justified by the work he must do, as the mother by the child she will bear."[74]

7

In early February 1888, GM's essay on Turgenev and the book version of *Confessions of a Young Man* were published. The intellectual seriousness and boldness of the *Fortnightly* essay should have alerted readers to the irony in Moore's characterisation of the bold and silly young hero of the autobiographical novel. In the essay, Moore stakes out his mature aesthetic position. He explicitly turns away from *La Terre* and Zola as a whole ("the physiological school") and from *She* and Rider Haggard ("the school of adventure"): indeed, they were on a par:

> As there is no difference (thought being abstracted) between a spot of perspiration and the killing of a negro, it will be seen that Mr. Rider Haggard is a disciple of M. Zola, when M. Zola is at his worst . . . For it is thought, and thought only, that . . . elevates or degrades human deeds and desires; therefore, turgid accounts of massacred negroes and turgid accounts of fornicating peasants are in like measure distasteful to the true artist.[75]

The real names of the two schools, he went on, should be "the thought school" and "the fact school" (a revision of his earlier classification of the "literary and illiterate schools"). Turgenev was the great master of the first. Greater than

Flaubert or George Eliot, he was only less than Balzac because of an "irritating reserve" from his "excessive delicacy and certainty of touch." GM also had a fellow-feeling for Turgenev as another landowning aristocrat who "looked on and judged both [the serf and the gentleman] as a scholar and a philosopher, without small-beer cynicism or that air of which Thackeray could never divest himself, of having been in society [only] after the success of one of his books." Though a pessimist "who is convinced we turn and turn in a little circle until overtaken in the great oblivion," Turgenev concludes that since live we must, we should be "inclined towards kindness and pity." He was also a "personal artist" undeterred by that "vainest of all delusions," the "impersonality of the artist" preached by Flaubert. Turgenev could not invent stories, so he had to put his personal friends into his books, or to develop the stories they told him – but with the aim of subtlety, not gross travesty. Only Henry James came near Turgenev in subtlety, and James drifted into good breeding, becoming "merely social, and, notwithstanding his great qualities, too often like a fashion-plate." Through the essay on Turgenev, Moore charts his own place amid the constellation of his significant contemporaries. Like the Russian, he sought a personal, thoughtful, lordly, and subtle art – one that cared for truth, while never believing that it can be finally found.[76] All that keeps GM's portrait of Turgenev from being a self-portrait is that Moore leaves out the shameless mischievousness of his own queer character.

The queerness of that character was on full display in the autobiographical novel that came out at the same time as the essay. In the *Confessions*, Dayne brags that he is "feminine, morbid, and perverse – above all, perverse." By turns, he is the know-it-all raconteur, the idiotic *naïf* without knowledge of grammar, the lover without a lass, the lover weary of the woman of thirty, a Carlyle raging about cultural decay and a satanist whispering of sweet decadence.[77] Above all these pranks of "Amico Moorini," GM's name for his silly side, there is the voice of a man past the age of thirty and well aware of the approach of a death from which there would be no waking.

Throughout, Moore never let his readers forget that in his own opinion he was something better than an English gentleman, that middle-class product of public schools, well mannered and earnestly employed. The hero of the *Confessions* was an Irish landlord of great estate, with a valet, a good annuity, ancestors distinguished in history and letters, with the willingness to fight a duel and the training in marksmanship to win one. He was not of the new commercial gentleman class, but one of the old rank.[78] Indeed, he defiantly did not meet the Rugby school standards of the new class: he was sent down from public school with the worst of records, and from a Catholic school at that. He was not even Christian, much less manly; and he does without any of the genteel virtues of the drawing-room Lancelot. He is tactless, sexually exploitative, and abusive to the fair sex, when he is not in ecstasies over the personal charms of one particular woman.

The *Athenaeum* review shows how an Oxbridge-educated gentleman responded to the hero of *Confessions*: Edward Dayne was "a disagreeable young man, of bad education and vicious habits." "If Mr. Dayne had been educated, he would have learnt that one of the uses of education is to take the conceit out of a man, and he would have discovered that much of his originality was commonplace."[79] The only other review of *Confessions* in a major monthly, however, was favorable: William Sharp in the *Academy* thought this "brilliant and clever" book "much the best thing Mr. Moore has yet done: the production of a man of wide culture, and containing scarcely a single page void of something suggestive, amusing, daring, or impertinent."[80] The first reviewer would have preferred that a good education had rubbed out that impertinence, and with it, all that was amusing, daring, and broadly cultured in the book.

8

The most perceptive review of *Confessions of a Young Man* was written by James Davis ("John A' Dreams"), then cooling his heels in Monte Carlo. The story of how Davis ended up there is part of the genealogy of the style of *Confessions*. In Monte Carlo, Davis was a refugee from English law. The previous March, 1887, the *Bat* editor had been brought up on libel charges twice in one month, and both times in the court of Sir Henry "Hanging" Hawkins. The first charge was for saying the actor-managers of St James's Theatre had staged a series of flops, and for that Davis had to pay £150 and costs.[81] For savaging horse-owner Robert Peck in the 1 February 1887 issue of the *Bat*, Davis was next sentenced by Hawkins (a member of the Turf and Jockey Clubs) to a £500 fine, three months in Pentonville Prison, and a formal retraction of the libel. In the *faux*-contrite retraction, Davis said that he wouldn't call Robert Peck a thorough rogue, and then went into an elaborate, point-by-point, hair-splitting comparison of Peck with a thorough rogue.[82] Having served his time, Davis published a brisk, observant essay – on the lines of travel journalism – about his visit to Pentonville: its rooms, cuisine, leisure-time activities, etc.[83] Then the incorrigible editor wrote some nasty paragraphs concerning Miss Reynolds, a woman with a past on the stage, on the event of her marriage to Sir Henry Hawkins, keeping it up in the following weeks by twitting Hawkins for trying a docket of cases in record time in order to clear his desk before his honeymoon with the former actress.[84] Still irate with Hawkins, on 3 January 1888 Davis published a long-announced "Letter to a Notable Sportsman", in which he gave a full review of the judge's career in court and on the track. Lawyers went over the text, so there is no open libel in it, but the article is full of Swiftian insults, such as "No one who knows as much about you as I do can respect you more than I do." In a survey of all English judges, Davis determined that the average number of death sentences per judge was 5.4; Hawkins had hung 28. Alas for Davis, a few weeks later in yet another poison-pen letter to a "Notable Sportsman," his paper accused the Earl of Durham of having driven his first wife into a mental asylum. Durham sued, and the case was remanded to the court of Sir Henry Hawkins. Davis did not wait for the result, and fled the country. In the meantime, he handed over to Augustus Moore the office, furniture and machinery of the *Bat*,[85] and Augustus, using the capital from a successful libel suit of his own against critic Clement Scott, brought out the same paper, with the same staff, under a new masthead: the *Hawk*.[86]

So it was in the *Hawk* that Davis's review of *Confessions* was published. Davis said he felt like the parrot the sailor left with his monkey: after all its feathers had been cleverly plucked out, the parrot cried, "Oh, we've been 'aving a 'ell of a time." GM had taken from Davis's sharp, cute, caddish paper all that was interesting, and turned it into literature, making the "most original, the hardest, most audacious, most rigid thinking our generation has seen." It was a *Sartor Resartus* for the end of the century. GM had caught the cadence of Baudelaire's poetry, and learned to make "a scene or figure stand out with a perfection of illusion that makes his art resemble a painter's," far more "hard and brilliant" than that of his master, Pater. Moore's cynicism was a put-on: "he really has no admiration save for things that are healthy and beautiful." Finally, Davis warned "the canting, gorging, creeping, flattering brotherhood" of critics to watch out what they say about GM: "he has a wickedly keen scent for humbug . . . and his wit is as acid as Heine's."[87] To the youthful, caddish, hyper-male sass of the *Bat* style, GM had given a literary character. Moore owed something else to Davis too: from his example, GM learned, if not to stay away from "personalities," at least to stop just shy of libel. Only one time was Moore brought to court on libel charges, and then unsuccessfully, but he made dozens wish there were a justice stronger than his pen.

9

In spite of the small number of reviews and a cold response in February for Swan Sonnenschein's traveling agent from book dealers ("'Wouldn't have his books in my establishment, for any consideration!' 'No, thank you! We had his last!'"), Moore was still confident of the value of *Confessions of a Young Man* because of the private praise of Pater, J. M. Robertson, W. E. Henley, and other men of letters.[88] He had no hesitation in sending it to Dujardin for translation and publication in the *Revue indépendante*.

At this time, Moore made a small but momentous change in the text: he instructed Dujardin to remove the name "Edward Dayne" and to substitute "George Moore." Using a pseudonym, GM now decided, had been "a failure of courage which, I must admit, partly spoils the truth of the book."[89] With this stroke, the autobiographical fiction became a fictionalised autobiography. GM took upon himself the silliness of his character Edward Dayne, and gave to Edward Dayne the interesting and always developing future of "George Moore," the author. Elizabeth Grubgeld illuminates the importance of the step

GM was now taking.[90] He was beginning a lifelong project of constructing the "author function" "George Moore" as his chief creation. He would not just write individual consumption commodities, one novel after another, good or bad, to be ascribed to "George Moore," the name on the title page. He studiously elaborated a complex and developing identity for public consumption, manifested in letters to newspapers, public enactments of a studied role, five autobiographies, autobiographical characters in novels, and imaginary conversations. This "George Moore" was first put into books under other names, like "Harding" in the novels of the early 1880s, or "Landlord M—" in *Parnell and His Island*; but with the French edition of *Confessions of a Young Man*, he began to appear as "George Moore," and would more and more manifest himself as himself. Oddly, this fictional self was not a wish-fulfillment; indeed, he is consistently, at least in some ways, unattractive, even repellent. He has cold blue eyes, weak shoulders, and a body it is surprising a number of women could have loved; he is vain, sometimes insensitive to the poor, cruel to relatives, and, on principle, unashamed. (Indeed, "George Moore" lacks the fellowship, courage, and frequent generosity of GM.) And "George Moore" is perpetually interested in, and bewildered by, "George Moore": why should he be as he is?

Because, he concludes, of his peculiar "instinct." In the early 1880s, GM, then a student of Zola, believed that people could be explained in terms of their environment, heredity, and instinctual nature. According to this way of thinking, the self is not really free, and GM can be no more than "Landlord M—" from County Mayo. Then, in 1887, he came under the influence of Schopenhauer, who explained there was a world of will and a world of idea: in the latter we seemed rational, moral, far-sighted, and apparently free; in the former, we were simply expressions of an ongoing and impersonal life-force, a great "instinct" bent on reproducing itself. GM found the pessimism of this view of humans as theorising animals strangely exciting, but he was restless with its definition of instinct. He developed his own version of "instinct" into an amoral analogue of the daemon of Socrates – a transcendental impulse within one's nature. Moore believed this instinct always led him right even when it led him, for instance, to be callous to his mother, because it brought him to be himself, "George Moore." Many people, however, apparently had no such superhuman guiding instinct; they were the dupes of all-too-human instincts, which made them, for all their hypocritical idealisations, greedy, lustful, and foolish. An unsettled dialectic develops between GM's conception of humanity as a thing made by its past and its species-being, and his own inward sense of himself as a thing made by himself, basically a dialectic between determinism and freedom. Moore acts sometimes as if his "instinct" is a real entity, and part of a serious rethinking of life from end to end, and at other times as if it is a colossal put-on, meant to make fun of the hopeless human aspiration to understand our existence.

In the letter to Dujardin that requests the names be switched in his manuscript, GM was clearly aware that this was an act of courage required by the genre of confession: one had to be an open book before the public, defiant of their mockery or anger. Anger and mockery were inevitably going to be the result of a French publication of *Confessions*. His tell-it-all account of Parisian personalities might entertain Londoners, but once it was published in Paris's leading avant-garde monthly, and read by the very characters in its pages, there were bound to be doors closed to GM that once had been open. Duret was telling him as much in letters, but, though nervous, Moore went straight ahead, and the French serial began to appear in March 1888 and continued through August.

On 17 March, Moore made an attempt to forestall anger by writing directly to Zola about the *Confessions*, especially about the yet-to-be-translated chapter "The Synthesis of the Nouvelle Athènes," the mother-lode of witty abuse of the arch-naturalist. For something meant to be an apologetic explanation, the letter began strangely with a paragraph withholding approval from Zola's *La Terre* (just then being released by Vizetelly in an expurgated edition). It was not for him, GM said, to criticise such a book – time would take care of that – but he thought that Zola needed to renew his method of composition, so that he could again create memorably human characters like "Gervaise." GM then admitted that he had to warn Zola about a passage from his book soon to be published in the *Revue*: "When I speak personally, as I speak in the next number, I say about you what I have always said, but in the chapter entitled 'La Synthèse de la Nouvelle Athènes,' I formulate paradoxes with much violence, and there are things there disagreeable to all." Duret would not, Moore complained, understand that GM's real sentiments about Zola are expressed in the book, just not in that chapter; it represents the sentiments of others. "Daudet and Goncourt are acquaintances, and if they are offended I will regret it, but you are my friend, and believe me, my dear Master, it would be terrible for me to offend you in any fashion. I have a hope that you will understand 'La Synthèse de la Nouvelle Athènes' as I understand it and not as Duret does."[91] GM would have been on safer ground if all the barbs at Zola had indeed been confined to that one chapter, and safer still if Zola and Goncourt never read the book. But they did, and so did many others; it was a popular number in the *Revue indépendante*.

For the time being, GM was happy to think his work was the talk of Paris. A few days after his tactical letter to Zola, he wrote buoyantly to Maurice Moore, then in India, about all of his plans. The *Confessions* were coming out in Paris; in London *Spring Days* was about to begin. Pater's letter about *Confessions* ("My dear audacious Moore") and Sharp's *Academy* review were further successes worth sharing with his brother. He had begun riding over the Downs on Maurice's pony or Colville Bridger's hunter; he turned away from marriage once again, and now was even giving up his mistress – whether Dulcibella Bridger, Julia Frankau, or another, he does not say. "My life is given up more than ever to art . . . I am now in the plenitude of artistic life and I live in the

giddiness, the madness, the exaltation of unceasing creation" – a sincere statement of what gave George Moore joy in life. GM then laid out his own grand
design for a sequence of novels, including what he had called the "Don Juan
trilogy" about nineteenth-century male sexuality (*A Mere Accident*, 1887;
Spring Days, 1888; and *Mike Fletcher*, 1889), as well as the great novel that followed these, *Esther Waters* (1894):

> *Spring Days* is the prelude to a trilogy, the immediate and direct prelude to 'The
> World's Amusements,' that is the book about the young men in London; the
> book after will be a book about servants, from their point of view, and it is laid
> in the same house as *Spring Days*, and the servants pass on to London and work
> in one of the houses where the young men meet in 'The World's Amusements';
> the third book is about old people who see their children going wrong, their
> troubles and hopes and disappointments.

The timing of this letter – 20 March 1888 – makes it possible that the story
Moore gives of the early origin of *Esther Waters* (published in April 1894) is
substantially true.[92] In *A Communication to My Friends*, Moore recalled that
after the publication of *Confessions*, he came across a newspaper article that
asked if readers ever thought of the "manifold services that we demand of servants, to the performance of which we summon them by bell-pulls." Immediately, GM's mind took fire with an idea: what if one treated servants not as
comic characters, but as the main figures in the drama? He recalled that he
quickly came up with a plot centering on the struggle of a scullery maid to
protect her illegitimate child, begotten by a footman. Instead of George Eliot's
tale of Hetty Sorel murdering her child, GM would give the motif a "woman's
moulding," and have his heroine "living to save her child." With this heroine
fixed in his mind, he would let himself be led by her hand, "obedient as the
child she carries in her arms." He was so excited by his idea (which may have
freed up many of his own feelings about his mother, ever the servant to his own
future), he hurried to Catherine Street in order to sketch the book out for
Vizetelly. The old man listened, but he was troubled. "'Perhaps I shall never
see your book.' 'And why not? Half my pleasure in writing it –' 'The Vigilance
Society's man has been here purchasing one of our translations of Zola's novels.
That is the law. The prosecutor must prove that he purchased in the publishing house itself one of the books he has in mind to proceed against.'"

In fact, in December W. K. Stead had begun to beat the drums against Zola's
La Terre long before its publication.[93] Stead then asked Vizetelly for information about sales of Zola, and Vizetelly rather proudly told him that it was a bad
week when he did not sell 1,000 volumes of Zola (he had eighteen titles in
print), and, what was more, the translations of his firm, unlike others, were the
real thing, unexpurgated; all of this information Stead indignantly reported at
the end of March.[94] Vizetelly's account of the state of his business was, in fact,
both untrue and imprudent; untrue because Zola's texts had indeed been bowd-

lerised by Vizetelly's translators, and imprudent because Stead sat on the board of the National Vigilance Association. By 3 May 1888, Vizetelly would be sitting in Bow Street court listening to W. A. Coote, Secretary of the NVA, reading out passages from the "wicked, scandalous, and obscene" *Nana*, *Piping-Hot!*, *The Rush for Spoil*, and *The Soil*. At the end of the performance, Magistrate Vaughan committed Vizetelly to trial, and soon the government, under parliamentary pressure, took up the prosecution.

10

When Vizetelly was summoned to court, GM was in Paris. Having finished the newspaper serial of *Spring Days* in late April, he headed directly for the Hôtel Continental and the Salon at the Palace of Industry.[95] He wrote to Zola on 8 May agreeing to come to Médan with Alexis in order to discuss two matters: the long-delayed preface Zola had promised to write for *A Mummer's Wife*, and the chapters of *Confessions of a Young Man* being published in the *Revue indépendante*. Slightly panicked, GM said he had shown the passages to faithful Alexis, who laughed at them, and promised everything would be all right. Still swearing his opinions about Zola had never changed, GM signed himself "Your student and very devoted George Moore."

Before going to face Zola at Médan, GM was a guest of honor at a party given by Dujardin to celebrate the publication of *Confessions*. The walls of the offices of the *Revue indépendante* were covered with paintings by Jean-Baptiste Armand Guillaumin (1841–1927) (Guillaumin's first one-man show). Mallarmé, Méry Laurent, Verlaine, and Villiers de l'Isle Adam were among the guests.[96] In a conversation recalled in *Avowals*, GM told Villiers how much he admired *The Eve of the Future*, and, wanting to buy a copy, found that the second edition had just sold out. This success was news to Villiers – "If after all this, good fortune has at last come to me . . ."[97]

Certainly, GM felt his own luck had turned. *Confessions* was making him the talk of Paris. Méry Laurent, past mistress of Manet and currently Mallarmé's love, sent for Moore through Dujardin. According to Moore, when he made his visit to her, she explained her great troubles in finding just the right man as an *amant de coeur*: a man in love with her, and with whom she was in love, a man with money and no distracting occupation, with time for dinner, theater, and dalliance. Ignoring the possibility that he himself was being considered for the post, GM agreed with her – he too had trouble finding just the right man for a "boon companion," but his requirements were a bit different. The perfect man had to like GM's company, and GM had to like his; additionally, he should not be married; should be a smoker, preferably of cigars; be willing to talk of art and literature into the small hours; and most importantly, be very intelligent. Indeed, any of Méry's own lovers would serve him admirably. She required her lovers to be great artists; he asked only that they be good conversationalists.[98]

According to *Memoirs of My Dead Life*, Méry Laurent then remarked that she wasn't the sort of lady that lifted her skirts in a garden, and led George Moore to her bedroom. Having arrived there, GM thought he was probably supposed to take her in his arms. Méry Laurent, the lover of Manet! But also now the lover of Mallarmé . . . and thinking about it, he delayed "till Mary wearied, and with a touch of annoyance in her voice said, 'I don't think I'll detain you any longer in my bedroom.'" Feeling now a right fool, GM wondered what stopped him, and fell to thinking of the image of Mallarmé starting out joyously from his grubby apartment in rue de Rome for a rendezvous at Méry Laurent's. Indeed, GM's tale concludes, Mallarmé very shortly did show up, and GM's ten-year-long dream of lying in the arms where Manet had lain came to an end.[99] It was good enough for him to be able to imagine that he could have. A desire that is gratified is darkened by the threat of the additional unknown consequences of fulfillment; the memory of a pleasure that was only imagined would never suffer alteration.

GM's new Paris *réclame* had its side of infamy too. On 8 May Goncourt read what Moore had written about him, those paragraphs beginning, "Goncourt is not an artist, notwithstanding all his affectations and outcries; he is not an artist . . ." and ending, "Hugo's vanity was Titanic; Goncourt's is puerile."[100] Astutely, Goncourt blamed most of the smart sharp *mots* on the spirit of *badinage* that emanated from Degas at the Café Nouvelle Athènes. Degas was just a constipated artist! Goncourt complained to his diary. A man of letters trapped in his failure as a painter! No temperament for art! How could George Moore say that I am not an artist? It is too beastly, Goncourt raged, me, not an artist! Who else then, of all modern authors![101]

GM was not likely to be invited to see Goncourt again. But on Saturday GM did still have to make the trip with Alexis to Médan. Letting Zola know of their scheduled arrival at 10.55 in the morning, Alexis added that the passage in the *Revue* did not seem so bad to him as it did to Duret.[102] On Saturday morning, Alexis and GM walked along the road from the station through fields of young corn, and Moore explained his plan for a sequence of novels on the position of the young man in the nineteenth century, and then a book on servants. Alexis did not neglect to make a sly gibe: "'I see you are devising a little Rougon-Macquart series.'"[103] This silenced GM till they reached the house and went up to "that dreadful room of his, fixed up with stained glass and morbid antiquities. [Zola] lay on a sofa lecturing me until breakfast." With an exactitude painful to Moore, the forty-eight-year-old Zola read over and over each of the satirical sentences: what could his dear pupil have meant by writing such a thing? Zola stepped out of the room, and Alexis whispered, "'Don't press him to write a preface. He'll not write it. His mind is made up. It was very unkind towards Zola and unkind to Charpentier.'" When breakfast came, and they had a walk in the garden, GM thought the ordeal had ended, but Zola led them back upstairs for another slow session of readings. GM's "heart blanched."[104] "'It is the law of nature,' [Zola] said, 'for children to devour their parents. I do

8. Zola in pajamas at his desk in Médan.

not complain.'"[105] GM tried to say he was just giving voice to the passing thoughts of an hour, and these thoughts would change again as consciousness changed. Zola disagreed. For him opinions were like heavy pieces of furniture, moved about with difficulty. But his opinion about GM was apparently undergoing such a change of position, and considerable strength was being applied to effect the move. What Moore had said about Goncourt, Zola warned, would prevent the young Irish author from ever returning to the *grenier* in Auteuil. What he had said about Zola himself made it utterly impossible for Zola to write a preface for *La Femme du cabotin*, in spite of his promise to his old friend and publisher, Charpentier.[106] GM thought the ordeal would never end. But at last Mrs Zola came up to say that the visitors might miss the afternoon train. On the way home, Alexis regretted that GM had ever allowed himself to criticise Zola's literary style. Moore sadly replied: "A man cannot do more than express his sorrow. *J'ai courbé l'échine et vous m'avez fouetté. Ne parlons plus de cet article malheureux.*"[107]

Within six years, GM realised that this day of shame, in which he took one whipping after another, would make a rich little episode in his ongoing confessions. He wrote it up as "My Impressions of Zola" for the 1894 *English Illustrated Magazine*, put that article into the 1913 edition of *Impressions and*

Opinions, then into the 1926 edition of *Confessions of a Young Man*, and further enriched the story in his last work, *A Communication to My Friends* (1933). It was a choice exhibition of the fact that he was ashamed of nothing but to be ashamed, and that he finally owed more to Manet than to Zola. In May 1888, however, GM was less philosophical; he posted an angry caricature of the French author back to London for publication in the *Hawk*. It begins: "M. Zola, as a man, is not much to look at . . . He is not exactly hump-backed but for all that his ears are on the same level as his shoulders."[108]

If Moore was now out of favor with the naturalists and the whole older generation of French novelists, he was thereby something of a hero to the younger crowd and to the symbolists. Mallarmé, for instance, asked GM for help in translating Whistler's *Ten O'Clock* into French, and GM made a number of changes in Mallarmé's manuscript in order to capture the sense of Whistler's weirdly rhetorical idiolect.[109] On the same trip to Paris, GM was introduced by Dujardin to the work of the Théâtre Libre, which was to have a lasting effect on his ideas about reform of the stage. He saw a production of Tolstoy's *Dominion of Darkness* at a suburban theater, Le Bouffe du Nord,[110] and then André-Léonard Antoine's production of Théodore de Banville's *Le Baiser* ("The Kiss") starring Mlle Richenberg and Coquelin. To judge by Moore's review of *Le Baiser*, he was bowled over by the verse and the acting in the play. It is about an aged fairy in a wood who, to regain her youth, must convince an innocent young person to give her a kiss.[111] GM liked the plot sufficiently to pass it on, fifteen years later, to Douglas Hyde, who based "The Tinker and the Fairy" on Banville's plot. GM may have resigned, or been fired, as manager of Zola's export office in England, but he would continue to trade in cross-Channel aesthetic trends in the years ahead, in drama and painting, as well as literature.

II

When Moore got back to Freshcombe Lodge, he wrote an article, partly sparked by his visit to the Théâtre Libre, on English theater to be entitled "Mummer Worship." It was commissioned by Harry Quilter for the *Universal Review*. Quilter, a rather fatuous art critic who sported checked pants and loud jackets, had an office in the same building as Swan Sonnenschein, and was trying to launch an international monthly to outshine all others.[112] On his behalf GM had been urging Huysmans, Zola, and Villiers to contribute; large fees were promised. Quilter had permitted GM to contribute on condition that he write something that would "attract attention." No problem there – Moore went after the stars of the London stage with a vehemence that could be forecast to blow through the society and theater columns like a hurricane. After seeing a draft in mid-June 1888, Quilter got cold feet and tried to tame GM's diatribe.[113] Even amended, the article is ferocious.

In July Moore added material to *Confessions* for the French edition of the book, additions that were to be carried over into the 1889 English edition. A key change was a new opening chapter in which he told of his paradoxical exhilaration at the funeral of his father, an undisguised Oedipal anecdote that may have been triggered for him by his recent face-off with Zola (it is the law of nature, Zola had remarked, for the sons to kill the fathers).[114] Another momentous self-recognition came through in a new Chapter 14, a dialogue between GM and his Conscience. When Conscience accuses him of being so persecuted by a desire to astonish that he has exhibited himself "in the most hideous light you can devise . . . The man whose biography you are writing is no better than a pimp," GM quotes Manet, "I am ashamed of nothing – I am a writer; 'tis my profession to be ashamed of nothing but to be ashamed."[115] There is little sign in this summer's work that he was in any way crushed by his reprimand from Zola; if anything, he seems to have been liberated into a deeper sense of his very different and unique selfhood.

In midsummer, Moore turned to what was conceived as the final volume in his Don Juan trilogy of *A Mere Accident*, *Spring Days*, and *Mike Fletcher*. A jolly junket to the Goodwood races by coach from Worthing became the basis for an episode in Chapter 8 of *Mike Fletcher*.[116] By 9 August he was already "deep in my Don Juan," the working title for the book.[117]

Moore does not seem to have been aware of what a terrible challenge was just then being mounted against the type of literature he wished to write, something even more oppressive than the ban by circulating libraries. On 10 August 1888, the slow processes of the Chancery court heaved another stage forward when Vizetelly was forced to appear to answer charges for publishing three obscene books – *Nana*, *The Soil*, and *Piping-Hot!* The prosecution was led by Herbert Asquith, later Prime Minister. He showed more political ambition than literary judgement in pronouncing Zola's novels "the three most immoral books ever published."[118] Vizetelly was committed for trial; the trial date was set for 18 September, but was then postponed until 31 October 1888.

Three days after Vizetelly's court appearance, GM left on the Dover boat for Dieppe, where he stayed from 13 to 18 August at the Blanches' Chalet du Bas Fort Blanc, a house overlooking the sea. Blanche lived with his mother and father, Dr Emile Blanche (1820–93), author of a biography of Victor Hugo, and psychiatrist for Gérard de Nerval and Guy de Maupassant.[119] Each morning, along with an old friend, Jacques-Emile Blanche played Wagner for four hands, then he began work in his studio, where the walls were decorated by Renoir with scenes from *Tannhäuser*. On this visit, Blanche's guests included not just Moore, but also the Wagnerian Dujardin and the painter Henri Gervex, who took GM for a walk about Dieppe and also for a session of landscape painting. Dujardin himself was busy translating the new parts of *Confessions of a Young Man* into French. On his return from Dieppe, GM thanked Blanche profusely and urged on the painter the essential importance of being bold: "Courage, one must not be afraid, courage. The picture is not more difficult to paint than my Don Juan is to write, and you are better equipped for the battle than I am."[120]

On 22 August GM got a letter from Swan Sonnenschein about "Poor old Vizetelly!"[121] It was time for GM to reckon with the possibility that courage might not be enough in the battle in which he found himself. There could be no doubt that Moore was in danger, even if he was alienated from Zola and following a new path in fiction. What is more, he felt loyalty to Zola's publisher Vizetelly, if not to Zola himself.[122]

On 22 September GM entered the fray with a letter published in the *St. James's Gazette*. GM did not think it was right to throw the fate of Vizetelly's books, or his own, to the judgement of "twelve tradesmen" on a jury, so he made a surprising "Plea for a Literary Censorship." Moore said he would be happy to be judged by his peers – any three novelists one would care to name – but not by twelve tradesmen. It would be no loss if they condemned *La Terre*, "a very dull book," but the National Vigilance Association could make out the same case against *Madame Bovary* and *Mademoiselle de Maupin*. In morals, they were the same as Zola's novel; "they differ only in literary excellence." This letter did little to exonerate Vizetelly, publisher of *La Terre* as well as the novels by Flaubert and Gautier.[123]

Moore also worked behind the scenes to help Vizetelly. In September, he went straight to W. T. Stead, principal wire-puller of the Vigilance Association. In a series of letters and meetings behind closed doors in Stead's office, GM addressed the editor out of the fullness of his mind.[124] They sat on a window-seat facing the Thames in the *Pall Mall Gazette* offices, and man to man, GM said he admired Stead's "courage in speaking in the teeth of prejudice, ignorance, and danger"; he could even admire the manliness of Stead's national-interest arguments against the justice of Irish Home Rule; but he could not admire his moral puritanism:

[I]n all concerning morals I think you are mistaken. Women are lustful and the preservation of the race depends on the lust instinct. Individuals may be moral but a nation cannot be moral without ceasing to exist. I am not at all prepared to say that it would not be well if the race did cease, but that is Buddhaism [*sic*], and I have not heard you yet accused of Buddhaism. To rage against immorality seems to me like going down to the sea and asking the waves to retire, no good can be done in this direction for as I have said, lust is life and collectively life is lust. I readily understand how the spectacle of the world's lust must shock some minds, if I did not I should not have written "A Mere Accident," but no good can be done in morals. Your bullets flatten against the rock of the desire to live. I am talking Schaupenhauer [*sic*], his book is a sad book, but it is a terribly true one. I have written all of this because I have had it a long time on my mind, because although I am an adversary, I am a friendly adversary, because I see much to admire in you and because with all its faults I like the P[all] M[all] G[azette].

Stead was not quick to understand an argument with which he did not wish to agree, and he turned very grim at the idea that "Life is lust." As the vigilante campaign continued, Moore tried to persuade Stead that it was beneath him to allow the NVA to prosecute publishers of books like those of Flaubert and de Gourmont – surely, he could see that these were works of consummate art.[125] Yet Moore's private remonstrance with Stead did not succeed in bringing a halt to the prosecution of Vizetelly.

When the trial began on 31 October 1888, the jury groaned with disgust on cue when passages from Zola's novels were read out to them by the Solicitor General. *La Terre*, he told the jury, was "filthy from beginning to end"; he himself "did not believe there was ever collected between the covers of a book so much bestial obscenity," and "there was not one passage in it which contained any literary genius or the expression of any elevated thought."[126] Vizetelly's own counsel B. F. Williams lacked any courage or ingenuity whatsoever. After the first presentation of the case by the Crown, Williams advised his client to give up his defense and plead guilty. The judge summed up the evidence in a shockingly prejudicial way, telling the court that Vizetelly had published *The Soil* (*La Terre*) not just "for the sake of gain" but "deliberately . . . in order to deprave the minds of persons" who might read it.[127] The fine was £100, with £200 security for good behavior. Vizetelly was furthermore bound over not to publish Zola's novels "in their present form."

This condition in his sentence, as understood by Vizetelly, permitted his firm to republish Zola's books after the passages read in court had been deleted. Two months later, slightly expurgated, Zola's novels were reissued by Vizetelly, and he was then prosecuted once again on 31 May 1889. In the second trial, charges against him named more titles as obscene, including Flaubert's *Madame Bovary* and Maupassant's *Bel Ami*. This time the publisher was defended by a fat Queen's Counsel with the name of Mr Cock, a man with no knowledge of French, and no real desire to see the old man through his trouble. He advised his client to throw himself on the mercy of the court. Ailing and bankrupt, Vizetelly got little mercy. Moore's publisher was remanded to Holloway prison for three months. It was a grim era for authors and publishers of advanced literature. George Moore was marked out as a man of criminal association.

Chapter 7
Don Juan Jr. in the Age of the National Vigilance Association

I

Given the climate created by the National Vigilance Association, it is no surprise that Moore's attempt at an English novel in the vein of Jane Austen was described in the September 1888 reviews as "vulgar," "low and degrading," "too realistic," and, crushingly, "one of the most worthless novels . . . seen in twenty-five years of reviewing."[1] The journalists were reviewing the Vizetelly imprint as much as Moore's text. Even *Fortnightly* editor Frank Harris, to whom *Spring Days* was dedicated, wrote no note of thanks, and, when the two met, said that he knew GM meant to offer him a compliment, but . . .[2] It was a time of humiliation. For twenty-two years afterwards, GM was convinced he had perpetrated a folly, and tried to destroy every copy of *Spring Days* he could steal from friends. Then Edward Martyn read the book looking for *faux pas* with which to twit his friend, but instead liked what he found; so did George Russell ("AE") and Richard Best. So GM read it again himself and found it surprisingly full of "zest" and "as free from sentiment or morals as *Daphnis and Chloe*." Moore reissued *Spring Days* in 1912, and it then found a kinder reception.[3]

In the *History of the English Novel*, Ernest Baker, although overlooking the affection beneath the novel's satire, caught something of its quality:

> *Spring Days* is an excellent example of quiet, literal, unrefracting realism applied to an utterly commonplace subject, without satire, without irony, without any insinuation of the author's private view . . . Yet his petty world of shoddy, second-rate people inhabiting a residential place near Brighton, with its bumptious adults, ineffectual young men, and frivolous girls, is shown up in all its banality; and, without any jokes, the result is as good as *Punch*. Not its significance, but its insignificance, is the drift and point . . .[4]

Baker's "shoddy and second-rate people" are the fictional equivalents of George Moore, the Bridger family, and their neighbors. Doubtless, GM was aware of the Bridgers' lack of culture, but all that was missing had been made up for by their health and geniality. They were as comfortably placed in the social world of England as he was adrift in it. He forgave them with his eyes open to their faults, and they did him the same favor. An unaccusing yet undeluded air is the peculiar quality of the novel, summed up in the narrator's comments on one of his hero's disappointments: "All this, like much else in life, was ridiculous enough; but because we are ridiculous, it does not follow that we do not suffer, and Frank suffered very genuinely indeed."[5]

Mr Brookes has three daughters and a son, Willy, and, like "a comic King Lear," he frets over his disobedient children, who are constantly plotting to marry, or at least seduce, sailors, counter-jumpers, penniless soldiers, and others at rungs lower on the social ladder than Mr Brooke's level of county squire. Each of the characters, in the manner of Dickens, appears heralded by a personal flag: Mr Brookes always asks, "Was ever a man so cruelly tormented?" and then with resignation says, "it will all be the same a hundred years hence." The social upstart Berkins insists upon how much better what he has got (glasshouses, horses, statues) is than what others have. Willy is ever at his account books, saying he never involves himself in his sisters' affairs. Aunt Hester prates about the salvation of the Brookes girls. GM appears – minus any such hobbyhorse, but minus also any dignity – as Frank Escott, Irish heir-apparent of his cynical and wealthy uncle, Lord Mount Rorke. Frank was a classmate of Willy Brookes in school, and Frank's "rasping humours" go along with Willy's stolid reserve like a pony and a donkey put out to pasture together. By profession, Frank is a painter whom art lessons cannot make into a successful draftsman, and a perpetual storyteller without the stability or strength of character to become a novelist. Into Frank, as into a trash receptacle, GM deposited his impulsiveness, bravado, swagger, "harsh blunt manners," flash enthusiasms, effusiveness, capacity for self-deception, and inability to choose a single course of artistic expression. Like GM, Frank takes a room on Shoreham Green, flirts with his friend's sisters, shuttles to and fro between Brighton, London, and Paris, and ineffectually pursues affairs with bar-girls and society ladies.[6] Frank's class position makes him eligible in the eyes of Mr Brookes for the hand of a daughter, but when he theatrically proposes to Maggie Brookes, she turns out to prefer a London bank clerk on vacation in Brighton. His other entanglements are with Lady Sevely, a woman of thirty, and Lizzie Baker, a Gaiety Bar girl. Lady Sevely angles to make a lover of Frank, but he spoils his chances after she lightly teases him about an earlier romance of his. Suddenly defensive, he answers her "in the grossest manner, forgetful that he was making formidable enemies for himself."[7]

The subplot in which Frank Escott courts Lizzie Baker may have grown out of Manet's *The Bar at the Folies Bergère*. In this painting, a sad, blank, beautiful, impassive bar-girl, her hands on a marble counter stacked with champagne, liqueurs, and oranges, looks directly at the viewer and past a top-hatted, mustachioed customer, whose inquiring gaze is reflected back at us, along with the crowd at the spectacle, from a tilted mirror behind the lovely serving-woman. When the novel first introduces Lizzie Baker, she is in just such a position at the Gaiety Bar in London's Strand. Behind her "there were shelves charged with glasses and bottles, gilt elephants, a hideous decoration" – and Frank Escott is the top-hatted gentleman importuning her. Frank is aware that he appears to be just another of the young men of various classes released from the theater, all dressed alike in black and white. In the new urban consociation of men on the make, Frank's distinguished Irish parts are quite undetectable.[8] Certainly, his distinction is lost on Lizzie; she prefers another young man, a soldier.

Frank feels sympathy for Lizzie Baker and others like her, as Manet evidently did when painting *The Bar at the Folies Bergère*: "Breathing for hours tobacco smoke, fumes of whisky and beer, listening to abominable jokes, the subjects of hideous flirtations; and then the little comedy, the effort to appear as virtuous young ladies . . . It is at once pitiful and ridiculous."[9] Lizzie has to develop "her bar manners and her town manners, and she slipped on the former as she would an article of clothing, when she lifted the slab and passed behind. They consisted principally of cordial smiles, personal observations, and a look of vacancy which she assumed when the conversation became coarse." It is just that look of vacancy that Manet represented in his final masterpiece; it is the stunned look of a person becoming an urban commodity. In Moore's novel, he tells the story of a man who tries to win his way into the heart of that beautiful, vacant-faced girl. Frank Escott eventually does Lizzie a kindness by going to her bedside when she falls ill, and, in a remarkably big-hearted act for Frank, writing her former lover on her behalf.

Whether Moore himself fell in love with a "Gaiety Girl," whether that love was requited or not, and in what fashion, whether he showed the magnanimous concern of Frank Escott for Lizzie Baker, are unanswerable questions. Certainly, GM like Turgenev tended to elaborate narratives from his own experiences or those of his friends. The following letter of farewell or dismissal, written on 28 October 1888 from Freshcombe Lodge, was sent to a person apparently of a lower station in life, yet unnamed and unidentified:

What you thought of my letter, whether it made you laugh or cry, whether you burnt it or preserved it matters to me not at all, but I am sorry you failed to understand it. There is no use going into details, suffice it to say that latterly your society has become to me unbearable; I write this so that you may not think it surprising if I do not come to see you when I am in London. We have been very intimate, this intimacy must cease, that is all. You cannot remember who you are, you cannot remember who I am, so for the future we must meet as acquaintances not as friends. I do not care unless you do to press this matter any further. Yours truly, George Moore.[10]

2

On 24 September Moore sent Dujardin some revisions of *Confessions* for the French edition ("I mean to be fair to Zola"). He added a report on his current literary standing in England: "My last book *Spring Days* is pronounced to be very bad, an absolute failure, whereas my article in Quilter's review is a great success. It is being a good deal talked about and Quilter is much pleased."[11] "Mummer Worship" is a polemic hot with all the scorn an aristocratic author can feel for the tribe of celebrity actors. The basic argument had three points: that acting, if an art at all, is the lowest art; that the public cannot tell good from bad acting, but applauds that which is most advertised; that the actor, "like a priest or sacred ape," is applauded not for what he does but for what he is.[12] In its slashing demystification of the star system, Moore gives full rein to his lordly contempt for the actor as social upstart. He ridicules Mrs Kendal for pretending to be as good a mother as an actress: "Five years have not passed since we heard for the first time that a favourite actress nursed her children, read prayers, and gave tea and tracts to naughty chorus girls." Now actors write books about themselves, and the public buys up edition after edition. When actors sing in drawing rooms, they ask "to be received on an equal footing with the guests, whose presence was not paid for." They are even claiming intelligence. Meanwhile, the actor is as immune from ordinary courtesies as he was before he claimed a high social position: "As rarely as of old does he answer a letter, pay a visit, keep an appointment, or tell the truth . . . He parades upon the river amid our wives and daughters his beauty, his mistresses, his vulgarity, himself." This was sure to get the attention of Sir Henry Irving, the Bancrofts, the Kendals, and other celebrity actor-managers. In this essay, GM was playing to the hilt the part of Matthew Arnold's "barbarian" – the aristocratic, high-spirited immoralist who bridles at the "Hebraic" moralism of the middle-class philistine.

Sir Henry Irving, dean of the actors' guild, rounded on Moore with counter-attacks, both private and public. Privately, Irving wrote to F. C. Burnand, editor of *Punch*, defending the dignity of actors – "I would certainly not have bothered about either Moore or Quilter . . . had not statements of these learned pundits been copied all over the country." Wouldn't Burnand, Irving asked, "put 'em all right" with a "a word or two" in *Punch*? Closing his letter, Irving invited Burnand's daughters to call on Irving's star actress, Ellen Terry. In such a manner, the populist press was both closed to Moore and marshalled against him. Irving also told people, people who then wrote articles, that Moore was just taking revenge because many years ago Irving had snubbed him when GM attempted to push *Martin Luther* into the notice of the breakfasting actor.[13] Irving was partly right that Moore was settling scores for an old insult; partly, Moore was also trying to clear the decks for a full-blown discussion of the reform of the English stage, inspired by his interest in the

Théâtre Libre. Yet another important motive of Moore's attack was his anger at the hypocritical and ignorant philistines of England, who slavishly adored pseudo-genteel actors while persecuting an honest and dignified gentleman, Henry Vizetelly. He was out of sorts with his age, and letting people know about it.

On 13 November 1888, two weeks after Vizetelly's trial began, Sonnenschein informed Moore that the additions he proposed to make for the second edition of *Confessions* were completely unacceptable. Not only would they be so extensive as to require resetting the whole book, but the new Chapter 12, with its assault on the hypocrisy of the English readers, would "in no case . . . be advisable." "It is of course clever, but would give offence to the very people you should be, and we are, desirous of conciliating towards the book."[14] Compromise and conciliation, however, were not Moore's strategies of dealing with the National Vigilance Association and the mob spirit of intolerance it had excited. How was one to cope with statements like the one by NVA advocate Samuel Smith, made on the floor of Parliament, that it would take a very religious young man to read a page of Zola and not commit a sexual offense within twenty-four hours? An army of "prurient prudes" was in the field, and someone had to fight them.[15]

3

Moore ultimately managed to get his way with the new edition of *Confessions*. Apparently, he convinced the English publisher Sonnenschein that by allowing GM to alter the text Sonnenschein could circumvent the American edition pirated by August Brentano. Some months previously, in the spring of 1888, the New York novelist Clara Lanza had been asked by Brentano for an opinion on the advisability of putting out an American edition of *Confessions*.[16] A progressive writer herself, Lanza was enthusiastic about the book. Brentano, rather than simply stealing the book outright, used the threat of piracy to induce Sonnenschein to send him printed sheets at less than cost, and to pay a tiny royalty of 25 shillings to Moore. After Brentano quickly sold out the first two issues of 500, Sonnenschein tried to raise his price per copy for a third issue.[17] Thereupon, Brentano reprinted the same text but with Americanised spellings under the heading "Authorized Edition," and paid neither Sonnenschein nor Moore a cent.[18] By bringing out a wholly revised second English edition, Moore could discredit the claim that the Brentano version was in any way "authorised," and Sonnenschein would have a chance to arrange a profitable American copyright for his new text.

Another aspect of Moore's plan was to whip up an "English authors versus American publishers" controversy around the current debate in the United States Congress about international copyright law. On 8 December 1888, Moore printed a long, detailed account of the transactions with Brentano in the

London *Athenaeum*, concluding that all American publishers may steal English novels, but only Brentano puts a fraudulent statement ("Authorized") on the title page to deceive the American public. G. H. Putnam came to the defense of American publishers, writing back to the *Athenaeum* that Brentano may have been a liar and a thief, but the older established American firms were honest. On 5 January 1889 GM dared Putnam to name two US firms which had not pirated English novels. The United States had the chance to sign the international copyright agreement, and refused: the nation of slaves and slaveholders did not yet stand "within the morals of civilisation." To Brentano, who had been defending himself in the *New York Herald* by saying that he intended to pay a 10 percent royalty on his edition of *Confessions*, GM said, "Please send me a cheque for twenty pounds." Brentano had further sneered that he had been hesitant about publishing Moore's racy books in the USA "from motives of delicacy"; Moore whipsawed Brentano by begging him "to postpone talking about his morals until he [has] left off picking my pocket."[19] GM probably thought himself the dignified voice of English authors, and an able advertiser of his own wares too,[20] but this controversy made him enemies throughout the New York publishing world. His next volume, *Mike Fletcher*, was rejected by every major American publisher to whom it was submitted before being brought out by a small house, Minerva Publishing.

4

A by-product of Moore's tangle with Brentano was an important epistolary relationship with Clara Lanza (1859–1939), the wife of the Marquis Manfredi Lanza. After contacting him in her role as Brentano's editorial advisor on *Confessions of a Young Man*, she forwarded to Moore a newspaper article about her own work, and was not behindhand in adding a photograph.[21] Her second letter was thick with compliments, and in return Moore wrote confidentially to her about his own life and plans, especially for the "Don Juan trilogy" about John Norton, Frank Escott, and Mike Fletcher: "I might call the book *The Seekers of Oblivion*: one seeks oblivion in religion, another in the fireside, the family, another in love."[22] He also quickly began to make use of Lanza as his New York agent: would she see if Brentano would publish, in addition to *Confessions*, an expurgated *Mummer's Wife*? She followed up by sending him her novel *The Righteous Apostate* (1883), which on 23 September 1888, he praised, criticised, and then proposed turning into a play, with GM doing the scenario, Lanza providing the dialogue. Her representation of love he thought a little "tepid"; how about something more "feverish"? He was, he admitted, taking the "liveliest interest" in her. It especially pleased him, he mused, after a day riding on the Downs and dreaming up plots for his novel, to return to Freshcombe Lodge and watch Colonel Bridger admiring her photograph.[23] Moore was thrilled by the most attenuated forms of eroticism: sex through the transatlantic post, or voyeurism redoubled, as in seeing the image of the image of Lanza in the lustful eyes of his male friend. She took a reciprocal pleasure in her powers to excite the famously advanced novelist. She sent him another photograph, more recent, and taken, she explained, after she had lost weight.

Though their collaboration on the play ran aground, the two fed their growing relationship by mutual log-rolling. She published an admiring article on GM as "the head of English realism"; he arranged for Lanza's stories to be published and her novels noticed in the *Hawk* and the *Speaker*.[24] He occasionally excited himself enough to suggest going to New York to meet her in his own person, but he was equally curious to worm out of her confessions of times past when she had been "fascinated" by another man: "Every woman worth anything has been."[25] He freely gossiped about dropping one mistress, setting his cap for another American novelist, Gertrude Atherton, and talking with travelers from New York about the looks and personality of Clara Lanza herself. He let her know that he was scripting their relationship on the pattern of Flaubert's correspondence with George Sand; indeed, he imitated Flaubert by addressing her as "*Chère bon maître*."[26]

After thirty letters had passed between them within a year and a half, GM began to get very personal indeed. On 12 November 1889, he returned from a weekend hunt at a country house with Frank Harris, a model for Mike Fletcher, and a hero in Moore's imagination. The party of guests sat up until four in the morning talking of love. Harris was brilliant. There were many people staying in the house, and they were all held spellbound. "I talked about you," Moore wrote Lanza, "but none could realise how two people who had never seen each other could be perfect friends . . . They were astonished when I said that there was no one whom I trusted like you." Moore explained on another occasion that if he liked a woman he talked of her; if he did not talk of her, he did not like her. If that was not perfectly conciliating to Clara Lanza, the subject of country-house dissertations, she was probably right to be uneasy. Harris may have been developing for the guests at the country house the epicurean thesis of his *Life and Loves* – women are like fine meals: you do not know a woman until you have eaten her; once you have eaten her, she will never be able to do without you, and you may go on to another. The stage would then have been set for GM to present his counter-truth: real sexual intimacy may require no physical contact whatsoever. He explained to Clara Lanza that ever since that country-house parliament of love, he had been brooding over what seemed to him a new thought:

> I have been thinking of the sexual side of our friendship. The word startles you but there is no other word that expresses my meaning. For it is quite true that the friendship which sprang from intellectual sympathy, pure and simple, has become coloured and modified by the knowledge that you are a woman, by the sympathies of sex. For you are certainly to me a woman, and I know very well

that were you a man you would not interest me as you do. Of course, there are people who regard sexual feeling only in its simplest form, but you are not one of those common lovers; you know as well as I know that sex is full of mysteries and subtleties . . . For the really healthy [person], sex never ceases and is full of magic quite unknown to the vulgar. You are to me always a woman. I see the blonde hair on the neck – *la nuque est de santal sur les vives fissions d'or* . . . I see your hands and feet and the movement of your skirt . . . Search your own heart and ask yourself if you would take the trouble you do take if I were not a man. I think you would not. And yet we have never seen each other, probably never shall.[27]

This letter issues from the core of Moore's sensibility, and it connects with something characteristic of his work as an author. He was predisposed to refinements of erotic desire, rooted in actual relationship, but elaborated apart and away from basic family-founding acts of procreation or any immediate obligations of making up a life in one place together with a woman.[28] The sexual impulse to rarify and prolong and decorate a desire was interwoven with the literary impulse itself. Yet his literary work – whether in letters like this, memoirs based on his romantic relations, or novels about love like *Evelyn Innes* (1898) – was not wholly a sublimation of the desire; it was also an intensification of that desire. With Moore, art relies neither on the fulfillment of the sexual impulse, nor on its frustration; in his case, art is the protraction into the future of a past desire, or into the present of a future possible desire, so that its beauty might be endlessly re-examined, and safely re-experienced without the terror of failure, abruption, or decline after fulfillment.

By 1890, Clara Lanza and Moore were on sufficiently confidential terms for her to tell him that she was writing a pornographic story for money. After the "Cleveland Street Scandal" scattered lords to the continent and shut down a house of assignation for homosexuals, she asked what his own attitude was to men who love men. Homosexuality was so widespread, GM replied, that it was hypocrisy for the English to make a fuss over the Cleveland Street affair, but, as for himself,

I see no reason why those who prefer to drink salad oil to champagne should not be allowed to do so . . . The charm of nice women is so sufficing, so infinite, that the perversion necessary not to see it is to me as unfathomable as belief in the mystery of the Trinity.[29]

The vividly oral descriptiveness of that salad–oil image must have raised the eyebrow of the marquise, but what she really had to watch out for was the jeer treating Catholicism and homosexuality as comparable forms of irrationality. Her relationship to Moore ultimately came to grief in 1906 after she turned Catholic and he turned Protestant.[30]

5

While *Spring Days* was being condemned and "Mummer Worship" debated, Moore finished his draft of "Don Juan, Jr." and requested Sonnenschein to serialise it in *Time*. On 4 September 1888, Sonnenschein let GM know that Walter Sichel, the monthly's editor, would have to approve of the manuscript. Sichel's office was on the top floor of the building on Paternoster Square, just above the rooms used by Harry Quilter for the *Universal Review*. Into this garret, Sichel recalled, "a tall, pale, slender man, in bearing languid yet immoderately youthful, approached . . . with a manuscript of a novel entitled 'Don Juan Junior.' His name was Mr. George Moore. In vain did I assure him that ours was a strictly family magazine designed for homesteads that would shiver at the very name of his romance. He could not agree. Why not a Don Juan Junior in South Kensington, just as there had once been an 'Oedipus at Colonus'? Why not? He seemed never to have heard . . . of the puritan fathers . . ."[31] Sichel did not, however, reject the novel out of hand, and Moore said he would not insist on the title. Yet shortly after sentence was passed in the Vizetelly trial on 31 October at the Old Bailey, the firm rejected Moore's new novel for publication as either a serial or a volume.[32] On 5 November Sonnenschein reminded GM that it was 1888: even if Byron had written his own *Don Juan* now, it would not be publishable – "Do take my advice; burn your new MS. If you intend to write for the public in the future, you will never repent it."

Moore was an example of what Yeats called "the antithetical man," an intellectual at war with the customs of his epoch. Just days after Vizetelly was fined for publishing Zola's novels, at the height of the national hysteria about the French novelist, GM chose to sign a highly complimentary review in the *St. James's Gazette* of Zola's new work, *Le Rêve*.[33] An article in the 1 November 1888 *Times* that reported the Vizetelly sentence (£100 fine, £200 security) declared that it was impossible for anyone "to ascribe the publication of such works [as those of Zola] to a high literary purpose or to any motive worthy of respect."[34] Moore began his review by saying that both the press and jury were altogether mistaken. Zola was indeed a high literary artist, and one who had written no realistic novels at all. There are only two or three such books in a generation – works like *Pride and Prejudice*, *Tom Jones*, *Madame Bovary*, *Vanity Fair*, and a few others. People have mistakenly looked at the matter of Zola's books, not at their form. Zola's genius is not his descriptive power, but his "power of lifting detail into such intense relief that the illusion of life is more vivid in his work than in those of any other author." He had, Moore argued, invented a form of literature all his own, but one that only he can successfully employ; in other hands, it is "narrow and sterile, like the form of Racine." With *La Terre*, Zola had written a book as brutal as something by Swift; this year, with *Le Rêve*, he writes another as purely imaginative as the work of Shelley. Romance is not a matter, Moore urged against Andrew Lang, of pirates and

magic potions, but it springs from "the eternal aspiration after such overflow-
ing measure of strength, fortune, and love as life has not for the giving."[35]
Moore drew upon all of his forensic ingenuity as he tried to get English readers,
at a most difficult time, to see literature in ways that were literary and appreciative, rather than ethical and repressive; and he did so on behalf of Zola,
though he himself was no longer a friend or follower of the French novelist.
Moore's article on *Le Rêve* also came out when, next to Zola himself, Moore
had the worst name among novelists – on 18 December 1888, the Cambridge
Union passed a motion to remove his books from its library – yet GM simply
would not be quiet.[36]

6

In January 1889 Moore gave up on the experiment of living at Colville Bridger's
rabbit farm in Sussex. Without the stimulation of the city, he was beginning to
lose interest in his own work, which was still *Mike Fletcher*. After its rejection
by Sonnenschein in late 1888, Moore rewrote parts of the novel, possibly introducing the descriptions of life in the Temple, his new place of residence near
the Strand in London. GM at first found quarters at 2 Pump Court in the
Middle Temple, in rooms that William Geary shared with Edward Martyn.[37]

In these historic quarters for men of law, situated across from the Inns of
Court, many prominent writers had lived – William Congreve and William
Wycherley, Henry Grattan and Wolfe Tone, Charles Dickens and Edmund
Burke.[38] The Temple was still infested with writers who neither practiced nor
studied the law. Arthur Symons, W. B. Yeats, and Havelock Ellis would all come
like Moore and Martyn to live in the Temple. It was sequestered and quiet like
the grounds of a university, yet it was located conveniently close to the editorial offices on Fleet Street and the stalls of West End theaters. Edward Martyn
especially liked the place on account of its associations with the Knights
Templar, a brotherhood of knights who took a vow in the twelfth century to
protect pilgrims on the way to Jerusalem. The Knights Templar built a round
church in imitation of Jerusalem's Dome of the Rock, and the Temple Church
then became a center for merchant-soldier priests. Martyn fancied that it was
still a shelter for elite male initiates for whom the world would serve as
monastery; Moore himself found an escape in the Temple "from the
omniscient domesticity which is so natural in England." For both Moore and
Martyn, one of the Temple's charms was "young male life . . . and the absence
of women."[39] By April 1889 Moore had moved a few hundred meters to the
east of Pump Court, where he settled into another set of Geary's rooms, 8
King's Bench Walk, Inner Temple (erected to designs by Wren in 1677). GM's
garret apartment was at the top of three flights of stone stairs. Its low-ceilinged
sitting room looked out onto the Inner Temple Gardens that reach down to the
Thames. The small bedroom faced another building at the rear. In this cramped

and hot but conveniently located quarters, Moore would remain for the next six years.

At the time Moore left Sussex, his beloved Mrs Bridger was ill with cancer. He managed to persuade her to allow him to bring in a London doctor, but that doctor could do no more than predict that she might at best live a year. She did not live so long as that. Before winter was over, Moore was alarmed enough by reports of her decline to get on a train and go to her bedside. She lingered a while – at lunch, GM thought with despair, "She is dying upstairs while we are eating jam tarts" – but one day, after a ride on the Downs, Moore returned to find she had passed away.[40] He helped the family write the required black-bordered letters, and then went back to London, seldom to return.

In early February, Harry Quilter opened the pages of the *Universal Review* to Robert Buchanan for a massive attack on Moore, "The Modern Young Man as Critic." Its title is an obvious echo of the title of GM's autobiography.[41] Moore had first gotten on Buchanan's nerves with *Literature at Nurse*, where one of the novels by the "lettered Scotchman" is put in the pillory; in *Confessions of a Young Man*, GM had another rip at Buchanan: "Mr. Buchanan has collaborated with [master of melodrama] Gus Harris, and written programme poetry for the Vaudeville Theatre; he has written a novel, the less said about which the better – he has attacked men [the Pre-Raphaelites, or "Fleshly School of Poetry"] whose shoestrings he is not fit to tie, and, having failed to injure them, he retracted all he said, and launched into slimy benedictions."[42] Buchanan knew how to conduct a polemic himself, and the first thing he did was to bring a £5,000 libel action against *Time* which had serialised *Confessions of a Young Man*. This action frightened editors from publishing counterattacks by Moore.[43] Then, with GM's hands tied, Buchanan launched a second wave of assaults in the *Universal Review*.

The premise of "The Modern Young Man as Critic" is the old reliable chestnut of reactionaries – the world is going downhill, and what are young men coming to? In Buchanan's day, the Young Man "dreamed wildly of fame, of fair women, of beautiful books," and he worshiped God. Now the Young Man is likely to be a pessimistic follower of Schopenhauer, Zola, and Ibsen, who doesn't write literature so much as "criticism run to seed." As examples of this new decadent type of author, Buchanan examines Henry James ("Superfine Young Man"), Paul Bourget ("Detrimental Young Man"), Guy de Maupassant ("Olfactory Young Man"), and William Archer ("Young Man in a Cheap Literary Suit"), but these men, some of them not so young, are just blinds for his real object of attack; he saves George Moore for the last, "the Barbarous Young Man," "the Young Man of No Culture," "the Bank Holiday Young Man" (an epithet Edward Martyn later used on Moore). All that matters to the "Bank Holiday Young Man" is horseplay, indecency, and thumbing his nose at respectability. Things get very rich when Buchanan asserts that Schopenhauer has led to Jack the Ripper by way of George Moore, because not one of them maintains the necessary chivalrous respect for the fair sex.

Buchanan repeated this argument with further bluster in "Is Chivalry Still Possible?" in the *Daily Telegraph* of 22 March, and four days later he turned the heat up by telling the story of a seventeen-year-old girl of good family who was corrupted by the new literature. First she lost her faith, then her virtue. Moore, who was a far cry from a rapist, much less a murdering rapist, was taking the shape in Buchanan's polemic of a threat to the nation's womanhood. With the disembowelment of East End prostitutes continuing through the fall of 1888, with the police still in full pursuit of the "Ripper" week after week, and with the second Vizetelly trial coming up in May 1889, Buchanan's March 1889 charges against Moore fed the popular hysteria about "pernicious literature."

It probably would have been wise for Moore to ignore these articles, as James did, or to brush Buchanan off with a sophisticated demurral, as Lang did.[44] But his blood was up already, and the Vizetelly trials would keep him in a state of rolling rage for some years yet. By 4 April he had persuaded Henry Labouchère to print "Is Buchanan Still Possible?" in *Truth*.[45] This merrily choleric article begins by redrawing the distinction between French and English attitudes to vice: both relish it equally, GM says, but "The French talk of vice with laughter, we talk of vice in low and unctuous tones." Regarding the various species of Young Men listed by Buchanan, Moore asks if Buchanan really thinks his own *New Abelard* as good as James's *Portrait of a Lady*, or his *Master of the Mines* the equal of Maupassant's *Une Vie*. No, his only reason for writing was to get revenge for Moore's *Confessions*. But Buchanan would never really win the respect of readers, because he lacked, Moore said, the essential thing, sincerity: "Grand master of all that is prurient in purity, of all that is mean in man . . . meditate on the fact that your poems are forgotten, that your novels are read by servant-girls, that your plays are only heard by the patrons of the Vaudeville Theatre, and that your critics are an occasional acting manager and a music conductor, who, before the evening performance, discuss your chances of being the next Poet Laureate." Like the bare-knuckle boxing then popular among gentlemen, literary quarrels in the late nineteenth century were a blood sport, and Moore loved them.[46] Their fight continued for several more rounds, and Buchanan did not win, but GM lost a good deal of dignity in the course of his victory over a rancorous and very articulate opponent.

7

In May, Moore made his annual trip to Paris, then in a tumult of preparation for the Universal Exhibition, held in honor of the hundredth anniversary of the French Revolution. At a musical salon, he met a flirtatious and coy American widow, Gertrude Atherton (1857–1948), dressed in "a décolleté gown of black velvet and a head-dress [she] fondly believed made [her] look like Pauline Bonaparte."[47] Her fantastic caricature of Moore as a man with "a long colorless face that looked like a codfish crossed by a satyr" does not help one to understand why she went along with him to a secluded dining room where they could be undisturbed. Moore talked about his transatlantic intimacy with Clara Lanza, and Atherton spoke, it seems, of her troubles with reviewers who found her novels daringly suggestive. That was invitation enough to provoke Moore to call on her a few days later at her host's apartment. She tried to put him off by saying that her people were conservatives who did not approve of writers, and anyway she was soon going into retreat at a French convent. Then I will join you, appears to have been Moore's reply. She preferred that he await her in London. Once she did arrive in England, she declined his invitations to tea at 8 King's Bench Walk.[48] Her intrigues, it transpired, were all mental,[49] and she was disposed to make much of little in her autobiography.[50] Her behavior puzzled Moore – he thought he was literate in the semaphore of sex – and he spilled a good deal of ink in later letters to Clara Lanza with speculations about whether Atherton was really hot or really cold.[51]

In addition to making this new acquaintance (who was never to be more than that), Moore looked up old friends in Paris, including Degas and Alexis. GM had a commission from the *Magazine of Art* to write about his memories of Manet and Degas,[52] and he may have run Degas to cover at Blanche's, at the Halévys', or at Madame Hortense Howland's. Madame Howland was an elegant Parisienne whose wealthy American husband had left her with a good annuity and a house in the rue de la Rochefoucauld,[53] where Degas was a regular ornament at her weekly gatherings. It was not just for copy that Moore wanted to find Degas. GM attributed a kind of oracular genius to Degas, and took his own bearings from the maxims of Manet's old friend. That May, Degas made a remark about the English paintings in the Paris exhibition that served as guide in Moore's later painting criticism in the *Hawk* and the *Speaker*: "I am disappointed with your English school: it seems to have lost a great part of the naiveté which distinguished it in '60 and even in '78, and without which art is worthless. You come over here and learn to draw from the nude, and acquire the trick of professional French painting (*la bonne peinture*), and then you return to your own country neither fish, nor fowl, nor good red herring."[54] The point was not for the English to mimic French Academic painting, or even French Impressionism; they had to achieve their own relationship to nature and the tradition of great art. English traditions were rooted in the Dutch masters, not in the Italian Renaissance, as French painting was. This conversation with Degas enabled GM to turn against his studio training – that is, his failure at being trained in a studio – and the whole débâcle at Julian's Academy, indeed, to turn against Academicism as a whole. While he would advocate the commitment to greatness and to personality found in the French Impressionists, he would not urge the mimicry of a technique or the devaluation of earlier epochs of British art. Moore is famous as an advocate of modern French painting, and properly so, but in his fosterage of British Impressionism he would often praise pictures that bore no resemblance to what was fashionable in Paris. His greatest allegiance was to the personal geniuses of both Manet and Degas.

That May, GM was brave enough to tell Degas that he wanted to write an article about him. Even broaching the subject was dangerous. Degas hated invasions of privacy by journalists; indeed, he did not have much time for writers of any sort. To his friends the Halévys, Degas once expressed relief that a mutual friend had escaped the life of a journalist by emigrating to Canada. Halévy said he did not know that the man had been a journalist. "He might have become one," Degas snapped. Now when Moore suggested publishing his "Souvenirs of Manet and Degas," Degas swore that he would not allow it. GM was nervous, knowing how morose and irascible the old painter was growing, and knowing too the "exaggerated tone" it was his own habit to affect in writing of contemporaries,[55] but Moore was by his nature bound to do the article he had it in mind to write. After Degas refused further help, he turned to Blanche for notes on the reclusive Impressionist's habits of life and memorable remarks.[56]

On this visit to Paris, Moore also called on his old friend Paul Alexis,[57] now living atop Montmartre on "La Butte" with Marie Monnier, the woman he had fetched back to Paris on his one visit to London in 1884, and whom he had finally married in 1888. At the time of Alexis's London visit, he and GM were collaborating on a version of W. S. Gilbert's *Sweethearts* they entitled *Le Sycomore*. It had been accepted by Georges Porel for production at the Odéon, and was still awaiting performance. In July 1888, Alexis began to try to interest Antoine in doing the play at the Théâtre Libre. Though Antoine thought the play *"délicieuse,"* he was worried about the expense of an indispensable stage forest.[58] However, by May 1889, during GM's Paris visit, Antoine had changed his mind, and scheduled *Le Sycomore* as the Théâtre's forthcoming spectacle. This production would not come to pass either; in fact, the little trifle wouldn't be on stage anywhere for another five years, but at the time that GM hired a coach to carry him up "the white torridities of Rue Blanche" to La Butte, Alexis was full of false hopes of a theatrical windfall to support his growing family of Marie and two infants. Coming to the door, GM was a bit disgusted to be greeted by a servant with a baby. "Another baby," sighed the Irish prophet of non-procreative sex and the coming apocalypse of overpopulation.[59] Awaiting the return of Alexis, he sat in the study of the house, built on a sheer hillside, garden after ruined garden descending by steps to the vast brick plain of Paris. He had time to examine Paul's books – yellow-backed copies of all the volumes of the naturalists – and his furniture, including the crib Zola had sent after the birth of Alexis's first child. It was evidently a moment of great contentment for GM to sit in the study of his old friend, whom he knew inside and out. Here GM felt at home, contented because he was at home in two cities, with two sets of friends, two reputations, two languages, and two selves, each of which was all the more cosy for having the other as a closet into which he might retreat. And he was happy to reflect that if Paul Alexis was the most true-blue naturalist, GM himself was the youngest of the naturalists and the oldest of the symbolists.

Upon his return home, Alexis read to GM from a draft of *Madame Meuriot*, specifically the chapter about "chez Nina de Villiard," a description of a bizarre nightlong party with Villiers, Mendès, Mme Rattazzi, Forain, Manet, and twenty others making characteristically bohemian appearances. "It's better than Guy de Maupassant!" Moore cried.[60] He liked it so much he stole parts of it for "Ninon's Table d'Hôte," as he would also steal Alexis's story of the "Death of Lucie Pellegrin" for his own "The End of Marie Pellegrin." Later, prior to the story's translation and 1907 publication in *Revue bleue*, GM felt obliged to explain "why I undertook to rewrite one of Paul's stories, and the best he ever wrote." GM personally knew Pellegrin at Alphonsine's restaurant – Marie was the name, not Lucie; Paul had only heard of her from the women around the Café Rat Mort in the Place Pigalle. GM had been to at least one party at Nina de Villiard's such as Alexis described in *Madame Meuriot*. As GM wrote from experience, guided only by Alexis's clever, Parisian sense of the point where gossip and literature meet, he considered that he ought to be acquitted of plagiarism.[61] Anyway, as a writer he was a migrant worker, who seasonally moved to Paris to harvest in other men's fields – Zola, Dujardin, Alexis, and Huysmans – but, more and more, taking only that on which he could convincingly put his own stamp.

8

On 30 May 1889, the second trial of Henry Vizetelly began. The passages objected to in the first trial had been removed before the reissue of the books, but the NVA had little trouble in locating equally objectionable passages in what remained. In Moore's view, the case and its handling were packed "with subterfuge, evasion, lies, hypocrisy, cunning," and the whole affair was an "ill-smelling midden, humanity at its foulest." He was shocked that a man who poisoned his nieces could obtain the best advice the Bar could offer, but no one would step forward to defend the elderly publisher of the best French fiction, no one except Mr Cock, who took a high fee, then said he could not go on with the case, and told Vizetelly to plead guilty. After the trial, Moore visited his former publisher in Holloway gaol, and Vizetelly, suffering from a serious stomach ailment, complained that "there was a good jury, and I should have been acquitted if Counsel had gone on with the case, but . . . I was in great bodily pain . . . and thought all the world was against me."[62] Thirty years later, when writing *Avowals*, Moore was still sufficiently stirred to throw himself into imagining a long defense before the jury of Vizetelly.

Once Vizetelly had been sentenced to three months in Holloway as a Class 1 misdemeanant, Ernest Vizetelly and George Moore collected names for a petition to the Home Secretary to ask the Queen for a remission of the old man's sentence. The signatories are largely a list of Moore's acquaintances of the period, including Gosse, Symons, Norman MacColl, Havelock Ellis, Olive

Schreiner, Edmund Yates, Frank Harris, William Archer, Harry Furniss, Max O'Rell, Frederick Greenwood, and remarkably, W. H. Smith's reader, William Faux.[63]

Moore even sent a copy of the petition to W. T. Stead, the *Pall Mall* editor whose "Maiden Tribute of Modern Babylon" got the whole persecution started. GM had been trying to cultivate Stead by intermittent letters throughout the past ten months, beginning with his Schopenhauerian declaration that *life is lust, and lust is life.* In April 1889, GM had noticed an editorial by Stead on "The Overflow of Mankind," and saw an opening to use his opponent's own weight and strength to throw him. GM quite agreed, he wrote Stead, that no "remedy for human suffering will be found in democracy or socialism"; no remedy is possible except the control of population. Next to overpopulation (here came the jujitsu move), the other immoralities are as nothing: "That a young man should take a young girl on his knee seems to me of no moment; that he should marry her and have a dozen children seems to me of great moment . . . all philanthropy except that of not bringing any children into the world seems to me superficial."[64] In that round, however, Moore gained no real victory on the moral issue.

In June, when GM sent the Vizetelly petition, he again tried to construct a bridge of manly understanding to Stead. You are a brave man, GM offered, if not wise. For at bottom, if one were to speak the truth, wasn't the "Maiden Tribute" just as much a work of pornography as anything Zola wrote? Indeed, it was "deliberately obscene." But of course everyone had noticed that it had stopped child prostitution! Seriously, Moore went on, literature, moral or immoral, does not affect the conduct of human life, yet organisations which judge it and interfere with people do, and for the worse. While Moore said he could admire Stead, liked him in fact,

> I hate the Association, I believe its influence is pernicious. I hate all interference in private life. To protect unfortunate children is one thing, to bring a man into contempt because he has a mistress is another. So long as people are healthily immoral, no one has a right to interfere . . . It is infinitely preferable that a man and a woman should live in illicit union and produce no children than that their union should be legitimate and they should bring ten unfortunate creatures into the world, the poor little half starved mites that we see in streets and alleys.[65]

Reflecting on the prosecution of Vizetelly for publishing *Madame Bovary*, GM was speechless with rage: "comment is impossible." Moore offered to develop the line of thinking in his letter into a *Pall Mall* article, and to allow Stead full comment. Let them have it out. Or would Stead submit now, and simply add his name to the petition? Stead would not do either thing. Nor would the Home Secretary, Henry Matthews, agree to place the matter before the Queen after Moore presented the completed petition.[66] Moore lost the fight, rounds one,

two, and three, and so Henry Vizetelly, old and tortured with an intestinal stricture, spent the rest of the summer months in prison.

9

Moore himself, however, remained at large. He finally found an English publisher for *Mike Fletcher* – Edmund Downey, the Waterford man who had
been editor of *Tinsley's Magazine* when GM's first short story was published.
In September 1884 Downey had struck out on his own with Osbert Ward
and founded a publishing house specialising mainly in "Irish humour" and
romantic Irish fiction aimed at tourists and expatriates. *Mike Fletcher* was
definitely not in Ward and Downey's line, but Edmund Downey was always
ready with a helping hand for an Irish writer in London.[67]

Having put his publishing affairs in such order as he could, GM wrote an
anti-English appreciation of Balzac (not just better than trivial Thackeray and
pedantic Eliot, but superior to Shakespeare as well), published in the October
Fortnightly.[68] He turned next from abuse of the English novel to abuse of its
theater. The background to Moore's intervention into theater controversy goes
back to the start of the Ibsen movement in England, and involves his relationships with his friend William Archer and his brother Augustus Moore. In June
1889 GM's friend William Archer had initiated a performance of *A Doll's
House*, starring Janet Achurch and Charles Carrington, at the Novelty Theatre.
In the course of its run, a mounting war of reviews spread through the press,
A. B. Walkley declaring that "The great intellectual movement of the day has
at last reached the theatre," and Clement Scott raging that Nora is "all self,
self, self! This is the ideal woman of the new creed, not a woman who is a fountain of love and forgiveness and charity . . ."[69] Archer kept the Ibsen furor going
by assisting in the production of *Pillars of Society* on 17 July at the Opéra-
Comique.[70]

Although Archer had written for the *Hawk*, its editor Augustus Moore now
steered the weekly on a course of perpetual attack on Ibsen. *A Doll's House* was
"Ibscene"; *Pillars of Society* was "dull, deadly dull, and . . . no more like life
than the melodramas at Princess's Theatre." Augustus attended the opening at
the Opéra-Comique and noisily prattled away during the performance. When
asked by a musician to be quiet, he loudly said, "My dear sir, you want to listen,
I want to talk; let us both amuse ourselves in our own way. I don't ask you to
talk."[71] This rude attack on the new etiquette of realistic theater – darkened
hall, continuous playing of scenes, a hushed spell of quiet maintained in the
audience, and low-key acting on stage – earned Augustus a vilifying article in
the *Pall Mall Gazette*. Augustus's paper parasitically feasted on the star system
and the backstage gossip of the commercial theater; many of its staff writers –
like J. H. MacCarthy and Cecil Raleigh – wrote cosy reviews of old-stagers,
and collaborated on melodramas. Augustus himself had been a manager of a

touring company. He did not like Archer's high Scottish moralism about the decay of London theater; it was bad for business.

George Moore, however, agreed with Archer rather than his brother on this issue. GM was always predisposed to the modern, the realistic, and the revolutionary in art; when new movements were breaking out, he lent his weight to the breakage, not to holding the door closed against the new. Furthermore, he knew a bit more about realistic theater than many people in London, having been to Antoine's productions in Paris, quite enough to allow him to play the role of expert. When the proofs of *Mike Fletcher* began to arrive, GM visited Archer to ask him to read the text (giving him a broad writ "to strike anything that seems to you unseemly"), and spent the afternoon listening to Archer talk about Ibsen with J. M. Robertson.[72] In turn for help with his proofs, Moore wanted to join Archer in the fray against the current standards of the British stage. For the *Hawk*, GM wrote an article slating Beerbohm Tree for pompously talking of the reform of the stage, and then producing *A Man's Shadow*, Robert Buchanan's adaptation of the "the crudest and most curdling French melodrama" to be found.[73] This was a sweet opportunity for GM: in a single stroke he got to help a friend (Archer) and hurt an enemy (Buchanan). But his advocacy of the new drama was putting him at odds with his brother.

Moore was also gathering notes for his "servant book," ultimately titled *Esther Waters*. Polled by his old *Tinsley's Magazine* friend Tighe Hopkins for his view on whether periodical writers should sign their articles (first-rate authors should, was GM's opinion, and he usually did sign), GM added that he was "hard at work on my book on servants. I spend the afternoon with a Hampstead cook and my evenings with a footman. I find it very hard."[74] This is highly Moorish humor, but it might just be true as well: Gilbert Frankau recalled GM interviewing the family wet-nurse when he was a child.[75] GM also made a trip to Brighton in September 1889, and may well have spent time taking notes on Buckingham House, the model for Woodview in *Esther Waters*.

In October, Moore wrote a long article published in the November issue of the *Fortnightly Review*, "Our Dramatists and Their Literature," which did for the playwrights of the English stage what "Mummer Worship" had done for its actors.[76] On 12 October, GM told Clara Lanza that he was "getting rid of a good deal of gall" in this article.[77] The article begins: "No first-rate man of letters now writes for the stage." It then went serially through a list of English playwrights – W. S. Gilbert, F. C. Burnand, George Sims, Robert Buchanan, Henry Arthur Jones, and Arthur Wing Pinero – inspecting the credentials of each to the title of man of letters, and discovering that every one came short, far short. The essay is in GM's satirical mode that combines hauteur with lampoon. Throughout it run images from the turf. Jones, for instance, aspires high but always falls, "a country bumpkin on a racehorse."[78] It takes a gentleman to ride a winner. Playwrights compared with other authors are like racehorses without native speed, and thus turned over to the steeplechase, or worse, to be coach hackneys. Authors who are worn out go to the stage just as old horses are turned out to grass. The underlying ethic is that of the track: blood, speed, competition, winners, losers – the sport of kings. But now in England, by this ethic, all is hackneyed and vulgar. Having finished his article, Moore accepted its implicit challenge to himself, and wrote a scenario for a five-act play (*The Strike at Arlingford*), which he sent to Beerbohm Tree.[79]

"Our Dramatists" excited a lot of attention among those who wrote for the press and the stage, giving George Moore a notoriety that piqued Augustus Moore: "In the name of Heaven, why [so much fuss]? I can see very little that is new in it. It reproduces everything I said years ago . . ." So on one page of the *Hawk*, Augustus attacked his brother George, while on the next page appears a signed article by George Moore about Stevenson's *The Master of Ballantrae*.[80] Readers must have thought it strange – an editor attacking his best contributor, a brother going for a brother in public. The following week, GM made a demure defense of himself, against Augustus and others, by saying that, in essence, all he argued was Swinburne's claim that the intelligence of Elizabethan England was poured into the drama, that of today goes into the novel and the poem.[81] George did not join in fratricidal journalism, but the relations between the brothers were beginning to show public signs of strain.

Mike Fletcher, dedicated to Augustus, came out in November, right after "Our Dramatists" had been published, when a whole Fleet Street of writers would have liked to give Moore a drubbing. The novel itself proved to be less popular than *Spring Days*; that is to say, it was not popular at all. Moore himself gave up hope for the book with remarkable speed. Though in the past it had been his custom to make sure all his literary friends and most editors got copies of his books, this time he did not even want any presentation copies from Edmund Downey.[82] On 13 November 1889, he wrote Clara Lanza: "*Mike Fletcher* is not good. I wish I had known that it was not good, I would not have published it. The articles I write attract a good deal of attention . . . but my fiction is not up to the mark; my subjects are not good; that is about the truth of my failures."[83] He was pleased, however, with his new subject and vowed to take his time over it: "*My next book will be more human*: I *shall* bathe myself in the simplest and most naive emotions, and shall not leave them – the daily bread of humanity."[84] *Esther Waters* had its birth as a cure for the cynicism of *Mike Fletcher*.

The reviews of the novel were not so terrible as Moore's own disappointment suggests. True, William Wallace called it tedious and clearly inferior to *A Mummer's Wife* (which Wallace evidently forgot that he had detested in an earlier *Academy* review).[85] Yet in a surprisingly fair account, the *Athenaeum* admired "the unique effrontery of [Moore's] realism" and his deliberate lack of humor; the style was "crisp and incisive"; the matter full of "original ideas about art, literature, and sensuality." The problem was that the vignettes and character sketches, while excellent, were not part of a really engaging plot – just an ABC of decadence: "vice, ennui, suicide."[86] Yet Moore lost hope before any reviews had appeared, much less reports of sales (which turned out to be good enough), as a result of the reactions of Augustus Moore, to whom it was dedicated, and Frank Harris, the model for the title character.[87]

It had to have been embarrassing for GM when Augustus, to whom the novel had been dedicated "in memory of many years of mutual aspiration and labour," slated the book in the *Hawk*. Augustus began by admitting that he was not an ardent admirer of the author. GM had known "little worry and work" yet he was a pessimist; Augustus himself had "laboured much and lost all" yet was "an optimist of the most pronounced type." Mike Fletcher is really no Don Juan: he is never even shown sleeping with a woman: "bar talk, Mike Fletcher is the purest character in fiction." The real Don Juan of today, Augustus says, "is good-humoured, good-natured, good-looking, and good company, and he does more than he says."[88] One suspects that Augustus saw *Mike Fletcher* as a critique of himself and his way of life, and he was hitting back with the poisonous knowledge a family member possesses of where a hit will hurt the most. The subtext of his review needles George Moore about not being handsome (compared with Augustus), not being successful with women (compared with Augustus), and not being discreet (compared with Augustus); his older brother was – the portrait went – an idle, whining scion of a once-great family, without a good practical sense of reality.

In December of 1889, a frost fell on relations between George and Augustus. GM furthered the estrangement by showing disapproval of Augustus's conduct of his newspaper. Since taking over the *Hawk*, Augustus had run Jimmy Davis a close second in the business of unsavory libel, though unlike Davis he kept himself out of court by apologies and cash settlements.[89] Augustus's ugly divorce from his showgirl wife – he charged her with adultery on 20 June 1888 – dragged the family's name through the dirt, to George's disgust. Worse yet, Augustus was in a public brawl with actor Charles Brookfield on the same day he petitioned for divorce.[90] In October 1888 he lost his job as editor of the *Hawk* at £5 a week, and then was rehired by the new proprietor W. Morley Pegge in December.[91] Augustus ingeniously rebuilt the advertising budget of his weekly by opening a "Financial" desk in the City, which reported on prospectuses for new mining and manufacturing firms. Rather dangerously, the new firms were then invited to take out advertising space in his paper. If they did not, they understood they might have to contend with the considerable powers of abuse Augustus held in common with his brother. Rumors were also afoot that Augustus had arranged a half-share sale of the *Hawk* to Frank Harris, so that this hairy little adventurer could employ the weekly in a libel campaign against G. E. Buckle, editor of the *Times*, whose job Harris wanted.[92] Augustus had not then been so entirely exposed as a scoundrel as he would one day be, both to his brother and to London at large, but even when Augustus was writing his review of his brother's *Mike Fletcher*, he was a man with a very sore ego and few known principles – but widely known as a cuckold, a libeler, and a borderline blackmailer.[93] Compared with the seaminess of Augustus's life, George's mode of existence was one of high propriety. Indeed, GM's improprieties required the frame of a decorous dinner-table at Lady Jeune's or a prose style modeled on French masters. In *Mike Fletcher* that style was deployed in a rather bleak inspection of the lives of Augustus Moore and Frank Harris.

10

Mike Fletcher reunites the characters of Moore's earlier novels, as he continued to attempt to evolve a self-subsistent literary world, mirroring the real world, in the manner of Zola's Rougon-Macquart series. John Norton is back from *A Mere Accident*. He lives in the Temple, experimenting with his "theory of life": "the world as monastery." One of his friends is Frank Escott from *Spring Days*, now the editor of a paper like the *Bat* and *Hawk*, called "The Pilgrim." His staff includes Harding (from all the earlier novels) and Thompson (from *A Modern Lover*). The title character is also a writer for the journal; Mike Fletcher could have been an artist – indeed, he could have been anything – but something has gone wrong in him and he is nothing more than a part-time journalist. Mike Fletcher is the sort of man with whom a woman shares her sensuality though she shares it with no other, and by means of his amorous experiences Mike has come to believe there is no virtue. One of the women he seduces – indeed, draws on to suicide – is the wife of Lewis Seymour from *A Modern Lover*.

Mike was born, like Frank Harris, of poor parents in Ireland: "You cannot imagine the yearnings of a poor boy," he tells Frank Escott: "you were brought up in all elegance and refinement. That beautiful park! On afternoons I used to walk there, and I remember the very moments I passed under the foliage . . . and lay down to dream . . . I used to watch the parade of dresses passing on the summer lawns . . . And I wondered what silken ankles moved beneath her skirts . . . I thought I should never hold a lady in my arms. A lady! All the delicacy of silk and lace, high-heeled shoes, and the scent and colour of hair that coiffeur has braided."[94]

Class envy drives sexual rapacity in Mike. When he was young, he was hideous, and did not believe women could love him. Now, he will never give them money, a present, or even a flower, just to prove to himself that they are not doing it for what they can get out of him; it is for what he gets out of them – vindication. He has a passion for destroying principle and degrading anything dignified. When he comes to London, his "eager, impatient nature" draws him, as Harris too was drawn, to journalism, and he becomes the essential male creature in the Strand during that last great age of unquestioned male dominance. Mike Fletcher exults that he arrived from Ireland poor and now (like Frank Harris) enjoys the benefits of wealth: "I have made myself what I am . . . I get the best of everything – women, eating, clothes; I live in beautiful rooms surrounded by pretty things. True, they are not mine, but what does that matter? If only I could get rid of this cursed accent, but I haven't much; Escott has nearly as much, and he was brought up at an English school. How pleasant it is to have money!"[95] For all his front of *arriviste* self-regard, Mike is haunted by self-contempt and self-doubt. He is hideously afraid people will find out that he takes money from women. He manages to live with the fact that he is a sponger and gigolo, but he cannot get over the fact that he was low-born; he wishes he could whisper to himself, "I may lose everything . . . but the fact remains I was born a gentleman."[96] Moore was fascinated by Frank Harris as a phenomenon. Harris had all the intelligence, energy, self-knowledge, and all-round ability a man could want, yet he had no character at all and no real achievement worth speaking about.

What is brilliant about the novel is not really its programmatic design, though that design is an ambitious one. GM clearly meant John Norton to represent the way of the world as idea, and Mike Fletcher the way of the world as will, in a thesis-novel about two theories of life, with Frank Escott taking the middle course of marriage to former bar-girl Lizzie Baker. The plan was schematic and recondite, and because all three roads lead nowhere, the feeling a reader is given is one of balked contemplation on the problem of how to live.

Astute in the study of his models, GM created three powerfully damning central incidents. In the first, Mike Fletcher attempts to rape Lily, a girl not long out of her convent school, whom he has tempted to his apartment in the Strand. He would prefer not to rape her, but when she tries to leave, "an occasional nature in him, that of the vicious dog . . . snarled," and he wrestles her until she breaks loose, throws a glass at him, screams, and climbs the casement to throw herself out of a window. Then with the passion of an orator, Mike talks romance all over again until the girl allows him an embrace. His vanity is briefly satiated; his lust is not. Some time later, Frank sees Lily again at a party (now chaperoned by Alice Barton, from *A Drama in Muslin*), yet she will have little to do with him. He curses himself for not having raped her when he had the chance; then "she would now be hanging on his neck."[97] Mike is persuasive, but part of his rhetoric of seduction is the threat that he will turn mad dog on his companion if she fails to be complaisant.

In the second incident, Mike talks with Lady Helen, Lewis Seymour's wife, about Schopenhauer: he agrees with the philosopher that life is miserable, but disagrees that suicide is wrong. The great advantage of life is that one can end it whenever one wants to. When he doesn't show up for his next assignation with Lady Helen, she kills herself. Arriving late, he takes her handkerchief as a souvenir, and later wears it in his vest pocket. In the final incident of the three, after failing to convince himself that "every human being was as base as he was," Mike Fletcher concludes that one cannot live "without wife, without child, without God," and kills himself.[98]

Mike Fletcher is a judgement on Schopenhauer, on the "young man" in a century of male privilege, and on Augustus Moore and Frank Harris in particular. That George Moore imagined that either one of them could like the novel is astonishing – it is a cold, ruthless, ugly portrait – but perhaps no more surprising than that he thought English readers of 1889 were prepared for a philosophically oriented look at male rapacity. Of all Moore's books, it is the only one that has remained completely unrevised and unrepublished. It was left in the oblivion into which it quickly sank. At the end of the decade, what seemed to have disappeared with it was Moore's reputation as a rising novelist.

Chapter 8
Three Reformations: Of the Stage,
Modern Painting, and George Moore

I

A writer of great ability could hardly have been in worse shape than George Moore was at the end of 1889, having completed his scheme for a "Don Juan" trilogy during the age of the National Vigilance Association. Not just his old enemies but his old friends condemned *Mike Fletcher*. Even he himself did. Not everything could be blamed on the stupidity of the English public or the conspiracy of the circulating libraries. Part of the fault was his for shoddy workmanship; part was his too for defects of character. For one who thought of himself as an artist among commercial hacks and time-serving romancers, GM had been writing too much too fast. Only in the cases of *A Mummer's Wife* and *Confessions of a Young Man* had he revised his text over and over, bringing out new editions with a view to posterity. As a person of great taste but no training – Wilde's quip that GM conducted his education in public was right on the mark – there needed to be a great gap between a first draft and a final product if his work was to be successful.[1] What's more, there was something wrong with the man, wrong with his heart, wrong therefore with the style in which he regarded life. That style was elitist, sneering, purely scampish; it had not sufficiently transcended the ugly masculinity of the caddish club in which it had been born – the offices of the *Bat* and *Hawk*, an air of acrid cheroots and brandies and soda, only partly alleviated by the fading fragrance of the atmosphere of the Café Nouvelle Athènes.

The reception of *Mike Fletcher* caused Moore to take stock of himself. As usual, he confessed himself to a woman, Clara Lanza: "Frank Harris says [*Mike Fletcher*] is not nearly so good as *A Mummer's Wife*. It is very disappointing to hear this. He says it is full of good things but it is nevertheless unsatisfactory." GM immediately goes on in this letter, in a passage quoted in the previous chapter, to make a resolution to change the sort of fiction he is writing and the sort of feelings he is indulging: "My next book will be more human. I shall bathe myself in the simplest and most naive emotions and shall not leave them

– the daily bread of humanity."[2] Clearly, he reckoned that he had to move his own being into a different relation to the lives of ordinary people; he had to escape the dialectical knots of a philosophy of pessimism which he could not untie; and he had to feel his way forward slowly. The plan for *Esther Waters* was conceived in March 1888; the book would not be published until April 1894. The interval was partly spent reworking the style, and partly remaking the man.

Nothing could be further from the case than to think, however, that Moore disappeared into a cork-lined room or an Irish castle in order to decant first a new self and then a masterpiece. Over the next five years, between the publications of *Mike Fletcher* and *Esther Waters*, Moore wrote at least 169 articles and stories, a play (*The Strike at Arlingford*, 1893), a second novel (first published in a periodical under a pseudonym, *Vain Fortune* by "Lady Rhone") and that book in three widely variant editions (1891, 1892, 1895) – staggering productiveness, much of the work still fresh and readable in the gatherings of *Impressions and Opinions* (1891), *Modern Painting* (1893), *The Untilled Field* (1903), and *Memoirs of My Dead Life* (1906). In sum, Moore wrote five books and part of a sixth while taking his time over the seventh.[3]

G. B. Shaw was amazed by "the incredible industry" of GM.[4] Shaw himself was a powerful and prolific pressman, yet in the early 1890s Moore and not Shaw was arguably the most consequential literary journalist in London. The canny editor of the *Scots Observer*, W. E. Henley, instructed his staff to study George Moore in the *Fortnightly* and *Pall Mall Gazette* because "that way leaders lie."[5] GM's scorching, logical, audacious, and sometimes beautiful articles not only attracted attention to a paper; they started controversies that other journalists used to give dramatic continuity to their daily editorial pages. In occasional articles in the *Fortnightly Review*, *Pall Mall Gazette*, *St. James's Gazette*, the *Magazine of Art*, and the *New Review*, and weekly articles in first the *Hawk*, then the *Speaker*, Moore struck out on his own line (the Parisian Irish line) in matters relating to the English stage, English painting, and English literature. He wanted to educate a readership into the appreciation of the kind of culture he then wanted to create himself. But he also used his weekly articles as a laboratory in which to conduct experiments in writing the self, a new self, one who would become the invisible and objective painter of the human drama of *Esther Waters*.

In his weekly article in the *Hawk* on 3 December 1889, written right after he accepted the failure of *Mike Fletcher*, Moore was still confounded by his ire at militant philistines. In the present condition of England, he complained, governments may rise and fall because a policeman mistakes a shop-girl for a prostitute, or if a government hesitates to prosecute the publisher of Zola, or to close "music halls in which light women assemble."[6] Women cannot meet men for the purposes of lovemaking, that liberty is not to be allowed; but the "New Protestants" demand that women be given the same liberties of labor as men, even to become soldiers and policemen. If a man speaks to a woman going about her business on the street, they say he should be put in prison. How very strange! It is not apparent that Moore has altered his support for women's equality since writing *A Drama in Muslin*; he just cannot go along with the puritanical plan to reconstruct human nature with sex left out. The mob vengeance against great men like Sir Charles Dilke (and soon against Charles Stewart Parnell) for their human loves was rooted in humbuggery.[7] "Such excessive virtue," GM believed, "is inconsistent with the exigencies of human life, and the preaching of it results only in making Protestantism a synonym for hypocrisy." Taking it upon himself to speak for English Protestants, he admits on their behalf what they would be unlikely to admit on their own: "That we are the hypocrites of the world is the judgment of the world; that we owe our hypocrisy to Protestantism is, I think, probable."[8] The political correctness campaign against male libertinism had turned into a quixotic, puritanical rejection of human nature, with the result that everyone was constrained to pretend to be what they weren't, unsexed souls instead of imaginative animals.

GM's relationship to religion was taking another turn on its axis. There is no time on record when he was certainly a believer in God. In Paris, he had been a wild pagan, celebrating the classical love of physical beauty, and sometimes playfully indulging in sacrilegious sports with Catholic imagery, in line with Swinburne's high-camp pornographic blasphemies. Back in London, Moore then developed a prosy rationalist atheism in *A Mummer's Wife* and *A Drama in Muslin*. By the second edition of *Confessions*, his life in Sussex with the Bridgers had given him an ironic fondness for village Protestantism, so clean and homely and rational, though his outward amused indulgence of it did not imply inward conformity to it. On his return to London, he found the NVA packed with Protestant clergymen; the Salvation Army was staffed by evangelists as well. Too many people were threatening to save souls by killing pleasures. This prosecutorial "New Protestantism" forced him to reevaluate Catholicism, which in the late nineteenth century, under Cardinals Newman and Manning, was making a fair bid for the affections of aesthetes in England. In "There are Many Roads to Rome," the balance sheet added up for Moore in favor of the old religion all down the line.[9] Catholicism, he had come to think, is "more human" than Protestantism; Protestantism is too moral. Catholicism wants to bring about an absolving confession of sin, Protestantism wants to abolish frailty. Catholicism encourages celibate orders in lovely contemplative retreat from the world, Protestantism distributes birth control information. Catholicism gives "a noble and beautiful turn to life," Protestantism is "hysterical, hard-faced utilitarianism." Catholicism is gentlemanly, ceremonial, and educated; Protestantism is "pusillanimous, querulous, prurient, and fanatical." He concluded that "the high road of common sense now leads past Cardinal Manning to Rome." (Most of GM's preferences for Catholicism over Protestantism, however, have to do with its appeal to the sense of beauty, not to common sense.) George Moore was never himself going to be a pilgrim on that road to Rome, but he reckoned that an atheist must live in the world as it is, and therefore can find that one rather than another religious organisation promotes qualities that make this world more livable for him.[10] Moore's problem – not yet tackled, or even sighted – would be to find a way, without submitting to the prevailing hypocrisy, to bring himself into a sympathetic relationship with what was human, natural, and lovable in the English people, granted their Protestantism and even their hypocrisy.

In a 25 March article, "Pruriency," Moore's word for what Quilter had called "Morality" in a *Universal Review* article, GM raged once more against the whited sepulcher of Protestants after the death of God. Quilter's moralism was "Christianity without Christ"; Mona Caird's New Woman feminism was "morality without marriage"; and Tolstoy's new philosophy was "optimism without gaiety." That a genius like Tolstoy was falling prey to Western utopianism was more infuriating to Moore than the lapses of others. Tolstoy wanted to change nature; human nature was not good enough for Tolstoy; yet how could an artist hate beauty, sex, and beautiful music? Tolstoy's answer to adultery, having grown tired of its pleasures, was that men should marry women who are not attractive, who smell bad; then keep them in the family way. What an appalling commitment, GM thought, to "the desolating tide of children." So what was Moore's counter-gospel? A touchstone sentence from Gautier: "O beautiful, visible world, to me at least thou art visible and more divine than all the gibbeted psychologies of Christendom." Yet if life on the terms in which it is given to humans sufficed for Moore, he had not just to feel, but to make felt its beauty. That would require more than his righteousness without religion; it would take an act of imaginative generosity.

2

An editor putting together an anthology of poems by painters asked Moore for a contribution, and GM offered him "To a Consumptive Girl," from *Pagan Poems*, and recently quoted in *Mike Fletcher*.[11] The request put it in his head to rewrite the poem as a story for the *Hawk*. GM aimed for the manner of Turgenev, and nearly got it – an older man's wise and lovely meditation on youth, love, and *lacrima rerum* (the pity of the world) – with the additional quality of Moore's own strange freedom from falsely saying that he feels what one is supposed to feel. The article begins with GM recalling Paris in the 1870s, and his friend the debonair painter Henri Gervex, "whose light cynicism and *abandon* dissipate sorrow" – a hint of the background of mournfulness in front of which Moore stages his all-too-human efforts of expressive play. The story continues that one evening he ran into Gervex outside Tortoni's, and accompanied him on an evening with "Mlle. D'Avray," an actress infatuated with Gervex.[12] After an opera by Bizet, the three went to the home of the mademoiselle for dinner. Moore dearly loved "to walk by the perambulator in which Love is wheeling a pair of illegitimate lovers." Admittedly, he was sore with envy of Gervex. Had a woman so beautiful as Mlle D'Avray ever loved him, he would not be so indifferent to her coaxing as Gervex seemed to be, but then, old Moore reflects on young Moore's pain (while drawing on Keats's "Ode to Melancholy"), "a week of intimacy would dissipate all the poetry that allures you now; the glitter and exultation that now possess you is in yourself, not in her." After dinner, they all go to a small café, where GM noticed among the other bar-girls and broken-down cocottes (women who seem conscious they are now where Mlle D'Avray might one day be, when the curtain falls on her hour of maximum beauty) –

> a girl whom I cannot call a waitress – a thin, strangely thin girl, delicate beyond measure, and touched with languor, weakness, and a pensive grace, which moved me, and I thought her pale, deciduous beauty enhanced and accentuated by the Medici gown she wore. The cheeks were sunk, the deep grey eyes were filled with sweet wistfulness, and her wavy brown hair fell over the white temples, looped up low down on the neck after the fashion of a Rossetti drawing.

After this frank gaze from a connoisseur, she is asked by Moore if she would like a drink. No, her doctor has told her she mightn't drink, but could she have a piece of raw beefsteak? He paid for her nutriment, and after a few bites she came over to talk. Wasn't that accent English? GM asked. "I am Irish," she answered; "I am from Dublin." So, she was like himself, an Irish person in Paris, wholly submerged in another life, yet she was dying – consumptive, no doubt about that – and he had his health. "I have seen a hare beating a tambourine on a showman's barrow," Moore thought with surprise, but what strange accident brought this animal from its meadow and forced such a fate upon her? She told him her story of leaving Ireland to become a French au pair, then falling for a student too poor to feed her and too handsome for her to leave, so now she must work in this smoky café that was killing her. "The doctor said she might live if she went away south. But she had no money, so she supposed she must make up her mind to die." GM told her how he would like to take her to Algiers, feed her, and put some color in her cheeks – but not too much color, "'for your cheeks are beautiful in their pallor.'" She laughed at the morbidity of his affectionately ironic aestheticism, but a coughing fit came upon her, and she said, "'I must not laugh.'" After the café closed, when walking home alone in the cold moonlight, GM stopped on the Pont Neuf, looking into the mysterious depth of space, and "thought of the dying girl to whom I had spoken of health . . ." The whole vignette, from the consumption, and reflections on how to live, down to the very hare, is quietly reminiscent of an urban "Resolution and Independence," Wordsworth's great meditation on a dignified old man who lives by gathering leeches from mountain ponds. Moore's mind was full of a poem of his own, but he was "conscious of the barbarism of writing it, conscious also of the folly it would be to refrain from writing it . . . I could not take her to Egypt any more than I could take the hare from the showman and restore it to its native meadows." When he returned days later

to the café, she was gone. And now, GM concludes, she is "forgotten utterly
. . . Perhaps I alone think of her – I, who only saw her once."

In this story, one finds Moore's uniquely swift interchange of literary allu-
siveness and idiomatic simplicity, whimsy and poignancy, self-parody and self-
importance, bathos corrected by pathos, pathos by irony, and irony by truism.
He has broken free of the frugal, objective reportorial style he learned
from Zola; from the dogmatic, rude fanfaronade of his polemical articles; and
from the caddish, thirsting-to-astonish japes of the *Bat*-bred style of the *Confessions*. Now he has a way of writing that is straight from the strippings of his
own strange blood, a syntax the pulse of which is his pulse, and a view of life
that is the hard-won work of much thought. There can be no doubt that he has
registered the existence of this beautiful consumptive Irish waitress in a keen
and sympathetic way, that he has felt the beauty and pathos of her sole self, a
beauty inseparable from the sad conditions in which she is perishing, and that
he has also felt the urgings of a desire to go out to her, whether in mercy or in
lust, but that he has not acted, only reverberated with all that was there to
be felt.

What makes the style new in Moore's work is the quality of its pity, the way
the episode is finally "bathed in the simplest and most naive of emotions, the
daily bread of humanity."[13] GM's relationship to pity had fluctuated over the
years. In *Pagan Poems*, there are febrile, cold-hearted rejections of tubercular
girls and of a beggarwoman – "You are useless . . . Life ignores you . . . You
were blackballed out of life. There is nothing for you here, Nothing."[14] In
Confessions, he occasionally identified with the pseudo-satanic aestheticism of
Gautier, delighting in the fantasy of the world as a bloody gladiatorial theater;
he distanced himself at that time from both Christianity and socialism as identical and unrealistic expressions of pity, not of intelligence. In *Parnell and His
Island*, the rejection of progressivism is repeated, when he concludes that his
pictures of Ireland's poverty were like the images on a Japanese fan, calculated
to wake "fictitious feelings of pity, pitiful curiosity and nostalgia for the
unknown," not for the purpose of remedial action.[15] Schopenhauer may
have been the one that caused Moore to reexamine the question of pity. For
Schopenhauer, *Schadenfreude* – joy in anther's discomfort – was the worst trait
in humanity, and pity was the best, "the true source of genuine justice and love
of humanity."[16] Schopenhauer, however, does not believe that the fundamentally awful conditions under which humans suffer can be rectified, or even
ameliorated. Moore, like Schopenhauer, feels the grandeur of a sympathetic
recognition of fellowship in suffering, but he leaves Schopenhauer behind and
comes close to Nietzsche in two other ways. First, he is more splenetic than
Schopenhauer in his attitude to those like Tolstoy who, out of pity, would try
to take humans out of the web in which we are entangled, the woof spun before
our birth. Second, like Nietzsche Moore is disposed to ground his affirmation
of life even in the very conditions of suffering; strength and sweetness flow
from the embrace of tragedy. The Irish waitress's own bravery in telling her

story over and over again, like Wordsworth's leech-gatherer, telling it with a dignified sad simplicity, is worthy of record among the things that make life worth the living. Such tales are the wonders of this beautiful, visible world, more beautiful than "all the gibbeted psychologies of Christendom."[17]

One might complain that there is still something inadequate, even callow, in Moore's response to the consumptive girl, something with its root in that which gave rise earlier in his life to the line in *Pagan Poems*, "Heigh-ho . . . My life has been a very pleasant one."[18] Yet Moore's new prose setting for his youthful poem is vastly more subtle than its first state: a pitiful girl recalled after many years, against the background of sorrows about a self not satisfied with its lot, and mixed with a humor that spares himself no indignity and steals from the girl no glamor. The ultimate sense of inadequacy to the suffering of another is made philosophical. There is, he thinks, no way to compensate adequately for birth into a low estate, heartbreak, disease, poverty, and the obligation to toil. All that can be done is to fully register by means of style the being and the beauty of the other who suffers, so that justice, beauty, and pity can be held together within the same thought, without a grandiose profiteering on another's pain, the sort of genteel aesthetic *Schadenfreude* of a melodramatic artist.

3

The stylistic qualities of pity – call it *cold pity*, or *beauty envisioned by regret* – were cultivated by GM in other articles in the *Hawk* in early 1890, as he felt his way forward into a new mode. The story of the waitress had been entitled "Notes and Sensations," and in another story with the same Impressionistic title, published on 11 March 1890, he told about the end of Marie Pellegrin. It is modelled on the story by Alexis, but Moore contributed his own brand of pathos, concision, and humor. "In Blue Silk and Brass" also works this vein of comedic and poignant memoir.[19] A third tale first published under the heading "Notes and Sensations" is again in the style Jean Noël calls *mémoire fantaisie*, but in this case the fantasy element is given free comic rein, and the poignancy appears in the gap between what did and did not happen, between life and literature. The story may have sprung from his abortive courtship of Gertrude Atherton in May 1889. In it, GM meets a pretty American widow at a ball, writes her a rondel in French "good enough to win a heart already won," then takes her for a day in the country. Caught in a downpour, they seek shelter at a grand château, the owner of which assumes that they are married, and since the Paris train has left, gives them a bedroom for the night . . . "a very pretty, though a painful dilemma for a young woman to find herself in, particularly when she is passionately in love with the young man." Or such would be the story in the hands of an "accomplished story-teller." Not being so accomplished, GM has to admit that in the narrative written by nature, the rain stopped, they went back to Paris, she gave him her garter the next day before boarding the steamboat to America, and he promised to write, but didn't. Now he guesses she is married to a Chicago meatpacker who "fills her life with happiness from end to end." Yet she will sometimes think of him, because "life is written on weariness with the indelible ink of regret."[20] Beauty is again secreted not from a wish fulfilled, but from the unfulfillment of our wishes by the course of nature and fate. The stories it falls to GM to write are those in which literature hovers over a part of life, one that aspires to the qualities of romance, but does not reach it.

In his reinvention of himself as a writer, Moore was showing in his *Hawk* articles a growing yet still incomplete consciousness of the qualities that made his stories different from those of other great storytellers. In "Le Revers d'un grand homme," for instance, he meditates on *The Letters of the Duke of Wellington to Miss J.* "Miss J" was a lovely young English evangelist who set out to convert the randy Duke and then would allow herself to be neither seduced nor put off.[21] Given this premise, how, Moore asks, would James, Zola, Daudet, and Maupassant develop their narratives? James would have the Duke make absent-minded advances, repelled by the lady in an absent-minded way; the Duke would make vague efforts to get free, until his death and her return to Boston. Zola would have the Duke become her lover, her remorse would then take her to many lavishly described cathedrals; after the Duke took another mistress, she would distribute tracts in the lowest dens of vice: "the book would end with the description of the Duke's funeral, interwoven with the description of the death of the lady on a Kensington hearthrug." With equal accuracy, GM burlesques the manners of Daudet and Maupassant, and then gives his own solution:

> Miss J. would succeed in entangling the Duke sufficiently to make it imperative he should marry her. It would be pleasing to show the glory of Waterloo fading in the ridicule that would follow and fasten on the absurd marriage; above all, it would be delightful to determine how far this lady's religion was true, by testing it in the crucible of court life, and the book should be called "Le Revers d'un Grand Homme."

Moore here thinks of himself as a novelist who loves to gourmandise over the delicious, painful comedy of love, religion, and society. In fact, what he is best at is not writing in any particular way a novel around this premise or that. What he does well is to model reveries upon the many forms in which the poignant human comedy may be stylised, and the ways in which life will always have a remainder that is wonderfully inexpressible, a surplus of humanity outside language, and a surplus of existence outside humanity.[22]

Later in his life, Moore would sometimes realise where his true strength lay – that is, in a narrative form that combines memoir, narrative inventions, critical appreciations, and speculative philosophy – but he never got over wanting to be a great novelist and a great playwright, writing widely applauded novels and plays in a personal but still conventional fashion. Max Beerbohm – who knew Moore well, and caricatured him mercilessly – summed up this oddity of his achievement: "Genius, he assuredly had; not, I think, in his specifically creative work; but in criticism, yes . . . I saw [his novels] rather as experiments, made with admirable skill and patience and, as the years passed, on an ever-increasing scale – experiments which, though all the proper materials had been collected . . . somehow failed of that final result for which they were made: creation of authentic life." While his novels often were missing something, his other writings, Beerbohm acknowledged, certainly did have that "vital magic."[23]

4

At the same time that Moore was engaging in these experimental narratives, he used his weekly space in the *Hawk* for other purposes as well, sometimes literary criticism, as in another critique of the racist pogroms of Rider Haggard's African novels.[24] Yet the major theme of his 1890s journalism was the reform of British painting. He wanted to shake up the British Academy, rally support for the ambitious young painters of the New English Art Club, and clarify the relationship of contemporary painting to the Old Masters. On the whole, he advocated the scholarly, allusive, modernist forms of Manet and Degas. In November 1889, Moore did not have time to write the exhibition catalogue for the "British Impressionists" show at the Goupil Gallery, 116–117 New Bond Street, but he promised to do something for his friends Philip Wilson Steer, Walter Sickert, and others by means of his *Hawk* column.[25] He was one of only four reviewers of the Goupil Gallery show, out of forty-nine, who strongly supported the London Impressionists.

Moore had met Steer in the Cock Tavern, near the Temple, the resort of W. E. Henley's *National Observer* staff as well.[26] The two became friends, visited back and forth, and GM was delighted when Steer made him a present of a painting of a girl in a large black hat.[27] Steer had also been to the Académie Julian, changed his preferences from Julian's salon style toward the Impressionists' manner, and come into the society of Blanche and Walter Sickert. Together, Sickert and Steer were now the key figures in the New English Art Club, after 1888 more and more simply a society of British Impressionists, with Sickert's work following in the path of Degas, and Steer's in that of Monet and Seurat.[28] Moore was charmed by the apparent respect these young painters showed him, and further charmed because he saw in their heroic dedication to art the realisation of that band of English "Moderns" he had imagined in a *A Modern Lover* (1883). Now a real alternative to the Royal Academy was coming into existence.[29]

In histories of British art of the late nineteenth century, Moore has usually been described as a main interpreter of French Impressionism to the English, and, along with the more scholarly D. S. MacColl, the principal advocate of the British Impressionists. Certainly, he was more sympathetic to the work of Steer, Sickert, Whistler, and others than most English art critics, who bowed the knee instead to the titled painters of the Royal Academy, classicising decorative artists like Sir Frederick Leighton and Sir Lawrence Alma-Tadema.[30] There can be no doubt that Moore materially helped Steer and Sickert, James Guthrie, John Lavery, and Mark Fisher. He made their names prominent to the public, exemplified for readers how to look at their pictures and to appreciate qualities for which no price had yet been set by the market. He exposed the fragility of the high prices currently being paid for Frank Dicksee, Alma-Tadema, and other luminaries of the Royal Academy. That prices for works by Monet and Degas were starting to skyrocket seemed to confirm that Moore's taste was in general going to stand the test of time; maybe he was right that Manet would also one day be judged a master, and Whistler too; even that these new painters of the New English Art Club had that "quality" in their "handling" of which Moore confidently spoke.[31]

Alongside his publicity for their careers, Moore was judiciously critical of the work of the New English Art Club, even of the pictures by his friends Steer and Sickert. Sickert later admitted with embarrassment that they were "genuinely elated or depressed" according to GM's judgements in the *Hawk* and *Speaker*.[32] Elie Halévy, in London during November 1890, visited the painters of the New English Art Club at D. S. MacColl's house and, after listening to the conversation, concluded that Halévy's friend Degas reigned over modern English art, or at least over that group of artists "ruled over by George Moore."[33] Moore expressed his authority over the young British Impressionists in an apodictic style of judgement. Concerning a Goupil Gallery exhibition, for instance, he ridiculed the ephemeral aestheticisms of the French avant-garde, and regretted that Steer's *Knucklebones* – though powerful as a painterly representation of children, shingles, and the sea – was so obviously derivative of the pointillists in its handling of the stony shore, and of other painters in other parts of the picture. It is as if Albert Moore painted the children, Monet the sea, and Pissarro the shore.[34] In the same review, GM points out that Sickert doesn't always succeed with his extremely difficult Degas-inspired subjects, involving shadows, artificial stage lights, reflections in mirrors, and oddities of perspective. *Little Dot Hetherington at the Bedford* had been a success; the new pictures, he judged, were not.

In addition to the critical cast of his appreciations of the British Impressionists, Moore aimed to influence their work in one consistent way. Surprisingly, he hectored them about avoiding the direct imitation of contemporary French painting. GM's authority was Degas, who just the previous May had remarked that English painters, as a result of French training and emulation of French fads, were losing all that made them distinctive. Degas had an honest appreciation of eighteenth-century English painting: from his horse pictures, it can be seen what he learned from Gainsborough and others. In Moore's article on an RA exhibition of Old Masters, he drives home the importance of Degas's lesson about the distinctive value to contemporary painters of the Old Masters and national traditions. Gainsborough, Moore says, "thank heavens, knew nothing of France, or Italy." He was self-taught and thus "free from the cant of school." GM praised Holbein for not being French; he drew "by the character," not by "the masses of light and shade" in the academic French fashion. An exhibition of Old Masters, "Expert Moore" advised, is where young English painters should come; they need not pack their bags for Paris.[35]

This particular praise of Old Masters and English painting is in line with Moore's charted course as an art critic. He celebrated the picture of a bull by Troyon, and an exhibition of English hunting pictures, saying love of sport "almost redeems our hypocrisy and cant," and, *mirabile dictu*, makes him "glad that [he is] an Englishman."[36] GM liked the work of his friend Mark Fisher from the start, but he barked even at Fisher for not being sufficiently English. Moore could coldly appreciate the drawing and painting of George Clausen in *The Mowers*, but declared he wouldn't hang one of Clausen's pictures in his own house – they were too derivative of Bastien-Lepage, that "Bouguereau of the modern movement," as Degas maliciously quipped.[37] "The French studio has destroyed all the naiveté, all the sincerity," and Moore pronounced, "the great English tradition of the eighteenth century is ended."[38] In the summer of 1890, GM developed his memoirs of Julian's Academy into a slashing attack on the commercialisation of modern French painting, broadened a few weeks later into a wholesale rejection of any artistic training in "Is Education Worth Having?"[39] Some of his greatest praise was for the Dickensian black-and-white artist, Charles Keene. Keene was uneducated, never went to France or any-where else, yet he was, GM judged, a draftsman who had achieved the greatest quality of all – "national character."[40] This praise may seem absurd to those who think of Moore as the great advocate of Manet and Degas. Yet it is not strange coming from the author of *Esther Waters*, straining during these years to immerse himself in the qualities of English life. In an appreciation of the Dutch landscape painter Ruysdael, Moore surmised that he liked Ruysdael so much "because I desire above all things to tell the story of life in grave simple phrases, so grave and simple that the method, the execution, would disap-pear, and the reader, with bating breath, would remain a prey to an absorbing emotion."[41] There isn't a better description of the stylistic virtues of *Esther Waters*.

Moore's advice to young London painters to attend to the Dutch traditions of draftsmanship, the taproot of English painting, has been overlooked recently, but the young painters of the New English Art Club did not miss the drift of Moore's articles.[42] Steer repeated the same lesson in a lecture to the Art Workers' Guild in 1891, and Steer and Sickert both ultimately developed lessons learned from Monet and Degas (respectively) in the direction of English antecedents.[43] In May 1891, however, it was premature of GM to claim

9. *Portrait of George Moore* (1891), Walter Sickert.

to have influenced contemporary art in this direction – "the French method of painting acquired in the last twenty years is being assimilated, is being Englished."[44] Sickert, for one, was still unconvinced, and secretly seething at Moore's admonishments.

In 1891, Sickert did a portrait of GM first exhibited in the November show of the New English Art Club (now in the Tate Gallery). Moore sat only two times, apparently for sketches in pencil. Sickert did not need any further studies, his purpose not being accuracy or beauty but stinging satire.[45] It is even more of a cartoon than Manet's oil sketch that was dubbed "the drowned fisherman"; Sickert's picture was described by Henry Butcher at an RA banquet as the image of "an intoxicated mummy."[46] Moore's big wondering eyes are blue pools in a muddy seascape of oil; the hair is an unkempt mess of brushstrokes; and a big yellow mustache droops over a partly opened and astonished mouth. The subject looks as if he has just missed a joke at which everyone is laughing. The portrait is in keeping with Sickert's resentment at being advised to do in painting what Moore had lately decided was best for him to do in writing. Moore remained a good sport about having been the occasion of an original use of oil portraiture, not to ennoble, glamorise, or even depict the sitter, but to abuse him.

5

While GM's press campaign on behalf of the new "British Impressionists" had its contemporary impact, the articles about painting by Moore which have the most lasting significance are those about Degas and Manet. There are no good books about either of these great artists that do not cite Moore, partly because he writes pregnant criticisms of their work, but still more importantly because he records their words, appearances, and manners of being as he knew them. He put his faith in the illustrative value of the anecdote. After reporting a conversation with Manet about Morisot, he commented, "This anecdote will give a better idea of the value of Berthe Morisot than seventy columns of mine or any other man's criticism."[47] It has often been deplored that George Moore betrayed the confidence of his friends by writing about them, but if he had not done so, we would know less about many key figures in modern literature and art. Certainly, there would be hypocrisy in an art historian deploring Moore's tactlessness while employing his quotations from Manet and Degas as interpretive keys, more still in a biographer finding fault with Moore's combination of the private scoop with the profound conclusion, the exposé with the exposition.

There was a price for GM's outspokenness, of course, and he paid it. In October 1890, when he finally published in the *Magazine of Art* his long-bruited study of Degas, "A Painter of Modern Life" (the title is stolen from Baudelaire's article about Manet), Moore lost the friendship of the living artist he admired above all others. He knew beforehand he was running that risk. Indeed, in the article itself, he quotes Degas's threats:

> To those who want to write about him, [Degas] says: "Leave me alone; you didn't come here to count how many shirts I have in my wardrobe?" "No, but your art, I want to write about it." "My art . . . Do you think you can explain the merits of a picture to those who do not see them? . . . My opinion has always been the same. I think literature has done only harm to art."[48]

By way of self-defense, Moore expatiates on the good fortune that enabled the mutual friend of Zola and Degas "to snatch out of the oblivion of conversation two such complete expressions of artistic sensibility" as the sentences he uses to illustrate the contrasting temperaments of the French novelist and painter. GM's article on Degas contains priceless revelations about, for example, Degas's attitudes to his nudes. He told Moore that his bathtub scenes show "the human animal taking care of its body, a female cat licking herself. Hitherto the nude has always been represented in poses which presuppose an audience, but these women of mine are honest, simple folk, unconcerned by other interests than those involved in their physical condition. It is as if you looked through a keyhole."[49] Degas may also have told Moore that "a *danseuse* is just a pretext for a drawing,"[50] but there was more to Degas's nudes and studies of little girls in tights than experiments in form or medium. Degas was revealing the character of his misogynist voyeurism, his hunger to see and depict what women are when they think that they are unseen.

"The Painter of Modern Life" infuriated Degas. To us, it reads like wonderfully sympathetic commentary; to him, it took one unforgivable liberty after another. It described a visit to his private studio; it mentioned the financial failure of his once-prosperous family (a mortal shame to the dignified bourgeois Degas); it reported his private jokes, even about painters with whom Degas wished to remain on friendly terms, this one about Whistler, for instance: "My dear friend, you conduct yourself in life just as if you had no talent at all." And comparing their capacities for wit, GM reported Degas as saying that Whistler's conversation with him was characterised by "brilliant flashes of silence." Degas tried to patch things up with Whistler by abusing GM as a scandalmonger.[51] Whistler then demanded that Degas, and Mallarmé too, should cut GM – just an infamous courier, and a miserable specimen of an ignorant type.[52] Degas then did cut Moore, utterly. Even years later, he would not dine at the Halévys' if Moore was to be a guest.[53]

Moore continued to show reverence for Degas, and he continued to write about him with equal honesty, as when he described Degas's work as "small, confined, scattered; there is no view; it is never like looking out of a window, it is more like poring over the text of a book . . . the direct outcome of great knowledge and admiration of the works of the masters."[54] This allusive, enigmatic, and modernist conception of the great artwork, practiced by both Manet and Degas, was what Moore esteemed most highly in his own writing, and what he advocated most consistently, over pointillism and other new aestheticisms, to the British Impressionists of the New English Art Club.[55]

6

In an odd way, the break with Degas was perhaps not altogether inevitable. It may have been to a degree a contingent accident of another aspect of Moore's periodical writings over this period. For while it is necessary to speak separately of Moore's development of a new style of reverie in narrative, his advocacy of young painters and interpretation of old ones, his steady slow progress through the composition of *Esther Waters*, and his theater journalism, in fact he was doing all of these things intermittently, during different days of the same week, and even different hours of the same day, and one thing naturally reacted upon another. His interest in draftsmanship and Old Masters certainly influenced the clarity of narrative line and the homage to Dickens and Fielding in *Esther Waters*, and so too his theater journalism had a rippling effect on his personal relationships, even on his relationship with Degas, who knew nothing of Moore's attitude to theater.

Moore had been meddling in theater business through the 1870s and 1880s – writing plays like *Worldliness*, *Martin Luther*, *A Fashionable Beauty*, and, currently, *The Strike at Arlingford*, and carrying on a stinging critique of English actors, theater management, and playwrights. In May 1890, he took Arthur Symons along on his annual Paris visit. Symons had stepped into the role of Moore's London *bon ami*, previously occupied by James Davis and then Edward Martyn. Symons had rooms in the Temple, shared Moore's interest in keeping track of trends in French literature, and, aside from being a beautiful boy "of somewhat yellowish temperament," won GM's affection by deferentially serving him with the "*cher maître* attitude."[56] In Paris, the two of them attended a performance of Ibsen's *Ghosts* at Antoine's Théâtre Libre.[57] They were fervently excited by Ibsen's play in Antoine's production, though it bored many of the other guests. Quickly, they hatched plans to campaign for an equivalent "free theatre" (free from convention, free from commercialism, free from censorship) in London. Symons broached the idea in the *Pall Mall Gazette* on 5 June, and Moore charted plans for such an operation in a four-part article in the *Hawk* that ran from 17 June to 8 July. Coincidentally, J. T. Grein was mulling over the possibilities of an English "free theatre" for new English plays in the 31 May issue of *Life: A Weekly Journal of Society*.

Moore's opening *Hawk* article described the first reading of *Ghosts* he had been to at the home of Edward Aveling and Eleanor Marx. Even performed in such circumstances, the play amazed him: "I watched, even as a child watches the fly that chance has thrown in a spider's web." Antoine's performance simply redoubled the effect of what Moore thought was the greatest scene in modern drama, the final scene between mother and son. He had never felt "so divine a horror"

as when the mother, declaring that she cannot do what is asked of her [and give her son poison to end his suffering from congenital syphilis], breaks into the natural cry: "I who gave you life!" The son answers: "A nice kind of life it was you gave me." Then the mother, overcome, rushes from the room. She is followed tumultuously by the son, and the stage is left empty – empty and not empty – for its emptiness is the symbol for the horror we feel, the blank stage becomes at once the symbol of the blank insoluble problem which is life. And when the mother and son return – their exit was no more than brief venting of their anguish in animal movement – and continue the scene, the terror moving among the spectators becomes suddenly unbearable, and each one and every one is ready to rise to his feet, and cry to them on stage, "Say, oh, say, that it is not true."

Why can't London have a theater for plays like this? he wondered aloud.[58] Surely there were a thousand persons dissatisfied with commercial plays, people of sufficient wealth and distinction to subscribe £5 a year for twelve interesting "literary dramas." What was such a play? Moore's definition is important:

a literary drama was a play with no comic scenes in a serious story; with no faultless hero; no plot "that is not tied and untied by the action of the senti- ments, and not by fortuitous accidents, letters, sudden deaths, etc."; one with a "logical development of character: bad people shall not suddenly become good people." All that was needed was a man to organise a society.

By the time Moore wrote his 24 June article, he had met that man, J. T. Grein. For his "encouragement and instruction," Moore then summarised his *Hawk* articles in a booklet on the history of Antoine's Théâtre Libre from March 1887 to the present. Antoine's theater had many aspects, but only a few of these did GM wish to replicate in London. The Théâtre Libre was an ensemble of actors, initially tradesmen and amateur actors, who wanted to attract attention by staging new pieces mostly by previously unproduced dramatists. At first Antoine's troupe played in small rented halls because they had neither big audiences nor expensive sets. Their plays had short runs, and so they were able to put on about forty different shows a year. Unable in the beginning to rely on ticket sales, Antoine appealed for subscriptions. When the company became more successful, the actors got an annual salary and a share in profits. Eventually, they were able to build their own theater, which intro- duced modern stage machinery to eliminate pauses between acts, dropped the big saloon in the lobby, put the seats in rows in front of a "fourth wall" proscenium stage, and offered low ticket prices.

Many types of theater could be derived from this complex model, and many theaters were, including that of Dublin's Irish National Theatre Society. GM's notion of what an English "free theater" would be is really a high-society author's literary theater. He did not care about creating a permanent acting company, or doing ensemble work; he did not propose building a new kind of theater for a new kind of representation; and there was nothing of the prole- tarian, naturalist, and progressive character of the Théâtre Libre in his own proposals. What he proposed was to take subscriptions from wealthy literate playgoers, rent an existing theater, hire assorted actors for one-time perfor- mances, and create a monthly play to be as "celebrated in the Press as our annual exhibitions at Burlington House or the State Balls at Buckingham Palace."[59] In short, highbrow art for highbrow audiences. The aspect of the enterprise most important to Moore was to stimulate the production of really literary plays by authors such as Meredith, Hardy, Stevenson, "Michael Field," and perhaps even Julia Davis Frankau. (Astonishingly, Moore thought *A Babe in Bohemia*, her lampoon of himself and the *Bat* bohemians, might make a suitable play.)[60] In his announcement of the founding of the Independent Theatre Society ("Théâtre Libre" was judged to be too *risqué* a title), J. T. Grein thanked GM and fell right into line with the highbrow cast of his proposals. Grein liked the Novelty Theatre as a site to rent, because of its large foyer, where so many of the subscribers, who "will be known to each other," can meet "to discuss the play."[61] Grein said he did not want to be told that the general public would not like plays written by "prominent men of letters" in London; it's not for the general public, he snapped, that the presentations are being provided. In many ways, the Independent Theatre Society would establish the guidelines for the strangely elitist, anti-popular, and literary character of the Irish Literary Theatre and Annie Horniman's Abbey Theatre.[62]

George Moore was thrilled that "all things [were] tending towards a Théâtre Libre" and quite proud of the part it had been his honor to play in its foundation.[63] Augustus Moore, however, immediately threw cold water on the idea on the same pages of the *Hawk* in which George Moore tried to build a fire under it. Augustus said he had been a play-reader for Gus Hare and Wilson Barrett (prominent actor-managers) and in that capacity had read hundreds of manuscripts; there were no good plays that went unproduced. And he had been an actor-manager of a traveling company, and he could say the current English system was in good shape. The English did not need or want grim boring plays by Ibsen. The Dutchman Grein had no right to come over to England and set up shop; he was just trying to put on his own poorly translated dramas in double-Dutch and then embezzle the subscription fund. This extremely nasty, fratricidal critique was a subject of comment in the *St. James's Gazette*, so GM wrote to dissociate himself from his brother's opinions, stating simply that he only stood by comments in the *Hawk* that appeared over his own signature. The cold dignity of this letter further infuriated Augustus. He published his own statement that he "strongly object[ed] to any articles which have appeared in this paper being used to induce anyone to subscribe a shilling to such an enterprise" as an English Théâtre Libre.[64] The quarrel between the brothers then escalated another notch when GM warned Augustus that by challenging Grein's honesty, he was effectively calling GM a thief as well, and if he ever did it again, they could not remain friends. Augustus did it again.

Why did Augustus drive off his brother, a contributor to his nasty little weekly, who was at the time writing the best journalism in London? Augustus obviously resented the differences in the nature of their lives that had resulted from the old law of primogeniture or law of entail. GM did not get much from his estate rents, but he received a competence. Augustus had to scramble for presswork, while GM simply took up what interested him. Augustus probably was especially irritated by the propaganda for Ibsen because the *Hawk* had always been closely tied to the fortunes of the commercial London stage: the regular staff did reviews, provided gossip, wrote celebrity biographies, created skits, and moonlighted as authors for the stage. GM was running down the whole crew of them, and the ship they sailed, lock, stock, and barrel. There is no sign that George ever asked Augustus to run the Independent Theatre Society, or even consulted him, a courtesy Augustus might well have thought was owed him as a man of experience in theater.

Augustus's life had been spinning out of control for the previous few years. In addition to blackmailing companies into advertising in his paper, he had been involved in a dark libelous vendetta against a man named J. A. Chandor, a Dutchman like Grein, or like Grein at least in being a Dutchman. Early in

1890, Augustus had accused "Mr. John Arthur Chandos, alias Chandor, alias Captain Carlton," of conspiring with W. T. Stead to morally assassinate Colonel Hughes-Hallet so that Chandor could take his parliamentary seat.[65] Augustus also printed details of charges the wealthy American Mrs Clara Bloomfield Moore made against Chandor after his involvement with Mrs Moore's daughter: theft by fraud, seduction of a young girl, then of her sister, skipping out on hotel bills, theft of jewelry from girls he seduced, blackmail, and false claim to being an officer in the army.[66] Chandor then apparently tried to countermine the *Hawk* editor through an amazingly complicated trap. First, Chandor wrote salacious letters to a young girl under a false name; second, he placed newspaper advertisements under that name to arrange a rendezvous for sexual purposes; next, he sent a mysterious note inducing Augustus to show up at the appointed place of assignation, which was under watch by Scotland Yard after a tip from Chandor.[67] Augustus considered the mysterious note of invitation –

A lady wants very much to make your acquaintance. Be outside at the Avenue Theatre on Saturday at three. She will be walking up and down with a letter in her hand. Say, "Venus, I think." She will reply, "Montmorency, I believe." The rest depends on yourself.

– and hesitated. Augustus was all too aware he had enemies, and that the Vigilance Association was entrapping men who approached women in the street, so he sent Jimmy Glover in place of himself, just to suss out the scheme. It was only with difficulty that Glover, taken in the trap, himself escaped charges. In a new dirty trick during August, Chandor offered to pay the legal expenses of an actress if she would bring libel charges against Augustus for some chaff printed in the *Hawk*.

While Augustus was at daggers drawn with his brother George, and caught up in cloak-and-dagger conspiracies against his fellow-scoundrel Chandor, on 7 September, chatting in the Drury Lane lobby during an intermission of George Pettit's *A Million of Money*, Augustus suddenly spied the mustachioed little painter, James McNeill Whistler, striding toward him squeaking, "Hawk! Hawk!" and then bringing his raised cane down on Augustus with the words, "Thus I chastise you!" Augustus blanched, then lunged at or stumbled over Whistler, who fell to the ground, as respective friends of the two combatants pulled them apart. Both then hastened off to newspaper offices to dictate their versions of the combat.[68] However, Augustus had not gotten out of the door before he was attacked a second time, now by the actor Horace Lingard, who claimed Augustus had insulted his wife Alice Lingard in the *Hawk*.[69]

Whistler wasted no time at all in writing to Mallarmé: "Hello, *mon cher ami*, here is the latest news! You can take a certain pleasure in that it is the brother of George Moore who has received this beating!" Whistler included a copy of the account of the battle just published in *Whirlwind*, a little paper run by his followers, which had made Augustus the winner of its "Ugliest Man" contest. Whistler wanted Mallarmé to circulate this account in Paris, where it would most hurt GM. Mallarmé obliged.[70]

Augustus produced his own report in the *Hawk*, entitling the article, "The Gentle Art of Making a Goose of Oneself." It is full of contemptuous condescension to Whistler, "this little withered-up old man . . . who has fondly fooled himself he is a great *chef*." Augustus apologised with broad irony for slapping Whistler after receiving only a light tap from his "twopenny-halfpenny cane." "For this I am very sorry, as also for having knocked him down, for I hope I did not hurt him seriously, and trust I only gave him a slight shaking. They ignominiously threw him out of the theatre, which I think was quite needless . . . he could not have hurt anybody: there were no women present."[71] This was all well enough, and quite in keeping with contemporary standards of journalistic abuse, yet Augustus began his article with a quotation from Degas about Whistler, which can only have derived from George Moore: "'Whistler, you behave yourself just as if you have no talent at all.'" That made it seem to the many French intellectuals who read the tide of articles on the fight – in the *Star*, *Globe*, *St. James's Gazette*, *Stage*, *Sporting Times*, *Sporting Review*, *Topical Times*, *Evening News*, *Echo*, *Referee*, etc. – that GM helped his brother write the article and thus shared his brother's character and views.[72] It is highly probable that GM had nothing to do with penning the article about Whistler. The brothers don't seem to have been any longer on speaking terms. Furthermore, Jimmy Glover does not mention GM as having been present when he and Augustus returned that night to the *Hawk* office to rush their account into print. Still, GM could not decently disavow his brother under such circumstances, yet the fact is they were never further out of sympathy with one another than in September 1890; indeed, they never fully made up their breach, even in the last months of Augustus's life in 1910.[73]

On 4 October, the *Echo de Paris* published a highly colored account of the Whistler/Moore combat that was absurdly favorable to Whistler; it was written by Mallarmé's friend Octave Mirbeau, for which Mirbeau was lavishly thanked by Whistler.[74] When Mallarmé saw Degas in late October, Degas had seen GM's "Degas: Painter of Modern Life" in the *Magazine of Art*; he had also become acquainted with Augustus's use of his own quip to attack Whistler. Degas, speaking of "the entire Moore family" to Mallarmé, said, "Nothing can break my friendship with Whistler!"[75] But his friendship with George Moore was another story: that was at an end.

The end of GM's weekly articles for the *Hawk*, and of Augustus's reign as its editor, were also fast approaching. On 30 September 1890, Augustus printed GM's final offering to the paper. Justin MacCarthy became a poor substitute for GM as a weekly columnist. Then in October his blackmailing efforts caught up with Augustus. Other small papers run by Harry Marks, Colonel McMurdo, and Mr Perryman – the *Financial Observer* and *Financial Times* – had gotten into the same game of merchandising protection from libel. On 7 October 1890,

Augustus began to quarrel with his competitors by calling Perryman, editor of the *Financial Observer*, a "subsidised thief" and "blackmailing ruffian." Perryman called Augustus that and more in the issues of the *Financial Observer* for 11, 18, and 25 October and 1 November. Augustus sued for libel, but by December had lost, and was ordered to pay costs – a terrible humiliation: the court had agreed he was a ruffian and thief. The *Hawk* limped along – still ragging J. T. Grein, GM, and the Independent Theatre Society – until it was sold by a liquidator in August 1892, and Augustus was fired by the new proprietor, J. Arthur Chandor.[76] Chandor then used the paper to hound Augustus, especially at the time of his prosecution for rape of a lady's maid in May 1893. Chandor paid the legal costs of the victim, and printed column after column of greasy, gloating accounts of the legal proceedings, along with a full-page "Chronological Epitome of Moore's Career," listing many of the sordid events from the previous fifteen years of that broken man's life. Those offended by GM who judged him the lowest of the low presumably never met his brother.

7

In spite of his falling out with Augustus, and then with Whistler and Degas, GM went right ahead with his plans for the Independent Theatre Society. First he had to locate "unconventional," "original," and "literary" plays worth producing. This took him to the door of Katherine Bradley and Edith Cooper, two women who wrote verse plays under the name "Michael Field"; they had been great devotees of Ruskin, and now were friends of Symons.[77] GM met the two-women author at Louis Chandler Moulton's "At Home" on 21 July 1890, and he was tickled by their tricks of identity:

> I daresay you saw I was much interested in you – my face . . . tells all my feeling better than my pen. I was sorry that Mrs. Moulton took me away (the observation is addressed to only one side of Michael Field), just as you kindly asked me to stay. I tried to get back, but Oscar Wilde was on one side and someone else was on the other side of Michael Field and – Forgive me my very obvious joking . . .[78]

It is a perfectly Nineties vignette: the double-lived Oscar Wilde – his friend Bunbury was away in the country – between the sides of a man who is two women, one of them very fetching. If only William Sharp was there (and he may well have been), who shared his soul with the lovely, passion-torn, yet nonexistent Celtic poet, Fiona Macleod, the possibilities of gender-splitting, interlacing sexualities would have been nearly complete. The "singularity of the talent" in "Michael Field" was what fascinated George Moore: did that secondary personality have the identity of a man, a man and a woman, a woman, or two women? He couldn't sort it out.[79] At Moulton's party, Moore praised

Michael Field's play *William Rufus*, and thought it a possibility for the Independent Theatre. The following Saturday, he went to visit the two women on his way to Dulwich Gallery (later, one of his favorite places of resort), and offered them advice about play construction. They found him the best conversationalist they had ever met, and they had met Wilde,[80] though a later description in their diary of GM at William Rothenstein's studio is not very appetising: "His smile is like sunshine on putty, his talk sticks to one with the intimate adhesiveness of the same material – it approaches the surface of one's personality softly and there it is, on one."[81] On 27 October 1893, the Independent Theatre Society would finally produce one of their plays, *A Question of Memory*.

To Edith Cooper, GM made an insightful confession. In writing one of his own dramatic scenes, he said, he had conceived of the situation quite perfectly, "but when I wanted words, they would not come."[82] He had admitted the same discovery about his limitations to Clara Lanza: "although I can sometimes describe a scene in a novel, I cannot write a scene in dialogue. Had it not been for the assistance of Arthur Kennedy, I never could have written 'The Strike at Arlingford.'"[83] Not to be able to write dialogue is a significant drawback for a playwright, yet GM persisted in trying to write a success for the stage throughout his life.

The shortcoming did not prevent him from being a capable critic, plot constructor, and script-doctor of plays for which others supplied the words. When the Independent Theatre project was getting underway, Moore wrote to William Archer: "You and I will have to decide what plays are to be done. That will be all."[84] However, GM did a good deal more than that: he wrote letters to potential subscribers, took a hand in stage management, doctored Teixeira de Mattos's translations of Zola's *Thérèse Raquin* (Royalty Theatre, 9 October 1891), reconstructed Symons's dramatisation of Frank Harris's story, "The Minister's Call," censored Archer's translation of Brandes's *The Visit*, proposed to John Gray that he translate Banville's *The Kiss* (Avenue Theatre, 4 March 1892), and recruited actors. J. T. Grein was admittedly more than the titular head of the Society – he also took care of the business end and the legwork – but GM was the driving force for the first years of the Independent Theatre Society. Yet there was a question as to whether he could write a play on his own.[85]

While the Independent Theatre Society was awaiting the arrival of new English playwrights (Shaw – the only great talent discovered – would make his first appearance as an Independent Theatre Society playwright with *Widowers' Houses* on 9 December 1892), GM and William Archer set up a program of foreign dramas, like Zola's *Thérèse Raquin* and, spectacularly for the Society's first production, Ibsen's *Ghosts* (Royalty Theatre, 13 March 1891). For *Ghosts*, there was an audience of 175 subscribers, including Meredith, Hardy, Pinero, Shaw, Archer, and Henry Arthur Jones, an overflow of single-ticket buyers, and a small army of dramatic critics. Nearly as many newspaper reviews were published as there had been spectators – 500 reviews and articles, most of them vilifications of the author, the play, and the audience – "long-haired, soft-hatted, villainous or sickly-looking socialists, well-known propagandists of atheism" accompanied by "spectacled, green-complexioned, oddly dressed females of unhealthy aspect" (from the *Licensed Victuallers' Mirror*).[86] Augustus Moore was less funny but just as vicious in the *Hawk*; Clement Scott, writing in many papers, behaved as if he had seen the Antichrist. Since Zola, no artist had been able to drive the English into hysteria like Ibsen.

It took Moore some months to launch his counterattack. The *Pall Mall Gazette* published his two-part article "Our Dramatic Critics" on 9 and 10 September. The first, witty, and ungrammatical sentence establishes the key in which the whole essay is conducted: "Like a waiter, the equipment of a dramatic critic is a suit of dressclothes."[87] GM had been around Augustus Moore and the staff at the *Bat* enough to know the life of the drama critic inside and out; indeed the way of life throughout "mummerland" was familiar to him: "a land of eating, drinking, idleness, and cigarettes, a land flowing with champagne, rustling with skirts." He describes the visit of the critic to the pretty villa owned by an actress, a woman "peculiarly suited to a teagown," "photographs of her in all positions . . . she explains them . . . and the critic finds her tale of successes more interesting than the actors'." The article is devastatingly funny.

While GM meant to get his own back on Augustus Moore and Clement Scott for their brutalisation of *Ghosts*, he unintentionally ruffled the pride of his close friend and colleague, William Archer. In the November *Fortnightly*, Archer, a Scotsman, declared that no one had ever tried to buy his goodwill, and he was not to be influenced by afternoon teas with pretty actresses.[88] In fact, Archer had been spooning with Elizabeth Robins all through the recent months, and had then praised her acting; furthermore, she was only the most recent of his infatuations. George Bernard Shaw knew all about Archer's amours, and on 7 November, Shaw twitted Archer for being hypocritical in his *Fortnightly* article.[89] "How if I were to tell the world," Shaw threatened, "that I have hardly once dropped in on you unexpectedly at Queen Square without disturbing a *tête-à-tête* between you and some pretty actress or another . . ." Shaw then suggested that Elizabeth Robins herself write a *Fortnightly* article with the *Hawk*-like title: "How to Get at William Archer, By One Who Has Done It."[90]

Archer's anger at Moore for "Our Dramatic Critics" was nothing compared with that of others, who continued to write letters to the *Pall Mall Gazette* throughout September. The most cunning stroke of revenge upon GM for his assaults on English actors, playwrights, and critics came about when the *Pelican* interviewed playwright and critic G. R. Sims in its "Notable Pressman" series on 27 February 1892. Sims admitted to being a conventional playwright himself, but said he still supported the Independent Theatre Society. He would just like to see it do what it was supposed to do, and produce "unconventional plays by English authors," "not translations of foreign failures." He would give the Society £100 if George Moore himself would produce an original play of his own invention. The *Pelican* reporter then hotfooted it to 8 King's Bench Walk to ask if GM would accept this generous offer. At first ruffled, GM soon accepted the challenge – after all, he had a manuscript of the four-act *Strike at Arlingford* in his desk – though he was very careful to define what he understood by "original" (not a translation) and "unconventional" (psychological in approach, uncommercial in its handling), so that his play could possibly pass muster.[91] He promised to get to the matter (he wanted to rewrite *Strike* as a three-act drama) as soon as he had completed the book he was writing. Meanwhile, the critics of London sharpened their pens.

8

Moore was a courageous person, but his courage was not inconsistent with terror. Even beyond "Our Dramatic Critics" and other "manslaughterly" articles, he had set up an impossible situation for himself by means of *Vain Fortune*, a novel he had recently serialised. After *Mike Fletcher*, he was having trouble finding a publisher for his fiction, so he agreed to write the novel with Ella Hepworth Dixon for *Lady's Pictorial* (Arnold Bennett's employer) under a pseudonym, "Lady Rhone," and on the sworn promise that it would contain nothing offensive.[92] Dixon fell ill, and Moore then became the sole author. The theme of the story was something much on his mind: "Is not an insufficient talent the most cruel of temptations?"[93] He worried to his brother Maurice, "I have the sentiment of great work, but I cannot produce it."[94] The novel made public Moore's private terror when facing the challenge from G. R. Sims to write an original play of unusual literary merit.

Vain Fortune tells the story of Hubert Price, a playwright living in the Temple whose career had begun with *Divorce*, a drama in a new psychologically complex mode that succeeded in spite of attacks from critics who feared that Price meant to reform the stage. Hoping to make a masterpiece of his second play, *The Gypsy*, Price suffers writer's block. His days are spent trying to make a little money by turning out imbecile journalism. The actor-manager Montague Ford (who is based on Beerbohm Tree) decides to encourage Price with a new production of *Divorce*, although the great critic Stiggins (modeled on Clement Scott) deplores the idea – there should be no unhappy endings on the English stage, and also no science, darkness, or novelty. Montague Ford has trouble locating Price. He has sunk to living from slum to slum on the Tottenham Court Road, without any money, and still stuck on his fourth act; suicide seems to him his best course of action. At last, Ford locates him, *Divorce* is restaged, but though it is fairly successful, Price realises it is only the work of a "half genius": "he had not the strength to write the *chef d'oeuvre* which nature in perverse cruelty had permitted him to see dimly."[95]

The plot takes a surprising turn when Price receives a letter from a solicitor, explaining that an uncle had disinherited his young ward, Emily Watson, for refusing to marry him, and then had died, leaving everything to Price. Freed from poverty, Price graciously settles money on Emily, allows her to stay in the country house, and moves in with her and her governess, Mrs Bentley. Emily is developed as a neurotic, jealous, adolescent girl, somewhat, GM fancied, on the pattern of Amy Levy, a talented poet who had recently killed herself. Emily falls in love with Price in spite of his indifference to her febrile charms. What's worse is that Emily is distressed by the fact that Price spends a lot of time talking with Mrs Bentley about his play; to *her* charms he's not indifferent. Both Mrs Bentley and Price "humor" the girl by denying their mutual attachment, until they suddenly elope together. While in a London hotel, contemplating going to bed (Joyce borrowed the scene to conclude "The Dead"), they learn that Emily has committed suicide, and a pall is cast over the possibility of even marital happiness for the failed genius Price.

There are good things in the novel – there are good things even in GM's worst books – but *Vain Fortune* is more a symptom than a success. It has ripping satire on theater critics; a good portrait of Emily; a new scenic form of presentation, as if it had been half envisioned as a stage piece; and a great deal of anguish about creative sterility – odd, in that Moore had written in the previous months some of the best prose he would write in his whole life, the periodical writings that later went into *Memoirs of My Dead Life*, *Impressions and Opinions*, and *Modern Painting*, but perfectly understandable in light of the failure of *Mike Fletcher* and Moore's dread of an even more humiliating failure with *The Strike at Arlingford*. In spite of the shortcomings of *Vain Fortune* – not remedied by two rapidly produced new versions of the narrative for the American and then English volumes – Moore was initially pleased just to have written a book no one attacked.[96]

The story had one very sincere admirer, and her affection for its author must have done something to restore Moore's confidence. Ada Leverson possibly became acquainted with the author of *Vain Fortune* through her friend Julia Davis Frankau (Frankau joined GM on the Committee for the Independent Theatre Society).[97] Ada was the witty, twenty-nine-year-old wife of Ernest Leverson, forty-one-year-old son of a diamond merchant.[98] Following her relationship with Moore, Ada would become a close friend of Oscar Wilde, who called her "The Sphinx"; she stood by Wilde during his time of trial when few others did. By the time of the final 17 October serial of *Vain Fortune*, the relationship between Ada Leverson and George Moore was well begun. She then wrote him to "tell how utterly enraptured I am with your last chapter in *Lady's Pictorial*."[99] There was enough arrant flattery in the letter to cause GM to pay a Sunday visit to the wife of Ernest Leverson. GM paid court to Ada by asking about her own spare-time literary activities. While Leverson aspired to be a writer, she had not yet published. He asked to read her work, and, writing again to "Dear Mr. Moore," she sent him a "little paper."[100] She had, she admitted, been thinking of him constantly – couldn't he visit again soon? What is possibly the next in the undated series of letters is addressed to "My dearest." She is desperate: a family sojourn in the country will separate her from him for some time. "I adore you," she pleads. Another letter to "Darling" George Moore followed a dangerous visit to his rooms in the Temple. Could he still care for her after that day? When she closed her eyes, she would still "see you, & . . . hear your voice of reasonable persuasion & feel your enervating kisses & your sympathetic hands." That letter begins with an appreciation of a manuscript chapter from the American revision of *Vain Fortune* written in late December 1891, and ends with a response to GM's advice about her three-part story. Now this was the sort of relationship that was perfect for GM – love sandwiched in literature. GM wanted to parade around with Ada Leverson at the Earls Court Exhibition. She was naturally afraid of being found out by her husband or brothers-in-law, and preferred to meet in the darkness of Madame Tussaud's: "ghastly and fantastic . . . but safe."

In early 1892, Leverson began to publish in *Punch* and *Black and White* the smart, brisk little stories on which she had been working with GM.[101] It has been said that the catalyst for her becoming an author was Oscar Wilde, later the dearest friend of "the Sphinx," but in fact it was George Moore who first encouraged her, as she encouraged him.[102] All he needed was a student to make him feel like a teacher, and that student's complete love to make him feel like a man. It must have made him well again to read, "Darling, you cannot think how fondly I love you. You have always been most sweet & good to me. You are a perfect & ideal lover." How their relationship ended is unknown. She frequently spoke of her fear of scandal. He never exposed her in any way in his subsequent amorous writings (possibly a sign of respect for one of the wittiest women in London), but he did ignore her frequent requests to "burn this letter." At the end of the affair, he tied her letters up in a little packet and stored them in his escritoire.

Another encouragement to GM was the reception of his collection of essays, *Impressions and Opinions*. Initially, Moore could hardly find a publisher for the book. Edmund Downey, publisher of *Mike Fletcher*, turned it down, as other publishers must have done too before GM arrived at the bookshop of A. T. Nutt, who occasionally issued a book.[103] Although poorly printed and designed, the volume was respectfully noticed in the press. The *Speaker* pointed out that the essays were not English essays, which ought to be "gossipy, familiar, full of amenity, slightly provincial"; instead they were, like French essays, "urbane, colder in feeling, more deft in structure . . . and slightly pedantic." Like other reviews, the *Speaker* regretted GM's "lack of restraint" in going for "personalities," especially in "Mummer Worship."[104] In the *Academy*, Symons declared it was the most interesting such book since Pater's *Appreciations*, an impressive-sounding compliment, but *Appreciations* was published little more than a year earlier.[105] The review that really turned GM's head, the one he sent to his mother, was the review in the *Athenaeum*.[106] It noted that he tended to use "therefore" as just "a superfluous introduction to another dogmatic canon less self-evident than the former"; still, GM's dogmatically delivered intuitions were "acute and brilliant." Finally, the *Athenaeum* reviewer recognised George Moore as a writer who "should put away all that is less [than] worthy of an eminent career."[107] That sentence, and the fact that the *Athenaeum* gave him the lead article, went home to Moore. He should, he realised, think of himself as a man of achievement, not someone like Hubert Price in *Vain Fortune* for whom success might have been imagined, though it never had and never would come to pass. The reviews sometimes concluded, painfully, that GM was a better essayist than a novelist, but GM was recharged with courage: "I shall disabuse them of that idea presently. There is more in me than they think."[108]

But whether there was a good play in Moore remained an open question. After Beerbohm Tree rejected *The Strike at Arlingford* in November 1890, GM put the play away until Sims's challenge caused him to take it out again.[109] By December 1892, having been pestered for months by needling advice in the theater press to get on with taking up the challenge, he was back at work on recasting the four-act play into three acts.[110] He quickly ran into trouble with the dialogue, as he expressed in his mephitic colloquial manner: "You can't fart higher than your arse, that I know." By January 1893, he was courting Elizabeth Robins to star in the play as the sexy, manipulative Lady Anne; Janet Achurch he had in mind for the pure-hearted proletarian heroine, Ellen Sands. If he could get this cast, he would have the two best Ibsenite actresses in London for his play, and the acting could carry the script.[111]

Robins, however, told him frankly she had no great interest in his play.[112] He wheedled and flattered her – it disgusted him that it was necessary for authors to beg for help from actors, but he did it. She allowed him to come and read the first two acts of the play to her on Sunday, 15 January 1893 (he had not written Act III yet), and she then submitted to his persuasions. But on Tuesday, 17 January she changed her mind again, saying she preferred to take the part of Hilda in *The Master-Builder*, as translated by William Archer, her intimate friend, and about to be published by a second suitor, William Heinemann.[113] Archer was feeding her the proofs of Ibsen's play slip by slip, at the same time that GM was hectoring her with his own needs.[114] It was maddening for Moore – he was boxed out in a love triangle. If he could not get the right cast before 21 February, the date set for the performance, and the descent of hundreds of London critics like birds of prey in black, he was ruined. He begged her to allow him to send the last act, finished by Thursday, 19 January. He tried to bait Robins with jealousy by saying that if she would not do it, what would she think of Janet Achurch in the flashy, histrionic part of Lady Anne? When Robins wavered and said she might just do it after all, Moore offered to drop Achurch from the cast altogether, because the play did not "want two good-looking women."[115] He was struggling mightily with the vanity of a fairy sprite, and he lost the fight. By the time Robins had read the last proof-slip of Archer's translation of *The Master-Builder*, she had "fallen in love with it," and with its translator: psychologically, she was playing Hilda to Archer's Solness. On 26 January, Moore wrote in despair to his close friend Lena Milman, "I don't know what I shall do. Tomorrow morning I am going to see your friend Miss Achurch." But what did it matter? He had just read *The Wild Duck*, and Ibsen's dramatic genius had, Moore said, "taken all the conceit out of me."[116]

The Strike at Arlingford went on as scheduled on 21 February 1893 at the Opéra-Comique, a day after Elizabeth Robins performed in *The Master-Builder* and during the run of Wilde's *A Woman of No Importance* at the Haymarket – tough competition on both sides. The failure to find the best cast took its toll on Moore's play, as many reviewers admitted. Archer claimed to see through the bad acting into "the large simplicity of great drama," but one suspects he was standing by a friend, toward whom he felt guilty after robbing GM of the appropriate actress for *Strike*. Archer went as far in recompense as to say that Moore's play was better than Shaw's *Widowers' Houses*, even though Moore's economic analysis of the labor situation did not meet Fabian standards.[117] Shaw himself hated *Strike* as an encroachment on his turf, and wrote GM "to warn him that his sociology is not what it might be."[118] GM had worse things to hear from critics who were not on the side of the realistic drama. Those persons whose only equipment was a tuxedo had a proper feast on the fact that *Strike* was neither very literary nor very original, the key terms of Sims's challenge.[119]

Moore tried to invigorate the play before its publication (June 1893), rewriting it again and again in proofs, hoping to snatch a book victory from the jaws of a stage defeat. For all his efforts, it remained a tame treatment of the Edward Aveling and Eleanor Marx relationship, so palely reflected as to be almost unrecognisable. John Reid, a golden-tongued orator and an intellectual in the vanguard of the proletariat, is the Aveling figure; his sweetheart, Ellen Sands, an idealistic daughter of the people, evokes Eleanor Marx. As representative of a miners' union, Reid is brought face to face with Lady Anne, the mine-owner. They had met, and romanced one another, at an earlier time – when he was eighteen years old, Reid had been her father's secretary. Then, he was a gentleman; now, in Lady Anne's view, he simply pretends to be a worker. Lady Anne is in league with a capitalist, Baron Steinbach, who is organising all mine-owners against the unionised workers. Ellen Sands persuades Reid to turn the workers against the deal offered by the capitalist syndicate. Then Lady Anne takes Reid for a walk.

By Act II, Steinbach has checked the books of Lady Anne's mine. In fact, she cannot afford to meet the workers' demands and still run the mine. Steinbach proposes to her that they show Reid the books: he's an educated man and can see that the union would be killing the goose that lays the golden eggs. But she believes that her own approach, sexual intrigue, will be necessary as well. In a tête-à-tête with Lady Anne, John Reid explains that the break-up of their youthful romance taught him the meaning of class difference; then, through Ellen Sands, he found something to live for – leadership of the ragged army of the poor. Following this scene is an answering tête-à-tête between Steinbach and a journalist, in which Steinbach defends capitalism against the sentimental alternative of socialism. It is the best scene in the play. Capitalism, Steinbach says, is founded on three things society calls virtues, and three it calls vices: thrift, industry, and forethought are the virtues; and greed, gambling, and the craving to be best are the vices. "Do you think," he asks, "that a system founded on six instincts inherited from the beginning of time can be overthrown?" According to Steinbach, "the misery of man is incurable . . . Misery and vice are antecedent to capital; they exist because Nature believes them essential in her design."[120] One can see why the Fabian propagandist Shaw hated the play.

It is a pity that a character as good as Steinbach is wasted on a play with a sometimes clunky plot and often stagy dialogue. The denouement sees John Reid breaking troth with Ellen Sands, and submitting to the temptation of Lady Anne. His faith is lost in another way too: he knows that the strikers' demands are unreasonable and ultimately self-destructive, and that communism is a failed philosophy. He goes out to persuade the angry mob to submit to terms, fails in his eloquence, and commits suicide, while Lady Anne makes off to Italy with Steinbach. GM could hardly understand, nor could Archer explain to him, why the play was so much inferior to the work of Wilde or Pinero. Finally, however, after he had given it his best, he acknowledged to Archer that "the play is wanting in mystery . . . it is a world without air."[121]

9

By the time he was reworking the acting text of *Strike* for publication as a book, GM also had parts of *Esther Waters* ready to offer to monthlies and newspapers for serialisation. Even after the success of *Impressions and Opinions*, his market value as a novelist was poor: "No reasonable offer will be refused," he told his agent, W. M. Colles.[122] He still had "part four" to finish and a title to discover. "Mother and Child" had been the working title; in May he was thinking of "Traveller's Rest," the name of the pub where Esther after twenty years of wage-slavery finds a temporary home with her child and the child's father William Latch. "Esther Waters" probably did not come to him as a title until he realised the value of highlighting the contrast between his plain heroine and the fancifully named *Tess of the D'Urbervilles*.[123] So deeply was he buried in his novel through the spring and summer of 1893 that he cut his annual trip to Paris, though he hoped to be able to celebrate the book's conclusion with a trip to Bayreuth in August.[124] By July, he had finished Chapter 31, the great narrative version of William Frith's *Derby Day*.[125] Working "long, long hours" through the heat, he had William Latch in the Brompton Hospital on 20 August, dying of consumption, and hoping to save his family's bacon by one last great bet on a horse.[126] Esther Waters was indeed leading her author like a mother who has taken a child by the hand. He was writing so fast that the nib of his pen never left the page; new sheets were thrown on top of ones on which the ink was still wet.[127] The story in which he was caught up was all he could write about in letters to friends like Lena Milman, D. S. MacColl, and Gosse. In spite of his frenzy, he was wise enough to decide to hold the text back from publication until the following spring; he wanted to let it ripen, to mull it over – no more impetuous, torrid transfers of "copy" into hardbound volumes.[128]

The most telling of all Moore's letters about his intentions in the novel was sent to his brother, Maurice. He explained that he was making "one more effort, the most serious I have made yet, to do a book – you know what I mean, a real piece of literature":

The servant-girl is approaching completion. I think it is better than *A Mummer's Wife*. I have been writing on this book for nearly three years and am still in love with it. Is it possible I am mistaken? It is immensely long. It contains a description of the Derby, 30 or 40 pages – no racing, only the sweat and boom of the crowd – the great cockney holiday. The people I love and understand – the dull Saxon. Flesh of my flesh, bone of my bone – how I love that thick-witted race. I have a great literary project in view – I want to paint the portrait of the Saxon in his habit of instinctive hypocrisy. Pecksniff done seriously, and, if the feat does not seem impossible, with love. This extraordinary civilising agency – the Bible in one hand, the gin bottle in the other; the Cotton Factory behind him starting from the cricket field. Do you understand? A great project but one of enormous difficulty, I am afraid unrealizable. But dear me, is it not shocking – I cannot write to tell you that I long to see you without the spectre of literature grinning and barking all the while.[129]

Esther Waters is such an objective narrative – the author has put an iron bit in his own mouth and kept the reins tight throughout – that a reader could hardly have intuited the guileful intentions of the author without a letter like this one.[130] Though a very English book (with a disciplined, French finish), the English people in it are seen externally, from an Irish point of view, as "dull Saxons," "the hypocrites of the world" – "Pecksniff done seriously," not as Dickens did him in *Martin Chuzzlewit*. In spite of both seeing and seeing through the Saxon as only an Irish writer can do, Moore communicated as well both his humorous appreciation and his serious respect for the qualities of the English, with whom he knew he shared, as an Anglo-Irishman, a bond that was more than cultural; the English were both alien and "bone of his bone." By keeping this complex of perspectives undeclared within his novel, by becoming an invisible and impersonal narrator, GM managed to introduce into the canon of English novels a very deep critique of that Protestant hypocrisy that had for so long infuriated him, along with a fair-minded rendering of what was dear to him in the same religious tradition. He must have savored the fact that three chapters of his novel were going to be serialised in the *Pall Mall Gazette* – even editor W. T. Stead would not realise the ways in which he was being had.

10

While *Esther Waters* was going through press (much revised on the proofs by GM), Moore's relationship with Lena Milman was coming to a climax of irritation. Moore had known Milman (1863–1914) before his affair with Ada Leverson, indeed since he first moved into King's Bench Walk in the spring of 1889. The friend he enjoyed in common with Edward Martyn, William Nevill Geary, had introduced GM to this only child of Lt.-Gen. George Bryan Milman, Commandant of the Tower of London since 1870. As Geary recalled, she "lived in a large room overlooking 'the Pool.' She and I had ridden and danced together, but she had refused to marry me. She was a lady of singular charm and distinction and highly educated. She asked me to bring to the Tower Moore who was then rising to fame. He came and they made friends at once."[131] After their first meeting, Moore, evidently concerned for the good opinion of the lady in the Tower, sent her a copy of the new edition of *Confessions of a Young Man* with the proviso that she should understand he did not, and no sane person could, believe all the things he wrote in his books.[132] As the years passed, she would invite him to tea upon her returns to London from frequent travels, and she introduced him to friends of hers, such as the novelist Florence Henniker (1855–1923), sister of Lord Houghton, Lord Lieutenant of Ireland.[133]

In early 1893, GM's relationship to Milman began to heat up, at least from his side. Geary thought Moore was caught up in one of the most serious affairs of his life, though "neither were 'in love.'"[134] In love or not, GM was pressing his suit, taking Milman to galleries, plays, and Temple balls, in addition to their regular meetings for tea in the Tower, but he was never certain of where he stood. Returning from the Tower, he worried, Had he stayed too long? Might he ask her to go out of town with him?[135] She sometimes accused him of being cross, but he was only sulking after being thwarted in an attempt at some mild intimacy.[136] He tried to get over to Paris for a meeting in May 1893, but she left that city early without notice, and he was bitterly disappointed: "Really I think you might have written."[137] In May 1893 *Modern Painting* was published, and she was indignant with him for saying in "Sex in Art" that women did not often paint or write works of genius, because they couldn't transcend shame. They would never dare to make a full sexual confession (perhaps appropriate to Milman's own case). GM dodged her anger by saying the article "was only written to tease . . . the *Westminster Gazette* and that lot who tease me by saying women would make better policemen than men."[138] Miss Milman then headed off to Dublin for a stay with Florence Henniker and Lord Houghton in the Vice-Regal Lodge in Phoenix Park; among the party was GM's rival, Thomas Hardy.[139]

When on her return Milman talked of her admiration for Hardy, Moore was deeply wounded. Hardy's *Tess of the D'Urbervilles*, the sensational novel of 1891, was just a "bundle of anecdotes ununited by a philosophic idea, and therefore (to me) void of artistic interest."[140] Indeed, while writing *Esther Waters* that summer, he was involved in a passionate contestation of Hardy's tale. GM was also writing of an unwed mother, jilted by the father of her child, who later reencounters him as a suitor just when there is another man in her life. Moore, however, felt his book would be reality, not romance – no fantastical scenes of sleepwalking brides crossing bridges over rivers in spate. He would write Esther's confession to Fred Parsons (Chapter 23), knowing that Hardy hid the confession of *Tess* under the skirts of a summary.[141] Perhaps sensing GM's deep rivalry with Hardy, Milman seems to have subsequently kept rather quiet about the other lion in her drawing room.

In July, Moore wanted to make a declaration of love to Lena Milman, but he knew beforehand she would just find it "tiresome." Would she consider a trip with him to Folkestone?[142] In a chilly reply, she did not even take the trouble to refuse his suggestion. She was an enigma: attached to him, pleasant, interested in his affairs, but chilly and dissatisfied too. "You said that women have to pretend to be satisfied with the lives they lead. Your life seems about as pleasant as any I can imagine; the chains you wear are of your own forging. But then I know so little of you; notwithstanding study, you remain as enigmatic as ever. But I suppose when you are quite alone with your own thoughts, you give way. There are moments when life must appear to you arid and bitter and you then become as weak as another."[143] She did not like him to write to her in such intimately supposititious terms, and let a silence lapse between them, until GM had to write a make-up note, and he did so in a rather self-piteous way: "True that I might tell you how much I miss you, how I long to see you, but you do not encourage such confidences, so I refrain."[144]

GM was trying, and failing, to take his relationship with Milman to a new plateau. He got so impatient that, on a September visit to France, he had a passionate affair with a pretty eighteen-year-old heiress, as he confessed, or perhaps bragged, to his brother Maurice:

> I have had a most delicious love adventure . . . Generally my loves are mature but this one is a young girl of 18 – I think the most beautiful girl I ever saw in my life. Beauty generally doesn't fetch me, but this one did. What she could see in me to rave about I cannot think. I have been wondering ever since – a blasé roué like me, rotten with literature and art, to which Wagnerism has lately been added. Wagner's operas are now my great delight . . . my golden-haired siren is an heiress; she wanted me to marry her but I said that would be dishonourable, that I never went after a girl for her money. Only five days but when a lady is

amorous and the aunt is complacent or witless a good deal can be done. "J'ai rêvé dans la grotte où engage la sirène." That women may lose their virtue certainly makes life worth living.[145]

One cannot be sure if Robert Becker is right that the golden-haired teenage heiress was Maud Burke, later Lady Cunard, then seventeen years old and traveling in Europe not with an aunt, but with her complacent mother. It would be strange, however, if GM could not distinguish, even after only five days, between a mother and an aunt.

While GM was away, unknown to him Thomas Hardy was rapidly gaining ground on the outside in the pursuit of Miss Milman. After her return from Dublin, Milman was seeing Hardy now and then through the summer. On 4 September he sent her his photograph at her request, and, after many requests from Hardy, she sent him her own portrait (very pretty, he coquetted, but he preferred the original). Hardy was aware of the race he was running. On 9 November, he admitted to her, "I feel rather jealous of George M!" [146] He need not have worried. GM was getting quite fed up with Milman as a love prospect. She had told him that "nothing seems more despicable than following one's inclinations." How utterly wrong, from GM's point of view! "If one does not follow one's inclinations, the result seems to me to be complete sterilization. It is only those who are wanting in strength who do not follow their – will you allow me to substitute the word *instincts*? . . . All my sympathies are with the instincts and their development. Instinct alone shall lead us aright."[147]

They continued their relationship, unhappily stalled for GM, happily so for Milman. As usual, Moore got the woman in his life to start writing. Since Milman knew Russian, he wanted her to translate Dostoevsky and Turgenev.[148] By promising to revise the text and write an introduction, he succeeded in getting Milman a contract from Bodley Head to put Dostoevsky's *Poor Folk* into English, the beginning of her career as a writer. She continued to see Hardy, and Moore continued to abuse *Tess of the D'Urbervilles*. In December, she finally insisted that he never speak of Hardy's book again.[149] It was a promise he made but could not keep.

I I

After handing over the corrected proofs of *Esther Waters* to the printer, Moore went to Paris to spend Christmas with the family of his new friends, William and Sybil Eden. Before his departure, he had been speaking with Arthur Symons in the Temple of an unknown correspondent, John Oliver Hobbes, who some months earlier had asked Moore's opinion of whether Hobbes's novel, *Some Emotions and a Moral* (1891), would make a good play.[150] John Oliver Hobbes, Symons informed him in December, was the pen-name of a very beautiful American heiress, Pearl Craigie (1867–1906). Earlier, GM had written John Oliver Hobbes that his story would not make any kind of play at all; now, he wrote a second time to Pearl Craigie a letter full of the warmest interest in her.[151] She invited Moore to the family mansion at 56 Lancaster Gate, just across from Hyde Park. At first, she looked a little dowdy to him, but as they talked of a play they might write together, she proved so witty that he felt "almost an idiot" by comparison.[152] In London, it was said she was the only rival to Wilde in the making of epigrams, and her appearance improved considerably in his eyes as he listened to her talk.[153] She wrote him almost daily asking him to call, and he began to spend many hours at Lancaster Gate. He was fast falling in love. This seemed to be a woman with all the grace and intelligence of Milman, but with a lot more eagerness to press forward into passion than the lady in the Tower. True, Pearl Craigie hinted in the beginning that "sex relations did not appeal to her," but GM reasoned, "such hints are so common among women that one attaches no real significance to them."[154] In fact, Pearl loved to talk of sex; all her books were about flirtations; she was an artist of the teasing allusion. Why would she entice, if to no end?

Moore should have done more research on "John Oliver Hobbes" after hearing from Symons that this author was a rich and beautiful woman. She was indeed rich. Her father was John Morgan Richards, a Yankee who had made a massive fortune by selling Carter's Little Liver Pills to the British as a cure for whatever ailed them; he was the first in Britain to use picture-posters to sell such an article of trade.[155] Her mother was a bit of an embarrassment to her daughter: Mrs Richards talked to unseen Prophets of the Bible while visitors were present, and once dispatched a telegram to Rome reading: "Pope, Vatican . . . Stop War. Richards."[156] She had a large placard on a wall inside the mansion that read: "What would Jesus say?" One can picture Henry James staring at this sign with a furrow in his great-domed brow, while Pearl came into the room in a teagown, and hurriedly said, "Oh, that's just mother's."[157]

An only child, Pearl received an excellent education, including the study of Greek and medieval literature at University College London. She made, however, a big mistake in 1887: she married Reginald Craigie, a handsome, hard-drinking diner-out of the sort the *Bat* and *Hawk* were written for. He was wealthy, vulgar, and syphilitic. In May 1891, he left her with a son John, bruises, and possibly a case of venereal disease. She went home to the family mansion in Lancaster Gate. After her separation from Reginald Craigie, Pearl began to move toward high-class Brompton Oratory Catholicism, and away from her parents' Yankee Protestantism. Retreats to a suburban convent enabled her to cope with guilt, nervousness, and despair. When she emerged from seclusion, it would be to a rapid round of social engagements at the edge of royal circles, occasionally passing through the more fashionable artistic spheres of Gosse, Hardy, and James (who may have used Pearl as a model for Milly Theale, heroine of *Wings of the Dove*). Max Beerbohm described Pearl Craigie as "The pretty and pleasant little woman of the 1890s [who] was of all climbers the grimmest, of all wire-pullers the most indefatigable and undiscourageable, and of all ladies who ever put pen to paper the most brazenly conceited."[158] She thought herself a better novelist than George Eliot, and miles superior to the standard "New Woman" writers of her era, such as Mona Caird, George Egerton, and Gertrude Atherton.[159] Craigie herself was opposed to women's liberation. The fashion reporter for the *Queen* was welcome at Craigie's musical "At Homes" (Pearl was a talented pianist). This was a woman on the make in social and literary London, not hesitant about using her charms, but only up to a point. Natural frigidity (as she thought), a wretched marriage, a weak heart, a sexually transmitted disease, social ambition, and religious devotion all came between her and the adulterous bed.

GM had very little idea of what he was up against when "J. O. H. Craigie" asked him to come for a *séance de collaboration* at 56 Lancaster Gate on 6 January. On the 11th, she invited him to a dinner on the 31st, where he could meet the family, and Reverend J. E. C. Welldon, headmaster of Harrow, whom she was sure GM would like. (In fact, Moore hated Welldon, an NVA supporter who as recently as October 1893 had been attacking Zola and old Vizetelly.)[160] More fetchingly, Craigie, having read *Esther Waters* in proof, said that it was "extraordinarily beautiful and will never lose its fascination (I do not say this because you are a man and I am a woman and I like you, for I have no manners and false compliments choke me)."[161] After months of chilliness from Lena Milman, this candid expression of warmth looked very promising to Moore. A week later Craigie sent him tickets to a box for the Saturday night performance of *Twelfth Night* at the Haymarket, so she was ready and willing to be seen in public with George Moore. GM was still rather a scandalous figure, but he was also the celebrity author of *Modern Painting* and a director of the advanced and fashionable Independent Theatre Society.[162] After the play, GM stayed for two hours with Craigie at Lancaster Gate, and then, accustomed to Milman, feared he had overstayed his welcome. Craigie wrote to reassure him: "Please never stay less than two hours!"[163] She made a date to go with Moore, then the *Speaker*'s art critic, to the Grafton Gallery the next day (Thursday, 25 January 1894), where, while looking at pictures by Whistler, Alfred Stevens, and Albert Moore, they ran into Lena Milman.[164] Craigie was merciless in her description to GM of her rival: "I am trying to remember when I met some of the Milmans. The poor nervous little soul I spoke to yesterday I have never seen before in my life, and she in love?" GM later recalled the moment with pain. Only Rousseau, the great confessionalist, could relate . . .

> how an old friend seeing us walking in a picture gallery had recognised [Pearl] at sight as her enemy and turned faint. Jean Jacques' pen would reveal more than a simple aspect of the subject, and I do not doubt he would interpret the exquisite relish with which [Pearl] enjoyed the pain she had given, and the pleasure it was to include in the letter she addressed to me the same evening . . . : "Is your friend in love?" I think I hated [Pearl] for a moment, for I knew the woman she spoke of slightingly to be a true friend, and when I asked her what she thought of [Pearl] she said, "A mean little mind, with a taste for intrigue."[165]

But GM could not break with a beautiful witty woman who seemed to love him in favor of a wiser one who did not, and Lena Milman anyway was just then leaving London for four months.[166] On that day Pearl gushingly thanked GM for his photograph: "You must tell me where to hang it, and how often I am to think of you when I look at it. That to me is the choicest of presents." This piece of hot flirtation was deleted from the published version of the letter in her father's biography of Pearl, a general whitewash of her sexual come-on to Moore, and one that has slanted biographical accounts of the relationship. The petting, the tendernesses, the compliments – "what a marvellous book [*Esther Waters* is] . . . immeasurably greater than the stroke of any present-day writer" – dizzyingly inflated his ego, and saved the vain man from having to keep it inflated himself.[167] She knelt before him; she exalted him: "You were so perfectly right about the comedy [they were writing together], and I was so perfectly wrong . . . I have such a primitive instinct about the superiority of the masculine intellect that I could make mistakes all day for the mere pleasure of being corrected! Is this weak? I hope not." She troweled it on so thick one may regret both that GM liked it and that he did not suspect its sincerity.

Through February, they worked together on their play, *The Fool's Hour*; they went to concerts by Arnold Dolmetsch in Dulwich (which gave GM an idea for a new novel, *Evelyn Innes*);[168] they met in galleries; they dined out; they saw *The Land of Heart's Desire* in April at the Avenue Theatre, with author W. B. Yeats striding back and forth in the dress circle wearing a black cloak and sombrero;[169] they traveled in closed coaches; they socialised with Henry Harland, Aubrey Beardsley, Arthur Symons, and the new *Yellow Book* set (which was to publish Act I of *The Fool's Hour* in its inaugural April edition); they attended the famous *Yellow Book* dinner at the Hotel d'Italia on 15 April (and chatted with Olivia Shakespeare, later Yeats's mistress).[170] Craigie wrote Moore nearly every other day – fifty-five letters survive from January to May 1894 – usually inviting him to visit or go out with her. The temperature of her salutations rises day by day:

"Dear Mr. Moore . . . Yours affectionately" (6 February);
   "My dear George . . . I wish I did not like you so much, Pearl" (7? February);
   "Dearest . . . Yours affectionately" (12 February);
   "Dearest . . . O, to be an unconscious sinner for five and twenty minutes; I miss you, Good-night, Yours affectionately, Pearl" (14 February);
   "Dearest . . . Men as men can be so repulsive – and women too, I know – but you are nice; Yours always affectionately, Pearl" (15 February);
   "Dearest . . . I dare not warn you how long it takes me to dress; Fate and your Guardian Angel must deal with that question; Always, dearest, yours affectionately, Pearl" (18 February).

While writing from a safe distance in Paris, Craigie led GM up this staircase of intimacies to hints of the marital bedchamber. Upon her return to London, she began to balk: she was, she said, "fearful of [her] own best impulses." "My thoughts are too mature for my body." "I talk about things I do not believe in to people who do not believe me." This strange confession of self-division and self-distrust came on 8 March from one who still signed herself, "always yours, dearest, affectionately." She hinted that she was going into a nervous collapse.[171] Yet still they met daily, or almost daily, for work on their play.

In late March or early April, *The Fool's Hour* ran aground on Act III. One day while walking with Moore in Hyde Park, Pearl said that her close friend, Ellen Terry, "'would like to play in a one-act comedy'"; could GM suggest a subject?[172] Moore, eager to tie Craigie to him by means of another collaboration, rapidly borrowed a plot from a French comedy, and, telling her of its origin, drafted a scenario and rough dialogue for *Journeys End in Lovers Meeting*. Pearl then embellished the dialogue with her epigrams and flirtatious phrasings.[173] GM thought things were going well again.

12

In Moore's experience, success in love both fed and fed upon success in literature. The confidence necessary to write came from the affection of intelligent women, to whom he always told his novels before he wrote them; and the still greater confidence necessary to offer himself as an object of physical affection, so strangely made as he felt himself to be, came from times of success as a writer. All the stars were favorable for art and love in the March and April of 1894. The first reviews of *Esther Waters* were terrific: in the *Daily Chronicle* Lionel Johnson (another Temple dweller) described Moore, on the basis of his new novel, as "among the half-dozen living novelists of whom the historian of British literature will have to take account."[174] GM's greatest triumph came in the *Speaker*, where Arthur Quiller-Couch (somewhat coached by Moore), made an extended comparison of *Esther Waters* with *Tess of the D'Urbervilles*, and concluded that Moore's story was more heroic, probable, philosophical, and sane than Hardy's great novel.[175] The sentiment was widely and rapidly copied in other reviews, even in America: *Esther Waters*, the *New York Times* reported on the front page, was "a genuinely great book," "a bigger work than Hardy's *Tess of the D'Urbervilles*."[176] Neither Hardy nor Moore perhaps ever received a review that made a greater impression than Quiller-Couch's of *Esther Waters* – bitter for one, sweet to the other.

Best of all, on 7 April 1894, right on the heels of these laudatory reviews, W. H. Smith banned *Esther Waters*. Indignation spread through the columns of newspapers. Moore had "photographed nothing unnecessary to the telling of a sad rather than a sordid story." Indeed, "the anti-gambling societies should circulate the book by the thousands." "Esther Waters' Homes for Girl Mothers" were to be set up. GM had written a reformist tract, it was held, "with not a note of cynicism in it." The great English race is treated by Moore "with a reverent sympathy."[177] Even the *Athenaeum*, while complaining that a proper

English novel should be more humorous and less serious, orchestrated, and unified than *Esther Waters*, allowed that it was an "eminently moral" book which should not have been banned.[178] Moore must have had a grim laugh over the fact that his book should have been both attacked and defended in moral terms. Could a book be great, the debate went, that showed a woman "living with a man without benefit of marriage"? Was it right for an author to give a picture of a lying-in hospital?[179] One minister said he would not recommend *Esther Waters* to his parishioners, and thanked W. H. Smith for keeping it off the railway bookstalls.

Moore had no moral intention; his intention was to write a great novel, and one illustrating the Schopenhauerian theme that the life-instinct overrules all other proprieties and moralities. More than in any previous narrative, he kept himself and his score-settling reflections on his friends and enemies out of the story – though certainly there are "studies" of his acquaintances (Mrs Barfield is evocative of Mrs Bridger and Mrs Moore; Esther is a wet-nurse for a society woman something like Julia Davis Frankau and then becomes the servant of a kindly authoress resembling Lena Milman, but Moore dropped from the manuscript his own persona, Mr Bryant).[180] On the whole, however, the novel is written with unique restraint: the narrative is meant itself to do the work of analysis, commentary, and atmosphere. He hoped to be a pen through which life would tell its story.

The life-instinct, the drive to survive and perpetuate the species, impels Esther Waters throughout her long circular life-journey from the Sussex country house of the Barfields and back again. In the upstairs/downstairs world of that house (half Moore Hall, half Buckingham House), the footman William Latch gets her pregnant, an event that forces the otherwise kindly Mrs Barfield to turn her out. Esther walks about looking for help in vast indifferent London. After lying in at a charity hospital, she rents herself out as a wet-nurse to a bourgeois society wife until Esther realises her own child is dying at a baby-farmer's (nineteenth-century "day-care center"). It is a question of a life for a life, her baby or the bourgeois baby, and Esther nobly tells her furious employer where to get off. Then after a few brutal, badly paid jobs as a house servant, she gets a safe post with a kindly authoress. Esther can then afford to foster her boy out to a good woman in the suburbs. Esther gets a chance to marry a man of no sex appeal, but a decent fellow who was one of the Plymouth Brethren like herself. While she considers marriage, William Latch comes accidentally into her life again. She is still properly furious at having been abandoned by him, but he has money, kindliness, and good looks, and she reckons that a boy should be with his own father and she should be with the man she loved according to the flesh, not the one to whom she is tied by religion and respect. She and William take over the Traveller's Rest, as much a quiet betting shop as a drinking nook. After a time there, their business suffers from police and evangelical harassment, so William has to become a tout again. Standing out of doors in all kinds of weather drags him down into sickness and death. Esther returns to Mrs Barfield and her Sussex house (by then the family estate has been ruined by horse-racing). With satisfaction, Esther Waters sees her now fully grown son join the Army and go off to risk his life for the Empire. The novel has one bright steel thread through it: Esther's heroic commitment to raise that son in spite of all odds, and the odds were great. It is a commitment that is instinctual, beautiful, and ennobling.

While GM intended his book to be neither moralistic nor demoralising, in the fight with W. H. Smith he gave a statement to the press that he "wrote *Esther Waters* in sincere love of humanity, out of a sincere wish to serve humanity." [181] Considering his effort to bring about in himself a change of heart as well as a change of style after *Mike Fletcher*, the statement had a weight of sincerity behind it. Yet still he was being abused by righteous English puritans. All his old anger about being blackballed by the circulating libraries ever since *A Modern Lover* came surging back in him. He went to see William Faux, reader for W. H. Smith. Everything about Faux was *faux*: "A tangle of dyed hair [that] covered a bald skull, and as he smiled, his false teeth threatened to jump out at me." Faux said that *Esther Waters* might very well be "good literature," but subscribers of W. H. Smith would be unaccustomed "to detailed descriptions of a lying-in hospital."[182] GM tried to argue but got nowhere. Then he went to an accountant and had a record drawn up to show how much money W. H. Smith and Co. had lost by banning his best-seller. This account he sent to the partners of the firm, with the remark that it was not good business "to ban books likely to be recommended by Gladstone" (as had been the case with *Esther Waters*). The monopoly of the fiction market formerly held by the two chief circulating libraries was collapsing anyway, with fewer and fewer three-decker novels being written, and more high-quality authors issuing their books in an affordable one-volume format. Once the partners had seen the balance-sheet drawn up by GM's accountant, the circulating libraries stopped automatically banning the books of George Moore.

13

On 1 May 1894, GM, for the time London's literary lion, wrote to his brother Maurice, then stationed at the military camp at Boyle, County Roscommon: Pearl Craigie, "the most charming woman in the world," would be visiting the Lord Lieutenant in Dublin on 11 May. Couldn't Maurice invite her to spend a few days afterward at his house? Craigie, he guessed, could deposit her maid at the Boyle hotel, if Boyle had a hotel. GM would himself slip over to Ireland at the same time. Of course, Maurice would have to talk with his wife about the set-up, and then could he send GM word? GM later admitted he was pressing Craigie to become his lover; he was "frantic" for it.[183] Riding home from the theater in the darkness of the family brougham with Pearl, he essayed attempts on her person that evoked responses he could not easily read.[184] When writing one of his many accounts of this relationship, he changed the end of the following sentence –

By some word or letter, sometimes even by acts, she would dissipate suspicions, I might almost say the belief, that my courtship would come to nothing

– to read: "By some word or letter, sometimes even by acts, she would dissipate suspicions, I might almost say the belief, that my courtship would bring me to her bed."[185] In the first version, he thinks he'll fail, so she encourages his hope; in the second, he thinks he'll get into her bed, and she *discourages* the same hope. Both statements may have been true, alternately, day by day. One Sunday morning, for instance, she begged him to come for a long visit at 4 p.m.; they would skip their walk in Hyde Park: "This is the day for a warm room, lamps, and tea (and love) – Always yours affectionately." Yet on a Sunday afternoon, in John Morgan Richards's house, with the lamps on, the tea service arrayed, the servants just beyond at the buzzer, and the sign on the wall saying, "What would Jesus say?" what kind of love was Moore going to get up to?

On 5 May, they were trying to decide on whether to go to a Wagner concert or a performance of *The Wild Duck* – GM was for the latter, she was committed to the concert, but no fissure is apparent in the relationship.[186] Apparently it was on 8 May, three days before she was due to leave for Dublin, that GM called at Lancaster Gate to hear what Ellen Terry thought of their comedy, before they went out together to the St James's Theatre. He also talked with her about the plans for a rendezvous in Ireland. When GM mentioned the word "Ireland," her face darkened, and throughout the play that evening her manner became more artificial. He knew something was wrong, and in the brougham on the way home he pressed her for an answer. Finally, she got it out: "I don't think I want to see you any more." The words gave him "miserable pain." He tried to persuade her to let this casual mood pass. Or was she just worried about the problem of seeking a divorce petition? She simply did not wish to see him any more, that was all. At last she agreed to walk with GM in Hyde Park. Why was she breaking it off? Why? He could not understand. He was "dumbfounded, heartbroken, miserable." Then, turning toward her, he saw on her face a look of quiet satisfaction, even a smile; yes, she was laughing at him, "enjoying my grief as she might a little comedy of her own invention, conscious of her prettiness in black crepe de chine, with a hat to match." He let her walk a bit ahead, and with his left boot kicked her in the backside, "nearly in the center, a little to the right."[187] Astonishingly, her reaction was, it seemed to him, to become still more proud, proud that she had had the power to make GM put off all conventions "and become, as it were, another George Moore." [188]

She did not explain, and he could not know, that Pearl Craigie, pressed a little too closely anyway by GM, had changed direction and aimed now to captivate a more distinguished, handsome, and proper gentleman than George

Moore. This new man was Lord Curzon, star student from Eton and Oxford, government minister, and bachelor reportedly on the lookout for an American heiress. A year later, GM learned about her infatuation with the man who was just about to be named Viceroy of India. To Nevill Geary, Moore explained that he had been mercilessly dropped by Craigie because "When a woman falls in love, every previous thought or promise or obligation dissolves like a burnt thread; I was driven out by a handsome lordling."[189]

On the night of 8 May 1894, however, GM could not be so philosophical. He went to the Alhambra Music Hall, picked up one of the flower girls who strolled the lobby, and, for the night, she was the anodyne for his pain.[190]

Chapter 9
From Celibate Lives to the
"One Great Love"

I

A few days after the Hyde Park interview, Pearl Craigie was on the boat to Dublin, and GM, his hopes dashed of a rendezvous at a garrison town in the Irish midlands, decided to make a night crossing to Paris on 12 May 1894.[1] Lena Milman was there; she, maybe, would make him feel less alone.[2] Before going, he sent an inquiry to Ellen Terry about *Journeys End in Lovers Meeting*: while he had heard that the Lyceum Theatre intended to produce the play at the end of the month, he had heard nothing directly from Terry, though GM was the co-author. Would she write to him, he asked, at the Hôtel Continental, Paris? He had lost Pearl, but he did not mean to abandon his stake in a possibly profitable one-act. The day after his crossing, he met Dujardin just before midnight at the hotel on rue Castiglione, and walking the streets of Paris, told his old friend of his great triumph with plain Esther and his astounding loss of the rich Pearl.[3] He was groping for a way to transform blinding, confusing pain into a masterful, intimate narrative. He looked for and could not find the lovely Sybil Eden, wife of Sir William; he could have talked to her, he later confided, of his true subject, "the burden of life." He was too sick at heart for Lena Milman to cure him, though she was willing to let him row her about a lake in the Bois de Boulogne. He gave up and returned to London before the end of his usual fortnight in Paris.[4] Maybe he could write himself out of agony; most likely, it was just then that Moore began a story about a wealthy frigid woman, "Mildred Lawson."

One afternoon at the Temple he suddenly remembered that he had invited friends to dine the following evening, but had not yet ordered dinner. He ran up the Embankment to the Savoy Hotel, and while standing in the restaurant a small, young, golden-haired woman of twenty-two came forward in a grey and pink shot-silk gown, a gown he never afterwards forgot – it had all the evocative charm for him that the madeleine had for Proust. In a bright American voice, she impulsively insisted that the forty-two-year-old author join her party for lunch. GM was reluctant, "for I was minded to return to my writing, the only cure for my sickness. She must have divined it, and her kind heart must have told her she could cure it, or it may have been that some book of mine stirred her imagination."[5] They had met before. He recalled the time he "first saw her cross the room in a white dress, her gold hair hanging over her shoulders"; even then, he felt a look of recognition from her, the man loving first according to appearance, the woman through her imagination.[6] Meeting again in late May 1894 at the Savoy Hotel, the young American girl seemed as "instinctive and courageous as a sparrow-hawk." She came forward and "put her little hand, like a fern and white as a lily," into his own.[7] He followed her to the table, she arranged to sit next to him. He then unfurled his lines of talk, a wild display of plumage, until she suddenly exclaimed, "George Moore, you have a soul of fire!"[8]

She was Maud Alice Burke of San Francisco (?1872–1948), a Gold Rush heiress.[9] Her father, possibly an Irish immigrant, opened a successful California mine in 1849. After his death, her mother, Alice Valentine (1845–1905), married Colonel James Frederik Tichenor. Maud then lived with General Horace W. Carpentier (1824–1918), another successful gold-miner, and mayor of Oakland, California. Maud traveled extensively in Europe in the company of a Mrs Harris, and sometimes with her mother. In December 1893, the San Francisco *Examiner* reported that Maud Alice Burke was secretly engaged to the dashing Prince André Poniatowski, a Parisian exile from Poland and the descendant of King Stanislaus. Poniatowski was a friend and neighbor of the Blanches in Dieppe and lover of the Duchess of Caracciola, by whom he had a daughter, the beautiful Olga. In the 21 February *Examiner*, the Prince confirmed his intention to marry Maud and denied he meant to barter his title for her money; it was a love match, he explained. The Colonels Tichenor and Carpentier, stepfather and protector, both had their doubts. On 29 April they gave a statement to the press announcing their disapproval of a match between wealthy little Maud and the older, titled roué. Two weeks later, the engagement broken, Maud sailed for Europe with her mother.[10] She was not long in London before making the acquaintance of, or renewing her friendship with, the literary lion of the hour, George Moore.

It is not easy to trace the early progress of the relationship between twenty-two-year-old Maud Burke and forty-two-year-old George Moore. He often wrote about her in his stories and novels – as the "beloved girl" in "Resurgam," Doris in "The Lovers of Orelay," Elizabeth in "Theme and Variations," "Spring in London," and "Lui et Elles" (in successive editions of *Memoirs of My Dead Life*), Elizabeth again in *Vale*, at certain moments Evelyn in *Evelyn Innes*, and both young "Héloïse," lover of Abélard, and "Lady Malberge," lover of the knight and hermit Gaucelm d'Arembert in *Héloïse and Abélard*. There is psychological unity to these discreetly fictionalised portrayals, and often the circumstances match some of the facts available, but one cannot date events precisely from the fictive reminiscences. There are some

10. Maud Burke
Cunard; photograph
taken at a ball.

letters in print between the two, and there were many more in manuscript – by
her count, more than a thousand. In the last decade of his life, GM told various
writers planning his biography that these letters were the key to his life; he told
Maud the same thing, and begged her to allow herself to become part of his
story.[11] Both before and after his death, however, she absolutely refused to release
them to a biographer. On her own death in 1948, she willed 276 of Moore's letters
to Sacheverell Sitwell, most of them from the later years, and usually ones that
reflect favorably on her dignity as a tender and considerate friend (not a sensual
and changeable mistress). The Sitwell collection was admirably edited and published by Rupert Hart-Davis in 1956. The missing stacks of letters have not been
located and probably were destroyed.[12] Yet there is no way to keep Maud Burke,
later Lady Cunard, later still "Emerald" Cunard, hidden within the life of
George Moore, though Joseph Hone did his best to honor her wishes and respect
her threats in his official biography of the author.

Moore left London for Sussex after the performance of *Journeys End in
Lovers Meeting*, but before he parted from Maud Burke they must have made
promises to write one another or exchanged travel plans. He was able to look
forward to meeting her on the continent at the summer's end. He had found a
long-lasting anodyne for his pain, but one that periodically, through the rest of
his life, he would find it a pain to do without.

2

In Shoreham, Sussex, GM stayed for some time in Adur Lodge with the Bridger sisters, Dulcibella and Florence. It was a beautiful rich-blooming spring. He appears to have needed, and gotten, a good deal of petting from his old friends. He also wrote a friendly letter to Ada Leverson, to whom he had inscribed a copy of *Esther Waters*. Lena, Dulcibella, Ada – having been dropped by Pearl, GM was picking up one stitch after another to knit himself together again.

He also began to contemplate writing another play. Archer had issued a rather condescending appreciation of *Journeys End*, asking why the authors did not apply their talents to a more serious and lengthy drama.[13] In Sussex, Moore "thought of a subject for a three-act play."[14] That subject was probably Colville Bridger and his rabbit-ranch on the Downs. Colville's sisters used to tease him, and worse than tease him, for his improvident, impractical schemes.[15] One of the schemes GM mentions in *Hail and Farewell* was a plan for how to catch the rabbits without shooting them: Colville would plant the Downs in furze, then mow lanes in the furze, and finally net the rabbits when they crossed the lanes. The possibility that the dignified Colonel Bridger was mad may have arisen. The situation is precisely reminiscent of *The Heather Field*, a play written by Edward Martyn from a synopsis by Moore.[16] It concerns an idealistic gentleman farmer at odds with the woman of the house because of his expensive and unsuccessful plans to clear the heather from a field as a land reclamation scheme. She finally has him committed to an asylum.[17]

Five years later *The Heather Field* was one of two plays – with *The Countess Cathleen* – on the opening bill of the Irish Literary Theatre (May 1899). It was only shortly after Moore's return from Sussex that he met for the first time the author of the other play, W. B. Yeats.[18] In *Ave*, Moore described how the meeting came about.[19] He had been at the home of J. T. Nettleship, a painter of lions and visionary Blakean scenes, and a friend of GM's from the 1870s. (In the early 1870s, Nettleship, along with Arthur O'Shaughnessy and John Payne, had been the lover of the remarkable Helen Snee, the lovely literary wife of a traveling salesman.)[20] At Nettleship's rooms, GM picked up a volume of poems – probably *The Countess Kathleen and Various Legends and Lyrics*, with a frontispiece by Nettleship. GM found himself "seduced by the strain of genuine music" in the poems. Nettleship had long wanted to bring together his two Irish friends – to watch the ensuing cockfight, was Moore's guess at Nettleship's intention. After reading the poems, Moore allowed the artist to set up a "tryst" (Moore's language about WBY is often mischievously homoerotic). At the Cheshire Cheese in Fleet Street, Nettleship and Moore found "the poet in front of a large steak"; he hardly bothered to acknowledge Moore. Surely, Moore was known to Yeats – he forbade his sisters Lily and Lolly to read his copy of *A Mummer's Wife*.[21] GM guessed that someone had told Yeats that at the Avenue production of *Land of Heart's Desire* in April, GM had ridiculed the author for striding pompously up and down in his black cloak and sombrero. (Such impresario-ship seemed to GM *déclassé* and pushy.) Merely to start a quarrel, Nettleship brought up the subject of Blake's designs, and the *Speaker*'s art critic, though knowing little of Blake, obligingly charged, "all my feathers erect." But WBY easily parried, and Moore discovered that the mystic was a fine dialectician. Indeed, in the following argument, GM became aware that Yeats could have killed him "with a single spur stroke," but declined to finish him off.

Yeats changed the subject to drama: what were the chances of getting a play – presumably *The Countess Cathleen* – produced in London? So Moore told him about the Independent Theatre Society, G. R. Sims's challenge, and *The Strike at Arlingford*, pausing to explain his notion that an author should not show himself in the theater while his play is being performed. In general, though thirteen years younger than GM, and without a great deal of achievement behind him, Yeats left the impression that he regarded it as a condescension on his own part to meet with the author of *Esther Waters* at the Cheshire Cheese. Moore, however, liked Yeats. He fancied brilliant, truly literary men who seek to astonish, and reflected that if Yeats pompously paraded in black, didn't all middle-class Irish writers in London seek to attract attention by their clothes? Wilde in velvet, Shaw in a Jaeger suit, now Yeats in the get-up of a "Bible reader." GM wanted to continue the acquaintance, but the two did not cross paths again until more than a year later.

3

In early June, GM may have attended a production of *Journeys End*, yet, given his views on authors taking bows in public, it was probably only Mrs Craigie who took bows and accepted congratulations at the Lyceum; indeed, she may have been inclined to forget about the embarrassment of her compact with Moore. Yet GM was not going to surrender his rights in the play. On 11 July 1894, GM met with Ellen Terry at the Lyceum to negotiate the sale of *Journeys End in Lovers Meeting*. It had proved to be a curtain-raiser worth putting into repertory, and Terry wanted exclusive use of the text. Moore had trouble explaining that he could not sell her the French plot, only the version done by himself and Craigie.[22] While Terry was obviously ceding his co-authorship, just a week later the Lyceum produced a second playbill that diminished GM's role, simply stating that he suggested the situation from the French of Caraquell, while Mrs Craigie was given credit for sole authorship. Moore was outraged: "I cannot find words to express my astonishment at the place my name takes on your programme. I assume the explanation of the collaboration comes from Mrs Craigie: it could have come from no one else. But I fail to understand why you should have accepted her explanation without consulting me. Will you please have new programmes printed tomorrow on which my name shall appear in the same place as it did on the original programme."[23] Craigie was apparently writing him out of more than her life. Her version of the collaboration was that GM suggested a situation, and didn't even make that up himself, while she wrote all the words the actors spoke; Moore's version was that he had written nearly all of the piece, and she merely added her epigrammatic "little liver pills" (an allusion to her father's stock-in-trade). Moore marched to the Lyceum to talk with Henry Irving's right-hand man, Bram Stoker; and Stoker, GM claims, obliged his fellow Anglo-Irishman by having new bills printed.[24] Now the story becomes murky. It may be that Terry explained to GM that it would be ungentlemanly, and probably would lead to scandal, to force the issue of a second set of new playbills and that, since GM would be paid half the fee, he should offer Craigie the right to sign the play as her own – in short, he should make her a gift of what she had stolen.[25] And that was the end of the affair until 1904.

4

In August 1894, Moore made his first pilgrimage to Bayreuth for the Wagner Festival. *Parsifal*, *Tannhäuser*, and *Lohengrin* were scheduled for performance. His companion was Edward Martyn, a Wagnerian of old standing; Edouard Dujardin was another annual pilgrim, and a close friend of the arch-Wagnerian and Nazi philosopher Houston Stewart Chamberlain who married Wagner's daughter. George Bernard Shaw, the perfect Wagnerite, had been making heroic claims for the German composer for years, and in July 1894 Shaw also made the trip to Bayreuth.[26] Although his friends were Wagnerians, Moore had stood apart from their admiration until July 1892, when Edward Martyn convinced him to come along to Drury Lane, first to hear *Rheingold*, then *Tristan and Isolde*.[27] Hearing the last opera, Moore took the plunge: "Words cannot tell my delirium, my madness."

Before their departure for Bayreuth, Martyn imposed rules of the road: GM was not to make up to "English and American women that congregate in the Continental hotels." Martyn was especially worried that such an acquaintance might turn out to be a "woman whose sole morality [was] to yield to every impulse of the heart." Edward's morality was to yield to no such impulses. The two oddly matched Irish Catholic landlords went through Germany looking at cathedrals and listening to boys' choirs before arriving at the small festival town of Bayreuth with its unique Festspielhaus on a hill on the outskirts. The 1,650 persons who filled the steeply banked seats of the amphitheater, with a sunken orchestra pit and deep double-proscenium stage, would sit still in reverent darkness through the performances which, uninterrupted by applause, ran from four in the afternoon to ten at night, with intermissions between the acts. During the intermissions, Moore could walk around the wooded hilltop with two musical ladies, probably Milman and another, or go into the village with

Edward in search of a seat in one of restaurants at the Golden Anchor or the Sun, the only two inns.[28] Moore loved the combination of picnic and pilgrimage at Bayreuth, the cultic celebration of an avant-garde artist, the whole upper-class bohemianism of the musical holiday.

From Bayreuth, Moore and Martyn went on to Munich for more music. It is possible they spent part of the time during their travels drafting *The Heather Field* together. When they came to that task, GM gave Edward his head, yet still stayed in the saddle. Moore later told Yeats that he had written nothing, but had told Martyn what was to go into every speech.[29] The hero Carden Tyrell became far more like Edward himself than Colville Bridger: Carden had an attachment to young Kit, for instance, and a Strindbergian relationship to the hateful regiment of women that has no echo in what is known of Colville Bridger.[30] GM was given a part too, as the undeceived rationalist, Barry Ussher. Ussher suggests that Carden, "such a queer creature," should never have married; no woman was suitable to one of his kind, and his "latent, untamable nature [is] not to be subdued." When Carden snaps, he has visions of fauns and hears silver voices of boys choiring of "speechless longings."[31] The element of deeply devious humor in GM's having brought about Edward's self-revelation should not be missed. Moore reveled in that sort of machination.

By 29 August 1894, Moore had become bored by these games with his Galway friend. He wrote Clement Shorter, editor of the *Sketch* and the *Illustrated London News*, that Munich was a "furnace" and Germany was "dreary" except for the hours of Wagner's operas; living in silence because he knew no German was awful.[32] He later told Vincent O'Sullivan (who often misses the depth of GM's clowning) that he had felt so poorly he went to a German doctor. Moore was suffering, the doctor said, from having to keep silence: "The doctor was right. As soon as I got back to Paris I felt quite well."[33]

In fact, Moore felt better, much better, before he got back to Paris. In Munich he made plans to break his tour off with Edward, and head for Hôtel Splendide in Aix-les-Bains by way of Dresden (more Wagner there).[34] In the first week of September, he rendezvoused with Maud Burke in Dresden. Edward took a poor view of this development. He may have deployed the high moral tone about a middle-aged author rotten with literature running after a little American coquette chaperoned by her mother, but it was enough to put Edward out that he himself was being jilted, and his plans for companionship at the Köln boys' choir were spoiled.

After following Maud, her mother, and Mrs Harris to Aix-les-Bains, GM apparently spirited Maud away from the hotel and her minders, so that the two could admire the beauties of Lac Bourget unchaperoned. Thirty years later, Moore was deeply wounded that Maud seemed to have forgotten they had been there together.[35] He certainly had not forgotten. It may have been there that they went for those walks in the hills he described in a rejected chapter of *Memoirs of My Dead Life* – "through the woods, through sunny interspaces that I remember for many a pleasant frolic in the warm, fragrant grass. I remember the tasselled branches of the larches, the blackbird in the underwood, the thrush on the high branch, and the mocking laughter of the yaffle . . . but [Maud] remembers nothing."[36] Walking in the hills, she would come to a stop: "'Let us sit here,' and after looking steadily at [me] for a few seconds, her pale marmoreal eyes glowing, she would say, 'You can make love to me now, if you like.'" He was aware that the details of this story might be regarded as "somewhat base to worldlings," "an errant lust" rather than "an inspired love story," yet to him her "cold sensuality, cold because it was divorced from tenderness and passion," was beautiful, beautiful like a dryad, the inhuman female spirit of the forest.[37] Ten years later, he told Maud as much: "You are a hard woman in many ways, but if you were less hard I don't think you would have held me captive."[38]

From Aix-les-Bains, GM probably continued to follow Maud and her mother south to the coast of Provence. That is the story as given in "The Lovers of Orelay," a highly literary erotic epyllion, but nonetheless touching on the truth at a number of points. In 1906, he wrote to Maud that "I am writing the 'Avignon' episode"; he told Richard Best that "Orelay" was Avignon; and Oliver St John Gogarty claimed to have been to the hotel – probably the Hôtel de l'Europe – where the proprietor offered to show him the particular bedroom in which the lovers stayed (a suspiciously folkloric certitude about that assurance).[39] The Avignon episode comes about when the hero is invited to accompany a young woman on a final romantic adventure before her marriage. They go to the coast of Provence, but he finds himself thwarted at every turn by the company of her elderly female companions, nice oblivious women certainly, but still serving too effectively as chaperones. Eventually, he convinces the heroine Doris to allow him to meet her in a small town on the rail line back to Paris – "Orelay," or Avignon. In scenes that come closer to the painting of Boucher than to anything in English literature, GM discovers that he has neglected to pack his silk pajamas, and he could not possibly do what was expected of him without them. A search of shops is made, but pajamas are regarded in Provence as a newfangled garment, probably an immoral one, and all he can find is a nightshirt. Next he worries about sleeping in the same bed – "after the love feast . . . to sleep, perchance to snore."[40] Finally, the root cause of all fears: he suffers male performance anxiety. What if his "eagerness should undermine his bodily strength"? But her beauty and kindness save him "from the misfortune dreaded by all lovers." She was, he lovingly recalls, like "a little white ferret" in the bed, with a pretty movement when she rolled her hips over.

Yet if George Moore and Maud Burke did go to Provence together in September 1894, and if they did stop at Avignon on the train back to Paris, and then slept in the same bed, and if Moore escaped the misfortune dreaded by men, it is still doubtful that before her marriage Maud permitted him to have full sexual intercourse with her. In "Lovers of Orelay," he speaks of her (prior to Avignon) as having "given a great deal of herself while denying me much," so that their love affair became "too one-sided to be borne."[41] That this state of affairs continued up to the time of her marriage is confirmed by a letter Moore wrote years later to Nathaniel Hawthorne's granddaughter, Hilda, when he was playing the part of her "father confessor": "Surely you know that love is possible without incurring any risk whatever; if love were so restricted, how should I have managed . . . For a whole year I was the lover of an American girl and when she was married she was a virgin (technically)." He quoted for Hilda's instruction a French writer he was reading in 1894, Marcel Prévost, to the effect that the dangerous savor of an incomplete love, all-but love, is more poignant by a hundred times than the facile happiness of a completed act of ordinary love (from Prévost's *Les Demi-vierges*, the "Half-Virgins"). GM found it necessary to explain in a subsequent letter to Hawthorne how safety and pleasure were to be reconciled: "kisses need not be confined to the mouth and . . . kisses placed within the nest of love are more intimate and exciting than the mere act of love which grocers and their mates perform at midnight in the middle of a four-poster."[42] Art is art, GM liked to say, because it is not nature; the same for him was true for the art of love. In both cases, his gifts were linguistic.

On their travels through France back to London, evidence suggests they stopped again at Barbizon for the *fête de Marlotte*, a charity benefit held in an inn famous for having Corot and Monet as guests.[43] The subject of marriage came up, according to the rejected draft of *Memoirs*. Maud said if they married, they should be very happy . . . for six months. GM had no choice but to agree: he knew her ambition was to "shine in society . . . to form a salon and gather clever men about [her]." Quoting Nietzsche, Moore describes them as two ships lying side by side in a harbor, but each destined for other ports.[44] So together they talked of possible husbands for her. In London, she took his advice and leased a little house in Chelsea.

Such is the story. There is nothing to contradict it, and only a few pieces of evidence to confirm it, and some may be no evidence at all. In a late October 1894 letter to Lena Milman, written after a testy exchange over tea, Moore told her never to bring up again the slanders she reports as being circulated about him; such talk could, he said, never hurt him. Indeed, if it was about George Moore and a pretty young American he had lodged in a Chelsea hideaway, he may have enjoyed the rumor. More substantively, in his first extant letter to Maud, GM sends his "Dearest" some French verses he titles "Barbazon," a memorial to their times together in France. He had published the poem in the 15 January 1895 *Pall Mall Gazette* as "Nuit de Septembre," but had tried to improve it. The last stanza, he wrote, "describes you":

> O seule maîtresse, viens; j'aime
> Le clair de lune de tes yeux,
> Pur et triste que le ciel même,
> La blonde odeur de tes cheveux.

Blonde odour of your hair! The echo of *Pagan Poems* is not difficult to trace. The verses were offered as a reminder "of one who, whatever his faults may have been, certainly loved you dearly."[45]

In February Maud Burke was to return to America, but before leaving she asked if he would always remain her friend. Were their "bodily relations . . . to be continued"?[46] On 18 February, she was gone, and in a letter to Clara Lanza his mind followed Maud's progress across the Atlantic: "I have seen a good deal of Miss Maud Burke last year and this year. She told me that she knew you . . . . Miss Burke is now on the Atlantic, about the middle I should think. She will arrive in New York at the end of the week. If you are there you may be disposed to call; she always speaks nicely about you."

Once arrived in New York, it was not long before Maud Burke met, received a proposal from, and agreed to marry Sir Bache Cunard (of Cunard Steamship Lines). The wedding took place on 25 April 1895.

5

The beginning of the hour of love was not the end of the time for writing in the case of George Moore; there was no end to writing for him except death. While he was caught up in his courtship of Maud Burke, he also busied himself with two different literary projects, a novel with a musical background, *Evelyn Innes*; and a collection of novellas about three varieties of people who do not have reproductive sex, *Celibates*.

He began to work out a plan for *Evelyn Innes* as soon as he finished the proofs of *Esther Waters* in January 1894. On 30 January, he took Pearl Craigie to Dowlands, the new home of Arnold Dolmetsch at 172 Rosendale Road in Dulwich, for a concert of fifteenth-century English music played on the original instruments. Moore found enormously engaging the strangely tuned instruments, the domestic charm of Dowlands with its music room hung with viols, lutes, and violins, and the beauty of Dolmetsch's daughter Helene.[47] Others in the mid-1890s, including Shaw, Yeats, and Symons, were enthusiastic about the new performances of old music. By both his research in the British Library and his concerts, Dolmetsch was virtually recreating Renaissance and baroque music in England.[48] On the day of the January Dolmetsch concert, Moore wrote to Gosse: "I am contemplating an outline that will take at least six years to fill in."[49] He continued to develop the plan in conversations with Craigie – "What scenes for you at your best!" she cooed – but he may not have yet worked in the twist by which Evelyn periodically leaves the bed of her older lover to hide out in a convent, as Pearl herself would sometimes retreat into the Convent of the Assumption.[50]

Over the summer of 1894 and at the Wagner Festival, GM continued to treat his life as his research. Moore often did not write about the life he had lived; instead, he began to live the kind of life he wanted to write about. In this case, that would be the life of an aristocratic Wagnerian with a lovely, gifted young mistress for whom he had artistic plans. By the time GM got to Munich in August 1894, he had "several sketches" and was trying to make the right choice. Would Evelyn be a sweet daughterly violist, like Helene Dolmetsch? A woman of religiously blocked sensuality, like Pearl Craigie? A Wagnerian opera diva living out the passions of the multitude? A woman of fiercely pure eroticism, the sort that when it comes over her forces her to lie down, like young Maud Burke? If he could connect music, eroticism, and the religious passion, and put it all into a Wagnerian high romantic and high society myth, what a grandiose thing he would have authored! It could be as deliberately scholarly as Huysmans's *En route* and *Là-bas*, with a similar focus on the flesh and spirit as explored in Catholicism, but with a female center of interest and a gloriously rich Wagnerian setting, neither of which Huysmans had attempted.[51] But he was nervous, as he admitted to Clement Shorter in late August: "I am hesitating about the subject of a long novel . . . So much depends on the choice of subject and I intend to write more deliberately than ever. If I am lucky in my choice I shall do better than *Esther Waters*." Passing through Paris on the way back from Aix-les-Bains and parts south, he visited his old friend Mary Robinson Darmestetter. Mary told him of a "little actress who had scruples of conscience about her lovers, and had gone into a convent. She could not stop there because the nuns were all so childlike."[52] That anecdote helped him jell aspects of his tale.

Back in London in October, Moore made a new acquaintance who was going to have a vast influence on the novel. Moore is such a deeply foxy man that one cannot be sure if he stumbled upon this particular woman or if he obtained an introduction to her by deliberate design. He wrote to W. T. Stead saying that he wanted to write a novel in which a large part of the story would be set in a convent of cloistered nuns, and he needed to talk to a woman who had been in such a place. H. W. Massingham – previously, one of Stead's writers – had told GM that Stead might know of such a woman who could use some money. In a following letter on 10 October 1894, GM assured Stead that he would not "write a word that would give offence to any nun of any order . . . To do so would ruin my book."[53] So Stead put GM in touch with Virginia Crawford, the woman who had been involved in the terrible divorce case in 1886, when Stead dragged Sir Charles Dilke down. After the trial, she had moved to 105 Marylebone Drive and taken a part-time job on the staff of Stead's *Pall Mall Gazette*. At that time, Stead had introduced her to two knights always ready for the rescue of fallen women, General Booth of the Salvation Army and Canon Lidden, both prominently involved in the National Vigilance Association. In 1889 she veered away from these Protestant evangelists and was accepted into the Roman Catholic Church by Cardinal Manning. For a time she lived as a tertiary of the Order of St Francis (lay member not subject to the strict rule of the regular nuns). Still, when "pressed by the world," she would retreat into St Mary's Abbey at Mill Hill, London. Her vocation became

both writing about religious art and ministering to the poor.[54] Stead had published the story of her saintly life-after-Dilke in an 1890 pamphlet, *Has Sir
Charles Dilke Cleared His Character?*

Moore evidently never asked Stead for an introduction specifically to
Virginia Crawford, but he could well have known about the Stead/Crawford
relationship from Massingham. The very Protestant Stead seems a strange
resource to call upon for introductions to any other former inhabitant of a
nunnery. It is possible that intrinsic to Moore's emerging plan for *Evelyn Innes*
was yet another deep critique of the foundations of the National Vigilance
Association. One of those foundations is the belief in the purity of spiritual
virtue and the viciousness of sex. Moore could write a novel sympathetically
exploring the sensuality of spirit and the spirituality of sensuousness
within the life of the star witness and prize convert of the National Vigilance
Association.

By 14 March 1896 Virginia Crawford had become a key informant for *Evelyn
Innes* – to Sybil Eden GM referred to Virginia as "Evelyn Innes, that is to say,
the woman who suggested the story."[55] Viriginia and GM were to pass into a
lifelong friendship without first going through the bedroom (though they once
contemplated a rendezvous in Rouen).[56]

6

While Moore was evolving the subject of *Evelyn Innes* (composition did not
begin until late summer 1895), he was writing the three novellas that make up
Celibates. In late December 1894, "Mildred Lawson" was already with the
printer, and Moore was bearing down on the composition of a new story, "Agnes
Lahens." In order to carry on with it, he broke off his engagement to spend
New Year's Day with Sir William Eden and his family at Windlestone, County
Durham.[57] By 7 February, he was still making promises to get away from
Celibates and see the Edens, by then in Boulogne.[58] On 21 February he had taken
up "Mildred Lawson" again to rewrite the ending after Lena Milman judged
it to be an unsympathetic, undramatic, cold tale – and it is (while by means of
such qualities being also a stunning story). It was a touchy business for Lena:
she was worried that the frigid woman so coldly depicted in it might have been
herself, though Moore assured her it was "not drawn from one model." "I
wished to represent in Mildred a woman living in the shallows of vanity just
as in *Esther Waters* I represented a woman living in the deepest human
instincts."[59]

What Moore really represented in "Mildred Lawson" is the case of Pearl
Craigie from his own point of view, which, by means of the strain of composition, he had managed to make dispassionate, merciless, and precise. Occasionally he revised away the most personal statements of his diagnosis, such as
the following:

She even asked herself if she desired to meet a lover who would inspire in her that personal passion which she had heard of from Edith. She did not know; she shrank from concluding and thought that such mutualities and corporeal usage would always be repugnant to her. She did not think that she could ever accept them. Nor could she think that she would love the man who inspired such desire in her, if such a thing were possible. She thought she would hate him for it.[60]

It was wise of GM to delete this theory that Craigie hated him because he inspired erotic desire in her; the story was evidently a contrary case. He changed the passage to an expression by Mildred of her contempt for the one option open to women: "Marriage, marriage, always marriage – always the eternal question of sex, as if there were nothing else in life." Here Mildred transparently pretends to be a feminist, and, like Pearl, only pretends.[61]

In the beginning of the narrative, Mildred, daughter of a wealthy suburban family, decides to take up painting though she has no genius for it. She induces her London art instructor Ralph to fall in love with her, then leaves him. Traveling to Paris, she works at Daveau's Academy (much like Julian's), while writing love letters back to Ralph in England (just such as Pearl wrote from Paris to GM in February 1894). Ralph crosses to see her, and she is forced to say she wrote more than she intended, and sends him packing. She is conscious that she does not want to marry; she just wants "the nicest men in love with her."[62] In addition, she seeks a little success in art, because even a little success "goes a long way in society" (a little success like a Lyceum curtain-raiser?). Next she goes to Barbizon, where her prim, wealthy turnout catches the eye of Morton, a talented Impressionist. He drops his mistress to pursue Mildred, and dreams of kissing her (in a draft, she gives him her lips easily, but then spurns him when he tries to come into her bedroom; in the final manuscript, she does not give him even so much as that, and her story of Morton's midnight stealth is made to be a lie). Running away from Morton, she next takes up with a famous French socialist couple, the Delacours (possibly based on Paul LaFargue, husband of Laura Marx).[63] Just as John Morgan Richards bought the *Academy* as a shop window for his daughter Pearl's articles-in-trade, Mildred buys the Delacours' paper so that she may write for it. Her brother is forced to come over to Paris to attempt to rescue her from being completely bilked by the socialists. She tells him she has become not just a socialist but a Newmanite because her safety in life, what protects her from suicide, is religiously guarded chastity. Her brother leaves Paris with his mission unaccomplished, but she soon turns up at home again. Mrs Delacour had accused Mildred – quite falsely, Mildred protests – of having an affair with her husband, and the marriage had broken up. In London, she learns that Ralph, her art instructor, is now ailing. He had threatened to die of a broken heart, and she is a little disturbed by her wish that he might do so. She pays a call and finds him with his model, Ellen Gibbs. Ralph admits to Mildred that the two are lovers, but that his heart really belongs to Mildred. He asks for a kiss; she refuses it. Bitter at his unfaithfulness, she delays a while to send flowers to the sick man. Next comes a letter from Ellen Gibbs: Ralph is dead; would Mildred care to view the body? The pure and the impure woman stand beside the corpse of their man, and Ellen lets loose: "Why did you take the trouble to do this? You were not in love with him . . . Women like you make virtue odious." Mildred keeps protesting that nothing happened between her and Ralph. "How that one idea does run in your head," Ellen retorts. "I wonder if your thoughts are equally chaste . . . I read you in the first glance . . . your eyes tell the tale of your cunning, mean little soul."

Moore continued to perfect the tale in future editions, adding new details from subsequent developments in Craigie's life and in his own, just to give more sting to the details that are purely fictive. It is a classic in the literature of hatred, an *ad feminam tour de force*, though not much loved by reviewers then or by many scholars since. An exception was Harry Thurston Peck who described it in an article on "The Rise of George Moore" (published in June 1895 in the *Bookman*) as the best thing GM had done, ranking with Stendhal, Balzac, Flaubert, and Thackeray – though "the type is too new in society . . . to have much appeal." Another notable exception was James Joyce, who in 1904 began a translation of *Celibates* into Italian, and, settled in Trieste, gave "Mildred Lawson" to Nora Barnacle to read.[64] More typical of the reaction to "Mildred Lawson" was the review in the *New York Times*, which spoke of the story as "not nice, and it seems to have no serious purpose."[65] The London *Bookman* complained that the story "tortures every sensitive mind . . . wounds, and keeps the wounds open for tedious scrutiny . . . brings no opiate at all, and but little promise of future relief; [and] . . . gives too much comprehension of human suffering and sin."[66] It is doubtful if the type of heroine or the etched-in-acid style will ever have wide appeal, yet "Mildred Lawson" is a first-rate piece of character assassination.

The other two stories that make up the collection, "Agnes Lahens" and "John Norton," are suited to the style and theme of "Mildred Lawson." Stylistically, GM intended to allow himself "only . . . an indication" in representing character, not fully painted portraiture; each touch was to be deliberate and necessary, and the narrative was minimalist in its detail.[67] This sparing draftsmanship caused him to improve *A Mere Accident* by deleting much that was unnecessary about John Norton's late Latin scholarship, and "John Norton" gained further by being set between stories treating varieties of people who do without sex. The last story – "Agnes Lahens" – is a preliminary investigation of the subject of *Evelyn Innes*. It concerns a young girl home from a convent who hates the look of life in her parents' home – the mother is caught up in a seven-year-long affair, the kindly bankrupt father lives in a maid's room and dresses in clothes he bought from the butler. Judging that the celibate life is better than the lives she sees about her, Agnes returns to the convent at the end of the story. Several reviewers, while admitting the insidious strength of the stories, received a fright from the book – "*Celibates* suddenly arouses a sense of disgust and a doubt whether life is worth living at all."[68] That may very well have been how GM felt in the sudden dusk of his romance with Pearl Craigie, and even through the brief hours of his affair with Maud Burke.

7

Since 1893, Moore had been spending a lot of time with Sir William Eden (1849–1915) and his wife Sybil. Eden had been Master of the South Durham hounds; he was an affectionate but irascible friend, a hater of dogs and children, lover of women, untamed child at heart, father of a future Prime Minister, gifted boxer and wingshot, and talented watercolorist. He made a profession of lordly British arrogance: "Walk," he taught his sons, "as if you had bought the earth."[69] Moore praised Eden's watercolors in the *Saturday Review* as "worthy of the title of *amateur* [a 'lover' of art]."[70] GM was making a place for Eden in *Evelyn Innes* as Owen Asher, the lover of his heroine, and he needed to keep his subject under watch. The Edens invited GM to join them and their children for Christmas of 1893 in Paris at 4 rue de Presbourg.[71] The Edens were spending more and more time abroad to reduce the expense of keeping up Windlestone, their massive sandstone country house, standing in an 8,000-acre estate in Durham. William Eden still continued to spend what he could in collecting pictures of his beautiful wife by great artists. Swan, Sargent, Sickert, Blanche, and Herkomer had all done her (several on GM's recommendation); now Eden was persuaded he must have a Whistler, but he did not have the ready money. While in Paris Moore met with Whistler to negotiate on Eden's behalf for a portrait of Sybil, a small one, for a reduced price. Whistler charged £500 ordinarily, but, after meeting with GM (the two were again on friendly terms because of GM's advocacy of Whistler's pictures in the *Speaker*),[72] the artist agreed to do a small watercolor sketch of a head for £100 or £150. The terms seem to have been aristocratically vague, a matter of honor between gentlemen and artists.

In January 1894, Whistler began a minute oil portrait, eight inches by twelve, of a full-length figure on a sofa, in a golden brown dress, against a brown background: *Brown and Gold: Portrait of Lady E* was Whistler's title.[73] For him, it was not a representation of a woman, but a piece of self-expression, a statement of his own personal, harmonic vision of color. He could not help painting with ardor, trying to make it into a masterpiece, a *"prix."*[74] He was still fussing with it on 14 February, when Eden, wishing to return to England, stopped by the studio and handed Whistler an envelope, while bidding him farewell. After Eden departed, Whistler tore open the envelope: "Herewith your valentine – cheque value one hundred guineas. The picture will always be of inestimable value to me, and will be handed down as an heirloom as long as heirlooms last." Whistler was outraged. Eden had not consulted him about the price; he had just paid the minimum, or near it, and not even paid it openly.

Whistler wrote back immediately: "My dear Sir William, I have your valentine. You really are magnificent! – and have scored all round." Detecting irritation, Eden hurried back to the studio and offered another £50, but Whistler declined: "The time has gone by." Thereafter, Whistler kept both the picture and the check. Eden made requests for one or the other; his solicitors made requests; then, on 8 November 1894, Eden sued. In December, Whistler returned the check on the advice of solicitors, but now it was Eden's turn to say, "The time has gone by." He wanted the portrait.

For the trial in Paris, GM was named as a witness for the claimant. Whistler was delightedly, manically raging with egotism and machinations. Mallarmé and Degas were again to be brought into a conspiracy to rout the vulgar sportsman and his henchman, "Expert Moore." Whistler's secret plan – shared with too many friends – was to paint out the face of Sybil Eden. Then, suddenly, in the trial the bouquet would be revealed to the world: Whistler had painted in the face of a woman who would be seated beside him in the courtroom. For Whistler, it would be his disastrous *Ruskin* v. *Whistler* trial done over, and done triumphantly.[75]

Moore, on the other hand, had no appetite for trials whatsoever. He never liked public speaking – possibly as a result of Oscott traumas. He liked to say he was the only Irishman who could never make a speech. If public speeches were traumatising, trials were worse. It had been less than two years since his brother Augustus was in the dock for the rape of a servant girl. Augustus had paid a visit to the residence of Mrs Edith Gardner, possibly a courtesan, and finding her out, dragged the eighteen-year-old maid, Kate May, onto the dining room floor and had sex with her instead. Mrs Gardner returned and demanded an explanation of the maid, who said she'd been forced.[76] The newspaper accounts of this unsavory trial (involving ugly investigations into Kate's sexual history) identifed Augustus as "the brother of the novelist, George Moore."[77] During the trial, GM wrote Duret: "I am more unhappy than I have ever been. I am overwhelmed."[78] Augustus escaped prison, but he lost what little was left of his good name. Approaching the Whistler–Eden trial in Paris, Whistler may have been looking for a reprise of the Ruskin trial, but GM was dreading a disaster like the Augustus Moore trial.

Moore slipped into Paris by 5 March 1895 and out on 7 March.[79] The court heard evidence through 6 March, and, though with little assistance from Moore's feeble testimony, the court decided for Eden, and ordered Whistler to deliver the portrait as originally painted with a penalty for delays, and to pay 1,000 francs in damages. Before and after the trial, Whistler was waging battle on a second front in the *Pall Mall Gazette* and had fired some insults at GM. Whistler believed himself a past master of the put-down, but he may not have known that GM was raised on the sport of personal abuse in G. H. Moore's house. On 11 March GM counterattacked, sending the *Gazette* the following letter to Whistler for publication, a letter rapidly wired to the Paris papers as well:

Dear Whistler,

I am reading a wonderful book, *En Route* by J.-K. Huysmans and have no time to consider the senile squalls which you address to the papers and which you are obliging enough to send me. There is so much else in life to interest one. Yesterday I saw an elderly eccentric hopping about on the edge of the pavement, his hat was in the gutter and his clothes were covered with snow. The pitiful part of the whole thing was that the poor old chap thought that everyone was admiring him.

Very truly yours,
George Moore

P. S. If a man sent me a cheque for a MS, and I cashed the cheque, I should consider myself bound to deliver the MS, and if I decided not to do so I should feel I was acting dishonourably. But everyone has his own code of honour.

This was very bad from Whistler's point of view. He had squared up to Eden on a point of honor. Now he had lost the legal issue, lost money in the fees and penalties, and lost respect in the London press. He was looking ahead at bankruptcy and a public auction at his Tite Street house in Chelsea. He sent Moore a challenge to a duel by way of his seconds, the poets Francis Vielé-Griffin and Octave Mirbeau. Moore simply answered: "Mr. Moore begs to acknowledge the receipt of Mr. Whistler's letter of the 12th. In Mr. Moore's opinion, Mr. Whistler's conduct grows daily more absurd." In front of the irritable and pompous Vielé-Griffin and Mirbeau, Moore dropped the challenge into the wastepaper basket. The seconds waited around a week without seeing any movement toward the field of battle by GM.[80] When a *Daily Chronicle* reporter asked GM why he refused the challenge, Moore replied that Whistler was "too old and near-sighted" for such doings.[81] Besides, he explained to his friends at the *Speaker*, he could not shoot the jester Whistler, or the egotist Whistler, without killing the genius Whistler.[82]

8

Although his lover had left him, and he had been dragged into a ridiculous trial and public scandal with Whistler in early 1895, GM was a lucky man in one way. At the beginning of the year, the "neglectful but affectionate son" wrote his mother a really tender letter – "How good you are! You seem to be incapable of selfish thought or feeling. I cannot say as much for myself. I feel my own selfishness very acutely."[83] On 23 May 1895, just after he returned from a fortnight in Paris, he received a telegram from Maurice Moore summoning him to Ireland immediately; his mother was dangerously ill.[84] On the boat over from Holyhead and the train to Castlebar, he found it terrible how the past had rearisen, evoked by Irish landscapes all in bloom. He had not seen the country of his birth for ten years. More terrible still was his feeling that he wished that his mother might die before he arrived. Confessing this in the story "Resurgam," he acknowledged that such an emotion "will seem hard and selfish to some," but they must understand there are "not only many degrees of sensibility, but many kinds." His own strange sensibility could not bear another death like Mrs Bridger's – agonised, long-drawn-out, inevitable. So when his brother collected him at the station and said, " 'I have bad news,' " GM admits thinking, " 'Not altogether bad news.' "

In "Resurgam" GM says that he tried to grieve over his mother, but the sudden thought of Maud Burke, now Maud Cunard, came back to him: "the wound gaped again, and it was impossible to staunch the bleeding . . . The most beautiful thing that had ever appeared in my life, an idea which I knew from the first I was destined to follow . . . had appeared to me, had stayed with me for a little while, and had passed from me." In a contemporary letter to Sybil Eden, he writes of his mother's death, "I was and am heartbroken. There are moments when one forgets and then it all comes back again, all the flood of sorrow."[85] So he was not unmoved, but he very well may have yearned to possess feelings that would be a proper tribute to the love his mother gave him. Still, his sense of failing to feel to the degree he thought he should feel, and to the exclusion of all other emotions, may be an acknowledgement of what she meant to him that is comparable in force to conventional mourning.

GM walked out on the Kiltoom peninsula, as he told Sybil Eden, to the family "burying ground at the end of a long wood stretching into the lake, a beautiful soft merelike lake, the warble of the lake mingling with the songs of innumerable goldfinches, the long grass swept by the shadows of the larches and the beeches." There, according to "Resurgam," he found the carpenter, Michael Melia, preparing a new shelf in the vault. Melia, a small tenant with only a house and garden, seems to have had the character of the gravedigger in *Hamlet*.[86] He noted that there was only enough room left for GM, his sister, and a brother (an observation noted in the Eden letter too). But they did not have many children; the Moores were dying out. Did GM have his heart set on any particular place? The mason pointed out the casket of GM's namesake and grandfather, George Moore (1770–1840), and said he had heard they were both writers. Being put on the same footing as his largely unpublished and utterly forgotten ancestor gave GM a shock: " 'That country boy took it out of me as perhaps no poet had ever done!' "

At that moment in the story (it took him six years to evolve the vision of life from the funerary experience), GM knew he never wished to be laid into such a crypt, among such a moldering family, while the words of priests fell upon him. He had a vision of his own funeral, presided over by tutelary spirits of his choosing, Wagner and Nietzsche. From the forest around Lough Carra, let his mourners fell timbers and build a pyre 50 feet tall out on an island, with himself on top lying on a pile of all his books. Let concert bands play Offenbach and Mozart's *Marriage of Figaro*, followed by the "Ride of the Valkyries" while the

11. Moore Hall.

mourners, dressed in gay apparel, feast and drink. His funeral would be a beacon fire calling Ireland from Catholicism to its pagan future. Or if public burning of human remains were illegal, he would like to have his ashes deposited in a copy of an ancient urn, depicting on its outside a bacchanal from which "one dancer, more pensive than the rest, steals away to the river bank, to cut a reed and found music within." Where should the urn be put? Where would it be safe? At last he thought, let them sink it in the sea so that in millions of years after the earth is covered in oceans, the seas will recede and "my tomb shall stand on a high rock in the solitude of an extinct sea, of an extinct planet." Then the sun would burn up into other suns, until the point toward which things were moving had been reached, and the tide would flow out again, with all the succession of life once more, plants, fish, animals, maybe even a George Moore writing a story called "Resurgam." "It is like madness, but is it madder than Christian doctrine [revised later to read: 'Palestinian folklore']?"[87]

Nietzsche played a key role as midwife to a new view of life for Moore.[88] The "myth of the eternal return" taught Moore once again, as Manet had taught him, to accept every aspect of himself, to want nothing about himself to be different, so that he could vanquish guilt and regret by acknowledging his wrongs while seeing them at the same time as part of all that brought him to be the person who made that acknowledgement. He came to accept even his so-called heartless impulses, those that made the son on the death of his beloved mother weep instead for the loss of his lover; all the impulses that grow in that garden of instincts he wished to cultivate and make flourish. Their fruits, after all, had made his mother take notice of what a wonderful child she had borne. In response to Nietzsche's affirmation, "Only as an *aesthetic phenomenon* is existence and the world eternally justified," Moore answered, Amen.

After the funeral, GM stayed with his agent Tom Ruttledge in Westport for a few days to take care of legal business.[89] Ruttledge suggested that GM should break the entail on the house and property of Moore Hall, so that, as sole, unencumbered owner, he would be free to dispose of it in his own will as he wished.[90] It was possibly because of GM's quarrel with Augustus Moore that he wished to overstep the usually automatic descent of the property to the next-oldest son or his children upon the death of an owner without children himself. True, Maurice – two years older than Augustus – would have been next in the line of inheritance, but Maurice was a soldier and might be killed in foreign combat. In fact, the one who would finally suffer by this change in the entail was not Augustus but Maurice Moore. Yet at the time of Mary Blake Moore's death, GM and Maurice were the fondest of brothers.[91] George invited Maurice to live at Moore Hall as its lord and master, and with the expectation that Maurice's sons would inherit the place; meanwhile, the housekeeping bills for Maurice's family would be paid out of the estate earnings.

9

While in Paris during May 1895, GM received a letter from Maud, who had recently become the wife of Sir Bache Cunard. Evidently, her letter scolded him for not writing to her in New York (he said two letters went astray), and for not answering by return of post her letter from Nevill Holt, Cunard's country house in Leicester. Of course he wanted to see her again, he said, and he would be back in London to meet her on 20 May. GM's letter is rather cross; he seems unsure of what tone to take. He says he has bought her a bottle of French perfume. Would she also "care to have a yard of scented flannel? . . . it scents underwear beautifully."[92] Without transition from this comically intimate considerateness, he passes on to the visit he has planned with Huysmans to hear nuns sing plainchant, and the first performance of *Tannhäuser* he had attended the previous night. When he saw Maud back in London (perhaps just before he was suddenly called to Moore Hall), he reports that he was shaken by his doubt as to which way she wanted to take their affair – into friendship, or adultery. To his shame and deep regret, as he tells it in *Theme and Variations*, he did not promptly take her in his arms and kiss her; instead, he talked of literature and she behaved like another man's wife.[93]

The correspondence between the two must have picked up over the summer, after Moore's return from the funeral of his mother. If, however, there were meetings between the two, intimate or otherwise, in June or July, they are undocumented. He was working on *Evelyn Innes* and dining frequently with Sir William Eden at Boodle's, the London club for country gentlemen Moore had joined. Eden was to be his model for the man-of-the-world hero in *Evelyn Innes* (Eden hardly returned the favor in describing GM as "white, fat, and maggot-y").[94] Eden tickled Moore by giving him "artless, natural" notes about his life and love affairs. Sybil Eden seems to have been tolerant of these; she herself was not above an innocent flirtation with GM.[95] In early August, GM wrote to Sybil that Lady Cunard was headed to Scotland for a shooting party and would like to escape. Lady Cunard could be reached, he explained, at Durris, Aberdeen. Would Sybil be willing to arrange a visit to Windlestone, the Eden estate, for 12, 15, or 20 August? If Sybil would write, Lady Cunard could be counted on to answer at once, he promises. A few days later, he wrote accepting Sybil Eden's invitation to join the Windlestone party on 20 August 1895. He was eager for that day to come round. On 14 August, he confided to Maurice Moore that "My young lady is trying to get away from her husband for a time – a week's adultery we agree would be charming. Some good friends of ours are doing their best but it is difficult to arrange."[96] The cavalier, confident tone of this letter raises the possibility that GM and Maud Cunard had indeed resumed their intimacy earlier that summer.

Moore never published accounts of what happened on that occasion at Windlestone; he could be discreet in certain circumstances. There is a letter to Maurice written from Windlestone in which GM denies he is going to marry Pearl Craigie now that she's divorced, or that he's going to marry anyone: "I am too much interested in other people's wives to think of getting one for myself."[97] He was at least very much interested in the wife of Sir Bache Cunard.

In March 1896, Nancy Cunard was born, seven months after GM and Lady Cunard met at Windlestone, and more than nine months after Moore's return to London from Ireland. He was never certain that he was not the father of Nancy Cunard. When Nancy was old enough, and troubled enough, to ask, GM replied that he was not sure; only her mother knew; and when Nancy then said she'd put the question, GM exclaimed, "Oh my Lord! Never ask your mother that!"[98] But Maud may not have known for sure either. What did become clear was that in later years he would often act like a father to her, and like a daughter she would look up to her GM.

10

On 13 October 1895, GM met Arthur Symons and Aubrey Beardsley among the company gathered for one of Edmund Gosse's Sunday dinners (from 1895 Moore was Gosse's most regular guest).[99] Symons and Beardsley were back from a September visit to Dieppe and Paris music halls, studios, and casinos,[100] and they were planning a new post-*Yellow Book* aesthetic monthly, the *Savoy*. Late one night, probably in the second half of October, Moore came round to Symons's rooms at the Fountain Court in the Temple, perhaps to give him his inscribed copy of the two-volume Leipzig edition of *Esther Waters*.[101] He found W. B. Yeats had moved into the room previously occupied by Havelock Ellis, the better to carry on his courtship of Olivia Shakespeare beyond the watch of his sisters in Bedford Park.[102] In a composite scene from *Ave* inventively drawing on later meetings as well as this initial encounter in the Temple, Moore says that Symons had not yet returned from the music halls, so the novelist and poet talked of the story in which WBY found himself entangled, the pages of which lay all about the floor. He simply could not decide what language to put on it. Do you mean to write it in Gaelic? GM asked. "A smile trickled into his dark countenance, and I heard him say he had no Irish." What WBY meant was that English was soiled by its use in newspapers; only in dialects did the language run pure, like a mountain stream; Yeats wanted a dialect for his story, an idiom flowing from the habits of Sligo peasants' lives.[103] Here was an aestheticism new to Moore. He was fascinated by Yeats's praise of peasants, by the curious notion of putting style on something like icing on a cake, and by the rejection of a whole urban London culture by one living within a stone's throw of Fleet Street. He tried to help Yeats disentangle a knot in his narrative – Moore liked nothing better than getting his finger into another person's pie.

Walking back to his garret in the small hours of the night, Moore thought with delight that he had found a new "boon companion," that essential intimate male friend. As GM sized up his current male friends, Edward Martyn, his Wagnerian fellow-traveler, was unpleasantly "obsessed by a certain part of his person which he speaks of as his soul"; it caused Edward to force his diet, Mass-going, and misogyny on others. William Eden was unsatisfactory too: a valet was essential to Eden, while a mildly effeminate literary companion was essential to Moore.[104] Yeats was as literary and as lovely as Symons, yet he was a far better talker; indeed, his talk seemed to GM far better than his writing. Or that is how Moore told the story in *Hail and Farewell*, fifteen years later when he wanted to queer the poet's pursuit of fame.

The teasing, hinting homosexuality of Moore's language about his "boon companions" rarely becomes explicit, but just during this period of his renewed acquaintance with Yeats, Moore published an extraordinary *symboliste* homoerotic fantasy. The occasion is a literary response to Wagner's music. GM imagines himself sitting in a Paris tavern; into it comes the spirit of Wagner, a dark-eyed bohemian playing ravishing strains on a violin, with his black eyes all the while fixed on the Irish writer:

And I listen overpowered, a strange being that I myself do not know; a strange germination progressing within me, thoughts and desires that I dread, whose existence in myself I was not aware of, in whose existence I did not believe and whose existence in myself I would fain deny, come swiftly and come slowly, and settle and absorb and become one with me . . . I pause horrified; but I may not linger: I am hurried on, repudiation is impossible, supplication and wringing of hands are vain, God has abandoned me, my worst nature is uppermost; I see it floating up from the depths of my being, a vicious scum: but I can do nothing to check or control . . . I am the prey of that dark, sensual-eyed Bohemian and his abominable fiddle, and seizing my bank-notes, my gold, and my silver, I throw him all I have, I bid him cease, and fall back exhausted.[105]

One might make much of these desires (*"Sodomita Libido"* is the name a trembling Huysmans gives this love) that Moore dreads and wishes to deny but to which he finally submits, but one must be careful: it is a fantasy and a highly literary one. Voluptuous and satanic literary responses to Wagner's music were an established genre, going back to Baudelaire's "Richard Wagner et Tannhäuser à Paris" (1861), Mallarmé's "Hommage à Richard Wagner" (1885), Verlaine's "Parsifal" (1886), and Huysmans's "L'Ouverture de Tannhäuser" (1893).[106] Indeed, Moore's purportedly intimate reaction to Wagner's music sounds like a translation of an untraced original in the files of Dujardin's *Revue wagnérienne*. If so, why did Moore excavate it, and at just this time? Oscar Wilde was sentenced on 25 May 1895 to two years in Pentonville Prison on charges of criminal love, and with his usual angry imprudence, Moore might well have published his fantasy, and published it again four months later, as a taunt in the face of an hysterical English public. When everyone else was running from any association with homosexuality, it would have been like Moore to embrace it, in literary terms at least; yet it would be surprising if he embraced it in any other sense, however attractive he found the dark young poet Yeats.

Shortly after Yeats moved into the Temple, Moore met Lady Augusta Gregory. Moore and Gregory both attended a performance of Wagner's *Valkyrie* on 21 October at Covent Garden. Lady Gregory was coming out as a literary hostess in a large way at her Queen Anne's Mansions flat in London, and on 4 November 1895 she invited GM to tea along with poet and imperial governor Sir Alfred Comyn Lyall. Less than a week later, she met with her Galway neighbor Edward Martyn to talk about landlord–tenant conflicts on their estates; in July, Martyn's steward had been fired upon at Lady Gregory's Coole Park gate. She was also socialising with Neville Geary, Martyn's Pump Court roommate, Moore's lessor at King's Bench Walk, and close friend to both of them.[107] A key link remained to be forged among the future leaders of the Irish Literary Theatre: Lady Gregory had not yet attached Yeats to herself. All of the players were in position, but it would not be until the summer and fall of 1896 that the curtain opened to find them plotting together to bring plays to Dublin.

In the meantime, GM tried to interest a London producer in *The Heather*

Field. The play was evidently finished around February 1895, and Moore gave it to George Alexander, the producer of *The Second Mrs Tanqueray*. Although Alexander saw there was no money in the play, he agreed to produce it on account of its merits; but then he found better things to do.[108] Next Moore tried it on William Archer for the New Century Theatre (managed by H. W. Massingham and Elizabeth Robins). Caught up in his own translation of *Little Eyolf*, Archer still had not read *The Heather Field* by January 1896; when he did, he was not impressed.[109] The New Century had a drawerful of plays of similar quality, Archer felt; the play GM was pushing was built around a good idea, but it was written "without a trace of specifically dramatic instinct or talent."[110] As a result of Archer's rejection, Moore's professed opinion became that the *The Heather Field* was a wonderful play and *Little Eyolf* a silly one. He went with Robert Hichens to the 23 November 1896 star-studded performance of Ibsen's drama, and afterwards gave a short critique of the plot, which involves a crippled child drowning, after which a crutch is found floating. Did Hichens notice that the whole play centered on one question? No, what question was that? Hichens asked. "Why didn't they have a nurse?"[111] When Moore came to write a preface for the book version of *The Heather Field* in January 1899, he ridiculed Archer's taste with his customary bludgeoning violence.[112] Moore cared a lot about this play signed by Martyn, and from early 1895 to late 1896 he craved to see it produced in a London theater associated with the Ibsen movement.

II

In the fall of 1895, after his rendezvous with Cunard at Windlestone, GM began looking for a new flat.[113] His motive seems to have been the same one that took WBY from Bedford Park to Fountain Court, and from there to the double bed at 18 Woburn Buildings: to have a place where he could meet his mistress. He tells of a lady, possibly Cunard, climbing three flights of stairs to his King's Bench Walk garret and finding him in his undershirt. She was shocked, but kindly forgave him, saying "With me it is all or nothing."[114] Still, he realised he needed a place where he could invite her to dinner; certainly, he had the money to live in better style than he had so far lived in London.

In early 1896, Moore left the Temple for a large flat with a spare room and his own servant at 92 Victoria Street, not far from the railway station.[115] The broad street was then "lined with lofty 'mansions' let out as 'flats' and large blocks of [legal] chambers."[116] Lewis Hind, who edited the *Academy* for its proprietor John Morgan Richards, visited Moore at his Victoria Street "mansion" and was astonished to find no books in the place. What did GM do with his time: look at his pictures by Manet, Monet, and Morisot? Tread his Aubusson carpet? "O, I write till it is time to go out to dinner," Moore answered Hind. "Writing bores me less than anything else." There were few books in the place because Moore normally read only a little of a book before he drew his conclusions from it, then he passed it along to a woman friend, such as Lena Milman, Mrs Charles Hunter, Sybil Eden, or Maud Cunard.[117] Hind and Moore went to Boodle's for a meal, and Hind was again confounded by the astonishing man. No one at Boodle's knew him as the author of *Esther Waters* and other notable books, but as Moore of Moore Hall, County Mayo.[118] Hind may not have thought of Moore this way, but GM himself never forgot it. "'If you did not know me, if you just saw me in the street,'" he once asked Sickert, "'what should you guess me to be?'" Sickert considered where to place the dart. GM continued "with a touch of impatience," "'Should you not guess me to be an English country gentleman, who had come up to London to see his lawyer?'" Sickert laughed hysterically.[119] But GM was more and more living up to the style of his class: he pursued millionairesses and titled wives, set himself up in a large flat in Pimlico, visited a tailor with Eden, wrote at his club, took tea with titled folk, spent weekends at country houses, and rode to the hounds with the other gentry.

During the Christmas holidays of 1896 he visited the Hunters and Edens in Durham. He was enthusiastic about Mary Hunter's arrangement of private theatricals, enthusiastic as well about getting up on a horse again and joining the New Year's Day meet with Sir William Eden's hunt, the South Durhams, at Selaby, the Hunter estate. Before mounting, he noticed one young gentleman, Mr Farquhar – an "ominous gnome-like creature." Hearing GM was to go on a hunt, three people had had presentiments he would be shot – an upstairs maid at Windlestone, GM's own servant, and Gosse. (Never the easiest friend or master, GM may have been the subject of wish-fulfillment dreams.) Now Moore himself was worried. He begged Charles Hunter not to let the young man shoot, but Hunter just laughed. Later in the day, the ominous youth fired a shotgun in Moore's direction, and, after a ricochet off a tree, one of the pellets pierced GM's right eyelid. Mary Hunter brought him over to Dr T. A. McCullogh, who found the retina displaced; the extraction of the "shotcorn" was "most painful."[120] After lying in a darkened room for two days, GM was visited by Mr Farquhar, the ominous gnome, who had come to beg forgiveness. "Oh, go a-way," Moore cried, "I do not ever want to see you. You are an id-i-ot. For heaven's sake, go a-way." Hearing this story from GM's lips at Gosse's on 27 January, Max Beerbohm was staggered by Moore's failure to say the English thing – "My dear fellow! It is nothing! Sort o' thing that might happen to anyone." And Beerbohm finally decided Moore's way was better; it was better not to offer false forgiveness. After all, once GM had uttered his contempt, he spoke to Beerbohm of young Farquhar in a perfectly good-humored way. In fact, vanity coming to the rescue, GM concluded, "the eye is rather a pret-ti-er color" (though it left him with proper sight in only one eye and a disconcertingly wandering stare).[121] Moore did not behave like that middle-class thing, an English gentleman; he acted according to the broader license of an Irish landlord.

12

After Yeats and Moore had left their lodgings in the Temple, GM kept up the relationship. He had made room in his plan for *Evelyn Innes* for a character study of an effeminate Celtic mystic with dreams of Wagnerian success for his works on stage (as opera, however, not theater). Indeed, GM was going to pay WBY the compliment of having this character, Ulick Dean, become the second lover of Evelyn, and, on the lines that enabled Flaubert to say, "*Madame Bovary c'est moi*," this was the deepest of compliments from the author of *Evelyn Innes*. In June 1896 he gave Yeats's story "Rosa Alchemica" "a wild ulogy" (WBY's spelling). Moore sometimes met with Yeats at Gosse's Sunday parties (for instance, on 5 July 1896),[122] but it is doubtful that Moore joined the Yeats, Symons and Martyn party at Tillyra Castle during August.[123] Yeats's visit to Galway in 1896 was to prove significant, as it drew him into the orbit of Lady Gregory, four and half miles down the road from Tillyra at Coole – perhaps one should say the meeting drew Lady Gregory into WBY's orbit of folklore-gathering, literary-political log-rolling, and progressive Unionist cum pacifist Nationalist cultural politics, all of which was to bear important fruit one year later at another summer meeting in Galway.[124]

During the intervening months in London, Lady Gregory cosseted Yeats, fed him at teas and dinners with the great and good in her acquaintance, and took up work as his typist and publicist. She invited GM to dinners show-casing Yeats on 28 March and 11 April 1897; he too was proselytising for WBY, even to the already converted Lady Gregory.[125] Moore reviewed "Mr. Yeats's New Book," *The Secret Rose*, in the *Daily Chronicle* and praised it, mostly for not being Robert Louis Stevenson. A little apologetically, Moore thought readers would have to allow Yeats his belief that when you look into the dark-ness there is always something there; witches were as necessary to him as a servant-girl had been to Moore. What GM was not yet ready to accept was the principle that an author should look after the words, and the ideas (or story) would take care of themselves; GM believed the opposite.[126]

So in early 1897 Moore was an enthusiastic observer of Yeats and a useful ally to him. He did not join the summer party at Tillyra, Coole, and Duras in July of 1897 when the "Celtic Literary Theatre" was proposed. Moore was in London in June and July writing *Evelyn Innes*, with a break for a furtive trip to a country house with Maud Cunard.[127] From the very start, however, he was part of plans for that theater. He was mentioned in the letter "To the Guaran-tors" drawn up at Coole as a contributor of future plays. During July, he was kept informed by means of letters from Martyn, and probably counted on by everyone for his experience as a stage manager and publicist.[128] The whole notion of mounting literary plays impossible for a commercial stage, and unde-sirable to a common audience, by means of an appeal from authors to wealthy people of taste concerned for the nation's reputation was taken over, lock, stock, and barrel, from GM's campaign for the Independent Theatre Society in the early 1890s. An early name contemplated for the organisation was "the Irish Independent Theatre Society."[129] The vital new element was the "Celtic" (Irish, Welsh, Scottish), and later simply Irish, focus: Dublin was to become the Mecca to which Irish literary Londoners would make pilgrimages once a year.

In that regard, it would be rather like Bayreuth. On 26 July 1897 Martyn left Galway to join GM on the way to Bayreuth; Dujardin, Symons, and Havelock Ellis were also making the pilgrimage.[130] They were all turning from Ibsen to kneel before Wagner, whose works possessed "that hieratic character which it is the effort of supreme art to attain," to quote Symons, possibly quoting Yeats quoting Pater. Martyn brought along a scenario for a new play, *Maeve* – a less realistic and more mythical play than *The Heather Field*. Both Symons and Moore were to put their hand to the manuscript, gently but perhaps decisively.[131]

Dujardin arranged an introduction to Cosima Wagner, the composer's widow. Moore presented her with a specially bound copy of *Esther Waters*: "And does he think she will read it?" snapped Aubrey Beardsley on hearing news of this gift.[132] Moore is likely to have met Houston Stewart Chamberlain, husband of Wagner's daughter, dear friend of Dujardin, and author of the idol-worshiping *Wagner in Excelsis*.[133] A year later, during the Dreyfus affair (GM was a mild Dreyfusard, respectful of Zola's courage), Chamberlain would convert Dujardin to his poisonous race theories, informed by Gobineau and Darwin, but driven by a new spirit of German imperialism and anti-Semitism.[134] Moore became interested in Dujardin's subsequent researches into the life of Jesus (the proto-Nazis wanted to prove that the first Christian was not a Jew), but he remained uninterested in Chamberlain's race theories, whether applied to England, Germany, France, or Ireland. His vanity extended only to cover his individual person, not his class, race, or nation – "It seemed to me that myself was my country," as he reflected when a boy at Jurles's military training school.[135]

In November, Moore was bearing down on the conclusion of *Evelyn Innes* (proofs began to come back from Unwin's printers in early January) while Yeats and Martyn were in Dublin negotiating for permission to stage plays outside of one of the patented theaters. Martyn wrote asking GM for a copy of the manuscript of *The Heather Field* (interestingly, he did not have one of his own), and for permission to put GM down as one of the committee for the "Celtic Theatre."[136] Yeats may well have begun to unfold for Moore the plans for an Irish Literary Theatre around the time of Gosse's Sunday afternoon party on 9 January 1898, when the two were among the five guests asked to remain for supper.[137] Perhaps Martyn and Yeats, the fat owl and the lank dark rook, even came to call on GM at 92 Victoria Street, as famously narrated in *Ave*, Volume 1 of *Hail and Farewell*. Although Moore was to telescope chronology and play with perspective in that work, there is no reason to doubt the element of hilarity in GM's subsequent rendering of his initial response to the idea of bringing literary dramas to Dublin, "of all the cities in the world." Edward,

GM wrote, spoke of a "Celtic Renaissance": "I am glad to hear of it . . . the Celt wants a renaissance, and badly; he has been going down in the world for the last two thousand years."[138] GM did not initially care tuppence for Irish nationalism or even Irish theatre, but he did care a good deal to get *The Heather Field* (and other plays he might write) put on stage before an appreciative audience in some English-speaking city. What's more, Edward seemed inclined to guarantee everyone against any loss of money. WBY and GM could agree on that being a very nice development.[139] Finally, in *Ave* GM speaks of his desire "to secure a good part in the comedy which I foresaw."[140] *Hail and Farewell* was beginning to write itself from January 1898.

What Yeats thought of Moore at this stage may be judged from the confidential conversation Lady Gregory copied into her diary of 1 March 1898 after a private dinner with the poet at her Queen Anne's Mansions flat.

> George Moore is a good natured fellow with an absorbing love of literature, who has reasoned himself out of all the moral codes as other people reasoned themselves into them – His tongue is terrific – He has quarrelled with Zola & with Mrs. Craigie & has only one word with which to describe both, that of pig! He was never looked upon by Mrs. Craigie as anything but a clever and agreeable man who was rather a distraction to her to have following her, but he was never her lover – He was reading his new novel to Symons the other day & said, "Mrs. Craigie won't like that remark about her" – "What remark" said Symons – "Why that it is unpleasant to meet your mistress afterwards & find her both middle aged and middle class" – "I did not know that applied to Mrs. Craigie" said Symons – "Well, she will!" says G. M.[141]

Augusta Gregory never approved of Moore, and indeed was made jealous by his affection for Yeats. Yeats himself, however, more tolerant of the moral eccentricities of artists, was at first an unresisting victim of Moore's "terrible gift of familiarity."[142] Besides, just as Martyn's money had its spiritual value, Moore had, Yeats estimated, "a mind that can be of service to one's cause." Furthermore, in the early days of their relationship, Yeats had respect for Moore's "courage and explosive power."

Yet Yeats was startled and disconcerted by the portrait GM gave of him in *Evelyn Innes*. The story is about a Wagnerian diva with two lovers, and one of those lovers, Ulick Dean, is a portrait of Yeats that was easily recognisable to London reviewers – one of them pointed out that the only difference between Yeats and Ulick Dean is that the first is a poet and the second is a composer of operas.[143] Dress, hair-style, mannerisms, living quarters, mystical chicaneries, conversation, style of masculinity, and Celticism are all carefully indicated features of the poet. Moore wrote the novel at the height of his infatuation with Yeats, and he often sees the poet through the eyes of his heroine Evelyn. After Evelyn has begun to desire Ulick, she leads him into a conversation about chastity: if he were to become her lover, would he have to surrender his spiritual life? Dean says that a sect of mystics in which he is involved advises its members to accept the married state, so that partners can "aid each other to rise to a higher spiritual plane."[144] This is not what Evelyn had in mind. She is not sure Ulick likes women at all, but he is very sympathetic to her, and his magic arts, mental abstractedness, and spiritual airs fascinate her. Carried away by the "strange rhythmical chant of his about the primal melancholy of man, and the remote past always insurgent in him," she wonders, why won't he kiss me? He could kiss me now. But Ulick was a thousand miles away.[145] Finally, they do make love when she seizes the initiative between the acts of *Tristan and Isolde*. He assumes that once they have made love, she will be his and his only, forever. ("A romantic" at the time, Yeats "thought one woman, whether wife, mistress, or incitement to platonic love, enough for a lifetime: a Parsifal, Tristram, Don Quixote.")[146] That is not Evelyn's plan.

When GM read to Symons and Yeats from the proofs in April 1898, they told him his latest novel was wonderful, on an even higher plane than the phenomenally successful *Esther Waters*.[147] However, early in June after Moore gave them presentation copies of the published novel, Yeats indicated that there was a flaw in the narrative. How could his heroine have loved someone so effeminate and unassertive as Ulick Dean?[148] The moment was propitious for throwing Moore into a panic . . . it was just before the reviews arrived, and he never had the least idea whether he had written a masterpiece or a laughable flop. He had been thinking that with *Evelyn Innes* he had run Balzac a close second and knocked Huysmans into a cocked hat, but now he immediately agreed with Yeats. Yes, surely he had failed to come up to his original, and he had made the narrative simply illogical: no one like Evelyn could have fallen in love with anyone like Ulick.[149] Although when the reviews did come out, some (such as the one by Quiller-Couch) were very good, and sales were excellent, GM immediately set about revising the novel, demanding of his publisher Fisher Unwin that the changes in the characterisation of Ulick go into the second printing, demanding next a complete resetting for another edition for still more changes, made with the help of Yeats, and at last changing Ulick entirely, remodeling him on George Russell instead of Yeats.[150]

There never was anything wrong with the novel that the correction of Ulick, making him more passionate and less mystical, would fix. Almost all the revisions, therefore, were useless and damaging. The problem was not with Ulick as a character; it was with Yeats as a man. The novel may have been "a complicated insult," as the poet's father suspected, but it was an unconscious one.[151] GM had shown up the poet in prose, revealing, as only a talented realist novelist could, just how the mystifications of WBY's personality beguiled women, and men too. Yeats comes off as the consummate sexual tease, attractive to many of both sexes, but unable to satisfy the one woman he loves. When it came to love, he was a young boy in the arms of Evelyn, frightened before, doting afterward, and ultimately lovelorn. This is not how Yeats wished to be seen; thus, the advice and Moore's wild goose chase.

In fall 1898 and winter 1899, Yeats began to make use of GM's powers in a way that would be a service to his cause. As part of the publicity for the spring 1899 opening season of the Irish Literary Theatre (ILT), he wanted Moore to whip up a controversy by means of his preface to the January 1899 Unwin edition of *Maeve* and *The Heather Field*. Moore obligingly brought into the sphere of debate WBY's own play, *The Countess Cathleen*, which GM judged had the only "actable blank verse" since Shakespeare, but he also inclined to believe that Yeats's dramas were better suited to be opera scenarios than plays for the stage, rather like Ulick Dean's Celtic opera "Conla and the Fairy Maiden" in *Evelyn Innes*. Indeed, at the October 1898 Leeds Festival, GM tried to interest Gabriel Fauré in composing music for the playlet.[152] Yeats was quite pleased with Moore's enthusiasm in taking up the role of John the Baptist to his own Messiah, and in letters to J. B. Yeats, William Sharp, Lady Gregory, and T. P. Gill, the poet eagerly looked forward to GM's preface.

When the preface came out in mid-January 1899, it instantly succeeded in one of its objects: it drew blood from William Archer, who replied in "Mr. George Moore as a Dramatic Critic."[153] As Max Beerbohm astutely illustrated the trap in a cartoon, the Irish novelist was trailing his coat before the sparky, tartan-clad Scotsman with one hand, while holding in the other his shillelagh for the start of the fun. (For Oscar Wilde, the cartoon perfectly captured Moore's "vague, formless, obscene face".)[154] Archer said GM never started the Independent Theatre Society, Grein did; GM never helped in the defense of *Ghosts*, Archer did. Furthermore, Yeats's play is poetry without drama, and Martyn's is Celticism without poetry. This was just what the doctor ordered, and both GM and WBY then had a go at Archer in the *Daily Chronicle*. Great publicity in London's biggest selling newspaper! To Archer's challenge that Martyn and Yeats had yet to prove their power of appealing to an intelligent public, GM – too explicitly expressing his own and Yeats's private views on the subject – replied, "Mr. Archer must know that the public is, was, and always will be, a filthy cur, feeding upon offal, which the duty of every artist is to kick in the ribs every time the brute crosses his path."[155] Archer then lost his composure, and threw a punch below the belt: "When I consider the similarity of Mr. Bernard Shaw's processes to Mr. Moore's, I begin to wonder whether there be not after all something in race," as if there were any significant racial difference in the descent of either Anglo-Irishman from that of another British citizen.[156] Beerbohm later upbraided Archer: "when you reach the point of calling people like Shaw and Moore feeble, you must have somehow gotten off the proper and safe track of controversy"; it was absurd to speak of "those two trenchant and interesting brains" as "feeble."[157] Yet it signaled a victory to Moore when Archer lost his urbanity.

Moore's next job for Yeats was to lend a hand at the stage management of the plays, Yeats himself having many theories but little experience as yet with play production. On 28 January 1899, WBY introduced GM to Florence Farr

12. George Moore trailing his coat before William Archer, by Max Beerbohm; *Daily Chronicle*, 30 January 1899.

(Ibsenite actress and past mistress of Shaw; verse-chantress and future mistress of Yeats). Yeats had put Farr on salary from Martyn as the ILT stage manager. Upon being introduced, GM complimented Farr and tried to get her to go to dinner with him. Farr ordinarily was, as Shaw said, "too good natured to refuse" a man, but she still did not fancy a night alone with the "boiled ghost" (her friend's description of GM) and tried to get Martyn invited to join the party of two.[158] "I tell you [Edward] knows no more about managing a theatre than a turbot from the North Pole," Moore barked.[159]

By 5 March, with the 8 May opening night looming ahead, Edward Martyn was morose about the quality of the actors Farr had cast for his play, and about slow progress at rehearsals. He called on Moore for help in his hour of need, and the two visited a rehearsal, hilariously described in *Ave*. They found Yeats explaining his theories of cantillation to the actors, while Florence Farr sat on the ground plucking a Dolmetsch psaltery, and chanting again and again, "Cover it up with a lonely tune." The leading lady, meanwhile, "walked to and fro like a pantheress."[160] To illustrate for the actors an invocation of the spirits of hell, Farr lay on the floor and spoke into the grate. (Moore's own preference was for simple, quiet realistic acting, as in the style of the Théâtre Libre.)[161] After such a rehearsal Moore and Martyn went to Lady Gregory's for dinner, where they found Yeats. After dinner, Moore "made an attack on Mrs. Emery [Florence Farr], & deposed her . . . Yeats taking it quite well, but put out."[162] Moore marched off the next day to clubs popular with actors and gathered a professional cast, including May Whitty and Ben Webster, Edward signing the checks, while Yeats and Farr were to be dispatched early to Dublin to stir up interest in the coming attractions (this had the advantage of keeping them away from rehearsals).[163]

Before they could get away, however, Martyn had an attack of conscience. He submitted *The Countess Cathleen* for the approval of Monsignor Gerald Molloy, Rector of Morehead Catholic University.[164] Monsignor Molloy found fault with the play. This would not be difficult for a Catholic to do. The play's premise is that God looks on the motive, not the deed, when judging actions; it also assumes that souls are worth different prices and a countess's soul may be worth a great deal more than a peasant's. And it involves a scene in which a soulless peasant kicks apart a domestic shrine to the Virgin. Edward announced that he wished to withdraw his money, his play, and his countenance from the first season of the Irish Literary Theatre.

On 22 March 1899, Moore, Yeats, Lady Gregory, and T. P. Gill (a Catholic nationalist editor) all had lunch with Martyn. Yeats was willing to make compromises, Gill made light of the difficulty, no doubt Lady Gregory smoothed things over with diplomatic brilliance, but Moore was explosive with rage. Such servility in his friend, such unreasoning subordination of art to religion, touched his fuse and he blew up and blew up again. Edward's conscience! Part of it was in his stomach, the rest up his ass.[165] Yeats feared that GM's fury was then more dangerous than Martyn's piety.[166] Moore went home to write an article for the *Nineteenth Century* to be entitled, "The Soul of Edward Martyn." Through the intensive fence-mending labors of Yeats, Martyn was relieved of his compunctions by the advice of two more priests and some light editing by the author. The play was back on schedule. Moore was crushed. On 8 April 1899 he told Yeats, "It was the best opportunity I ever had. What a sensation it would have made. Nobody has ever written that way about his most intimate friend. What a chance! It would have been heard of everywhere."[167] Moore sent the draft manuscript to Martyn as a letter, no longer extant; Martyn remembered it a year and a half later as "most insulting."[168] Presumably it was a satirical *De profundis* and may well have trod on very dangerous ground – Martyn's interest in young choirboys. Martyn got the letter when in Dublin in early April, and immediately sought out Yeats and Farr. Mopping the "large sweat upon his forehead," he began: "I withdraw again."[169] WBY condoled with him about Moore; then Moore was persuaded to apologise, so things were once more on track.[170]

Moore stayed in London with the actors (he was also busy bringing out a revised edition of *Esther Waters*), so he missed the Dublin controversy over *The Countess Cathleen* whipped up by F. Hugh O'Donnell and his pamphlet *Souls For Gold!*. Since GM judged Edward Martyn fit for an asylum on account of his theological objections to the play, it was incredible to him that Dublin was full of Edward Martyns. When he arrived at the Antient Concert Rooms in Dublin halfway through the production of *The Countess Cathleen* on 8 May 1899, he did not know what to make of the howls of protest from Catholic students in the audience,[171] or of the presence of twenty or thirty big Dublin policemen. "Into what land have I drifted?" He considered that the play, at bottom, shocked no one's feelings;[172] it just gave people an opportunity to pretend that their feelings were shocked, and to manifest sectarian tension.

What must have been most amazing of all to Moore was the passive and uncritical applause for *The Heather Field* on the second night of the performances. The "cheering was loud and long-continued" for Martyn at the curtain (Moore seemed doomed to be involved in the writing of plays for which others received ovations).[173] "Here is a play," the *Freeman's Journal* proclaimed, without "the remotest suggestion in it from beginning to end of the disordered eroticism which is responsible for so many stage successes in London and Paris." It is a ridiculous comment. No one noticed that the character Barry Ussher ("landowner, student, philosopher, etc.") is as explicit as he could decently be in saying that the hero is homosexual. Carden Tyrrell, he explains, was not fit to marry women and was only happy among boys during his schooldays. No one noticed that Carden treats Miles Tyrrell, the Trinity College student (safely coded as a younger brother), with the confidential familiarity with which a man would treat a wife, or that he treats nine-year-old Kit (safely coded as a son) with the wistful eroticism of a paedophile. Even without these disguises – regular aspects of Wilde's own plays, by the way, where the dandies all marry in the end – probably the ILT audience would not have noticed that the "heather field" itself symbolises not so much "idealism," "romance," or "madness," as the instinctive attachment of Carden to men. Even given the fact that the play was not legible in such terms to Irish audiences in 1899 and the meaning had to remain GM's poignant but private joke, it remains surprising that no one brought up the fact that the play is also about, for, and in favor of landlords, improving landlords with a vision of national good, of course, but also landlords harassed to the point of madness by their tenants and local government boards. *The Heather Field* is an Irish literary drama because it was written by an Irishman and performed in Dublin, but it is not a nationalist or democratising play by any means. This passed unnoticed amid the controversy over *Countess Cathleen*. The play's success was possibly aided by the facts that Martyn was Catholic, that the pre-performance publicity told people it was a patriotic work, and that a local man had written a proper realistic drama of a very serious sort (and with no smut visible to the masses). Irish audiences were a volatile, complex, and subtle body, one not well understood by Moore (or even

Yeats), but GM loved a fracas and he was eager to learn more about his forsaken countrymen. In less than two years, he would decamp for a ten-year perch at 4 Upper Ely Place, Dublin, the better to study them all and take his part in the casual comedy of the Irish Literary Revival.

Chapter 10
The Irish Literary Theatre

I

Why did George Moore, like a cosmopolitan Lord Jim, make a standing jump from all that he had known for the last thirty years into the strange seas of Dublin political life? There is no mystery about why George Moore left Paris and went to Moore Hall in 1880 and left it for London a year later. He did not want to be a Mayo land agent but a great English writer. Why he left England in early 1901 was, however, a complicated mystery even to himself. In *Ave* Moore says it was a miracle that sent him to Ireland: like Paul on the road to Damascus, GM on the Hospital Road toward Chelsea had heard a voice. Three times the voice of Cathleen ni Houlihan said, "Go to Ireland!" so he felt he must obey. (Yeats had visions, why shouldn't GM?)[1] While no miracle, the web of instincts, ambitions, loves, and resentments that actually pulled him by the gathering force of many little tugs toward 4 Upper Ely Place, Dublin, creates a kind of awe at the mysteriousness of the human animal. It involved falling out with Lady Cunard and falling in with the young painter Clara Christian, a brotherly tie with Maurice Moore and a more than brotherly link to W. B. Yeats, an ambition to be a playwright with an audience and a fascination with literary adventures (such as the possibility of being the father of a new literature in an ancient language), a sense of rejection as an Irish Catholic by English culture and the hope of acceptance within Ireland as a distinguished national figure. Within and above these threadlike factors there was the hovering design of the great spider spinning its self-pleasing thread even while being suspended by it. More and more, GM began to see life in the guise of an unfolding comic pattern, in which, with just a little assistance here and there, human specimens might be caught up in their own exertions, there to await one's delicate inspection.

The lurches Moore made away from London and forward to Dublin can be measured by the sequence of his public declarations at celebrations of Irish Literary Theatre performances. The first lecture followed the performances of

The Heather Field and *The Countess Cathleen*. On 11 May 1899, editor T. P. Gill and the *Daily Express* put on a dinner at the Shelbourne Hotel for those involved in the productions. In a set-piece tableau from *Ave*, the young *Daily Express* journalist Ernest Longworth, in the chair next to Moore at the head table, gives him little dossiers of Dublin gossip on his fellow guests: T. W. Rolleston, once a Trinity College poet and Home Ruler, now neither; Robert Yelverton Tyrell, drinker and classical scholar at Trinity; Douglas Hyde, Trinity alumnus and President of the Gaelic League, and for Moore the ultimate "Catholic-Protestant" – "cunning, subtle, cajoling, superficial, and affable";[2] J. F. Taylor, florid in face and oratory; Standish O'Grady, Carlylean in prose, imperialist in politics, and Celticist in culture.[3] It was an upper-class, mostly Trinity, constructive Unionist or National Party elite.

Gill opened with a speech that put some distance between himself and Yeats on representations of the Irish Famine, and then called Edward Martyn "a dramatist fitted to take rank among the first in Europe." The ovation greeting this puffery made Edward's moonlike head swell – "happy as a priest at a wedding" and "slightly triumphant . . . over Yeats," Moore noted.[4] Yeats rose to continue the battle over the interpretation of *The Countess Cathleen* before GM, nervous about all courtroom and public appearances, had to get to his feet to read a prepared speech.[5] He was in formal dress, "cut-throat" collar, peg-top trousers, and long-tailed black coat, but to the curious young author, James Cousins, both "his pasty face and vague eyes," and "straw-coloured hair that looked as if it had been pitchforked on," "contradicted his clothes."[6] Moore apologised to the guests for reading his speech, apologised for being in Ireland, and apologised a final time for having been so long out of Ireland, then bent his head and plunged onward. Beerbohm, who was present, agreed with GM's own assessment that he was the only Irishman who could not make a speech. Indeed, "he could not passably read a speech." "Well do I remember," Beerbohm wrote later, "the woe-begone way he murmured into his MS."[7]

Yet Moore had something to say for himself. He had gone to Paris, he explained, because that was where art was to be found in the 1870s; for the same reason, he went to London for the 1880s and 90s.[8] Now the Muses were taking flight again, and next they would alight in Ireland, because – and this is the interesting part – art always follows in the wake of struggles for power and wealth, when the time comes that humans begin to ask what the wealth and power are for. Then, individuals can pursue art for its own sake, that is, for the discovery of the beautiful, which accommodates the species to its existence. It was time, he said, to forget class and sectarian conflict, to recognise that the Land War was over and that the Parliament in Westminster was no longer the theater of meaningful acts. The Irish Literary Theatre, the Cooperative Movement, the Loan Exhibition of Old Masters from Irish country houses, and the Gaelic League were signs of a renaissance in Ireland, a spring tide of art.

Most of this is party-line cultural nationalism, sponsored by Hyde, Plunkett, and Yeats, but Moore gives the story a new twist. Usually, the Irish Revival is read as a prologue to the Easter Rebellion; GM read it at the time as an epilogue to the Land War.[9] The peasants had won that war, but the Ascendancy now had a chance to win the peace, by giving the Irish people forms in which to exercise their new franchise on identity. As Augusta Gregory put it, the directors of the Literary Theatre were not working for Home Rule; they were preparing for it. While Home Rule was inevitable, it was not inevitable who would rule at home, or how the citizens would domestically get along with one another.[10] The language of peace and liberty rhymes with a language of containment.

Moore would probably have been better advised to sit down while the people were still applauding his prophecy that Ireland would be the next Periclean Athens and Medician Florence. But he went on: he said he had only done this terribly disagreeable thing, come from London to make a speech, in order to proclaim Yeats as a great poet, comparable to Victor Hugo – why stop there? – comparable to Shakespeare. England had fallen into an imperialist nightmare, honoring generals who slaughtered Arabs with machine-guns, atrocities celebrated in the bloody-minded poetry of Kipling; but "the Celt was celebrating in a poor wayside house the idealism of Mr. Yeats." Moore finished reading his speech and sat down. J. F. Taylor, himself a terrific speechmaker, took the floor. Taylor used his Corinthian irony on a Moore "kind enough to return to Ireland" now that Ireland had "raised herself to his level." The Irish people, Taylor wanted to put on record, had always been the best of races. Nonsense! Moore thought. All races were the same, all dust, but he did not dare to speak without notes, and WBY would not on his behalf deny the existence of race; indeed, Yeats would have agreed with Taylor that there were racial differences and that these were in the favor of the Irish, or some segment of the Irish.[11]

GM's panegyrics got both the praiser and the praised in trouble. Edmund Gosse scolded GM for blasting Kipling and booming Yeats (Shakespeare for our time) in the preface to the May 1899 revised edition of *Esther Waters*. Yet Moore was unapologetic: "why should I acquiesce in the general opinion? Is not this a shameless truckling to the newspapers?"[12] The *New York Times* judged Moore's assessment "preposterously wrongheaded," but Moore said he "must insult the public somehow."[13] Yeats himself seems not to have been averse to a high public estimation of his value; he thought well of himself too. Soon enough, Yeats and Moore, Shakespeare and Shakespeare, would begin to collaborate on plays, and there would then be many impediments admitted to that marriage of true minds, not least who was going to be allowed to be the *prima donna* and who the *primo uomo*.

2

In the summer of 1899, Moore made another pilgrimage to Bayreuth with Edward Martyn; a third member of the party goes entirely unmentioned in

Moore's account of the trip in *Ave* – Edward's friend and fellow-member of the Catholic Ascendancy, the tenth Earl of Westmeath, of Pallas, Loughrea.[14] On 1 August 1899, the travelers left London for Bayreuth by way of Aix-la-Chapelle, Mainz, Boppard, Nuremberg, and Rothenburg.[15] Upon their arrival, according to GM's story in *Ave*, the driver wanted to take them to a room with a view, GM wanted one with a clean privy, and Edward required lodgings near a restaurant and chapel. All these amenities were not to be found in one place, and so a fracas broke out, described by Moore at hilarious length. In Bayreuth, the Irish landlords circulated among the fashionable crowd gathered for performances of the *Ring*, *Parsifal*, and *Die Meistersinger*. On 14 August 1899 they ran into Pearl Craigie, flirting with a young Guinness until the arrival of Lord Curzon, and on 16 August Moore's party joined forces with Arthur Symons and Havelock Ellis; they then made their devotions to Madame Cosima Wagner.[16]

Over the course of their journey, three sources of trouble cropped up between GM and Martyn. First, GM budgeted himself to £1 a day on his travels (this journey cost him £45 over six weeks); Martyn had much more to spend.[17] Second, and far more seriously, after the success of *The Heather Field*, Martyn was flush with a sense of himself as Parnell and Ibsen rolled into one. "His" realistic dramas were going to be the salvation of Ireland. So even before they left for Bayreuth, Moore's own vanity was irritated. Martyn had sent GM the draft of a new play, and GM says he wrote back, "There is not one act in five . . . which, in my opinion, could interest any possible audience – Irish, English, or Esquimaux." Having thrown cold water on Martyn's hopes, GM suggested that perhaps he could help straighten out Martyn's mess of a play on their way to Bayreuth, thus reminding Martyn of the complete dependence of the amateur on the professional writer. But Martyn was now getting touchy about Moore manhandling his manuscripts, and, evidently, no miracles were worked on this trip.[18] There was one final source of trouble: GM always arranged for female companionship on his travels; Martyn wanted none.

It would not, however, be Maud Cunard that Moore was meeting on this journey. In spite of the little pyre she made of her past, some letters survive to show that things had not been going well between the possible parents of two-year-old Nancy. In a letter of 10 February 1898, GM despaired of the time that had passed since he had last seen Lady Cunard. She was evidently jealous of his friendship with Lena Milman, yet he needed someone to live for besides "Evelyn Innes."[19] Maud promptly invited him to tea four days later, but the mercurial man's melancholy was too black to let him accept the invitation.[20] There were possibly other invitations that he did accept – little feasts of love in London hotels, when he knelt over her bed "like a saint at the Sacred Table," as he puts it in the rejected chapter of *Memoirs*.[21]

Moore also sought meetings with Cunard outside London. During the late 1890s he had assembled titled acquaintances and arranged a summer and fall itinerary through country houses. Thus, he mapped his life upon that of Lady Cunard. Her set became his set: Lady Randolph Churchill (formerly Jennie Jerome); Adela, Lady Essex; Sybil, Lady Eden; Lady Algernon Lennox; Leonie Leslie (formerly Leonie Jerome); and Mary Hunter (sister of composer Ethel Smyth). Like Lady Cunard herself, they were cultured, beautiful, rich, and often American ladies, but they bored him, and though he made them listen to versions of his emerging narratives, he suspected he was wasting time that might have been given to writing. They seemed to him driven by "an exasperated desire to escape the tedium of leisure."[22] "Sex was the object" of their parties, but too rarely did GM land in the same house for the same weekend with Cunard, when he might have been able to cross the hall to her bed-chamber for the odd night of love.[23] When fortune did seem to smile on him and the two were houseguests together at Windlestone, she apparently once asked him to excuse her – he would surely understand – and not come to her room – she was minded to entertain, for the time, a certain young man with skinny shanks.[24] Though no moralist, this capriciousness was hard for Moore to understand. He was possessive, but did not possess her. He came to regard their relations as too painful to continue, or, as those relations were hardly continuous, too painful to hope for their resumption, and one significant tie to England was cut.[25]

The woman Moore was to meet on his 1899 trip to Bayreuth he apparently first encountered in the studios and Chelsea apartments of his friends, the British Impressionists – Henry Tonks, P. W. Steer, William Rothenstein, and Walter Sickert. Clara Christian (1868–1906) was a former student of Tonks's at the Slade School; when Moore met Christian, she was a contributor to New English Art Club exhibitions. Moore, describing Clara under the pseudonym "Stella" in *Hail and Farewell*, says that she grew up in a wealthy Putney family, one of two children, both staid. The Christians originally came from the Isle of Man, with one branch of the family settling in County Waterford, Ireland, and another in Llanwnda in Carnavonshire, Wales. Clara often visited the same Welsh shire northeast of Bangor when she wished to paint landscapes.[26] While still at the Slade School, she met Ethel Walker (1861–1951), and the two painters set up house together at 33 Tite Street in Chelsea.[27] Both were gifted – Walker later became an OBE and, according to her *Times* obituary, "the most important woman artist of her time in England," especially well known for her portraits of young women, done in a style reminiscent of Sickert.[28] Together, the two women had traveled in Italy and Spain; in August 1899 they were visiting the museums of the Low Countries.

GM had persuaded Martyn to interrupt their return to London in Antwerp, so that they might see Rubens's *The Descent from the Cross* and other Dutch pictures. There, at a certain cathedral, Moore had arranged to run into Christian, who was traveling with her lover, Ethel Walker.[29] GM very much relished this episode in *Ave*, a new romantic plot – two couples traveling from Antwerp to Ghent and then Holland, one couple male, the other female, but one member of each same-sex couple heterosexual. In one turn of GM's narrative, Ethel ("Florence") stands to gaze with GM upon Clara ("Stella") and appreciatively informs him that "no more perfect mould of body than Stella's existed in the flesh – perhaps in some antique statues of the prime, though even that was not certain."[30] GM and Clara then gravitate to one another, and the others are left to themselves, doubly unlinkable.

Martyn broke off his tour at Bruges to return to Tillyra, but Ethel Walker saw the journey out, unhappily. As was his habit, budding romance inspired Moore to write bad French verses – which, after he rejoined Martyn at Tillyra, he promptly arranged to publish in Gill's Dublin *Daily Express* on 30 September 1899, the first of a sudden spate of contributions to an Irish revival.[31]

3

Moore had arrived at Tillyra by 29 September, and soon afterwards forced discussion of Martyn's play, *The Tale of a Town*, a burlesque satire of political pretenders in post-Parnell Ireland and, oddly, also a satire on women in general. According to *Ave*, Edward protested that the new scene GM wished him to write was not truly Irish (Moore would henceforth often be told in Ireland that he was not Irish enough, as many were plunged into colonial paranoia about vanishing quantities of Irishness). Since Martyn would not do so, Moore wrote out the scene himself, causing Martyn to beg, "almost hysterically, . . . 'Leave me my play!'"[32] So Moore passed the play to the other director of the Literary Theatre, Yeats, then Augusta Gregory's guest up the road at Coole, and Yeats pronounced it "entirely impossible." In *Ave*, Moore says he felt he could see in Yeats's face a fuller judgement on Martyn than on the play itself – "Your soul is inferior, beneath my notice; take it away," and the observation is a nice foreshadowing. What WBY showed he felt about Martyn, he would within a year feel, and show that he felt, about Moore too.[33] But for now, the novelist and poet were leagued together in demanding an overhaul of Martyn's play. Martyn was distressed, but he said, for the sake of Ireland, "Do with it as you like; turn it inside out, upside down."[34] The revision of *The Tale of a Town* went forward in his own house, a betrayal almost more than Martyn could take, especially after Yeats moved into a room at Tillyra in late October.[35] Yeats and Moore, Augusta Gregory noted, made "too much mystery over [their revisions], & it vexed [Martyn] till he 'hated the sight' of both."[36]

Martyn was not the only one who found the balance of intimacies upset by Moore: Augusta Gregory and George Russell ("AE") both regarded Moore as the evil Svengali in the life of their fair poet, especially when GM began to reconstruct Yeats's mystical play, *The Shadowy Waters*. Apparently responding to an emergency call for help, George Russell wrote Augusta Gregory on 12 October 1899 that he would do what he could to intercede with Yeats and prevent the alteration of his verse drama; indeed, he would "strangle Moore if

13. W. B. Yeats and George Moore at Coole (*c.* September–October 1900).

necessary" (once GM went on to Dublin, George Russell let Augusta Gregory know, "I gave him my mind on the Shadowy Waters").[37] Moore next blithely butted his way into Augusta Gregory's relationship with Douglas Hyde by offering to help Aran islander Tomas Ua Concheanainn (1870–1960) frame a narrative for a life story to be published in Irish. Moore did not mind if his name was kept out of Concheanainn's autobiography. *An Claidheamh Soluis*, the League organ, would have smelled a rat if George Moore were known to be in any way involved.[38] Next, on 17 October, the night after WBY had dreamt of the Irish queen Grania, GM asked him to collaborate on a play based on the ancient saga of Diarmuid and Grania.[39] Since Ulick Dean (i.e. Yeats) writes a *Tristan and Isolde*-style opera called "Grania" in *Evelyn Innes* (1898), the idea did not originate with the spirits of the night.

When the news was broken to Augusta Gregory that Yeats and Moore were going to collaborate on a play, her face clouded. As told in *Ave*, Gregory took GM for a walk about the house and grounds of Coole, illustrating how much she had done to create an atmosphere in which Yeats could write poetry. Collaboration with Moore on a prose drama would only be a distraction from that poetry. Then she murmured "something about a man of genius and a man of talent coming together, speaking quickly under her breath, so her scratch would escape my notice at the time."[40] (This notion about the bad offspring that must come from misalliance apparently did not apply to her own subsequent collaborations with Yeats.) In *Ave*, Moore understated the pain she gave him by such a remark. Her claws raked the delicate integument of his artistic vanity, and the area of the wound remained sensitive.

For the time being, however, the spirit of artistic brotherhood offered by Yeats was sufficient balm. At Tillyra, the two authors began to replace Martyn's play piece by piece. Yeats thought Moore's "tremendous" new scene for *The Tale of a Town* "will make . . . our theatre a national power."[41] Moore, carried forward by "boundless enthusiasm," also drafted with Yeats a scenario for *Diarmuid and Grania*. At the end of October, GM left Galway for the Shelbourne Hotel. There he wrote out a version of the dialogue act by act. According to an arrangement that WBY explained to his sister, GM was to send this rough version of *Diarmuid and Grania* to Coole so that Yeats might put it into "[his] own language," or that language he and Augusta Gregory thought fitting to the characters. By 6 November, Moore already had an early draft of part of *Diarmuid and Grania* ready to hand over. Thus, in spite of Gregory's warnings, Moore was leading Yeats away from verse and into prose drama. In a letter to Gregory, GM tried to lay the blame for the interruption of *Shadowy Waters* on the necessity of repairs to Martyn's play, not on his own collaboration with Yeats on *Diarmuid and Grania*. The scratch was still tender, and he feared more of the same. Moore also tried to turn the tables by complaining to Augusta Gregory that Yeats was forcing him from his proper work by demanding further revisions to *A Tale of the Town*: "my sanity must be considered," not to mention an old friendship with Martyn.[42] "Martyn is sound" for the time being, Moore told Yeats on 2 November, but "I dare not venture further changes" to *The Tale of a Town*.[43]

But he did venture farther. The very next day Moore dropped Martyn's misogynistically conceived female characters, and began to enlarge the part of the protagonist Jasper Dean. Martyn's humiliation was incidentally publicised when, after he refused to help, Moore turned to T. P. Gill and AE for political allusions to paste into the plot.[44] All Dublin would soon know what Moore was up to, and that Moore was in charge. Every character was to be somebody in public life, so that – this was to be the fun for the audience – anyone in public life just might be a character in the play: Alderman Lawrence might be John Redmond; Ralf Kirwan might be Standish O'Grady; Ferguson, Tim Healy; Foley, William O'Brien; and everyone and his neighbor could be Jasper Dean – Lord Castletown, T. P. Gill, T. W. Rolleston, Martin Morris, Horace Plunkett, etc.[45] *The Tale of a Town* was becoming a very different play from what it had been in early September. Moore tried to mend fences with Martyn, by working the press on behalf of Edward's other play – *Maeve*, scheduled for performance in February with Alice Milligan's *The Last Feast of the Fianna*, and the revised *Tale of a Town*. Before leaving Dublin, Moore also obtained from W. F. Bailey a possible remedy for Edward's gout, as if to say that he had not forgotten his friend's pain.[46]

In London, Moore arranged to meet up with Yeats for further *séances de collaboration*. Moore loved the way he could get under someone's skin in the process of co-authorship, and in a letter to Yeats, he plumbs Yeats's psychology:

> Here is the solution of the difficulty. [The hero] leaves the second woman because she falls in love with him. He wants (like all of us) to adore, not to be adored. When the God descends from his altar, the worshipper goes to another church . . . You see how it leads up to your end, religion. There the God never descends from his altar to worship the worshipper.[47]

By this ventriloquistic palaver, Moore at last was coming close to understanding why Yeats turned aside from the chances he got, as an entrancing magelike poet, to sleep with female admirers, why especially he neglected to sleep with Maud Gonne – what Joyce called "the spiritual-heroic refrigerating apparatus, invented and patented in all countries by Dante Alighieri."[48] Stephen Dedalus needs to keep Emma Clery on an altar to the Virgin, and there Maud Gonne must stand too. From what Moore evidently knew of Paris, another man had lain with Maud Gonne, namely the anti-Dreyfusard journalist Lucien Millevoye, so why shouldn't WBY? Yeats did not like to hear such talk from Moore, but he was falling for what he later called GM's "terrible gift of familiarity."[49]

The spirit of contagious creativity Moore generated – the pace, vehemence, and cheek of his sense of authorship – exhilarated Yeats. GM's highly communal sense of the enterprise of authorship – learned long ago from Bernard Lopez at the Hôtel Quai Voltaire – was just what was needed for the start of a literary revival. Under GM's leadership, *The Tale of a Town* became a play that was socially authored by a whole fleet of cultural activists, all charged with the idea that they could by means of their own literary endeavors make something happen. In early January 1900, Yeats wrote Gregory that the play was now "extraordinarily fine . . . a splendid and intricate gospel of nationality and may be almost epoch-making in Ireland."[50]

4

In early January, rehearsals of Martyn's *Maeve* were already underway, and Martyn was predicting that his own play would be better than *The Heather Field*, not to mention *The Tale of a Town*, a play now spoiled in his judgement by Yeats and Moore; indeed, he meant to publish his original text to prove its superiority to the revision.[51] Yet Symons, J. B. Yeats and family, and Moore himself were in agreement with WBY that *The Tale of a Town* had been turned into something that was "really literature."[52]

When Augusta Gregory arrived in London for rehearsals of the play (retitled *The Bending of the Bough* after Martyn refused to sign or co-sign it),

Yeats began to take up an apologetic tone about Moore in the letters he wrote to Augusta Gregory, as if he were fatigued by his friend, or only put up with him "for the sake of Ireland." Begging off a date on 20 January with Augusta Gregory, he explained that "Moore has insisted with his usual vehemence (I tried to keep that evening in the hope you would be in London & could let me dine with you) – on my meeting an actress who is to hear & perhaps act Grania" (*sic*).[53] Still, could he show up at Lady Gregory's apartment for tea or supper the next day? He came, and stayed for both tea and supper. Certainly it was difficult for Yeats to keep in with Augusta Gregory if he was going to be so close to Moore – whether because she loved the one man or because she hated the other it is hard to say, as both were the case. She went to Yeats's Monday evening gathering at 18 Woburn Buildings on 22 January, and there was GM again. A fuss occurred because he wanted to alter Alice Milligan's little play, *The Last Feast of the Fianna*. With her deadeye wit, Augusta Gregory indignantly observed that GM was "resolving himself into a syndicate for the rewriting of plays." *The Heather Field*, *The Tale of a Town*, *Shadowy Waters*, *The Countess Cathleen*, and *Diarmuid and Grania* – it was alarming the amount that he had co-written and rewritten and superintended the rewriting of.[54] Then Moore almost started another fight in Yeats's rooms, because Florence Farr believed Yeats had promised her a part, but found that GM had already assigned that particular part to another. Just who was the maestro here anyway? And what part would Augusta Gregory herself be able to play as patroness or muse to a maestro, if Moore was going to sweep all before him?

Another complication was that she was beginning to identify with the fate of poor Edward, her Galway neighbor, the left-out friend whose talent is overlooked or downplayed. Augusta Gregory dreamt that Yeats told her that her business was not to write but to create an atmosphere. Martyn's business seemed to be to guarantee the Irish Literary Theatre against financial loss, while Yeats and Moore did the men's work of writing.[55] Martyn took Gregory to dinner and a play on 24 January, and poured out his troubles. He had been very badly treated, he complained, only Augusta Gregory had been good to him at all; but he was delighted that Hermann de Lange, stage manager for *The Bending of the Bough*, dispraised the play. De Lange and Martyn wished to drop the Yeats/Moore version and substitute Martyn's original text, but they could only do this on the agreement of a majority of the ILT Society "committee." Martyn wanted Augusta Gregory to count herself as one of this committee (her membership was news to her), and vote with him – which was more treachery to Yeats than she had stomach for.[56] Two days later she attended a rehearsal, and judged that under De Lange *The Bending of the Bough* was going efficiently, but noticed that Martyn was driving Moore to breaking point by deprecating the play in loud whispers to her.

The high-tension crossed wires of affection nearly broke loose in a blaze of sparks the very next day, 27 January. Yeats came to dine with Augusta

Gregory. He was angry with Martyn for making trouble and with Augusta Gregory for taking his part. According to her diary, Yeats

> says Moore claims no one can have more than one conscience, & his is an intellectual conscience – & no one with that can forgive Martyn's want of intelligence – I say if I have but one conscience it is a conscience of friendship – . . . Then he declares that Moore wrote most of 'The Heather Field' & 'a gr part of "Maeve"' – (a new story) – says Moore told him so & he believes him – (all very well, but he doesn't believe [Moore] when he attacks Miss Gonne's morality).

Augusta Gregory was indeed fighting for her friend, but the "friend" was Yeats as much as it was Martyn, and the enemies were both Moore and Maud Gonne. Augusta Gregory had a genius at managing relationships, and she kept Yeats by sacrificing Martyn. A few days later, she persuaded Edward not to publish *The Tale of a Town* as it could not hold its own against *The Bending of the Bough* as *literature*, and she delivered that drastic if true judgement in such a way that Martyn accepted the outcome quietly, at least for two days.[57] Then, nettled by Moore, Martyn went on a stampede and threatened to withdraw his financial guarantee from the upcoming performances, causing Yeats to consider the likelihood that he could draw upon the large reserves of Annie Horniman (an Order of the Golden Dawn member, his admirer, and ultimate owner of the Abbey Theatre). First, however, Yeats tried to rope Martyn back into the stable by telling him that his money did not matter: lots of people have money, but the possibly fine plays Martyn might one day write for his country did indeed matter, so he should stick with the Irish Literary Theatre.[58] When you want to get someone to do something, always appeal to what is best in them, Augusta Gregory wrote in her diary; the strategy worked for Yeats too, with a revision to "what they fancy is best in them."[59] "I'm not taken in – I'm not taken in by you and Yeats and . . . the old proselytizer in the background," GM has Martyn crying in *Salve*, but taken in he was for the time being, and the more glory to him for it.[60]

5

Moore disappeared for a few days to Nevill Holt to visit Nancy and Maud Cunard, but when he reappeared at Augusta Gregory's Queen Anne's Mansions apartment on his return to London, he once again threw her into a fright.[61] She had just been persuading Yeats in Moore's absence that for the sake of peace there had to be a "general" in the Literary Theatre, and that absolute ruler should be Yeats (the newspapers were full of demands for an authoritative general to take charge of the war in South Africa). Now on 4 February 1900 Moore came in with his preface to the Unwin edition of *The Bending of the Bough* and an idea for a speech at the banquet scheduled to follow the Dublin performance. The projected speech would bring together condemnation of English imperialism in Africa and praise of Irish as the language of a great future literature. With his characteristically immoderate enthusiasm for a new idea, Moore was "taking the Irish language under his protection." Moore projected "a wild scheme for having 'Shadowy Waters' translated into Irish for next year's theatre."[62] This was a breathtaking blow to Augusta Gregory: all Yeats's beautiful poetry, and all his talk of *style*, swept away in one blithe political gesture, and a gesture it would be hard to stand against, since the Irish language was a sacred cow for Irish nationalists. Furthermore, the Irish language was supposed to be Augusta Gregory's own special area of expertise; she was the only member of the Literary Theatre who could read or speak it at all. Anyway, she tartly noted, *Shadowy Waters* in Irish "would appear to the audience as 'Three Men in a Boat' talking gibberish."[63] Since Moore was generally conceded to be the master hand at plot, character, and construction, but ungifted in the writing of dialogue, his status would lose little and gain a great deal if the phraseology was left to Irish translators.

The origins of Moore's enthusiasm for the Irish language go far deeper than an intention to wrongfoot Yeats, who at this stage was still his "boon companion." The story of how he came to take the same line on the Irish language as Reverend Michael P. O'Hickey, Maynooth Professor of Irish, and D. P. Moran, editor of *The Leader* – that is, the position that Irish literature is simply literature in Irish; the rest is denationalising English literature – seems to begin right under Augusta Gregory's roof at Coole during the previous October.[64] He then wanted to lend a hand to her work in the Galway chapter of the Gaelic League: he would guide Aranman Tomas Ua Concheanainn in writing his autobiography. He may even have paid lip-service to Hyde's efforts to convince people that to be Irish everyone should learn to speak Irish, write Irish, and think Irish (but not drink Irish).[65] By the end of October 1899, Maurice Moore, stationed at Castlebar, County Mayo, had been drawn into support of GM's new enthusiasm. Maurice invited Hyde to come out and propagandise for the Gaelic League among Moore Hall tenants.[66] When GM turned up in Dublin in November, he probably discussed the Concheanainn autobiography with Eoin MacNeill, the League Secretary. According to George Roberts, for a short time a member of the Gaelic League, when he proposed inviting George Moore to become a member of his branch, the teacher, "a middle-aged buxom woman from the Aran Islands," "threw up her arms in horror." If GM did not become a regular member of the League at the branch level, he opened a parley directly with the executives in the central office: Hyde, MacNeill, and Father Finlay. Moore was delighted that, after he had knocked and shoved at it heavily, the door was opened enough for him to jump right into the thick of things.[67]

Moore's enthusiasm for the Irish language and hatred of the Boer War became intertwined in early November 1899, when Maurice Moore was ordered away to South Africa just as the two brothers were beginning to work together in the patriotic language movement. For George and Maurice, it could have been a return to the glory days of the nineteenth century when George H. and Augustus Moore made the Moore colors fly at the track, and when G. H. Moore carried the flag for Ireland in Parliament. But the dream of a revival of Moore family glory was interrupted by imperial policy in November 1899.

Seven months earlier, on 24 March, British subjects in the Rand petitioned Downing Street for protection against Dutch nationalists in South Africa, and the London newspapers began to beat the drums for the rescue of Englishmen, or, more especially, for the rescue of their women and children, that old cry for military action used during the Indian Mutiny of 1857 and during General Gordon's invasion of the Sudan.[68] On 9 May 1899, the imperialist high commissioner, Sir Alfred Milner, took up the petition on behalf of the British government, and both sides prepared for war. At that time, Moore was complaining that the rising tide of imperialism was floating high the poetry of Kipling and prose of Haggard (as in GM's Shelbourne Hotel lecture of 11 May 1899). In October, Boers attacked and drove 10,000 British infantry into retreat at Ladysmith, where they lay under siege from 1 November. These defeats forced the call-up of Maurice Moore, the Connaught Rangers, and some 70,000 other troops, who were shipped off to fight the 20,000 Boers (like Irishmen, mere farmers, according to the Dublin propaganda).[69] Maurice, a new recruit to the National movement, was not happy to go; he had come to feel that the promotions he was due after twenty years' service in India and Africa never arrived because he was an Irish Catholic.[70] And GM hated to see him go: "You have seen enough of foreign service," GM cabled from the Shelbourne Hotel.[71]

When GM got back to London, he brought his unhappiness about English politics with him. He was out of sorts with his old friend, Philip Wilson Steer. First of all, he hated Steer's new portrait of him. It was always difficult to paint a man like Moore, a tragic soul in a comic body, as he said himself. Examining Steer's portrait, Moore complained that "the features are mine but the face is without character of any kind."[72] Steer must start over with a new canvas. At a dinner with Tonks and Steer, GM railed against Britain's imperialist war. Tonks sympathised, but to Steer England was at all times "all right as she is."[73] This deep patriotism, instinct in Steer's heroic English landscapes, further enraged Moore against his old friend. Yeats and Ireland were leading him away from what he had been, and into being something different. If his fundamental ideas were to change, Moore felt his friends must change too.

Meanwhile, all through the negotiations leading up to the February ILT performances, Augusta Gregory was receiving late-night off-the-record briefings on British military strategy from her young friend at Queen Anne's Mansions, Paul Harvey, a secretary in the War Office. The plans of January 1900 only led to more reverses in the field, reported in thick black newspaper headlines. In

January the Boers foolishly tried to storm Ladysmith and took serious casualties; Sir Redvers ("Sir Reverse") Buller then attempted to lead British forces to the rescue of Ladysmith and suffered several defeats, including a terrible one on 24 January 1900 at Spion Kop, where 1,700 British soldiers died. Meanwhile, Yeats and Moore were hoping for British defeats, but with a difference: Moore's brother could have died in any one of them. "I live in a sort of nightmare when I think about it," George wrote Maurice. "I pass whole days without reading a paper. I look at the placards furtively and hurry by."

So when Moore burst into Augusta Gregory's rooms, "more *gaedhilge* than Hyde," with his idea about the necessity of de-Anglicising the Literary Theatre, even de-Anglicising Yeats, it was part of a larger agonistic polemic for him.[74] It would soon take new shapes, but for the moment it was a way of fighting an England that had never returned his affection and now was stealing his dearest brother.

6

Augusta Gregory was maintaining the position in private conversations with Yeats that *The Bending of the Bough* was "not really a good play." And Yeats finally agreed with her one evening in mid-February that "a play we produce ought not to depend on political allusions for its success" – a strange turnabout, since he had helped introduce those allusions into *Bending*. The same night, Yeats left Augusta Gregory to pick up Moore on his way to lecture on Shelley and moon symbolism at the Fellowship of the Three Kings. Arthur Machen thought Moore appeared out of place in the room in the Adelphi overlooking the Thames, while enthusiasts debated why the moon should be a symbol for chastity since it changed all the time.[75] The next day, Augusta Gregory went to a *Bending* rehearsal in the day and a performance of *Floradora* at night: her son Robert was bored by the first, and loved the second. Yeats felt otherwise.[76] *Floradora* was a farce with smart songs, a bit of *risqué* plot, and lots of pretty women in short dresses. Its author was James Davis, GM's old friend from the *Bat*, now making a new fortune writing such operettas under the name "Owen Hall" (debtor's pun on "owing all"). Moore doesn't mention *Floradora* himself. New ideas, new friends: *Floradora* gave way to a mystics' seminar on moon symbolism.

On Saturday, 17 February, Yeats, Augusta Gregory, and Moore set off together for the Dublin performances, and GM was in such good form that even Augusta Gregory had to like him: "G. M. very amiable & really agreeable."[77] On their arrival, Yeats and Moore went to 6 St Stephen's Green to an "At Home" given by the National Literary Society for their welcome, where Yeats chanted a lecture about symbols.[78] On Monday, 19 February 1900, Martyn's *Maeve* opened at the large Gaiety Theatre in a double bill with Alice Milligan's *The Last Feast of the Fianna*, a "twenty-minute peep into the legendary past of the Ossianic period of

Irish folklore."[79] Martyn's play was about a boyish-looking young woman who dreams of old Ireland, faeries, and especially a young Greek/Irish faery lover boy; she is then led into the mountains by an old crone who is Ireland, because the heroine would rather die than wed her wealthy English suitor. This plot was eventually sorted out by the audience into a political allegory (such as *Cathleen ni Houlihan* was to be) when the crone, Peg Inerny, cries out: "I tell you Ireland can never be subdued." What they made of the "procession of boy pages" and "choir of rose-crowned boys" one cannot guess.[80] Martyn was called out three times to take his bow at the end. "It may be called a success," Augusta Gregory concluded in her diary, but the *Irish Times* the next day pronounced it "a complete and unadulterated failure."

The good news/bad news story of the following days was that *The Bending of the Bough* was unquestionably a great and growing success. "The applause was tremendous," Augusta Gregory had to admit. "Author, author" was shouted again and again, but GM kept to his rule not to take curtain calls or show his face in the theater, so the first night Yeats took it for him, and made a speech; another night Hyde did the honors. The *Irish Times* carped about Ibsen-for-the-Irish (we don't need that!), but the *Irish Daily Independent* called *The Bending of the Bough* "the most remarkable drama that has been given to the nation for many years . . . a brilliant play," and the *Daily Express* review showed that the play was very well understood: it concerned the "Financial Relations question." Debate over the Childers Commission in 1897 had revealed that England took more out of Ireland in taxes than it put back in services. The review explained that Moore "ingeniously associates [with this debate] all the current feelings about the preservation of the Gaelic language, the cultivation of Irish literature, and similar topics, and a more subtle appeal to the sense of tragedy in the frustration of ideal aims and the abandonment of a spiritual mission."[81] Hyde thought, "No young man can see that play and leave the house as he came into it."[82]

Extraordinarily, Augusta Gregory and Yeats soon set their faces against the play and wanted no others like it. It was too "political" in a special Irish sense of the word (though the mystifying Hyde denied that there was anything political about the Irish Literary Theatre performances, any more than about Gaelic League activities, since they were not affiliated with a parliamentary party and remained open to both Unionists and Nationalists). *The Bending of the Bough* is not, admittedly, a great play; Moore himself looked upon it as just something literary people would not have to be ashamed of while they watched it.[83] Yet all the early plays of the ILT were significant as patent molds for subsequent Irish plays, illustrations of the possible representability of Irish life. By staging contemporary problems in realistic settings, even presenting the very images of public people of different classes and religions, *The Bending of the Bough* made dangerously explicit the divisions within Ireland. What was needed, Augusta Gregory appears to have felt, was a form of theater that might allow these differences to be reconciled, or put under erasure, in a symbolic space. A verse or romantic prose saga, for instance, or a picture of peasant life rendered in a poetical dialect, perhaps based on folklore, would serve very well. Lots could be done very subtly in such genres, and lots would be done by Yeats and Augusta Gregory at the Abbey Theatre. The path opened up for Dublin by Moore and Martyn to a modern European urban social drama remained largely untraveled, in spite of the great popularity of the first performances of *The Heather Field* and *The Bending of the Bough*. James Joyce was sufficiently impressed by seeing *The Bending of the Bough* to write his own first play, *A Brilliant Career*, upon similar municipal themes, and Fred Ryan's socialist *The Laying of the Foundations* (1902) echoes Moore's title and treatment; however, after 1902 (with the exception of two plays by Padraic Colum) verse-dramas, comedies, and dialect folk-plays held the stage at the Abbey against all comers until 1909 when the Cork Realist school of Lennox Robinson and T. C. Murray picked up the dropped stitch.

7

William Kirkpatrick Magee (1868–1961) provides a vivid picture of Moore in Dublin during the week of plays. Magee went to a conversazione on 24 February 1900 at Leinster Hall arranged by Augusta Gregory as a way to attract buyers to an exhibition of paintings by Jack Yeats.[84] Magee had been a schoolmate of W. B. Yeats in 1883, a winner of the Vice-Chancellor's prizes for both verse and prose at Trinity College (1889–93), and the son of the Presbyterian Superintendent of the Irish Mission, still trying, with considerable difficulty, to dispel "the baleful shadow of Romanism" from the city of Dublin.[85] Employed from 1895 as sub-librarian at the National Library of Ireland, the better to continue his spare-time literary activities, Magee had taken the upper-class, Anglo-Irish pen-name "John Eglinton" from Eglinton Street in Kingstown (Dun Laoghaire), where his father lived. John Eglinton was known as an essayist (*Two Essays on the Remnant*, 1895) of whose work readers would have liked to see more than Magee cared to produce. His prose combined the controversialist energy of his father with the urbane, liberal Britishness of his favorite professor, Edward Dowden. When Magee first met Moore at the Leinster House exhibition, he appeared to GM to be "a thin small man with dark red hair growing stiffly over a small skull . . . the face somewhat shrivelled and thickly freckled. A gnarled solitary life, I said, lived out in all the discomforts of a bachelor's lodging . . . a Thoreau of the suburbs."[86] Meanwhile, Magee was taking the measure of Moore:

> He was at this time turned forty [forty-eight, in fact], erect and coldly genial, and but for the curious appearance of his sloping shoulders he looked, with his bowler hat and cane, more like an army officer than a distinguished writer. He had offered himself as a champion of the Gaelic Revival, and had announced his

intention to establish himself in Dublin, an accession of strength to the literary movement over which Yeats was in high exultation, though the romanticist and the satirist were soon to quarrel: 'the Aristophanes of Ireland' was the phrase with which Yeats hailed his new ally . . . Moore looked me up and down (rather insolently, I thought), rapidly as it seemed to me comparing me with the probably favourable accounts he had heard from AE, and in a strong harsh voice which impressed me disagreeably, told me he had read my articles in the *Daily Express*. He did not say what he thought of them, and I for my part could think of nothing to say, so that he turned off at once to be introduced to some other hole-and-corner man of letters.

This was the frosty, inauspicious beginning to what would be one of the most serious friendships in the lives of both Magee and Moore. GM was to be, Magee later reflected, "the most familiar of my acquaintance, peering curiously into my privacy, and opening his soul to me more I believe than to others: a soul in contact with some perennial source of caustic insight and salutary disillusionment, yet one that craved for affection."[87]

On 22 February 1900 a celebratory luncheon was held at the Gresham Hotel for the Irish Literary Theatre.[88] Moore gave the speech he had rehearsed on the Holyhead–Kingstown boat. Next on the program for the Irish Literary Theatre, he announced, would be a collaboration between himself and the great "racial" poet who was his friend, W. B. Yeats. Together, they would write a play about Diarmuid and Grainne. In addition, Yeats's *Land of the Heart's Desire* (1894) (not *Shadowy Waters*) would be presented in an Irish translation by Hyde (Moore broke off to say that Augusta Gregory would be the only one of the directors to understand it, an ad-lib compliment she appreciated). Moore foretold a time in which all the great literature of Ireland would be in Irish, English having been degraded by commerce and war. Irish-speakers should look into their hearts "fearlessly and without shame" and write sincere autobiographies. Those who are simply too old to learn Irish should force their children to be brought up in it, he declared, and he, while having no children, would see that his brother's children learned it. This caused nervous laughter.[89] Undisturbed, Moore went on reading, as Declan Kiberd puts it, with "an intensity that bordered on absurdity, with a sincerity that seemed . . . to come close to parody":

> I have written to my sister-in-law, telling her I will undertake this essential part of her children's education. I will arrange that they have a nurse straight from Arran (laughter), for I am convinced that it profits a man nothing if he knows all the languages in the world and knows not his own.[90]

The entire speech was printed in the next day's *Freeman's Journal*, which judged it a very important statement; the *Daily Express* thought it was a joke.[91]

The next day GM wrote to Maurice in South Africa, sending him the newspaper clippings: "Yesterday there was the lunch and I made a long speech, which was reported almost word for word. It will interest you for it contains many ideas which I learnt from you and I think it will do good. The last sentences caused a good deal of laughter. I knew they would and yet I meant them seriously. Evelyn will be astonished when she reads them this morning. I hope she will consent to the arrangement."[92] Maurice was himself "learning Irish in the Transvaal under a rock amid the shriek of shells."[93] Enthusiastic about his brother's speech, Maurice wrote his wife Evelyn that she should fall into step with George's plans for a nurse from Aran.

The plays over, the directors of the Literary Theatre all returned to their London apartments, save Edward Martyn, who went west and created a furor by refusing to allow "God Save the Queen" to be sung at a Tillyra dinner party. Lord Clonbrock, the Chief Secretary, consequently tried to force Martyn's resignation as Justice of the Peace and Deputy Lieutenant in Galway. On 12 March, Moore came round to Woburn Buildings with a project to create some trouble on his own.[94] He had written a letter to the *Times* and all the Dublin newspapers about Queen Victoria's upcoming royal tour of her western province, the first state visit to Ireland since the Famine. Moore said the Queen was only coming now to recruit Irishmen as cannon fodder for the Boer War, "with 'the shilling' between her finger and thumb, and a bag of shillings at her girdle" ("not in the best taste," Augusta Gregory thought). With cold bitterness, Moore pointed out that the five Irish regiments in General Buller's forces had taken most of the losses from the Boers.[95]

The plan was that GM would call for "some sort of protest," and then WBY would write follow-up letters suggesting a counter-demonstration on the hundredth anniversary of the Act of Union, to coincide with the Queen's visit on 2 April.[96] Yeats was really enjoying running this controversy with Moore, who was obviously a world-class troublemaker. WBY went to the theater and a gallery with Moore and listened to the author of *Modern Painting* aestheticise; they dined together at Augusta Gregory's; they added barbs to one another's letters to the editor. This was one of the peaks in their friendship. Controversy was sport for Moore, and he had found an able and happy hunting partner in Yeats.

Yet Augusta Gregory found the violent rocking of the boat was making her queasy: her good friend W. H. Lecky turned angry on 3 March at the "silly speeches" of her friends, and withdrew as a guarantor of the ILT on 4 April; Enid Layard was alarmed that Augusta Gregory had introduced her to a man who could write such letters.[97] Moore was being cut by his "smart" friends too, yet "he is in fine spirits as a result," WBY instructed Augusta Gregory.[98] At one of Gosse's Sunday dinners, Moore vituperated against Kipling for writing *Times* letters advocating the hanging of Boer farmers. By way of apology for the force of his remarks, GM said to Mrs Gosse, "Someone must tread on the beetles." She may have wondered if it could be right to do so with such evident pleasure.[99]

The "Queen letters" of Yeats and Moore were judged by many (Horace Plunkett, for instance) to be outside the bounds of decency, somewhere between very bad manners and treasonous disloyalty. Yet the letters ably turned the tables by a reasoned assault on Loyalism in an Irish setting. Yeats developed an idea that was to form the germ of *Cathleen ni Houlihan*. There are, he wrote, ignoble and noble loyalties – Irish loyalty to Queen Victoria is ignoble, and Irish loyalty to the old-woman-who-is-Ireland, Cathleen ni Houlihan, is deeply noble.[100] In his own letter, published in the *Freeman's Journal* on 16 April 1900, Moore addressed himself to fellow Irish landlords. They were fools, GM wrote, to be loyal to the English Parliament, which by a sequence of peasant-pleasing land bills had reduced their rents and enabled tenants to buy up estates, and which soon would compel the last few flourishing landlords to sell up and move out. England's South African difficulty was the Irish landlords' opportunity, Moore claimed, if only they would join the National Party. Nationalists would treat patriotic landlords well, while England showed them no gratitude whatsoever for their past loyalty to the Crown. At present, however, "the Irish landlord stands on the steps of the Kildare Street Club and cheers the Government that is robbing him; every cheer encourages the Government to further robbery, and still the landlord cheers. A strange spectacle it is, truly, of a man cheering himself out of existence. At a hundred pounds a cheer the Irish landlord, if he begins at noon, can be a pauper in the evening."[101] Edward Martyn took the next step on 10 May 1900, writing to the *Tuam Herald* with a proposal for a "National" Landlord Party. The Irish Literary Theatre Committee was becoming openly nationalist and political.

Moore's *Freeman's Journal* letter suggested that the landlords would be wise to help turn American opinion against the British. Remarkably, in May 1900 Moore proposed that he and Yeats should go on a barnstorming lecture tour of the USA as Gaelic League missionaries and anti-war protesters. On 2 June 1900, Moore proposed a lecture series to the promoter James Pond, offering for instance a lecture on "The Intellectual Bankruptcy of England."[102] Moore could no longer bear to be in Mafeking London, with mobs in Trafalgar Square cheering the victorious British slaughter of Boers; he was ready to move to Ireland or set sail for America.[103] Sincere as GM may have been about the evils of Empire, the value of the Irish language, and his own recovered Irishness, it seems strange that he could have thought himself capable of a lecture tour; strange too that Douglas Hyde should have encouraged him, and that Yeats could have seriously considered joining him.[104]

On 24 May 1900 George Russell and Augusta Gregory conspired to break up the planned lecture tour – AE asserting that "Moore is altogether too extravagant a writer and a critic," and it would damage "Willie's reputation as a serious thinker if he makes himself responsible for Moore."[105] Yeats hated to be "bemoralised" by Russell, but on 5 June said he would follow Lady Gregory's advice against going with Moore to the USA.[106] Yeats was brought to agree that he "must keep from mixing up my name" with Moore's somewhat more tarnished name. Furthermore, Yeats "could not forgive anyone who spoke" as Moore had done "against Maud Gonne." "It is so hard not to trust him," Yeats mused, like a half-seduced girl, yet "I am afraid he is quite untrustworthy." Then, taking the step from being the used to becoming the user, Yeats concluded his explanation to Augusta Gregory: "one must look upon [Moore] after all as only a mind that can be of service to one's cause."[107] If the poet had written, "of service to oneself," then the statement would be even more shocking, but since Yeats intended to use Moore for Ireland – as a propagandist and occasional playwright – the deliberate exploitation of a friend appeared to be virtuous. It is still surprising that he thought he could make an instrument of Moore without paying a price for it. The workman should always know his tools.

8

Through the summer of 1900, Moore proceeded full speed ahead with his Irish language campaign. On 9 July, just back from a visit to Clara Christian in Llanfairfechan, he telegraphed the Gaelic League office concerning Balfour's Intermediate Education (Ireland) Bill, formally offering his services to have it amended. He could, for instance, "set an agitation on foot" to pressure the Board of Education to make Irish the language of instruction in Irish-speaking districts, but he would do anything else the League asked.[108] They suggested or he proposed the following steps: (1) put on a play in Irish;[109] (2) give prizes to tenants of his estate for Irish speaking or composition; (3) arrange publication of the poems of Douglas Hyde, as translated by Augusta Gregory, and introduced polemically by Moore;[110] (4) have his nephews taught Irish; (5) propagandise for Irish-language instruction.

Moore carried out this plan of campaign in short order, writing Evelyn Moore on 14 July with instructions to hire a local Irish-speaking woman to "speak Irish all day to the children," so that Irish could be their language of instruction when they began school.[111] On 18 July, his letter on Irish-language education appeared in the *Times*. Clearly, for Moore the value of the language was in two areas, and in those areas only: first, small languages were "catchments of the soul," reservoirs of a certain sort of life not otherwise expressible, therefore it was "of world-wide interest" to preserve them. Second, English was a fine language of commerce, but no longer of literature. Moore's emphasis on art was not Gaelic League doctrine; instead, it echoed Yeats's praise of rural Irish dialect. Moore had bought into the idea that a modern writer's thought would be purified by a baptismal bath in Irish.[112] In a pseudo-sympathetic reply to the *Times*, Gosse teased GM, "In Cheremissian I feel, under a happier star, I could have been a stylist."[113]

The stars all seemed favorable to Moore at the time. He collected Clara Christian on his route to Dublin, where on 19 July he read his *Times* letter at a protest in the Rotunda. According to *Ave*, the prior speaker, a priest, annoyed Moore by praising Irish as a language in which no heresy had ever been uttered (no heresy for GM meant no literature). Another speaker, a republican, volunteered his willingness to "shoulder a musket" (why not a pike? GM wondered).[114] Earlier Moore had been so enthusiastic about joining that he had not taken the time to get to know what or whom he was actually joining. It rapidly appeared that many Irish enthusiasts had ideas unlike his own, even unlike any ideas of which he had recently heard. While in Dublin, he evidently made a date with George Russell (then painting fairies with Yeats at Coole)[115] to go on a September bicycling expedition to the neolithic passage graves of New Grange, where Moore too might be introduced to the gods of ancient Ireland.

In July 1901 GM was ready to turn his attention back to the composition of *Diarmuid and Grania*, interrupted the previous November for the sake of *The Bending of the Bough*. When that play had been performed, Moore debated surrendering to Yeats's urging on 1 March 1900 that he pick up *Diarmuid* straight away, but T. Fisher Unwin wanted GM first to write *Sister Teresa*, the sequel of *Evelyn Innes*; furthermore, *Harper's* had made an offer for serialisation of the novel.[116] Weeks later, Moore was deep into *Sister Teresa*, too deep to accept Monet's invitation to Giverny, and Virginia Crawford's offer to meet him nearby in Rouen (Moore had been seeing Monet at the Savoy Hotel, from which Monet was painting Waterloo Bridge in every possible light). By 8 May Moore finished a 60,000-word draft; so he turned around and began to rewrite.[117] Intermittently, while campaigning for the Gaelic League in July, GM met with Virginia Crawford (a model for Sister Teresa) and rewrote Chapters 6–9 of *Sister Teresa*, in which Sir Owen Asher desperately tries to keep Evelyn Innes from immuring herself in a convent and becoming Sister Teresa. By 16 August GM had wrapped up the novel, leaving Sister Teresa in the convent, a singer who has lost her voice and a nun who has lost her faith in the sacraments, but still a woman with a questing spirit, wishing to taste life better by putting it aside.[118] Once he brought the two-volume tale to its harbor, Moore wrote new scenes for *Diarmuid and Grania*.[119] By the end of August 1900, he was ready to go bicycling with Russell.

They were an odd couple, the saint and the sinner, both Christian heretics. Previously, Russell had taken up a guarded tone when speaking of Moore, and earlier in August, at Coole, he was particularly disgusted by Moore's conception of Grania in the new draft scenes. He guessed, rightly, that Moore was "building her character upon some of his queer Lady friends" ("Grania . . . is you," GM wrote to Lady Cunard), but, according to Russell, "most of the women in Ireland" had throughout history been "pure."[120] For Russell, his own mission was to keep Moore away from Yeats, holding him at bay by pretending Moore was a ridiculous person.[121]

Yet the joke could work both ways. On the bicycle journey, from 11 September to 13 September, Moore asked a thousand questions and listened with apparent wonder to Russell's oracular lectures about Druids with a mystic knowledge of Hinduism, still expressing their wisdom by means of ghostly

14. *Portrait of George Moore* (1900), George Russell (AE).

emanations from Mother Earth. The earth itself was a *zoön*, a living being and a divine one; it was useless to look for God in heaven:

> I look with sudden awe beneath my feet
> As you with erring reverence overhead.[122]

Wide-eyed and delighted, Moore watched AE practice the new American science of psychometrising "through which ancient places are made to deliver up their spirits."[123] Russell believed he was with wonderful rapidity fulfilling his promise to Yeats that he would "drive Irish mythology and idealism into Moore."[124] A portrait of Moore was done in an hour, "and it is clearly the work of one who has been with the Gods," GM says in *Salve*, "for in it my hair is hyacinthine and my eyes are full of holy light."[125] Moore returned from the odyssey round the neolithic tombs with a great respect for the mystic's pedal power, as he himself was compelled to wait with his bicycle (bought for the occasion) at the bottom of the sacred Hill of Tara, seat of the ancient kings of Ireland. He began to think Russell would make an even better Ulick Dean than Yeats, and during the fall of 1900 he once again rewrote *Evelyn Innes*, cutting it by a third, airbrushing Yeats out, then overpainting Russell in his place.[126] Surely he belonged in literature, whether romantic or satirical remained to be discovered. As a result of their Quixote–Sancho Panza quest for earth-spirits, Russell's enmity toward Moore had turned into something very different. Perhaps, as W. K. Magee suggests, "he even divined the essential innocence of Moore's mind, of which an invincible ignorance of the sacrosanct element in life was part."[127] Russell made himself Moore's constant companion after GM moved to Dublin.

9

Moore put his bicycle on the train and headed west to Coole for further story conferences over *Diarmuid*. In August, Yeats had explained through his amanuensis, Augusta Gregory, that it would take him a month to revise a draft of Act I that Moore regarded as all but finished (sent by GM on 30 July 1900); GM rejoined that in two weeks he himself could write Acts II and III.[128] This was not a good start, and the two were in for a quarrel over who was the top man. After pedalling into Coole for a three-day visit on 15 September, GM began to alter Hyde's Irish-language one-act, *Casadh an tSúgáin* ("Twisting of the Rope"),[129] offered £100 for the next season of the ILT, and sat down to a story conference with Yeats.[130] Augusta Gregory and Yeats wanted to establish the register in which the dialogue would be written: peasant dialect? biblical? modern conversational idiom? Not the idiom, at any rate, of *Esther Waters*, traces of which WBY discovered in GM's manuscript.[131] His feelings bruised,[132] GM seems to have spoken roughly of the concept of "putting style on" one thing and another.[133] A number of words were placed on the Index Expurgatorius by Yeats – *ocean*, *soldier*, and *mountain* must be replaced by *sea*, *swordsman*, and *hill*, and all "picturesque" descriptions of nature were stigmatised as anachronistic. Such painterly, Corot-like descriptions were famously among Moore's best things.[134] Disputes about the lexicon became so fierce that it was decided that GM would decamp and bivouac at the Shelbourne Hotel, while Yeats worked at Coole. Further collaboration would be attempted through the post. This failed too, so GM came back to Coole on 27 September supposedly for a few days, but he stayed several weeks; then the collaboration shifted scene to London on 26 October.[135]

In Dublin, Russell saw the draft and suggested to Moore that "Diarmuid is supposed to be a man,"[136] but the biggest ongoing problem was with the character of Grania. In October and early November, the co-authors, with lashings of mutual flattery and calculations of massive profits at the London box-office, managed successfully to get on with their work except on the point of Grania's psychology. Moore had truly conceived her as a Lady Cunard figure: a hot-blooded, cold-hearted woman who puts a love-spell on young Diarmuid at her marriage feast to Finn, then after years of love in a valley with Diarmuid, gets a hankering for Finn again. The singing gets into her breasts, and she can do no other than her desire dictates. That phrase about "singing in the breasts" was too much for Lady Gregory,[137] and Yeats thought it needed Celticising too, but Moore, while now "fairly docile about words," believed he knew more about passionate women than either of them. Perhaps the phrase was an original piece of bedroom poetry by Maud Cunard.[138] At any rate, he would not surrender it, and Yeats stood by his guns as the one with the final right of revision, the master of all fights about "style." Moore did not like "the picture of you the pedagogue, [me] the pupil." "Yeats is so dictatorial I can't stand him," he complained to Augusta Gregory on 14 November, saying he could not surrender the singing in the breasts.[139] He came up with a new compact for peaceful collaboration: wherever Grania spoke "of her intimate self," GM should write; wherever Diarmuid spoke, let Yeats speak for him – that was Moore's demand. Augusta Gregory was urging Yeats not to see Moore, just to be firm. On 17 November 1900, Yeats put the question to the arbitration of Arthur Symons.[140] Face-saving alterations were made, but the song remained in the breasts of Grania.[141] Moore was satisfied and went back to behaving, Yeats said, "like an angel."[142]

The issue was partly Moore's autobiographical investment in the play, but more largely his desire to be treated with respect. Symons, who always treated Moore with "the deferential attitude of the young Frenchman to the older artist he admires," was the perfect man to untie the knot.[143] On 10 December, the last act was passed for publication by the two authors, and negotiations began in earnest with Mrs Patrick Campbell for a gala London or Dublin performance.

10

In the midst of his October ructions with Yeats, Moore received an article he had encouraged Maurice to write about the British conduct of the war in South Africa. Kitchener had given orders to burn churches, loot homes, and punish the families of Boer soldiers; British soldiers raping Boer women went unpunished by their commanders. After Boer Generals De Wet and Botha turned to guerrilla tactics, the British command gave further orders that no Boer prisoners be taken; women and children were to be gathered into concentration camps; the farmland was to be fenced and cleared, section by section.[144] On 18 October 1900 GM contacted W. T. Stead through their mutual friend Virginia Crawford. GM could provide Stead with an article about British atrocities written by an officer in the field. "Publication of this article on top of the elections," Crawford told Stead on Moore's behalf, "would be a fine stroke and would help to redeem English opinion from the savage rage it has drifted into."[145]

Stead, then editor of the *Review of Reviews*, was not such an odd choice to receive this bombshell, even though he and the National Vigilance Association had ruined the market for GM's sort of literature in the late 1880s, and even though he had until recently been an ardent imperialist. Stead's imperialism had been wedded to his Low Church, puritanical idealism. What he had already heard about British methods against the Protestant Dutch South Africans had enraged Stead against the government. By 3 November GM had persuaded Stead to issue Maurice Moore's article (though Stead did not then know the author's identity, and feared it would be thought too literate to have been written by an officer) as a broadsheet mailed to all the clergymen in England, entitled *Hell Let Loose: How We Are Waging War in South Africa.*[146] There was an immediate demand in the December *Blackwood's Magazine* for the name of the "Officer in the Field" who signed the articles, but Stead protected his sources. On 25 November, GM had another article from Maurice to pass on, and the ex-Zolaist and ex-NVA leader met on the 26th to discuss a joint strategy. Lord Roberts, British Commander-in-Chief, was denying the charges of the "Officer in the Field" and an investigation of the leak was set afoot. In early 1901 Maurice sent a third letter which concerned Kitchener's order to kill De Wet's Boer soldiers once they surrendered. London papers refused Stead's offer of this new bulletin, or to print any further charges until the author was named, so GM dictated the third letter to a *Freeman's Journal* reporter, and its 15 January story ("No Quarter!") was then picked up by the *Times.* When Maurice's reports were reprinted in Cape Colony in the February *South African News*, the editor, Edward Cartwright, was tried and sentenced on 23 May to a year in prison; a word from Stead about the true authorship and provenance of the article could have saved his fellow-journalist, but Stead again refused an appeal to name his sources, and saved GM from obloquy and Maurice from court-martial.

Though frightened, GM took a real pleasure in making life unpleasant for the British Empire.[147] He had tried to win respect in London as an English novelist, and thought he had earned it with *Esther Waters*, but his next books were once again badly treated. Furthermore, his "public was not nourished like that of other authors by descriptions of [his] personal life": no interviews in the *Sketch* about the high tone of life at 92 Victoria Street, no charming anecdotes about the lofty ancestral past of George Moore of Moore Hall. No matter what he did, the bad odor of Paris and Catholic Ireland clung to his clothes, at least to the sniffy English. In *Communication to My Friends* (1933) Moore recalled that Gosse accused him of just wanting to see his name in the papers. "Naturally," GM replied. "Everyone does; you do, and you find your name; I do, and I don't find my name. Why not?"[148] Would he end up like Manet, his life poisoned by a sense of injustice? He was moved when Yeats and Martyn told him that he would not have to put up with such prejudice in Ireland; he would be honored there as a famous Irish author from a great Mayo family.

But were they right? In December 1900, at the time of meetings between Moore, Yeats, and Mrs Patrick Campbell about a production of *Diarmuid and Grania*, Yeats put up Moore's name for election to the Irish Literary Society

(ILS) in London, an organisation that had never excluded anyone. Yet both Barry O'Brien and Sir Charles Russell swore that they would blackball Moore – O'Brien on account of *Parnell and His Island*,[149] and Russell because Moore humiliated him in the newspaper controversy over depiction of a convent school in *A Drama in Muslin*. Russell had also heard that even as an Oscott schoolboy GM was called "Heathen Moore." Other Irish clubmen were unforgiving about GM's disrespectful "Queen letters"; and some feared that in the event of his admission, the Irish Literary Society would not really take in Moore, but Moore would take in the Society, annexing it to one or another of his headline-grabbing outrages.

Yeats stood by his collaborator: "I do not think a man of letters should tolerate a slight of that kind passed upon a man so eminent in his order. One owes some loyalty to literature."[150] Yeats was the heart and soul of the Irish Literary Society in London, yet he was ready to resign over the issue, comparing Moore's position in Ireland to that of Byron in England and Burns in Scotland. How shameful would it look to later generations to blackball "one of their chief men of letters" for his "morals"? [151] Yeats's willingness to stand up for Moore as a distinguished author scarred over the wounds recently opened, but the ILS fight did not cause GM to feel confident he would be more welcome in Dublin than in London. Both capitals were part of Victoria's empire of respectability.

Mrs Patrick Campbell had a clear preference for London as the site for the first performance of *Diarmuid and Grania*, but Yeats and Moore felt it was essential for an Irish Literary Theatre play to open in Dublin. She suggested she would, after all, agree to do it in Dublin, then said that she could not. Mrs Pat stopped "flirting with the option of an Irish premier," more especially flirting with Yeats, as soon as Moore asked her on 26 December 1900 to put up a good-faith guarantee of £200.[152] By 4 January Moore had made a deal with F. R. Benson, a Shakespearean actor-manager, to stage the play in Dublin the following autumn, and that business complete, Moore crossed to Ireland to consider settling in a new home.[153]

By 14 January 1901, GM had gone to the Gaelic League offices and told Douglas Hyde that he was coming to live in Ireland so that he could join the fight for the Irish language. Hyde "laughed that vacant little laugh" which GM found so irritating; Hyde in turn was amazed at how "touchy" GM was – what, he wondered, had he done?[154] Hyde sometimes feared Moore might "do much harm," and evidently betrayed his unease.[155] He had shown no jubilation at the return of the sinner to the fold, no welcome at all in fact. GM wanted to be useful somehow and welcome somewhere – as in the *Freeman's Journal* office, when he dictated the final letter from "An Officer in the Field" about British atrocities in Africa.

Joseph Holloway, the Dublin theater diarist, noticed GM at the annual conversazione of the National Literary Society on 14 January, telling a funny story to Edward Martyn just as the lady reciting "The Priest's Boy" came to the pathetic death scene.[156] "Dear Edward" and GM renewed their friendship. In an official smoking of the peace pipe, Moore accepted Martyn's suggestions for minor amendments to *Diarmuid and Grania*, while Martyn heartily approved of putting the play into performance (though he did not offer to foot the bill).[157] Together, the two old friends "sacrificed Yeats on the altar of reconciliation," in Gregory's phrase.[158] However, GM returned Yeats's favor in standing up to the ILS for him. Moore called on D. P. Moran, editor of the *Leader*, to tell him to stop attacking Yeats for not being a simple, Irish-speaking Catholic balladeer.[159] Talking to Moran like a father to a son, GM said a great writer like Yeats could no more change the way he wrote than he could change the shape of his nose by trying. Putting a Yeats volume into Moore's hands, Moran pointed out a passage and demanded, "Do you understand that?" "I don't," Moore replied after a moment, "but I take it that it is my misfortune that I am unable to grasp his meaning." Moran was not to be brought around: "what the country needs is an Anglo-Irish Burns," he declared, "not an Anglo-Irish mystic" of "inordinate egotism."[160] In this busy week, Moore may also have visited a Royal Hibernian exhibition, subsequently calling at the studio of the sculptor John Hughes, who was modeling statues for the new Loughrea Cathedral.[161] Things seemed to be happening in Dublin. It had painters, sculptors, journalists, witty women who put on conversaziones, and a movable feast of fights. GM could be at home there.

During the week, GM hired cabs for a general tour of Dublin properties to let – including a house with a moat in the suburbs of Rathfarnham and fashionable Georgian houses in Merrion Square. It was George Russell who found just the right perch for him: 4 Upper Ely Place, quiet, central, and Georgian. It stood near the end of a cul-de-sac, just up the rise from the National Gallery and National Library, only a block east of St Stephen's Green, and with a view from the upstairs window of a nunnery. Its front had recessed arches and pilasters in low relief. There was, his future neighbor Oliver St John Gogarty noted, an old street lamp over the central arch. Soon, under the fanlight, the door would be painted, by GM's order, a republican green (all the other doors on Ely Place were white).[162] Opposite the house was a half-acre garden with three or four apple and pear trees; that garden belonged to the occupant of number 4.[163] This was a far better lodging than any Moore had taken in London. It implied a dignified, central place in the life of the city, in an area familiar to him since childhood when he stayed with his aunt in Merrion Square down the hill toward the River Liffey. And George Russell shaped up as the essential boon companion. Moore would take the house.

There remained one problem: what was he to do for female companionship in a place like Dublin? The lucky man was able to persuade Clara Christian that she would find the Dublin hills just the thing for her palette, and that he had found a perfect house for her, Tallaght Lodge out on the Rathfarnham road. In late March, he said goodbye to London friends, and by April he was settling in, hiring a cook and servant, employing housepainters, putting a gardener to work across the street, and, with equal dispatch, taking charge of literary affairs in the capital. He tried to get George Russell to carry on with a novel he had dropped,[164] and in mid-April, when Douglas Hyde stopped by, Moore insisted that Hyde act in the ILT production of *Casadh an tSúgáin*. After Hyde refused to either sing or dance, Moore helped him rewrite the part to make it unnecessary for the President of the Gaelic League to perform these frivolities.[165] Hyde mentioned to a friend his unhappiness that Moore was bringing over an Englishwoman as his mistress; Dublin was not Chelsea or the Strand, and Irish scandal might be hurtful to her. Moore himself prepared for Clara Christian's arrival by ordering from abroad a pair of fancy corsets. A postman unfamiliar to Dublin's new arrival delivered the package to F. C. Moore, a clerk in the Land Commission office (Church Temporalities branch) at number 5, Ely Place South. Fortunately, this other Moore had read *A Mummer's Wife* and was able to redirect the package correctly.[166]

The local attitude to the famous author and his books was captured by a conversation of two workmen who had come to mend the drains in front of 4 Upper Ely Place. They were overheard by GM's neighbor at number 3, Stephen Cunningham, who told the story to Sir Thornley Stoker, Moore's friend a few doors down at Ely House. After having dug a hole, the workmen took a seat at either end of it, and one said to the other:

> "Do you know the fellow that lives in the house forninst us? You don't? Well, I'll tell you who he is: he's the fellow that wrote *Evelyn Innes*." "And who was she?" "She was a great opera-singer. And the story is all about the ould hat. She was lying on a crimson sofa with mother-of-pearl legs when the baronet came into the room, his eyes jumping out of his head and he as hot as be damned. Without as much as a good-morrow, he jumped down on his knees alongside of her, and the next chapter is in Italy."

According to Yeats, the sisters who lived at number 5 bought a copy of *Esther Waters*, tore it up, put the tatters in an envelope, marked it "Too filthy to keep in the house," and stuffed it in GM's letterbox.[167]

The problems Moore had with hiring a suitable cook and redecorating his house became the great gossip of Dublin. Though "not fond of changing," he admitted to Virginia Crawford that he had gone through "six cooks in three weeks"; there is even contemporary corroboration of the tale that one cook called in a policeman after listening to Moore's verbal assault on her culinary arts, whereupon Moore led the policeman to the dining room, crying out in a tragic voice, "Is there a law in this country to compel me to eat that abominable omelet?"[168] Moore seems to have been going in for an exaggerated burlesque of the Ascendancy gentleman with a Servant Problem (in the grander Irish houses, the servants were brought in from England, Irish ones being thought impossible, but English ones often proving very hard to keep).[169]

GM saw Dublin as a stage on which to playact; his old delight in astonishing people flowered in the Irish climate. He especially played up the role of a sham Whistler on the Liffey, cosmopolitan aesthete, tyrant, and "character." Apropos his troubles with cooks, he explained to Susan Mitchell that his tastes were simple – "that just as Whistler had narrowed down his colours to a couple of tones, so he had narrowed down his carnal appetites to a couple of dishes – an omelette – but it must be properly made, a chop – but it must be properly cooked." Whistler was again invoked in a dispute that arose when Moore's pro-British neighbors complained in late May about his green door, "a beautiful pale green."[170] Most of Moore's neighbors at the Merrion Square end of Ely Place were either land agents or solicitors; at his quieter southerly end of the street, GM's neighbors were Mrs M. A. Webb at number 5 and Miss Rynd at number 2, and Stephen ("Martin" in *Salve*) Cunningham at number 3.[171] Not on speaking terms with the novelist (Cunningham avoided him for years to come), the neighbors objected through the landlord to Moore's politically green door. Moore replied in a letter to the landlord that his house decorations were a Whistlerian symphony of which the door was a keynote – pale green wall-paper in the foyer, a darker green in the dining room – number 4 was a "nocturne in green." If he changed the door, he must change all the furniture, and repaper the walls, the bill for which – £200 – would have to be paid by the landlord.[172]

Another source of entertainment to Dubliners was Moore's social form of composition: whatever he was writing, he talked about, asked for help with, subcontracted parts to specialists, etc. Rather than read a book himself for purposes of research, he would prefer to talk to a person who had read the book. His first project in Dublin came from members of the Gaelic League. When he asked them how he could be of service, they said, "Attack Professor Mahaffy" – that is, John Pentland Mahaffy, Senior Fellow of Classics at Trinity College, and former teacher of Oscar Wilde. Mahaffy was a Unionist who earned the enmity of the League by saying "all Irish language textbooks were silly or indecent," or religious; such remarks did not prevent him from being appointed a Commissioner of Intermediate Education, in charge of deciding if Irish was to be part of the national curriculum. According to Yeats, Moore replied to the Gaelic League's request for an attack upon Mahaffy: "I will. I have come over to be useful. You say he is doing mischief. That is all I want to know. I met him once."

Not knowing Mahaffy, Moore invited his friends to gossip about the famously witty professor: Gill gave him a tale about Mahaffy as a squireen and place-hunter who flattered the Queen ("a title astonishes him as it does a valet"), but was snubbed on her visit to Dublin. Yeats, staying with GM in mid-May, no doubt fed him other stories, such as the reply of the Provost when Mahaffy claimed he had once been whipped for telling the truth – ". . . seems to have been very effectual, Mahaffy." Moore's daily visitor George Russell, who wanted to make Moore's article one in a series, probably contributed as well.[173] Academic gossip may have been provided by Professor Tyrell: Mahaffy, the impatient "understudy" to Provost Salmon; Mahaffy, author of just the sort of scholarly works a classics professor with a taste for countesses would write. In "The Culture Hero in Dublin Myths," Moore presents himself – a new-comer to Dublin – simply as "the first of the Dublin folklorists, a humble col-lector and interpreter of popular tales."[174] The terrible body-blows delivered to Mahaffy are in the style of "Plain Words to Party Men" that James Davis used to produce for the *Bat*, yet the cagey Moore stayed clear of the libel law by not affirming that any of the Mahaffy tales were true. Indeed, he archly claimed, they were so outlandish they had to be false. Moore the folklorist divides the "daily spite of this unmannerly town" into cycles, as Standish O'Grady had divided Irish heroic tales into Red Branch and Finn cycles. The article con-cludes by imagining a Gaelic poet of the future drawing upon Mahaffy, more lackey and valet than professor, as material for a light comedy entitled "MacGafferty."

AE was delighted that a new Voltaire had arrived in Ireland, who "whenever [Archbishop] Walsh or [Cardinal] Logue said something stupid in the papers, [would] show them up in the most ridiculous light, terrifying them into silence" (the "them" here sounds like the Catholic hierarchy, not Trinity College). Hyde, however, was somewhat shaken by the slaughter of a reputation carried out at the Gaelic League's command. Maurice Moore was ashamed that his brother should have treated another gentleman in such fashion. It was, indeed, a fine "How do you do?" from Dublin's newest resident to one of its most famous characters. GM himself later regretted, when his Dublin company began to bore him on his Saturday night "At Homes," that he was unable to invite Mahaffy, author of *The Art of Conversation*.[175]

II

Yeats secretly claimed to look upon Moore "after all as only a mind that can be of service to one's cause," yet the poet still treated Moore to his face as a friend. Yeats was GM's houseguest at Ely Place (9?–20 May). While there, WBY found reason to begin to worry about the independent line Moore was taking in relation to literature in Irish.[176] By 14 May 1901, the two men had located an "old theatre . . . in Abbey Street" that could be bought for £800 – only £300 was required as downpayment. "Our plan is to have a Gaelic theatre," Moore told Virginia Crawford.[177] On 17 May, Moore had Yeats invite people who might be interested in the project mooted by the recently deceased William Rooney, a *United Irishman* poet and friend of Maud Gonne – an Irish theater in Dublin that would periodically tour the provinces. D. J. O'Donoghue, W. A. Henderson, Frank Fay, and W. G. Fay were all invited. Less than four years later these were to be, respectively, the enthusiast, business manager, actor, and stage-manager of the Irish National Theatre Society in Dublin's Abbey Theatre.[178]

An initial problem in carrying out a plan for an Irish-language Abbey Theatre was that although the Fays were good amateur actors and Gaelic League sympathisers, they did not know much Irish.[179] Even if they learned to speak Irish or Irish-speakers learned to act, Moore did not want to go forward unless the theater was blessed by the Gaelic League, and the Gaelic League did not want to go forward unless the whole operation was blessed by the priests, which ultimately would of necessity involve priests blessing Moore, an unlikely outcome.[180] A final problem was that Yeats was not really enthusiastic for a theater of that kind: "I have always felt that my mission in Ireland is to serve taste rather than any definite propaganda," he confided to Augusta Gregory.[181] Yeats's dominating, persistent purposefulness enabled him ultimately to recruit the Fays to his vision and to get Annie Horniman to buy him the Abbey Theatre as an art-and-no-politics theater, when the building could have been had for a song as an Irish-language theater, by Griffith, Gonne, and the *United Irishman* crowd (Sinn Feiners), the Gaelic League (Irish Irelanders), or Martyn and Moore (European Catholic aesthetes).

12

After an August trip to Bayreuth (Moore propagandised for the Irish language to the bemused American journalist James Huneker),[182] GM returned via Paris and London to Dublin to assist at the rehearsals of *Diarmuid and Grania* and *Twisting of the Rope*. In Paris, he tried to get Augusta Holmes, an Irishwoman and Catulle Mendès's mistress of former years, to compose music for the play, but she could not oblige. Then GM hurried to London on 4 September because Edward Elgar showed interest in composing horn music for Diarmuid's funeral (the play was becoming ever more like an opera).[183] No sooner had Moore gotten to Ireland than he had to answer questions to a *Freeman's Journal* reporter on why an Englishman was composing music for an Irish play.[184] Moore's explanation was that Elgar was a Wagnerian and there were no adequate Irish composers, not a reply "An Irish Musician" appreciated in his letter to the 16 September 1901 *Freeman's Journal*. Irish-born alternatives to Elgar were suggested, including the scalawag Jimmy Glover. Moore was in his element in a newspaper controversy like this: "I was very stern," he explained to Hyde, "for a newspaper is like a dog, no use until it has been thrashed."[185]

GM was in charge of stage management for *Casadh an tSúgáin*. That worried Hyde somewhat, because he feared that Moore would not know enough to keep Hyde's Gaelic League play from being hijacked by actresses from Maud Gonne's radical Inghinide na hEireann ("Daughters of Erin"), the most recent skirmish in Hyde's long, doomed battle to keep revolutionary politics out of the League.[186] On 28 September, Moore found the cast, handpicked by Hyde, waiting for him at Ely Place, and rehearsed them for three weeks with "as much attention as the most conscientious *régisseur* ever gave to a play at the Théâtre

Français."[187] The actresses were a "scratch lot," Hyde admitted, and on 10 October GM hired W. G. Fay for "three or four pounds" to help rehearse them.[188] By the 15th things were running smoothly with *Casadh an tSúgáin*, but at the Gaiety the English actors from the Benson company were having trouble with pronunciation of Irish names in *Diarmuid and Grania*: how were they to say *Caoelte*? Yeats proposed "Wheelser." On stage, the actors variously addressed this character as "Wheelchair," "Cold-tea," and "Quilty."[189]

On opening night at the Gaiety Theatre, 21 October 1901, the audience was largely recruited from Irish-language enthusiasts, so the big hit of the evening was *Casadh an tSúgáin*, in comparison with which the language of Yeats and Moore, like the accents of the Benson troupe, seemed fraudulent.[190] Holloway, who like many did not understand Irish, still felt "a thrill of pleasure through [his] veins" as he listened to the " 'old tongue' " in *Casadh an tSúgáin*.[191] While Holloway did not care for Mrs Benson's "eternal attitudinizing" (perhaps a sexist opinion?), he thought *Diarmuid and Grania* "a beautiful piece full of weird suggestiveness but lacking here and there in dramatic action." The "weird suggestiveness" was perhaps owing to the fact that Yeats had filled the play with omens, potions, forebodings, blood bonds and pledge-breaking, prophecies from a spinning wheel, and a haunted wood. The initial reviews were generally favorable, though the *Evening Herald* took the same line as Holloway, and proposed that Diarmuid should have taken a rod and beaten "Mrs. Tanqueray, B. C." [192] One of the chief forms of interest for the audience, according to James Cousins, was the attribution game: " 'Ah, that's Willie' . . . '[that's] dirty George.' " This worry over the "author-function" – the desire to interpret the play in light of one or another author's complete works – led to a creeping worry in later accounts over whether Ireland's Grania might not be George Moore's Evelyn Innes in a Celtic toga.[193] GM reported to Maurice, "they first of all enjoyed the play, and having enjoyed it they repented in sackcloth and ashes, and I really believe that the repentance was much greater than their enjoyment."[194] Martin Ross, for instance, blamed Moore for Grania being "excessively French in her loves," and for Diarmuid's "backhairy" comments to Grania while he's dying.[195] Moore and Yeats did not make the safest choice of legend to dramatise, as the Irish audiences protested that an Irish heroine would not leave one man for a second one, much less the second for the first, even though that is the heart of the ancient story. Still, the plays sufficed as an occasion to manifest patriotism, and during the intermission political ballads were sung in chorus. Best of all, the little Irish play (prototype of all stranger-in-peasant-cottage plays) put to shame the big three-act English drama.

At the performances, WBY distributed an issue of *Samhain* containing his epitaph to the three-year experiment of the Irish Literary Theatre; something different, he announced, needed to come next.[196] After the performances, GM appealed for public support for a permanent national theater, one that would perform plays in the Irish language. Interestingly, both WBY and GM were prominent in the audience at a 7 November meeting in the Rotunda on "Our Duty to the Language Movement."[197]

In a mind-bending gambit on 13 November, Moore gave a long interview to the *Freeman's Journal* in which he stipulated that this new theater should have ecclesiastical censorship and plays by priests, even if it took a papal decree rescinding the rule against priests frequenting such houses of entertainment. "The intelligent censorship of the Church will free the stage from the unintelligent censorship of the public," "the mamas and the papas who write letters to the papers."[198] You could not expect to run a theater like a brewery, Moore complained; it would have to be supported, whether privately or publicly, but such a National Theatre would give people an interest in the town, and it would save some of the £150,000 a year Dublin pays to bring in English traveling companies like the Bensons. He himself, he said, had had to pay for Hyde's play, and rehearse it too; it was time for a millionaire or the Dublin Corporation to do something.

The ploy did not work. Just a page earlier, the editor of the *Freeman's Journal*, very suspicious of Moore, spoke up in favor of family censorship, the free market, and obedience to the Archbishop (but no playwright priests). The interview also alarmed a member of the intellectual Contemporary Club, who was overheard by J. B. Yeats to say, "Who is this George Moore? . . . Who asked him to come here?" And WBY himself was, of course, horrified at the notion of clerical censorship. In his autobiography, Yeats remembers Moore pleading, "But my dear Yeats, Archbishops are educated men. If there is some difficulty about a play, I will call upon him. I will explain. He will approve the play. No more mob rule."[199]

What was the point of this strange ploy? Moore was trying to outflank Edward Martyn, who had Archbishop Walsh's stated support for his efforts to clean up "the present scandalous condition of the Dublin stage." In a speech reprinted in the *Freeman's Journal* prior to the *Diarmuid and Grania* production, Walsh called Martyn's work in the ILT "the only real hope" for clearing up the "prolific source of corruption" and "evil suggestiveness" of the stage. The support of His Grace for a National Theatre was qualified, however, by a demand that it exhibit works that "no self-respecting Irishman, no self-respecting Irish lady . . . need be ashamed or afraid to go to." Some people at least pretended to be ashamed to have gone to see *Diarmuid and Grania*.[200]

Martyn was also making trouble for his fellow directors through the *Leader*. Martyn funded the weekly, he was granted space in it for his campaign for a Palestrina Boys' Choir, and invariably its editor Moran spoke highly of him but had low blows for Yeats.[201] Within weeks, Martyn would publish an article in the *Leader* claiming it was up to Catholics to regenerate Ireland, "and those few Protestants who had become so Irish as to be indistinguishable in national aims from Catholics."[202] The sectarian campaign in the *Leader* was a serious nuisance. Moore, evidently thinking of his father's friendship with Archbishop MacHale, thought he could easily get round Walsh and neutralise Edward Martyn and his henchman, D. P. Moran. Moore, however, neglected to reflect that his father had been at least a nominal Catholic, and indeed, more than that: he had gone to Mass, and he had been proud of his religion. His eldest son, on the other hand, was a notorious heretic, and the difference between them was likely to be significant to Archbishop Walsh.[203]

In the 15 November 1901 *Freeman's Journal*, Yeats courageously declared that he would have nothing to do with a George Moore theater under the censorship of a priest: "I believe that literature is the principal voice of conscience, and that it is its duty age after age to affirm its morality against the special moralities of clergymen and churches, of kings and parliaments and peoples." That is just what Moore thought too, but GM was, as Yeats sized up the situation on 19 November, living in the present: "we would both be more popular if I could keep from saying what I think & he from saying what he does not think."[204]

13

The sort of Irish-language theatre George Moore had in mind can be estimated from a collection of short stories he began to write in September 1901. George Russell had been calling for Moore to be Dublin's Voltaire, but one evening W. K. Magee ("John Eglinton") made another suggestion: that Moore become Dublin's Turgenev. The two men were returning from the Provost's House at Trinity College, where Magee had introduced Moore to Professor Edward Dowden, the scholar of Shakespeare and Shelley, an old friend of John Butler Yeats, and one of Magee's own heroes, especially since Professor Dowden had awarded the young collegian Magee the Vice-Chancellor's prizes for prose and verse several times in the early 1890s. Magee was described by Stanislaus Joyce as "a dwarfish, brown-clad fellow, with red-brown eyes like a ferret, who walks with his hands in his jacket pockets and as stiffly as if his knees were roped up with sugauns [hay ropes]" (the hostility of this portrait may be due to the fact that Magee's father, Hamilton, was the Presbyterian minister in charge of the Dublin Mission for the conversion of Roman Catholics).[205] Yet the son was, if not friendly to Catholicism, an agnostic with no passion for evangelising of any sort, unless it be for modernity in general. He was, like Dowden, literate in several languages and widely cultured. For him, to be British was to be European. After taking Moore to visit Dowden, it was in keeping with Magee's cosmopolitan perspective to suggest that the Mayo gentleman novelist was best suited to become Ireland's Turgenev, producing something like a *A Sportsman's Sketches*.[206]

The idea appealed to Moore's taste and vanity; Turgenev was one of his heroes. He decided to write the tales in English, then get Tomas Ua Concheanainn to put them into Irish.[207] Finally, he would convince his new friend, the priest and economist Father Tom Finlay, to publish them in his brother's Jesuit journal, *New Ireland Review* (which had already printed Moore's February 1901 ILT lecture, "The Irish Literary Renaissance and the Irish Language").[208] Finally, the whole series from The *New Ireland Review* could be published as a Gaelic League textbook, and would henceforth serve as a model for Irish-speaking authors on how to construct a modern European short story. The plan was grand, even grandiose, but for Moore culture was not something that just happened; it was a thing made, and made by men like himself just as a book would be made.

The human material in which the author of a cultural trend had to work could prove intractable. Father Peter Finlay, editor of *New Ireland Review*, right away turned out not to be the easygoing worldly priest for whom Moore might have wished. In the February 1900 issue Finlay laid out the limits of his tolerance in the way of culture. He did not insist that "books and pictures and visitors [to a Catholic home] and the rest should be limited to what is religious, but I do mean that none of all these things should be such as religion must condemn." In the Church's judgement, Irish people should be, he lectured, "sober, industrious, practically crimeless, and eminently religious."[209] Yet for the time being, Moore clung to the idea that "One can only get the better of the clergy by setting the clergy against the clergy."[210]

Fired by Magee's suggestion that Moore become Ireland's Turgenev, GM says he went home and rapidly wrote "The Wedding Gown" from a story Dick Maitland had once told him. The writing must have been made easier by the fact that Moore had published an un-Celticised version of the tale in the Christmas issue of the 1887 *Lady's Pictorial*.[211] The *New Ireland Review* published it as "An Guna-Posta" in January 1902. It fell within the circle of what religion need not condemn.

One can see how Moore thought an Irish theater might work. He would write scenarios, even whole plays, about contemporary Irish life. In a manly friendship with an intellectual priest, he would talk over the plays as he wrote them, fitting his deeply naturalistic view of life around the dogmatic objections of the clergyman. Then the plays would be put into Irish for a municipal theater where they could do their artful demystifying work. Subsequently, he would publish the English text so that the plays might be staged in New York or London, just as he would publish the English text of *Untilled Field* in New York, London, and Leipzig. The plan was grandiose, but not absurd. *The Untilled Field*, as an interlinked collection of short stories about sterility in modern Ireland, was James Joyce's model for his first book, *Dubliners*. An Irish-language theater run on similar principles might have scattered seed with unpredictable blooms.

The ways in which GM's subsequent stories ran foul of Father Finlay's requirements illustrate the rocky road a permanent Irish-language theater probably would have traveled. Once Moore had gotten excited about painting "a portrait of Ireland," he gathered information about the strange land from his nearest friends. George Russell, for instance, bicycled all over the country as an Irish Agricultural Organisation Society organiser, and in each parish he had to work with priests, some of whom he liked; but Russell was a Northern Protestant before he was a theosophist, and priests often got on his nerves or simply tickled him. He gave Moore the story sequence about the priest who tried to build a "Playhouse in the West" for an Oberammergau festival, so that the people would not have to depend solely on Department of Works projects – famine roads that went nowhere, ports in harbors too shallow for ships, etc. In GM's story, a local girl cast as Mary in the sacred play gets pregnant on the way home from rehearsal; tied up in a shed by her own mother, the girl dies and the infant is aborted. This gives birth to the superstition that the playhouse is haunted by faeries; no one will again go near it. The priest's effort at rural regeneration thus came to nothing.[212] The same charming priest – he loves to knit – figures as the hero of a second story, "A Letter to Rome." This time the priest has a new brainstorm for local improvement, and he writes it up as a Latin epistle to the Pope. The cure for Irish emigration and the sure path to strengthening Catholicism, he explains to His Holiness, is for priests, who have the best houses and incomes, to marry; he himself has no one particularly in mind, but he would, for the sake of the Church, do his duty.

One would not be surprised if Father Gerald O'Donovan (1871–1942), Martyn's friend from Loughrea and Moore's regular visitor on O'Donovan's weekly trips to Dublin, supplied other stories about the Irish clergy, such as those that led to "Patchwork," "The Wedding Feast," and "The Window."[213] O'Donovan had trouble with the hierarchy and favored a less sectarian, more joyful version of Catholicism than, for instance, Father Peter Finlay. In "Patchwork," the puritanical, patriarchal young Father Maguire refuses to marry a couple of lovers because they don't have the full fee for a wedding service, so they celebrate their nuptials anyway, and he has to get the wiser, less doctrinaire, old Father Stafford to help him patch up a ceremony after the fact. In "The Wedding Feast," the sexy, spirited Kate Kavanagh is commanded by Father Maguire to marry one of several boys in love with her, and marry him immediately, but she bolts for America from her own wedding feast. In "The Window" the priest does his best to terrify an old woman to give up her little fortune from an egg business for his church-rebuilding project, but the tough old creature will not give it to him except to pay for a stained-glass window of her own choice, and she chooses a very stereotypical design. When the window is put in place, she stands entranced in front of it seven days a week, hearing music played by painted angels with harps – popularly acclaimed a miracle, to the disgust of the priest but also to the enrichment of his building campaign. The story evidently involves a parody of the miraculous apparitions in 1879 at Knock, County Mayo, afterwards the main site of Irish pilgrimages.

The stories are not absolutely anti-clerical, but they depict the priests as men – therefore, often misguided, impassioned, and egotistical – and as men in a second sense, that is, fearful of the sexual and mystical powers of women. The hostility of the Catholic Church to love, sexual love between men and women, brought about in Moore a mounting irritation as he contemplated the condition of Ireland. Moore had begun to write the stories for Father Finlay on the assumption that a sophisticated Jesuit and a Catholic landlord intellectual could work together in a worldly fashion, just as his father G. H. Moore had worked with his friend Archbishop MacHale. But MacHale and his like had lost out to Cardinal Cullen and a new sort of priest, more ultramontane and dogmatic. Under Cullen's regime, they introduced to Irish Catholics the devotional practices of the rosary, perpetual adoration, novenas, vespers, devotions to the Sacred Heart and to the Immaculate Conception, the Feast of the Assumption, jubilees, processions, and retreats; confession and Mass were made central to Sunday worship in Catholic churches, and regular attendance was sharply policed. The folk practices of local beliefs – holy wells, local pilgrimages, and stations (worship held in cottages rather than churches) – were largely replaced by modernised Roman worship.[214] Catholicism became a substitute for all that the Irish people had lost of their original customs and language: to be Irish was to be Catholic in a redefined sense of the practice. Under Cardinal Cullen's "devotional revolution" (as Emmet Larkin named it), in the half-century following the Famine the number of priests, monks, and nuns had risen from 5,000 to 14,000, while the population declined by a third.[215] Twenty-four cathedrals and more than 3,000 churches were built in the century after Catholic Emancipation (1829). To support its clerical staff and building campaign, the Church consumed about 15 percent of that share of the total wealth of Catholics available over subsistence.[216]

This massive change in the character of Catholicism and Irish life largely occurred over the decades that George Moore lived out of the country. Like a Rip Van Winkle, GM opened his eyes to find his homeland utterly changed. The music of harp and violin practice penetrated his house at Ely Place from the convent behind it; out for a walk, he met "seminarists all along the pavement, groups of threes and fours; and full-blown priests flaunt past me – rosy-cheeked, pompous men, dangling gold watch-chains across their paunches – . . . a black queue stretching right across Dublin, from Drumcondra along the Merrion Road."[217] The change may have been too gradual for some others to notice, but it had made its full impact on the returning novelist. Moore's perceptions were further sharpened by his sense that in Ireland the clergy were taking the place once occupied by landlords, his own class, and he did not like that. His collection of stories records the impact that the "devotional revolution" had on him. Its two salient charges against the clergy are the ones formerly made against landlords: that the Church had enriched itself at the expense of the people, and that Ireland would never thrive under its oppression.

In *The Untilled Field*, the tales about artists in Ireland or exiles returned are always tales of dissatisfaction, tales of Ireland as a prison run by jailers who are priests. "In the Clay," a story about the sculptor Rodney (modeled on John Hughes), for instance, shows him driven out of Ireland and his best work smashed after he persuades a lovely young woman to pose nude in a study for some religious statue.[218] By the time Moore had the collection complete, its theme was clear to him: "Catholicism and nationhood are incompatible." Roman Catholicism cannot be appropriate, he decided, for every country and every race and every person: "people have to make their own religion as they have to make their own arts . . . and . . . they must find their own salvation."[219] A collection that had begun in a collaboration with Father Finlay and the Gaelic League thus ended up being an attack on Roman Catholicism that, even in Irish as *An T-Ur-Gort,* was banned from the display window of the Gaelic League office.

14

Moore was, however, to have one last hurrah for the Gaelic League and his conception of an Irish-language theater. On 2 January 1902, there had been a showing of Russell's *Deirdre* in George Coffey's drawing room. This was the play Russell wrote to prove he could do better than Yeats and Moore combined when it came to dramatising the Celtic myths. Russell himself took part in the performance, while Moore "pervaded the outskirts of the proceedings" – and found little there to take seriously.[220] The Fay brothers, however, were sufficiently encouraged to put *Deirdre* into rehearsal with *Cathleen ni Houlihan* (idea by Yeats, dialogue largely by Gregory) for a spring performance under the aegis of Maud Gonne's Inghinide na hEireann. At the same time that the *Cathleen* rehearsals were going on, GM planned to build on the success of *Casadh an tSúgáin* with another play written and acted by Douglas Hyde, but this time performed in Moore's garden at Ely Place for the delegates to the Oireachtas, the annual Gaelic League convention. As Declan Kiberd points out, a "Gaelic Lawn Party" is a contradiction in terms, but how was the language to become the spoken tongue of modern Ireland if it was not taken out of the cottage? Moore relished the revaluation of both peasant language and aristocratic entertainment: he suspected his Gaelic lawn party "would annoy Dublin society very much; which will add considerably to my pleasure."[221] On 13 February 1902, Moore had begun to egg on a reluctant Hyde to write a play about a fairy, and the play he had in mind was, effectively, Banville's *Le Baiser,* an 1887 high-society piece of Parisian pastry, and then an 1892 Independent Theatre Society Aesthetic production, as translated by John Gray, original of *Dorian Gray.* To do this play in Irish – as a lawn party – for priests, peasants, and clerks of the Gaelic League! Moore was ecstatic with delight.

Moore would not take "no" as an answer from Hyde. The party could be held whenever Hyde liked; Moore undertook to provide "the garden and the teas and the ices and the stage and the rest of it" (including the play's plot). All Hyde had to do was write the dialogue and act the main part.[222] By 24 February, Hyde, suddenly enthusiastic, was dining with Moore to make plans. Hyde finished the play in mid-March, GM had it translated, and on 24 March he wrote to Hyde: "Your play is a masterpiece, nothing could be nicer"; the next day he began to harry the author with suggestions for improvement.[223] One of Moore's contributions to the Irish Revival was his regular insistence that all virtue is correction of form – "these little ends of sentences want little finishing touches," he advised Hyde, "if you wish the thing to be *quite perfect.*"[224]

GM also wanted more daring from Hyde, always the safe man. *An Tincéar agus an tSídheóg* concerns an aged-looking fairy who will be freed from the curse of a wicked queen and regain her youth if, without telling him her story, she can persuade a man to give her a kiss on the last day of her life. After rejection by a hunter and a farmer, she gets into a serious parley with a tinker. Moore wanted the fairy to say, "No, not on my hand, no not on my forehead, it must be on my lips," and the tinker to answer, "Well, there is no sin in this kiss, there is no theologian who would find fault in it."[225] Moore didn't get these little inflammatory additions, but he did push Hyde to apply the "finishing hand" to the text, had it printed, prevailed over Eoin MacNeill to have it distributed by the League, and Father Finlay to publish it in the *New Ireland Review*.[226]

The play was performed on Monday, 19 May, with little Sinead Flanagan (later Mrs Éamon de Valera) as the Fairy, and big Hyde as the Tinker.[227] Signor Michael Esposito composed special music and conducted the orchestra in the garden. Moore was "in a great stew" lest it rain, and a heavy shower fell at noon, but then the sun came out, and GM with nothing else to do stood about helplessly smiling. Trinity College people stayed away because of Moore's attack on Mahaffy, but the large crowd richly enjoyed themselves, or enjoyed themselves like the rich.[228] This was Moore's idea of a delightful Irish theater, and indeed it was, but it lasted for only one performance.

The real action, it transpired, had already happened elsewhere in Dublin. Six weeks earlier, on 2, 3, and 4, April AE's *Deirdre* and WBY/Lady Gregory's *Cathleen ni Houlihan* were staged by W. G. Fay's Irish National Dramatic Society at St Teresa's Hall, Clarendon Street, with Maud Gonne in the title role of *Cathleen*. The hall was packed: the Daughters of Erin crowd loved the pastel fantasy of Celticism in *Deirdre* and they loved still better the simple hair-raising propaganda of *Cathleen ni Houlihan*. Neither was Moore's cup of tea. On 3 April Yeats agreed with him, but as the applause grew from day to day for plays that were poetical, Irish, and in English, he began to warm to the Fays' work, and by the 5th Yeats already loved the way "they simply stood still in decorative attitudes and spoke."[229] This was not Moore's favored Théâtre Libre style of naturalistic acting, but for Yeats it was a new style, and a promising one for his verse plays. By 5 April Yeats was getting help from Moore on "Cuchullin" (a draft of *On Baile's Strand*, 1904), with a view to making it "simple enough for Fay in the end."[230] He was eager to write for these actors who had bravely arrogated to themselves the name "National Dramatic Society." Would Moore join them too? But the Fays could not speak Irish, and idealistic romance had never been GM's strong suit . . . Yeats and Moore were headed in different directions, and the sound of their tearing apart would be long and loud. Still, GM was well settled in Ely Place, and he was taking notes on what was coming to pass.

Chapter 11
George Moore in Dublin

I

In the third week of June 1902, Yeats, on his way from London to Coole Park, stopped for four days with George Moore at Ely Place. Excited by having seen the Irish actors perform *Deirdre* and *Cathleen ni Houlihan* in April, Yeats had already drafted a miracle play entitled *The Hour-Glass* for the Fays' company, and he had given it a plot of the sort he thought might "propitiate Holy Church" – or at least not cause Cardinal Logue to issue a warning to Catholics to stay away from his play, as Logue had done in 1899 with *The Countess Cathleen*. For that matter, just the previous autumn, Archbishop Walsh had withheld his blessing from *Diarmuid and Grania*.[1] Moore, however, had recently been reading Nietzsche and was not in a mood to propitiate. Since the Fay productions, he himself had located a mine of plot motifs – they might be turned into short plays or short stories; it was too soon to say. In origin they were unquestionably Irish, and Catholic too, but if dramatised, they were bound to irritate cardinals, archbishops, and Catholic nationalists.

At his Gaelic lawn party on 19 May, Moore had struck up a friendship with Kuno Meyer (1858–1919), who brought high German scholarship to the study of Celtic languages and a year later would found the School of Irish Learning in Dublin. Meyer told Moore some very intriguing stories, one for instance about an ancient Irish poem with the curious title, "God's Grandfather."[2] On 25 May 1902 Moore received in the post Meyer's translations of both "The Hag of Beare" – the song "of the last years of her who has been loved by many men" – and a newly rediscovered Irish love story from the ninth century, "Liadin and Curithir," "very charming" as Lady Gregory described it, very erotic as George Moore later retold it in *A Story-Teller's Holiday* (1918). These gifts excited Moore to invite the German scholar to stay as his guest at Ely Place when Meyer returned to Dublin in June to serve as the assessor for the Intermediate examinations in Irish.[3] Then they could talk at greater length about

Meyer's new discoveries in the ancient literature of Ireland; it seemed just the sort of material Moore was born to exploit.

When Yeats arrived at Ely Place, the two writers were able to make common cause with Augusta Gregory, W. K. Magee, Douglas Hyde, and Arthur Griffith on a Monday journey to the faery-haunted Hill of Tara, once the seat of the High Kings of Ireland. In June 1902 it had become the site of excavations by an English Protestant named Groome. He believed the English race was the lost tribe of Israel, and that he would find the Ark of the Covenant buried under Tara's "Fort of Synods."[4] This commando raid of intellectuals on the sacrilegious doings of a true believer had the bank-holiday sort of zaniness Moore seriously relished, as, for all that, Yeats did too, with the "Connaught cocasserie" side of his nature; with the heroic side, he was in high indignation at "Tara uprooted."[5] The party, once arrived, found the landlord "sitting on a hillside with a gun and a glass of whiskey, two bailiffs, and a number of dogs." The group, consequently, returned to Dublin and wrote a letter to the *Times*.

In Dublin at Ely Place the next day, 24 June, Moore kept Yeats from going to meet Frank Fay about theater business by insisting that he stay after dinner to help entertain Moore's guests.[6] Furthermore, when Yeats proposed that Moore write a folk play for the Fays, something like *The Pot of Broth* or *The Hour-Glass*, GM says he "rose from [his] chair, relying on gesture to express my abhorrence of this scheme." No great French writers, so far as he knew, used folklore or wrote in patois. "But not liking to be left out of anything, I consented, at last, to write half a dozen plays to be translated into Irish." Yeats demurred: why in Irish? Wouldn't it be enough if Augusta Gregory translated them into Kiltartan (her version of local peasant speech)?[7]

That is the story from *Salve*; however, Yeats and Moore did agree to collaborate on a play of another kind, destined neither for the Irish language nor for folk-drama. It was to be based on a real character named Philip Francis Little about whom George Russell had told them. A poet, Little had cast away all the customs of society. He lived on Dalkey Island and prophesied to the passersby. He had "got it into his head that he could only find God where there was nothing." Earlier, living at home with his parents, Little would sometimes find some outrageous idea coming into his head, and something would say to him, "You think so! Why don't you say so? You are a coward!" "I'm damned if I am," he would say, and out the idea would come.[8] Because of his outspokenness, Little's family paid him £150 a year to live away from them. Russell saw Little as the hero of a pastoral comedy, "a modern Pan playing [his pipe] in the fields to the flowers and talking to their spirits." The aim of the comedy Russell meant to write was to make the audience "go away happy in their hearts."[9] Moore saw possibilities in Russell's anecdotes about Philip Francis Little, but for Moore Little would not be a new Pan but a contemporary Jesus, someone who comically shows up Christianity by taking its tenets seriously, a

Zarathustra of the Dublin suburbs. Certainly, the aim of any play Moore would wish to write on the theme would not make the Irish audience go away "happy in their hearts." In June and early July, when Yeats had his eye trained on the Fays and the needs of the new Irish National Dramatic Society, it is unclear how he himself envisioned the fable of Philip Francis Little taking shape on stage. Perhaps with divided expectations, Yeats and Moore agreed to a new collaboration on the subject of Little. Within a week, that is by 3 July 1902, Moore had sent ahead to Yeats at Coole "a little scenario you may be able to develop." A scenario was a very useful thing to Yeats, whose great gifts did not include the gift for plot construction, just as among the talents of Moore there was hardly a penny's worth of skill in stage dialogue.[10]

With a protest, Russell abandoned the Little *donnée* to the "vulgarising" touch of Moore and Yeats.[11] Russell then began to talk to Moore of the Shakespeare/Bacon controversy. The popularity of this topic in Dublin is shown by the Library scene in *Ulysses*, where Stephen Dedalus launches a fantastical theory about Shakespeare's wife, friends, and dead son Hamnet turning up translated in the mirror of the plays. All those listening to Stephen – Richard Best, W. K. Magee, and "Buck Mulligan" (or Oliver St John Gogarty) – also have a richly academic acquaintance with the life of Shakespeare. The challenge to his authorship of the plays touched a nerve for contemporary writers: what might the relationship be between a writer's life and works – more particularly, between being well born and born with genius? Those who held that Bacon was the true author seem simply to have been horrified by the astonishing achievements of education and democracy in their own time. Here these testy young Catholics from the National University, "proud and impecunious," were jostling aside the Trinity College graduates like Best and Magee, and showing off all sorts of "seedy hauteur" and flash intellectual style.[12] Furthermore, the possibility of collusive, secret dual authorship was exciting, especially in a town that had seen Martyn's *Tale of a Town* come before the public as Moore's *Bending of the Bough*, and *Diarmuid and Grania* play out the uneasy marriage of Yeats and Moore. In the Library scene of *Ulysses*, a further twist is given to parallels between the Shakespeare/Bacon case and that of the playwrights of the Irish Literary Revival when Susan Mitchell's witticism is circulated "That Moore is Martyn's wild oats," and, Stephen Dedalus reflects, "Shakespeare Bacon's wild oats."[13] The witticism makes co-authorship into another kind of sexual adventure, one to be hidden, best forgotten, as socially compromising.

Soon after Yeats's departure from 4 Upper Ely Place, Moore himself began to take a suspicious interest in the "question of Bacon and Shakespeare." The latest twist of the new theory, as Gogarty summarised it, was that the common actor from Warwickshire "runs off with the credit and the true author [Bacon] finds himself in a position where to prosecute would only make him more suspected and embarrassed."[14] Moore himself had secretly co-authored aspects of Martyn's *The Heather Field*, and to a lesser extent, Martyn's second play,

Maeve; furthermore, in the process of "resolving himself into a syndicate for the re-writing of plays," as Lady Gregory put it, Moore had had a hand in the restructuring of Yeats's *Shadowy Waters* and *Cuchullin* (as *On Baile's Strand* was then called). On 5 July 1902, J. B. Yeats, visiting the novelist, was astonished to find GM quite taken up with the theme of double-authorship and stolen glory. In the case of the "Little" scenario, would Moore be the aristocratic Bacon and Yeats the pilfering actor? Was Moore, Yeats, or Russell himself the "onlie begetter"?

2

After Yeats's departure for Coole, Moore had plenty of amusements remaining in Dublin, between his story factory upstairs at Ely Place, his quarrels with neighbors down the street, his widening circle of friends among artists and writers, many of whom consorted at his Saturday night "At Homes," and his prowling about Gaelic League and National Theatre premises. GM continued to "put the finishing hand" to the English edition of *The Untilled Field*. His practice now was to dictate first to a shorthand reporter, and later to improvise from a typescript of the previous dictation, through many iterations. It was a method of composition made possible by the typewriter and the women's movement, that he, like Henry James and other turn-of-the-century novelists, richly enjoyed after decades alone beside the inkbottle. One of his Irish stenographers, Anna Kelly, remembers Moore looking like "an artful middle-aged baby" but being a generous if demanding employer:

> I liked him. I found him hard to work for but it was good for me to begin hard, because I never got it so hard again in my life. It was my first job, and I had to write shorthand at incredible speed, and I don't know how on earth I ever did it. It was there I first got to know his ways as a writer, and he was the hardest working writer I've ever met before or since. I hadn't met many before, but I've met many since. And although he always worked very methodically, he loved it. There was nothing else in life he liked better, than to write and write and write. He used to slave to polish his style . . . He dictated, corrected and recorrected. He'd spend half a day on one paragraph, and after lunch we'd tackle that paragraph again, and maybe next morning when I'd come in we had to face the whole thing again. The table was crowded with bits of paper, all scribbled on, crossways, diagonally and everything . . . Sometimes he must have written at night. He couldn't keep away from it . . . And he had to write in company . . .
>
> He sat still as a Buddha, and his hands would be folded across his stomach. Then, after a few sentences, the rhythm would come to him, the hands would unfold, and they'd begin to move, waving to and fro, keeping time to the rhythm. He had a wonderful sense of words. They came just in a regular flowing stream – not a turbulent stream, but a very gentle stream . . .[15]

The last accents of the truly great talkers of the nineteenth century can be caught in the works produced by means of the twentieth-century art of dictation, when an old mode of life and new methods of labor briefly met.

Sometimes as Moore would go over his manuscripts with a pen, he found the caterwauling of his neighbors' pets a nuisance; to make matters worse, the cats seem sometimes to have buried their scat on his own premises. These were grounds for new hostilities in the ongoing war of Ely Place, and attacks were made upon both the cat-owners, the Misses Drew (who had joined the opposition in the matter of *l'affaire porte verte*), and the cats themselves. For the latter, according to Yeats, GM set a trap; for the former, he composed and disseminated a limerick:

> The [cats] of the dirty Miss Drews
> Are suffered to do what they choose:
> Until they're called in
> With hysterical din
> While I am wiping my shoes.[16]

In July 1902, Moore's close friend, the Dublin painter Walter Osborne, drew for the amusement of another neighbor, Sir Thornley Stoker at number 8 Ely House, a little sketch of GM coming from the door of 4 Upper Ely Place and lifting his hand in alarm while a cat on the sidewalk, its bottom down and tail sharply lifted, prepares to pay its compliments.[17]

In August, Moore called at the dingy rooms in 34 Camden Street where the Fays were rehearsing their players in Yeats's *Hour-Glass*. Joyce, Russell, John Butler Yeats, and Joseph Holloway were also frequent onlookers at the mummers. Joyce had accosted Russell to inquire ironically if the theosophist in a long beard might be the new Messiah. "I wouldn't be his Messiah for a thousand million pounds," Russell told Sarah Purser: "He would always be criticizing the bad taste of his deity."[18] Instead, Russell referred Joyce to Yeats ("your clan more than . . . mine") and to Moore. The previous autumn Joyce's younger brother, Stanislaus, had already knocked on Moore's door at Ely Place and handed the maidservant a copy of a pamphlet, one of Joyce's first publications.[19] "The Day of the Rabblement" gave the following analysis of Moore's current literary standing:

> Mr. Moore has wonderful mimetic ability, and some years ago his books might have entitled him to the place of honour among English novelists. But though *Vain Fortune* (perhaps one should add some of *Esther Waters*) is fine, original work, Mr. Moore is really struggling in the backwash of that tide which has advanced from Flaubert through Jakobsen to D'Annunzio: for two entire eras lie between *Madame Bovary* and *Il Fuoco*. It is plain from *Celibates* and the later novels that Mr. Moore is beginning to draw upon his literary account, and the quest of a new impulse may explain his recent startling conversion. Converts

The latest . Sur le tapis .

*" There is a sweet little Cherub who sits up
aloft watching over the life of Poor Jack."
One of Moore's Melodies.*

15. George Moore
encounters a cat outside
4 Upper Ely Place,
Walter Osborne; from a
letter to Sir Thornley
Stoker, 19 July 1902.

are in the [language] movement now, and Mr. Moore and his island have
been fitly admired. But however aptly Mr. Moore may misquote Pater and
Turgenieff to defend himself, his new impulse has no kind of relation to the
future of art.[20]

"Preposterously clever!" was GM's comment to Russell on the booklet. The
sneer about Moore "drawing on his own account" in *Celibates* – employing for
a second time modes of expression from *Esther Waters* and a plot from *A Mere
Accident* – indicates that Joyce had picked up the Flaubertian, modernist
principle in Moore's work (a new style with each new book), and then judged
that Moore did not measure up by that principle. Joyce's devastatingly well-
informed analysis of GM's literary position in Europe may have pushed Moore
away from stories for Irish translators and toward the experiment with stream-
of-consciousness in *The Lake*, his follow-on story from *The Untilled Field*. The

broadside did not, however, predispose Moore to have Joyce invited to his Saturday night "At Homes," an omission frequently resented by Stephen Dedalus in *Ulysses*, and by Joyce himself in Dublin. Furthermore, the arch-mocker Oliver St John Gogarty ("Buck Mulligan") had gotten to Moore before Joyce, and evidently run him down as an "impossible person."[21] When Russell showed Moore some of Joyce's poems, GM returned them with what Ellmann calls "the derisive but acute comment, 'Symons'!"[22] These verse echoes of an echo of Paris symbolism, GM presumably reflected, hardly earned Joyce the right to sneer.

Unlike Joyce, the other young intellectuals hanging about at Camden Street, writing plays or acting in them, were awed by Moore. James Starkey (Seumas O'Sullivan) (1879–1958) and a friend followed GM one evening after a Gaelic League lecture at the Rotunda. After Moore went into a tobacconist's shop, they went in; after he bought two cigars, they tried to buy two of the same brand, but a week of their wages would not pay for them. Still, they went away rejoicing that they had been close to the author of *Esther Waters*.[23] Starkey, later a poet, publisher, and editor, was then one of the Fays' actors in the new Irish National Theatre Society. Frank Fay, an admirer of the French stage, brought Moore in to drill the cast on their accents when reading French verse. T. G. Keller recalled the "anxiety displayed in securing some cigars to offer him . . . [but] when the wise Moore, running no risks, emphatically and politely refused to smoke, a wave of depression obscured the horizon of the company."[24] For their better education, Moore, "lecturer on French letters to the youth of Ireland," recommended the example of Verlaine – a Catholic, alcoholic, homosexual, and most elegant poet.[25] Edward Martyn proposed to de-Anglicise Dublin by removing its "English" pubs and installing sidewalk cafés of the continental type; Moore had his own vision of the Parisification of Dublin: he wanted to foment bohemian rebellion against the respectability of the new Irish Catholic bourgeoisie.

The Boer War peace had been signed on 31 May 1902, and Maurice Moore returned from Africa to find that George, less than two years earlier an ardent Gaelic Leaguer working hand in glove with Father Finlay, was now declaring that Catholicism and literature were incompatible. It had ever been so, George affirmed, characteristically trailing his coat. What about Dante? Maurice asked. GM waved aside the Middle Ages and all of Spain as having no bearing on the question. This anti-Catholic effrontery was a problem for Maurice, who was otherwise proud of George's landlord superiority to good manners. Maurice idolised their father G. H. Moore as a great Catholic patriot; could he continue to respect his older brother if GM was neither?[26] Literature and Catholicism might indeed prove to be incompatible where George the writer and Maurice the communicant were concerned. The situation was delicate because George owned and paid the upkeep on Moore Hall, where Maurice, his wife, and two sons lived and hoped always to live as the representatives of a great Catholic landlord family of County Mayo. For the time being, the two brothers, still friends, let the matter rest.

3

Moore took the train west for the Galway *feis* (arts festival) held on 30–31 August. In St Patrick's Temperance Hall, he found Edward Martyn serving as a judge of the traditional music contest. Moore, no longer an Irish-language enthu-siast, soon wearied of the "peasant" contestant making noises to "uncouth rhythms" – worse yet, it was one peasant after another and all singing to the same jigs and reels. In *Salve*, GM tells how he inveigled Martyn away from the singers and Yeats away from Augusta Gregory for a walk over the Salmon Bridge, where Yeats, boy naturalist, explained the life-cycle of the salmon. Then the three walked down beside the River Corrib and out onto the long Claddagh jetty. Edward wearied, but Moore continued to the very end of the pier, where all alone the aging roué was granted a vision of Ireland. He saw three girls, their skirts kilted up, wading into a tidal pool:

> [A]s if desiring my appreciation, one girl walked across the pool, lifting her red petticoat to her waist, and forgetting to drop it when the water shallowed, she showed me thighs whiter and rounder than any I have ever seen, their country coarseness heightening the temptation. She continued to come towards me. A few steps would have taken me behind a hillock. They might have bathed naked before me, and it would have been the boldest I should have chosen, if fortune had favoured me. But Yeats and Edward began calling, and, dropping her petticoats, she waded from me.

Of all the fantastic *aislings* – Joyce's seaweed-bestrewn wader, Yeats's girl-hag Cathleen ni Houlihan, and Martyn's *bel canto* boyish Maeve – Moore's naiad is certainly the most funny and profane, and perhaps the most human.

At this Galway *feis* an incident occurred that was recalled by Yeats in *Auto-biography*. Moore, Yeats, and the other guests of honor lunched in a restaurant full of priests. Father Considine, the truculent President of the Galway Gaelic League, the Most Reverend Dr MacCormack (whom Moore once heard give a sermon on the "degrading passion of 'loave'"), and Father O'Hickey, the fierce ideologue from Maynooth, were all attending the festival.[27] So too was a Limerick priest on the Irish Literary Society committee, Father Michael Moloney, who struck up a conversation with Moore about the Reverend's favourite topic: "'I have always considered it a proof of Greek purity that though they left the male form uncovered, they invariably draped the female.' 'Do you consider, Father Moloney,' said Moore in a voice that rang through the whole room, 'that the female form is inherently more indecent than the male?' Every priest turned a stern and horrified eye upon Father Moloney, who sat hunched up and quivering."[28]

Yeats might enjoy the fact that Moore made trouble for priests, but by the end of the Galway *feis*, the two co-authors had a serious falling out. It remains unclear whether the fight started because Yeats said that he wanted to write a play on GM's "Little" scenario by himself, or because GM said he wanted the scenario back for a novel, but Moore definitely threatened Yeats with a lawsuit if he developed the idea on his own.[29] George Russell heard all about it when Moore got back to Dublin, and, evidently delighted that nothing good came of his stolen goods, kept Augusta Gregory in the picture:

> I know that Moore had threatened WBY with an injunction, and have been very much amused over it. Indeed, I have been very much amused over it. Indeed, I have enjoyed myself exceedingly over it all . . . I believe Moore is engaged in one of his little jokes at Willie's expense. In fact, to use slang, he is "pulling his leg." I cannot believe he is serious in threatening an injunction, and if I was WBY I would write my play and never bother my head about Moore. Of course, if what Moore asserts is true – that the main idea of the plot and scenario is his – then I think Willie ought to invent something else . . . I can't at present think it is anything more than what [Moore] calls himself one of his little bits of "play acting."[30]

This is an important letter. Moore was a *provocateur*, was known to be, and knew himself to be. He relished making scenes and elaborating preposterous dramas in order to exhibit the characters of people in a new light. These were not practical jokes which, after a brief painful period, are broken up in general laughter. They were protracted sleights in which one might, even while acutely aware that a trap was being set, still be "caught" by a sudden self-betrayal of one's deeper being.

In early September, Yeats decided he would steal a march on Moore and quickly write the play, get it published in the *United Irishman* and copyrighted by John Quinn, and then stand ready to accuse Moore of being the plagiarist should he himself do anything with the scenario; at least, Yeats could then defy his threats of a lawsuit. Yet Yeats did not really intend to write the play alone; his new collaborator would be Augusta Gregory (with Hyde and John Quinn helping out too). Within fifteen days of beginning, that is, by 19 September 1902, they had a text for *Where There Is Nothing* (Yeats's title). The authors' party at Coole came up with "Paul Ruttledge" as a name for the play's hero, and since Moore's land agent (and friend) was named Tom Ruttledge, it may be that they intended the sort of complicated insult Moore himself loved – the obscure aggression of a work of art that appropriates some incidental features of one's life and leaves the heart unrepresented. Lady Gregory and Yeats may well have laughed at the prospect of Moore's discomfiture as he tried to discover their meaning. It was such an easy thing for the poet to collaborate with one who submits, who literally takes dictation, who is always ready with the right word or the next turn in the story, who knows the Irish scene, and who does not ask to sign the play in the end; working with Augusta Gregory was nothing like working with Moore.[31] In early October, Russell was delegated to scold Moore for his antics and order him to back down, but it was too late.

Moore had already gone on to threaten the Fays with an injunction if they produced the play Yeats & co. had by then written.[32]

By the second week of October, Moore was quite possibly seriously put out, all playacting aside. A large conspiracy had been constructed at Coole to drub him. Russell was threatening to cut him if he did not give up; New York lawyer Quinn was offering free counsel to Yeats for a legal action. Furthermore, Quinn had paid a visit to Ely Place and seen Nietzsche's *Also Sprach Zarathustra* on the library table and, suspecting that was the clue to GM's planned development of the new Messiah scenario, he sent Yeats *Zarathustra* and a three-volume Nietzsche so the poet would not be left in the dust. (These gifts had spectacular effects on Yeats and his work.)[33] Hyde was sworn to secrecy by Yeats even while he was meeting with GM and Maurice Moore on Gaelic League business, and on 22 October, Hyde carried out his own surveillance during Moore's dinner party for Hugh Lane at Ely Place.[34] They were all co-ordinating their efforts through the post, with Gregory and Yeats in the war room at the Coole headquarters. These people had been Moore's friends and fellow-workers. Now he was being sealed out. It made him angry: "Publish the play and be hanged!" he wrote Yeats in the second week of October.[35] And what was it all for? After *Where There Is Nothing* was published in the 1 November issue of the *United Irishman*, Russell regretted the whole business: the play was "clever, nothing more . . . I don't like it at all . . . Where there is neither love nor wisdom there is nothing."[36]

At the 27 October opening performances by Fay's company of *Pot of Broth* (by Yeats and Gregory) and *Laying of the Foundations* (by Fred Ryan), Moore would not go near WBY, and continued to cut him for two years. He refused to read *Where There Is Nothing* in the November *United Irishman*, but he quizzed Russell about it:

Does the hero change his clothes? Yes.
Has he a brother? Yes.
Then it is exactly the same thing, absolutely mine!

In fact, Yeats's play did follow Moore's 3 July 1902 plot outline very closely.[37] Moore said he felt towards Yeats as towards a man who had dined at his table and then stolen some spoons from the set of family silver, one of his classic aristocratic put-downs of the social climber Yeats.[38] Yeats himself had begun to suspect as early as mid-October that he had been "caught in a strange sort of spiderweb of George Moore's spinning." Years later, he came to realise that he had been "young, vain, self-righteous, and bent on proving myself a man of action. *Where There Is Nothing* is a bad play," while Moore might have made a masterpiece, Yeats thought, from the theme.[39] This is full of insight, but it is odd that Yeats did not realise that Moore did make a masterpiece of the idea: the idiot Messiah is the leitmotif of *Hail and Farewell*, and the break with the conventional brother is its conflictual center. Furthermore, the whole cruel farce over the scenario (who's a plagiarist, who's an "original" genius?) simply liberated Moore to write whatever he liked about Yeats and Gregory in his autobiographical *tour de force*.

Thinking of Yeats, Moore began to dwell on Nietzsche's metaphor in *The Gay Science* for his own relationship to Wagner: "star friendship." On 4 November 1902, GM besought William Archer to translate the passage for him directly from the German:

> We were friends and we have become strangers, one to the other. But it is well even so, nor do we wish to hide our strangerhood or to dissemble as if we were ashamed of it. We are two ships each with a goal and a way; and our ways may draw together again and we may make holiday as before. And how peacefully the good ships used to lie in the same harbour, under the same sun . . . but soon the mighty sway of our tasks laid on us from of old sundered and drove us into different seas and different climates . . . The law that is over us decreed that we must become strangers one to the other so that just through this estrangement we should reverence each other the more, and the memory of our past friendship becomes sacred. There exists no doubt a vast invisible curve and orbit and our different goals and ways are parcel of it, infinitesimal segments. Let us uplift ourselves to this thought! But our life is too short and our sight too restricted for us to be friends except in the sense of sublime possibility. So let us believe in our stellar friendship though we must be enemies on earth.[40]

4

Depressed and grouchy at Yeats's high-handedness, Russell's siding with the old friend against the new, the twit Joyce's begging for Paris letters of introduction, Maurice's gentlemanly Catholicism, his friend John Hughes's sojourn in Paris,[41] and all the priests of Ireland, Moore was dying to get out of Dublin at least for a time.[42] Christmas was coming round, always a sad season for bachelors, but before he could get away, while riding his bicycle in the city, the front wheel got caught in a tram line: "extraordinary the fall that these little machines can give one," he moaned to Mark Fisher on 31 December, "worse than any fall from a horse." Trying to break his fall, he had put out his arm and dislocated the right shoulder; one piece of broken bone remained floating about in the tissue.[43] Unable to write with his right hand, he kept on with the left. By February he was able to get away to Paris, from which he sent Virginia Crawford one of his left-handed letters, begging her to come over to meet him.[44] He went down to Fontainebleau to see Dujardin at his grand house Le Val Changis, and came away with an idea of doing another big story for *The Untilled Field*, but using Dujardin's method of interior monologue (this became *The Lake*).[45] There is no evidence that GM met Joyce in Paris, though it was at this time that Joyce, seeing a copy of Dujardin's *Les Lauriers sont coupés* on a railway bookstall, and knowing Dujardin to be a friend of Moore's, bought the book and discovered the new method of representing the moment-by-moment flow of consciousness, *le monologue intérieur*.

Sickert, however, did run across GM, "divine in Paris," and, in a letter to Steer, ridiculed Moore for talking up Tonks and Steer as men already well known in Paris, and speaking of Corot as an unheralded artist, while trying to buy a bad Renoir portrait for £200.[46] For Tonks, Steer, and Sickert, GM was a source of amusement – they would go to him as to a play – but in Sickert's case there was a streak of cruelty and dislike in his cachinating laughter at Moore, not to be found in the tolerant geniality of Steer or the ironic tolerance of Tonks. GM was missing his London friends, and on his return to Dublin, he wrote Tonks an affectionate letter, on 26 March 1903: "The spirit of the old masters seems to have revived in you, and without a suspicion of plagiarism." With Moore, love generally emerged as aesthetic appreciation.[47]

Back in Dublin in March, Moore needed to rebuild a little world of sympathetic friends. He was locked out of the National Theatre crowd by Yeats; he could not just go on *épater la bourgeoisie d'Irlande*, or at least, not do that alone. Moore lived in the heart of south Dublin, near its universities, library, gallery, and government buildings, while Yeats paid only periodic visits there, staying in hotels when a play was in rehearsal or some other business called him from his winters in London or summers at Coole. In addition, Moore was, if a man of unusual manners – compulsively telling improper tales about his love life – also gregarious and capable of quick and deep intimacy with men. With his Saturday "At Homes" and his habits of gallery-strolling, library-reading, play-going, and taking long walks around the town with one friend or another, he made himself a prominent figure in Dublin, and a personage both more visible and approachable than Yeats. The history of the Literary Revival is most often told from the point of view of Yeats, of the National Theatre, or, less frequently, of Joyce, but Moore certainly gathered around him, in the wake of his quarrel with Yeats, most of those Dublin artists and intellectuals who were the poets, actors, painters, critics, and on-the-spot organisers of the cultural life of the country during the years of the Revival. Certainly he elicited from them their observations of Yeats, his growing haughtiness and sense of position, and Moore was no doubt quick to feed their sense of injured merit. In collecting about himself the most stimulating companions he could find, he was not, however, solely driven by the desire to recruit an army that could take the field against the ranks of Yeats and Lady Gregory. With whomever Moore found himself, he was fascinated to take the measure of their strangeness, and to urge them toward its expression; he could not be with a person without exhorting that person to write or paint or sculpt. The aesthetic life was for him life itself.

When Father Gerald O'Donovan was visiting Dublin from Loughrea, he would drop in on Moore, and for the benefit of Moore's biographer Joseph Hone, O'Donovan gave a list of those people he saw coming out of 4 Upper

Ely Place as he was going into it: "Miss [Clara] Christian, very often, Edith Oldham, Maurice [Moore] (not often), Hughes (frequently), Thornley Stoker (frequently) . . . Kuno Meyer, Mark Fisher, Edward [Martyn], Willie Orpen, Gill (once or twice), [Hugh] Lane, [W. F.] Bailey, a queer fellow, named, I think, Cunningham [Moore's neighbor], Ruttledge (his agent), [George] Coffey [President of the National Literary Society and officer in the National Museum], Charles Gatty, Faulkiner (I think), John Quinn, and a host of others."[48] Moore's acquaintance in Dublin during the years he was brewing *Hail and Farewell* thus included key figures in the professions, the government, and the arts. With some of them he developed deep friendships.

Although O'Donovan does not list George Russell among Moore's daily visitors, for seven years Russell spent his Saturday nights with Moore, often taking his companion and fellow-worker, the wit Susan Mitchell.[49] As Russell fell out with Yeats over his high-handedness with the theater workers, he fell in with Moore. GM's friendship with Father O'Donovan deepened as O'Donovan's exasperation with the Church hierarchy increased. Father O'Donovan made trips up to Dublin as often as twice a week, as, for instance, when he came in March 1901 to give a lecture at the Maynooth Union on the necessity for priests to employ Irish architects and artists in church building, and not rely on "pushful commercial travellers from Birmingham and Munich," a subject that found its way into "The Window," a story Moore wrote for *The Untilled Field* in the fall of 1901.[50] O'Donovan was also, willingly or not, a sitter for the portrait of an idealistic priest in two other stories, "The Way Back" and "In the Clay." After April 1901, O'Donovan had to be in Dublin regularly to arrange for the stained-glass windows of the Loughrea Cathedral. Clara Christian was the first on O'Donovan's list of those he met most often at Ely Place – that the English mistress and the Irish priest met without catastrophic embarrassment for either may indicate how far out of the grooves of the Catholic clergy O'Donovan had already run by 1902. His irritation with the older type of clergyman would climax after Dr O'Dea replaced the congenial Dr Healy as the Bishop of Clonfert. When O'Donovan had been a seminarian at Maynooth in 1894, O'Dea censured him for reading books deemed unsuitable for a priest in training.[51] In September 1904, O'Dea ordered O'Donovan to stick to his parish duties and give up propagandising for a new Church in a new Ireland, so O'Donovan threw up his post and, armed with letters of introduction from Moore, went off to London to try his luck as a journalist.[52]

By April 1901, O'Donovan had commissioned another Dublin friend of Moore's, John Hughes, to model a statue of the Virgin for Loughrea Cathedral, and Moore used to stop by the studio of Hughes in the Metropolitan School of Art in Leinster House to aestheticise. When the sculptor-schoolmaster was feeling especially hard up, Moore tried to fortify his spirits by the example of the prosperous portrait artist Nathaniel Hone: "Hone just missed being a great artist," GM judged; "a man may struggle against poverty, but no man can struggle against wealth" (perhaps a reflection on how the Land

War had turned poet Moore into a productive novelist).[53] Hughes was a faithful guest at GM's Saturday nights until the sculptor left for Paris in November 1902. It may be that Hughes told the tale that young Beatrice Elvery, later Lady Glenavy, modeled in the nude for him when he was trying to get the figure right for his lovely statue of the Virgin, an adornment still of St Brendan's Cathedral in Loughrea. Moore rapidly turned the idea to account. Two stories in the first edition of *The Untilled Field*, "The Way Back" and "In the Clay," deal with a young woman, Lucy, who is driven from Dublin when it is discovered that she posed in the nude. The sculptor, "John Rodney," leaves Ireland too, because the passion that inspires all art has there been reduced, he believes, to the mere act of begetting children. The supposed original of Lucy, Lady Glenavy, later agreed that "John Rodney" is a picture of Hughes, but, while "flattered and pleased," she had to deny being the model for either Hughes's statue or Moore's story.[54] However flattered, she cannot have liked the bit in "The Way Back" in which Harding, Moore's own favorite persona, meets up with Lucy in London, and while trying to steer the girl straight and put her worried family at ease, rolls over in his mind another idea – why not take the waif to bed himself? It would be so easy! What has become of him, he wonders, that he should let such an opportunity pass?

In the evenings after a solitary dinner in Dublin, Moore would call on two friends not listed by O'Donovan in his letter to Hone, yet who contributed greatly over the years to Moore's Dublin entertainment and his continuing education, Richard Best and W. K. Magee, both sub-librarians at the National Library. Moore would turn up at the counter before closing time and simply ask for "something to read." Gradually, by praise of Matthew Arnold (one of Magee's heroes) and appeals for help in his own education, Moore overcame the frosty start to his relationship with Magee. Magee introduced him to *Don Quixote* (certainly an influence on *Hail and Farewell*, as Moore and Martyn take the places of Quixote and Sancho Panza, and Irish nationalism does duty for chivalry), Rousseau's *Confessions* in English (a trigger for the unbuttoned and philosophical style of autobiography in *Memoirs of My Dead Life* and *Hail and Farewell*), and R. L. Stevenson's *Travels with a Donkey*, perhaps a model for the mellow amble of Moore's late style.[55] These fruitful hints do not include Magee's famous earlier suggestion that Moore write a book like Turgenev's *A Sportsman's Sketches*, a suggestion Moore followed up in *The Untilled Field*.[56] Ordinarily, after the library closed, Moore would put aside his reading matter, the two men would go for a walk, and Moore would discourse about how some scene in Cervantes or Stevenson *should* have been constructed. Magee found to his surprise that he was coming to like Moore:

> A bond was established between Moore and any one who had caught a glimpse of his inner nature, and there came to be such a bond between him and myself. A clairvoyant receptivity made of him a delightful companion at such moments,

when not only words of felt experience came from him, but it was a privilege to cast any sincere thought or genuine observation of one's own into his mind, where it was instantly apprehended and appraised.[57]

Once Moore remarked to Magee that he had a feeling of being disliked by people, and it came to him as a pleasant surprise to find that sometimes he had been mistaken, a sample of one of these genuine glimpses he granted to a few people into his inner nature.[58]

In addition to visits to the library, other Dublin amusements for Moore were to check at the Shelbourne Hotel to see if there were any interesting visitors to the city, or to stop by Sarah Purser's new stained-glass workshop, An Tur Gloine, in order to whip up a fight about religious art or art by women. The sharp-tongued Purser was one of the few people who could fight Moore to a draw, and she spiked his guns effectively when she quipped, "Some men kiss and tell; Moore tells but doesn't kiss."[59] His closest friends were Bram Stoker's brother, the surgeon Sir Thornley Stoker (who lived a few doors down at the grand Ely House), and Walter Osborne (1859–1903), a New English Art Club (NEAC) painter who had returned to Ireland from France in 1892 in order to support his sister's orphaned children by means of portrait-painting, when his genius hankered after tender, delicate treatments of trees and gardens. However, Osborne's new mode of life led him to give poignant expression to group portraits of children with uplifted faces, liquid eyes, and the beauty of frightened fawns. An athletic man who loved to cycle, Osborne suddenly died on 24 April 1903 of pneumonia after riding home coatless from a dinner at the Stokers', and Dublin seemed suddenly smaller to Moore.[60] "I am really heartbroken," Moore wrote Mark Fisher. "He was one of my greatest friends and cannot be replaced, but I cannot go on writing about him: it only brings it up again."[61]

Moore did not remain without fellowship; he was a point of interest in town for Dubliners. John Butler Yeats moved into Osborne's studio at 7 St Stephen's Green, and soon the poet's father and his former friend were enjoying one another's company. GM had "the most stimulating mind I ever met," JBY thought; "I always feel better morally for being with him" – an unusual but not a careless use of the word "morally."[62] JBY attributed the quality of Moore's mind to the fact that he learned nothing at school; consequently, he was always able to keep his own point of view. The National Librarian R. I. Best is another who spoke of Moore's fellowship as a tonic: "In his company one had to forget the exorbitant claims of Irish things for a space, & to enter into the wider air of the world of art."[63] In July 1903, the NEAC painter William Orpen came to Dublin, and on his recurrent visitations as the artist-in-residence of the Metropolitan School of Art, he would be an aesthetic friend for Moore.[64] Orpen, who did two portraits of Moore, came to depend upon the writer's company; it was "a blow" whenever, on his visits to Dublin, he found Moore to be off in London or Paris.[65] Finally, Moore was able to lure Mark Fisher to come and stay with him for a week at the end of May in 1902. By day Fisher and Clara Christian painted landscapes together in the Dublin mountains.[66] It is noteworthy that this set of friends is overwhelmingly drawn from the Anglo-Irish Protestant artistic-intellectual class fraction in Dublin; only O'Donovan and John Hughes were Catholic, and O'Donovan would soon defrock himself.

Even though GM might gather a circle of like-minded friends around him, he could not get his anger at Irish Catholicism under control. Virginia Crawford was about to enter a convent, and he excluded her "liberal" Catholicism from his condemnation, but in Ireland there was "a black Catholicism which begins at the North Wall and ends at Galway – a Catholicism that is the ruin of Ireland."[67] The Gaelic League and Irish press in general took no notice of *An T-Ur-Gort (The Untilled Field)*, except for a maddening comment in the *New Ireland Review* that it was shocking that Moore should write as he did about Catholic Ireland, while "himself a Catholic."[68] He was no Catholic! Enraged, he was provoked to a powerfully succinct avowal of his Nietzschean creed, given out in a June letter to Dujardin: "I have absolutely renounced all my Celtic hopes. Of the race there is now nothing but an end left over, a tattered rag, with plenty of fleas in it, I mean priests. The only end of life is life, and the only end of art is to help us to live, and so soon as we put our hope in another world life becomes ugly and art passes out of existence."[69] Nietzsche helped him see the way in which ideals (or idols) may deprive life of meaning, and the way in which art may serve as a heightener of our sense of existence, but Moore is also speaking here with the heart's simple force.

If one is to understand his later conduct, one has to reckon with the seriousness of George Moore's hatred of repressive, otherworldly religion. For him, it tyrannically cheated humans of the only life they have to live, and of the deepest joys that they can feel, the joys of sexual love and that praise of the visible natural world which is art. The "black Catholicism" he found in Ireland upon his return to the country was certainly a far more powerful force than the Catholicism his father knew. The priests trained at Maynooth were still rigorous in their attitude to the sins of the flesh, but the parish priests, the missioners, and redemptorist preachers were more given than in the past to threats of tortures of hell and purgatory, and to promises of relief for those in purgatory through processions, pilgrimages, adorations, and Masses (which might be purchased). The Church also used a good deal of parishioners' money for the support of those who chose the celibate life. It had control over the education of children in the national schools. Moore was not the only writer to be alarmed by the character of Irish Catholicism at the turn of the century. In *Ireland in the New Century* (1904), Horace Plunkett gave offense by his patriotically framed critique of the economic effects of the new Catholic habit of life; in *A Portrait of the Artist as a Young Man*, Joyce recreated his experience of the Church's haunting domination over the education of children; Yeats and

Gregory had a hard time keeping a politic silence about the religious pressures under which the National Theatre had to conduct its business. But Moore would not hold his tongue: from his arrival in Ireland until his departure, he threw his force into a challenge to Ireland's new Catholicism.

He would no doubt have liked to make carnivalesque use of the stage of the Irish National Theatre in this cause, but after the quarrel with Yeats, his remaining theatrical ally was Martyn, the most unlikely of men to join any anti-Catholic enterprise, and highly alert to GM's deep games of subversion. For the third week of June 1903, Edward Martyn hired the Queen's Theatre (usually taken by traveling companies playing melodrama) in order to stage *A Doll's House* and *The Heather Field*. Moore came in to do the stage management and to quarrel over every jot and tittle with Edward. The audience was not the hushed assembly one might expect in a concert hall and hope for at an Ibsen production; they whistled, chirruped, chattered out loud, banged the doors going back and forth to the lobby bar, and sometimes made rude remarks. A couple next to Holloway jumped up in Act III of *The Heather Field* and the husband exclaimed in terror, "Begob, she is trying to put her man into an asylum!"[70] GM did not mind the bad acting on the part of players and spectators; "I keep no memory of them," he reflected twenty years later, "only of the exultant happiness in which I returned home" from *A Doll's House*.[71] If only he himself could write a work to shake the foundations of Church and Family! Padraic Colum met Moore for the first time just coming away from Ibsen's play: "Shakespeare, Sophocles – what are they to this man?" Moore exclaimed.[72] Martyn's money was not badly spent on these productions. Ibsen was certainly to be an influence on Colum and many subsequent Irish playwrights.[73] But there was little chance that without a company, a regular theater, and a coherent publicity campaign, Martyn and Moore would be able to mount an alternative to the folk-dialect dramas of Yeats's Irish National Theatre Society.

In spite of all those who came to and went from Ely Place, and gathered together there on Saturday nights, Moore looks rather lonely in the beautiful portrait he commissioned young William Orpen to paint in the summer of 1903. Alone by the window, slightly hunched and resting on one elbow with his hand supporting his head, he seems sad, visited by something more than exhaustion.[74] Creatively, however, Moore was on the rebound in mid-1903. Writing *The Lake* over and over, telling the story of how a priest thought himself out of Catholicism after unconsciously falling in love, was like mimetic magic: if he could tell it right, maybe it would happen. He was also delivering himself of wise and hilarious opinions in a series of six essays for *Lippincott's Magazine*, later published as *Avowals* (1919); "books, painting, and myself are the subjects," was his preview for Sybil Eden.[75] Saturday-night discourses at Ely Place were having a splendid effect on his critical prose; the new style was reminiscent, worldly, unhurried, refined, and serpentine in the sinuous dance of its ironic poses.

16. *George Moore, at 4 Upper Ely Place* (1903), William Orpen.

5

On 21 July 1903, Dublin was set awhirl by a visit from the new King, Edward VII. In the course of the tour of his province, the King stopped at Maynooth, the Catholic seminary, and the bishops made him welcome by hanging up his racing colors and pictures of his horses. In protest, Yeats wrote a letter to the *United Irishman*. Moore decided to write a letter to the *Irish Times* publicly renouncing his religion, in so far as he may be said to have had one. How was a man to cease being a Catholic in Ireland, except by becoming a Protestant? In *Salve*, GM says he laid the case before Clara Christian: he could not live in Ireland bearing "the brand of Catholicism" on himself, yet if he were to convert, it would surely give his brother pain and Maurice had suffered enough in life. A protest against the bishops' reception for the King was an excellent pretext for cleansing himself of the stigma. Clara, however, suggested it was time to leave Ireland and his brother in peace.

Yet when Maurice came up to Dublin to talk about the redecorations of Moore Hall he was overseeing (at GM's expense), the brothers had an awful row.[76] Maurice denied saying that he ever told GM that it would be "a great grief" to him if GM declared himself a Protestant. The real fight was about the faith not of GM but of his nephews, Rory and Toby. GM argued that Maurice's wife Evelyn, a Protestant, should have a say in how her two sons were brought up. Indeed, GM should have a say: "I cannot allow [your] children to perish without saying a word in their favour." Maurice was forcing one truth on the boys to the exclusion of all other truths, when everyone knows, GM argued, that there is no single truth in life. Maurice, in GM's account, declared that he depended on George's honor not to try to corrupt Toby and Rory. "It is no part of my honor to withhold the truth," George makes himself reply, "or what I believe to be the truth, from any human being. The fact that you happen to be their father doesn't give you the right over their minds to deform and mutilate them as you please."[77] As told in *Salve*, they had an utter falling out and did not afterwards perfectly mend the break, though they tried.

After *Salve* (1912) was published Maurice read it in shock and rage, then wrote his own story of their religious arguments; indeed, he wrote three sputtering, vehement versions of that story. According to Maurice, GM was not especially apprehensive over the embarrassment to Maurice his change of faith might cause, and indeed Maurice was not especially embarrassed by George's turnabouts, and the brothers continued to be friends. Maurice was subsequently quite willing to take up George's suggestion and put the two boys into Pádraig Pearse's Irish school for the young Cuchulains of tomorrow, but GM, after a tour of inspection, did not like what he saw. So Maurice then went ahead and enrolled Rory in Downside, a Catholic boarding school run by priests.[78] The school fees were charged by Maurice to the Moore Hall expense account, he thought with George's encouragement. These fees were to become the source of dissension later on. In the summer of 1903, instead of showing concern about Maurice and his family, GM contemplated with absurd delight, his brother later wrote, "the shock his apostasy would be to the whole Catholic community & the pressure that would be brought on the episcopacy to reconsider its loyalty [to King Edward VII]. Then also there would be the joy in the Protestant hearts at the accession of so eminent a man. The Protestant Archbishop of Dublin must of course perform the ceremony. What a fine advertisement it would all be to his vanity."[79] No doubt, GM did fancy ham-acting a plot by Huysmans from *Là-bas* in which this time the *Protestant* Church angles for the exquisite soul of one of the nation's great men.

Even before the visit of Edward VII to Maynooth, GM had been preparing for his conversion by reading the Gospels in light of Dujardin's scholarly treatise, *La Source du fleuve chrétien* ("The Source of the Christian River").[80] Indeed, GM was also beginning to take an interest in the writings of biblical modernists like Abbé Alfred Firmin Loisy. In *L'Evangile et l'église* (1902; "The Gospel and the Church") Loisy dared to say that the historical Jesus never had in mind anything like the Roman Catholic Church or its teachings. It would be better, Loisy concluded, for the Church to preach a message of hope and drop its dogma and claim to infallibility. For such views, Loisy was excommunicated in 1908, along with another modernist, the former Irish Protestant George Tyrell. If Moore was to achieve excommunication, however, he would have to do it for himself. He wrote to Archbishop Peacock of the Church of Ireland that he had come to see, while living in Ireland, that "Christianity in its purest form is to be found in the Anglican rather than in the Church of Rome"; could he join up? There was no reply for some time, and then Moore received a note referring him to Revd Gilbert Mahaffy, just down the street at 13 Ely Place, and the Rector of St Peter's parish.[81] Russell was worried that Moore was playing with fire: "they will ask you to pray, Moore, to go down on your knees, things you have never done in your life, and you will feel very much out of place."[82] Indeed, the ceremony of induction (practically nothing in the rather Calvinist Church of Ireland) made one of the funnier scenes in *Salve*; GM was hoping he would not have to go much further than saying he thought Jesus a very interesting character, so he was startled when asked to affirm the resurrection of the flesh. His notion of a Protestant had been an English atheist in favor of morality and independent judgement.

After this ordeal of an affirmation of faith, Moore got the editor of the *Irish Times* to publish a lengthy letter on 24 September 1903 entitled "Mr. George Moore and the Roman Church." It gives a political rather than a theological reason for his change of faith. After the Archbishops' welcome of the King, Moore wrote, "no choice was left to me, if I wished to remain an Irishman, but to say goodbye to Rome."[83] His letter charged Rome with betrayal of Ireland, time after time: in the fifth century, an archbishop cursed Tara, seat of the High Kings; in the eleventh century, a Roman bishop invited Henry II to invade Ireland; the bishops betrayed Parnell, and now an archbishop, ambitious of getting a cardinal's hat, deserted the Irish national cause. Home Rule, he claimed, "will only serve Protestant interests"; that was why Rome opposed it, and every right-thinking Protestant should favor it. The Roman Catholic Church anti-Irish? Home Rule a benefit to Irish Protestants? The print must have seemed to swim in the eyes of readers, so strangely did Moore stand contemporary opinions on their heads. "Irish" and "Catholic" had come to seem synonymous terms; Moore said they were contradictory. It was mad! As mad as George Bernard Shaw (whose preface to *John Bull's Other Island* would take up strikingly similar lines of argument).

The news of Moore's conversion was copied as far away as New York, where in November Yeats was interviewed by a *New York World* reporter. Just how devoted a Catholic had Mr Moore been? Yeats could hardly stifle his laughter as he spoke of the important political principle involved.[84] In Dublin few seemed to care whether an atheist like Moore called himself a Protestant or a satanist; he would always be a Catholic, good or bad, doubtless in fact very bad, and thus a person to whom no one should give ear. One who did write in response to GM's *Irish Times* letter made an Aesopian comparison with a gnat (GM) announcing his departure from the horn of a bull (the Roman Church), which did not know it had been there, and did not care about its departure.[85] The main topic of Dublin controversy in October and November 1903 was Synge's first play, *In the Shadow of the Glen*: surely no Catholic Irish wife would leave her old husband and walk off with an itinerant! There was *A Doll's House* in an Irish cabin. That was an outrage worth fighting about.[86]

6

In November, Moore escaped Dublin for Paris for the second time in the year. His secretary forwarded to him fascinating and funny letters from Cecile Gabrielle von Hoenstadt, Baronne Franzi Ripp, of Vienna.[87] After he wrote from the Hôtel Continental, the Countess was perplexed to conclude from his accommodations that he was not, as she believed, a priest.[88] As one of his devoted readers, she proposed a new plot for *Sister Teresa* in which Evelyn stays in the convent but has furious fits of jealousy that all her former lovers are consoling themselves with others; jealousy drives her to write her amorous reminiscences into four successive sweet volumes, "especially very exciting things about the two years in Paris you have ubersprungen [skipped over] to my greatest sorrow." Gabrielle wrote that she would love to accept his invitation to Paris, but, being recently divorced, she was closely watched; why didn't he come to Vienna? That is, if he was not in fact a lady novelist writing under a man's name. In a postscript, she adds that she once thought of writing to Tolstoy, but forgot about it; Moore is thus her first literary lover. With this letter following so fast upon his recent conversion, GM could have been forgiven for believing that maybe there is a God after all.

In reply, Moore boldly called her "one of my women," but then immediately began to worry about what she would think of him as her man if they met. She probably had some fantasy image of a handsome author; she did not imagine the reality, a middle-aged man who spent his life smoking cigars over manuscripts while his bottom broadened out. "My dear Baronne, I am not horrid; I used to think I was when I was very young but since then I have found out that I am not . . . [but] I would not undertake the journey you propose – . . . Imagine presenting myself and watching your face not daring to ask you if you were disappointed. I am not fatuous or courageous enough." Then he asked for her photograph.

The bold little twenty-eight-year-old Countess answered that of course she was "one of your women . . . and besides I am in love with you." On 11 December, she was miserable, pouting; all she wanted was "to sit with you in a dark room and kiss you fervently." Furthermore, she requisitioned from Moore a "Kreutzer Sonata" (but with a happy ending!), as well as a volume of Evelyn Innes's "lettres to her lovers (and confesseurs)." From Sir William Eden's London apartment at 12 Waterloo Place, GM wrote back in early December inviting her to come and sit by the fire with him in "Sir Owen Asher's rooms": she can be Evelyn, he can be Sir Owen. If only he were younger, he lamented, while shaving five years off his age, or she were older. She told him to stop hoping he would in hard cold fact manage to become her lover. How disappointing, Moore replied: "Chastity is a mean vice and I hope you do not labour after it."

In almost daily letters through December, she kept up the delightful, subtle, flirtatious, calculating chatter in three languages, and GM kept up his demands for a photograph, a revealing one if possible. "My secret hope has been," she replied on 20 December 1903, "you would forget all about it. I always look dreadful and affecte or swollen and greedy on photografs. I am much mieux que this. I don't look so toothachish in reality." She was confident he would look all right to her, so long as he was not "too Frenchy." "You see, I don't like the French. They are guindes and fussy and their hair is oily." She was glad he had gotten rid of his beard but wished he had not entirely gotten rid of God too: "We could say the same little prayer every day at the same hour, you in Dublin, I in Vienna. The liebe Gott will like it I think – he will smile good-naturedly and stroke his long beard. You know, I hope that he has a very long beard. He may have and ought to, but you were right to put off yours." In the sweet war of epistolary romance, she was overrunning his defenses. What brilliance! Her letters, he thought, were like his *Confessions of a Young Man*. Would she translate a story from *The Untilled Field* or a chapter from *Evelyn Innes*? he asked on 21 December. Somehow, this baroness had to get into literature. She did not like the idea of translating: "I think only governesses do it, pas?" And what was the point of translating a book at all – just so the ignorant can read it? "Is it the money you want or the fame? Is it both?"

In January they elaborated detailed plans – where to stay, what to wear, how to open the conversation – for meeting in Paris, Vienna, Venice, Munich, a regular Cook's Tour of Sexual Fantasy. Having seen his photograph ("your nose is very long," and "you have what I call a horse face"), she thought on 12 January 1904 that she would no longer dare to write him naughty letters. "You need have no fear that anyone will see your letters," Moore fibbed (he was reading them to friends at dinner parties), "so write the thoughts that pass through your mind however 'naughty' they may be, and I hope they will be very naughty." She could not provide pornography on the day of her reply, 25 January: "I promised my friend, you see. I told him in what manner I had written to you and he wasn't pleased at all. Indeed, I think he was *furious*. He has such dear, gentle ways that one never knows. But 'hysterich,' 'impossible,' 'indecent' were the words he used." Soon enough, she returned to teasing her favorite novelist: "Mr. Moore, do you quite know how wonderful you are? . . . do you know what I did last night? Well, no, I didn't exactly *do* something, but I was thinking of you and it was so nice!" This quite wound up the old man: "One should never refrain from pleasure and you say you have refrained. Was the thought of me really sufficient? I wish I had been by you – you great tall Gabrielle . . . I look forward to seeing you, to admiring you, to –––. You can fill up that blank with the word you prefer, several will be equally true." On a trip to Paris in March, she obtained a favorable report of GM from Catulle Mendès: Moore was "un aimable compagnon d'une élégante allure, parlant bien le français et écrivant de bons livres dans le goût naturaliste . . . un parfait galant." In April, she was rather shocked that the perfect gallant did not jump at her invitation to meet her in Munich. Would he ever fill in that blank with some signature proof of love? But the aging would-be amorist was satisfied with her letters and a photo of herself in which she does not, he judges, wear stays; he simply could not go see her for a week and then leave. No, he wanted to finish *The Lake*, and then to write a comedy.

What he did not say is that the comedy was to be about a woman named Gabrielle who writes to her favorite novelist, and, not daring to visit her himself, he sends in his place Sebastian, a young poet and his secretary.

7

Throughout this bombardment of love letters between Irish author and Austrian reader, Moore's relationship with Clara Christian continued, but to what destination seemed unclear. His friends teased him from fall 1903 to spring 1904 that he must be about to tie the knot, but no more than ever did GM have any intention of marrying; however, Charles J. MacCarthy did, and Clara Christian seemed the ideal choice of wife to Dublin's city architect.[89] The state of Dublin gossip about the matter is captured in the play GM wrote about the baroness in September 1904. Would famous author Davenant/GM stay in Malvern/Dublin, go to London, return to Paris, or get married? He had been meeting Rose/Clara since coming to Malvern:

Lady Thurloe: Do you think he cares for her?

Miss Rice: I don't think there is any doubt he likes her very much, but a man may like a woman very much without wishing to marry her.

Lady T: Or without being able to make up his mind to ask her.

Miss R: I suppose she is in love with him, for though Burchell [Charles Mac-Carthy] has asked her to marry him at least twice, she has refused.

Lady T: Poor Rose! If he should just sell his house, pack up his things, and end his days in a café! If what you say should happen, do you think she will marry Burchell?

Miss R: Perhaps Mr. Burchell will lose patience and marry somebody else.[90]

In the play, Rose becomes cross over Davenant's glorying in the letters he receives from a German countess. Davenant then brings Rose and Burchell together at his dinner parties. In *Vale*, GM similarly represents himself as speaking in MacCarthy's favor when Christian brought up the fact that MacCarthy had proposed.[91] There were more than enough reasons for Moore not to marry Christian, or Christian Moore, but two require mention. First, he says that she told him (and why would he make such a story up?) that he did not make love to her enough; this certainly gave him a fright that he was losing his virility.[92] Second, Lady Cunard wrote Moore, whistling her little leitmotif, and unable not to answer the love call, he went to visit Nancy, Maud, and her mother Mrs Tichenor at Nevill Holt on 20 June 1904.[93] Christian departed for a tour of Italy, and upon her return married Charles MacCarthy on 11 January 1905.

During Moore's June visit to Nevill Holt, he was welcomed as an old friend by Maud's mother and daughter, and as a lover by Maud herself – "You make a poem out of your body . . . you are at once the poet and the poem." Sir Bache furiously fashioned silver coconuts in his workshop at such times. Then Moore arranged for a second visit on 13 August 1904, his "last cruise" he called it to Gogarty.[94] Sir Bache "Bang Bang" Cunard was off shooting grouse in Scotland, and GM hoped to enjoy himself with the wife and an occasional brace of birds sent back by the husband – or this was the crass face he put on the affair for the benefit of young Oliver St John Gogarty.

Moore had been trying to employ Gogarty on several pieces of shifty business he was plotting. Over the previous months, GM had attended the Irish National Theatre production of *Shadowy Waters* (14 January 1904) and several rehearsals (6 February, 13 July), always upsetting the actors by making them imagine what he must be thinking. "When he is there I cannot help feeling the futility of our efforts," Frank Fay complained to Maire Garvey.[95] Gogarty and Joyce, living together in the Martello Tower in early September 1904, did not think any more of the "folk-smoke" of the Irish National Theatre Society (INTS) than Moore did. Yeats thought Moore was scheming to get back into the theater company and stage-manage plays himself, so he planned to bar Moore from attending any more rehearsals.[96] Gogarty himself, after very little squeezing from Yeats in the Nassau Hotel, spilled the beans that Moore had written an article for W. K. Magee's new journal, *Dana*, "Stage-Management in the Irish National Theatre," and was twisting Gogarty's arm to sign it.[97] As Gogarty refused to sign the article (though he probably helped write it), Moore used as *nom de plume* "Paul Ruttledge," main character in *Where There Is Nothing*, the play Yeats hijacked a year earlier. The September article dispraised Willie Fay's abilities as compared with those of Antoine; in fact, the article said, Fay did not even know the ABC of staging, his blocking of the characters in *Shadowy Waters* "remind[ed] one . . . of three little boys and a little girl reciting a story in front of a barn door." So why did Fay productions get good London reviews from people like Beerbohm?[98] That was just the sort of condescension given to "any little bushman who came over to London with his boomerang," Moore gibed. Still, he felt obliged to say Fay was to be admired for succeeding on his own, with little support . . . "but that after all cannot be said of a man who has found an admirer to buy him a theatre."[99]

That dry little locution was noted in a frenzy of rage by Annie Horniman, until then enjoying herself with Yeats at Coole Park. The "dissenting English spinster," as she called herself, was not in love with a dirty little Catholic former electrician! She had not bought Fay a theater! Then she thought with horror that everyone in Dublin would know it was not Willie Fay she loved but Willie Yeats; the Abbey was to be her very special gift to him. Her icy letter of correction to the December issue of *Dana* only underlined the reading she put on Moore's sentence. GM certainly meant to cause trouble, but he unloosed a hurricane against poor W. G. Fay. Horniman was not content until she ran him and his brother out of the Abbey Theatre in 1908.[100]

The second piece of business Moore had in mind for Gogarty was a still stranger kind of ghost-authorship. GM was back in contact with Pearl Craigie, and it occurred to him that she might help him make a good comedy out of the letters of Gabrielle. Craigie was game enough to invite him to come and stay at Steephill Castle, the family summer place on the Isle of Wight. As he prepared to set off on 2 September 1904, Moore wrote to Gogarty, himself then planning a trip to Vienna, to come to Ely Place and collect Gabrielle's address: "It would be really a pity of you not to see the lady for her sake and yours. You will come back with a pretty story which I may be able to turn into literature afterwards. I beg you to answer this letter at once."[101] The scenario of the comedy Moore wished to write involved Davenant/GM's young male secretary, a poet like Gogarty, going off to meet the Countess posing as the author of all Davenant's books. Once again, Moore was busily trying to script an elaborate plot involving many of his friends as attendants, clowns, heralds, juvenile male leads, dark ladies, and gossiping nurses, so that he might later have suitably literary material to dramatise as memoirs. He came to be a dab hand at plotting a tale in literature, but he was even better at staging "situations" in life, especially of the sort that cause an audience at a French farce to gasp in dread at an imminently fantastical cock-up prepared in Act I and finally tumultuously sprung in Act IV, something delicious, devious, maniacal, and elegantly immoral.

Craigie had come back into Moore's life when they both happened to be dinner guests of Edmund Gosse on 5 June 1904. It was later Moore's contention that they made a deal the following month: Moore would waive his sporadically reasserted claim to *Journeys End in Lovers Meeting* (which Craigie published under her own name with Unwin) if she would help GM with his new idea. By 7 September he was with her at Steephill Castle dictating to a shorthand writer at the pace of an act a day.[102] After three days he was done, and Craigie said there was little for her as co-author to do except edit out some repetitions and look after the details of getting the comedy on stage.[103] (Moore was pleased; he did not like it, he told Dujardin, when his "fair collaborator . . . wanted to hold the pen instead of the other instrument.")[104] GM continued to stay on at Steephill Castle after the playwriting was complete. In the course of his long stay he sometimes visited Virginia Crawford, out of the convent again and staying on the Isle of Wight with her sister (she had been helping GM by writing the letters of Rose to the priest for insertion into *The Lake*). In the course of his stay, GM and Craigie had a serious late-night talk, and, according to GM's story to W. H. Heinemann, Craigie then asked him what he thought her chances would be of marrying Lord Curzon, if Mary Leiter Curzon, then ill, should pass away.[105] Certainly, earlier in the summer, Craigie had been staying with the Curzons, and her letters about the former Viceroy of India may bear an interpretation of a continued interest on her part.[106] Moore never liked the pompous, ramrod-stiff Curzon; "she gave me up for the second footman" used to be one of his favorite lines of mock grief at having lost Craigie in 1894.[107] But it appears to have been neither such a remark about Curzon, nor one of the spiteful remarks Craigie was herself accustomed to make about GM's relationship to Virginia Crawford, that caused a new blow-up between Craigie and Moore; instead, Moore's conversation about religion set off explosions with the Richards' guests.[108]

There were further explosions – a chain reaction – when Craigie took the play off to London producer Arthur Bourchier (1851–1928) and began to rehearse it in early December as her own work. That is where Moore drew Yeats back into the picture.

8

A few days before the December opening of his Loan Exhibition of Modern Art at the Royal Hibernian Academy in Dublin, Hugh Lane stopped by 4 Ely Place one evening and asked George Moore to write an article or give a lecture on the French paintings in the exhibition. Lane had a long-range plan to "do something for Ireland" at his aunt Lady Gregory's suggestion. He would raise a subscription to buy the loan collection now being exhibited; that collection would then become the foundation for a modern art gallery in Dublin. If the collection were given to the city, Lane believed the Dublin Corporation would be shamed into building for it a handsome gallery. A Ladies' Picture League was formed, with Countess Markiewicz as secretary, Mrs Noel Guinness as treasurer, and Lady Gregory as driving force.[109] Lane roped John Butler Yeats into giving a lecture, and William Butler Yeats into taking a seat on the platform at several lectures. Lane approached matters like this, Moore remarked, like Napoleon preparing a plan of campaign.[110] Moore, however, at first resisted the attempt to be recruited into the ranks of what he took to be another man's campaign for personal immortality, but an appeal to his vanity ("but you are the only one in Dublin to have actually known these painters") was enough to overcome his resistance. Lane, always in a hurry, bade him goodnight abruptly and left.[111]

The lecture Moore gave on Thursday night, 8 December 1904 in the Large Exhibition Room of the Royal Hibernian Academy was hardly the piece of high-culture, high-minded patriotic puffery Lane might well have sought. Moore cut loose with a vehement, swingeing interpretation of the meaning for Ireland of the art of Edouard Manet, centering on Manet's portrait of Eva Gonzales. F. S. L. Lyons aptly called this lecture Moore's "epistle to the Philistines."[112] The *Irish Times* reported, in tones of distaste, the lesson for the day: "The doctrine upon which he insisted with almost painful reiteration last night was, 'Be not ashamed of anything but being ashamed.'" Joseph Holloway was puzzled by the talk: Moore "almost raved over the unshaded arm of a lady in one of [Manet's] exhibits . . . and propounded many strange things such as 'an artist should be almost unaware of any moral codes to succeed.'"[113] The *Irish Times* critic was worried: what would be the result for respectable society if this doctrine were accepted? Moore had given the audience a taste of shameless bad manners by ridiculing the National Gallery collection, apparently with the Gallery's director, Walter Armstrong, in the audience. Moore publicly exposed Armstrong for refusing to buy a Manet for £10 some years ago that today sold for £1,000. In fact, he went on remorselessly, a young man wandering into Armstrong's "dull and commonplace" collection would say to himself, "if this is painting, painting is depressing work, and I would prefer to be a clerk in a brewery."[114] Very "ill-advised" sentiments, the *Irish Times* felt compelled to say, "very ill-advised."

Joseph Holloway was astonished to see WBY on the platform with Moore; he had thought the two were still "at daggers drawn" over the disputed scenario and "the *Dana* affair."[115] On 3 December 1904, however, Moore and Yeats lured one another into a condition of guarded friendship, each for his own purposes. In his inveigling way, Moore asked Yeats to help him – one man of letters to another – with a certain problem. It concerned the ownership of a scenario. Another author, the very unscrupulous Pearl Craigie, was threatening to steal the play Moore had written all but all of, then entitled *The Peacock's Feathers*.[116] Craigie had recently made a deal with the producer Bourchier and was running down Moore with his own publisher, T. Fisher Unwin.[117]

17. *G. Moore Giving his Memorial Lecture at the RHA* (1904), John Butler Yeats.

Yeats suspected some sort of trick on Moore's part. Yeats himself had taken a plot Moore chose to regard as his own property, had given the play a London production, and complained to Unwin that Moore was an impossible person. Now Moore was sending Yeats away with the page-proofs of *The Peacock's Feathers*, in order, Moore said, to determine whether it was good enough to fight over.[118] This indeed was the very question about *Where There Is Nothing*: was it a play worth the price of a friendship? Rightly suspecting a mindtrap of truly Mephistophelean intricacy, Yeats nonetheless involved himself. He had in mind several uses for Moore. First, Yeats wanted Moore to give up his share of the rights in their co-authored *Diarmuid and Grania* so that the National Theatre Society could produce the play in an altered form; second, Moore was just the man to help whip up a controversy for the Municipal Gallery campaign.[119] So the two authors entered into a *rapprochement*, but guardedly.

One key to understanding what was in GM's lecture for Yeats, and just for Yeats, is his comment on this episode in *Hail and Farewell*. He writes that as soon as the applause died down after the lecture, Yeats got up to propose a vote of thanks, and the audience considered the figure of the poet "lately returned to us from the States with a paunch, a huge stride, and an immense fur over-coat." Yeats began, Moore says, to "thunder against the middle classes, stamping his feet . . . and all because the middle classes did not dip their hands into their pockets and give Lane the money he wanted . . ." Then, with one of the beautifully cruel turns in the trilogy, Moore goes on with *faux* wonderment: "And we asked ourselves why our Willie Yeats should feel himself called upon to denounce his own class."

Like *Hail and Farewell*, Moore's 1904 lecture itself contains warnings about the dangers of class pretension to the artist, warnings that might well have made Yeats squirm in his chair. The first thing Moore had to do when he went to Paris, he said, was to send his valet home: "his presence stood between me and myself; I wished above all things to be myself . . . Myself was the goal I was making for, instinctively if you will, but still making for it." For this end, he declared, "All conventions of politics, society, and creed, yes, and of Art, too, must be cast into the melting pot; he who would be an artist must melt down all things . . . Art is a personal re-thinking of life from end to end" – a spirited paraphrase of Nietzsche's "you must become who you are," that difficult, demystifying, self-deconstructing experience, in which you want to become what you do become and do not want anything about yourself to be different; then "the final seal of freedom" is attained, because, in Nietzsche's phrase, "one is no longer ashamed of oneself."[120] Moore and Yeats were both Nietzscheans, but there was a basic difference between the self-assurance of an artist with all the property of a landlord and none of the proprieties, and the self-overcoming of an artist with all the proprieties of a landlord and none of the property. Yeats never had a valet to send home.

When in Moore's lecture he compared Renoir with Manet, he was staging his own imagined relation as landlord with Yeats as middle-class pretender. Manet's art, he says, has "the birthmark of easy circumstances and the culture thereof"; Renoir, a Parisian workman, had not sufficient talent "to redeem his art from the taint of an inherited vulgarity."[121] Though Manet was, Moore said, "born in what is known as refined society," "in dress and appearance" "an aristocrat," he knew enough to "avoid polite society."[122] If you would become who you are, you needed instead the company of *ratés*, dabblers, however poor and miserable, so long as they were artists. The new Yeats of the overcoat and the paunch had cut the *ratés* of Dublin, the minor poets, Abbey actors, Dublin journalists, and local painters, who tended now to gather at Moore's Saturday nights or Russell's Thursdays. Yeats had cut this crowd – AE's "canaries" he called them – and he was now thinking himself the man of the house at Coole, acting up to the manners of Lady Gregory's set and Hugh Lane's country house set. He was trying to keep in the good graces of English millionaires like Horniman and American millionaires like Quinn. Moore, on the other hand, was making his appeal to the bohemian artist figures of Dublin, not people with a national ambition but at least with a truly artistic one.

These sentiments of 1904, copied into *Vale*, are petty and spiteful, and ridiculously premature as an obituary on the genius of Yeats as a poet. But occasionally, the petty spite of Moore the man connects with what is noble in Moore the writer. While wrong in his valuation of Yeats, he was right in his statement of his own values. Moore really did admire in Manet what he himself wished to become: a person of courage, candor, and shamelessness, with an almost childish innocence. J. B. Yeats noticed this quality about Moore: "he is always like a man tumbled in among us out of some distant planet where everything is different from what it is here." "I like George Moore," JBY explained to Rosa Butt, "because he is more humane than anybody else. Everybody else wants to put fresh chains on humanity. He wants to strike them off . . . He is besides always quite sincere and honest . . . I always feel better morally for being with him. Compared to him, I find most people humbugs, addicted to dishonest practices and thoughts."[123] Assuredly to the genuine distress of family and friends, Moore was willing to sweep aside the old values and to laugh at morality, in order to arrive at a new estimate of human life and new molds for human feeling. In all his aristocratic bohemianism and priestly devotion to an agnostic individualism, Moore is an essential modernist. He spoke to Dublin out of a complete identification with the intellectual movement that takes in Rousseau, Baudelaire, Dostoevsky, Flaubert, Manet, Degas, and Nietzsche. It was their texts he drew upon when overwriting Manet's portrait of Eva Gonzales with his own gospel of shamelessness.

To Edward Martyn, Moore's words did not have to do with class, but with sexuality. After the lecture Martyn told Moore that although parts of the lecture interested him, "Every now and again . . . you said something that hurt me as much as if someone had shoved a pin in the very quickest part of my body." This painful prick was from "that detestable phrase, 'To be ashamed of nothing but to be ashamed.'"[124] It was "the most anti-Catholic" phrase, Martyn thought, that had ever been uttered; it would ever after ruin his appreciation of Manet's pictures. These are strong words, and they made Moore's blood boil. For him, Martyn represented the "frozen orthodoxy of Ireland" better than anyone. Moore had known since the early 1880s that Martyn hated women and loved young boys, but Martyn was ashamed; he dared not. Instead, he did his best to dedicate himself to holy renunciations and sacred sublimations. He established boys' choirs, stained-glass works, literary theaters, and national exhibitions, always after taking advice from the Church hierarchy. What was the use of all this self-improvement built upon self-denial? To Moore, it was an outrage on nature. For his own part, he told his audience the story of his meeting with Manet as a sort of homosexual pick-up, after which comes love-at-first-sight. Finding the young jonquil-haired Irishman at the Café Nouvelle Athènes, Manet asks George to come to his studio in the rue d'Amsterdam, and begins one of his three portraits of his new friend. Moore spent the rest of his life trying to become the something that Manet saw in him. It was his boast, and not his shame, that he loved Manet.

Although the lecture was supposed to serve a fund-raising function for a Dublin gallery, Moore's treatment of this object in his lecture is highly ambivalent. Moore had always been bad-tempered and wrong-headed about cultural philanthropists – had he gotten his way in 1892, there would have been no Tate Gallery.[125] He had also opposed the Chantry bequest to the National Gallery, again on account of the vanity and bad taste of the gentleman collector. Moore brought up both of these two earlier misconceived (as he thought) pieces of vain (as he thought) philanthropy in his lecture, a lecture supposedly offered to support a third such piece of philanthropy.[126] He had to admit, however, that Lane had wonderful taste. So, after some growling, it seemed that Moore finally came down on Lane's side in favor of a Museum of Modern Art for Dublin.

At the same time, GM wanted to distinguish between his reasons and those of Lane, Gregory, Yeats, &c., for why a museum would benefit Ireland. For them, such a museum was another store front for their educational mission of cultural nationalism.[127] For Moore, however, neither nationalism nor education nor even Irishness seemed valuable anymore. Once he may have thought so; once he had been part of the Irish Revival; no longer. For him, what might give such a gallery of paintings value was the fact that it was not national, but international; not educational (as he understood education), but disruptive; and not Irish, or even French, but individualist. It would not lead to a native school of Irish art or teach Irish artists how better to admire a sunset at Malahide; it would not educate anybody.[128] Moore was splenetic on this point: "the folly of the twentieth century is the desire to educate . . . we never meet anyone who will admit that he cannot educate somebody else." Then what was the good of a Museum of Modern Art? What the gallery could do, Moore declared, is send young men to France. There they could find some such café as the Nouvelle Athènes, better than any Oxford or Cambridge. The gallery, in short, would be an aid to emigration; it would thus, for the few, spell an end to nationalism and a beginning to internationalism.[129]

And finally – this was Moore's most important and alarming point – the gallery would be the beginning of the end of Catholicism. "Art," he concluded, "is but praise of life." Religion, however, and especially dogmatic Catholicism, was a condemnation of life, of instinct, and thus of art. Revisiting the trope of the flight of the Muses that he had used in his first Irish Literary Theatre speech in May 1899, Moore explained that since the fifteenth century in Italy when artists turned their eyes toward pagan Greece, the Enlightenment (an artistic more than philosophical movement for Moore) had been slowly spreading northward, bringing an end to the Dark Ages of dogmatic belief. It was returning pagan joy in existence to one country after another, and Ireland's turn would come some day too, Moore promised – Oh, not soon, not probably for a hundred years, but the heresy of modern art might begin to free some few young men from "the deadly fingers of the Ecclesiastic."[130] Moore was ready to tell the future artists of Ireland, "Go to Paris, young man."

From the beginning, then, Moore's endorsement of a Museum of Modern Art hinged on its being a force for revolutionary atheism and instinctual liberation. Within a few weeks, he had begun to doubt that it could ever serve this purpose. In the movement to raise funds, those who campaigned included a number of schoolteachers, several respectable Home Rulers, Royal Hibernian Academicians, and many titled folk, such as Lady Ardilaun, the Earl of Mayo, the Countess of Fingall, the Countess of Drogheda – a whole *Burke's Landed Gentry* of charitable donors. Was this the sort of respectable, well-meaning movement with which Moore wanted to associate himself? When Augusta Gregory wrote to ask him if he would add his name to "An Appeal from Irish Authors" for subscriptions (already signed by Yeats, Russell, Somerville & Ross, and several others), GM refused. "My mind is full of doubts," he replied, "and I could not sign the enclosed unless I were convinced the pictures would benefit Ireland."[131] His doubts remained: the armies of the conventional had closed ranks, and their force was too great even for the revolutionary spirit of Manet. His pictures were being turned into articles of commerce, trophies in a museum, a lesson in the curriculum.

Moore's lecture at the Royal Hibernian Academy was his last public speech before he left Ireland in 1911 and issued *Hail and Farewell* from a London publisher. After that lecture, he resorted to more devious and literary forms of subversion of Irish respectability, Irish nationalism, and Irish Catholicism.

9

One of Moore's interventions into the cultural life of Catholic Dublin was even more bewildering to the citizens than his Manet lecture had been to Joseph Holloway. In January 1905, Moore was working on "The Lovers of Orelay", his autobiographical reminiscence of the joys of love he found with "Doris," that is, Maud Burke before her marriage. According to Gogarty, Maud Cunard was so angry at Moore for writing it that she said she would never see him again. This story is not supported by those letters she chose to preserve; however, she may well have been irate, and Moore may well have replied, as in Gogarty's story, that if she ever wanted him again, all she had to do was hum a bar of Schubert's "O Tannenbaum."[132] Yet Moore's epicurean sex comedy was written out of a deviously polemical impulse as much as a gossiping, belletristic, or pornographic one.

"The Lovers of Orelay" was conceived as the heart of an autobiography of the author as a former lover (now that age had come upon him he had only, as Yeats described the condition, "Vague memories, vague memories").[133] *Memoirs of My Dead Life* (1906) came to be the title of the book, but originally its chapters were called "Moods and Memories," a series of articles Moore published to support *Dana*, a new Dublin journal, launched in February 1904 by the

18. George Moore and another, as "the Lovers of Orelay," Henry Tonks.

Arnoldian W. K. Magee and the Marxian Fred Ryan. They thought of *Dana* as a modern forum for the tolerant intellectual discussion of issues usually kept under wraps because of the high level of sectarian tension in Ireland. James Joyce thought their intellectual tolerance was simply "an amusing disguise of the proselytising spirit."[134] In his diary, Stanislaus Joyce was severe on the subject: Magee thought it "his mission in Ireland" "to prove to his Protestant grandaunts that unbelievers can be very moral and admire the Bible."[135] Moore himself thought of the monthly simply as an "anti-clerical journal" like *La Revue des idées*.[136] In late February 1904, Moore provided the *Dana* editors with money, letters of support to English editors, and the privilege to republish articles from Dujardin's Paris review.[137] GM's greatest contributions to *Dana*, however, were the six articles he astonished Magee by handing over in March. Moore was able to produce them so quickly because most of them had already been written. They had been published in the *Hawk*, *Speaker*, and *Pall Mall Budget* in the 1890s. At that time, they were part of GM's aesthetic-erotic rebellion against English Protestantism and the National Vigilance Association. Slightly rewritten, then supplemented with new chapters, they would serve very well as an instructive outrage to Catholic sensibilities.

Some of the changes Moore made to the original texts show the new anti-Irish-Catholic spin he wished to give the epicurean sensibility that the stories celebrate. To the *Hawk* version of Moore's recollections of the Blanche family, he added for the August 1904 *Dana* article a paragraph about Madame Blanche's custom of going to morning Mass, which always caused breakfast to be postponed: "*La messe!* How gentle the word is, much gentler than our word, mass, and it shocks us hardly at all to see an old lady going away in her carriage, *pour entendre la messe*. Religion purged of faith is a pleasant, almost a pretty thing. Some fruits are better dried than fresh: religion is such a one, and religion, when nothing is left of it but the pleasant, familiar habit, may be defended, for were it not for our habits, life would be unrecorded, it would be all on the flat . . . without perspective." This bland, painterly, and worldly treatment of faith is as deliberately offensive to Irish Catholics as he could make it. Another added touch is even more precisely targeted at the repressive Irish version of Catholicism. The chapter presents Moore as a "Beau Brummell of the emotions" who, in middle age, is trying to recall the women he loved in Paris. He works to come up with a cycle of seven, seven women for seven visits to Paris, so that for a whole week he may "meditate on art and women," occupied "with what I once heard dear old M'Cormack, Bishop of Galway, describe in his sermon as 'the degrading passion of *loave*.'"[138] Not degrading at all, was Moore's subversive claim, but inspiring, indeed ennobling, even when the love in question did not lead to the altar and the home. Dead loves, maybe especially those, were equally worth delectation for having made life worth living.

This theme was also the serious fruit comfit at the center of the frothy comedy of "The Lovers of Orelay." After resuming his affair with Lady Cunard in the summer of 1904, Moore wrote to his lover in late October 1904 that he must see her again because "you make me feel alive, and life is what we are all after. You are a light, I am but an accumulator and my supply is running low."[139] This parasitical, onanistic dependency on Maud Cunard will hardly seem to many a flattering form of attachment, but he knew it for what it was and displayed it without shame for the reader's entertainment and instruction when he wrote the story in January 1906.[140] Wouldn't the shock of "the mamas and the papas" be just a result of the custom of the time and an undeveloped aspect of their humanity? In "Lovers," GM discusses with Doris the oddities of sexual shame – in Western Europe, women uncovered their bosoms in the evening; in China, they uncovered their feet. Doris mentions that Empress Eugénie, a most civilised woman, went without drawers. What now was sin was once meritorious, and would be so again. Here GM comes upon his theme: "At the bottom of his heart every Christian feels, though he may not care to admit it in these modern days, that every attempt to make love a beautiful and pleasurable thing is a return to paganism. In his eyes the only excuse for man's love of woman is that without it the world would come to an end." And why shouldn't it end, since to the Christian the only use of the world is to supply hell with fuel; very few indeed could get to heaven, if the rules for membership were strictly enforced.[141] This passage strikes the tone that JBY loved in GM, that of a man dropped down from another planet, who finds all accepted customs arbitrary. Fundamentally, Moore could take a Martian view of earthly love because he was a homosexual man who loved to make love to women. He loved their dresses and underdresses, their "little ways," their acceptance and sympathy, their effortless evasion of his understanding, and their sympathetic amorality, since to them too moral codes might seem arbitrary repressive inventions of other people, different people, men.

One of the most profoundly unsettling aspects of "Lovers of Orelay" is its psychological contrariness to the normative structure of heterosexual narratives in England, Ireland, and America. The English novel, as Michel Foucault noticed, is a forward-looking tale of heterosexual desire that ends at the home and the altar, before desire is consummated, or else desire is consummated in the inter-chapters, between the lines. There was yet to be written a literature that was fondly reminiscent over acts and bodies and over the meaning of our secrecies – or not so much their meaning, for they may have no issue, as their being-in-the-mind. It might, Foucault thought, fall to homosexuals to create these nostalgic sex narratives: "it is the recollection rather than the anticipation of the act that assumes a primary importance in homosexual relations."[142] Such a literature might be found already hinted in the French side of the Russian novel, for example in Turgenev's *First Love* or Nabokov's *Ada*, and with vastly greater depth of consciousness it would appear in Proust's *Remembrance of Things Past*. Moore's own *Memoirs of My Dead Life* is one of the first fruits of this literature in the English tradition. Readers of the 1904 issues of *Dana* may be forgiven for not knowing what to make of Moore's moods and memories.[143]

However beautiful he might make his memoirs, there may still be something incompletely satisfying to many people about either religion or love as a *dried fruit*. Moore's 1905 novel *The Lake* is a stylistic *tour de force*, a remarkable example of a different way to handle the *monologue intérieur* from the one employed by either Dujardin or Joyce, but the philosophical naturalism it celebrates never fully envisions a life of fruition for its hero, Father Oliver Gogarty.[144] On his long walks around Lough Carra, Father Gogarty slowly comes to be aware that he had fulminated from the altar against the pretty parish music teacher, then pregnant, not because she had wickedly sinned with a passing lover, but because the priest loved her himself. He writes to her in London where she has gone to have her baby, and her own brisk, academic but free-spirited letters to the priest make up a fragment of an epistolary novel interleaved with the first English stream-of-consciousness novel. The letters jar on Gogarty's meditations. Her fundamentally natural view of life forces him into reckoning that his own life has never really been lived. He plans his escape from the priesthood and from Ireland, leaving his collar and habit folded up on one side of the lake and a new secular suit on the other. One night he takes a naked swim through the lake and walks away to a new life. While this fable is beautifully realised, there is something odd and anticlimactic about the fact that in the end Moore's hero, Father Oliver Gogarty, goes off to America to become a journalist (rather as Father O'Donovan set off for London in the autumn of 1904 with letters of introduction from Moore to editors and publishers).[145] Gogarty never comes close to entering a real human relationship with a woman; instead, he has entered into a real relationship with the letters of a woman and her image. A reader may justly feel that Gogarty will always be a celibate, a secular priest who has lost the confidence to preach to a congregation on how they must live.

This occlusion of the woman herself in the course of a meditation on the woman was also a feature of Moore's Royal Hibernian Academy lecture. There is something remarkably absent from Moore's profound reading of Manet's portrait of Eva Gonzales. What is missing is Eva Gonzales herself, or any hint of a female presence. Moore reads the painting of Eva Gonzales as Manet's expression of himself. Manet's absence from the picture is felt as present in every sweeping brushstroke, in the frank modeling, in what Moore called Manet's refusal to make the arm of Gonzales beautiful. But Eva Gonzales was Manet's only known student;[146] she was the daughter of a writer father and musician mother, raised in an artistic milieu;[147] Manet's praise of her progress was the despair of Berthe Morisot; one of Gonzales's paintings, *La Loge*, hangs in the Louvre; a strangely matching painting of a boy and girl by the sea hangs in the National Gallery of Ireland.[148] As much as Moore did see, he was blinded by his birth, nature, and disposition, he was even blinded by the wonderful Impressionist pictures that hung on the walls of his house, from seeing that there might be some purpose more serious to the life of a woman he loved, or an artwork he admired, than a Pateresque heightening of sensation, a Beau Brummellism of emotions. Moore's gratitude to women is real, but it is often for the memories of sensations that they have given to him. The critique of his epicureanism is not that pleasure is its goal, but that self-pleasuring is both its means and its end. While the good fairy gave him the sight of what was invisible to his married brothers and sisters, the bad fairy dimmed his vision of the purpose of their lives. "Other men have wives, children, religion, god," he wrote passionately to Lady Cunard; "I have my star, ideal, my ideal of light, loveliness, and grace which I follow always and which I see shining when my eyes grow dim."[149] By such language he meant to refer to Maud, Lady Cunard, née Burke, but he was possibly, when his eyes grew dim, seeing something other than the human in her full possibility.

10

The campaign for a Museum of Modern Art in Dublin continued long after the inaugural Loan Exhibition. Moore, however, continued to waver about the advisability of beautiful pictures being provided for the Catholics of Dublin, thus setting himself apart from his friends Clara Christian MacCarthy (who contributed a Degas and her own *Meditation*) and J. B. Yeats (who supplied vigorous letters to Irish newspapers), as well as setting himself directly against W. B. Yeats and Augusta Gregory. GM began to create some serious trouble in August 1905, a few weeks after returning from Castlebar, County Mayo, where he had served his turn as High Sheriff.[150] On 3 August 1905, a Dublin *Evening Mail* reporter came by Ely Place just as Moore was occupied in the extermination of snails that were slowly devouring his mallows. Using the occasion to intervene in a dispute between Hugh Lane and Colonel Plunkett (Director of the National Museum), Moore pronounced the Corot that the Prince of Wales had donated to the collection to be a fake. The original purchaser of the picture, J. Staat Forbes, admitted privately, GM told the reporter, that it probably was not an original. Forbes bought the picture "in the same way he would have bought Corot's boots as a curiosity. It would have been certain that Corot wore the boots, but in this case the boots were never worn by him." It could be by a Hungarian artist named Mezzoly, or by a hundred others; by anyone but Corot, that at least was certain.[151]

This interview, when printed the next day, embarrassed Hugh Lane of course, but Moore too because Lane's many friends fell upon Moore in outrage. GM tried unsuccessfully to retract his words, but they had been perfectly caught in a shorthand report.[152] All he could do was to give a second interview in which he transferred the fault in choosing the Mezzoly/Corot from Hugh Lane to Walter Armstrong, Director of the National Gallery, as Armstrong had a special taste, GM suggested, for high-priced fakes: the National Gallery of Ireland specialised in them. Moore showed the interviewer around his own private collection at Ely Place – a David portrait bought for 30 shillings, a Constable for £3, a Manet oil for £80, and a Manet sketch for £10. They would also have passed by portraits of GM by Orpen, Tonks, and S. C. Harrison, Steer's *Girl in a Hat*, a sunset by Daubigny, a Thomas Couture picture of Rachel, Mark Fisher's *Land of Wine and Roses*, a Morisot, a Monet.[153] Having established his credentials by this tour, Moore then denounced with barefaced hypocrisy the "unspeakable malignity" of Dubliners who would use the false Corot to damage Lane's project. In fact, Moore had inside his gut a slowly moving but ineradicable worm of disgust for what he took to be the self-righteousness and vainglory of Lane and his supporters.

Soon a parliamentary Committee of Inquiry came to Dublin to investigate the teaching of art, and Moore made an alarming witness on 11 October 1905. He began by asking the Committee first to "find out whether art can be encouraged or repressed . . . I should like you to enquire into the origin of art, and, facing that question boldly, I should like you to ask yourselves if you really believe that the cause of art can be advanced by the collecting of pictures, and presenting them to the nation."[154] The collector (he did not name Lane in particular) "insists that the nation shall build a gallery to house his treasures." "It is generally assumed that art is being neglected if the industrious collector is

not provided with immortality in the shape of thirty or forty feet of gallery."
But do such exhibitions of the vanity of the rich inspire new painters? "We
find that art comes suddenly and swiftly, and that nobody has any clue as to
how it comes." Certainly art is not the result of classes in schools. What was
the use of a Metropolitan School of Art that processed between four and five
hundred art teachers a year?[155] It was grotesque. He went there one day to chat
with William Orpen, and among the hundreds of students, all paid a pound a
week by the taxpayers to come to class, he found "a Christian brother labori-
ously trying to turn a piece of clay into the shape of an apple, not because he
wanted to do it, or because he had any interest in the matter, but because he
wanted to be paid for teaching other people to take other lumps of clay, and
make them more or less like apples."

The National Gallery he judged to be a waste too – what could be the use
of culture in contemporary Dublin?

> Whatever education and culture there is in the country is leaving it; Ireland will
> soon be given up wholly to small farmers; out of these, no doubt, an aristocracy
> will emerge eventually – hundreds of years hence . . . The National Gallery is
> proof of the little interest Ireland takes in art. The National Gallery is the most
> perfect image of the Sahara that I know. Now and then one sees a human being
> hurry by like a Bedouin on the horizon. True, that the pictures that are bought
> for the National Gallery are generally worthless. Sometimes the pictures are
> ridiculous forgeries . . . They are nearly always without artistic interest . . . How
> can I expect Sir Walter Armstrong to give much attention to his gallery? No one
> goes there, except when it rains. Ireland is given over to officials, graziers, and
> priests.

While he was at it, he asked why Ireland should have a school of stained glass,
such as Sarah Purser ran in An Tur Gloine: it was just "spending money on
religion – or religiosity, I should say." And that, for Moore, was the very opposite of art. He was disgusted that so much of the wealth of a poor country, in
the course of its transfer from landlords to peasants, was being sucked up into
the vast building schemes of the Catholic Church.

For someone who had meditated for years on Matthew Arnold's "The
Function of Criticism at the Present Time," the 1865 essay on the conditions
that make for an artistic masterwork – "the power of the man and the power
of the moment" – Moore was giving one more turn to the always turning screw.
First, in London during the mid-1880s, thinking of the drama and the novel,
he had imagined that free trade and free expression were the key conditions for
a creative epoch: if one could only get rid of Mudie's monopoly and the NVA's
censorship, all would be well.[156] Second, propagandising in July 1890 for the
Independent Theatre Society, Moore held that it was not free trade but freedom
from commerce through a subscription theater that would open the way for
new Ibsens in London. His third position, taken in his May 1899 Irish

Literary Theatre speech, remained anti-commercial, but with a new nationalist twist: Moore declared that the muses had flown westward to Ireland away
from the industrial obsession with money and the gross traffic in popular sensation to be found in England. Money seemed less evil a year later. Again speaking in Dublin at an Irish Literary Theatre banquet, he thought the Muses
arrived when wealth changed hands and people began to gild the furniture. At
the Royal Hibernian Academy in December 1904, Moore found his way to a
fifth speculation on the subject: art would arise in Ireland only when the
Catholic Church subsided there, and people felt free to praise life.

Now, in October 1905, he judged the conditions for artistic production to be
a complete mystery. It was not generated by trade, suppressed by puritans,
bought for money, found in the land of the humble or the houses of the rich,
or taught to children in schools. Art could neither be stopped nor encouraged,
but came as it list to certain aristocratic souls who in certain magical circumstances fed one another's genius. When asked by a reporter how he could
contemplate leaving Dublin with the Celtic Renaissance at its height, Moore
replied crushingly, "There is no literary revival. There is only one man,
Mr. Synge, and he has written only one really beautiful play, 'The Well of the
[Saints].'"[157] (After Moore read the *Playboy* in February 1907 and saw it
performed in 1909, he would increase the total of masterpieces to two.)[158] GM
felt he had known one great creative epoch, the Paris of the 1870s and
1880s, the Paris of Mallarmé and Manet, Zola and Degas, and dozens of
others, including even Dujardin and Moore. His Irish companions who displayed their arts on Saturday nights at Ely Place did not measure up. GM
wanted to inspire his fellows to new works – he was always trying to get a man
or woman friend started on a play or a story, always quick to do propaganda,
contribute to magazines, buy paintings, commission portraits, and join theater
societies, but try as he might, he could not find the secret of another Nouvelle
Athènes.[159]

By a prophetic accident, one can see in *Homage to Manet* by William Orpen
what finally became of Moore and of the inspiration of Paris in the 1870s.
Orpen was close to both Moore (they spent Christmas Eve 1905 together) and
"Petticoat" Lane (Orpen's term of endearment for the cross-dressing Lane).[160]
Orpen wished to pay tribute to Moore and the Manet tradition in English art,
and to praise Hugh Lane for purchasing examples of Manet for artists to
admire. Orpen himself, living with Lane at 5 Bolton Gardens, admired the portrait of Eva Gonzales that hung there so long as negotiations continued in
Dublin for a municipal gallery. As a gesture of affiliation to his own school,
Orpen painted Manet's painting, the rooms at Bolton Gardens, and then, in
late February 1907, Moore sitting at a table in full discourse on Manet. He later
added other figures who stood for modern painting in Britain through the two
previous decades.[161] The documentary painting commemorates an actual event,
when GM, on a May 1906 visit to London, dined at Wilson Steer's with Henry
Tonks, D. S. MacColl, Will Rothenstein, and "the New English kin."[162] GM

19. *Homage to Manet*
(1909), William Orpen.

needed little prompting to read to them from his address at the Royal Hibernian Academy just off the press as *Reminiscences of the Impressionist Painters*. This
audience, fit but few, loved it. Most of them were bachelors, and men of a
certain age; they had all spent time in Paris; they all had about them a sort of
aristocratic bohemianism, now declining into respectable Tory eccentricity.
There is an odor of cigars about Orpen's picture: it depicts a mutual admiration society of the old aesthetes, with Tonks, Steer, Sickert, MacColl, and Lane
all gathered about a table: "with whatever silent protests their minds register,"
they "listen attentively and with respect," while Moore sits in the foreground
reading his lecture, and the grand picture by Manet of Eva Gonzales rises up
in the high-ceilinged room, flooded by light from a magnificent window beyond
the frame.[163] Five years later, it was into the masculine clubbish society of these
friends and to London itself that GM retreated, closing the green door at 4
Upper Ely Place for the last time, and settling in for his final decades as the
Sage of Ebury Street, Belgravia.

II

In the remaining years of his residence in Dublin, Moore fed upon his memories of his meeting with Yeats and Martyn and the whole adventure of his Irish

missionary activity up to 1905.[164] He began an autobiography in early 1906 as a pamphlet to follow his printed Manet lecture, a stirring farewell to Ireland. He continuously expanded the conception – a volume, two volumes (*Hail*, then *Farewell*), and finally three volumes: *Ave, Salve, Vale*.[165] The title oddly came to him lodged between his love for Clara Christian who had just died and Maurice Moore from whom he was now estrauged. Christian died in childbirth on 7 June 1906 just before Moore was due to write about a New English Art Club exhibition for the *Saturday Review*. Into the review he poured his perhaps too literary but still sincere grief. Her painting of a wild cherry tree in bloom took him back to Tallaght Lodge in April a year earlier, and brought to mind a poem by Catullus:

> Hail and Farewell: "*Atque in perpetuum frater ave atque vale.*" The death of friends never fails to recall this noble line written, as everybody knows, two thousand years ago by Catullus on the death of his brother. He journeyed over land and sea to visit his brother's grave, and after weeping over the cold ashes he wrote a poem which none can read today, even in a prose translation, without weeping . . . No poet has found a more perfect expression for the resigned grief we feel – which we must feel – for those who have just gone.[166]

Now that Clara Christian MacCarthy was gone, he wrote, "it will be harder than ever for those of us who care for Art to live in Dublin." Oddly enough, the spirit of resignation, the narrative of a journey over land and sea and then back again, and the theme of the death of brotherhood, would all structure not the saddest story ever told, but one of the funniest.

Parodically structured as a new gospel, with Moore as Messiah,[167] GM's trilogy had one main truth to prophesy: the kingdom of heaven was personality, not population. This truth came to him, he says, after his return from a visit to "Doris" (Lady Cunard), when a lady came to see his pictures. Taking her into his arms, he had a fainting spell, and the frightened woman had to call for a glass of water for him. With shock, he realised he had "become the equivalent of the priest, the nun, and the ox. Chastity is the prerogative of the prophet, why no man can tell." Moore had "come into the most impersonal country in the world to preach personality – personal love and personal religion, personal art, personality for all except God." Moore fantasises that when his condition becomes known, women from around the country will come to him as to a new prophet. How may we escape the burdens of childbearing? they will ask.[168] Eighty years ahead of his time, Moore's message to the Irish would be contraception.

It is not possible to identify with certainty the woman who was the first witness to this moment when the man fainted and the heavens opened. Perhaps she was Viola Rodgers, a young journalist who first met Moore while she was attending, with many other Americans, an Oireachtas art exhibition at the Royal Hibernian Academy.[169] She wanted to write an article about Moore for *Cosmopolitan* magazine, and after lunch at Ely Place, she says in her memoir that he showed her his Aubusson rug and his Impressionist pictures; she makes no mention of fainting spells.[170] He began a flirtatious correspondence with her on 10 September 1907 that did not end until his death. In a letter of 14 September 1907 he begged her to allow him to talk in naughty ways to her – "allow me my little whimsical turns of thought, do not stamp upon me for the little joke, do not frown."[171] In her, he found a woman to give him in his later years the intimate affection of a lover without either a requirement or permission for lovemaking.

The woman in question, if she exists, may also have been Honor Woulfe, an American of Irish Catholic descent, in her mid-twenties, originally from Waco, Texas, who ran an Austin bookstore where Moore's works were sold. She made a European tour that took in Dublin and Ely Place, where she consulted Moore about a play she wished to write. Years later, the evenings she came to visit Moore rose "up in memory – a glitter of white shoulders and a fleece of soft pale brown hair."[172] On one such evening at Ely Place, something occurred for which Moore tried to apologise on 2 March 1908:

> A little misunderstanding arose between us in Dublin and the fault lay neither altogether with you nor with me. About this misunderstanding, which I regret, I propose that we shall never speak again. That will be the better way. You have apparently forgiven me and I have nothing to forgive. You were mistaken that was all and – but enough has been said.[173]

If this letter suggests that the "lady from Texas" and the Irish novelist had relations which were never sexual, that suggestion is contradicted by GM's musings upon one of her letters written ten years later. Moore was then back in Dublin at the Shelbourne Hotel, Honor's address at the time of their first meeting. "The letter before me," Moore wrote, "is the letter of a woman to a man whom she knew to be a man, and this letter is the letter of a man to a woman he knew to be a woman. A sexual memory is a wonderful memory, it transcends all other memories and I am sorry for those who have not tasted the poetry of sex . . ."[174] With Woulfe Moore kept up a lifelong friendship and correspondence, though not so prolific of letters and visits as his relationship with Rodgers.

Moore's Dublin encounter with Honor Woulfe did lead to the remarkable story, "Euphorion in Texas." It concerns a woman from Austin named "Honor." She makes a special trip to Dublin in order to conceive a child by the author of *Sister Teresa*, because through her son she wishes to become the mother of Texan literature. The story dwells on the awkward and delicate negotiations between the nervous American on her foreign mission to "render a great service to her country" and the even more nervous author, deeply flattered that she "did not make application to Meredith, Swinburne, Yeats, Henry James, or Gosse" (two of these authors were dead or nearly so, two were possibly inclined toward their own sex, and the remaining one was Yeats). Frightened down to his boots by the request from Honor, Moore says he was sustained only by his "natural and inveterate desire of the strange, the odd, the bizarre." But he leaves no doubt that he managed all right over the next six weeks, and she left with what she'd come for, Euphorion, child of love and art, whom Moore years later imagines growing up as a young cowpoke who plays Wagner on a piano in Waco.[175]

In addition to this story, another fictive fruit of this affair unblessed by real offspring was a story-cycle about monks, nuns, and lovers in medieval Ireland, *The Story-Teller's Holiday* (1918). Kuno Meyer had given Moore the idea by telling him that in ancient Ireland it was believed that the standing of the saved in heaven was fixed by the amount of temptation a man had successfully withstood. Moore saw possibilities, and probably he first spun them out at François Jammet's French restaurant on Nassau Street near the corner of Trinity College, where Meyer, Moore, Magee, Richard Best, and Russell sometimes dined together.[176] For the after-dinner entertainment of Honor Woulfe, he also told these stories of nuns virtuously tempting monks with "the temptation of the thighs" and "the temptation of the breasts," with trials of naked leapfrog or naked dancing to hornpipes, and of monks undergoing with the shepherd's daughters the terrors of *virgo subintroducta*, until it would become necessary to plunge themselves into the cold cistern before resuming the ordeal. All of the stories are about desire that comes short of procreation, of orgasm, and usually even of erection, but mounts ever higher in the mind when denied another outlet. The tales originally seem to have been aids both for self-stimulation and for seducing the imagination of a fine woman from Texas away from the ordinary courses of love and into its byways and *culs-de-sac*. She remembered him as being "inwardly hesitant . . . if not actually trembling," yet Honor Woulfe says nothing about Moore fainting on her.[177]

Hilda Hawthorne, granddaughter of the novelist Nathaniel Hawthorne, was not the woman who made Moore faint, but she may have inspired his brainstorm that his mission in Ireland was to be its new father-confessor and prophet of contraception. At the suggestion of her father, Julian Hawthorne, an old acquaintance of GM in 1880s London, Hilda wrote Moore a fulsome letter of praise for his books in January 1907, "a sudden touch of a friendly hand in the loneliness of life," as Moore described it in his reply.[178] Within weeks, safely divided from the New Yorker Hilda by the Atlantic, he was writing her *risqué* letters, such as a long and intimate account of an affair that had misfired in his youth. In turn, she shared with him the details of an affair she was having with a Hungarian. Excited, he urged her to "treat me as a confessor." The confessor soon wanted naked photos of Hilda, and she was not too shy to oblige. By and by, she became eloquent on the subject of nude swimming and confessed her desire to be rid of her virginity (she was thirty-six) though she feared pregnancy. "Surely you know," Moore wrote back on 14 September 1907, "that love is possible without incurring any risk whatever; if love were so restricted, how should I have managed . . . you must be poking fun."[179] Taking a long view of his own love life, he judged that love is best as an imperishable memory, the terrors of failure and the inevitability of decline being then already passed through. He was full of wonder when Hilda confessed that while she enjoyed kisses with her Hungarian friend, she was afraid of the consequences of male orgasm. "I cannot understand," Moore answered, "how it is that natural instincts did not tell either of you that kisses need not be confined to the mouth and that kisses placed within the nest of love are more intimate and exciting than the mere act of love . . . It would be a sad thing indeed if love were limited to the mere act which grocers and their mates perform at midnight in the middle of a four-poster."[180] Love for Moore only becomes an art when it ceases to be reproductive. He is happiest when sex is polymorphous: that is, when it is transferred from genital intercourse to touch and talk, to sight and speculation, where it can be indefinitely prolonged through thought.

In August 1913, a meeting in Paris with Hilda Hawthorne became unavoidable. At this time, she may have learned that George Moore by then was a voyeur and tactilist (he liked to touch, palpate, caress). If she was disappointed, the relationship was resurrected once distance again intervened.[181] Their sincere mutual confidence and real intimacy depended on each for the other being an imago and not a bodily presence. Moore was a great reader of character and an inveterate author of stories, yet life had come to exist for him chiefly as a literary stimulus: all relations had become literary relations, all codes a matter of style.

12

Whether it was in search of friendship, adventure, literary material, or a new muse with a gift for dialogue, Moore involved himself in an elaborate relationship with yet another female correspondent, Emily Lorenz Meyer, a Bostonian married to a German in Hamburg, who wrote to Moore in late 1906, just weeks before Hilda Hawthorne took the same step. He quickly got up to the same tricks with her as with Hawthorne – one curious request after another: for pictures, for details of her love life to be retailed to GM as "father confessor," for signs of sexual interest in himself, and for places and times of assignation up and down the capitals of Europe, always to be put off by him once suggested by her, or dodged by her if insisted upon by him. Moore, however, had another use for Meyer: he wanted to engage her to translate *The Peacock's Feathers* – the play he wrote with Pearl Craigie, now retitled *Elizabeth Cooper* – into German and, furthermore, to arrange for a performance in Hamburg.

Craigie and Moore had carried on a quarrel as vicious as it was petty through 1905 about the ownership of their two co-authored plays. Moore wanted to sign *The Peacock's Feathers* alone, and evidently offered in trade that Craigie could publish under her own name *Journeys End in Lovers Meeting*. Craigie, of course, had already published and produced that 1894 play, time and again, as her own, so she had little to gain from the bargain.[182] She put *The Peacock's Feathers* into production, altered its text as if it were all her own, and then prepared a new edition with Unwin of *Journeys End*, to be signed once again solely by herself. GM became apoplectic. Why shouldn't "Fishy Onions" – his contemptuous pun on "T. Fisher Unwin" – bring out the book straightaway under Moore's name instead of Craigie's, with an explanatory preface? Craigie and Moore then conducted a fierce argument by means of letters to Unwin. Craigie spoke of Moore as "not a gentleman and he is mad . . . Seriously, I believe his brain is touched . . . Tales reach me from Dublin. I am sorry for him, because it is now a case of mental disease."[183] GM from the start wrote his own letters with a view to the publication of the whole correspondence when the affair had sufficiently ripened. "No one writes nowadays except for publication . . . You surely can have no objection," he wrote to the publisher.[184] Moore was his father's son in the vigorous handling of such duels, though his father fought with men. Finally, however, Moore let the matter drop, yet in March 1905 he also dropped Unwin as his publisher: throughout their seven years of business together, Moore had truly treated Unwin according to his maxim that publishers are like dogs, no good unless whipped. It was W. H. Heinemann who brought out *The Lake* (1905), *Memoirs of My Dead Life* (1906), and many of Moore's later books, as well as the Uniform Edition of his collected works in 1933.

The Peacock's Feathers then sat, untouchable by Moore and untouched further by Craigie. On 18 August 1906, Craigie suddenly died of cardiac arrest (only a month after her rival, Mary Leiter Curzon, had herself passed away).[185] As soon as Moore read the account of Craigie's death in the *Irish Times*, he put back in the drawer the little project he had taken up of turning *Esther Waters* into a play, and took out *Elizabeth Cooper*. "I hope that her executors will allow me to write the comedy in my own way," he wrote Maurice. "The subject is mine and the writing is mine."[186] Even before he had settled that question of copyright with Craigie's father, Moore set to work fiddling with the play in September, and was still rewriting parts of it when he answered a letter in December from Mrs Meyer in Hamburg.

Moore did not get around to bringing Meyer into the complicated charade of *Elizabeth Cooper* until 1 October 1908. Then the play inspired by Cecile Gabrielle von Hoenstadt, and partly plagiarised from her letters, which had subsequently been reenacted by Moore in his relationship to Hilda Hawthorne, would be imaginatively rehearsed once more with Emily Lorenz Meyer: "I have just finished a comedy on a subject which cannot fail to interest you," he began; "it is about a lady who admires a man's novels and writes to him asking if he will meet her" – just what Meyer had done. After a full account of the plot, and a request that Meyer locate a producer for the play in Hamburg, Moore breaks off: "Six women have come in to see me, they are all strangers to each other, and the parlourmaid has let them all in – in a sort of flock – so it is impossible to continue this letter."[187] In a spirit of farcical boasting, Moore in effect admits he keeps a string of secret relationships going, and can keep them all going smoothly only so long as each stays secret from the other. Indeed, a lapse in such confidentiality brings about the comedy of embarrassment in *Elizabeth Cooper*. As AE remarked, Moore loved to playact, and the type of play he most loved to act was bedroom farce.

In March 1908, Moore had taken *Elizabeth Cooper* with him to Paris in order to go over it "microscopically" with Dujardin, who was also afflicted with the belief that he could write money-making plays. Dujardin came away from his *examination du texte* with the belief that he would be able to adapt Moore's text for the Paris stage. Once Meyer had begun her own German version, Moore tried to get her to use Dujardin's French improvements. At the same time that he wished Meyer to get on with her work, he did not wish her to go forward too fast, because a German production, while highly desirable if it were to be the only production, was to be avoided if it were to precede, and perhaps even prevent, a sensational and money-making Paris production.

Dujardin also had to be kept on his toes, lest he become distracted by his occasional desire to write an opera. In February 1909, while in London with Howard de Walden, Moore finally met with Pearl Craigie's father, John Morgan Richards, at the Reform Club to discuss the rights to the play. Richards did not give them away, but he agreed to let Dujardin adapt the play, so long as Richards was paid half of the one-third share GM was to receive from the profits. (At their meeting, Richards in turn asked Moore to give him Craigie's letters for the biography Richards was trying to write about his daughter, and that, after he failed in his efforts, he paid Clement Shorter to ghost-write.)[188] When Dujardin's attention to the play wavered, Moore warned him that the great American businessman John Morgan Richards might become impatient and find an English producer, in which case the grand première of *Elizabeth Cooper* would occur neither in Hamburg nor in Paris, but in London.[189]

Of course, it was ridiculous to expect the play to be a major success anywhere – it is a trifle, and an awkward, labored trifle. Thus *Elizabeth Cooper* appeared to chilled, polite audiences in London on 23 June 1913, in Paris as *Clara Florise* on 24 February 1914, and in London again as *The Coming of Gabrielle* on 17 April 1923.[190] William Archer was harsh in speaking of the play as the "most inept childish twaddle imaginable," but no one who saw it in any language, under any title, had much good to say for it. Why then did Moore spend nearly twenty years working on the play and trying to get others to work on it for him? He kept on with it largely because writing the books he cared about – his fiction, essays, and autobiographies – was hard and lonely work; he wanted some frivolous and sociable entertainment on the side. What most entertained Moore was writing itself, or the many fabulations of his inescapably literary being. The imbroglios caused by collaboration and play production were the equivalent of "light literature" in his life, the free and somewhat pointless expression of a drive to devise plots. The serious side of his nature – his skepticism, self-bewilderment, bleak sense of mortality and necessity – he kept for the books he was writing. This serious side appears even in the comic trilogy he was working on simultaneously with *Elizabeth Cooper*, *Hail and Farewell*.

13

After being nearly killed along with Lady Cunard by a runaway automobile raking through a society crowd at Bayreuth, GM returned to Dublin in September 1910 to finish a complete draft of *Ave*, first volume of *Hail and Farewell*.[191] He wrote his brother Maurice that he planned to "leave this dull country" "in February at the latest,"[192] but the dullness of Dublin was probably not his main reason for departing at this particular time. He had been saying that he was going to leave Ireland for at least six years, because his imminent departure is already a theme of *The Peacock's Feathers* (begun in September 1904).[193] On 6 December 1905, he gave an interview to the Dublin *Daily Mail* in which, playing the Irish landlord for whom "all the best people" choose to live in England or on the continent, he said that he had stayed as long as he could bear it, until he found himself "the one solitary person who was in Dublin for any other reason than he had to be," and once he himself left for Paris or London, the only people remaining in Dublin would be government officials. A month later, he wrote his old friend William Archer that he had made up his mind to settle again in London.[194] By the summer of 1906, he had set a departure date for the autumn, but when autumn came, Moore remained. He could not, though he wished to do so, "get away from 'copy,'" the rich Irish material he must mine for his trilogy.[195]

One of Moore's announcements of imminent departure formed the subject of a chapter of *The Plough and the Cross*, a novel by W. P. Ryan. "Geoffrey Mortimer," "the famous novelist who had mildly shocked two continents," shows up at the editorial offices of a magazine much like Ryan's *Irish Peasant*, wearing GM's "habitual look of ennui and solemnity tempered by resignation, as if the small sins of Dublin bored him, while at the same time he understood that it was beyond her power and courage to sin boldly." He has come to say goodbye before catching the boat for Holyhead. Avuncular and well-meaning, GM thinks the editor's fad of running a weekly paper an understandable way to kill time in a country like Ireland, but the editor's idea of also managing a little farm, "in a land where nobody tills or consumes home produce," is insanity. If the editor has the price of a ticket, he should do as the famous novelist is doing – go to London, or better yet, Paris, where ideas matter. Eventually, the patriotic editor will wake up and "see Ireland as she really is – a certain number of silly sheepfolds attached to a certain number of priests' houses."[196] If he doesn't watch out, he'll end up excommunicated by the priests and butted by the sheep. That was, GM thought, roughly speaking, his own fate, and it was to be Ryan's too. In December 1906, after Ryan printed articles saying that if Ireland was to modernise it had to allow lay people a role in the management of primary education, Cardinal Michael Logue wrote to the proprietor of the *Irish Peasant* that the paper was "poisonous and anti-Catholic." The Cardinal said he would be forced to denounce it and forbid the people to read it. The proprietor immediately closed the paper.[197]

Each year Moore repeated his threat to leave Dublin, but he could not do so until he finished *Ave*. Then, whether he liked it or not, he had to get out of town. Things might have become too exciting for him there once his book was published. By September 1910 he had a finished manuscript of *Ave* (it was published in October 1911), and sketches of both *Salve* and *Vale*, the final two volumes. He would need some safe, peaceful place in which to perpetrate them.

GM asked for and got an invitation from Maurice Moore for a last visit to Moore Hall – a stay for three days in January 1911 – time enough for the brothers to have one more bitter wrangle over religion. Maurice Moore wanted to help the Blake family overturn Uncle Llewelyn Blake's 1908 will leaving £60,000 and the family house, Ballinafad, to the Church, in order to found a college for the African Missionary Brothers; Maurice was furious that their mother's childhood home was going out of the family and into the hands of the Church.[198] GM had himself been outraged by the zeal with which the clergy pursued aging Catholics to bequeath house and fortune to the Church, in return for a promise of daily Masses for the relief of their souls in Purgatory. He leveled this charge against the "spiritual advisor" of Stephen Cunningham, Moore's neighbor at 3 Smith's Buildings, Ely Place. The former owner of the Ship Hotel, Cunningham had scores of friends in the newspaper business and throughout Dublin, but he lived alone, a bachelor and only surviving child of his parents. He became haunted with terror after months of insomnia and a subsequent addiction to sleeping potions. In *Salve* and *A Story-Teller's Holiday*, Moore hypothesised that Cunningham had been persuaded by his priest to will his fortune to the Church, and then pressured to go into John O' Gods mental asylum in order to withstand the temptation of drink. Whatever the motive, after saying to his housekeeper, "They'll never get me there," Cunningham bought a long leather strap and on 22 April 1908, hanged himself from his attic banister.[199] While it was suppositious and slanderous for Moore to blame a hypothetical priest for Cunningham's fate, many families were indeed bringing actions against the Church for avaricious practices with elderly people of property. GM, however, refused to join in Maurice's own indignation about Llewelyn's disposal of Ballinafad, their mother's birthplace. GM claimed that Maurice, to be consistent, should be eager even for Moore Hall to go to the priests, since he claimed to believe in Purgatory and Masses for the dead.

Implicit comparisons between Llewelyn and GM, Ballinafad and Moore Hall, might well have nettled GM. Maurice's indignation about the fate of Ballinafad rested on the assumption that ownership of the historic family house did not truly lie within the free disposition of the title-holder, but that its ownership by right passed to the next of kin. By such logic, Moore Hall would have to go to Maurice Moore and his sons at the death of GM.

The brothers were openly divided about the immediate future of Moore Hall and its outlying estates. GM had tried to persuade Maurice in July 1905 to let him sell the family lands (but not Moore Hall) under the provisions of the 1903 "Wyndham Act," but Maurice thought there was a future in Ireland for a patriotic Catholic nationalist landlordism, the dream of his father G. H. Moore.[200]

Though Maurice found enough sentimental reasons to prevent the sale of land at that time, in September 1906 he did go along with the felling of a number of the ancient trees, a beech 103 inches around near the garden, for instance, and a spruce 82 inches around. When the wood of an old estate goes to a timber merchant, the future of the estate is not likely to be long.[201] In January 1908, GM pushed forward the sale of outlying lands at Dollardstown through the Land Commission, but at the same time as the trees were being felled and land parcels put up for sale, Maurice was redecorating the Georgian house. In April 1909, GM sent an £8 cheque to pay for curtains, and said it would be the last he wrote for refurbishment, but in July 1909 he was again shocked by the bottom line of the Moore Hall annual accounts. In the previous two years he had put £1,000 into the property, and his rents had fallen from £800 to £500 a year; meanwhile, Maurice was urging him to invest another £1,000 in his Ballintubber property, perhaps for one of Maurice's "improving landlord" schemes, local sawmills and the like. Maurice seems to have fantasised his brother's wealth and expenditure to be vast. In fact, according to a July 1909 letter from GM's bank manager, he spent £387 from July through December 1908, and £453 from January through July 1909, when he showed a balance of £984. For the first half of 1909 his earnings from royalties, at least those deposited, amounted to £104 3s. 9d.[202] Money worries led him to ask Edward Martyn to buy a Nathaniel Hone painting he had not so long ago bought for himself – "I have to buy a new typewriter and my income decreases."[203]

So George offered Maurice £40 for "your saw mills or any other project that takes your fancy," but warned that this was the last: "I don't want to speculate in saw mills; I speculate in literature." It was time for George to sell the land and pay off the Scottish Insurance Company mortgage, and for Maurice to look for a paid position and stop chasing the Gaelic League will-o'-the-wisp, advice that, however practical it might be, was most unpleasant for Maurice to hear. At the dawning of the Home Rule day, Maurice envisioned his sons in a new Ascendancy under the banner of an Irish-speaking Catholic Ireland, a fixed fantasy that irritated his brother. Maurice occupied himself with "the raspberry bush and the goat in the ram park," GM sneered, but he ought to be "seriously alarmed":

The property won't last out even my lifetime, that is to say if I live a long while and there will be nothing I'm afraid for your children and Moore Hall will go the way of New [Brook] or be turned into a nunnery or monastery. You always put on the philosophic air when I speak of the probable future and say, "the future is hidden from us." But the future of landlords isn't in the least hidden from us.[204]

That future had been spelled out in the title of the last book by one of GM's anti-clerical friends, Land War hero Michael Davitt – *The Fall of Feudalism in Ireland* (1904).[205] Even as Maurice pictured his young son Rory riding a hunter over the estate he had inherited, pulling up to express in Gaelic a kindly interest in his tenants, both landlordism and the language had been virtually dead for decades.

The two bad stars of the brothers' relationship – religion and land – came into alignment in December 1910 at the funeral of a third brother, Augustus, and the conjunction had a disastrous influence upon GM's January visit to Moore Hall. Augustus had been suffering for some time from both diabetes and a painful intestinal ailment; now the end was in sight. Maurice had gone over to London to say a final farewell (George admitted he had not the courage to face a deathbed). Just as Augustus passed away at the end of December, GM received in Dublin a letter from Tom Ruttledge, his agent, explaining why Moore Hall expenditure was so heavy: "you are paying for the education of Maurice's boys," up to the amount of £130 a year.[206] Indeed, the tuition for Rory had been folded into the estate accounts since 1904, and this wasn't an Irish-language or a Protestant education, but education by Jesuit and Benedictine priests. That news outraged GM: it turned the shamelessly honest artist into a Tartuffe. His Oscott education by priests had been horrid; the education of all Irish children in National schools by priests was, he thought, just as bad; the education of his nephews by Jesuits or Benedictines in boarding schools was more of the same. He wrote to Maurice at Augustus's house, 19 Sackville Street, making no mention of Augustus's death and funeral, to complain about this shocking cause of his dwindling income. How could his money have been given to priests, and for clerical education? Maurice knew GM hated Irish Catholicism, education, and priests; now Maurice was giving him the bill for supporting all three of these evils. Maurice read the letter quickly, and to GM's vigorous reproaches, added another. Maurice mistook "dwindling" for "swindling." Immediately, he fired off a violent reply.[207] George's visit to Moore Hall was shaping up to be a frightful settling of accounts.

GM himself wrote a public letter that only made things worse. In its obituary, the *Irish Times* identified Augustus as having come from "an old Irish and Roman Catholic family." George Moore instantly wrote a letter of correction, saying that his family had been Protestant until the late eighteenth century, when his great-grandfather, George of Alicante, began trading in Spain, and changed his religion for commercial reasons. His grandfather, George the historian, was an agnostic. His father, George the MP, went to Mass and was notionally Catholic. So there were no centuries of Catholicism in the Moore family. Then came this ominous sentence: "I hope the next generation will be Protestant. I shall have no hesitation in leaving any money I may have on the condition that my heir carry on the Protestant traditions of the family."[208] Years earlier, Maurice had accepted GM's declaration that he would leave his estate to his nephew only if that nephew were a Gaelic-speaker, but obviously he was forced to treat with contempt this public demand that his own son change religion for the sake of money.

This was the situation in mid-January 1911 when GM took the train west for a visit to Maurice and his family at Moore Hall. Even before his arrival, GM pressed for a sale of the estate to the Land Courts under Augustine Birrell's 1909 Land Acts. The terms on offer were not good, but were, in GM's judgement, only going to get worse after January 1910 with Lloyd George's Liberals in power and dependent on the support of the Irish Parliamentary Party; they would preside over "a papistical pandemonium [that is, Home Rule] in which a unionist and a protestant [that is George, *c.* 1911] will have no chance whatever."[209]

GM was not an entirely bad guest. He praised Evelyn Moore's coffee. He went with the boys, Rory and Toby (then on school holiday), on an excursion to Castle Island, taking his turn at the oars. Yet when he asked about their schooling, he became very worked up over what he heard. It was terrible that money taken from the estate should be paid to priests for such teachings. Rory, in order to become his heir, should be raised as a Protestant. James Reilly, the new steward, saw the brothers walking up the long lawn toward the house, GM in a bowler hat and a suit, Maurice in gaiters. "The Colonel's face was flushed, and George's gestures were deprecatory."[210]

The two brothers walked over the estate to examine Maurice's improvements, which GM treated sarcastically: "My dear Maurice," he has himself saying in *Vale*, "it is sad to see ancient Ireland passing away before our eyes. But we cannot rebuild ancient Ireland, and it is clear to me that as soon as I am gone, Moore Hall will be pulled down to build cottages in Derrinanny and Ballyhooly, or the house will become a monkery or a nunnery. Which would you prefer?"[211] On the subject of the boys' education, Maurice promised to reimburse GM for the school fees and take over future payments, for that education would certainly continue to be a Catholic one. The future of the estate was then on the table, and in discussions with Tom Ruttledge it was decided to sell the Ballintubber and other outlying estates through the Land Courts, but for the time being to keep Moore Hall. It was also agreed that Maurice would vacate the house and move to Belgium to see his sons' education.

It must have been a bitter thing for Maurice to have his brother arrive as a houseguest and then during his stay break the estate up for sale. There went Maurice's residence, his labor, and his legacy; the imaginary landlord had in a fashion been evicted. On the third night of his brother's stay, Maurice proposed that he and his brother had better see each other no more. George sadly agreed; his wild loathing for Catholicism had poisoned even his love for his brother. He was aware as he departed that his old age, fast falling on those slumped shoulders, would be comforted neither by brother, nor nephews, nor wife.[212]

14

After a farewell dinner in Dublin at the home of the Land Commissioner W. F. Bailey, along with Russell, Susan Mitchell, Ernest Longworth, W. K.

Magee, *Irish Times* editor John Healy, and Dena Tyrrell (daughter of Trinity scholar Robert Yelverton Tyrrell), Moore set off for London on 5 February 1911, ten years after he had come to live in Dublin.[213] Russell was distraught: "I miss him very much," he confessed to John Quinn; "Moore was so much alive all the time, and the Irish people who write whom I meet here are anaemic people, or if they are not anaemic they have prejudices and no ideas . . . There is nobody broad or bold enough to take his place."[214]

By April, Moore had taken a house at 121 Ebury Street, a "little hole in which to carry on my authorship."[215] Now marked by a blue plaque, the undistinguished house stands in a long street of such houses, behind Victoria Station and about halfway towards Sloane Square. To place it more meaningfully in the geography of Moore's later life, the Belgravia address is in between his masculine companions in Chelsea – Steer, Tonks, and St John Hutchinson – and his lady love, Maud Cunard, who would establish herself as a celebrated hostess in the house of a former prime minister at 7 Grosvenor Square. At 121 Ebury Street, surrounded by his pictures, pacing on his Aubusson rug, GM soon was back at work telling the story of his days in Dublin, fixing his friends in the photographic bath of his finest style of portraiture.

Hail and Farewell is at once a classic and a book in a new form: a novel with real characters going under their real names. The propriety of keeping up distinctions between eavesdropping, tale-bearing, and omnisciently reported dialogue, between privacy and publicity, on the whole between life and literature, is transgressed with breathtaking cheek. As Yeats noted on his first reading of *Ave*, "there isn't the smallest recognition of the difference between public and private life, except that the consciousness of sin in the matter may have made him unusually careful," because the book is "curiously honest" and never "petulant."[216] From the start, Moore planned it to be "a book everybody will think disgraceful, but which will sell longer than any of my novels."[217] The disgracefulness of the book was sometimes said to be its unreliability, but Moore's ability to recall conversation with considerable accuracy has been validated by the recent publication of Lady Gregory's *Diaries* and the early volumes of Yeats's *Collected Letters*. The greatest outrage of the volume is not that Moore lied, but that he told unseasonable truths, not that he was inaccurate but that he was indiscreet and thus unkind. He did not see Yeats, Gregory, Martyn, Lane, or Gill as they would expect to be seen by a sympathetic friend. The book is generally not libelous – Moore had learned from the best barristers and from the sorry example of James Davis how to stay out of court – but it has a sly, elegant, insinuativeness that seems at every moment about to become libelous, like that of a dreadfully intelligent elderly aunt gossiping at a formal dinner, incited to ferocity by the nervousness of her kin and the laughter of the guests. Since the genre of *Hail and Farewell* was comedy, to be translated onto his pages was to be traduced, to be pushed out on a stage "where motley is worn," in Yeats's phrase.

The theory behind the comedy concerned relations between Nature and Art. Nature itself was taken to be a greater novelist than Balzac or Tolstoy, and

Nature's *métier* was to show up the vanity of human ideals, the psychological costumes in which the funny little creatures playact their lives. In fact, we are greedy beasts driven by sex, food, and the will to power. Moore made himself the chief article in evidence of this naturalistic truth by means of merciless self-satire. "George Moore," the author-function, had a friend, "Amico Moorini," who lived a life that provided the author with endless insights into the silliness of the human species. Having satirised himself, GM next did the same to others. Hone rightly points out that Moore overlooks a difference between his own case and that of those others: he got to pick what frailties he would exhibit; "his neighbours were not given the choice, and it may be added that he had the schoolboy's genius for divining what was most likely to tease and humiliate."[218] Another thesis of the trilogy is that human idealism comes down to life imitating art. So, for instance, T. P. Gill was one person before he grew an Henri Quatre beard; afterwards, he thought himself a Florentine prince and prospered in Dublin as one.[219] The beard had a great career. Gill and Plunkett, working together to introduce new and sometimes wild schemes for the improvement of Irish farm-life, find themselves simply reenacting a novel by Flaubert, the absurd *Bouvard et Pécuchet*. The two real heads of Irish departments can only improvise from what was before imagined about two fictive clowns.

The plot of the trilogy as a whole is really a conceit: Moore comes to Ireland on a mission, like an aesthetic St Paul or St Patrick; but his aim is to save the Irish *from* Catholicism. There is some truth in W. K. Magee's observation that this conception was insufficiently sincere to carry the weight of three volumes: "it is perhaps permissible to say that [Moore's] career as an apostle petered out in the joyous exercise of his faculty for characterization, with the result that through whole tracts of his three volumes the story is left standing."[220] Yet a reader hardly wants more of either sincerity or the mock-gospel plot. *Salve*, with its long haggle with Maurice over the history of Catholic literature, is the least entertaining of the volumes precisely because a reader becomes alarmed that GM may really believe that Roman Catholicism is pernicious, and that he must save Ireland and his nephews from their misguided faith. The best parts of the book are: the set-piece tableaux (like the Irish Literary Theatre banquet), the clever play with leitmotifs, the aesthetic and philosophical speculative sports, the effortless visualisations of Dublin, Galway, Mayo, London, and Paris, the hilarious recollections of boyhood and youth, and, especially, the long gallery of character-portraits. Through the whole trilogy (a theme first sounded in the "Overture" to a decadent Big House, "Mount Venus") there repeatedly sounds a requiem to the Irish Ascendancy, passing away amid eccentric plans for regeneration, while the Roman Catholic Church builds an empire on its ruins. Yet the accuracy of this representation of the political realities of the country – realities Maurice Moore refused to accept – was largely lost on contemporary readers. They were mostly concerned with the way Moore appropriated details of the lives of his acquaintance into his largely satirical project, made them over into literary characters, usually under their own names, and hidden only by vivid descriptions of their own faces.[221]

From 1907 to 1911, all his friends knew that Moore was writing a book in which they were characters, yet they could hardly stay away from the author. In a 16 January 1907 letter to Julian Hawthorne (Nathaniel's son, Hilda's father), GM spoke of Dublin not as home but as his "workshop"; its life was his "copy," waiting to be converted to literature.[222] He used his Saturday "At Homes" along with his "treacherous gift of familiarity" to lure his models under his gaze. Magee pleads in extenuation of his complicity, "He gave us dinners, far better dinners than we were accustomed to, and . . . unwonted wines."[223] Come in, said the spider to the fly, and James Starkey ("Seumas O'Sullivan") came to Ely Place one evening before others had arrived. Starkey was just back from his third visit to Paris – the very theme and lesson of Moore's Royal Hibernian lecture. "Moore had undoubtedly," Starkey recalled, "the faculty of 'drawing out' in conversation those in whom he was interested." Now Starkey expatiated on his Paris revels: he said he had a plan to write an essay taking off from Wordsworth's "Yarrow" poems: "Paris unvisited, Paris visited, Paris revisited." Moore listened, smoking his cigar, and, unlike his guest, seldom lifting the wine-glass to his lips. A few Saturdays later when Starkey returned to Ely Place, in the course of the evening Moore read out to his visitors a witty new chapter of *Hail and Farewell*. It began with a fantastic description of Starkey's profile as reminiscent of a Syracusan coin; then came the "effect of that 'Syracusan' profile on the ladies of Paris, the adventures into which it led its owner," etc., with the young Irishman before, during, and after Paris. That evening, Starkey just laughed at the genuinely funny chapter. Later, he returned and suggested to Moore that it might be better "to omit the personal element – the mention of my name, for instance."[224] The chapter was dropped.[225]

Most of Moore's acquaintances were neither so ingenuous nor so lucky as Starkey. In late February 1908, Moore dropped in on Maud Gonne in Paris after her divorce from John MacBride. After drinking a cup of tea, Moore turned to Gonne in a businesslike way and said: "Now I want you to tell me all about it, just why did you get married? I can understand the separation but I want to hear all about that too."[226] Is it for that book you are writing? she asked, then tried to turn the conversation to the weather, but one way or another (the acoustics of Dublin are famously perfect for spite), he got what he needed about Yeats and Gonne. According to Moore's theory, the early poetry of Yeats was excessively ethereal, famished of reality, adolescent, even effeminate, and, by 1910, withering up before it had fruited, largely because of unrealised desire, as he explained in *Vale*:

I continued to meditate the main secret of Yeats's life, until one day we happened to meet at Broadstone Station. We were going to the West; we breakfasted together in the train, and after breakfast the conversation took many turns, and we talked of her whom he had loved always, the passionate ideal of his life, and why this ideal had never become a reality to him as Mathilde had become to Richard [Wagner]. Was it really so? was my pressing question, and he answered me:

"I was very young at the time and was satisfied with . . ." My memory fails me, or perhaps the phrase was never finished. The words I supply, "the spirit of sense," are merely conjectural.

"Yes, I understand, the common mistake of a boy"; and I was sorry for Yeats and for his inspiration which did not seem to have survived his youth, because it had arisen out of an ungratified desire.[227]

Yeats was rocked by such disclosures in *Vale*. This premature epitaph underestimated the stores of energy left in the poet; worse yet, Moore betrayed his past friendship with Yeats; worst of all, he showed Yeats himself betraying the confidence of Maud Gonne.

George Russell knew that Yeats was going to get the worst of the satire and, in October 1908, Russell wrote John Quinn that "one half of Dublin is afraid it will be in [*Hail and Farewell*] and the other is afraid that it won't." He himself would be glad if he were safely out of it. He had never quarreled with Moore.[228] Indeed, Russell himself had over the years of Moore's residence in Dublin considerably added to GM's stock of knowledge about Yeats. W. K. Magee recalls that Moore took the place in Russell's life occupied by Yeats before those two old friends fell out in late 1905 over the privatisation of the Irish National Theatre Society. On Moore's Saturday nights at Ely Place, he milked his favorite guest on a weekly basis. "Moore himself was perfect on these occasions – amused, evocative, appreciative, in his own way as inexhaustible as Russell in reminiscence and invention."[229] As for Susan Mitchell, Russell's editorial assistant at the *Irish Homestead* and frequent Saturday evening companion (Violet Russell stayed at home with the children), Moore, "who froze up at all facetiousness, used to find her witticisms, uttered in her plaintive contralto voice, rather fatiguing."[230] He may have enjoyed the performance less than others did when Mitchell "sang with much 'go' . . . her 'Wearing of the Green' song about George Moore," her party piece at recital times.[231] Russell's sense of safety at Ely Place was rattled when Moore remarked in the spring of 1909, "Russell, I have just written 2,000 words about you." Russell asked if he might see them. "No," "the fiend" answered, "you will see them later on."[232] After the publication of the first two volumes, *Ave* and *Salve*, Russell made a winter 1913 visit to London and dropped in on Moore at 121 Ebury Street. Russell jokingly claimed not to be satisfied with his own portrait given thus far in *Hail and Farewell*; he had been made into "the blameless hero of a young girl's novel."[233] Moore conceded that he still had the last pages of the final volume, *Vale*, to write, and he would see what he could do about hunting up some little sin to humanise his friend.

In fact, in that final volume, Moore dramatises a conversation with Magee on this subject of possible sins for Dublin's saint. Magee says Russell is an unhappy man and Moore had better "be careful about what [he] said about AE's home life."[234] Moore showed the first draft of the passage about Russell's humanising sin to Ernest Longworth, and Longworth warned him that it was of "the utmost importance not to give offence in this quarter." GM rewrote the section, and the bowdlerised, hinting version is what we have in *Vale*. It simply says that Russell's human shortfall is that he sometimes neglected his wife – propped up a book at the dinner-table and didn't talk to her, didn't bid her goodnight, and didn't make much money. Yet what is indirectly hinted many knew. That's why Longworth and Magee told Moore to be careful; that's why Russell let it be known before publication he was "on the watch."[235] Even before the book came out, Moore received an unpleasant letter from a Mrs Baker, possibly the painter Frances Baker, warning him not to say anything that might hurt Russell. Moore was enraged at this shocking attempt at interference with a literary work; he told Mrs Baker he would never speak to her again.

What was the source of all this tension surrounding the question of Russell's domestic life? Simply put, the sainted man had for years been in love with the former resident of the J. B. Yeats household, Susan Mitchell (1866–1926), Russell's fellow editor of the *Irish Homestead* and a witty poet (e.g. *Aids to the Immortality of Certain Persons in Ireland, Charitably Administered*, 1908). Their love affair was an open secret in Dublin. For instance, after the couple came to see John Butler Yeats off on the boat to New York, JBY wrote to his friend Rosa Butt, "I am sure they are a great happiness to each other. I think everyone is glad that it is so. Mrs. Russell never knows anything about anybody and finds her children and life generally a bore (but this is all for your faithful bosom. You must not betray them. You and I make each other happy)."[236] Just because AE loved Susan Mitchell, and Susan AE, was no reason, of course, for Moore to slyly allude to their extradomestic happiness, much less to bring Mrs Russell into contempt among that group of Dubliners who were in on the secret.

Edward Martyn had better reason to be shocked by *Hail and Farewell* than Russell did. Moore divulged Martyn's homosexuality; he danced around it, planting his brightly beribboned darts like a mincing banderillero around a stumbling bull. Moore promised Martyn that "on the subject . . . there is not a word in my book, I assure you," but this is true even less than that there is nothing about Russell's marital infidelity in *Vale*.[237] Edward's queerness is the running joke of all their encounters – woman-hating, boy-loving, priest-obeying dear queer Edward is the book's virtual laughing stock. GM portrays himself as standing below Edward's window in Dublin, his heart "faint as a lover's," whistling a Wagner motif as his secret signal for "dear Edward" to descend, touch, and allow him to enter. Alarming as this regular serenade was to the men passing out of the pub opposite the tobacco shop above which Martyn lived, GM soon makes it clear that Edward, sitting on the couch in all his fat, is not really GM's type, nor does Edward care for men like

George. What then? Inside, Edward keeps a small harmonium, *Salve* continues – "one can only think it serves to give the keynote to a choir-boy." Every Saturday night, before the Sunday performance of his specially endowed Palestrina choir at Dublin's Pro-Cathedral, Edward takes a boy home to listen to his singing.[238]

Martyn put up with a lot from Moore, but he could not put up with *Hail and Farewell*. Nevill Geary, Martyn's Temple roommate, seems right when he wrote that "Every word Moore wrote of Martyn makes one love Martyn more, and that is a noble tribute to a friend," though Max Beerbohm is closer to capturing the sport involved when he says: "I see Martyn . . . as a fast featherbed on which Moore, luxuriously rolling and pommeling and crowing and (it goes without saying) stark naked, is borne towards immortality."[239] The outing of Martyn may have been sympathetically perpetrated but in Dublin in 1912 few took this view. Furthermore, Edward took himself seriously as Sinn Fein's first President, Gaelic League board member, and especially as a perfectly pious Catholic; no reader of *Hail and Farewell* fails to laugh at "dear Edward," and the laughter of men and women at the homosexual in the closet cannot be good to hear. Years after Martyn's death, Yeats might rhetorically ask, "What drove him to those long prayers, those long meditations, that stern Church music? What secret torture?"[240] but how could his old friend George Moore show off his secrets in that way during his own lifetime?

Moore also "outed" Hugh Lane as a homosexual transvestite, after portraying his aunt, Augusta Gregory, as a proselytiser in her youth who went in for cultural missionary work during her widowhood. Gregory read this libel in a chapter published in the January 1914 *English Review* and, writing from Hugh Lane's London house, promptly threatened Heinemann editor Sydney Pawling with a lawsuit unless changes were made prior to publication of the book version of the episode.[241] Lane followed up with a similar threat of legal action while Moore was out of the country on a visit to Palestine. Upon his return Moore was enraged at the alterations made in his text by Pawling. Why shouldn't he say that Augusta Gregory used to find young Lane trying on dresses out of her clothes closet? Was there anything so very malignant about suggesting that this feminine taste for refinement was the secret of his commercial success as a picture dealer? Didn't all Lane's close friends know that he loved to dress up in fancy costumes – Spanish mantillas with castanets, Turkish outfits with long skirts, etc.?[242] As for publication of the facts, Lane himself had enjoyed listening to Moore read his "wonderfully clever, remorseless" pages on "dear Edward" to Tonks, Steer, and Lane just a few months earlier.[243] Writing to Augusta Gregory, Lane said he had pressed Steer as to how Moore got the cross-dressing story: Moore recalled that it "was told him by [Lady Gregory]! Later on, he said, 'now that I come to think of it to be *quite* accurate it was Yeats who told me, which is the same thing!'"[244]

Moore, however, may have known about Lane's disposition from other sources as well, from William Orpen, for instance, who as early as 1906 teased

Lane about his affairs: "I went out yesterday afternoon with a friend of yours, I won't mention names – a male friend – critic, of the drama – lives in Mayfair – do you know him – Because I'm anxious to find out a little more about him. My knowledge of life leads me to believe [?etc.]. I'll have my doubts of you soon . . ."[245] (Subsequently, the letter identifies Lane's friend as Max Beerbohm.) Orpen himself was also hideously flustered when he was found by Tonks and Moore alone with Lane at Lindsay House, Cheyne Walk, at eleven o'clock at night in 1912 – "a terrible moment in my life," he told his mistress, Mrs St George. Would his idols Tonks and Moore now have their doubts about Orpen? It was like a game of sardines: how many grown men can fit in one closet? With an author like Moore prowling about the private homes of London, Orpen could have ended up with his own funny part to play in *Vale*, funny to others, that is, but not necessarily to Orpen, any more than their magnificently sly, comic presentations to the purchasing public had been entertaining to Russell, Susan Mitchell, Augusta Gregory, Hugh Lane, W. B. Yeats, or Moore's other erstwhile friends and immortal characters.

It is not becoming for authors and readers of biographies to become self-righteously indignant about the invasion of privacy, especially when the thief of secrets turns them into a book that will always be read with delight. As Robert Ross admitted in the *Times* review of *Salve*, "it would be hypocrisy to deplore an absence of reticence and good taste in the presence of such irresistible reading."[246] The oddity of one's own complicity in Moore's transgressive arts comes out clearly, along with other strains often hidden, in Violet Martin's account of her response to *Ave* in a letter to Augusta Gregory:

> I have been affronted by what he says of you – by his languid approval as much as anything else – There is a leisurely superiority that must be trying – as much as the franker impertinence – yet, leaving my friends out, if I can, how penetratingly well written it all is – The scene by the lake at Coole is exquisitely done; whether Mr. Yeats may agree with me I know not – It is a pity that such a gift as his should be set in an earthen vessel – at it its best it is very hard to beat – & then comes a feeling as of tasting suddenly a lump of garlic – Paris, on top of R[oman] C[atholic] Mayo ancestry can produce these things – but this is for your private ear. The second rate R.C. with the French admixture is a blend peculiar to itself & betrays itself sooner or later – what hidden treason and philistinism this would be reckoned, but you know what I mean![247]

Augusta Gregory knew what Violet Martin meant, and sometimes felt as she did about Roman Catholics. It was precisely to explode all that goes without saying, the whole system of sub-codes about sex, respectability, religion, sectarianism, and class, that Moore wrote *Hail and Farewell*. To call its sensibility second-rate, *a fortiori*, to call it Catholic, is simply defensiveness on the part of Violet Martin. As writing and thinking, it is as first rate and free thinking as one could wish. Yet, having gorged upon the book, a reader is likely to feel guilty. Gossip and novels are alike practical meditations that establish the subtle moralities of everyday life, and it is customary and proper that they should each be conducted at some distance from their living human subjects, either out of earshot or under other names. By putting real people with their real names in a novel, even one written with genius, Moore invited his contemporaries to banquet on the living flesh of their friends. They wined and dined with delight, but later blamed the cook for their indigestion.

15

It is a wonder that Moore could have found it humanly possible to write a book that would put at risk so many of the natural ties of friendship on which he, like anyone, must have depended. True, he had once before had to leave Ireland after writing about friends and family in *A Drama in Muslin* and *Parnell and His Island*; and he had sacrificed many Paris friendships by publishing a French translation of *Confessions of a Young Man*. Perhaps nothing mattered to him but art, and it was just his bad luck that his peculiar gift was for the art of auto-biography. Before beginning the trilogy, he took stock of his own talent and decided he did not stand with the best novelists: "I do not feel that I can write novels as well as other people, I mean as well as Balzac or Turgenev, but I do think that I can write autobiography as well as anyone that has yet written it. And this last sentence will tell you how [*Hail and Farewell*] will be written – with perfect candour and complete shamelessness."[248] In a critique of *Father and Son* (a book Moore encouraged Gosse to write), Moore found just this one fault with his friend's classic autobiography: "That sense of decency, *which as a writer you should not have*, you could not overcome."[249] By his honesty and encouragement, Moore bound Gosse over as a friend for life, and, much as he might sacrifice himself and others to his art, Moore needed such friends as much as another does – maybe, being a bachelor, more than others.

There is also a secret side to the life of Moore, an underground river of affec-tions that may have been the strongest and most long-lasting of his feelings. All the time he was making friends in Dublin and all the time he was busy making strangers of those friends by the ways he wrote about them, it is quite possible his heart was still in England, at Nevill Holt, a place he might visit but not live in. Although Nancy Cunard recalls that Moore came to Nevill Holt "two, three, or more times a year during each of those Edwardian years," his name in the Cunards' visitors' book appears just ten times over nine years, each signature marking a stay of some length, often a fortnight or more, as Nancy grew from a lanky six-year-old to a poetically inclined schoolgirl of fifteen:

2 February 1902
20 June 1904, 13 August 1904

11 October 1907
21 April 1908, 6 August 1908
19 January 1909, 30 August 1909,
5 February 1910; 2 August 1910[250]

There were other meetings with Lady Cunard, of course – at Howard de Walden's Seaford House in London, at Baron Braybrooke's Audley End near Cambridge, perhaps at Sir William Eden's London residence, also in Paris and Bayreuth. In a diary, affecting the English of Pepys crossed with schoolgirl French, Nancy Cunard recorded a London meeting on 23 July 1910: "Father dyde leave todaye forre Ye Holte . . . GM et moys allames fayre une promenade a Sohoe."[251] It was, however, Moore's lengthy stays in the fictive form of domestic life with Nancy and Maud at Nevill Holt that he most relished. In the course of these visits, he became for Nancy "the central figure of childhood."[252]

On his return to Ely Place, Moore would reminisce by his own winter fire about a summer month spent in the grand Leicestershire house, his room beside the oak passage covered in oriental rugs, the chestnuts behind the house, "when lilacs by the dooryard bloomed," Nancy and her governess walking the grounds, the sheep grazing, the pleasant Protestant service at the local chapel where during one Sunday meeting Moore himself was the reader of the weekly Bible passage.[253] Maud Cunard was the answer to all his instincts, and he was almost ready to invent a god to thank for the blessing of her love: "I wonder what god selected me for . . . happiness and why he selected me . . . surely the most fortunate man in the world is he who meets a woman who enchants him as a work of art enchants. I find in you Manet, Berthe Morisot, Tourgueneff, Balzac, Shelley, and the works I cannot write but would, were I the George Moore that George Moore sees in front of him, beguiling him, luring him like a will-o-the-wisp. If I have failed to write what I dreamed I might write, one thing I have not failed in – you. You are at once the wine and the wine in the vase."[254] Heaven for him, he thought, would be Nietzsche's eternal recurrence stopped on a summer evening at Nevill Holt, with Moore seated in the great room before the tapestries, talking to a man friend about the charms of their hostess – just to live in her atmosphere, aestheticising about her image, and his own image as seen in the eyes of one who loved him.[255] Yet like Owen Asher in the second version of *Sister Teresa*, it was hardly enough to meditate on the 853 letters received from his mistress over the ten years of their affair, or think back over the nights of kisses; he longed to see her more often, and her refusal to give herself to him forever, as well as his own refusal to put himself on the line, opened him up to a deep and derealising sorrow.[256] She could "give her body unreservedly" but was "parsimonious about her soul." Nature had given her every lovable quality, "but not the capacity for loving." He studied her like a difficult text, a palimpsest, "something written over," but he could not possess her meaning; he could not co-author with her a common story of life.[257]

20. *Nancy takes G. M.
for a Pleasant Walk;*
sketch on Nevill Holt
letterhead by Montague
Eliot.

He took more and more interest in Nancy as she passed through the stages
of girlhood. He spoke kindly to her when she was a little girl of four or five
curled up with *The Violet Fairy Book* by the great stone fireplace. With grown-
ups, GM enjoyed a row, but with Nancy he was "ever benign" and "winning."[258]
She watched him like she watched no other – his mimicry, his mind working
with brilliant paradoxes, his detestation of common English salt for its admix-
ture of powdered bones for the sake of whiteness. To her, he was "a delight
and a wonder"; her *GM: Memories of George Moore* is written with devoted love
for the man.[259] When flustered by a flying wasp, she recalls being instructed by
Moore in his rich, curious accentuation, "Wel-le, if you will leave him a-lone,
hee will go a-way," the sort of wise, kindly thing every man has told a child.[260]
Together they went on long walks in the Holt wood to gather flowers or look
at her favorite secret places. Once, they sat on a gravestone together in the
churchyard, and she told him she wondered where people go when they die.[261]
They sometimes took the road to Medbourne village, and thus were not to be
found when county visitors stopped at Holt in hope of meeting the famous
author. Once, after his return to Dublin, he sent a gift of antique yellow straw
bonnets for Maud and Nancy.[262] On 16 September 1908 he sent another gift in
memory of his walks with Nancy: George Borrow's *Lavengro*, once a popular

work of literary vagrancy. He set Nancy little tasks, as if she was another of his many research assistants, yet they were sweet daughterly tasks – to learn the names of the wildflowers around Nevill Holt, for instance, or to gather nosegays. These flowers he then blended into the final revised edition of *Sister Teresa*, along with a pained meditation on the love affair with Maud that never led to marriage.[263]

The complications of Lady Cunard's love life became so great that in 1911 she was forced to bar GM from coming to Nevill Holt again, and soon enough she would leave the country house and Sir Bache Cunard for good, settling in London. When GM heard that his summers with Nancy and Maud were at an end, he wrote Maud: "It was a great privation not to have been able to go to Holt, of feeling, affection, sympathy. You and Nancy are my realities – all the others are shadows."[264] Ten short approximations to family life, one table at meals but separate beds, and all under another man's roof – this is not very much reality for marriage, fatherhood, or family, but it gave George Moore all that he was to get of the sweet sensations of natural love. While he betrayed the confidence of Dublin friends, in his fashion he kept faith with the memory of those visitations to Nevill Holt.

Chapter 12
Jesus of Nazareth and the Sage of Ebury Street

I

During his August 1910 visit to Nevill Holt, Moore stayed in touch with his old friend, Edouard Dujardin. He was eager for news of Dujardin's recent trip to Palestine, but had declined the invitation to come along himself. Of all the friends from whom he stole, Moore attested that he harvested most profitably in Dujardin's fields – there he found Wagner, *le monologue intérieur*, and, most recently, the higher criticism of the Bible.[1] In the 1890s, the former symbolist poet had made and partly lost a fortune as punter, gambler, and proprietor of sexy newspapers; in the new century, he made himself into a biblical scholar, following in the footsteps of his fellow Wagnerite, the proto-Nazi Houston Stewart Chamberlain.[2] Chamberlain wanted to prove that Jesus was not a Jew; Dujardin wanted to show that it did not matter what he was. Dujardin concluded from his studies in "Palestinian folklore" that it was only the great Church erected by Europeans through the centuries that truly compelled one's devotion, and not the origins of that Church.

Moore's own tangles with the dogmatism of Irish Catholicism caused him to follow the speculative excesses of French Catholicism with interest. In early 1904, he translated for publication in *Dana* Dujardin's essay on abbé Loisy, the modernist theologian who argued, among other things, that Jesus had not foreseen Christianity.[3] In the same year, Dujardin published a volume that further inflamed Moore's curiosity, *La Source du fleuve chrétien*. It treated the Hebrew Bible as simply a "National Epic of Imperialism," construed with "brilliant audacity by the priests of Jerusalem" in the fifth century BCE. "Israel" was not at that time a kingdom, nor would it ever be; it was "merely the myth in which the men of Jerusalem symbolised their ambitions."[4] Dujardin's historical argument, informed by the scholarship of the day, is written with racist flair and Gallic assurance for an audience of non-scholars. Where Dujardin says "no doubt," there are usually very good grounds for caution, or indeed, for believing otherwise. At the end of his study, the author concludes that "Jesus the Nazarene," if he existed at all, and Dujardin was inclined to doubt that he had, would just have been one in a series of post-Daniel prophets, "wonder-workers, healers of men and beasts, wandering from town to town, living by begging or rascality . . . feverish with hatred of the *goyim*."[5]

It is strange that Moore, one of the few modernist writers who was neither anti-Semitic nor imperialist, should not have been put off by the racist strain in Dujardin's analysis. Instead, Moore found the breezy speculativeness about the source of Christian cultures – where so little can be certainly known – con-tagiously exciting. What were the Gospel writers anyway, he must have thought, but storytellers like himself, writing under assumed names long after the fact, taking bits of the best of one another's writings, making up a good deal of likely matter on their own, and relying on reports and rumors of reports in order to make the best story possible? "Theologising" he discovered to be a wonderful new sub-department of *aestheticising*. As early as 1907, he thought himself scholar enough to refuse to admit Harnack's arguments for the authenticity of the Gospel of Luke; Moore held that it was a medley of writings, containing some of Paul's own manuscripts.[6] In a visit to the National Library, he heard from Magee that a study on crucifixion in the Roman Empire had raised ques-tions about how Jesus could have died on the Cross in only three hours. Moore's fancy raced on to conceive a plot in which Jesus lives to recant his blasphemous claims to be the Messiah; then, twenty years later, he meets up with St Paul, Jesus knowing nothing at the time of Christianity, and Paul knowing little of Jesus except for the "fact" of his resurrection.[7] Moore tempted Dujardin with the idea on 13 June 1908, and GM's scenario, "The Apostle," was published (and copyrighted) in the June 1910 issue of the *English Review* while Dujardin was in Palestine.[8]

The two arch-modernists had other fish to fry as well. On his voyage to Palestine, Dujardin had written another play, and Moore himself had recently prevailed upon the Abbey Theatre playwright Lennox Robinson to take over the job of dramatising *Esther Waters*.[9] While neither of these ventures might guarantee fame or fortune, Moore thought he had a line on a sure thing right at Nevill Holt. On 10 August, the young Thomas Beecham had paid a visit to the Cunard house, returning for another on 23 August. Moore alerted Dujardin:

> Here is a bit of news for you. We have here the owner of an orchestra, whose father sells pills which rouse music in the insides of lady's maids, and who places his purse at his son's disposal for the creation of a national opera. For this purpose, he is full of the idea of establishing a bi-monthly review . . . He is sleep-ing it out at present and I am on the watch for him, and as soon as he leaves his bed, I will talk to him about you as an *essential* collaborator.[10]

Within five days, Moore had gotten Beecham's promise to deposit 6,000 francs on 30 September, evidently as an advance for an opera scenario to be written by the Moore–Dujardin duo, now setting up as successors to Meilhac and Halévy.[11] Beecham, however, did not pay up on time and ignored dunning letters. Moore could not quite make him out. He was the first-born son of the great Protestant manufacturer who discovered – rather as John Morgan Richards had done, with "Carter's Little Liver Pills" – that one could, by means of advertising, make a fortune by selling something of no real value. Yet Thomas Beecham seemed, Moore judged, "more of a dreamer than a business man."[12] However watchful Moore was over Beecham, his bank account, and his late mornings in bed, he failed to see what had been going on at Nevill Holt. According to village folklore, workmen on the clocktower over the stable spied the lady of the house in a bedroom with young Beecham.[13]

2

There is no record of the first meeting of Maud Cunard and Thomas Beecham; possibly it occurred not long before she and Nancy attended a 21 July 1910 rehearsal of Beecham's *Summer Night*, when she was thirty-seven and he was thirty-one.[14] In 1909 he conducted an opera by Ethel Smyth, and perhaps by this route entered the circle of Ethel's sister, Mrs Charles Hunter, who held a salon at Hill Hall in Essex; Cunard and Beecham are said to have first met there.[15] Cunard, like Mary Hunter, would play the patroness for Beecham and his plans for a national opera, but she did more than that.

Maud Cunard was still birdlike and beautiful, of all birds most like the canary, if canaries could be witty and lustful. Beecham was a natty young man with his hair parted in the middle, a three-inch goatee, upswept mustaches, dressed in a three-piece suit with a polka-dot tie, which he wore with an elegant slouch.[16] He had looks, youth, charm, money, ambition, an unhappy wife, and a mistress (he was named in a divorce suit in October 1910). His musical tastes were cutting edge: Delius, Ethel Smyth, and Richard Strauss; in June 1911, he would provide the music for the Covent Garden performance of Nijinsky and the Ballets Russes, a sensation of the pre-war years. Maud was an enthusiast for all Thomas Beecham did, to the extent of using the Ballets Russes production designer, Leon Bakst, to decorate her London house.[17]

When Maud left Nevill Holt and Sir Bache Cunard behind and set up house in the grand style at a succession of prominent London addresses – first Cavendish Square, then 5 Carlton House Terrace in 1920, and 7 Grosvenor Square in 1925 – it was not in order to be closer to George Moore, but to advance the career of her new lover, Thomas Beecham. She would gather illuminati at her diplomatic luncheons, and, throwing off a remark like "Jealousy is the most terrible of passions, don't you agree?" she would turn to Arthur Balfour and say, "but you must come tomorrow night to my box for that masterpiece of jealousy, Verdi's 'Otello' – Thomas conducts it as no one else can," thus gaining the visible appearance of sponsorship by one of the great and good for a Beecham production. Or, supposedly to illustrate that English divorce laws were out of date, she reportedly asked the Lord Chancellor, Lord Buckmaster, how poor Thomas could be liberated from that horrid Lady Beecham.[18] Yet Beecham did not obtain a divorce, and kept a good front on his relations with Cunard.

Moore left no account of his discovery that he had been supplanted in the role of famous lover to Lady Cunard. Knowing no better, he left Nevill Holt with the "capricious" "fashionable lady" on 28 August 1910 for Munich, Bayreuth, then Paris.[19] Although she liked to live dangerously, and never aspired to be known as the good and loving wife of Sir Bache, Maud Cunard hated the vulgarity of publicity about her role as the mistress of Moore. She had rejected Moore's many attempts to dedicate books to her. So she may have been horrified at her name appearing alongside his in newspaper articles about a runaway automobile that slashed through crowds at Bayreuth (two were killed, he escaped entirely, while she was shaken and bruised).[20] Yet if something was wrong, GM still did not know it by the time of his return from the continent, for he then told Maurice that the story of his life was "a hundred *passades . . .* and one great love affair."[21] She was too dear a part of his imaginative life for him to let go. After the news came, he permitted her to move him into the role of dear old friend, fond fatherly figure to Nancy, and the household lion of Cunard dinner parties. She could never keep him, however, from thinking of her as his beloved. Indeed, she did not really try to do so. She kept up the flow of invitations, visits, letters (two-thirds of those extant follow her meeting with Beecham), and other tendernesses of which the world will never know. A letter following a summer evening spent together in 1911 seems to acknowledge a great change in their relationship. Moore copied out a poem he recited for her the night before, AE's "A Farewell":

> And ah, my bright companion, you and I must go
> Our ways, unfolding lonely glories not our own,
> Nor from each other gathered, but an inward glow
> Breathed by the Lone One on the seeker lone.
>
> If for the heart's own sake we break the heart, we may
> When the last ruby drop dissolves in diamond light
> Meet in a deeper vesture in another day.
> Until that dawn, dear heart, good night, good night.[22]

Quoting the phrase "We break the heart" looks like a discreet way of saying "You broke my heart."

Many years later, after the deaths of Cunard and Moore, Rupert Hart-Davis called on Sir Thomas Beecham to ask him about his affair with Lady Cunard and its impact on Moore. Attended by a servant in white livery and a wealthy, young American wife, Beecham was generous with cigars and glasses of sherry, but he affected to know Lady Cunard only as a "fairly remote acquaintance"; as for Moore, Beecham said they never spoke to each other after 1911.[23]

3

The wider world of London into which Moore quickly entered after settling in Ebury Street suggests his complaints had been genuine that Dublin cramped his style – that is, his social style. Within a short time of his arrival, he was dining, on 23 March 1911, with Gosse, Heinemann, and Sickert; hosting a wedding reception for Sickert (an anticlimactic event, as Sickert's fianceé had refused to marry at the Camden Street register office); meeting Arnold Bennett; spending part of the month of May playwriting and theologising with Dujardin in Fontainebleau; returning to London for the Ballets Russes performances of late June; in utterances that were "genuine, felt, spasmodic," praising the exhibition of watercolors by his old friend, Sir William Eden; and in late July hearing (then reporting) the confession of Somerset Maugham, "at once fortunate and unhappy," that Maugham had "pawned his soul" by writing plays for money, and now could not redeem it.[24]

It was probably in late summer, when Moore was going over the proofs for *Ave* (published in October 1911), that he found himself a fellow-guest with Henry James at Hill Hall, Mrs Charles Hunter's country house. The two novelists each came away with wicked anecdotes about the other. After going for a walk with Moore, Henry James was asked by another guest if he enjoyed it. James made a long speech, enumerated the many people he had known, and the delightful women, but he had never met, not anywhere, "anyone so 'unimportantly dull' as George Moore."[25] Moore held his own anecdote back until giving an interview to a reporter from the *Observer* in 1916, ten months after James had died. Moore recalled that he had asked his fellow-novelist if he would give him help with a troublesome passage in *Ave* by replacing a certain phrase in the proofs:

James rolled his eyes like a man in convulsions. Then he snatched the proof from me and started from the room with it. Finally, he came down, having composed a line and a half. It looked profound, but what it meant I had no idea. However, I put it in. When my secretary came to type it, she asked me if it was written correctly, as she could make no sense of it! Later, when the book was being set up, Heinemann came to me with the proof containing that sentence. "Will you please tell me what you mean by this?" said he. "Neither I nor my reader could make it out." I told him I couldn't and then explained to him who had written it.

I can never think of that without recalling my first meeting with that great French master, Jules Lemaître. At that time he had read nothing of mine, and he said, "Tell me, are you clear or are you obscure?"

"I am clear, Monsieur Lemaître," said I. "I have not talent enough to be obscure." That remark seemed to please him.[26]

Over time, Mrs Hunter learned to invite George Moore, Henry James, and Thomas Hardy for separate weekends.

21. Colonel Maurice
Moore, frontispiece for
An Irish Gentleman
(1913).

   In the autumn, when *Ave* was being reviewed, and *Salve* was coming along,
Moore amused himself by bullying Shaw and the Stage Society into a production of *Esther Waters* on 10 December 1911 ("It succeeded perfectly," GM
announced to Dublin friends, "but there is no public for serious plays").[27] No
more did London reviewers appreciate *Ave*: "The reviewers look upon my book
as a book of reminiscences, whereas I took so much material and moulded it
just as if I were writing a novel, and the people in my book are not personalities but human types."[28] To judge from comments in the *Guardian*, *Athenaeum*,
and the *Times Literary Supplement*, Moore's masterpiece was a petty, dull, long,
and scandalous book, and the reviewers did not look forward eagerly to the next
two volumes.[29] Such responses had the effect of hardening Moore's vanity, and
they gave him the idea of pricing his books so that only those who wanted them
badly would be in a position to have an opinion about them. The man who had
introduced the six-shilling novel to English literature had already vowed on 14
December 1910 that "no book of mine shall ever again be published under
7/6." He was headed in the direction of deluxe editions sold by subscription.[30]
He had a low opinion of mass literacy and the fiction produced for public entertainment. "You can teach people to read," he complained to Arthur Machen,
"but you can't give them brains."[31]

In spite of the frosty welcome given his play and his book, Moore was happily settled in London. He had so far lived half his years there, and there he would live the rest of them. He would go to exhibitions and concert halls, dine at the Café Royal (he is represented in Orpen's 1912 painting of the restaurant), and accept invitations to the parties of Mrs Hugh Hammersly, Mrs Charles Hunter, or Edmund Gosse. There he could meet and take the measure of the vivid, emergent personalities of the world of culture; there he himself was seen to be such a personality. On his return to London from ten years in Dublin, his reputation had been improved by absence; his age and fame had also made society hostesses less frightened of what was still disreputable in his behavior. From having been a dangerous modernist, he was aging into the status of one of the last remaining great Victorians.

In addition to his London circle of friends – Tonks, Steer, and Gosse, mainly – Moore offered hospitality to visitors. Dujardin visited him in April 1912, and again on 15 September; the two men liked to sit in Moore's parlor, "befogged with the smoke of . . . corpulent cigars," exchanging "choicest confidences."[32] W. K. Magee was induced to stay at Ebury Street in August 1912, and for his sake Moore hosted a dinner with the Gosses, thinking his two friends would appreciate one another – both rather astringent and conservative, liking old things best, careful in their opinions.[33] It transpired, however, that Magee was overawed by Gosse, and irritably self-conscious about his clothes; and Gosse tended to lavish his attentions on the titled, the famous, or the young and delicate. Moore could "fit in" better than many of his friends – in Paris, London, or Dublin – precisely by fitting in nowhere. After settling in London, Moore must have made contact with Gerald O'Donovan, the ex-priest, now married to the daughter of an English Protestant colonel. O'Donovan was working on his first and most famous novel, *Father Ralph* (published in May 1913), a bitter farewell to Irish Catholicism, framed in allusions to biblical modernism and rich in a large cast of mostly unspiritual priests – all very much to Moore's taste. Yet another old friend from Ireland came to visit at the end of January 1913 – George Russell. They had their ominous conversation, described in the previous chapter, about the addition of a "humanising fault" to Russell's character for the final volume of *Hail and Farewell*. During the visit, Moore introduced Russell to Steer, Tonks, and Laurence Harrison, and others of the New English Art Club. Russell was sad to see his old friend so well settled out of Dublin.[34]

4

In early 1912, George and his brother Maurice resumed reasonably friendly relations. Negotiations with the Congested Districts Board for the sale of Moore's properties in Mayo were going forward, and George sought his brother's advice and agreement. On 27 January 1912, GM received a proposal to purchase the Ballintubber estate for £21,027 in guaranteed stock, Bellymore and Kilgellie for £3,021 in cash, Ashbrook and Moorehall (the lands around the house) for £7,907 in stock, and Carrowlickeen and Aillemore for £12,660 in stock – £44,615 in total. The Board also made a demand for the 168 acres between Moorehall and Derrinrush wood; Tom Ruttledge, his land agent, advised GM to refuse to sell this parcel, as it would break up the home estate. The price offered for untenanted land – ten years' purchase – was judged by Ruttledge to be a poor one; the Congested Districts Board most wanted to get its hands on the Moorehall demesne, and offered twenty-three years' purchase for that parcel.[35] The suspicion was that the Board wanted not only to get land for the tenants but also to root out the landlord. On 6 February, GM asked Maurice, then settled in Brussels, if they could meet to talk over the terms of sale. Maurice was unhappy about any scheme that would make the estate unworkable in the future, yet that seemed precisely the intent of the Congested Districts Board. For the time being, GM fell in with Maurice's line of thinking.

The February 1913 visit of Maurice to London is unrecorded, but the brothers appear to have considered not just the matter of Moore Hall, but also the case of their youngest brother, Julian Moore. In the 1880s, Julian pondered an extraordinary variety of careers: military officer, consul in the Foreign Office, novelist, delegate to a convention of the Tenant League, policeman, and opera composer.[36] GM's habit was to play the father to Julian, a heavy father, by turns encouraging and sarcastic. In 1891 after Julian had spent a year working on an opera, GM asked his mother to "tell Julian I often think of him. I wish he would write telling me exactly how far he has got towards being able to write a song"; four months later, he advised the under-confident twenty-seven-year-old to "turn his attention to something practical."[37] Julian made little progress as a composer, and did not turn his attention elsewhere. GM resolved to regard his youngest brother as "delightfully insipid."[38] After the death of Mrs Moore in 1895, Julian moved to London and managed to publish brief articles on book collecting, architecture, and the art of illustration, but he did not get on in life.[39] He appeared to be eager to run through his inheritance, and in May 1896 GM offered to help him make investments with a life insurance company that would guarantee £3 a week; Julian replied by threatening George with violence.[40] GM assumed it was Julian's intention to beggar himself at the door of his oldest brother. At the time of Maurice's visit in February 1912, George was willing to arrange an annuity, but he was afraid to offend Julian: "If I ask him here, he will say [it was] merely to show him what a fine house I had. If I speak to him of literature he will think . . . I am merely proving to him my writings are better than his." GM thought Maurice might safely approach Julian. It was arranged that a regular allowance would be paid Julian through GM's solicitor, C. D. Medley.[41] By the time GM wrote "Wilfrid Holmes" in 1921, he had overcome his exasperation with Julian, if not his bewilderment: Wilfrid (patterned directly on Julian) seemed "one of those weak, timid, harmless souls, come out of the mould that Nature reserves for some great purpose known only to herself, mayhap the preservation of pity and compassion in the world."[42]

The Moore Hall sale was more difficult to bring to a satisfactory conclusion than the problem of support for Julian. GM wrote directly to Augustine Birrell, the Liberal Chief Secretary of Ireland, to complain about the hard bargain the Congested Districts Board was driving. Birrell replied with "a lot of blather-skite," urging GM to "haggle with the Board," rather than take his case to the Land Courts.[43] As George presented the quandary to Maurice, they had three choices and only three: cede grazing rights to the tenants but keep the Moore-hall demesne intact, get a slightly higher price for those parcels key to the demesne by haggling with the Board, or sell the house and estate immediately for a good price. Concerning the last option, GM explained: "Don't think that I wish to do this, I am quite as unwilling as you are. But if I don't sell it Moore Hall will be sold in the next generation, of that I am quite sure."[44] Maurice was not so sure: he wanted to sit tight and hope the crisis would pass; maybe the next generation – Rory and Toby – would live to preside at Moore Hall yet. On 14 June, GM got wind of gossip that Birrell had remarked on his case, "Well, it's a great shame to break up Mr. Moore's demesne, but the peasants want land and it better be done."[45] Moore always had contempt for Birrell as a lesser writer, whose *Obiter Dicta* (1884) was beneath his notice, and, with this evidence of Birrell's double-dealing (pretending to help Moore, while giving the go-ahead for the demise of his property), GM thought he had the Chief Secretary in an impossible situation.[46]

Over the summer, the Congested Districts Board increased its offer by £3,000 and surrendered its claim to the Moore Hall demesne. Both Ruttledge and George Moore agreed this was the best deal obtainable, but Maurice spoke of "a movement now on foot to persuade the Government to purchase the land-lords' property at a higher figure if the landlords will help pass the Home Rule bill" (introduced in the House of Commons 11 April 1912). Yet how could either one of the Moore brothers help pass that bill? Was Maurice going to promise "not to place your military knowledge at the service of Sir Edward Carson"? As a result of Carson's leadership, the Solemn League and Covenant to resist Home Rule had been signed by Ulster Protestants on 28 September 1912, and civil war seemed possible. Maurice would be among the first to offer his services to Eoin MacNeill and the Irish Volunteers, founded in November 1913, the beginning of a long period of engagement in Irish national politics for Maurice (later a senator under two Irish governments). Yet George had come to be in favor of a separate status for Ulster, and said so in a letter to the *Daily Mail*: Catholics and Protestants don't mix.[47] Even putting his newfound Loyalism aside, GM told Maurice in October 1912 that it was as difficult for him to believe that the government set store by the landlords' influence "as to believe in the Trinity, the Immaculate Conception or the Pope's Indulgences." Surely the time had come to sell all the outlying parts of the Moore estate.[48]

In mid-October, Maurice crossed the Channel to discuss the matter with George. During his visit, he arrived at Ebury Street one day when GM was out. While waiting along with F. M. Atkinson for GM's return, he picked up a fresh copy of *Salve* on the table and began to thumb through it. On page 255, he paused and read the following passage, in which George, the art critic, tries to understand the psychology of his brother by the study of his head. In the passage, GM exhibited what Beerbohm called the caricaturist's "sheer desire and irresponsible lust for bedevilling this or that human body."

> "A refined head," I said to myself, and it seemed to me I had seen, at some time or another, the same pinched skull in certain portraits of ecclesiastics by Bellini and the School of Bellini: "but not the Colonel's vague, inconclusive eyes . . . It is into Spanish painting that we must look for the Colonel, and we most find him in Velasquez, a somewhat icy painter who, however, relished and stated with great skill the Colonel's high-pitched nose, the drawing of the small nostrils, the hard, grizzled moustache. He painted the true Catholic in all his portraits of Philip, never failing to catch the faded, empty look that is so essentially a part of the Catholic face. Our ideas mould a likeness as quickly if Nature supplies certain proportions, and the Colonel – when he fattens out a little, which he sometimes does, and when his mind is away – reminds me of the dead King.[49]

Maurice was so shocked that he appealed to Atkinson; had he seen this book? Atkinson turned away and continued reading, as if he did not wish to be "mixed in a family affair."[50] When GM returned, Maurice upbraided him for the "bitterness and personal antagonism" of the whole passage, as well as for "untrue, probably libellous" individual statements. Evidently, George defended himself by saying he himself had always put up good-humoredly with caricatures – look at all Beerbohm's cartoons – and that he had spoken less well of his own appearance than of Maurice's – and look at what he had written about Yeats! Every caricaturist makes those he loves and those he despises equally ridiculous. Maurice needed to see the passage in the context of the whole volume.

On 24 October 1912, after further reading of *Salve*, Maurice renewed his outrage in a letter from his lodgings in Beaufort Street. "Yeats is not your brother; if Yeats were to write this of me I would not care a rap."[51] On the 27th Maurice spelled out his indignation once more. If GM really cared how Maurice felt, why did he not show him the passage in manuscript? "You were not prepared to sacrifice your little 'paras' on the altar of friendship . . . You wanted to put them beyond the power of recall, & chance the rest." It was especially stinging for Maurice to reduce GM's new form of autobiographical literature to "paras," anonymous newspaper paragraphs, usually gossipy and "humorous," provided for small sums by Grub Street journalists. Maurice tried to bring the letter back to issues of business by its close, but business as usual, much less friendliness, was becoming next to impossible between the brothers.

The reviews of *Salve* were, curiously, more unguardedly enthusiastic than those for *Ave*. A man with a thesis, according to Arthur Machen in the *Evening News*, was "a joy to himself and his fellow men," especially when the thesis, pursued with "infinite gaiety, ingenuity, and determination," was a ridiculous and offensive one, such as Moore's proposition that "literature is incompatible with dogma"; hence, a "Roman Catholic cannot be a literary artist."[52] Robert Lynd revised his earlier opinion of the first volume of *Hail and Farewell*; he now judged Moore's autobiography a piece of playacting, "malicious but not malignant."[53] In the *Times Literary Supplement*, Robert Ross held that *Salve* was the best autobiography since Gosse's *Father and Son*. As for its absence of discretion, "A sort of perpetual youth with which it is impossible to be indignant has for many years been one of [Moore's] extenuating circumstances and one of his passports to the good opinion of the younger generation."[54] One of those younger readers in *Smart Set* found in Moore's frankness "an irresistible charm," especially given his "extraordinarily limpid, liquid style . . . not a misplaced accent from end to end of him."[55] The good reviews cannot have made the book go down any better with Maurice; they did not count for him as an extenuating circumstance.

GM tried to retrieve the situation by helping Maurice with *An Irish Gentleman*. He read the manuscript, made suggestions, and then helped get it published. On 3 February 1913, T. Werner Laurie, one of GM's publishers, agreed to bring out the book. Laurie begged GM to provide a frontispiece photograph (as a companion to Maurice's portrait) and to write a foreword – "it would make an enormous difference to the reception of the book."[56] Moore agreed. The portraits of the two brothers, however, raised the touchy question of looks: Maurice had them and George did not. On seeing the portrait selected by Maurice (slim and keen-eyed in his colonel's uniform at age forty), GM's imp of the perverse caused him to tease his brother on 24 April: "So now we know the light in which you wish people to see you! . . . in all your youth and beauty, the darling of the garrison hacks."[57] Maurice was not taking any more from George, and gave him "tit out of proportion to the tat" by GM's measure.[58] Maurice defended his choice of frontispiece in an official and complete manner that only further excited GM's ridicule: "It looks to me as if some curls have been added, but on this matter expert evidence would have to be called."[59] He was needling the poor man into a fury. Meanwhile, George's preface to the volume was overdue.

Moore made a rapid and quiet trip to Westport, County Mayo, in April to formally propose a deal with the Congested Districts Board: he would sell his properties "except Moore Hall and the acres that surround the Hall."[60] Yet it would take months for the Board to make a firm counter-offer. On his return, Moore busied himself with arranging the cast for a Stage Society production of *Elizabeth Cooper* scheduled for the second Sunday in June. He got a young Edith Evans from William Poel's cast of *Troilus and Cressida* for the maid.[61] Then GM set to work on the preface for Maurice's book.

On 1 May, George Moore had written a preface that his secretary, Margaret Gough, did not like – it failed to include any of his own memories of his father, and Laurie did not care for it either, but on 2 May Moore wrote Laurie he could do no better, as Maurice had said all there was to say about G. H. Moore. The next day, Laurie was told that this letter of resignation was a false alarm; something would come; and on 6 May GM sent in his preface ("I hope it will please my brother – I am sure it will please you") and left for Paris.[62] The preface is vintage George Moore: clear, elegant, personal, ironic, and troublemaking. Along with some unqualified compliments to Maurice's writing, the preface pays tribute to G. H. Moore's brilliance at Oscott, his fine drawings made during travels in Turkey and North Africa, and his Byronic affair with a married lady. There is a very funny arpeggio on the dullness of politics in biography, and, more generally, on dullness as the necessary salt in any work of literature, with many varieties: "the choking sandy tracts in Shakespeare," "the second part of Goethe's *Wilhelm Meister*, pompous and sterile as the moon," Wordsworth who wrote "the beautifullest poems in the English language, and the dullest." "The dullness of the great writer is not the dullness of the ordinary; it is deeper, more intense, more virulent, and often more persistent."[63] The final paragraphs were about his father's death. In the galley proofs (June 1913), they read:

Politics, however, drew [G. H. Moore] away from Moore Hall again; the horses were sold and he went to England to compose speeches in the morning and deliver them in the House of Commons at night. But, as if determined to save him from becoming a dull parliamentarian, his tenants rose against him, declaring that they would not pay rent, and he went to Mayo to fight the first Rent Campaign. I remember the night he went away, and how he returned from the front door to give me a sovereign. He died killed by his tenants, that is certain; he died of a broken hear[t], perhaps by his own hand. My brother gives a letter which seems to point to suicide, and I would wish that this were so, for I like to think of my father dying like an old Roman, [*sic*] The facts are these. When his vlet [*sic*] came to call him in the morning he was breathing heavily, and when he called again my father was dead. His tragic death was the admirable end of a brave life, and in my brother's book he appears to me as wonderful as any character invented by Balzac or Turgenev.

IV

It seems to me that we have no cause to regret that he died in the year 1870, for if he had not died then what would have become of him? The anti-rent campaign would have brought him to utter financial ruin and might have caused his defeat at the poll in the next election, and this last blow he could have hardly survived. Nor were these the only misfortunes that awaited him. I awaited him – my unwillingness to learn anything, to go into the Army, to take up any profession that seemed to offer a reasonable career. I can see now the great trial I would have been to him for many years. He would have had to wait a long time for my novels and it may be doubted if any of them would have seemed a sufficient recompense for the years that preceded their publication, though he always used to say that even a very bad novel inspired in him some feelings of admiration, so difficult did the art of story-telling appear to him. He used to say that he could not understand how anybody could know how servants talked in the kitchen and in the pantry.[64]

The earlier draft that was sent to Maurice in May contained the sentence, "I am glad my father died without the help of sacraments." GM's cover note was apologetic: "If it doesn't please you I'll withdraw it, so no harm is done." Maurice did not like anything about it, but he found two parts of his brother's preface absolutely unacceptable: the faint insinuation of suicide and the assertion that his father died without the sacraments. Writing from Paris, GM cut the latter assertion ("it was wrong – it was bad literature"), but kept much of the rest as it was. Maurice remained unsatisfied: even if GM did not assert suicide, he invited inferences, loose talk. On 26 May, writing from the Hôtel Brighton, Paris, GM explained he was sorry about the whole preface: the best thing in it was the defense of dullness, "and that you don't like." "The irony of the passage . . . is not directed against you but Lord Morley and writers of biographies of Prime Ministers. I am a little tired of this perpetual controversy."[65] Still, he spent further time with the preface, and "left nothing in it to which you could possibly object." GM sent the revised copy directly to Laurie with instructions to pass it to the printer at once.[66]

GM returned to Parisian entertainments. He aestheticised with Dujardin about "Jesus, Wagner, and Dukas."[67] On 2 June, he was in good form at a party at Blanche's house, surrounded by paintings of famous people all painted by Blanche, and by books all dedicated to Blanche. There Carl Van Vechten met the "extraordinary person":

He called D'Annunzio a "hair-dresser," and said that he knew just what brushes and scents to use – There was a widow at the luncheon – a femme du monde – and turning to her he said, "How are you enjoying your widowhood?"!! And he once referred to his impotency in the most careless manner possible.[68]

Moore did not return from Paris until early June, just before Maurice's scheduled trip to Ireland. Maurice, still agitated, then came to Ebury Street with proofs of the preface, and found his brother with a scholarly friend and helper, F. M. Atkinson. Atkinson suggested a satisfactory alteration in a troublesome passage. GM cut the whole of the final paragraph – including the expression of filial guilt, "Nor were these the only misfortunes that awaited him [had my father lived]. I awaited him" – so that the preface ends with the praise (there was none higher for GM) that in Maurice's book, their father appeared "as wonderful as any character invented by Balzac or Turgenev." The amended preface still employed the word "suicide," though more cautiously than hitherto:

> My brother gives a letter which, I should like to believe, points to suicide, for it would please me to think of my father dying like an old Roman. His valet told me that he was quite well the day before; when he came to call him in the morning he was breathing heavily, when he called again my father was dead; and this tragic death seems the legitimate end of a brave life, and in my brother's book he appears to me as wonderful as any character invented by Balzac or Turgenev.

"I will give the proofs to Laurie," Maurice said, taking his leave, "and the book can now go through."[69]

Once in Ireland, and after talks with cousins and his sister, Nina Moore Kilkelly, and perhaps even with Oliver St John Gogarty, Maurice began to believe once again that GM had asserted that his father had committed suicide, rather than that GM "should like to believe" that he had done so.[70] He telegraphed Laurie to have a slip inserted over the first page of the preface, reading, in large print: WHAT THE PREFACER WRITES REGARDING THE MODE OF HIS FATHER'S DEATH MUST BE TAKEN AS EXPRESSING HIS WISHES, AND NOT THE FACTS. On 17 July 1913, GM opened a freshly arrived copy of *An Irish Gentleman* with a sensation akin to, if less than, the shock Maurice experienced on first reading *Salve* ten months earlier. It was the first George had heard or seen of the erratum slip. He instantly supposed that Maurice had inserted it in order to "get up a controversy" that would sell the book. "I cannot think of a more disgraceful proceeding," Moore wailed. It is a strange protest from the past-master of controversy and an artist in disgraceful proceedings.

Perhaps Maurice should have waited a day before answering, but he did not. His letter is neither suave nor clear-headed, yet, after much muddled defensiveness, he gives their ailing relationship the final stroke:

> I do not know if it is wise to make any answer to this sort of letter or the two last because I feel that silence and separation have become the only modes of possible life. The kindly good-natured George that I knew for fifty years is dead; for that George I still feel the same affection; the same gratitude for many kind actions. But for the altogether different person who has grown out of him, since about the period of Augustus's death [December 1910], or a little before, & who has inflicted on me so many unkind and unbrotherly blows, my feelings could not be the same. Prosperity & exaltation alter certain characters, & so I suppose it must be.[71]

GM answered with what, inferentially, must have been a moderate letter asking for further explanation (now lost), and Maurice went halfway to an apology –

his erratum slip was, he admitted, "merely a repetition of your words & . . . perhaps unnecessary" – before he turned and charged in full battle. Was it brotherly or even friendly of GM to do the following: (1) To walk into Sir Thornley Stoker's, and finding his own nephew there, to say to Lady Stoker in a theatrical voice, that he could not stay in the same room with a papist? (2) To break the entail G. H. Moore had made for Moore Hall, on all his sons in order of age (by which the property would have come to Maurice at GM's death)? (3) To write a book "ridiculing his brother & insulting his children"?[72]

Moore mentioned by reply that he had been generous in the past, even the recent past, but he did not explain that the change in the Moore Hall entail was by the advice of a lawyer and not his own initiative. To do so would have been of no use, for in principle he should then behave, and should have always behaved, as if there were no question as to who would inherit Moore Hall – regardless of the language his nephews spoke or the religion they practiced. Weary, wrong, and wounded, Moore accepted Maurice's grim proposal of "silence and separation."[73] With that separation, feelings on both sides hardened. Maurice had nothing to say to George, but much to say about him to others. George's heart was locked shut, bound in ice and fire. He barred Maurice from further use of Moore Hall. Ultimately, he rewrote his will so that none of his property went to Maurice, or to the sons of Maurice; the bulk of it was left to his sister Nina Moore Kilkelly, whose children were no less Catholic or English-speaking than those of Maurice.

The whole story is a terrible one. George and Maurice loved each other as much as any two brothers.

5

In the fall of 1913, Moore was bringing *Vale*, the final volume of *Hail and Farewell*, to its close. So much of his life had been given to the work, so much had he sacrificed to it, that he was sad to see it pass from his hands and into print. In his bleak, skeptical manner, he wrote Magee on 17 October: "*Vale* is nearly finished; only a couple more chapters to revise and what I am afraid I must regard as the most important work of my life will be finished. The word 'important' seems a ridiculous word. As if anything we could do could be called important! We die regretting that our ill-luck has come to an end."[74]

In order to keep up his courage while writing, Moore always relied on the approval of women. He would read to a favorite female friend the chapters as they came. In late 1913, he asked Nora Robertson, a friend from his Dublin days, if she would allow him to read her the last chapters of *Vale*, those about his final visit to Moore Hall. "A reading is a great help. It will take two evenings to get through them, an hour each evening after dinner."[75] Later, she described for Joseph Hone why she always had time for George Moore: "His interest in women was quite genuine . . . He was obsessed by his ugliness when he was

young & he told me how astonished he was when he found women were interested in him. He had always been the ugly duckling of the family . . . Women
were attracted to him, I think, because they felt he liked & understood the somewhat cramped position of women at that period . . . He was very sympathetic
to the suffragettes . . . That is all of much more importance than his little
vanities as a lady killer."[76] The profound insecurity inspired in little George
Moore by his mother's thinking of him as the backward, ugly one among her
sons never left the grown man.

By 11 December, he had sent his manuscript off to the printer. His old friend,
the wealthy Lord Howard de Walden, invited Moore to Chirk Castle in Wales
for the Christmas holidays. The efforts made to entertain the children, both
by the parents and the "numerous servitude," astonished Moore: "children
have a much better time than they used to have when I was a child." "But," he
admitted to Sylvia Gosse, "since I was seventeen I've done very well."[77] The
Gosses had also invited Moore for Christmas, and he began to write out his
greetings to each of them – Edmund, Sylvia, Tessa . . . – and then broke off,
"Indeed, I love you all very much." Left to search elsewhere for the comforts
of family, the lucky man found others to take him in.

6

Writing from Chirk Castle, Moore had made a date to see Lady Cunard in
London on his return (3 January 1914), but she stood him up: "you feared you
mightn't be amused all the while, and of course life is intolerable if it be not
always *at concert pitch*," he complained, with a snap of his alligator tail at conductor Beecham. He had wanted to see her because he was "going away to Syria
next month to see a monastery among other things, and perhaps to come
back."[78] His feelings were hurt, and he plunged himself into his next big project
– an epic prose narrative on the life of Jesus.

Before he could think of getting away to Palestine, he had some trouble on
his hands from Augusta Gregory. E. V. Longworth, whom Moore had known
ever since the Irish Literary Theatre dinner at the Shelbourne in May 1899,
had been going through the proofs of *Vale* and striking out sentences that might
result in libel actions, and Moore often took his advice – though he refused to
delete the confession of his own impotence, as without it the book would be
"nothing at all." Longworth, however, failed to scotch every source of trouble.[79]
Augusta Gregory had been horrified by the portrait of herself in "Yeats, Lady
Gregory, and Synge," the chapter appearing in the January issue of the *English
Review*, right on the heels of her self-promotional *Our Irish Theatre* (issued in
late 1913).[80] Utterly intolerable was GM's description of her as an "ardent soul-
gatherer" in her youth. Gregory rushed off a letter of remonstrance to Sydney
Pawling, Heinemann's editor. In fact, Gregory's mother, Frances Barry Persse,
had been a half-mad evangelical, and she had brought her daughters on visits

to the poor and sick.[81] Gregory's neighbor Edward Martyn was only repeating county gossip when he spoke of her behind her back as "the Old Proselytizer." Yet when Augusta protested to Pawling that she herself never read the Bible to Catholic tenants, she was telling the truth. From childhood Gregory loved the Irish peasantry and shuddered at her mother's Calvinism. She grimly explained to Pawling that it would damage her position as a director of the Abbey Theatre to be known as an "enemy of the Catholic faith," a "proselytizer," so she could not allow the statement to be repeated in the book version of the chapter.[82]

GM's riposte caught up with Gregory at her sister's townhouse at 22 Dominick Street, Galway City. He only meant to banter, he fibbed; it was terrible to learn that she had been persecuted for trying to convert Catholics. As a convert himself, "of course, proselytizing is to me a virtue."[83] He would be happy to rewrite the passage and send the revision to his American publisher. She then announced steps to go public with news of her victory by sending her letter of remonstrance to the English and Irish papers with a note claiming that Moore had "withdrawn the charge."

Not so fast, Moore warned Gregory in his 15 January reply. He wished she wouldn't write to the papers. Then as a man of letters he would have to reply, and that would "bring about an endless controversy, and will do you no good. I am an old controversialist and it seems to me you give yourself away in every sentence." A vision was opened to her of herself in the public stocks. Anyone who ever had a reason to dislike her, or even no reason at all, would join in the festival of abuse. She would try to defend the honor of her family, a family that was not altogether honorable, while Moore, conducting his side of the controversy from the lofty position of art, took each step with the advice of a solicitor. It would be awful. She admits, he warns her, that Mrs Persse and Augusta's sisters read the Bible in cottages, while she herself offered only "practical help" – "This will be read by [D. P.] Moran and his like that while your mother and sister read the Bible, you distributed tea and sugar." No, if she wished to write to the papers, she should just say, Moore advised, "I did not read the Bible, I did not seek to convert anybody," and then threaten anyone impugning that statement with a lawsuit. Moore apologised for not signing the letter – "but I must rush away to an appointment with my solicitor."[84]

Before going abroad, Moore rewrote page 217 of the first English edition of *Vale*. He gave Gregory's own reason for being against soul-saving (to take away people's childhood religion may undermine their whole relationship to God), but he insisted her mother was right: "we must not acquiesce in what we believe to be error." His real dart remained: Lady Gregory had the attitude at the Abbey of a cultural missionary who wished to take care of the souls of a childlike people, bringing them the benefits of her higher civilisation.

That business behind him, Moore put Magee to work at the National Library of Ireland, and Miss Gough at the British Museum, hunting for maps and travelogues of Palestine, so that he could read up for his journey.[85] Moore had been reluctant to make the trip to Palestine, but Elizabeth Aria (James Davis's sister) encouraged him to go, by saying that if he did not go at once, by the following year he would be too old to go at all.[86] He asked various people to come along, including Joseph Hone, before W. F. Bailey, the Land Commissioner in Dublin and a world traveler, agreed to come as "guide and mentor."[87] On 8 February 1914, Moore dined at the Gosses' along with Max Beerbohm and Robert Ross, and sat for a crayon portrait by E. S. Klempner on the 14th to go with the *Evening News* interview about his trip and new book. Lady Cunard and Nancy both made visits to wish him goodbye.[88] The sixty-two-year-old novelist then set out on 19 February 1914 to catch the SS *Macedonia* at Marseilles, taking along *A Sentimental Journey* as ship-deck reading, and, once embarked, regretting he was not, as Sterne had been, on board "a felucca, lateen-rigged."[89]

En route, Moore was full of a desire to talk of pagan goddesses rather than Bible stories – Dido, Medea, Proserpina, and Helen of Troy all showed up in his epistolary fantasia to Lady Cunard (and which goddess was she most like: abandoned mistress, witch, raped girl, or stolen wife?). He complained to Gosse that "nobody on board has the faintest idea of conversation." A passenger on deck remarked, "We should pass Sicily tonight." In reply, Moore asked if that was not the place where Proserpina was raped by Pluto while trying to gather asphodels. The passenger, more up on newspapers than ancient classics, replied that recently "a far worse fate had befallen a child in Paris."[90] Arriving in Joppa from Port Said, Moore was amazed at the rags worn by bedouins, the camels, and all the shops in which Nancy would love to linger if she had been traveling by his side.[91]

What Moore most wished to discover was a cave near the Dead Sea that might once have been inhabited by Essene monks in the time of Jesus, a location out of which his own Jesus would come to be baptised by John, and to which he would return after not quite dying on the Cross. GM made the journey from Jerusalem to Bethany to Jericho and into the Negev desert beside the Dead Sea – twelve hours in the saddle – finally along narrow mountain paths astride a mule, through "rubble, rubble, rubble," terrified that the mule would slip and they would both die.[92] The author, from a family of historic horsemen, wrote fondly about this mule in *The Brook Kerith*, where Joseph of Arimathea travels a similar road. Joseph had a great admiration for "the mule's sagacity," "a wonderful animal truly," as it led the way and gave no heed to Joseph's pulling on the reins, but climbed a bankside like a goat, and then from the slope "slid into the path almost on its haunches."[93]

At last, Moore wrote Eliza Aria, he had been led to what he had long imagined:

> I rode day after day before finding the monastery, passing by it again and again, but a wonderful monastery I found perched between a cliff and a cliff in the Brook of the Chariots, a chasm a thousand feet deep. A path three feet wide

winds round the abrupt cliffs under overhanging rocks and down ragged loose places where a horse slips along the edge of the precipice. I spent two days in this monastery one leg hanging over the edge beseeching my eyes to remember the ledges, fissures, caverns and projecting rocks, which I would never see again.[94]

It was Moore's luck to happen upon a cave near to, and very much like, those at Qumran, nine miles from Jericho, where the Dead Sea Scrolls were found by a young bedouin in 1947. Coins excavated at the site show that a sect flourished there in a period inclusive of the lifetime of Jesus; i.e. from 135 BCE to 68 CE. Among the scrolls found at Qumran are biblical commentaries by writers who believed they were living in an age foretold by the Prophets, the age of the imminence of the Messiah. These writings are cut from the same cloth as the teachings of Jesus. They amplify what was written in ancient times about the Essenes by Josephus, Philo Judaeus, and Pliny the Elder, Moore's own principal sources of knowledge.[95] Moore's picture of the Essenes – those athletes of virtue – has an uncanny accuracy: the Teacher of Righteousness (in *The Brook Kerith*, "the President"),[96] the long initiation period, the habits of bodily purity, the simple, strict code of laws, the solar basis of daily life, and the allegorical readings of the Hebrew Bible all appear both in the scrolls and in *The Brook Kerith*. The similarity is largely due, of course, to the pages from ancient authorities that inspired Moore, along with his vision of the caves beside the Brook of the Chariots, but he brought the sure instinct of a novelist to both texts and landscape. He returned to London (via Paris) in April full of excitement.[97] He had a great scenic narrative in his mind.

On 2 May 1914, already in full spate of composition, he was held up for want of a few facts about Arimathea, so he asked Assistant Librarian Magee to locate the ancient village for him – was it near Moab?[98] Joseph of Arimathea – known in the Gospels only as the man in whose tomb Jesus was laid after the Crucifixion – was to be the key stroke of genius in Moore's narrative. The first half of the book is seen through his eyes. Moore figured him as a young Marius the Epicurean of the biblical lands. The sensitive only child of a wealthy, pious Jew in the fish-salting trade, Joseph is by nature celibate and contemplative, faith-hungry yet skeptical. Somewhat like the historian Flavius Josephus, Moore's Joseph of Arimathea investigates the beliefs of Pharisees, Sadducees, Essenes (in whose monastery he first lays eyes on Jesus), and Alexandrian Platonists before encountering Jesus the wonder-worker and preacher. The new Messiah has worked his spell on the fishermen who work for Joseph's father – James, John, and Simon Peter. Joseph himself almost becomes an apostle, but Moore, turning his novel into an elaborate midrash, identifies him with "the rich young man" in the Gospels who is told to sell all that he has and give it to the poor, and with the young man who would take leave to tend to his ailing father, only to be told by Jesus: "Let the dead bury their dead." Joseph loves his kind, doting father, so he returns home and gives up hope of being an apostle. Going back

into trade after the recovery of his father, Joseph befriends the cultured ruler
of Roman Palestine, Pontius Pilate, and thus, within a few years, is able to rescue
the body of Jesus from the Cross for burial. Late that night, to Joseph's astonishment, the body shows signs of life. So it is in his house, and under the care
of his woman-servant, that Jesus is returned to health, and ultimately to the
Essene monastery. Shortly afterwards, Joseph himself, under suspicion by the
Sadducees because of the disappearance of Jesus from the tomb, is murdered
in the streets of Jerusalem by a Zealot. Through his inventive handling of the
character of Joseph, Moore was able to lay out the many sects and schools of
thought in Palestine, win the reader over to a human and Judaic point of view
on Jesus, and lead up to his criticisms of the antipathy to property and family
in the teachings of Jesus.[99] Moore's conception came to him quickly, but it
would take a year of hard work before he had completed the first draft, and
another ten months – until March 1916 – would pass in repainting, touching
up, and lacquering the finished work.[100]

7

In the spring of 1914, Honor Woulfe wrote Moore from Waco, Texas, alerting
him to the date of her visit that summer to London; she had paid him a call in
late January of the previous year. On that earlier occasion, GM attempted an
intimate line of conversation, which she was pleased to sidestep.[101] In the meantime, *Smart Set*, H. L. Mencken's magazine, asked Moore for a story – something indelicate, told with delicacy – and Moore's imagination had run on to
Honor Woulfe's visit years ago to Dublin.[102] She had once told him of "a rich
young woman of Chicago" who went to Munich in search of a certain professor so that she might convey through her body his intelligence to the New
World. What if that had been Honor's mission to Moore? What if they had had
a child? And thus "Euphorion in Texas" was written. Yet it proved a shade too
risqué for *Smart Set* in the America of Comstock's vigilance crusade, so Moore
gave it to the *English Review*.[103] By July when Honor arrived in London, the
story was in the bookstalls, and it is likely that Moore read it to her.[104] She says
he was "obsessed with a determination to see it developed into a long character study," and tried to convince her she was the one to write it. For years
Moore had been intrigued by the possibilities of a half-imaginary, half-real
diptych, in which a man would write of a woman, and a woman of a man, elaborating a deep game of desire. Besides, he needed a literary sideline to amuse
himself while he toiled at *The Brook Kerith*. Although Honor did not take
offense at his having made use of her name, her state of origin, her physical
description, and her intimacy with him, she did not want to write a long, fantastical narrative about how she came to be what she was not: the mother of his
child. She liked Moore. As she explained to Hone when his biography was
going to press in February 1936, she did not recognise GM in the anecdotes of

Whistler and Wilde, Susan Mitchell and Yeats, as ignorant, gauche, malicious, or sexually inept; she knew another Moore altogether, a "kindly Moore," "tender and genial."[105]

Still, if Honor Woulfe wouldn't ghost-write Moore's story for him, maybe another would. Encouraged by Moore, Ernest Boyd, having recently completed *Ireland's Literary Renaissance*, made an unsuccessful effort at writing in the voice of Honor in 1914.[106] In the winter of 1915, at a dinner party at Mary Hutchinson's London flat, Moore came upon another prospect. He was introduced to a wealthy young Quaker from Philadelphia, James Whitall, who began by saying, "I've come from America with the hope of meeting you." This is just how Honor introduces herself to GM in "Euphorion." When Whitall explained that he wanted to write, but had no subject, Moore was ready to come to his aid. Like Honor, Whitall would be able to tell how Moore's novels struck an American admirer, made one intimately acquainted with the author's personality as it emerged, first one side, then another, in the telling of stories, and finally caused the truly devoted reader to risk a great change in life – to cross the sea, leave family and Church behind, for a splendid personal gesture. The day after Hutchinson's party, Moore called on Whitall to propose a collaboration on these lines, in which he would hold the cigarette and Whitall the pen.[107] On 24 March 1915, Moore had a formal contract drawn up spelling out their respective duties (GM would be an invisible but active partner; they would split the money; Whitall had until December 1915 to finish his story).

Both men did their best for over a year, well past the December deadline, and Whitall was driven to his wits' end by Moore's mind-games, but "How Literature Came to Texas" was a poor thing in the end. There were two main problems: Whitall was not a woman, and he was a proper, Jamesian young man, with no gift for the mingled preposterousness and ingenuousness the novel required. To Whitall's dismay, in October 1916, Moore quashed its publication on the advice of Pawling, Heinemann's editor.[108]

8

Vale received the best reviews of any volume of *Hail and Farewell*. The press, especially in America, wearied of crying scandal and began to justify the book's candor in the name of literature. *Vale* was "the history of a soul's pilgrimage," according to the *Boston Evening Transcript*, "as delectable as any in the treasuries of literature." It was a "brave book," the *Saturday Review* decided, and better than any novel by Moore, for "No single novel can give the full personality of such a man." For Americans, he was "the most interesting of living British writers."[109]

Yet the living originals of the characters in *Hail and Farewell* began to take their revenge. At London dinner parties, Yeats retailed as little-known gossip GM's published confession of impotence.[110] In March 1916, when *Vale* came out, Yeats was in Washington, DC, where Ernest Boyd heard him telling stories of GM. Even in his better days, Yeats sneered, "Moore has never had a love affair with a lady, but always with women of his own class."[111] The tide of ridicule was rising.

On 11 November 1914, Edward Martyn launched a new theater company, and for its inauguration he staged *The Dream Physician*, a satirical farce about George Moore, transparently named "George Augustus Moon," who was played by Thomas MacDonagh's brother John, made up to look like Moore. Moon is a pretentious old Mayo journalist who publishes verse under a female *nom de plume*, "La Mayonaise." Much is made of GM's having praised Sir Arthur Guinness's Ashford Castle in a chapter of *Parnell' and His Island* in 1887: "Toady patron of Peerage/He writes up the Beerage." In another scene, GM's secretary, "a wild-looking woman," kneels in front of him with a mirror, while saying, "Your genius is as great as your beauty."[112] Martyn's play was said by a few to be funny on stage; on the page, only a crude desire to hurt is apparent.[113] Although Martyn saw little of his old companion after the publication of *Hail and Farewell*, GM continued to show an interest in Martyn's well-being, anxiously begging Magee three times to visit Edward in Dublin during his 1916 illness, pay Moore's respects, and report back to Ebury Street.[114]

Martyn did not have the wit or literary skill to wound as he had been wounded, but of Susan Mitchell this cannot be said. In 1915, George Roberts, editor of Maunsel Press, offered her Moore as a subject for a monograph in his "Irishmen of To-day" series, which included scholarly, respectful books on Yeats, Russell, and Plunkett.[115] Moore was quite happy to be included. He did not at first suspect malice on the part of Mitchell, who had written a complimentary review of *Elizabeth Cooper*. That, however, was before *Vale* was published, with its insinuations about George Russell's domestic life.[116] Furthermore, Russell did not turn against Moore immediately. Upon publication of *Vale*, he still "[couldn't] help liking Moore in spite of his bad taste."[117] Moore made a visit to Dublin in June 1915, and, on friendly terms with Russell and Mitchell, urged her to write about him frankly. Returning to Dublin a year later, he gave her the pages he had just written describing the bombed city after the Easter Rebellion because, he said, "you will find some bits that will help you."[118]

Mitchell was, however, finding all the bits she required from Yeats, Russell, and Maurice Moore. Over the past year, Maurice had been working with Roger Casement and Eoin MacNeill on raising and organising the Irish Volunteers, a "national" army of 150,000; the retired colonel became Inspector General of the troops. During his June 1916 visit to Dublin, GM ran into Maurice on the stairs of Plunkett House, at the top of which Susan Mitchell worked.[119] With a brother's insight into what would hurt most, Maurice had explained to Mitchell that in the case of George, "there was nothing nasty in him except his mind, he is a most respectable elderly gentleman" – in short, that all his love stories were lies.[120] Into a collection of facetious observations about GM harvested from Dublin talk, Susan Mitchell placed two theses: first, that Moore would not observe the difference between private life and published literature; second, that his own love life was fiction. "Some men kiss and tell, Mr. Moore tells but doesn't kiss," Mitchell wrote, repeating an epigram of Sarah Purser.[121] Yet it was a third remark that Moore elected to resent publicly. On the first page, she spoke of "George Moore, the little Catholic boy," and "the Catholic George Moore," along with an allusion to Wordsworth's "the child is father of the man."[122] To be called a Catholic by a woman of Protestant ancestry, when he never was a believing Catholic or a practicing Catholic, and had taken the most extreme measures to put distance between himself and Catholics, seemed to him a piece of wild bigotry, a social snub by someone who was in every way socially beneath him, except in the caste system of an old sectarianism, by which all Protestants were simply born better than any born Catholic. Though it was by means of drawing-room artfulness, she gave him the tar-and-feathers treatment for upstart Micks.

He was *not* being "sensitive to what is said of me," Moore exploded in a letter to Magee; it was just that "I don't like deliberate lies. I never was a Catholic boy, and I told them [Mitchell and Russell] so, and I know that the statement was made in the hope [of hurting?] me by D.D. [i.e. Russell] who thinks I did not appreciate his [torn away] enough in *Hail and Farewell*."[123] Mitchell's volume was an "absurd little book," not the full life-and-letters treatment he had expected. Truly, Mitchell's *George Moore* – as the first in the field – did a lot of damage where it most hurt, to Moore's lasting literary reputation. Later scholars often adopted both the scoffing style and the false notion that Moore's confessions were all fantasies.[124] Upon publication of the volume, Mitchell sent GM a letter "talking to me about her style," probably an ironic allusion to Moore's own characteristic justification of sin.[125] Her point was: See how he likes being the laughing stock. He didn't like it at all. Moore subsequently cut Russell once and for all. With the cloacal violence GM used when he was quite sincere, he explained to Magee that he was angry because the "Donegal Dauber holds up the little bitch's petticoats that she may do a pee on my doorstep."[126]

9

While Moore sank himself into the writing of *The Brook Kerith*, the war against Germany rocked London. Moore enraged Tonks with his occasionally affected opinion that, as a subject of conversation, his book was more interesting than the war.[127] As a contribution to the war effort, Tonks himself gave up painting to return to surgery at Hill Hall, which Mrs Hunter had turned into a place of convalescence for wounded soldiers. While GM continued in his habits of daily composition throughout the war, he was by no means neutral in his loyalties. He helped Peter Moore, the son of Augustus, get a place as an officer, and was very proud of his nephew for enlisting.[128]

At the end of 1914, Moore was drawn into public discussion of the war by his old friend, Kuno Meyer, then Professor of Celtic Languages at Berlin University. Meyer had published a manifesto in November arguing that Ireland should remain neutral until England was weakened, and then help Germany win the war by becoming the staging ground for an invasion. After its victory, Germany would give Ireland her Republic, if Ireland ceded to the German fleet control of the Irish Sea.[129] Meyer then went to America to propagandise among Irish republicans in New York and Chicago, at the end of his speeches offering the toast, "*A Dhia saor Eireann agus Almain* [God Save Ireland and Germany]."[130] On 8 December 1914, Meyer wrote a chatty letter to Moore from New York, speaking of the food, the climate, etc., and saying he had met Quinn and J. B. Yeats there, closing with an invitation for Moore to write him a "nice long letter" in return. GM smelled a trap: Meyer wanted to read out to his American audiences some expression by Moore of sympathy for Germany. Moore wrote a letter that was long but not nice, then published both Meyer's and his own letters in the January *Daily Telegraph*.[131] He himself owed a debt to France, he declared, so if France were fighting England, he should remain silent. Meyer in turn owed a great debt to England, and yet when war broke out between England and Germany he went straight over to America to stir up hatred against the country that had given him opportunity, money, and fame. Part of the antipathy Meyer was encountering in America, Moore wrote – every phrase like a hammer-blow –

> . . . may be traced to yourself; your audiences know you to be a traitor to the country that fostered you. I can respect the German soldier, the German officer, and the German spy, but I cannot respect you. Nor do I think that your own people respect the work you are doing or attempting to do. They pay you to do it, and are glad that you do it, but renegades, traitors, and apostates do not win respect even in the country that employs them . . . It is hardly necessary for me to add that I am taking leave of you forever, but not because of the German that is in you, but because of the man that is in you.

In April, Moore conducted an interview with the young American writer John Lloyd Balderston, who asked him, "What effect will the war have on Art?" None, because there would not be any more art, was Moore's discouraged reply. Throwing out a theory like George Steiner's in *After Babel*, Moore claimed that art depended on humans in one place imitating nature, or even copying one another's copies of nature, but not imitating the imitations of humans from another place. "If a shipload of Elgin marbles had landed at Yokahama in the 17th century, there would have been no Japanese Art." So much for international modernism. Anyway, Moore said, changing the subject, why was the USA preparing for war instead of fighting it? Why wait until England was defeated?[132]

One night in August, some weeks after a pleasant visit to London by Viola

Rodgers, the *Cosmopolitan* journalist he had met in Dublin in 1907, Moore leapt up from a dream in which he was fighting off an onslaught of German soldiers. "The light shining on the bedstead deceived me," he explained to Rodgers, "and thinking the bedclothes were on fire I threw myself forward to extinguish the imaginary flame and fell headlong from the bed across the hearthrug sustaining a pretty severe shock and breaking my wrist very badly."[133] Two months later he still could not write, but relied on dictation to continue composition.[134] Lady Cunard amused her friends with the story that she was proposing Moore for the VC, "on the grounds that anybody can be brave when they're awake, but to be brave in one's sleep is the *real* thing."[135]

10

While the characters of *The Brook Kerith*'s "mirrors to reflect Jesus," Joseph of Arimathea and his father Daniel, came easily to Moore, he struggled with Jesus himself.[136] At first, the more he studied the Gospels, the more the character of Jesus vanished into tables of legendary sayings and the different agenda of the four Gospel-writers. In April 1914, Moore began to "come over to [Dujardin's] belief that Jesus never existed on this earth . . . Stripped of his miracles, the Lord is a sorry wight."[137] In July, he was reading Paul's Epistles and Acts of the Apostles every day, and "discovering things in [them] which I did not know and which I fear others do not know; for instance, that Paul never looked upon Jesus as God – a divine appearance at most."[138] Only a few weeks later, however, Jesus had become real to Moore, as a shaping insight dawned on him: "Are you aware that Jesus was one of the most terrifying fanatics that ever lived in the world, that he out-Nietzsched Nietzsche in the awful things he says in the Gospel of Luke? . . . His spiritual pride exceeds any words but his own. How splendid his repentance, if I could only write it, not only for saying that he was God but for all his blasphemy against life, human duty and human love."[139] What blasphemy? Magee wanted to know. "For instance, that we must hate our fathers and mothers to be worthy of him." In Jesus, "great sweetness of mind and great harshness" are found in one person.[140]

How was GM to manage to create a character for Jesus after the Crucifixion, when he has been robbed of all his beliefs? First of all, Moore decided to introduce very few sayings by Jesus, and in those cases to create equivalents of the Gospel words. For instance "It is easier for a camel to go through the eye of a needle, than for a rich man to enter the kingdom of God" (Matthew 19:24) becomes "It is as hard for a rich man to enter heaven as for a cow to calve in a rook's nest" (it is better, he said, "to err on the side of homeliness").[141] In this way, he could match the style of late Jesus to his simulacrum of the early Jesus. Another narrative decision further simplified the problem. After the scourging and Crucifixion, his Jesus would enter a period of traumatic shock in which he said little, refused to think of the past, and lived for fifteen years mostly unto himself as an Essene shepherd in the hills. When he finally emerged from his silence it would be as a different man, so the problem of the continuity between the Gospel's Jesus and the novel's Jesus is both addressed and removed within the story. Finally, Moore realised that as soon as the aging Jesus does begin to rethink his relationship to God and life, he would have to do more than recant; he would have to go beyond his earlier thinking. In November 1915, Moore thought he had Jesus clearly in his sights. "In the first stage, [Jesus] perceived the futility of sacrifices and the Law – God is in the heart, etc. In the second, . . . after the Crucifixion, he saw God in the clouds and flowers and heard him in the wind. In the third stage (the night that Paul arrived), he realised that God must also be put aside – God is the last uncleanliness of the mind."[142]

What could Moore possibly mean by such language? Magee asked. Jesus learned from experience, Moore explained in December 1915, that "We go out to convert others with words of love on our lips, but we end up by cursing."[143] "Whether we seek a corruptible, or an incorruptible crown, the result is the same. We commit sin." Therefore, we must not seek moral victory over others. Morality is certainly a way to know God, and our only way, but God did not mean for humans to know him completely. As we cannot be sure of anything, we should be tolerant of others. One thing we can know – that God made the world for us to live in it, not to repudiate it. Moore suspected the philosophy with which he had provided Jesus was a Buddhist one, but did not know enough Buddhism to be sure. He did, however, know a bit of Schopenhauer and Nietzsche.[144] Moore's Jesus during his last twenty years traverses in swift steps the history of modern German philosophy in its own meditation on the Christian heritage.

Oddly enough, Moore enjoyed Paul. His Paul only affected to despise the sexual attractions of women. Eunice had been Paul's "thorn in the flesh," and Moore found a warrant in the Epistle to Timothy for allowing his readers to suspect that Timothy was Paul's son by Eunice.[145] Timothy is Paul's traveling companion in *The Brook Kerith*. Moore weaves his account of the meeting of Paul and Jesus into the story of Paul's final trip to Jerusalem as told in Acts 20–21 and Romans 15, where Paul causes a temple riot and is arrested. As a Roman citizen, Paul appeals from Jewish law to the law of Rome. At this point in the Gospel story of Paul, Moore invented an episode in which Paul, granted leave from prison while awaiting a ship to take him to Rome for trial, is pursued along with Timothy by a band of Zealots. Separated in the night from his dear companion, Paul finds refuge in a cliff-side cave with the very sect of Essenes that has for shepherd Jesus of Nazareth. To the Essenes, Paul seems a great complainer who loves to tell stories of his ill-treatment by Jews. He is irascible, slightly unscrupulous (all things to all men), and absolutely certain of his mission to preach life everlasting through the resurrection of Christ.

What Moore most liked about Paul was the adventuring side of his character. In a brilliant speech, Paul retells for the Essenes all the travels described in Acts of the Apostles and the Epistles. They listen enraptured, as if Homer were telling of the voyages of Odysseus, only Paul is both storyteller and hero, "the greatest traveller the world has ever known," one brother tells Jesus (who arriving late missed most of the tale).[146] The episode in which Paul hears from a brother that they know a man named Jesus – indeed, from Nazareth – and yes, crucified under Pontius Pilate – has an unsuccessfully repressed humor about it. And this from the supposed Messiah to Paul is too close to a joke: "'Christians?' Jesus repeated. 'Who are they?'"[147] But Moore rises to a grave simplicity in the recantation by Jesus to Paul:

> God has created the world for us to live in it, and he has put love of parents into our hearts because he wishes us to love our parents, and if he has put into the heart of man love of woman, and into the heart of woman love of man, it is because he wishes both to enjoy that love.[148]

Any kind of conversion, much less the one Paul has undertaken, seems wrong to Jesus, yet "It is natural to man to wish to make his brother like himself, thereby undoing the work of God."[149]

Paul at first thinks the shepherd is a madman who believes himself to be Jesus Christ, but later decides that it matters "not at all" whether the Essenes' shepherd is Jesus, or, furthermore, what the real Jesus did or said; the important thing is Paul's own vision. Sad that he cannot alter a course of events he himself had set in motion, Jesus offers Paul one last piece of advice: "There is but one thing, Paul, to learn to live for ourselves, and to suffer our fellows to do likewise . . . it may be that in years to come thy knowledge will be extended, or it may be that thou hast reached the end of thy tether: we are all at tether, Paul."[150] It is a good metaphor: one can see the tethers of other people, how their range of thought has a limit unknown to themselves, but one cannot see one's own tether, or know what is beyond one's comprehension. In *The Brook Kerith*, Moore extended himself as far as he was able, intellectually and ethically. Certainly, Joseph when he repents his celibacy for his father's sake, and Jesus when he repents his anger and failure to love his family, are both repenting that which Moore too had on his conscience.

II

With the proofs of *The Brook Kerith* sent to the binder, Moore went off to the Shelbourne Hotel in Dublin in June 1916. While seeing his friends (who were surprised to find him "very fat, all curves"), he wrote a series of articles for the *Evening News* giving his impressions of the ruins of the city after the Easter Rebellion.[151] He had thought *The Brook Kerith* might be the last book he would write, but those articles were to be the beginning of his next volume, *A Story-Teller's Holiday*. Another book was the only sort of holiday for Moore.

During his stay, Moore made the acquaintance of an author whose novels he had admired, James Stephens, then employed in the National Gallery.[152] A year later, when Moore returned to Dublin with a complete typescript of *A Story-Teller's Holiday*, Stephens, for a gratuity, "deftly improved [Moore's] Irish idiom."[153] Over the years, Stephens would help Moore again in this line (especially with *Ulick and Soracha*, 1926), and Moore in recompense tried to help Stephens too, with small payments, a flattering review of his poems in the *Observer*, and some manly advice.[154] Stephens was about to go to his first formal dinner party, and, according to his account given years later, he asked Moore's advice about what he should say to his female dinner companions. If Stephens were in England, Moore mused, he would talk of the weather, vaguely, then a few words on the soup, the meat, and, subsequently, the pudding. An Irishman usually talks of the cattle and the crops.

Ladies prefer to talk of the theatre and actors, especially the actors, and hats. So why not tell one woman how pretty her dress is. Then turn to the other hussy, and say that she is the most beautiful person in the room. Admire her rings: don't ask where she got them: never ask a woman where or how she got anything whatever; questions like that often lead to divorce proceedings. You may talk to them of their hair, their eyes, and their noses, but . . . don't say anything whatever about their knees. In especial, Stephens, do not touch their knees under any circumstances. The moment a woman's knee is touched, she knows infallibly whether a gentleman is really caressing her or only wiping his greasy fingers on her stocking.[155]

12

At the end of August 1916 the reviews of *The Brook Kerith* began to explode in the daily papers and the big monthlies. An enraged reviewer, Sidney Dark, started it off on 29 August in the *Daily Express* by denouncing Moore for resorting to "the scrawling of cheap impertinences [about] the divine personage." The style of the book, Dark said, was "contradictory, stilted, peppered with anachronisms, irritatingly mannered, blatantly vulgar."[156] On 31 August, Major-General C. Hardy proposed in the *Daily Express*, simply on the strength of the reviewer's evidence, that the Bishops of England should excommunicate Moore and the government should confiscate all copies of the book. Lord Alfred Douglas, Wilde's boy lover now grown into a married Catholic peer, took out a summons against Moore for blasphemous libel. The judge at Bow Street court refused the process by Douglas on 6 September because "it had been held over and over again that to assert in a book that Christ was a man and not divine was not necessarily blasphemy."[157] To Robert Ross (great friend of Wilde and enemy of Douglas), Moore confessed that he was "not altogether displeased by the prominence given to me and *The Brook Kerith*" in the daily press.[158]

To keep the pot boiling, Moore wrote a letter to the *Daily Express* accusing Major-General Hardy of libel. After the *Westminster Gazette* also crucified the novel on 9 September, Moore more amply, and mischievously, defended himself for making a man of Jesus. Renan's Jesus, GM declared, was nothing but an eighteenth-century *abbé*; Holman Hunt's figure of little boy Jesus in *The Carpenter's Shop* is better than the Jesus of Catholic prayer-books, that emasculated figure with a flaming heart and a lamb trotting at his heels, but Hunt's Jesus was still short of full manliness. Moore further asserted that the historicity of the Gospel of John was challenged by scholars of all sects, and that it was the only one of the four Gospels that firmly claimed divinity for Jesus. This less-than-emollient letter really excited the pedants, the preachers, the art historians, and the righteous of every description to have a go at George Moore. In the *Westminster Gazette* alone, sixteen letters were published over the next month about *The Brook Kerith*.

Yet meanwhile, in some highbrow papers and periodicals, the book began to receive the serious praise for which any author yearns.[159] On 14 September 1916 the *Times* called it "A Difficult Success": "this book is a tribute – there never was a stranger one – to the charm of Jesus." The *New Republic* titled its review, "George Moore At His Best"; Edward Garnett in the *Dial* said that as a drawer of character Moore belonged "in the company of Rembrandt." *The Brook Kerith* was "easily the most challenging piece of literature published in the present century," according to *Life*.[160] Finally, in November Moore got what he wanted: *Vanity Fair* acclaimed him as the best living English novelist. Music to his ears, and, with all the controversy, the novel sold 5,000 copies in the first month.[161]

13

In the autumn of 1916, Moore resumed the task of revising and reissuing his earlier books. *Spring Days* had already been presented in a fresh dress in June 1912, followed by *A Drama in Muslin*, denuded of some passages of "French" writing, smoothed out in syntax, and retitled *Muslin*, in September 1915. Over the summer of 1916, he reworked *A Modern Lover* as *Lewis Seymour and Some Women*.[162] In October and November, when *The Brook Kerith* controversy died down, Moore proceeded to make corrections to the 1904 edition of *Confessions of a Young Man* for the fourth edition, published in the USA in 1917. He then turned immediately to the task of bringing *A Mummer's Wife* up to the standard of his mature taste. Old Moore aimed to correct the gaucheries of Young Moore, and present to the world collected works of uniform expertise. With a copy of *Lewis Seymour and Some Women*, GM sent Gosse a triumphant note on 26 March 1917: "You wrote many years ago of my clever but imperfect novels and you wrote rightly – my novels were imperfect. Such however is the whirligig of things that I'm now sending you the only perfect stories in the

English language," as if perfection were the result of imperfections removed, rather than a greatness originally instilled.[163] Many readers obstinately preferred the works as they were first written, yet the regular reappearance of so many books by Moore did remind the public of the scope and significance of his work.

Upon publication of *Lewis Seymour and Some Women* in January 1917, a libel action was brought against Moore and his publisher by an actor with the stage name, Louis N. Seymour.[164] GM veered between delight and rage at this bizarre assault on his authorship. "Louis Seymour" had been a baby, and a baby of another name, when the career of the fictional painter "Lewis Seymour" was first traced in *A Modern Lover*. If the jury gave Seymour damages, Moore warned, then "A man called John Falstaff will be in a position to stop several plays,"[165] but after the Vizetelly trials, GM regarded juries as packs of lower-class animals, capable of anything when judicially solicited. The case was tried on 23 November before Justice Darling, with Sir George Lewis representing Moore. Lewis suggested that if Seymour won the case, he could next change his name to "Tom Jones" and sue the publisher of Henry Fielding's works, and thus begin to work his way profitably through all the great English novels. The jury returned a decision of no libel and no costs, but Moore and Heinemann had to pay their own costs, £275.[166] Disgusted by his brush with the public, GM resolved to "practise his art in dignified privacy," through subscription circulation, which was not subject to charges of obscenity, libel, or blasphemy.[167]

"It is very tiresome to have stories always in one's head," GM complained to Magee, but even in the midst of his massive effort at self-correction, fresh plots arose in his mind.[168] A passing reference in *The Brook Kerith* to Talmudic folklore about Adam's first wife, Lilith, bloomed into an enormous interpolation of Genesis 2–3, and parody of Books 9–11 of *Paradise Lost*.[169] For his own "Garden of Eden," Moore invented an aetiological tale to explain how Adam and Eve discovered the missionary position, a thing unknown to the animals and kept a secret by God.

In February 1917, GM set to work in earnest on other parts of what would be *A Story-Teller's Holiday*. In March, he remembered some of tales that he had long ago heard of ancient holy Ireland from Kuno Meyer, and that he had embellished for the entertainment of Honor Woulfe and other friends in his Dublin years. He couldn't now ask Meyer to refresh his memory, so he sought help from Richard Best, an Irish scholar in his own right: "And now another thing. Do you remember my speaking to you about two priests of ancient Ireland who were anxious to put each other to the test, and one said to the other he did not believe his fellow could lie with a woman with pointed breasts without sinning with her . . . I mention it just so that you may know the story. There were only a few lines and it would be kind if you would send them to me." While he was at it, Best might also write a synopsis of the story "about a man who lived in a tree" (Sweeney).[170] By 3 April, the premise of a test of virtue by sexual temptation had been carried over into a retelling of the tale of Liadin and Curithir. His mind was alive with the motif, and he recalled another tale invented in his Dublin years about a scholar in medieval times who comes to Ireland after travels in France. Couldn't Best give him some historical detail about convents and the sorts of mission holy men took? This traveling scholar asks for board and lodging at a convent house. The nuns, hearing of him as a man famous for chastity, test his virtue, one nun after another alone in his bedroom, giving him the temptation of the breasts, and the temptation of the thighs; they make him face them and feel them, but, exploring freely his body, they find him slack as a little boy – until the youngest, Luachet, discovers his humanity.

By 9 April, Moore had a frame-tale for his story-cycle.[171] George Moore, famous novelist, visits Dublin after the Easter Rising and then takes a train to Mayo, where he meets Alec McDonnell, a fern-gatherer and *seanachie*. The two men engage in a storytelling contest, the traditional versus the modern, with Alec telling the bawdy tales of holy Ireland, and Moore retelling stories from the Bible and European novelists – Balzac, Dostoevsky, and Turgenev. He thought of the book as both "poetical" and "highly sexed," his own version of Balzac's *Droll Stories*.[172]

GM did not have the stomach for the public outcry, and perhaps legal difficulties, regular publication of the volume would cause, so he issued the book privately by means of subscriptions. As treats circulated among friends, the stories were an immediate success. Arnold Bennett noted in his diary for 30 July 1917: "200 pages of George Moore's indecency, A Story-Teller's Holiday – very good."[173] On a weekend trip to East Grinstead with Heinemann, Gosse, and Haddon Chambers, Moore read his friends "The Nuns of Crith Gaille." Delighted, they thought it as good as anything Moore had done, and congratulated him on the decision that it be circulated privately.[174]

In November, though distracted and discouraged by air-raids on London – "the world will not be wiser or better whether I finish [the book] or leave it unfinished" – Moore decided to add another tale to the cycle, since the Dostoevsky pastiche seemed weak to him.[175] The new story was a solemnly told tale about a woman alone in the city who, at the point of starvation, dresses up as a man in order to get a job as a waiter, and thereafter goes through life as a man, a very lonely man, with nothing to live for but money. When well on in years and working in Morrison's Hotel, Dublin, "Albert Nobbs" is compelled to share "his" bed with a house-painter. In a midnight search for a biting flea, Albert strips down, and the painter, awaking, discovers Albert to be a woman. But so too it happens is the painter. She explains to Albert that to improve her lot in life, she left her husband and children, put on his clothes, and went to work. The solution to loneliness in life, Albert learns, is to take a wife; that's what the painter did. Albert's pathetic search for a wife among the cruel hotel housemaids is the core of "Albert Nobbs," one of the best

22. In William Heinemann's garden at Ockham (August 1917); George Moore, Edmund Gosse, and Haddon Chambers.

studies Moore ever made of "celibate lives" and a little-known masterpiece of the short story.

Unlike most of Moore's friends, Magee and Steer did not approve of *A Story-Teller's Holiday*. Moore defended himself to Magee: "In the works of every considerable author there should be an esoteric work. *A Story-Teller's Holiday* is mine. I should ask you why it is worse to write than to speak . . . Does the National Library contain no copy of Rabelais?"[176] Yet a vindication is neither possible nor needful for the book. Those scandalised by Moore will be horrified by the dulcet lubricities of the stories; many of those who like Moore will like *A Story-Teller's Holiday* very much indeed.

14

In early 1918, while writing the last parts of *A Story-Teller's Holiday*, Moore received a request to help a younger novelist whose first books he admired: D. H. Lawrence. Moore had already been of some little help to Joyce in 1916, by supporting his case for a Civil List pension; furthermore, he had given practical assistance to Magee, Stephens, O'Donovan, Robert Hichens, and many others, so it was not impossible he would lend a hand to Lawrence, especially as the younger man followed in Moore's path by trying to write in a grown-up way about sexual love among humans.[177] Lawrence had been a good student of Moore's work.[178]

Halfway through *Sons and Lovers* in September 1917, Moore contemplated doing an article on its superiority to the novels of James and Hardy.[179] At just this time, Lawrence was desperate to get his manuscript of a prophetic-philosophical sequel to *The Rainbow* published: difficult to do, as that novel had itself been suppressed for immorality. From Joseph Hone, Lawrence then learned that Moore was an admirer and therefore possible benefactor, so in January 1917 he sent a forthright request for help to the older novelist, along with the manuscript.[180] Yet just weeks earlier, Moore had soured on Lawrence, evidently having gotten his hands on a copy of *The Rainbow*: "Lawrence has lost his talent," he wrote Magee on 22 December 1917, "in philosophic and sex hallucinations."[181] Eight years later, Moore was asked by a newspaper interviewer if he was familiar with *The Rainbow*. "I read a page or two," said Moore, "I didn't care for it. Seems to me, about all there is to it is, 'she pressed him, and he pressed her, and they pressed each other.'"[182] Unsurprisingly, he detested the manuscript Lawrence sent, either an early version of *Women in Love* (published 1920) or perhaps even something in the vein of Lawrence's metaphysical *Psychoanalysis and the Unconscious*. Moreover, the landlord novelist did not much care for the graceless way in which the coal-miner's son thirty-three years his junior asked for a "puff preliminary."[183] A snub was in order. Replying with irascible promptness on 22 January, Moore spelled out his reasons for admiration of Lawrence's first two novels, then dropped this discouraging bomb:

> With regard to your later writings which you tell me, to quote your own words, are going begging, I should like to say that I believe some part of your difficulties may be attributed to your abandonment of the description of human persons with human fortunes for vague sensual abstractions . . . The poetry that attracts us in middle age is a poetry about things rather than ideas. Return then to your dahlias; I remember them much better than your ideas . . .
>
> If I may venture to criticize your writings in detail, I would say . . . I should like you to keep the classes separate. It is possible that miners' sons may retire into corners, while their mother is laying the kitchen table for supper, to discuss Shelley's poetry and Sarah Bernhardt. But it does not seem to me wise to introduce these incongruities into prose narrative for they destroy the atmosphere. I doubt very much discussion of Shelley's poetry and Sarah Bernhardt's French accent should ever find its way into English prose narrative, and if I feel certain about anything in this world it is that reapers from the corn fields should not indulge in aesthetics.[184]

"Every man is at tether," and Moore's tether shrank in his late sixties to narrow Tory conceptions of class.[185]

Moore's Toryism emerged in the second decade of the century as many Irish landlords threw in their lot with the rest of a declining British aristocracy. Just as when he represented himself with such zeal as a language enthusiast, an Irish Nationalist, and then a Protestant, Moore burlesqued the part of a Tory Unionist. In 1919, after the "War of Independence" got underway in Ireland

and the first Dáil Éireann was held by Sinn Fein (21 January), Moore wrote a series of four letters to the *Times* about relations between England and Ireland (17 April, 1 May, 8 July, 5 August). His leading idea was the same one held by Magee and many others: that the two countries belonged together as parts of European English-speaking culture. Yet Moore manifested this belief in a parody of the country-house crank. Since the Nationalist claim was that England and Ireland should be separate nations because they were separate islands, Moore proposed – with elaborate, old Tory fuss – that the whole problem could be solved by a channel tunnel. Nancy Cunard perceived, and richly enjoyed, this side of her beloved GM: "He would be funny without knowing it, pretty soon he would see how funny he must appear and then came some 'lively mumming' on top of that."[186] Moore's habit of playacting meant that he had to be approached, as Lady Connell said, "with circumcision."[187]

Moore made an amazingly crackpot proposal to the Prince of Wales at a dinner party of Maud Cunard's on 6 December 1920, only a few weeks before the Government of Ireland Act granted Ireland two parliaments, one in the north, one in the south. If the Prince would just go and live in Ireland for two or three months a year – the fox-hunting was excellent in Meath, and while there the Prince would just have to cast a few Irish phrases into his remarks – then he would reap an "unprecedented popularity," and "Sinn Fein would be sponged off the slate in three weeks or less."[188] This absurdity has to be seen in the context of the history of such absurdities. The power of the House of Lords to veto legislation had been struck down by Parliament in 1911, largely with a view to the passage of Irish Home Rule legislation. The effect of this change on the landowning classes in both England and Ireland was not only to make them less responsible for British government, but also to invite them to be irresponsible.[189] The titled people Moore moved among at country houses and in the salons of Mary Hunter, Lady Sybil Colefax, and Lady Cunard professed ever more eccentric opinions as the ordinary populace paid less attention to them. Moore's exhibition of such eccentricity delighted in its rage and irresponsibility.

For lines of argument that were sensible and constructive, Moore showed a fine scorn. His aversion emerged in his dealings with his helper in the preparation of his *Times* letters, T. W. Rolleston (1857–1920), a leader of the Irish Literary Revival in the 1890s and a moderate Unionist in 1919. The two men planned to issue their letters as a pamphlet, entitled *Ireland's Choice: Substance or Shadow?*, but ultimately Rolleston spoiled Moore's game by a stubborn show of earnestness: "alas Mr. Rolleston insisted in discussing Dominion Home Rule and as he would not give way I threw up the sponge. I did my best to persuade him that originality was not as disreputable as he thought but . . . to no avail."[190] Originality required having a minority opinion, even an opinion no one else would, could, or did hold.

In his August 1918 visit to the pleasant sea-coast town of Westport, County Mayo, GM did not make the ten-mile trip to Moore Hall: "the eyes of memory," he wrote Mary Hunter, "are best of all."[191] Living most happily in the past, Moore thought of Ireland simply as the setting for fantastical medieval romances, a place of love, nature, and narrative; modern republican Ireland was indigestible. Back in Dublin, the sixty-seven-year-old son of G. H. Moore discovered the place to be full of Sinn Fein "madmen." As a "confirmation of [his own] sanity," George Moore went to Phoenix Park, entered the Vice-Regal Lodge, and signed the Lord Lieutenant's visitors' book.[192] Perhaps he did not recall that in February 1885, George Moore had been regarded as too dangerous a fellow to invite to the Lord Lieutenant's dinner party; and perhaps he did – the wrong side was always Moore's side.

Moore's favorite reading had become *Imaginary Conversations* by Walter Savage Landor (1775–1864) – the work of a touchy old man who had seen many revolutions of the globe, and retired into staging courteous and scholarly conversations among the glorious dead.[193] Landor loved nature, and next to nature, art, but contemporary life is made to disappear in his writings. The lofty attitude of the dialogues appealed to Moore. He had already staged several "imaginary conversations" of his own in March 1916, in the form of interviews with John Balderston, written by Moore.[194] Two years later, he wanted to do something more perfectly Landoresque with Gosse, yet on seeing Moore's first draft, Gosse stormed: "You present me to your readers as a journalist come to interview you for some newspaper! This I absolutely refuse to allow you to do. You must not start by giving yourself *le beau rôle* and making me venal and ridiculous . . . Damn your infernal cheek! Don't think I am opposed to the scheme: it will be amusing, but you *must* behave like a little gentleman, or else I won't play with you."[195] Moore sulked at having his hand slapped, so Gosse said he was only chaffing.[196] The two proud old men of letters then collaborated with great amiability on two long "Imaginary Conversations," largely about the English, French, and Russian novel.[197]

Moore and Gosse each had a nose for the some of the more delicate truffles of literary history. One of the more capricious turns in their published talk occurs when Gosse, librarian to the House of Lords, tells Moore of a curious work of French eroticism he discovered while cataloguing a country-house library. Moore caps this tale with another he says was told him in Paris by Suzanne Lattés, opera singer and mistress of the Duke of Brunswick in the 1860s (GM actually got the story from Mallarmé).[198] The Duke composed a masque of love in which, dressed only in peacock's feathers, he promenaded in front of twenty-four ladies-in-waiting, who make up two choirs, soprano and alto. They sing verses of "Le Beau Coq" chorus after chorus, but fail to "instigate a whimsy in the ducal blood" or cause him to choose from the twenty-four, so they dance about him, plucking him slowly. Before the story quite reaches its climax, Gosse gets up to close the drawing-room window, and changes the subject.

Moore gathered his dialogues together with autobiographical writings he had published in periodicals since 1903 to form a new volume, *Avowals*, issued in

September 1919. Surprisingly, some leaders of the younger generation of writers were able to take pleasure in the way Moore's sensibility combined Young Turk, Old Tory, and French Dandy. Reviewing the volume in the *Times Literary Supplement* (*TLS*) Virginia Woolf noted that Gosse's temperate presence "brings out the fact that we are hearing [in Moore] the voice of a fallible, frivolous, occasionally aggravating, elderly gentleman who will not refrain from poking fun at the Athenaeum Club, or at any other object that takes his fancy." That the critic was not a disembodied, cultured Arnoldian impersonality, but a particular, fallible person, made *Avowals* for Woolf "the most delightful example of printed talk that we can remember to have met with in English." She admitted that Moore's critical judgements were "jealous and capricious" (he mocked James and Hardy), but at the same time she found them to be "penetrating and true."[199] Conrad Aiken was even more enchanted by the book: "It is my own feeling," he confessed, "that not in the history of English literature has there been a prose style so beautiful."[200]

15

Moore had one more big project left in him for the decade, which had already seen him publish nine new books and revised editions of seven others, a Balzacian rate of production. The idea of retelling in his own way the world's great stories made him wish he had added the tale of Héloïse and Abélard to *A Story-Teller's Holiday*. "A love that survived castration is very appealing," he wrote Magee on 19 July 1918, but "Abelard's didn't; an unworthy fellow else I should write the story."[201] By October, however, he had already begun to dream his way into the narrative, one that would place Héloïse rather than Abélard at the center. In November he had started Magee to work on research for him, the first of a team of assistants he employed on the project.[202] *Héloïse and Abélard* was planned on the big scale, an epical prose narrative like *The Brook Kerith*.

Moore worked himself hard through the spring and summer of 1919. He would not even stop in mid-May to sit for a portrait by his old friend, William Rothenstein: "Were Rembrandt to rise from his grave (I think) I should refuse."[203] He read medieval philosophy with F. M. Atkinson and Thomas Whittaker.[204] The boy who flunked out of Oscott also studied the history, architecture, and geography of twelfth-century Europe. He took a break in July to visit Viola Rodgers and to retrace the path of Abelard and Héloïse on their journey up the Loire valley to Nantes.[205] At the old fortress of Le Pallet (where Héloïse would give birth to Astrolabe, her son by Abelard), the local priest walked GM through the legend of the famous lovers.[206]

In August the progress of the story was again held up because Moore could not picture to himself a twelfth-century convent at Argenteuil (the school and final retreat of Héloïse), so he called for help to Virginia Crawford. As a former nun, author of *Fra Angelico* (1900), and translator of *The Legends of the Saints* (1907), Crawford had the intelligence and expertise he required; what is more, she had already worked effectively with Moore on *Evelyn Innes*, *Sister Teresa*, and *The Lake*. She was about to run as a Labour Party candidate for the St Marylebone Borough Council, so she could use the wages Moore offered.[207] At first, she wrote a description of the convent at Argenteuil, then Moore had her make architectural plans and drawings of the grounds as aids to his imagination.[208] Later, he called upon her to fetch Viollet-le-Duc's *Dictionnaire raisonné de l'architecture française du XI au XVI siècle* from the London Library and dig up a description of a dress for Héloïse. In the course of many letters and dinners, GM also used "Nia" Crawford as a sounding-board for his story. Whether Moore lured her into the complexities of psychological reenactment of the story under composition, as he had done with *Evelyn Innes*, it is difficult to say. On 26 January 1919 (six months before Crawford became deeply involved in collaboration), Moore had written Magee:

> Tomorrow I take a large batch of "copy" [for *Avowals*] to the publisher and tonight a really beautiful woman is dining with me. She dined here once before and did all sorts of delightful things to me after dinner. May she do them all again tonight. So today and tomorrow, collectively, is a red letter day.[209]

Crawford was indeed "a really beautiful woman," but, unlike Moore's mysterious guest, she had dined at Ebury Street more than once before. The woman who came that night, and what she did for Moore and to him, remain unknown. To judge from the character of GM's surviving letters from this period, he treated Crawford during the composition of *Héloïse* as a friend whom he regarded tenderly and respectfully, and from whom he expected patience and good workmanship, and no more than that.

In late August, Moore took time out for a drive into Sussex with Lady Cunard in order to visit Nancy, married in 1916 and already separated from her husband, Sidney Fairbairn. Nancy's houseguest was St John Hutchinson, an eminent barrister and husband of Mary Hutchinson, herself the mistress of Clive Bell. Moore was also a friend of the Hutchinsons; he first began to visit them at West Wittering, near Chichester, in 1914.[210] GM feared Nancy might be in love with his old friend "Hutch," and his suspicions made him at first an awkward guest. Yet Moore softened as he walked in the garden with Nancy. He urged her not to publish her poems yet. He also reminisced about love adventures on his recent trip to France. On this hot August day, Lady Cunard did not soften; she continued to cut a figure as "a polished termagant," in Hutchinson's phrase. "Her Ladyship" scolded Nancy, "You have *no* sense, knowledge, or experience, and you have *no* plan of life."[211]

It was a bad spell in the relations of Maud and GM with Nancy, and relations between mother and daughter would deteriorate further, until Nancy broke with Lady Cunard in January 1920, and went to live in France. In his fictionalised memoir, Dikran Kouyoumdjian ("Michael Arlen") described Nancy as moved by a "profound contempt for the Conservative Party, the usages of society, rhymed verse, and her mother."[212] Lady Cunard neglected Nancy as a child, then, becoming aware of her grown daughter's beauty, she wanted to reclaim Nancy's company for the sake of her value as a social ornament and a tie to the children of the aristocracy. That, at least, is how Nancy saw it. Yet the daughter's fury with Maud did not spread to GM. Although impatient that he did not always grant her the liberty he everywhere else professed, Nancy continued to adore him. Just a few weeks after the awkward meeting in Sussex, she was staying at Lady Cunard's house in London. She sent for Moore, and he came at once. The two stayed indoors and talked of *A Mummer's Wife* (she was reading it), her ex-husband (GM understood her point of view), and Moore's recent love adventures – "G.M. was gross at moments, but most lovable; *never* have I liked him so well," she wrote in her diary of 7 September 1919.[213]

For the rest of the autumn of 1919, Moore's dictation of *Héloïse and Abélard* surged onward at 1,500 to 2,000 words a day. He locked his daily compositions away at night in a closet in order to prevent himself from rewriting until he came to the end of the tale. By November he had completed an 800-page typescript.[214] That was a signal to turn around and begin all over again, recasting everything in language more perfect, with incidents more smoothly and slowly flowing onward, like a broad French river.

In July 1920, proofs came from the printer and Moore rewrote parts of the tale in the margins (and paid £100 in penalties for author's alterations).[215] Beauty of finish was essential to him. Magee, one of his proofreaders, was instructed to strike out anything hackneyed or modern. The novel "should be written in 18th century English as far as possible – pure English."[216] The labor of self-correction told upon the old novelist, and though he wished to get "the right quality on every sentence," he had lost the hardihood necessary to hunt out his own imperfections.[217] On 11 October 1920, Moore was so weary he could not choose which was the better of two sentences describing Abélard, and sent them both to Gosse, so that his friend might make the decision. Moore finished his work, and work it was, in December 1920.

The book was hand-set, printed on handmade rag paper, bound in two volumes, and limited to 1,500 sets in England, 1,250 in the USA – a truly deluxe edition.[218] *Héloïse and Abélard* had been sold at two guineas each (and $15 in the USA) to subscribers even before it was written. In a 25 January 1920 "interview" for the *Observer* (Moore wrote it himself), he is asked if such a price is fair to those who would like to read Moore's books but cannot pay so much. Moore got on his high horse: "I am not aware that I am under any obligation to the general public . . . to supply cheap literature. To put it simply, the general public has never done anything for me," except, he added, to take him to court for blasphemy, libel, or obscenity. Those who write for a mass readership ruin their books, he said, by picking a subject that might interest 100,000 readers, leaving out anything that would limit the sale, and putting in anything that would increase it. In this way, "the public may be looked upon as the author of nearly all the novels published in England, the novelist is a mere go-between." Anyway, he concluded, one throws away cheap books once they are read; his deluxe edition can be reread, or resold to advantage "in six months . . . for twice as much as the subscriber paid for it."[219]

Moore was perfectly aware of the rapidly rising prices paid by collectors for his early first editions. Through Gosse, he had met T. J. Wise, the clever bibliographer who made a good deal of money by forging first editions of nineteenth-century poets. Moore would not have been party to these scams, but he would still have learned from Gosse and Wise how to play the market and keep a weather eye on *Book Prices Current*.[220] From *A Story-Teller's Holiday* forward, GM essentially manufactured rare, signed first editions as the initial state of his novels, so that he as well as the collector profited. Private circulation paid well: Laurie gave him a £2,500 advance on the English edition alone.[221] When the "cheap" (10s. 6d.) Heinemann edition came out in 1925, Moore received another substantial cheque. It was an altogether professional exploitation of his status in the book market.

16

Before *Héloïse and Abélard* could be put to bed, Moore had to settle the matter of a dedication. He wished to present this work to Lady Cunard. Several years earlier, she had begun to allow Moore to believe she would be pleased to have a book dedicated to her, but after he sent to the printer an inscription to her at the head of *A Story-Teller's Holiday*, she made him tell the printer to break up the type.[222] Next, he begged her permission to write on the title page of a single copy of *Avowals*, "To Maud, the incarnate Spring, whom I love as the goats love the spring";[223] whether she finally allowed him to represent himself in relation to her as goatlike is unknown. She didn't care for his words on the flyleaf of the 1920 edition of *Esther Waters*, so before inscribing another copy of *Avowals* to her, he asked her to collaborate with him in the phrasing of acceptable sentiments. It was a touchy business: anyone could pick up the book off the table at one of her political lunches, and she wanted something she could display. The following piece of grandiloquence was judged appropriate: "To Lady Cunard. Time, the arch thief, has not robbed me of my soul, my affection for you, dear Maud. Yours always, George Moore. October 30, 1920."[224]

Just two months later, Moore asked if he might publicly dedicate *Héloïse and Abélard* to her, "as it is written with more reticence and is probably as good as anything I have written."[225] Alarm bells went off at 5 Carlton House Terrace, and Lady Cunard made a date to discuss the matter with Moore at Ebury Street on Christmas Day. She let him know he could not say anything that might in the least provoke people to make "vulgar remarks."[226] So, writing in French, Moore contrived "a bit of eighteenth century gallantry." Cunard carried the draft to Lord Buckmaster, the Lord Chancellor, for examination. He advised caution. She told Moore he could print his epistle dedicatory, but not her name, so *Héloïse and Abélard* (1921) is dedicated to "Madame X." In "Dramatis Personae," Yeats sneered that Moore "wrote a long preface to prove he had a mistress in Mayfair"; Moore may also have written it to discover what love of him might be left in the heart of Lady Cunard.[227]

Moore's "mistress in Mayfair" is nonetheless to be discovered within the text of *Héloïse and Abélard*.[228] A brief episode is dedicated to a troubadour named "Gaucelm d'Arembert." He is still devoted to "Lady Malberge," though in late life he has become a hermit. In the bed of Lady Malberge, he first came to know himself. Although other women later captured his imagination, and other men hers, he never wavered in his love. He was thirty-eight when they met, and she was twenty and married. They spent ten years together. They chose never to marry because she accepted his Courtly Love conception "that love could not exist in marriage," but by "stint[ing] our desires to blessed adultery, our love shall last to the end of our lives." She was never faithful to him. Even when lying in bed by his side, she once asked his help in obtaining a young man – "Thou wilt help me . . . for I must have you both" – and then surrendered her body to him. With sorrow, he accepted the fact that "thou canst not be else than what thou art, and if thou wert else I might not love thee." That was years ago; now he lives alone. Lady Malberge's castle servants sometimes bring him presents. She too comes to see him on occasion, but she "speaks very little of the days when we loved each other, and methinks she cares little to hear me remind her of them." Still, he is glad he possesses her affection, and he continues to believe "there is little that I might ask that she would not do for me."

It was true that she would at least sometimes do a little for him. In early July 1921, she had delivered to Ebury Street a Worcester china bowl. Moore penned an effusive, self-piteous, love letter thanking her for the gift, a letter she kept. He signed himself "Gaucelm."[229] GM was revising *Memoirs of My Dead Life* at the time, and on the proofs of "Resurgam" he crossed out a generalised passage about the effect upon him of Maud's 1895 marriage and wrote in the following: "But from too deep thinking of her, a madness crept behind the eyes, and with it the thought came and went that to know I should never possess her sweet scented personality again, never again hold the dainty oval face in my hands, so that I might plunge my gaze deeper into her eyes . . . My senses grow dizzy thinking of her."[230] The real loss of his lover did not come once, with her marriage or with the arrival of Beecham on the scene, but again and again, a long slow defeated yearning, in which he never gave up and she never gave in. They were linked by a desire he would not let die, a past she did not wish to recall, and a daughter she did not acknowledge as his.

Chapter 13
Hardy, James, Conrad, and Moore

I

In March 1920 George Moore was brought face to face with the question of what would be the value ultimately placed on his work. He was confronted with a proposal from Boni and Liveright, the New York publisher of the Modern Library series, for a library edition of the collected works of George Moore, fiction and non-fiction. At first, Moore was "terrified" at the scale of the venture. All of his books would have to be revised and prefaced, as in the case of the "New York" edition of Henry James. Not only the labor frightened him. What if his life-works should prove unmarketable? "Yet Americans," he reflected, "are not looked upon as madmen."[1]

The Americans in question were Thomas R. Smith and Horace Liveright. Smith was the former editor of *Century Magazine* (1914–20) and present owner of one of the finest libraries of illustrated pornography in New York. Since 1915, Smith had acted now and then as Moore's agent in the USA, until Moore caught wind of the fact that Smith was selling GM's letters and manuscripts to rare-book dealers.[2] In 1918 Smith was hired as editor-in-chief of Boni and Liveright by Horace Liveright, a charismatic, big-spending, art-loving young publisher. Liveright wanted a big name on his list, and right away in 1919, after publishing a limited, signed edition of *Story-Teller's Holiday*, he told Moore that he wanted to publish a trade edition of a work by "the greatest living English author."[3] In 1920 Liveright's ambition had grown: he wished to publish a 21-volume library edition of the works of George Moore. One side of his proposal was that W. H. Heinemann would simultaneously undertake to publish a "Uniform Edition" for English readers. They too would get a chance to take the full measure of Moore as a writer.

When Liveright arrived in London on a buying trip in January 1921, he had a list of works he wished to publish that included all of Moore's novels and many of the stories and articles that had never appeared in book form. Reprinting everything he had ever published was the last thing Moore wanted to do.

Bound by Gautier's maxim that the correction of form is virtue, GM wanted to bury parts of his past, not dig them all up. A revised edition of "George Moore," the author-function, would still require, by studious retouching, the application of the sort of "finish" to past works that he now gave to his current pictures of life. Sometimes wholesale overpainting was in order, such as that which had turned *A Modern Lover* (1883) into *Lewis Seymour and Some Women* (1917). Absolute substitution was another alternative, as when he had replaced *Impressions and Opinions* (1891) with *Avowals* (1919); only the later book would be reissued in the Liveright collected edition. GM turned for advice to his old friend Edmund Gosse, who agreed that Moore was not obliged to reprint or rewrite works of which he remained ashamed – *Mike Fletcher* (1889) for instance, and *Parnell and His Island* (1887).[4] The volumes of poetry and *Martin Luther* (1879) should also remain as they were, best forgotten. Moore explained to Gosse that he even wanted to leave out two very popular novels, ones that Moore had revised again and again but could never bring into line with his evolving standards of taste, *Evelyn Innes* (1898) and *Sister Teresa* (1901). They were not, he judged, part of his development; they were dead ends. Let them be forgotten. Yet GM gave in to Gosse and Liveright, and permitted these two novels to be included in the collection for their interest as milestones on his journey; consequently, they were reprinted in the form of their first editions. All told, the forty titles listed in Gilcher's bibliography as published up to 1920 were reduced to twenty-one in the Liveright library edition.

Publisher and author also wrangled over the style of publication. Now an avid connoisseur of the book, GM wanted to stipulate the typeface, line-spacing, margins, and overall proportions of the library edition, so that the volumes would be reminiscent of eighteenth-century book production, not, as he judged Liveright's taste, evocative of "modern Ohio."[5] No agreement would be signed until Moore had seen a "dummy copy," the model for all subsequent volumes. Ultimately, Moore decided his strongest position was to allow the scheme to go forward without a contract, so that he could stop it at any time.[6]

Another stroke in the art of self-creation was suggested by Phyllis Williamson, Mary Hunter's daughter. She put it into Moore's head that an old drawing of Moore Hall would make an attractive decoration for the title page of the new edition of *Memoirs of My Dead Life*, under preparation for Heinemann in January 1921.[7] Phillip Selden did a woodcut from the drawing, and Moore, to complete the desired effect, added a hand-lettered list of subtitles in the style of the eighteenth century:

Memoirs
of My Dead Life
Of
Galanteries, Meditations
and Remembrances
Soliloquies or Advice to Lovers,

- with many miscellaneous Reflections
on Virtue & Merit
By
George Moore of Moore Hall

Tipped into this edition of *Memoirs* is a colored daguerreotype, oval, of the sixty-nine-year-old author as a boy of nine. His elbow against a chair, he wears a large flowing blue tie in a bow above a white collar that spreads over the top of his belted coat (see illustration 4, p. 15). What thoughts would one day run through that sweet little head looking out on the world!

On 20 January, before Horace Liveright left London, it was Moore's plan to use the woodcut of Moore Hall as his imprint for each volume of the collected works, and "George Moore of Moore Hall" would write eighteenth-century introductions for all of them. Once he got the idea of constructing his image as a classic, Moore characteristically went on to parody the antique and time-less style. It did not cause him any hesitation that he had not spent a month in Mayo in the last forty years, and had never lived, or wished to live, as Moore of Moore Hall in any practical sense of the phrase. After all, if Moore Hall was not the place he lived in, it was a chief fact of his identity. Furthermore, the landscape of Lough Carra had been the cradle of his imagination. The gentle lines of overlapping, receding mountains, and the gradations of shade – dove-gray stone, chalky-blue lake, and greens from dusty distant heather to reeds thinning out into the lake from the dark Derrinrush wood – gave him the sense of beauty by which he lived. So, while the Selden woodcut and the fanciful eighteenth-century prefaces did not in fact become part of the prototype volume, Liveright's edition was to be called "The Carra Edition" and Heinemann's became "The Moore Hall Edition." The translation of a lost way of life – West of Ireland feudalism – into literature was to be complete.

Part of Moore's value for Liveright was that he was reckoned to have been a bearer of modernist individualism, one of the first of the avant-garde since the 1880s, a writer who made havoc of middle-class Christian values, and who created books that were at once a critique of conventional books and a formal advance upon them. Now the proto-modernist looked as if he was to be bound up as the Last Victorian – though he himself wanted to signal that he arose out of eighteenth-century values, not nineteenth-century ones. The apparent con-tradiction between modernist art and superseded forms of social life was no contradiction for Moore. For him, Manet had been an aristocratic gentleman like himself; Degas too was a man of wealth and taste. Like their beloved Vil-liers de l'Isle Adam, they fancied themselves the last living sons of ancient families, unable to mate successfully in the modern world, and trying to make beauty out of the new, highly resistant material of modern life. The values for which they cared – will, love, beauty, masculine friendship, aesthetic individu-alism – had to be implied by satires of modern circumstance or by pastorals of the garden, the park, or the mind. The sadness, humor, and alienation in their works belong to a scattered people in free fall from a position in life that has vanished, their descent billowed by the steadily deflating balloon of inherited wealth.

2

At the end of January 1921, Moore was also attending to the shaping of his self-image in criticism. In March 1920 T. Werner Laurie – Moore's principal English publisher aside from Heinemann – wanted to pay someone £300 to write a biography of Moore. But who should do the job? Arthur Symons was GM's first suggestion. His old friend from the Temple in the 1890s "went off his head" after his 1904 marriage, but then "recovered his senses in an extraordinary way" (but not so entirely as Moore believed). Symons "would be the very man," Laurie was informed, for Symons knew "how to do a portrait" and "will not waste his time relating *A Mummer's Wife* and *Esther Waters* over again." Yet Symons, whom GM had neglected for years, refused.[8] Then Max Beerbohm? Nothing doing, although in 1950 Beerbohm did publish an insightful essay on Moore.[9] Gosse? But Gosse, always alert to the presumption of superiority on the part of his old friend, declined to follow up *The Life of Swinburne* with *The Life of Moore*.[10] Who then would write a biography, Moore wondered, that was not workmanlike and academic, but "a work of art" that "might outlast me"?[11] The next man believed to be right for that task was, extraordinarily, D. H. Lawrence. "Lawrence is not doing much and might be glad of the job," Moore instructed Laurie. "Write to him on the subject for it is quite in the cards that you may get a masterpiece – my life would furnish him with what he cannot invent – a story."[12] (Any reply made by Lawrence is unknown.)

So Laurie proposed on his own behalf G. K. Chesterton. "Chesterton is not the man," Moore snapped; he is "a Catholic, a firm believer in the power of the priest to turn God into biscuits and wine every morning."[13] W. K. Magee urged on Moore the claims of Chesterton as a writer, but all Moore had to say was, "He likes belching." Magee argued that this was not really an adequate way of judging the man's prose, so Moore added, "Well, he told me he did," and this caricature of Chesterton's Chaucerian acceptance of the body finally struck Magee as a possibly discerning form of prejudice on Moore's part.[14] On 6 April 1920 Magee had married an assistant librarian of the National Library in Dublin; starting a new family, he did not himself at this time come under pressure to become Moore's biographer, though he would be put on the spot years later.

The matter was finally settled after Moore, upon reading a general article on his works in the July 1920 *London Mercury*, invited its author, John Freeman, to come to Ebury Street to discuss writing a study that was more about the man than his books, and that gave full expression to the literary impulse of the biographer.[15] Freeman (1880–1929) was an occasional critic and a prolific poet, a "Georgian" like his friends J. C. Squire and Walter de la Mare.[16] This would be his first extended prose narrative. Once Freeman accepted the contract, Moore fed him from August 1920 through April 1921 lunches, books, and insights, and then exhorted Freeman to be original, but *Portrait of George Moore in a Study of His Work* (1922), while respectful, is arch, overwritten, pompous, and inexact. It would not be the book by which Moore wished to be remembered. Moore judged his life to be delicious material for a biography, if told well and frankly. Certainly, it had served as his own best subject. Yet the matter of a suitable biographer would have to await another day.

3

In February, Moore took time to write a review for the *Observer* of Nancy Cunard's first collection of poetry, *Outlaws* (1921). The great event of Maud Cunard taking up with Sir Thomas Beecham had never inhibited Moore from seeing Nancy; indeed, he saw her more often afterwards than before, either at her mother's London house, or, more frequently now that Nancy was an independent woman, at Ebury Street. For a man in his sixties and a girl in her adolescence, they took a uniquely serious interest in one another. On vacations from her French boarding school in 1913, she would come to see him; later, during her débutante seasons, she would give in to his curiosity and tell him of her beaux. He called her to come for a visit just before he left for Palestine in February 1914; he wished she had come along on the journey. As her own interest in literature grew after 1915, she urged him to reminisce about the poets he had known and the nature of the writer's life. In 1916, Nancy published some poems in the Sitwells' anthology *Wheels*. Moore feared he might have hurt her feelings with a letter of criticism, so he followed it up with a warmer expression of confidence in her talent.[17] She wanted to grow up to be like neither Sir Bache nor Maud Cunard, but like George Moore, a writer who believed in freedom from convention.

Nancy married Sidney Fairbairn in 1916, and that led to a hiatus in her relations with GM, though evidently not because Moore disapproved the match. As a mentor, Moore was more eccentric in morals than in art. Alone with a lover after the war, Nancy sat with the young man under a tree and read out passages from *A Story-Teller's Holiday* (1918), not every parent's choice of "Soliloquies or Advice to Lovers – with many miscellaneous Reflections on Virtue & Merit." On a visit to Ebury Street, presumably in 1919 while he was writing *Héloïse and Abélard*, Nancy listened to him philosophise about the strange forms that love has taken throughout history, "the Love Courts of the Middle Ages," for instance – "Well," he concluded, indeed, "one may be unfaithful and yet constant."[18] And Nancy was after her marriage to Sidney Fairbairn . . . unfaithful, that is. The two remained together only twenty months. She was an ambitious, wayward, original, and troubled young woman. "If I were [GM's] daughter," she confessed to St John Hutchinson on 20 July 1919, "it seems to me I should become quite a different personality and a much more contented one." But was she his daughter? Her friend David Garnett thought so. In his opinion, Nancy acted as if she were Moore's daughter (with "a proprietary quality in her devotion") and looked like him: both had the same delicate complexion, "like a white-heart cherry."[19] Both also had downward-sloping features, comical in GM's case, intensely sad in Nancy's.

On 21 January 1921, Moore sent Nancy a personal letter of criticism about the poems in *Outlaws*, urging upon her the necessity of recreating all experiences in the course of writing about them: "even the most subjective . . . the most personal to the poet, must be recreated." Nancy was part of the Sitwell and Eliot set of experimental, and often obscure, writers of free verse, yet for Moore obscurity was not permissible if it arose from "pale or weak thinking."[20] GM's review in the *Observer*, published 27 February 1921, was less stinting in its praise than his letter had been. In *Outlaws* Moore discovered "much more genius than in the mass of her contemporaries, and much less talent." By hard work, the author could acquire handicraft, tact, judgement; she should write over her study door: "The correction of form is virtue." Lady Cunard was displeased: she thought GM's review of Nancy's book should be *all* praise. Not possible, Moore replied: the review had to "read like a genuine expression of opinion."[21] Moore repeated the lesson to Nancy by letter six months later: "Many years ago a poet said to me, and his words have often been with me: If you go out and amuse yourself when you can't write, your art life will waste into nothingness. An artist's life is in this like an acrobat's, he must exercise his craft daily."[22] GM treated Nancy seriously as a writer like himself, one with the highest aims, and not as a socialite with a poetic pastime.

Moore had hoped to see Nancy in Paris in April (he crossed on 4 April 1921), but she had taken a house near Dieppe, and their meeting was postponed until August. In Paris GM breakfasted with Viola Rodgers on 5 April, then passed on to Dujardin's house in Fontainebleau. He desperately wanted Rodgers to come for a visit during his stay with Dujardin, and believed he had her promise to do so. Every morning he crossed the garden in his pajamas to the letterbox in hope of word from her.[23] Having finally made a date, Viola called it off at the last moment. Moore had already placed orders for their dinner with the fishmonger and the confectioner. He did not spare her a description of his disappointment and the trouble to which she had put him in canceling his arrangements.[24] Viola did not let him down on 28 April. Sitting with her on the shelving lawn behind the long house, the trees full of birds, and visited by a "suspicious wasp," GM sketched for Viola the stories he was planning to write for a new collection, *In Single Strictness*.[25] His plan was for five stories, all about "men who do not care for women, and women who do not care for men," in order to replace *Celibates* (1895) in the library edition.[26] It was for him a day of bliss, and afterwards he came to feel that he loved Viola Rodgers: "I have never met so sweet a woman," he would write her months later, "and there are times even in the midst of all this writing when my heart is full of love. I ponder your body and soul and would not separate one from the other so much do I love them." (She indicated after his return to London that she preferred that their relations should henceforth be platonic.)[27] Leaving Fontainebleau on 2 May 1921, Moore stopped once more to see Viola in Paris, then returned with a bad cold to London on a train with Dr Oliver St John Gogarty. Moore listened indifferently while the witty doctor recited poetry and offered medical advice.[28]

As soon as he recovered from his illness, Moore began to dictate the stories of *In Single Strictness*. On 22 May he lunched with Arnold Bennett, and after speaking ill of James, Conrad, and Hardy (GM's now inevitable ritual to cleanse the air of evil spirits), Moore told his host one of the new stories, "very good and Moorish," Bennett noted with pleasure in his diary.[29] Moore was just as pleased with himself, but nervous nevertheless. Once he finished the book of stories, and added it to the revised works for Liveright (the Moore Hall edition of *Memoirs of My Dead Life* was just then receiving its final polish), "my books will be all a uniform style, none sinking below a certain level." On 8 June 1921 he wrote Magee, his literary executor, that he might "one day decide where that level lies – above or below the villager (Hardy), the sailor (Conrad), or the eunuch (James)."[30]

This joke, which was never funny, the landlord (Moore) did not tire of repeating throughout his last fifteen years, in conversations, letters, newspaper interviews, and books. Moore had an acute sense of the fact that the canon of English fiction for his era would have room for no more than three novelists, and the three most likely to end up there would be James, Hardy, and Conrad. People like Ford Madox Ford might name Moore as one of four or five "British novelists of the first flight," but ultimately that might not be a high enough standing.[31] The door would shut on Moore; it would also be shut on many of his fellow-strivers in the craft of fiction – Gissing, Schreiner, Mrs Humphry Ward, Kipling, Stevenson, Lang, Haggard, Bennett, H. G. Wells, not to mention Moore's women friends, Gertrude Atherton, Pearl Craigie, Clara Lanza, Amelie Rives, and "Frank Danby" (Julia Davis Frankau). Moore had devoted his life to the treatment of prose narrative as an art form; he cared for nothing else so much. How could he release his wretched anxiety that in spite of his social superiority, all his labor, and what he knew to be the quality of his books, he would still be forgotten by most readers of the indifferent later generations? There might have been better ways to vent envy and terror than by mirthless jokes about Conrad, Hardy, and James, but that was one way, and his way.

At the end of July, Moore had finished three stories for *In Single Strictness* – "Wilfrid Holmes," "Priscilla and Emily Lofft," and "Sarah Gwynn" – and was preparing for the fourth, "Hugh Monfert," by planning an expedition (made on 1 September) to St David's in Wales for notes on cathedral arches and the locality.[32] It was crucial that he should finally get the Martyn story right, after, by his own judgement, getting it not quite right in *A Mere Accident* (1887) and "John Norton" (1895). This time around Moore had decided to take the leap and simply make the hero come to consciousness of his love of men. He introduces the Martyn figure to a pair that resemble Mabel and Aubrey Beardsley.[33] Hugh Monfert marries the sister of his frail, aesthetic friend, seeing in her something of him, but once married, Hugh is unable to act the part of husband, abandons his honeymoon, and confesses to his bride's father that he loves the son, not the daughter.

About five years earlier, Moore had come to William Heinemann with an idea for a great novel, one with an ending he now considered for "Hugh Monfert." After the wedding of two young people of distinguished family, the hero realises his impotence on the bridal night. He makes a handsome financial settlement on his bride and leaves on a sailing ship for a world tour. "On board he meets a plump little sailor-boy and lives happily ever afterwards. 'There,' exclaimed Moore, is a plot for you!'" Heinemann told him it was not the plot of a novel that could be printed in England. "Why not?" Moore exclaimed with guileful naïvety. "It is simply a modernizing of the Greek practice which pleased and thrilled the male and in addition gave protection to the innocency of the Grecian women."[34] This burlesque frankness of treatment would not be possible if Moore was to get away with his desire to publish "Hugh Monfert." So GM larded the story with detail about medieval literature and architecture (relevant to a book to be translated by Hugh and the sister, and illustrated by the Beardsley-like brother). The style Moore employed is archaic in diction and gravid in tempo. At the story's ending, Moore felt he "ran away from the subject," merely letting Hugh Monfert melt away in hints that the destination for his voyage would be North Africa, one of the haunts of Gide and Wilde.[35] After publication, he had a new ending printed on six pages and sent it to friends; the ending was also changed for the second (Carra) American edition published in 1923 in order to suggest more strongly that in Laghouat Hugh would accept a young Arab boy's offer of love. In the revision, Hugh comes to a great moment of insight:

> [He] was thinking that he had been given to his mother as an animal to a trainer. Ideas, principles, beliefs, he said, are lashed into us by our mothers, our fathers, by priests, schoolmasters, and our lives are spent going through our tricks, our antics, in fear and trembling, till the original wild instinct breaks out in us and we fall upon our trainers and rend them.[36]

Putting coyness aside, Moore for a moment was speaking not just for Martyn (who on this subject would never choose to speak for himself), but also on behalf of all his friends whose desire was outlawed – W. L. Courtney, Max Beerbohm, Robert Ross, and many others – and no doubt Moore was defending some sympathetic instinct in himself too, though ever so indirectly and inexplicitly. The story in each published form was padded successfully as far as reviewers were concerned: the *TLS* praised Moore for handling the theme without satire or prurience; the *Fortnightly Review* approved its "unexpected gentleness and sympathy."[37] As a story, it wins three cheers for discretion, two cheers for bravery, but only one cheer for literary merit. Eventually, Moore dropped it for the Uniform Edition of *Celibate Lives* (1927) (revision of *In Single Strictness*). Martyn himself, the original of "Hugh Monfert," died on 6 December 1923. For Moore, he was a great character still in search of a story.

In Single Strictness would also include "Henrietta Marr," a final attempt to perfect "Mildred Lawson," the searing, spiritless tale of Pearl Craigie first published in 1895. Moore cut the first third of the original story, assigned to Mildred/Henrietta a doomed attraction to a Count who resembles Lord Curzon (he has a metal back brace and an ailing wife),[38] and then made the frigid, ambitious heroine commit suicide, as he thought Pearl had done, with a dose of veronal. At Henrietta's death, letters are found in the room that explain what has happened: Henrietta had written the Count a letter of condolence on the death of his wife that closed with a reminder of his promise to marry her should he ever be free. By return of post, the Count answered her very roughly – all Henrietta's dreams of a grand marriage were shattered. She killed herself in despair. One of Moore's admirers, Conrad Aiken, deplored the changes to the original story, thinking GM was in search of concentration and a dramatic ending.[39] In fact, he was just providing an update on the life of Pearl Craigie after 1895.[40] "Henrietta Marr" is the only story of the five that is pitiless, and it is utterly pitiless.

The best story in the collection, and the only entirely new one, is "Sarah Gwynn." A doctor in Ely Place, Dublin, has trouble finding a suitable cook, until an ex-nun is referred to him, Sarah Gwynn. She works out perfectly, except that when a month is up, she says she must leave his employment because the gardener has fallen in love with her. The doctor demands to hear her story before letting her go, and it is a remarkable one. The child of a mixed marriage in County Down, Sarah was driven by Northern bigotry to Dublin, where she becomes a communicant of the Catholic Church. Phyllis, a kindly woman met on the street, helps the young girl from the country to a factory job, but by and by Sarah learns that all the girls in the factory have to supplement their inadequate wages by street-walking. For weeks, Sarah endures the painful consciousness that she is being supported by Phyllis's prostitution. To escape being dependent on prostitution, whether that of herself or another, Sarah joins a convent in Wales as a lay sister. There she hopes she can alleviate the life of Phyllis by means of prayer, having no other power to help her. The convent falls on hard times, so a dwindling number of lay sisters are driven to working all day long for a large, aging group of choir sisters; no time is left even for prayer. Sarah becomes cantankerous and ill, so she is sent away by the Prioress with just a sovereign for years of work. Sarah returns to Dublin with one purpose in mind: to find Phyllis – either to take her place in prostitution, or help her out of it by supporting her through honest labor. Sarah has taken a job as the doctor's cook just for this purpose. Should she marry the gardener, it would be a selfish betrayal of Phyllis. The doctor, a Protestant, accepts Sarah Gwynn's choice in a spirit of awe.

Not only did Moore keep out of the story every trace of his anti-Catholic bigotry, he put into it a tender comprehension of the faith of one particular Catholic. His old friend from the 1880s, the arch-feminist Olive Schreiner, would have been proud of Moore for writing "Sarah Gwynn," with its sympathy for the fate of women – who could choose no course of life other than that of domestic, sweatshop worker, prostitute, nun, or wife. In 1926, Moore substituted "Albert Nobbs" for "Hugh Monfert," and reissued the collection under the title, *Celibate Lives*. This volume achieves a full treatment of themes uniquely Moore's own – the poignant, strange destinies of those for whom fulfillment is impossible in a heterosexual, marrying society, and the secret workings of sex in those who don't have sex. Aiken detected a "hypertrophy of manner" in the style, and certainly Moore in this book is very much himself, but it would be difficult to find in his late work a more finished example of his genius for storytelling. Hardy, James, and Conrad would not have thought of these stories, and could not have told them better.

4

Nancy Cunard invited Moore to spend a week with her at St Martin-Eglise (four miles inland from Dieppe), and GM booked a room at the village inn. The dinner tables were set in a large apple orchard sloping down toward the river; this was the pleasant scene of several meals with Nancy in the latter part of his stay.[41] Arriving on Saturday, 30 July 1921, Moore was at first distressed to find that Nancy had a young man staying with her for the weekend – a mere friend, she explained, and very cultured. But Moore became uncharacteristically conventional and worried that "people would talk."[42] On Monday, after two days of sulking by Moore, she had it out with him, and on a long walk through the Forest of Arques they resumed their sweet relations. GM spun out a courtly little fable of love lost and found that he hoped she might versify, but it was too Pre-Raphaelite for her taste.

Nancy was not the only woman for whom Moore wished to script a tale. The previous September, Moore had befriended Mrs Arthur Harter, née Ethel Maud de Fonblanque, a poet who first published in 1880. She now lived not far from Ebury Street at 22 Montpelier Square.[43] In October 1920, Moore outlined a little novel that he wished her to write under his direction. Entitled *A Love Conference*, it was to take the form of a conversation between two women, one of whom has had only a few lovers and is jealous of the other, who has had many. Together, they explore the art of love from "a woman's point of view." Drawing-room folklore is passed back and forth between the two characters, such as the maxim that the longest affairs are those that begin quickest.[44] GM evidently relished the ironies of a male author inscribing through a female his version of the secrets known only to women.

In story conferences at his home and at hers from January through October 1921, Moore coached Harter on how to weave two narratives, one past, the other present, undetectably together, and how to let the deeper story emerge from a conversation in which the women tell more of themselves than they mean to do.[45] She would read her draft manuscripts to him as she went along, and GM would suggest revisions and the next turn in the tale. They both enjoyed this collaboration. Ethel Harter missed him while he was in France during May, and he welcomed her return to Ebury Street in June "with open arms."[46] When the book was finished in October, GM judged it to be a "seller," "likely to do fifteen or twenty thousand" copies.[47] To GM's irritation, Werner Laurie passed up the chance to publish the novel; Sydney Pawling, now in charge at W. H. Heinemann, was happy to issue *The Love Conference* in April 1922.[48] On 12 February 1922, Moore brought to a close his "secret collaboration" with Mrs Harter, telling her curtly, "This year I have no time for any work but my own."[49] He had had his fun, writing a popular novel at one remove.

In the autumn of 1921, while he was in the course of supervising Mrs Harter's narrative, Moore did not actually neglect his own work. All the stories of *In Single Strictness*, once dictated, had to be rewritten on typescripts and proofs, according to his custom. In addition, Moore returned to *The Brook Kerith* and gave the whole text a thorough going-over for the sake of the fifth impression (published December 1921).[50] The diction was made simpler, more Anglo-Saxon; word repetitions were avoided; any accidental jingle (e. g. "he had thought would be fought") was corrected. Since the first publication of the novel, a new simple statement of his philosophy had come to Moore, and he put it in the mouth of Jesus toward the end of the novel. Moore's first try at this statement was, "It is better to love goodness than to hate evil"; thinking again, he judged the focus should fall not on moral abstractions, but on particular people, and wrote: "It is better to love the good than to hate the wretched."[51] He was proud of a commission from the *Sunday Times* to write an article on "Works of St Paul" for Christmas Day 1921, and, forgetting to attend a dance at Lady Cunard's house, he labored to make Paul's case as author of at least part of Acts of the Apostles – for Moore one of the world's great narratives.[52]

The Brook Kerith brought Moore back into touch with Frank Harris, now a journalist in America suspected of having been a German spy during the war. Over the previous twenty years, Harris had fallen into envious imitation of writers whom he had once published in his monthlies: Wilde, Shaw, and especially Moore. More recently, Harris had been writing "Contemporary Portraits" of men he had known; the key diagnostic feature was the nature of the subject's sex-drive, yet Harris's character was more that of a blackmailer than of a Freudian analyst. Of all these portraits, Harris liked the one of Moore the best because "I can put in the black shadows in Moore, and I think I have vigorously, which makes the portrait life-like."[53] Contemptuous of Moore's mind, masculinity, and manners, Harris could not understand how the man still flourished. While Moore was writing *The Brook Kerith*, Harris also aimed to write a book about Jesus, as did Shaw, and as would Robert Graves a little later.[54] All three of them, after reading *The Brook Kerith*, thought that it was a far cry from the greatest story ever told, and that they could do much better.[55] Harris also thought he could write better autobiographies than Moore – after all, he had more insights on more men and more dirty secrets about more women. Urged on by Moore and Shaw, Harris aimed "to see if a man can tell the truth naked and unashamed about himself and his amorous adventures in the world." *My Life and Loves* (1922–27), however, was not the book for which they hoped – simply volume after volume of obscene braggadocio. Shaw scolded Harris, "even George [Moore] does not imagine that force in literature is attained by calling a spade a f —— king shovel."[56]

Moore may not have read Harris's *Contemporary Portraits*,[57] but he heard from an editor that Harris had been deriding all that Moore had written since *Esther Waters*.[58] Moore believed that his success was making Harris's life miserable. Ever since their meeting in the mid-1880s, GM had been on the rise from a scandalous start, and Harris had been in descent from a brilliant beginning. Their trajectories crossed in the purlieus of the *Hawk* offices around 1890. Moore had once respected Harris; by 1921 he looked down on him. There was no point, Moore wrote Harris on 15 August 1921, even for the sake of old times, in meeting for lunch in Paris: "your erudition on food would interest me much more than your crude opinions about the sources of Christianity, of which, I regret to say, you seem to know nothing. But despite the food, the grudge would come between us, inspired by the Gospel of John, or Shakespeare, or 'The Brook Kerith,' or the German War, I cannot tell which."[59] Here was one imitator Moore would not acknowledge – Frank Harris was GM's black shadow, without the artistry.

In early February 1922, the proofs of *In Single Strictness* were returning from the printer. Liveright had come to London a second time, and publisher and author had at last signed an agreement on GM's terms for a library edition of selected titles. Moore was ready for a holiday with Nancy, who had moved once again, this time to Sanary-sur-Mer in the south of France. GM looked forward to stopping along the route in the ancient Roman cities of Provence – Orange and Arles – and in Montauban, birthplace of Ingres.[60] Passing through Paris, he met up with Barrett Clark (1890–1953), an American drama critic, playwright, and anti-censorship campaigner. As GM walked his young friend through the Louvre, Clark was fascinated by Moore's stories about great figures of yesterday, and sharp opinions about those of today. What lay on Moore's mind was the possibility that he had come upon a man who might be able to write a play under his direction. Maybe *Esther Waters* could be turned into something more stageworthy than its 1913 version, and one more blot on Moore's literary record could be removed.

23. George Moore and Nancy Cunard at Sanary (February 1922).

Traveling on alone, Moore made it through the villages of Provence to Nancy's villa in Sanary, a palm-lined coastal town near Toulon. He posed for a photograph with Nancy just days before his seventieth birthday. The two stand in a suncatch, coated against the mistral. During his two days with Nancy, Moore was crusty on the subject of free verse. For him, there was no such thing: "If it is not verse, or blank verse, with a regular metre, then it is prose. *Bad* prose if you like – but still prose."[61] This particular stricture was not a case of an old man forgetting the radicalism of his youth: Moore had not approved of Mallarmé's original experiment with prosody and obscurity in *L'Après-midi d'un faune* from which the modernist tradition of *vers libre* sprang. Yet the trendsetter of an earlier era had changed his attitude to literary movements: "Whoever follows the fashion loses all individuality," GM wrote Nancy after his departure. "It is necessary to be stiff-necked and obdurate and to treat one's contemporaries with contumely. In the great periods the artist took strength from his environment; he was concentric, but in periods of decadence like the present, the artist must be eccentric, stand aloof and disdainfully."[62] The year 1922 is not looked upon as a bad one for literature: *Ulysses* was published then, and so was *The Waste*

Land.[63] The final blossoming of modernism to which Nancy belonged was, however, to GM no more than the decay of forms.

In the course of Moore's return to London, he stopped to see Claude Monet, and the two surviving companions from the Café Nouvelle Athènes spent the day looking at Monet's huge pictures of water-lilies. Was this decadence again, or creativity that had never grown old? Moore expressed his astonishment to Gosse:

> For the last ten years [Monet] has been engaged on great decorations, water flowers and weeds and reflected trees – 10 or 12 foot canvases which he (a man of 81) wheels around and sets in line, a sort of parade recalling a drill, and thinks he is a young blood but that is an illusion, his blues are not however those of yore; of that I am sure, but I dare not think of the value of these vast schemes of decoration. Japan gave him a million francs for one of them and Japan made a wise choice. But it is difficult to discriminate between these paintings and wall paper, and I do not feel sure that a scene painter, certain scene painters, could not produce or reproduce these. A little time is required.[64]

GM was hedging: Monet's vast creations were too successful to dismiss, too strange to love. It was disconcerting. What to do but make a return visit to the Luxembourg Gallery? There he could look upon Manet's *Olympia*, a naked "brothel girl and the negress who brings her the great posy – a gift from one of her lovers who is doubtless dreaming of the part of her which her left hand hides." Manet's firm drawing, beauty of paint, and "exquisite appreciation of life" reoriented Moore to values that he could fully appreciate.

After his return from France, Moore stayed over in London only long enough to cook up a scheme with Leon Lion, an actor-manager with a great deal of respect for Moore the novelist. It was GM's dream that Lion's direction and Athène Seyler's acting would turn the failure of *Elizabeth Cooper* into the stage success of *The Coming of Gabrielle*.[65] "There is nothing I dislike more," he told Lion, "than defeat and traces of defeat."[66]

In the third week of April 1922, Moore returned to Paris. He visited Daniel Halévy, Mary Robinson Duclaux and her sister Mabel Robinson, but his chief companions were Mr and Mrs Barrett Clark.[67] He met the Clarks on 25 April for dinner at the Hôtel Quai Voltaire, where nearly fifty years earlier Bernard Lopez had dined with his young collaborator on *Martin Luther*, Monsieur George Moore. By 26 April 1922 Moore had engaged Clark to handle the drafting of dialogue for a new *Esther Waters*, while Moore did the rest.[68] On the 27th, Clark and his wife took GM to dinner at Michaud's. Moore invented some apocryphal Swinburniana for their entertainment, spinning out "a long imaginary story about a naked woman and Watts-Dunton [Swinburne's attendant in later life]. Should he publish it," Moore asked Clark, "and attribute it to Gosse?"[69] Clark was thrilled with this mischievous, majestic new friend, and set to work on the overhaul of *Esther Waters*.

On 29 April, GM left Paris to spend a month as a paying guest of Dujardin at Val Changis in Fontainebleau.[70] While he was there, Moore received a call from Millicent Fanny, the Duchess of Sutherland, a woman of "beauty and brains," as he barefacedly called her.[71] She collected him in her carriage for a long ride down poplar-lined roads to her own residence.[72] A day out was a relief from life at Val Changis. Moore and Dujardin made "irritable old cronies."[73] They had much to argue about: Germany, the Bible, drama, and other things. Dujardin's mistress, Marie Marguerite Chenou, a young Swiss woman, had had a baby, and the baby would cry, which kept Moore from being able to write.[74] Another woman-friend of Dujardin's, Jane Hugard, decided to become an actress rather later in life than was common; nonetheless, Dujardin was full of hopes for her success, which Moore delighted in dashing. After seeing her perform in Paris, Moore wrote Dujardin: "In Jane Hugard France has lost a good concierge."[75] In case this was not enough, Moore added later that he himself, though seventy years old, was taking up the violin – "You are always my good friend, and will be present when I give a concert three months hence, to hear *me* in Beethoven's 'Concerto.'"[76] So much did they grouse at each other that GM went back to Paris on 23 May, and threw himself on the mercies of the Clarks.

He would arrive at the Clarks' rooms late at night, sometimes in his carpet slippers, and talk. On and on went the story of the lonely old man's life – how he collaborated with Alexis on *Le Sycomore*, for a time accepted for production at the Odéon; and how a doorman at the Odéon when asked for a free author's pass to a performance of *A Midsummer's Night Dream* took George Moore for Monsieur Shakespeare himself;[77] how Pearl Craigie refused to sleep with him and he kicked her in the bottom. And one evening, he said he hoped Nancy Cunard was his daughter, but he just wasn't sure. The problem was much on his mind. Clark wondered about it too, so he asked Moore's oldest Paris friend, Jacques-Emile Blanche. Blanche said that GM had confided that Nancy was, indeed, his own child.[78] Yet this may have been no more than the temporary conclusion of a never-ending argument with himself, a supposition not confirmed, and perhaps unconfirmable, by Nancy's mother.

During this period, Moore did a good deal of fussing with Lady Cunard. She would invite him to one of her big luncheons, dances, or teas. He would reply that he did not enjoy any company but hers, or that he was too busy with his writing, or too tired from his writing, to leave Ebury Street. Why did she not come for a visit? Or take him for a drive to the beautiful little gallery in Dulwich? Where was the harm? Maud Cunard, however, wanted more than ever to preserve appearances. Once she took him along on a shopping expedition to Selfridge's, but in London she was generally more discreet than he desired.[79] In mid-August, she promised Moore that if he came to visit, she would accompany him to an exhibition at Burlington House later in the day. At Carlton House Terrace on 18 August, Moore found her drawing room occupied by guests, while the clock ticked on. He went into one of his patented sulks – silent, "unutterably blank."[80] The ladies talked of their daughters, broken marriages, and the difficulties of divorce. GM suddenly entered the conversation, saying that a woman might well hesitate in suing for a divorce for fear that her own affairs would be brought to light by the opposing counsel. Lady Cunard immediately "blew up like a hurricane."[81] She took it that Moore was implying – or divulging the fact – that Nancy had lovers. In fact she did, and several of them – Tristan Tzara, Wyndham Lewis, and others. GM was himself only beginning to be able to accept Nancy's sexual freedom as a fact. But he was not to allow that fact to come into view in the drawing room of Carlton House Terrace. On 18 August 1922 Moore did not get his day out with Maud Cunard at the Burlington House exhibition, and for a few days he was put in terror by the possibility that he had lost the chance ever to see her again. For Her Ladyship, Nancy's conduct, and whatever Moore knew about it, was unmentionable.

5

In the autumn of 1922, George Moore began to see a good deal of Mary Annette Beauchamp, Countess Russell (1866–1941), the English author better known as "Elizabeth" after the publication of her most famous novel, *Elizabeth and Her German Garden*. This book was inspired by the twenty years she spent on the Prussian estate of her first husband, Count Henning August von Arnim, who died in 1910. Returning to England, she married (1916) and then left (1919) the second Earl Russell. At the end of October 1922, on the day her novel *Enchanted April* was published, she attended a *causerie* for Paul Valéry hosted by Sybil Colefax, an intersection of French culture and London high society that was a likely venue for meeting Moore. Moore genuinely admired the writing of Countess Russell; he thought that *Enchanted April*, if she would just rewrite the second half of the book, would be better than his "Lovers of Orelay."[82] According to her diary, in early November 1922 Countess Russell began to see Moore frequently – on 3, 9, 20, and 29 November; 9 and 17 December (1922); 16 and 29 January; 9, 21, and 28 February; 4, 22, and 25 April; 26 and 29 May (1923).[83] They met, often alone, for luncheons, teas, and dinners, both at her house and at 121 Ebury Street. On 30 May Countess Russell left London for her chalet in Switzerland, and Moore was quite in the dumps after the departure of his "dearest Elizabeth."[84]

Moore himself stayed behind in the summer heat of London. He had to see after the production of *Coming of Gabrielle* in three matinée performances, scheduled to open at St James's Theatre on 17 July 1923. Getting a proper performance of this play had been his main literary preoccupation for the previous year. Eighty letters survive of the correspondence of Leon Lion and George Moore about details of the production. It is a wonder Lion did not go mad with Moore's anxieties and demands. GM treated play producers like publishers – with vigorous impatience. Only actors got it worse. Moore demanded a certain cast: Leslie Faber and Athène Seyler must be the lead characters, no one else would do. He had seen Seyler as "Mrs Traill" in a Phoenix Society production of Congreve's *Love for Love*, just the sort of eighteenth-century Anglo-Irish highly literary social comedy GM wanted his own play to be.[85] She was perfect for Congreve, so she would be perfect for Moore. Even for minor parts, GM was choosy: Viola Tree was unacceptable, not enough "*chien*" (or sassiness), so Lion found Miss Aimée de Burgh for the part of Lady Letham. Upon her arrival at the hall for rehearsal, Moore insisted that she sight-read the part so he could judge her worthiness. She passed the test, but a few days later during rehearsal Moore sarcastically reminded de Burgh that "a woman who is telling the story of her life to a man does not pay more attention to the flowers than to the story."[86] After rehearsal, he told Lion to pull Aimée de Burgh from the cast. Lion protested indignantly on behalf of "an artist of reputation and distinction"; when would the author stop adding to Lion's "countless difficulties"?[87] Then Lion felt it necessary to make cuts in GM's text. At the next rehearsal, Moore would not even look at the players' faces; his eyes were glued to the original manuscript, so that he could register the pain of each unsaid word.[88] So Lion restored the cut text, with the caveat that the actors would not have time to memorise the restored lines. GM relented, but having relented, still sulked.[89] In the run-up to the 17 July opening, Lion begged Moore to take a bow when the author was called at the curtain, or at least to be in the house. Nothing doing; GM wanted to keep to his old practice of being absent on such occasions; he stayed away until the second performance.[90]

This production occurred under the aegis of the Phoenix Society, an organisation of the same type as the Independent Theatre Society and the Irish Literary Theatre, in that it was founded in scorn of popular theater, and devoted to the rebirth of literary drama from its ashes. Along with Moore, T. S. Eliot was a major supporter: "the Civilised Class," Eliot said, needed to provide for its own entertainment.[91] The audience for Moore's play was thus a select one. But it was 92 degrees Fahrenheit on 17 July 1923, and *The Coming of Gabrielle* was not found to be a pleasant way to spend a hot afternoon.

Moore's friends who attended tried to soften the bad news by saying that Athène Seyler was very good in the part of Gabrielle, and if it were not for the heat, or the long waits between acts, or the facetious playing of Sebastian by Mr Hannen, or Leslie Faber's sickness, or the lower-class accent of Lady Letham, then the play would have been a complete success.[92] None of these factors touches on the quality of the play itself, which reviewers publicly described as inept, digressive, and bookish, before they addressed the question of "Why Novelists Are Bad Dramatists," to borrow the title of the article in the *Daily Mail*.[93] Over the previous year, Moore had poured an enormous amount of energy into trying to turn the failures of *The Apostle*, *Esther Waters*, and *Elizabeth Cooper* into successes. That he fully measured up to Hardy, James, and Conrad in the scale of his dramatic failure was no comfort at all.[94]

Writing to Countess Russell after he had accompanied Mary Hunter to the second performance of *The Coming of Gabrielle*, Moore insisted his play was simply a success not yet recognised. "The view of every journalist in London" was that the play had no "plot or characters or a single witty line," but "'The Coming of Gabrielle' seemed to me one of the most original comedies ever written and one of the most graceful – one that would have turned Musset green with envy; the comedy he had been trying to write all his life without ever succeeding. How differently we see things . . . The first critics of 'Faust' could only detect one tune in the opera – the soldiers' chorus. I do not believe journalists can quench a beautiful comedy, it will come up again."[95] Yet the play has not like the phoenix risen from its ashes. A little later, in solitary retreat at Woodgreen, the Hampshire cottage loaned him by Countess Russell, GM came up with a still stranger way of both defending his play and reminding her of an opinion they held in common:

London is empty without you; I miss you dreadfully and do not dare to think that you can miss me, yet I look forward to October . . . In a very polite article about "Gabrielle" a critic wrote: "It must never be forgotten that a play exists essentially in the representation." Did he write "essentially" or "primarily"? I am thinking only of the thoughtlessness of men: for half a century men have walked about trying to see life steadily and see it whole which is of course impossible, and for another half century men will write "it must never be forgotten," etc., without it occurring to any body that the critic might have written with just as much truth, "Women exist primarily in their clothes." But we know one or two, don't we, who think they do exist and more essentially outside their clothes than in them.[96]

The transition is swift but strange from irritation with newspaper critics to thoughts of women without their clothes. Yet to be permitted to adore the undraped female form was always Moore's great comfort, his way of experiencing the forgiveness of the flesh; even to sit alone and reminisce in the solitude of a country cottage was something of a salve for the pain of public rejection.

During his days in early August at the Hampshire cottage, Moore carried forward a new book of conversations and essays about art and literature, intended to replace *Impressions and Opinions* (1891) in the Carra Edition, and to be "*Avowals* over again, only more so."[97] Parts of the book, to be called *Conversations in Ebury Street*, had been published as he wrote them since August 1922 – further conversations with Gosse, and new ones with Granville-Barker and a fictional "Mr Husband" from America.[98] Moore already had 70,000 words toward the final volume when he arrived in Hampshire. After a long walk in the forest one day, he returned to find on Countess Russell's bookshelves "a book [he had] been wanting to read all his life," *Liber Amoris*, William Hazlitt's tale of a modern Pygmalion, written after he had fallen in love with a maid in his boarding house. It would be pleasant, he wrote Countess Russell, to conduct a conversation with the author of *Elizabeth and Her German Garden* on the subject of this book – to conduct it, write it, and publish it in *Conversations in Ebury Street*.[99] Countess Russell wrote back straightaway, evidently to the effect, Don't you dare! Moore then assured her that he would not "do a talk" with her without actually talking with her; "moreover, I should not think of publishing anything about you without showing it to you and obtaining your approval."[100] The conversation was never written, and Moore's relationship with Countess Russell remained private. After her return to London, Countess Russell saw little of Moore that fall – she was ill, then he was ill, and they were both pre-occupied with their different literary endeavors – but in 1925 the "brilliant and deeply intelligent Lady Russell" resumed her invitations to luncheons, dinners, and teas during her occasional visits to London.[101] They were not frequent enough for GM, and, after she built a cottage in the Alps, he begged for more affection in his last surviving letter to "Dearest Elizabeth":

> Your sweet and affectionate letters came like rain to a dry landscape. Why are you not like your letters? Instead of offering me a hug when we meet, you are restrained by some thing you do not like in my face, and now you are thinking: if he were here, wouldn't I give him a hug. It is true that the man far away is loved more than the man standing by. Janfre Rudel discovered this sad fact eight hundred years ago and was sensible enough to die in the arms of the princess of Tripoli saying, "to see is enough." You go away to live for months in a cloud-enshrouded Alp and relieving your feeling now and then with an affectionate letter for which I am truly grateful. But I should like to see you again.[102]

6

In the winter of 1922, James Reilly, the steward of Moore Hall, noticed a damaged spot on the portrait of "George Moore, the Historian," GM's grand-father – "the sad old gentleman in a white waistcoat that hung over the chimneypiece."[103] Damp had gotten into the big house, and decay was spread-ing. Moore sent Reilly careful instructions for the removal of the canvas so that it could be carried to London by Tom Ruttledge, who arrived at Ebury Street with the rolled-up canvas on 28 January 1923.[104] Moore believed, as he told Sybil Eden, that "My house on a hilltop in Ireland will become a ruin, and many houses in England will too; another fifty years will see the end of life as we knew it."[105] Yet he was delighted to have as an emblem the portrait of the writer of the family who had been born in GM's beloved eighteenth century, a man of the school of Gibbon.

Four days later, on 1 February, in County Mayo, a local regiment of IRA men came to Moore Hall in the middle of the night and ordered James Reilly to hand over the keys. The soldiers moved bales of straw into the house, and poured paraffin and petroleum about the place.[106] Furniture, fireplace mantles, and many items of value were carried out of the lower rooms and stacked on the lawn. The vestments and sacred objects were removed from the third-floor chapel.[107] Upstairs, the rest of the furniture was thrown out of windows, piece after piece, to be caught in a tree in the back garden or fall to the ground. Books and paintings were abandoned inside. Nine cartloads in all were looted and carried off. Then the house was set alight. After six hours, the roof fell in. The men still on the staff at Moore Hall did not come round until the next day, when it was too late. The Moore Hall carpenter heard of the fire in the morning, ran up the hill, and saw right away that all was lost; he sat down on a stone and wept.[108]

What exactly happened that night, and why it happened, is still a subject of talk in the area round Moore Hall. It is said that after George Moore barred Maurice from further use of Moore Hall (for helping Susan Mitchell with her book on GM), James Reilly could not actually carry out the banning order. Why, he had worked for Colonel Moore from early 1911, and felt like just an employee on the place.[109] So Maurice continued to pass time at Moore Hall when in Ireland. During the Anglo-Irish War (January 1919 to July 1921), Maurice gave Reilly an order that those who were fighting the English could be billeted there. After the Civil War broke out on 28 June 1922, Mayo was strongly pro-de Valera and anti-Treaty, while Colonel Moore supported the Free State government, by which he had been made a senator. He once again gave permission for Moore Hall to be used by the military – as a resting-place for officers of the government troops in their passages through the Mayo countryside, or as an observation post.[110] The anti-Treaty forces had been effectively overmatched by December 1922, but they did not declare a cease-fire until 30 April 1923, and guerrilla attacks – assassinations, burnings of "Big Houses" – continued. Thus Moore Hall became a target for the IRA "Irregulars," and the order to burn it, some local people believe, came from Éamon de Valera himself.[111]

George Moore of Ebury Street had no inkling that Moore Hall had been used to quarter troops. In GM's imagination, until 1 February 1923 Moore Hall lay quietly on the hill above Lough Carra, slowly decaying into a ruin like Castlecarra, Castlebourke, and the little pile on Castle Island. Stephen Gwynn wrote a letter to the *Observer* on 4 February protesting against the destruction of houses belonging to Free State senators and explained that "Colonel Moore was agent for his brother, Mr George Moore." GM replied severely. As anyone in Dublin could have told Gwynn, GM wrote, he and Colonel Moore had not been on speaking terms for many years. He himself had no opinion for or against Sinn Fein; "I am purely a man of letters, dissociated from Irish or English politics."[112] There is no evidence that George Moore ever did learn why Moore Hall was burnt.

Writing to Richard Best eight months later, Moore said he did not think he would ever be able to visit Ireland again: "The burning of my house forbids; I should crumble into dust the moment I set foot on the shore."[113] His mind began once again to turn away from the present toward a dreamy tale of lovers in Castlecarra a time long ago, before guns, automobiles, nationalism, and sectarianism, when all that was ruined was in its first flush. Ireland was covered in great forests, people traveled only by horse or on foot, and storytellers were abroad in the land. Yet three years would pass before Moore could turn this dream into a book, his fifty-first, *Ulick and Soracha*.

For the time being, in order to complete *Conversations in Ebury Street*, Moore wrote a poetic elegy for the Moores of Moore Hall inspired by his grandfather's portrait. When GM was a boy of eight, his parents took down another beloved portrait of his grandfather, an early one painted when he was a boy in green Spanish court dress, and compared GM with his grandfather, point by point. As he grew up, GM wanted to be like his clever grandfather who wrote books, the sixty-year-old man in the golden frame, in "the prim chocolate-coloured coat, one shoulder showing against the dead gold of the armchair, and the voluminous cravat swathing him chin-high."[114] Over the decades, GM found himself "becoming the portrait of my grandfather in old age" – "the high, round forehead, the large nose, the small, truthful eyes":

> For my eyes are truthful, I said to myself; they belie me if they are not; and I fell to thinking that though truthful they did not tell a soul as beautiful as my grandfather's. He brought, I said, a beautiful soul into the world and took it away with him, leaving little of it to his son, and none, I am afraid, to his grandson. But I regret nothing, for had Nature given me my grandfather's beautiful soul – a soul of almost Virgilian melancholy – I should have remained at Moore Hall, reliving my grandfather's life.

It was better, GM judged, that he had left Ireland for cities where he was more at home – Paris or London – and used Moore Hall only as a "dreaming house": "his spirit going forth at the end of the day's work to wander in the deserted corridors, in and out of the empty rooms, the doors opening before him, everywhere meeting pleasant detentions, finding one in an almost forgotten water-colour, another in a faded curtain of remembered pattern, and still another in a chess-board. . . ."

> [M]y dreaming house is gone, with only the portrait saved to hang on the first landing in Ebury Street in a little lobby, whence it looks out and catches my eyes as I come downstairs, a sort of fetch-light or corpse-candle, reminding me that my race is over, betrayed, scattered, and in exile. Every race has its day, it says, and every creed; every grief, every joy, dies sooner or later. Memory outlives the dead; it, too, dies, but we are powerless to crush or bury it; and were I to remove the portrait to a garret and turn its face to the wall, my grandfather's eyes would still haunt and oblige me to rehang it in the lobby, for I shall lack strength always to write to the director of a public gallery and ask him to relieve me of it.[115]

24. *George Moore the Historian* ("the voluminous cravat swathing him chin-high"), Thomas Wyatt.

7

For Christmas 1923, Moore crossed the Channel with Nancy Cunard so that they could spend the holidays together in Paris. He took her to meet Daniel Halévy, biographer of Nietzsche. For GM's entertainment, she invited twelve for dinner at the Rotonde, some of them members of the younger generation of families GM had known for years – Dolly Wilde (Oscar's niece), Marie Beerbohm (Max's niece), Iris Tree (daughter of Herbert Beerbohm Tree). Others included the poet Tristan Tzara, the sculptor Brancusi, and the dancer Nina Hamnett.[116] And just to please her beloved "GM," Nancy persuaded the singers Yvonne Georges and Clotilde Vail, whose hair when unpinned and shaken out fell all the way to her feet, to dress up in gowns specially chosen for his pleasure – one suggestive of a Renoir, the other of a Manet, allusions that he did not fail to appreciate.[117] In her memoir of GM, Nancy Cunard describes with lovely delight the amusement her Paris girlfriends found in flirting with the old man, and the pretty compliments he paid them.

When writing her book in 1955, Nancy Cunard decided to leave out one section that describes an evening that possibly occurred during these Christmas holidays.[118] Her friend Charles Duff hoped that she would include the section ("it is beautifully written"). Suspecting correctly that Rupert Hart-Davis would give her the same advice, Nancy did not show it to him.[119] "Questions of TASTE, of OPINION" stood in the way of telling the whole truth.[120] Yet she preserved it among her papers for readers of a later era.[121]

After GM and Nancy had dinner alone one evening, they returned to the sitting room of his hotel. Moore then raised a question he had raised before at Ebury Street, speaking the words in a "matter of fact tone, and even the preparatory gesture was confidential – a sudden aside in a long conversation," leaving her dumbfounded: "'I wish you would let me see you naked.'" While she stammered, he went on urging her, "'What is the ha-arm? . . . I am sure you have a lovely body. Now why won't you let me see it?'" She pleaded that she had a long scar down her side. As he knew, in 1920 and '21, she had had three operations; indeed, she had nearly died at the time.[122] Such a scar, GM replied, meant nothing – "'I knew a woman who had two. Her body was beautiful all the same and she had many lovers. Think what a pleasure it would give me to see yours.'" Nancy says that "At no time between us had there been any 'passages' – the word he sometimes applied to amorous tentatives – unless that delaying kiss, now on the cheek, now the lips, *un vrai baiser plantureux*, could be called such?" "'Why won't you give me this pleasure? I am an old man . . . Come now, what possible ha-arm can there be in that?'"

At this stage, Nancy Cunard interrupted her narrative of events in GM's Paris sitting room that night. How did he look in times long past? She asks herself what kind of lover George Moore actually would have been.

> "I was a dab hand at making love," he once confided, the racy expression arousing no disbelief *in me*. Others – some who knew him, yet more who did not – have disputed his love-making. But why? Why do they want him to have been impotent, for "impotent" these people are determined he shall have been – an idea no less slanderous than it is absurd. Thinking of GM as an impetuous, temperamental lover in his own times, I felt all the same that my naked body fitted our relationship at no point.

Yet, if their relationship was not that of lovers, there he was, still asking for the intimacy that is possessed without asking by spouses with each other, or parents with little children. "'I *do* wish to see you naked. I am an old man . . . Oh! Let me at least see your naked back.'"

> Now, . . . suddenly, something within me said: "Do this!" and without more ado, facing away from him, I took off all my clothes, standing motionless a few feet from where he sat. How lightly, how easily that came about. My clothes left me, lying in a graceful summer pool on the floor, as if they had slipped away of themselves. The night was warm and the mood serene. Without hesitation my long, naked back and legs were at last in front of him and the silence was complete. It would be full-on he was looking at them and I did not turn my head. The silence went on and on, so long that I wondered what exactly he was thinking. At length came a slow, murmuring sigh:

"Oh, what a beautiful back! As long as a weasel's. What a beautiful back you have, Nancy."

Then, never turning, I put on my clothes again with the same ease. What might he find to say now? He would often be thinking about my back, he said; perhaps he would use it.

Thereafter they resumed their natural friendliness with one another.

On 26 July 1926, GM inscribed for Nancy a copy of *Ulick and Soracha* (1926).[123] Toward the end of that story, she came to a passage in which the storyteller and harper Tadgh is near the end of his life, spending his last days on an island in Lough Carra. GM had indeed "used" her back, just as the old storyteller in his novel used the back of his young wife:

It is the back of the Irish peasant woman Brigit, married by the priest to old, nigh-moribund Tadgh, as the last months of the venerable harper's life go by on the island in the lake . . . A good sight of her naked! Tadgh pleads – that he may give shape, in his talk with the pilgrims who come to him for the great story of the lovers, to the body of the Princess Soracha. Thus, looking at Brigit, dies Tadgh.

So that when you read of the back that is like a weasel's with a dip in the middle, that back is mine as he saw it, with never a word or a gesture, but only a long, slow sigh to end the silence in the room.

It is possible that Nancy Cunard was *not* the daughter of George Moore, yet no other child could have so completely matched and even surpassed George Moore in the telling of this story, and such a wonderfully strange story it is. She tells it with his fearlessness, elegance, and affection, and with something more of his as well: a sublime, comprehensive refusal to judge.

8

On Moore's return to London, he invited John Lloyd Balderston and his wife Marion for dinner on 17 January 1924.[124] It was usually otherwise, with Moore visiting the Balderstons, late in the evening, uninvited, taking a chance that the young Americans were home, and would welcome him after his day alone at work. Marion Balderston recalled that in conversation Moore would make the long speeches, leaving other guests with little ones, but she was "flattered that this great writer came to see me."[125] Some years earlier, when John Balderston was a single man, Moore had involved him in one of the many attempts made to turn *The Brook Kerith* into a successful play.[126] Balderston had a collection of four dozen first editions of Moore's books; he also had collections of Conrad and James, shelved in alcoves on either side of the fireplace. While they were working on dramatising *The Brook Kerith*, Balderston announced that he was going to marry. "You will need some money," GM said.

25. George Moore: *The Old and the Young Self* (1924), Max Beerbohm. YOUNG SELF: And have there been any painters since Manet? OLD SELF: None. YOUNG SELF: Have there been any composers since Wagner? OLD SELF: None. YOUNG SELF: Any novelists since Balzac? OLD SELF: One.

"Take all those first editions to America and sell them. I will write a long inscription in each."[127] And so it was done. Moore then resumed his visits to the married couple. The only books prominently remaining in their flat were those by James and Conrad. "'I cannot understand,' Moore would say to Marion Balderston, 'why John is so taken in.'" Then GM would take down James's "In the Cage," a story about a postal clerk who falls in love with one of her customers, and read out a page with exaggerated inflections:

> This morning everything changed, but with a kind of dreariness; she had to swallow the rebuff to her theory about fatal desires, which she did without confusion and indeed with absolute levity; yet if it was now flagrant that he did live close at hand – at Park Chambers – and belonged supremely to that class that wired everything, even their expensive feelings (so that, as he never wrote, his correspondence cost him weekly pounds and pounds, and he might be in and out five times a day), there was, all the same, involved in the prospect, and by reason of its positive excess of light, a perverse melancholy, almost a misery.[128]

Out of breath from the long sentence, Moore would gasp out, "Now do you consider *that* literature?" Customarily a teatime visitor, Moore was finally routed not by the eminence of James or Conrad, but by the birth of a baby to the Balderstons in 1923. Thereafter, he would only come late, or would invite John and Marion (but not the baby) to Ebury Street.

It is no surprise that a great writer likes his own writing best, and dislikes the work of his best contemporaries. Has he not written books that make all others unnecessary? That is the driving aim of finding just the right word and catching life completely in one's net. Hardy, for instance, hated Moore and all about him, and did not communicate with Arthur Quiller-Couch for twenty years after "Q" rated *Esther Waters* higher than *Tess of the D'Urbervilles* in an 1894 *Speaker* review.[129] Yet Moore's serio-comic efforts to prove that James, Conrad, and Hardy did not know their own business could be annoying to his friends, especially when those friends were also friends of the man whose claim to fame Moore was just then attacking. Moore's gibes at Henry James and then the ghost of Henry James nettled Mary Hunter so much that she made it a condition of their friendship that Moore remain silent in the future on the question of James's merits.[130] Should GM annoy Edmund Gosse by his heavy lunges at the fame of old Thomas Hardy, Gosse would nimbly manage to take revenge by drawing Moore out into further vanities – and then ecstatically tease him, ridicule him, and pet him into silence.

In one chapter of *Conversations in Ebury Street*, Moore took another step: he did not just sound off to friends, he published a "conversation" in which he tried to demonstrate to John Freeman that Thomas Hardy wrote the *worst* English prose of the nineteenth century.[131] In the mid-1920s, Hardy's reputation as a novelist had fully recovered from the scandals of the 1890s over the immorality of *Tess of the D'Urbervilles* and the atheism of *Jude the Obscure*, scandals that had made Hardy stop writing fiction altogether. In the 1920s, a complete set of the Wessex novels was to be found in the libraries of country houses all through southwest England; his literary standing was well established in London too. According to Moore's lights, however, Hardy made absurd gaffes as a novelist. By selective quotation, Moore could show that Hardy wrote some very bad sentences, awkward and senseless, and by the sarcastic retelling of Hardy's plots – especially the scene of a sleepwalking Angel Clare bearing the wakeful body of Tess across the meadow and over a bridge – Moore could also make a case that the stories were improbable. Essentially, for Moore, *Esther Waters* is the correct version of *Tess*, and makes Hardy's tale obsolete. What is remarkable about the case for the prosecution in *Moore* v. *Hardy*, however, is not that it is just or unjust, perceptive or unperceptive, but that it is a complete surrender by Moore to envy of Hardy's reputation, and therefore ludicrous, even self-consciously so.

But Moore's indictment was not funny at all to John Middleton Murry, a young admirer of Hardy (and a friend of Lawrence too). In the April 1924 issue of *Adelphi*, Murry answered *Conversations in Ebury Street* with "Wrap Me Up in My Aubusson Carpet," cruelty paid in the coin of cruelty. Moore was simply envious of Hardy, it said, because Moore himself had no understanding of men or women, no understanding of life, and his own books would not last. Murry spoke with the voice that had always spoken against Moore: Low Church, liberal, moral, and earnest. There was something of the pulpit in Murry's denunciation of GM's vanity, aestheticism, and eccentric masculinity, something of the pulpit too in Murry's refusal to take any pleasure whatsoever in GM's unchristian virtues. No doubt, Moore's reputation suffered a good deal of harm from the attack on Hardy in *Conversations*, and more still from Murry's counterattack. How could Moore disturb the peace of the last years of Hardy, who through a long life had had to contend with every kind of misunder-standing and unfriendliness? It was simply scandalous, exclaimed Granville Barker, chastising Moore in the drawing room of GM's old friend Leonie Leslie.[132]

Thomas Hardy himself, eighty-three years old, and living at Max Gate, knew about *Conversations in Ebury Street*. Indeed, the thought that it would cause the public to laugh at him pitched the melancholy old man into a new fit of despair. So he read "Wrap Me Up in My Aubusson Carpet" with delight.[133] Thanking Murry with an offer of hospitality at Max Gate, Hardy claimed that he himself had never read a single book by Moore, having intuited, "half unconsciously," that Moore was one of those "negligible" writers. When "somebody once called him a putrid literary hermaphrodite," Hardy "thought [it] funny."[134] The increase of Moore's fame galled the old novelist, just as Hardy's fame galled Moore. In 1928, when Hardy lay in bed with pneumonia, he roused himself in the afternoon to dictate the following verses on "G.M." –

> Heap dustbins on him,
> They'll not meet
> The apex of his self-conceit

– and then died that evening.[135]

9

While Moore was slowly evolving the lines his story of *Ulick and Soracha* would take, he amused himself with several smaller book projects. One, hatched in February 1924, he completed by April for Nonesuch Press. This was *An Anthology of Pure Poetry*, poetry in which life is not approached through "interpretive codes," a poetry of things not ideas, objectivity not subjectivity, Art not Empire.[136] The idea originated in a conversation with George Russell in Ebury Street over ten years earlier, and off the top of his head Russell had been able to spin out a complete table of contents.[137] Moore's own knowledge was better of French than of English verse, so he engaged Walter de la Mare and John Freeman to collaborate in defining a standard of inclusion and gathering examples; indeed, Moore further delegated his remaining share of the work. He paid F. M. Atkinson £75 to help him assemble poems to fill up the pages of the little book, which David Garnett agreed to publish.[138]

The description of a "pure poem" given by Moore – "things not ideas" – might make the anthology appear to be an intervention on behalf of poetic modernism, rather like Ezra Pound's definition of the Image, or William Carlos Williams's "No Ideas but in Things," but the particular examples and collaborators Moore chose do not bear out this impression. Elizabethan songs, Romantic nature descriptions (but not Romantic meditations on Nature), and the works of Poe make up the bulk of the anthology; together they imply a tightly constrained function for verse – rhymed stanzas descriptive of nature or love, impersonally constructed. The latter Georgian poets – such as de la Mare and Freeman – liked the anti-modernism of GM's concept of the "pure" and "objective," but with this anthology Moore was really launching a novelist's subversive put-down of poetry in general.

Through the month of April in 1924, Moore was also working hard at a second project: a translation of *Daphnis and Chloe*, the fourth-century pastoral romance by Longus. GM did not know Greek, but he knew people who did. With their help, Moore felt sure he could do a better English version of a classical tale than could that "Oxford rag and bone shop, [Andrew] Lang and Co."[139] He obtained a typed word-by-word crib from a Mr Johnston.[140] Subsequently, GM judged he would prefer to work from Bishop Jacques Amyot's sixteenth-century French translation. In a flurry of letters written in April while GM was rapidly doing his version, he consulted W. K. Magee, who compared GM's language with the original. Moore found Magee's corrections "always to my taste."[141] The collaboration with Magee was delightful, and so was the story by Longus – pastoral, erotic, "odorous and fair as a flower," "the last effort of Greek genius."[142] GM's practice was to translate literally until he came upon something awkward; then he judged "it is allowable for an author to make it read gracefully."[143] He had no intention of writing something that could be used by schoolboys as a crib (though schoolboys would not ordinarily be set to translate a text about the first adolescent sex between a shepherd and shepherdess). On 17 April, Moore had as his guest at dinner Thomas Whittaker (a scholarly assistant on *The Brook Kerith* project).[144] Whittaker was irritated at the liberties Moore was taking with the Greek, and fetched a book he had brought by the Oxford Professor Richard Claverwell Jebb. Moore called Jebb's prose "a frightful farrago," "a medley of Greek and English . . . These scholars learn one language for the purpose, so it would seem, of dishonouring another."[145] A few days later, he asked Mary Hutchinson: "I have heard of Jowett, but who is Jebb?" A month's work, and Moore had added *Daphnis and Chloe* to his collected works, and settled old scores, he hoped, with the men who had been up at Oxford and the professors who remained there, Lang, Jowett, and Jebb. In a fashion, accounts were also put straight with the hairy-knuckled headmaster of Oscott College, J. Spencer Northcote, who in 1866 had written G. H. Moore that there was something "singular & extraordinary in [George's] backwardness."[146]

10

While Moore was working on *Daphnis and Chloe*, he received an Easter visit from Leah Rosenbloom, a twenty-one-year-old reader who had first written to him in January 1924, and paid him her first visit at the end of that month. She lived with her parents in Manchester and wanted to be a great writer like George Moore. "At the dawn of sex-consciousness," she felt she "really began to live" – just like Héloïse in *Héloïse and Abélard*.[147] She could not fall in with the Jewish observances of her parents. "A sensitive and ardent mind" betrayed itself, GM thought, "in every sentence" of her first letter, so he invited her to make her first visit to him on 26 January.[148] Would Moore turn out to be lover, mentor, father, or father-confessor? In over thirty letters exchanged through the next year, he gives her a great deal of literary advice ("Very few can do much in prose before 30, and the difficulty is to acquire the *patience of passions*"),[149] charts out a confessional narrative for her to write, provides her with a curriculum that includes Rousseau, Pater, and Moore, tries to find her employment with publishers and agents, sends her money for trips to London, and, evidently, makes a sexual approach to her in the parlor at Ebury Street, so that he was at the end everything that he ordinarily had been in such situations with women young and old.

After her Easter call at Ebury Street, Leah was nervous about making a third trip to London in August, though Moore wanted to set a date and pay her way. She already had a lover, a young Irishman, and any unfaithfulness, she said, she would forever regret. She could understand his "live for the day" philosophy, but it was not for her. Henceforth, she would come "as a friend, to talk to you, but please don't be disappointed."[150] She confessed that her conscience spoke accusingly to her: "'If you were old and ugly . . . [GM] wouldn't care two straws about your writing, nor even your friendship. At the back of all his interest in you is his sexual desire, and sex colours all his interest in you.'"[151] Her conscience may have been right about the root of Moore's interest in her, but Moore continued to give Leah Rosenbloom books, advice, and travel money after she had made it clear that he was not going to get any loving in return.[152] Her honesty of feeling had a distinct weight with him. Prior to her fourth visit to Ebury Street, around Christmas 1924, Leah thanked Moore for having planted her feet on the road of literature.[153]

Leah Rosenbloom was not the only young woman who came to Ebury Street to meet a distinguished novelist in his seventies and found what would conventionally be called a dirty old man. Ilka Chase, a niece of Horace Liveright, was taken to meet George Moore. As the three of them went in to dinner at

Ebury Street, she felt her bottom pinched. "I felt rather honoured . . . but it was embarrassing too." Further embarrassment came when she asked GM for his opinion of one of her favorite writers, Joseph Conrad. "I don't know, my child," Moore said testily, "I can't read Polish."[154]

Mary Somerville, an Oxford BA, used to visit Moore while he was writing *Daphnis and Chloe*, and afterwards she came to him for help when she herself was starting to write stories. With her, Moore was on good behavior because she was a friend of Edmund Gosse, and Gosse had warned GM that if he tried anything, he would be forbidden ever again to enter 17 Hanover Terrace – no more sweet and savory Sunday dinners *en famille* with Gosse. She enjoyed many "entrancing hours" alone with Moore thereafter, but in the lead-up to Mary Somerville's marriage in 1928, Moore lost control. He wanted to know her "physiological reactions to the experience of falling in love, and he would talk of nothing else." He was impossible, and she stopped going to visit him. Many years later, writing of her friendship with Moore, she concluded, "I *wish* I'd been able to manage him."[155]

K. A. Tolhearst gave Joseph Hone a transcript of her conversation with George Moore when she came alone for tea one afternoon, hoping to get advice on a novel she was writing. It was an evidently autobiographical story about a naïve young woman's life after she has been seduced and abandoned by her lover, a German. GM did not like the premise: "We are never seduced," he instructed Tolhearst, "we only seduce ourselves."[156] Tolhearst then tried to go on telling him the story: her heroine was so innocent she had no idea what had happened to her. This too GM found hard to believe: "To enjoy a man and not know it!" Sex is not always enjoyable for a woman, Moore's guest informed him. "This is shocking!" he cried in mock alarm. "The Germans are such pigs, they only think of their own pleasure." The best enjoyment, he philosophised, comes from sex with a stranger. Having gotten her mind to dwell on this subject, he was delighted. He told her how to rewrite the novel: as a first-person confession, on the model of *Confessions of a Young Man* – with complete shamelessness. However, Tolhearst wanted neither to throw away what she'd written, nor to write autobiographically about sex. He was alarmed: absolute truthfulness and endless commitment to revision are essential to the artist! Thereafter, evidently disappointed with Tolhearst as a novelist, Moore began to show more interest in her as a woman. With tea finished, he begged her to take an armchair, pull it up close, and make herself easy. There the transcript breaks off.

In 1934 "Lorine Pruette" (pen-name of a psychologist teaching at New York University) published "Leda and the Lion," a short story about a young American woman, a novelist, visiting a famous old writer in London.[157] Neither the woman nor Moore is named in "Leda and the Lion," but the "Lion" is working on "Aphrodite" (*Aphrodite in Aulis* was published in December 1930) while recovering from surgery (GM underwent surgery in February 1928). He asks her to tell him her story. Why doesn't she take off her hat and stretch out her legs? Why not sit on his knee and give him a kiss – just one kiss, for a very old man. No, thank you. They go back to the discussion of literature, but a moment later, "with surprising agility and strength," he is holding her in her chair and kissing her. "You have nice skin . . . I too have nice skin," he purred, like a connoisseur. He gave her a second kiss before she could register an objection to the first. Then he reminisced about his earlier lovers. "I never asked a woman to do anything, but when they wanted to do anything I was glad. What do you find most exciting?" He explained his own preferences in a way that "confirmed his French affiliations." When she asked him bluntly if he was suggesting that she should make love with him there and then, he waved away the possibility: "You know I can't; I *wish* I could. Isn't it the best thing in life?" She was not frightened by his fierce, monotonous lechery – he was too feeble to be dangerous – but she was horrified by an impending insight.

Was it from this, she thought, was it from this, from this that all those fine stories had come? And was it for this that he had learned with infinite labor to fashion his prose, learned the subtle art of shaping a book into final form? She thought it was so, that here was the last flaring up of the original fire which had driven him out into the world so inquisitively, and back into literature so determinedly. And suddenly she had a sharp, flashing glimpse of the importance, not of love, but of lust, in the world.

"Do you have a nice figure?" she heard him ask. "Let me see you undressed and I will tell you." "Do you have a nice breast?" Before she could answer, his hand was inside her jacket: "Ah yes," he said contentedly, "it seems very nice." She made him promise to behave, and he "behaved" by telling her of those kisses and caresses which his condition did not prohibit him from giving and receiving. They are not vice, he explained; only one thing is vice, and he only did that to two women, and that was after they made a specific request for it. "Lawrence mentions it," she answered slowly. Even when the subject had turned to sodomy, she remained transfixed in her chair, fascinated. Moore gave a glowing exordium on the pleasures men give women, and women men, which she interrupted by returning him to the subject of her story. He promised to fix it right up, if she would just call again. But she did not want to have him fix it; she wanted to write it herself. She would rather her body were outraged than her manuscript tampered with. He followed her to the door and out into the cold, begging her to return, and, lying, she said she would.

One final example of the continuation of Moore's goatishness into old age. The present writer purchased a copy of Nancy Cunard's *GM: Memories of George Moore*. When it was opened, the following unsigned handwritten slip tumbled out: "Doris Thorne told me in 1930 about her jaunt to Ebury Street so that her nubile daughter Dorinda could see the Great Man before God called him home. When Dorinda went close enough to his Bäkth [*sic*] chair, he pinched her in the most accessible spot."

II

In September 1924 GM visited W. K. Magee, his wife, and young son in north Wales. In 1920, Magee, then fifty-two years old, had surprised his colleagues at the National Library of Ireland by marrying the sub-librarian, Mary Louise O'Leary. A year later, Magee happily took advantage of a provision of the Anglo-Irish agreement offering early retirement to civil service employees. At last, he hoped he would have the time to find out if he could fulfill the dream of being a great writer, a dream that he had nourished since his student days at Trinity College Dublin thirty years earlier, when he won four Vice-Chancellor's prizes for verse and prose composition, and had hopes of matching his high school classmate Yeats stride for stride in literary success.[158] Yet he would emigrate before making the attempt to recover his youthful inspiration. During the Irish Civil War Magee had been wretched. Ireland seemed to have no room in it any longer for either the Protestant faith or the modern European sensibility. So at the end of 1923 he moved to the village of Prestatyn in Wales, "with the sea in front and rather inviting hilly country behind."[159]

Ever since 1911 Moore had sent Magee proofs of all his books, accompanied by the suggestion "there is nothing to prevent you from altering an awkward phrase."[160] The much-admired correctness of Moore's late style owes a good deal to the former Trinity College prizeman. Of the Dublin critics, Magee was one of few to break the "boycott" on praising Moore's works, and GM appreciated "the courage on your part to number me among Irish writers."[161] In a review of *Avowals*, Magee counted GM as one of "the four principal writers [Yeats, Wilde, Shaw, and Moore] whom the Anglo-Irish have given to English literature." In the course of his "varied and provocative authorship," Moore had made himself, Magee wrote, "the master of one of the most intimate and resourceful styles in modern English prose."[162] However, in the early 1920s, the long friendship of Moore and Magee nearly broke apart. GM was irritated in 1921 when Magee devoted long paragraphs of a review article to poems by Yeats and AE, but made only a cold, brief mention of *Héloïse and Abélard*.[163] Moore admitted his feelings were hurt, but his pitiful plea for consideration won no retractions from Magee. In 1922 Moore sent a gift copy of *In Single Strictness*, and Magee, the son of a Belfast Presbyterian minister, was outraged by "Hugh Monfert" – a filthy subject. Even after being told off by Magee in terms "too Christian for quotation," Moore still would not let the friendship die.[164] "You haven't written to me for months and months," GM complained in a letter of 10 August 1923, "perhaps because you don't like my literature. It doesn't in the least matter whether you do or you don't, for I'm not very sure whether I like it myself . . . "[165] This was going far more than halfway to meet Magee, yet Moore's offer was straightforwardly rejected. Their relationship had been based, Magee wrote, on the fact that he was the reader, Moore the writer. Now that Magee no longer liked what Moore wrote, the relationship had no further basis. No, no, GM protested; we are not just reader and writer; we are friends.

Besides, "dislike of the Irish character and Papistry" is "deep enough in us, strong enough, close enough, intimate enough, for us to be able to scorn our literary differences."[166]

Thereafter, Moore cannily recognised that Magee was distressed most of all by the failure of his high expectations of himself as a writer. The job of GM as friend was to bring the author out of the lifelong reader in Magee. After Magee confessed, "I have almost ceased to be a writer," Moore gave him a dose of drily understated encouragement: "We are altogether ignorant of what we are and very nearly as ignorant of what we are not, so I suppose you will write to increase your income, retaining your old habit of speaking of what you used to call your 'efforts' with contempt."[167] Once Moore got his friend a commission, he told him to "Write your own article; let it be Magee and nothing but Magee, and you'll please me and the office and your readers" – a very handsome exhortation.[168] "I believe you will take a high position in English literature," Moore assured him, "if you produce enough." "With you it is entirely a question of production and push."[169] Or, to put it another way, a question of self-confidence – and GM did his best to cultivate into something fruitful that hard seed of buried artistic pride in Magee.

To supplement Magee's small pension, Moore paid him well for his editorial help. He also concocted a variety of literary projects for Magee to carry out – translations from the German for W. H. Heinemann, a two-volume edition of Landor's works, and a translation of Homer into the style of Moore's *Brook Kerith*. These particular projects came to little or nothing, but a few of Moore's subsequent proposals did pay off, such as Magee's translation of Moore's letters to Edouard Dujardin (1929) and the selection of *Dial* essays published as *Irish Literary Portraits* (1935).[170] At an Ebury Street luncheon, Moore also persuaded his friend Viola Garvin to commission literary articles by Magee for the *Observer*.[171] Still, Magee habitually professed a reluctance to write, or having written, to publish; and having published, to collect and reissue his periodical work in volume form. "Inaccessibility," Ernest Boyd observed, is "an apparently essential feature of all John Eglinton's work."[172] Moore pictured Magee as the years went by sinking deeper and deeper into his armchair, while he rearranged and dusted his favorite ideas, "conscious of their familiar presences," but undesirous of writing them down, and out of politeness hiding his contempt for the literary efforts of his friends.[173] Whether Magee liked it or not, George Moore was one of those friends, the best friend the writer in Magee could have had.

In Wales that September of 1924, the two men who had known each other for twenty-five years took long walks in the hills (rending holes in GM's socks) and talked of the art of translation. Like other exiles, they also reminisced about old times and friends back home – Saturday nights at Ely Place, Best, Russell, Yeats, Moore Hall before it was burnt. The visit was a great pleasure to Moore, and he returned time and again afterwards.[174] On one of his visits, Magee took GM to see St Winifred's Well, at the time still believed by some pilgrims to have healing powers. There was a turnstile and an old woman operating it. When the two visitors were told the price of admission, GM asked, "And how much for the cure?" The woman glared at him. "At your age, you ought to know it is by the grace of God!"[175] Magee, who numbered himself one of Christ's more moderate adherents, but an adherent nevertheless, was delighted by Moore's discomfiture. On the way down the long hill from the holy well, Magee asked Moore if for him there was no transcendental dimension, no mystery to life at all. "Of course, there are many things in life we do not understand," GM answered, "and it is possible to admit that there are minds which understand more than others, but life is no less wonderful for the materialist than for the transcendentalist – for Darwin, if you like, than for Kant."[176] And Magee mentally conceded that in the startled eyes of Moore, life indeed was ever full of wonder.

In late February 1928, when Moore was lying ill in a nursing home, he sent Magee money to come to London by train so that they might talk. Magee came up by the early train. Together they reviewed their past:

> [Moore] is pleased to say that I have been "part of his life"; "and I am pretty sure," he added, rising on his elbow, "that I have counted for a good deal in yours!" It was true. This man, whom I judged at first to be completely alien to me, was to be the most familiar of my acquaintance, peering curiously into my privacy, and opening his soul to me more I believe than to others: a soul in contact with some perennial source of caustic insight and salutary disillusionment, yet one that craved for affection.[177]

The friendly streams of that acid insight were clearly not wholly welcomed by Magee. They ate away at Magee's sense of propriety in matters of religion, sex, and self-assurance; they deprived him of essential mental comforts. In those insights, he had unpleasant evidence of the reason for Moore's importance and his own lesser importance. The most profitable enterprise with which GM provided his friend – translating the letters to Dujardin for £300 – both gave Magee a chance to make his mark and strictly indicated that the mark made would be small, serviceable, and contingent. When, lying in his nursing-home bed, GM asked Magee to be his biographer, Magee procrastinated.[178] Not so little a person as a Boswell! he hoped. Why not a Johnson himself? And he finally refused. The decision is not regrettable: there was much about Moore's true life that Magee could not easily have faced.

12

In 1926, Moore encountered Austin Clarke (1896–1974), a young Irish poet with a difficult relationship to Yeats. Having lost his job at University College Dublin because he entered into a civil marriage (never consummated), Clarke settled down to work in London as a reviewer in 1922, though it would take him decades to work out his fury at the Catholic hierarchy for its repression of human sexuality. In a review published in the 22 July 1926 *Times Literary Supplement*, he marvelled at the "plenary power and invention" of *Ulick and Soracha*. It is true that the novel does not lack the power to please; in addition, with the help of Trinity College Dublin historian Edmund Curtis, Moore created a visualisation of an Ireland long passed away.[179] *Ulick and Soracha*, however, is not one of Moore's best books. It was a favorite of Clarke's because it showed the way to an imaginative space in Irish history that had not been previously camped on by Yeats; moreover, it offered an attractive picture of an Ireland in which sex and Catholicism could be comically reconciled. Inspired by *Ulick and Soracha*, Clarke wrote three similar romances, beginning with *The Bright Temptation* (1931) – stories of poets and lovers traveling around a medieval Ireland of abbeys, towers, and forests, an Ireland that is at once Catholic and sexy, with the beauties of both nature and Celtic Romanesque architecture. In his verse, Clarke had already begun to explore the possibilities of Gaelic prosody and ancient themes. Pleased by the *TLS* review, Moore looked into Clarke's poems – probably those in *The Cattle Drive in Connaught* (1925). "Lacking in rhythm they certainly are," he commented to Magee, "whether from hardness of hearing or jugglery prepense I cannot tell."[180]

Clarke had heard that Moore was an irascible old man, but in early August he let Ernest Longworth bring him to Ebury Street for dinner. On first sight of GM, Clarke noticed "that foolishness of the mild eye" (the eye that had been damaged by birdshot in 1897) and "that schoolboy pouting of the lip."[181] Yet Moore greeted the young man "with an indescribable air of great courtesy," and Clarke's fears of the old lion were "whisked away." GM thanked Clarke for the review, then explained that one episode in particular from *Ulick and Soracha* left him still unsatisfied: the telling of Ulick's ride to Castle Carra. "Narrative is like the river Boyne, the weeds keep spreading under the surface. We have to keep clearing them away, if the story is to run smoothly on its course." Passing to the subject of one of his frequent concerns – aired in many newspaper interviews – GM talked about overpopulation.[182] What, for instance, would be the effect of the modern metropolis on birds? Creatures seem now to adapt themselves to man, no longer to nature. Perhaps only the wildest birds still have an ear for music. What did Clarke think? Finally, GM came around to the subject of Clarke's poems. He made no secret of his reservations. There were, he pointed out, two missing accents in the first line of a stanza. This was unacceptable: "the lines in every stanza should match."

Clarke was pleased with Moore. In 1927, when Clarke was writing a dedicatory note for his new book, *The Son of Learning*, Moore hinted that he would appreciate a little statement of homage to his own medieval romance.[183] Eagerly, Clarke obliged. Unlike Yeats, Moore seemed happy to affiliate Clarke's work with his own.[184]

13

In the autumn of 1925, Lady Cunard agreed to sit with GM for one in the series of "portrait interiors" by John Lavery (1856–1941).[185] It was a pleasant arrangement among friends. Moore had been one of the first critics to hail Lavery's talent, praising *The Tennis Party* in the Salon of 1888 as better than anything by the leading painters of the Royal Academy. Lavery and Moore were both artists born in Ireland and settled in England; both Lady Hazel Lavery and Lady Cunard were daughters of American millionaires now established, with Lady Sybil Colefax, as the leading hostesses in London.[186] From October through December 1925 the friends gathered at the Ritz Hotel for sittings.[187] Lavery set up his easel before the windows looking upon a drawing room, at the far end of which was a large mirror. In the painting, the mirror throws the light of the window and the image of the painter, peeking over his canvas, back at the viewer. On the walls of the room hang six gilt-framed pictures. Statues rest on the tables, including in the far corner a figure of a dancing faun oddly reminiscent of Sir Thomas Beecham (he conducted the music for the famous Ballets Russes production of *Après-midi d'un faune*). In the shadowy lower foreground to the left is a deep, richly pillowed couch, and on it the white-haired, slim-shouldered figure of George Moore. Alongside him, her body turning toward him, is Lady Cunard. This couple are not in the center of the painting; the center is occupied by a table, stacked with books, and amidst the books a vase of flowers. Vast, blooming lilies rise to catch all the light in the room. They stand there as a sign of some otherwise unexpressed life in the scene. Although the painting was first entitled *A Salon*, the quiet scene upon which we peer is more intimate than the title suggests, even marital, like a portrait of "Mr and Mrs M," or even "Lord and Lady X." After the many hesitations on the part of Lady Cunard about accepting Moore's dedications of books to her, it is remarkable that she agreed to this memorial to, and silent confession of, their attachment.

On 3 November 1925, Sir Bache Cunard died. Since 28 October, Lady Cunard and Moore had been in Paris, taking a break from their sittings to John Lavery. Although staying in separate hotels, they breakfasted together, attended a concert, and evidently enjoyed their freedom from the eyes of London. Moore's letters of early November make no mention of the death or funeral of Sir Bache Cunard; instead, they are full of allusions to a luncheon Lady Cunard was arranging in Moore's honor.[188] It was to be hosted by "Amis de la France" on 10 November 1925. Moore hated such events, especially this one – he was mortified by the necessity of giving a speech, but he went through with it, he told her, because she wished it: "I loved you in the beginning and shall love you to the end."[189] The report in the *Times* names, among other guests, three French princesses, two English ladies, and Marshal Fayolle. Cunard wanted a high society success for her now more publicly acknowledged old friend, George Moore.[190]

26. *A Salon* (George Moore and Lady Cunard at the Ritz, 1925), Sir John Lavery.

On their return to London, she accepted with pleasure a letter of dedication, to be published along with *Ulick and Soracha*.[191] Lady Cunard applied her social energies over the next nine months to getting the British government to award Moore the Order of Merit. Balfour indicated he was favorable, but he made no speed toward actually doing anything.[192] Moore's old friend Edmund Gosse, a former Librarian of the House of Lords, was a pastmaster at quietly arranging for honors and awards to come to writers he judged to be deserving. In April 1926, for example, he was working with Moore to get James Stephens a Civil List pension.[193] Yet Gosse did not grease the wheels for George Moore; instead, he derailed the whole enterprise. According to Lady Cunard's report to Shane Leslie, the writer and son of Leonie Leslie, Gosse "flash[ed] on the Prime Minister, Ramsay MacDonald, all the most lascivious pages he could cull from Moore. Obviously they would prove too much for the British Public and for once Lady Cunard was thwarted."[194] Why would Gosse do such a thing to one of his dearest friends? Leslie believes it was because Gosse had tried all his tricks in order to get Thomas Hardy the Nobel Prize, and he was determined that Hardy's fiercest critic should not get the OM.[195] Gosse and Moore remained friends, but under a strain. Lady Cunard thought the OM was right for Moore; Gosse thought it wasn't; Moore himself did not care tuppence about this particular honor, but no doubt he did want his lover to be pleased and his friend to hold him in high regard.[196]

In early 1928, after Moore's health had been failing for several months, Gosse sent him a note saying that the Prince of Wales had "bought three of [GM's] books, a piece of good fortune" that should brighten Moore up, Gosse wrote. GM "suspected an irony."[197] Lady Cunard had been trying to interest the Prince in Moore's work, and Gosse was evidently still keeping watch on the progress of her ambitions for GM's elevation. Indeed, when GM entered a nursing home, Cunard arranged for the Prince to visit so that GM could inscribe for His Highness *Avowals* and *Memoirs of My Dead Life*.[198] According to a hospital nurse, the Prince was "enchanted" by Moore's conversation.[199] On 1 April 1925, the Prince attended the opening of Moore's comedy on the Shakespeare/Bacon controversy, *The Making of an Immortal*, a sign of royal favor that may have contributed its mite to the play's surprising success.[200] All this celebrity was pleasing to Lady Cunard, but her quest for it may have fouled the last years of the long friendship between Moore and Gosse. At the nursing home, GM tried to interest Gosse in a new collaboration – "five articles, French landscapes with a French book in each." "We shall have such fun," GM pleaded from his hospital bed; "I am as agile as an Italian greyhound going through hoops at improvisation."[201] Yet Gosse appeared strangely out of sorts. There were to be no more collaborations, no more Sunday dinners, and no more letters. Gosse died on 16 May 1928.

14

Moore was lucky in his health right into his mid-seventies. He had the bouts of mild influenza, colds, and intestinal complaints that everyone has, but it was not until September 1927 that he took any medicine for the first time "since Gregory's powders were forced upon [his] weeping childhood."[202] Virginia Woolf, meeting Moore at Mary Hutchinson's party in March 1926, was amazed at the feisty vigor with which the seventy-four-year old author attacked Conrad, James, and Anatole France: "I can't tell you how urbane and sprightly the old poll parrot was; and (this is what I think the brain does for one) not a pocket, not a crevice, of pomp, humbug, respectability in him: he was as fresh as a daisy."[203] A year later, however, Moore began to suffer through some very bad nights, and by 18 March 1927 he was driven to call upon a doctor.[204] A sugar-free diet was prescribed, which helped Moore's stomach but left his head feeling heavy. The composition of a new novel, *Aphrodite in Aulis*, dragged through the autumn.[205] GM thought a trip to Paris would freshen him up but put it off again and again, feeling too ill to make the crossing. In December 1927 and

January 1928, he suffered from stomach pains and one cold after another; his days were spent sniffing eucalyptus. The possibility of meeting up with Lady Cunard in a hotel in Falmouth spurred Moore to make a journey south in the last week of January, but he could not get rid of his "nervous indigestion"; upon his return, he looked "a melancholy spectacle."[206]

Moore consulted a surgeon, Sir John Thomson Walker, who judged that the answer to GM's problems was prostate surgery. Blood tests revealed dangerous signs of uraemia, an effect of kidney failure. The enlarged prostate cut off the flow from the bladder, causing renal damage. On Sunday, 19 February, five days before his seventy-sixth birthday, he was put in Lady Carnavon's nursing home.[207] The *Times* reported that an operation was to be performed shortly.[208] Yet the blood counts on his kidneys, though fallen from 170, were still extremely high at 140, so on 23 February surgery was postponed.[209] A few days later, it appeared momentarily that Moore had turned the corner and was on the mend, so on 25 February, Sir John Thomson Walker judged that Moore would be able to resume the writing of his novel; major surgery could await a fuller recovery of his kidneys.[210] Yet his condition worsened in early March. He was not clearly aware of events for several weeks. Later Moore heard from the doctor, "no man was ever nearer death than I was," yet he did not feel as he thought a dying man should – terrified. He did not even "care about which side the balance might tilt."[211]

Until March, Moore was able to keep friends posted on his illness – he wrote or dictated letters to Viola Rodgers, Countess Russell, and Mary Hutchinson. One friend sent a reading-desk with a mechanical book-holder to the nursing home.[212] Many friends came to visit – Gosse, Tonks (himself a former doctor), James Stephens, the Duchess of Marlborough, and, of course, Lady Cunard, who arrived whistling "O Tannenbaum."

In 1906, when Moore had written "The Lovers of Orelay," she had been furious with him for the free use he had made of their intimate life together. Evidently, she sent him away, but he said as he left that if she ever needed him, all she had to do was whistle a bar of "Tannenbaum."[213] After her first visit to the nursing home, he called for her again on the last day of February. That night, he wished to settle his affairs. She would inherit his paintings, furniture, and publication rights; in turn, she would have to take charge of appointing someone to see to it that his completed manuscripts were published, his other books were kept in print, and a biography was written – preferably by Magee. He begged her to reach an understanding with Magee during his visit to London.[214] It was a gesture by which he wished her to take responsibility in the authorship of works she had inspired.

In March, the old man rose and fell in the depths of illness. He underwent painful daily extractions of his urine. His blood count climbed to 250. Through his misery, Moore talked and talked to his nurse, May Cooper. "There have been many women in my life," the feeble patient declared, "but only one Lady Cunard."[215] Nancy Cunard came to see GM one day, and after she left, he spoke to the nurse of a question Nancy once put to him . . . Are you my father? Many years later, Nurse Cooper, from retirement in South Africa, wrote Nancy about GM's days of illness, and his recollection of the great question she posed to him. Nancy left a note about what followed on the occasion of her putting the question. Moore answered by saying only her mother knew. Well, then Nancy would ask Her Ladyship. "'Oh my Lord! Oh my Lord!'" Moore cried, "'Never ask your mother that . . .'" Then, in a kind of dreaminess, GM had ended, "'I wish I could think so, Nancy . . . but I fear not, I fear not.'"[216] In the nursing home, half out of his head with uraemia, Moore was evidently possessed of a different belief. Nurse Cooper looked down at her patient, "that great brain, and then the frail body."[217] Perhaps he "imagined things he liked to believe."[218] One thing he liked to believe, even on his deathbed, was that he was the father of Lady Cunard's only child, Nancy.

By 27 March 1928 Moore had recovered sufficiently to give a long interview to the *Evening News*. Moore said he had three hopes: to have his play *The Making of an Immortal* produced, to see it performed, and to finish *Aphrodite in Aulis*. He got his first wish promptly: the play was produced on 1 April, at the Arts Theatre Club, with a spectacular cast: Malcolm Keen as Burbage, Charles Laughton as Ben Jonson, Sybil Thorndike as Queen Elizabeth, and Leslie Faber as Francis Bacon. Even Sir Thomas Beecham lent a hand by arranging a madrigal for Sybil Thorndike to sing. The following day a reporter came to get a story about its triumphant author, then still lying in his nursing-home bed. With real popularity at last within Moore's reach, the sick and grumpy man was able to show little grace. He used his day in the sun to speak ill of Hardy and Conrad ("Anyone could write the sort of stuff [Conrad] wrote about barges floating in green-blue hazes"), and finished up by asking why popularity had to come after forty years of "hard work, boycotting, and spurning." And what was the cause of this popularity? Just a short play.[219] The next day, the *Daily Chronicle* reporter was summoned back to the hospital room, so Moore could explain that he never meant to insult outstanding living writers – writers like Kipling, Bennett, and James Stephens. It was unlikely, however, that the reporter would be able to explain that George Moore did not actually hold Hardy, James, or Conrad in contempt, but was just afraid of perishing.

15

On 21 April 1928, Moore left Lady Carnavon's nursing home and returned to 121 Ebury Street. For the rest of his life he would have to cope with an india-rubber tube inserted through a hole under his navel and into his bladder; this carried off his urine to a bag held to his body by a belt.[220] The removal of his prostate – a major operation – was indefinitely postponed. In spite of Moore's dependence on a doctor to regularly wash out and reinsert his catheter, he promptly planned a trip south to visit Magee and take the sea air. This placed considerable demands on his host to prepare for his arrival by identifying a doctor capable of dealing with the invalid's daily needs. Still, all preparations were managed, and in mid-August, Moore was able to spend a few days in a bed-and-breakfast in Bournemouth, Magee's new home – a change of air that gave him a "renewal of health."[221]

Moore hoped that a second trip to Bournemouth in mid-April 1929 would ready him for the long-delayed surgery on his prostate. Besides, he wanted to have some serious literary conversation with Magee about a collection of *Dial* essays he was urging his friend to make: *Irish Literary Portraits*. To be complete, Moore advised Magee, his book required "a carefully considered article on James Joyce." GM suggested an extended comparison between Joyce and Yeats as major Irish writers, and of two kinds. There are "those who think of art as a washtub, into which all the neighborhood dirty laundry may be thrown, and those who think of it as a vase that collects nothing except perhaps a little dust."[222] "Yeats belongs to the latter class, Joyce to the former. Yeats likes Joyce, so I have heard, and I am sure Joyce detests Yeats."[223] Still, Magee must write an essay about Joyce, and write it in his own way: "My opinion is not essential in this matter." So that they might discuss the matter, Moore offered to bring a copy of *Ulysses* to Bournemouth.[224] For his *Dial* letter for May 1929, Magee did write about Joyce's novel, and in a fashion that "excited [Moore's] literary instincts." GM decided he would try to read *Ulysses* himself, though there is no sign that he got very far with the book at this time.[225]

Upon his return to London from Bournemouth Moore met for the first time in many years with George Russell (AE). Ever since the fallout from the publication of Susan Mitchell's *George Moore* (1916), each had felt badly treated by the other. Monk Gibbon (1896–1987), an admirer of both writers, may have paved the way toward reconciliation by carrying the message to Russell that GM admired Russell's attacks on the new Irish censorship laws.[226] Visiting GM in London, Russell found him "looking very old and white and shaken" by his recent illness.[227] This meeting, however, seems to have been as far as their *rapprochement* went; there are no records of other meetings.

In August and September 1929, James Joyce was in England. In the full flush of fame, Joyce felt a curious need to make a "*rapprochement*" with "very old men" – Italo Svevo, Edouard Dujardin, and George Moore.[228] Although in his letters, critical writings, and *Ulysses*, he had often been sarcastic about the "genuine gent/ That lives on his property's ten percent," he had read GM's novels deeply and with profit.[229] His Trieste library included eleven books by George Moore, and Joyce read others before and after his Trieste period.[230] Furthermore, he wanted to ask a favor from Moore: a preface for an English translation of Dujardin's *Les Lauriers sont coupés*, the first example of *le monologue intérieur*.[231] It was a matter for Joyce of acknowledging his forerunners. GM was eager to see Joyce too: he wanted to gather notes for Magee's *Irish Literary Portraits*.

The two novelists had their first of three meetings in the first week of September 1929.[232] GM was evidently expecting simply an older version of the super-smart cad he had briefly met in Dublin twenty-seven years earlier. The new Joyce who appeared at 121 Ebury Street was altogether different, as GM reported to Magee on 9 September:

> Joyce is in London – he paid me a long visit. He was distinguished, courteous, respectful, and I was the same; he seemed anxious to accord me the first place. I demurred, and declared him first in Europe. We agreed that our careers were not altogether dissimilar, and he added, "Paris has played an equal part in our lives." This morning he sent me a book, and pleaded I had promised to accept a copy of the French translation of *Ulysses*. I was conquered.

It was extraordinarily kind of Joyce to call upon the old man and offer to send him the French *Ulysses*. Moore had demurred: "But Mr. Joyce, I can read English," and Joyce smiled a "Gioconda smile."[233] Moore was not so old as to have ceased to be Moore, and there is a streak of his mischievous genius in the letter of thanks he sent for Joyce's gifts – the French *Ulysses*, "Anna Livia Plurabelle" (an excerpt from *Finnegans Wake*), and a collection of critical essays on that work, *Our Exagimination Round his Factification for Incamination of Work in Progress*:

> When we look back upon our lives, our lives seem fateful. I never understood why I avoided reading *Ulysses*, for I was curious to read it, and when I was in the Nursing Home somebody whose name I cannot recall at the moment sent me a present of a reading-desk, and I wondered what could have put it into his head to send me such a useless piece of furniture. Now I know! I am reading *Ulysses*, and if you were here for a longer time and could dine with me, we could talk about the French, which I think wilfully exaggerated in places.
>
> Thank you for sending the book; I look forward to reading it all the winter.

The thanks are not without irony: *Ulysses* is the one book for which a reading-desk is necessary, the one book until *Finnegans Wake* becomes the second, which an old man must put aside a whole winter to read, and which requires trots and "critical guides" to be consulted alongside the novel itself.[234] Joyce returned to Ebury Street for dinner alone with GM on Saturday, 14 September. Moore was primed for some aesthetic sport. How was the action of Joyce's novel, GM led off, "advanced by associating the minor acts of Bloom with the acts of Ulysses?" "I see I am on the defensive," Joyce answered, and Moore apologised. Thereafter, Joyce sat "silent as a mummy." GM was disappointed and surprised: he had "always heard of him in Dublin as one of the most garrulous of men."[235]

GM tried to read *Ulysses* in French, but even with the reading-desk sixty pages was all he could manage – "I was doing no more than trying to follow Joyce in the dark." "It was like getting out of a cellar into the open air" when he shifted to the English text, lent him by Hutchinson.[236] Nonetheless, he had his doubts about the "inner monologue," and, were he to write them out, he let Joyce know on 11 October, they "should fill three or four pages."[237] There is no sign of what GM thought of the allusions to himself in the Library scene of *Ulysses* (Chapter 9, "Scylla and Charybdis"), if he got as far as that. In that scene, it is remarked that Ireland's national epic was yet to be written, and someone (probably "John Eglinton") says, "Moore is the man for it." He could do an Irish *Don Quixote*, with Martyn as Sancho Panza and GM himself as the "knight of rueful countenance" – a plain foreshadowing of the plot of *Hail and Farewell*.[238] This ironic treatment of his own trilogy as a weak precursor of Joyce's own "national epic" would surely have annoyed Moore.

GM was a cantankerous customer at all times, and in his final years more so. Illness left him with a life of complaint. He had been trying to write his own Homeric novel, *Aphrodite in Aulis*, since May 1927, all through the brainfog of a long illness; in October 1929, while reading *Ulysses*, he thought he was at last bringing *Aphrodite in Aulis* to an end.[239] Moore's novel is an historical romance about two brothers in the time of Phidias. One brother, a sculptor, falls in love with a woman because she has a rump that would be perfect for his statue of Aphrodite. The story "mingles the vulgar with the aesthetic, the trivial with the sublime," as the *Times Literary Supplement* said in its review; indeed, it reduces all the sublimations of religion and art to an origin in the male sex drive, even to voyeurism.[240] The *TLS* reviewer was excessively courteous to its elderly author in saying that *Aphrodite in Aulis* was "written with undiminished vigour and a yet increased artistry." In *Ulysses*, one also finds the trivial next to the sublime, the vulgar next to the aesthetic, and a man admiring the rump of a statue of Aphrodite, yet Joyce's novel is indeed written with truly undiminished vigor and artistry. In "Lestyrgonians," Leopold Bloom seeks an escape from terrible thoughts of Molly's first kiss, compared with his feelings about her present liaison with Blazes Boylan – "Me. And me now." Bloom's mind then turns to a cast of Aphrodite he has seen in the National Gallery:

> Beauty: it curves, curves are beauty. Shapely goddesses, Venus, Juno: curves the world admires. Can see them library museum standing in the round hall, naked goddesses. Aids to digestion. They don't care what man looks. All to see.[241]

A benign spirit of self-preservation may have saved Moore from making the comparison of his book with that of Joyce, and concluding, "Me, and me now." Moore never wished to be yesterday's man.

In a letter to Joyce of 10 May 1930, Moore backed away from the promise he had given to write a preface for *Les Lauriers*. "The human mind is not like a weathercock," GM began, "and cannot be diverted from one subject to another. I may live a few more years, and if I do I shall naturally devote them to my own work." Anyway, GM continued with gathering ire, there was nothing to be said about the "question which apparently agitates France, the discovery of the *monologue intérieur*."[242] At the back of GM's anger about the fuss made over the interior monologue and "stream of consciousness" is his own belief that, after having experimented with the technique in *The Lake*, he had gone on to discover a better way of passing from plane to plane of narrative – from dialogue, to the thought process of a character, to description, to the narrator's voice – without ever breaking the rhythmic flow of the story. This narrative practice, he believed, was not modernist, but part of the ancient craft of storytelling: "In England . . . we think [it] existed from time immemorial." Joyce was magnificent about this irritable letter. He replied "sweetly and suavely," then remarked to Sylvia Beach, "Old men have a right to their anger."[243]

16

In his last years, Moore was certainly a crotchety old man. That may have had something to do with the hailstorm of infirmities that fell upon him: bladder infection, lumbago, neuritis, sciatica, uraemia, and the inoperable swollen prostate. He was a difficult patient for his nurse, master for his servants, and friend for his acquaintances, but as death closed in, and being entirely cut off from his family, he needed friendship more than ever. It had been his custom for many years to dine on Saturday nights with Steer and the Hutchinsons at the Vale, the home of Henry Tonks, Slade Professor of Fine Art from 1917 to 1930. Mary Hutchinson was very dear to GM, and often asked him to bring whatever he was writing to read to the guests, a custom that irritated Tonks and put Steer to sleep. Moore was prickly about the subject. In January 1930, he told Mary Hutchinson that this week he would prefer not to read from his manuscripts: it would "bore [Tonks] too much. He is always so full of elegant and instructive conversation that it seems a pity to interrupt it."[244] Tonks painted a delightfully comical – but also satirical – picture of one such "Saturday Evening at the Vale," catching the responses of each of the guests to Moore's recitation, and another picture depicting Moore's sulk when "The Conversation Turned on Tonks."

Eventually, the two old friends irritated one another into a quarrel, and a silence grew up between them. On 4 September 1930, GM held out an olive branch: "The interval that divides us has become so burdensome and so long that I can barely believe I am going to see you again, and I am writing to ask you to assure me I am mistaken."[245] In his reply, Tonks evidently suggested that GM's infirmity would probably make it difficult for him to resume regular attendance at the Vale on Saturday nights. GM naturally suspected Tonks did not want him there.[246] Yet the two men, both sensitive and grumpy, resumed their friendly intercourse until late 1932, when Moore let a wounding word slip from his lips, and another silence came between them. Each man brooded in

27. *Saturday Evening at the Vale* (1928–9), Henry Tonks. George Moore reading to St John Hutchinson, P. W. Steer, Henry Tonks (*standing*), and Mary Hutchinson.

his tent, then one cold Saturday night, GM put on his biggest overcoat and set out for the Vale:

> I couldn't bear to think that we were at quarrel any longer, but the night was piercing and I dreaded cystitis and returned . . . Remember I am ill and that I barely know what I am saying. For the last three days I have had nothing but ill-luck with surgeons . . . Think no more of my casual word but come and see your old friend. We all have to forgive each other, for none is perfect.[247]

The strict master of the Slade School allowed his heart to soften, and made his visit to Ebury Street; GM did not die unbefriended. Tonks found Moore "the most trying friend [he] ever had," "but the great thing to remember," he wrote after Moore's passing, "is that he was Great."[248] Tonks was faithful to the last, and beyond: of all GM's friends, he was the most helpful to Charles Morgan, whom GM designated to write his biography; and after Morgan relinquished the job, to Joseph Hone.

17

In Charles Morgan, GM at last found a suitable and willing biographer. Morgan (1894–1958) was the *Times* drama critic, a mellifluous novelist, and an admirer of Moore's late style.[249] Moore gave Charles Morgan all the help, and all the freedom, a biographer could desire: "Spare nothing, so far as I am concerned," GM told Morgan. "Make your book true as only a novel can be true."[250] Nothing was held back from Morgan once he accepted the job. Moore's sexuality "doesn't in the least shock me," Morgan wrote later. "It was part of the nature from which his art sprang, is continually reflected in his writings, and is therefore of the utmost importance." Yet "even to suggest publicly to what extent he was a voyeur and a tactilist and the special coldness or detachment of his sexual approaches would . . . raise a British outcry."[251] An intimate biography of the sort they planned was unprecedeuted in the early 1930s.

The letters he had written to Lady Cunard, in GM's judgement, were essential. She was the heart of the story of his life. In December 1929, a luncheon was arranged at Ebury Street between muse, author, and biographer. Moore asked Lady Cunard to let Morgan see all his letters over the years. "All?" she replied. "Yes," he answered, "all. There must be more than a thousand." There were a great many more than a thousand, she said, and indicated she would require some time to think the matter over.[252] It was her first preference that the biography be published before GM's death, and written without access to the letters in her possession. But no proper story of his life could be told without them, GM believed.

The first meeting with Lady Cunard was unsuccessful, yet Moore assured Charles Morgan that sooner or later, certainly after his bequest to her, she would relent; if she failed to do so, Morgan promised to give the project up. As he continued his work, Morgan began to doubt that a biography along the lines GM wanted – "Literature in front, and a background of women!" – would be possible, even if Lady Cunard should have a change of heart.[253] Moore's men friends were generous, but Morgan's interviews with GM's female friends did not go well: "They have their pride to consider," Morgan reported to Tonks; furthermore, "they are acutely aware of the commercial value of whatever materials they possess."[254]

During the Christmas holidays of 1930, a disastrous quarrel blew up between Nancy and Maud Cunard that made it less likely than ever before that Lady Cunard would permit any biographer to make her a character in Moore's life-story. Ever since Nancy had left London for France a decade earlier, relations between the socialite mother and bohemian daughter remained frosty. Just as Nancy loved GM for being an apostle of individual freedom, so she detested Maud Cunard for being an imperiously conventional *arriviste*. Nancy's bitterness toward her mother pained Moore. In his periodic heart-to-heart talks with Nancy, he tried to play the go-between by praising his beloved Maud; afterwards, he carried cheerful news of Nancy back to Lady Cunard.[255] In 1930,

28. *The Red Dressing Gown* (1920), Henry Tonks; National Portrait Gallery, London.

29 and 30. Lady Cunard
and Nancy Cunard,
photographed by Cecil
Beaton. Mother and
daughter in clashing
styles, yet the same pose.

during one of their talks, Nancy raised the question of interracial love. Was it really any obstacle to love if one's beloved were white, red, yellow, or black? Moore supposed he could "'not do better' (in the sense of 'go further') than a yellow man."[256] She did not then tell him that for two years she herself had been in love with Henry Crowder, an African-American jazz saxophonist in Paris. This relationship turned Nancy into a militant: she intended to challenge racial prejudice in general. Ultimately, her quest led her to assemble the massive *Negro Anthology* (1936), an historically important collection of literature in English by people of African descent.

For the Christmas holidays in 1930, Nancy planned to come to London with Henry Crowder, and not for the first time, though she had concealed her new relationship from her mother. Word nonetheless got around. Just before Nancy's departure from Paris in late December 1930, Margot Asquith, Lady Oxford – a rival wit and hostess to Lady Cunard – came to a large Grosvenor Square luncheon. She threw out a loud greeting: "Hello Maud, what is it now – drink, drugs, or niggers?"[257] Confusion followed. Lady Cunard subsequently got on the telephone to ask Nancy's friends if it was true that her daughter "knew a Negro." Lady Cunard worked herself into a violent fury of indignation at the insult she felt her daughter was bringing upon herself and, perhaps more especially, upon her mother. On 23 December 1930, Sir Thomas Beecham sent Nancy the following telegram: SERIOUSLY ADVISE YOU NOT TO LEAVE PARIS FOR LONDON UNTIL YOU RECEIVE MY LETTER TOMORROW STOP IMPOSSIBLE TO EXPLAIN IN TELEGRAM BUT MATTER VERY IMPORTANT THOMAS BEECHAM.[258] Beecham was telling people, who told Nancy, that she should be "tarred and feathered," while Maud believed Nancy would not come to London with her black lover, for no hotel would accommodate him.[259] Yet Nancy Cunard did not mean to let herself be cowed. The couple stayed a month in a London hotel.

The atmosphere at 7 Grosvenor Square was combustible. Nancy did not at this time make her case to Lady Cunard. Instead, in a 24 January 1931 letter, at the time of her return to France, she frankly explained how things stood to George Moore, and gave him the job of preparing her mother for the crisis.[260] Eunice Sands, one of GM's regular visitors, called at Ebury Street after he had read Nancy's letter. He was "in a feverish state, 'shocked' . . . for the first time in his life." According to the report Sands gave Harold Acton who directly passed it to Nancy, Moore was "so pained that he had already summoned his lawyer to change some arrangement – by which he intended to leave . . . [Nancy] his Manets."[261] Nancy immediately challenged GM: had he cut her out of his will? In fact, Moore had long ago assigned those paintings to Lady Cunard. On 27 February Moore sent Nancy this short sad reply: "Dearest Nancy, I have made no change in my will, Always affectionately yours, George Moore."[262] With Nancy having taken sanctuary in France, and GM unable to travel, they never saw each other again.[263]

The war between mother and daughter got ugly. In late January 1931, Nancy received a letter from her bank stating that high taxation had forced Lady Cunard to reduce Nancy's allowance, and on 11 June, Nancy heard from Beecham that Lady Cunard had taken the last step: disinheritance.[264] Nancy's response was to publish the following Christmas a blistering, nearly homicidal pamphlet about her mother's conduct, *Black Man and White Ladyship* – including every detail of the family feud: the extended family, that is, including Beecham and George Moore.

The likelihood that Lady Cunard was ever going to assist in a possibly scandalous biography of Moore was always slim, but after the horrible open quarrel with Nancy, there was no chance at all. Lady Cunard either lost or destroyed the great majority of her letters from Moore; the ones she saved are mostly from the later years of Moore's life. Joseph Hone published just one of these in his highly discreet biography, and Lady Cunard "frightened [the publisher] out of his life."[265] In the immediate wake of the scandal about Nancy, Lady Cunard even backed away from being GM's literary executor. She acted as one who did "not wish to associate" herself with his literature.[266] To an old friend, Moore acknowledged that Lady Cunard "was the only woman he had ever known who had had the power to hurt him, and further that she had often done so."[267]

18

In 1931, the indomitable author began another novel – *Madeleine de Lisle*. It was planned as a story about an Edwardian book collector (modeled in part on T. J. Wise) and a nun who had once loved him. A. J. A. Symons helped Moore with details about the habits of a collector, and Virginia Crawford once more came to his assistance with lore about convents.[268] He worked as hard as ever, but the story would not come together. "I live in a state of terror lest I should find one morning," he confided to Crawford, that "the literary craft which was once George Moore has departed."[269] What more could death be than to awake one day to find that one's identity had fled?

In late 1932, Moore dropped *Madeleine de Lisle* and sketched out a different book, an autobiography to be called *A Communication to My Friends*. It is the sixtieth title in Edwin Gilcher's bibliography of works by Moore. Hilda Neal, GM's last secretary, was astonished at his assiduity. He would dictate a passage six times over, meanwhile urging her to hurry up and keep pace with him. She could tell he was terribly ill. More than once, he gave utterance to his very reasonable fear that he would die before the book was finished. Yet he had his comforts. When he got a phrase perfectly polished, he "smiled like a delighted child": "Now that is perfect English!"[270] Although his remarkable visual memory was not so sharp any longer, there is indeed in this last book the winning quality of old men's tales. They have been told so often that they have found their own perfect shape, and a truthfulness that owes much to wisdom and less to fact. Marvelously, Moore recovered in his last month his famous limpidity of phrase, a happy marriage between the spoken and the written word. *A Communication to My Friends* is the story of a man who received a call to be an artist, struggled to make himself articulate, and then fought for the freedom to be himself. The painful memories lasted longest – his first two decades as a novelist when his books were banned one after another by the circulating libraries, in a concerted attempt by the book trade to stamp him out as a professional man of letters. Indeed, he contemplated entitling his recollections "The Story of a Persecution."[271] In the first week of January 1933, Moore gave a report on the book to G. W. Bishop of the *Sunday Times*:

> The one piece of heroism in my wretched character is that I did not sue the [circulating] libraries for libel over *Esther Waters*. The book had been praised by Mr. Gladstone and it sold 24,000 copies, but I had set up in business as a man of letters, and, even though I was bound to win, I came to the conclusion that a court of law was not the place for a writer . . . It was not for many years that it was even admitted that I was an English writer . . . I am also telling the story of the prosecution of Vizetelly, which is one of the most disgraceful things in the history of English literature.

Moore sent Magee a batch of typescript on 7 January 1933, and another on the 12th – the last. It stops at the point where Moore recalls a drawing by Stephen Gooden for *Peronnik the Fool*, a last portrait of George Moore:

> A fierce blustering cock, screaming, perched on a key drawn in perspective, no doubt the key of the secret castle where the sorceress kept the knights she lured into her service, how he screams! A raucous scream, as if nobody knew except himself that day was near. What intensity in that eye, I continued, what life there is. Look again at his bony legs covered with a hard skin. Will my luck give me a publisher when I am among the gone who will ask Gooden to do four, five, or six pictures for my *Daphnis and Chloe*? Should such a thing happen, I doubt not that God will open my ears to hear the crowing of the cock.

On 14 January, Moore wrote Magee: "I am very ill today and feel inclined to abandon the project of writing anything more. I have written enough." A man from his publishers came to see him when he was bedridden, and rather unfortunately mentioned the style of Conrad. "The dying man sat straight up in bed and with great indignation cried, 'What! Style you call it! Why it is nothing but wreckage of Robert Louis Stevenson floating in the slops of Henry James.'"[272] A week was spent in misery, dulled by sleeping pills. Then, at seven o'clock in the morning on 21 January 1933, George Moore slipped out of life peacefully.

Moore had asked to be cremated and for his ashes to be taken to Lough Carra. On 25 January, a small party of mourners gathered at Golders Green Crematorium for a funeral service. Magee, Tonks, Steer, David Garnett, and Prime Minister Ramsay MacDonald were among those who listened as the elderly Irish Protestant minister, Canon Douglas, tried while very drunk to recall the words of the burial service, and mixed them up with the Lord's Prayer: "Ashes to ashes and dust to dust . . . Forgive us our trespasses . . . glorious resurrection . . . our daily bread in the life everlasting."[273] Steer and Tonks came home from the funeral of their best friend "helpless with laughter."[274] Not mentioned in the newspaper notice of floral tributes was "a large chaplet wreath of cistapalm and barberry leaves green and brown mixed with an inscription"; it was sent by James Joyce.[275]

The duty of returning the ashes of George Moore to Lough Carra was shouldered by his brother Maurice, who had, after GM's sale of Moore Hall to the Congested Districts Board, by purchase finally come into ownership of the burnt-out ruin. Now GM was also delivered into his hands. Taking his cue from GM's 1901 story, "My Own Funeral," Maurice had an urn made after a Bronze Age Greek original in the National Gallery.[276] The ashes were put in a packing case, shipped from London to Dun Laoghaire. Then, by the same route that George Moore had come with his mother sixty-three years earlier for the funeral of his father, the ashes were carried by rail west to Balla, County Mayo, arriving on 26 May. Virginia Crawford, Richard Best, Oliver St John Gogarty, Maurice Moore, Nina Moore Kilkelly, C. D. Medley (GM's literary executor), and a small number of reporters took the train with the remains of Moore. Word had gotten around that there was to be a "pagan" – that is, non-Christian – burial at Carnacun on the 27th. The parish priest, Father Batty Canavan, reportedly told his parishioners, "You may have heard that something is going on up the way, but you stay away from there. Pay no more attention to that than to a man burying his dog."[277] According to Gogarty, not enough local men could be found to row the mourners out to the burial site at Castle Island, so he himself lent a hand at the oars.[278]

The man Maurice Moore had selected to write the funeral address was George Russell ("AE"), with whom GM had rarely spoken in his last decade. Russell himself "funked" the journey, so Richard Best read out the brief oration – sonorous enough, but also a "masterpiece of double-meaning."[279] Watching the mourners, the former steward James Reilly saw only one of them weep – Virginia Crawford.[280] As stones were being piled up on the urn, Maurice Moore felt inside his overcoat and "produced a wooden crucifix," which he planted within the cairn.[281] Were GM's wishes for a pagan rite carried out? To use a West of Ireland saying, "They were, and they weren't." A visitor to the heavily thicketed little island can still discover on its shoreline that cairn, six feet across and four feet high, and in front of it a Celtic cross on a pediment, which bears these words of still somewhat begrudging forgiveness by friends, family, and nation:[282]

31. At the cairn of George Moore, Castle Island, Lough Carra. Richard Best reads the address written by George Russell. At the far right, Maurice Moore and Nina Moore Kilkelly. The woman in the background to the right may be Virginia Crawford.

George Moore
Born Moore Hall 1852, died 1933 London
He deserted his family and friends
For his art
But because he was faithful to his art
His family and friends
Reclaimed his ashes for Ireland.
VALE

Far from Moore's family and friends in Ireland, newspapers in Rome, Paris, New York, Toronto, Zurich, and other cities marked the passing of George Moore.[283] More than one critic expressed a belief that Moore had made himself, as Ford Madox Ford put it, "the most skilful man of letters of his day – the most skillful in the whole world."[284] Many different titles were named as the one book sure to live. *A Mummer's Wife, Confessions of a Young Man, Esther Waters, The Lake, Memoirs of My Dead Life, Hail and Farewell, The Brook Kerith, A Story-Teller's Holiday, Héloïse and Abelard, Daphnis and Chloe,* and *Celibate Lives* each had advocates. Some said nothing by Moore would stand the test of time.

19

Yet nearly 150 years after the birth of George Moore, there are still readers who discern in his books an exquisite pleasure only those books can offer, and there are scholars with the zeal to make his work better understood. In 1986, Robert Langenfeld recorded 2,355 books and articles published on Moore, a number that is larger now, and will go on increasing, for the interest of his books is permanent. One part of that interest is rooted in his life, that of a man who made himself, from the son of a Mayo landlord with little education, into an author who took a large part in the reinvention of art in his time. Bound by no belief, and guided by absolute confidence in his instincts, he had the courage to see things by his own lights. Nationality was for him an elective affinity, and, as a resident alien, he might observe, or make observations on, the customs of a country, but it always seemed to him that "Myself was my nation." He spelt out his feelings in the teeth of Victorian England and Catholic Ireland, regardless of the trouble it got him into, and into trouble it often got him, for men were not supposed to feel what he felt, or see what he saw. He had to fight to be heard, for the circulating libraries – the major form of distribution for novels – tried to drive him out of the trade for the first fifteen years of his career as a man of letters. Profoundly interested in Matthew Arnold's question about what makes great art possible – both the man and the moment, according to Arnold – Moore labored to create the conditions for literature of the highest order in England and in Ireland. Many of the women writers of the period went to school to him. Nearly every major figure of his era worked with Moore, tangled with Moore, took his impression from, or left it on, George Moore. Where he led, others followed and sometimes went further: W. D. Howells, Arnold Bennett, James Joyce, D. H. Lawrence, Ford Madox Ford, Austin Clarke . . . Modern English fiction as a whole would have been different without George Moore, for, along with Henry James, he was the first writer in English to treat the novel deliberately as an art form. He did not just write novels; he introduced new ways of telling stories to English literature – sometimes those were French ways, transplanted from Balzac, Flaubert, Zola, and Dujardin, but latterly Moore compounded suggestions from Turgenev, Pater, Sterne, and Landor with his own spoken idiom into a style without precedent.

His devotion to his craft was extraordinary, especially in a landlord who did not have to work at all. G. B. Shaw, who as a young man knew Moore in London only as a good-humored gentleman who told silly stories about himself and women, was astonished when *A Mummer's Wife* was published; then Shaw "began to understand the incredible industry of the man."[285] Moore often put his painfully acquired gifts to the service of telling the stories of those who were most unlike himself: the wife of an invalid in a boarding house, a household servant with a child to look after, a woman forced to dress as a man to earn a living, Jesus of Nazareth. It was from his meditation on Jesus that GM found in his sixty-ninth year a way to articulate to his Christian detractors a great simple lesson: "It is better to love the good than to hate the wretched." The story of his own life he told again and again, always guided by Manet's lesson: "Be ashamed of nothing but to be ashamed"; as a result, he is an essential witness to the Paris of the Impressionists and the Dublin of the Irish Literary Revival. Although he often embarrassed his famous contemporaries by his auto-biographies, he was hardest on himself, and contemplated the oddity of his own human existence in a spirit of a philosophical comedy. George Moore did without the conventional props of a man – wife, family, class, religion, and country – but his peculiar fidelity to the one great love of his life was a kind of monogamy in itself, and from Nancy Cunard he won a love that any father would crave from any daughter. "A man must be judged by what is fine in him, not by what is trivial," Max Beerbohm reflected. Beerbohm had bedeviled Moore's poor human figure in one cartoon after another, yet he put in print his admiration for the "fine things inside" George Moore: "his matchless honesty of mind, his very real modesty about his work . . . his loving reverence of all that in all arts was nobly done; and, above all, the inexhaustible patience of his and courage, whereby he made the most of the gifts he had, and earned for himself a gift which Nature had not bestowed on him: the specific gift for writing . . . Somehow, in the course of long years, he learned to express himself beautifully. I call that great."[286]

Editions of Works by George Moore

The following editions are cited in the Notes. Where different editions exist and no date is given, the edition cited is the one given in bold below.

Au Authology of Pure Poetry. Boni and Liveright: New York, 1924.

Aphrodite in Aulis. London: Heinemann, 1930, 1931.

"Apologia pro scriptis meis." General introduction, Carra Edition, vol. 1. *Lewis Seymour and Some Women*. Boni and Liveright: New York, 1922. xi–xxxiii.

The Apostle. Maunsel: Dublin, 1911.

Ave, vol. 1 of *Hail and Farewell*. Heinemann: London, 1911, **1937**.

Ave, vol. 1 of *Hail and Farewell*. Carra Edition, vol. 11. Boni and Liveright: New York, 1923.

Avowals. Boni and Liveright: New York, 1919.

Avowals. Heinemann: London, **1924**.

The Bending of the Bough, A Comedy in Five Acts. T. Fisher Unwin: London, 1900.

The Brook Kerith: A Syrian Story. T. Werner Laurie: London, 1916.

The Brook Kerith. Carra Edition, vol. 16. Boni and Liveright: New York. 1923.

Celibates. Walter Scott: London, 1895.

Celibate Lives. Heinemann: London, 1927, 1937.

Les Cloches de Corneville. Lyrics by George and Augustus Moore. Privately published, c. 1883.

The Coming of Gabrielle: a Comedy. Privately printed by Cumann Sean-eolais na h-Eirann, 1920.

The Coming of Gabrielle. Boni and Liveright: New York, 1921.

A Commmunication to My Friends. Nonesuch: London, 1933.

Confessions d'un jeune anglais. Nouvelle Librairie Parisienne: Paris, 1889.

Confessions of a Young Man. Swan Sonnenschein, Lowrey: London, 1888, 1889.

Confessions of a Young Man. Ed. Susan Dick. McGill–Queen's University Press: Montreal and London, 1972.

Conversations in Ebury Street. Heinemann: London, 1924, **1930**.

A Drama in Muslin, A Realistic Novel. Vizetelly: London, 1886.

A Drama in Muslin. Walter Scott: London, 1893.

Elizabeth Cooper: A Comedy in Three Acts. Maunsel: Dublin and London, 1913.

Esther Waters. Walter Scott: London, 1894, 1899.

Esther Waters. Boni and Liveright: New York, 1922.

Esther Waters. Everyman: London, 1994.
Esther Waters: A Play. Heinemann: London, 1913.
Evelyn Innes. T. Fisher Unwin: London, 1898, 1901, 1908.
Flowers of Passion. Provost: London, 1877.
Hail and Farewell. Ed. Richard Allen Cave. Colin Smythe: Gerrards Cross, Bucks, 1976.
Héloïse and Abélard. Two vols. Boni and Liveright: New York, 1921.
Impressions and Opinions. David Nutt: London, 1891.
Impressions and Opinions. Brentano's: New York, 1913.
In Single Strictness. Heinemann: London, 1922.
In Single Strictness. Boni and Liveright: New York, 1922, 1923.
The Lake. William Heinemann: London, 1905, 1906, 1921.
Lewis Seymour and Some Women. Heinemann: London, 1917.
Literature at Nurse, or Circulating Morals. Vizetelly: London, 1885.
The Making of an Immortal, A Play in One Act. London: Bowling Green Press, 1927.
Martin Luther. With Bernard Lopez. Remington: London, 1879.
Memoirs of My Dead Life. Heinemann: London, **1906**, 1921, 1928.
Memoirs of My Dead Life. Tauchnitz: Leipzig, 1906.
Memoirs of My Dead Life. Boni and Liveright: New York, 1920. Boar's Head: Cambridge, 1960.
A Mere Accident. Vizetelly: London, 1887.
Mike Fletcher: A Novel. Ward and Downey: London, 1889.
A Modern Lover. Three vols. Tinsley: London, 1883.
Modern Painting. Walter Scott: London, 1893, 1896.
A Mummer's Wife. Vizetelly: London, 1885, 1886.
A Mummer's Wife. Brentano's: New York, 1908.
Muslin. Heinemann: London, 1915.
Muslin. Carra Edition, vol. 3. Boni and Liveright: New York, 1922.
Pagan Poems. Newman and Co.: London, 1881.
Parnell and His Island. Swan Sonnenschein, Lowrey: London, 1887.
The Passing of the Essenes. Heinemann: London, 1930.
The Pastoral Loves of Daphnis and Chloe. Heinemann: London, 1924.
Salve, vol. 2 of *Hail and Farewell.* Heinemann: London, 1912, **1937**.
Sister Teresa. T. Fisher Unwin: London, 1901, 1909.
Sister Teresa. Ernest Benn: London, 1929.
Spring Days, A Realistic Novel. Vizetelly: London, 1888.
Spring Days. Carra Edition, vol. 4. Boni and Liveright: New York, 1922.
A Story-Teller's Holiday. Privately printed for subscribers only by Cumann Sean-eolais na h-Eireann, 1918.
A Story-Teller's Holiday. Carra Edition, vol. 14. Boni and Liveright: New York, 1923.
The Strike at Arlingford. Walter Scott: London, 1893.
Ulick and Soracha. Nonesuch Press: London, 1926.
The Untilled Field. T. Fisher Unwin: London, 1903.
Vain Fortune. Henry: London, 1891.
Vain Fortune. Walter Scott: London, 1895.
Vale, vol. 3 of *Hail and Farewell.* Heinemann: London, 1914, 1915, **1937**.

Notes

For further bibliographical details of works by George Moore see pp. 470–71.

Abbreviations

Bancroft	Bancroft Collection, University of California Library, Berkeley.
Becker	Robert Becker, ed. "Letters of George Moore, 1863–1901." Dissertation, University of Reading, 1980.
Beinecke	Beinecke Library, Yale University, New Haven, Connecticut
Berg	Berg Collection, New York Public Library
Bertrand	Ellen Clarke Bertrand Library, Bucknell University, Pennsylvania
BL	British Library
Bodleian	Bodleian Library, Oxford University
Brotherton	Brotherton Collection, Leeds University Library
Columbia	Columbia University Library, New York
Eglinton	*Letters of George Moore*. With an Introduction by John Eglinton, to whom they were written. Folcroft Press: Bournemouth, 1942.
George Moore in Transition	Helmut E. Gerber, ed. *George Moore in Transition: Letters to T. Fisher Unwin and Lena Milman, 1894–1910.* Wayne State University Press: Detroit, 1968.
George Moore on Parnassus	Helmut Gerber and O. M. Brack, Jr., eds. *George Moore on Parnassus: Letters (1900–1933) to Secretaries, Publishers, Agents, Literati, Friends, and Acquaintances.* University of Delaware Press: Newark, NJ, 1988.
Gilcher	Edwin Gilcher, *A Bibliography of George Moore.* Northern Illinois University Press: Dekalb, IL, 1970.
Hart-Davis	Rupert Hart-Davis, ed. *George Moore: Letters to Lady Cunard, 1895–1933.* Hart-Davis: London, 1957.
Houghton	Houghton Library, Harvard University, Cambridge, Massachusetts
HRHRC	Harry Ransom Humanities Research Center, University of Texas, Austin
Huntington	Huntington Library, Pasadena, California
An Irish Gentleman	Colonel Maurice George Moore, *An Irish Gentleman: George Henry Moore.* T. Werner Laurie: London, 1913.

Lady Gregory's Diaries	James Pethica, ed. *Lady Gregory's Diaries: 1892–1902.* Colin Smythe: Gerrards Cross, Bucks, 1996.
Langenfeld	Robert Langenfeld, *George Moore: An Annotated Secondary Bibliography of Writings About Him.* AMS Press: New York, 1987.
Letters to Dujardin	John Eglinton, ed. *Letters from George Moore to Ed. Dujardin, 1886–1922.* Crosby Gaige: New York, 1929.
Life of George Moore	Joseph Hone, *The Life of George Moore.* Macmillan: New York, 1936.
LWBY1	John Kelly and Eric Domville, eds. *The Collected Letters of W. B. Yeats.* Vol. 1. Clarendon Press: Oxford, 1986.
LWBY2	Warwick Gould, John Kelly, and Deirdre Toomey, eds. *The Collected Letters of W. B. Yeats.* Vol. 2. Clarendon Press: Oxford, 1997.
LWBY3	John Kelly and Ronald Schuchard. *The Collected Letters of W. B. Yeats.* Vol. 3. Clarendon Press: Oxford, 1994.
The Moores of Moore Hall	Joseph Hone, *The Moores of Moore Hall.* Jonathan Cape: London, 1939.
NGI	National Gallery of Ireland
NLI	National Library of Ireland
NYU	New York University Library
Reading	University of Reading Library
Rochester	University of Rochester Library
TCD	Trinity College Dublin Library
UCD	University College Dublin Library
Virginia	University of Virginia Library, Charlottesville, Virginia
Washington	Manuscripts, Special Collections, and University Archives Division, University of Washington Libraries, Seattle, Washington

Chapter 1 His Father's Funeral and the Birth of George Moore

1. Father Peter Conway to Mr—, 22 April 1870, *Ballinrobe Chronicle*, 30 April 1870: 1.
2. *Telegraph* [Castlebar], 20 April 1870; *Weekly Freeman's Journal* [Dublin], 23 April 1870.
3. *An Irish Gentleman*, 374.
4. James S. Donnelly, Jr., "Landlords and Tenants," in W. E. Vaughan, ed., *A New History of Ireland*, vol. 5: *Ireland Under the Union, I, 1801–70* (Clarendon Press: Oxford, 1989), 341–42.
5. See Gerard Moran, *A Radical Priest in Mayo: Father Patrick Lavelle, 1825–86* (Four Courts Press: Blackrock, 1994), 66–67, 85, 94, 105–7, 126–28.
6. R. V. Comerford, "Churchmen, Tenants, and Independent Opposition, 1850–56," *A New History of Ireland*, vol. 5, 407.

7. *An Irish Gentleman*, 373–74. Father Lavelle wrote Moore on 20 February 1870 that he had persuaded the tenants to pay what they owed, with future rent levels to be negotiated between themselves and Moore (NLI). See E. D. Steele, *Irish Land and British Politics* (Cambridge University Press: Cambridge, 1974), 296.
8. *Weekly Freeman*, 12 March 1870.
9. *An Irish Gentleman*, 350. Two Fenian leaders, O'Donovan Rossa and John O'Leary, reported that G. H. Moore took the organisation's secret oath. Yet his membership nonetheless has been doubted. In Joseph Hone's account, a meeting between Stephens and Moore took place, and probably in 1864, yet no oath was seen to be taken by the witness, John Devoy (*The Moores of Moore Hall*, 171).
10. R. V. Comerford, "Gladstone's First Irish Enterprise, 1864–70," *A New History of Ireland, vol. 5*, 437;

O'Donovan Rossa was arrested along with John O'Leary on 15 September 1865 in a police raid on the offices of the *Irish People*.

11. According to Comerford, "Gladstone's First Irish Enterprise," 444–46, after the failure of the 1867 Rising, the Irish Republican Brotherhood was guided by a supreme council, under a constitution, organised by William R. Roberts. At the time of this speech by Moore, there is a story that he kept in touch with O'Donovan Rossa in Chatham jail through a Highland Scottish warder (*The Moores of Moore Hall*, 180).

12. *Weekly Freeman*, 26 March 1870.

13. Ibid., 19 March 1870.

14. *Ballinrobe Chronicle*, 23 April 1870.

15. Ibid., 30 April 1870.

16. *An Irish Gentleman*, 374–77; *The Life of George Moore*, 37–38. For the matter of G. H. Moore being unable to make his last confession, see George Moore to Maurice Moore, Wednesday [May/June 1913], *George Moore on Parnassus*, 274–75.

17. "Father Lavelle's Sermon," *Freeman's Journal*, 27 April 1870; NLI Ms 897.ix; George Moore, *Confessions of a Young Man* (1972), 195–96.

18. Room plan of Moore Hall, from rough sketches supplied by Rory Moore; my thanks to Edwin Gilcher. Joseph Apply's name is sometimes spelled "Appley" or "Applely."

19. *George Moore on Parnassus*, 274–75.

20. George Moore, *Vale*, 31.

21. *An Irish Gentleman*, 371. Hone, however, quotes a letter from the Partry parish priest T. F. Conway in which he reports burying a widow who had died of starvation, two other parishioners the same day, and two the day previous (*The Moores of Moore Hall*, 136–37). Still, Moore's generosity and concern during this period earned him a good memory among those who survived.

22. *Ballinrobe Chronicle*, 23 April 1870.

23. *The Telegraph, or Connaught Ranger* [Castlebar], 27 April 1870.

24. Moore, *Vale*, 215; *Ballinrobe Chronicle*, 23 April 1870.

25. *Life of George Moore*, 39; NLI Ms 897.ix; *Ballinrobe Chronicle*, 30 April 1870.

26. *An Irish Gentleman*, xx.

27. *Daily News*, quoted in *Telegraph* [Castlebar], 27 April 1870.

28. The Athy family seat of Renville Hall, Oranmore, County Galway, was erected in 1826, decades after the marriage of Jane Athy to John Moore. See Mark Bence-Jones, *A Guide to Irish Country Houses* (Constable: London, 1988), 241.

George Moore of Alicante was descended from Thomas Moore of Barrenourgh, County Galway and Katherine de Kilikelly. (Tabular pedigree, in Spanish, of George Moore of Alicante; copy in NLI Ms 10566 [1]). At the end of the nineteenth century, Maurice Moore, along with two antiquarian cousins, Martin J. Blake and Dominick Browne, conducted a genealogical search with the aim of proving that the Moores were descended from Sir Thomas More; however, they came to grief, in that they could only conclude that a demonstrated relation of Sir Thomas More, "Thomas More of Leyton, Essex, living in 1606, *may* have been the man who married Mary Apadamn in the pedigree of Moore of Moorehall, County Mayo. But there is no proof whatever that he was" (Martin J. Blake to Maurice Moore, 4 February 1898, ibid.).

29. *The Moores of Moore Hall*, 20–21.

30. Ibid., 44.

31. When GM read the manuscript preface to his grandfather's work on the French Revolution in 1909, he saw in it "an anticipation of my own writing. My grandfather and I are one" (GM to Maurice Moore, 26 July 1909, *George Moore on Parnassus*, 170).

32. *The Moores of Moore Hall*, 114.

33. *An Irish Gentleman*, 104.

34. *The Moores of Moore Hall*, 134–35.

35. *An Irish Gentleman*, 150.

36. Ibid., 1.

37. Ibid., 326–27.
38. *Life of George Moore*, 32.
39. Comerford, "Churchmen, Tenants, and Independent Opposition," 408. Cardinal Cullen, leader of a devotional revolution in post-Famine Irish Catholicism, looked with nearly equal distaste upon Protestants, Englishmen, landlords, and Irish patriots (*The Moores of Moore Hall*, 160; Emmet Larkin, "The Devotional Revolution in Ireland," *American Historical Review*, 77 (1972): 625–52).
40. R. V. Comerford, "Conspiring Brotherhoods and Contending Elites, 1857–63," *A New History of Ireland, vol. 5*, 415–16.
41. Martin J. Blake, *Blake Family Records, 1300–1600* (Elliot Stock: London, 1902).
42. Gerard Moran, ed., *Galway History and Society* (Geography Publications: Dublin, 1996), 319–31.
43. Will of George Henry Moore, p. 10, Castlebar County Library, Co. Mayo, Ireland; my thanks to Padraig Sherlin.
44. The sons of Maurice Blake, however, either did not marry, or married without issue. Upon the death of Marcus C. B. Blake in 1886, Ballinafad was inherited by Joe Blake. Joe Blake himself never married. He took up residence at Towerhill, and gave Ballinafad to his younger brother Llewelyn, who married but had no children, and left Ballinafad in 1908 to the African Missionary Brothers.
45. J. H. Whyte, *The Independent Irish Party, 1850–59* (Oxford University Press: Oxford, 1958), 129.
46. Moore, *Vale*, 31.
47. George Moore, *Ave*, 118.
48. George Moore, *Salve*, 100.
49. Moore, *Ave*, 201–3.
50. Moore, *Vale*, 33.
51. *Life of George Moore*, 40, though this figure may be inflated. According to NLI Ms 895, ff. 832, in 1870 Moore Hall was yielding £1,000–1,200 per annum; in 1876, the assessed value of the property was £3,534 per annum; see Becker, 196; Moore, *Confessions of a Young Man* (1972), 53. In February 1883, according to the notarised accounts of Thomas Ruttledge, then the land agent for Moore Hall, the total rental for the estate was £1,780 7s. 9d., before a charge of £300 per annum for Mrs Moore's jointure and £240 per annum for the Moore children were paid (documents in Castlebar County Library, Co. Mayo).
52. Moore, *Confessions of a Young Man* (1972), 196.
53. Moore, *Ave*, 61.
54. Ibid.; Moore, *Salve*, 210–11; Moore, *Vale*, 223; Moore, *Salve*, 214. In *The Brook Kerith*, Joseph of Arimathea is laughed at by his granny for saying that when he grows up he wishes to be a prophet, but Joseph's father – unlike GM's – puts things right by treating as an impressive omen a subsequent dream of the boy's in which King Saul appears (T. Werner Laurie: London, 1916), 2–5.
55. George Moore, *Memoirs of My Dead Life*, 61.
56. Moore, *Confessions of a Young Man* (1972), 49; *Vale*, 225–32.
57. George Moore, *Avowals* (1919), 29; *Salve*, 231.
58. *An Irish Gentleman*, 307.
59. Ibid., 312; *Life of George Moore*, 22–23. Hone reports that St Mary's College, Oscott, was founded in 1794 by a group of nobility and gentry of the old faith, whose design it was that their sons should be educated in an atmosphere at once English and Catholic (*The Moores of Moore Hall*, 50).
60. Moore, *Ave*, 80.
61. Moore, *Salve*, 213.
62. Moore, *Avowals* (1924), 45–46.
63. Moore, *Salve*, 217. J. Spencer Northcote, the master at Oscott, wrote to G. H. Moore on 20 September 1866 that GM's backwardness was "singular and extraordinary. And the loss of that year or six months during which his health obliged you to remove him from school was very serious" (Becker, 1366).
64. Moore, *Ave*, 198.
65. Moore, *Confessions of a Young Man* (1972), 50.

66. NLI Ms 10566 (1).
67. J. Spencer Northcote to [G. H. Moore], 22 December 1865, Becker, 1364.
68. George Moore to My dear Papa [G. H. Moore], 25 January 1866, ibid., 91.
69. George Moore to My dear Papa [G. H. Moore], 28 January [1866], ibid., 93.
70. Moore, *Salve*, 282.
71. George Moore to My dear Papa [G. H. Moore], 5 July 1866, Becker, 92.
72. George Moore to My dear Papa [G. H. Moore], [July 1866], ibid., 93.
73. Moore, *Avowals* (1924), 47–49; *Salve*, 221.
74. J. Spencer Northcote to My dear Sir [G. H. Moore], 20 September 1866, Becker, 1366.
75. Moore, *Salve*, 221.
76. Ibid., 222–23.
77. Moore, *Ave*, 201–2. Moore does, however, record taking his first Communion (*Life of George Moore*, 23).
78. *Life of George Moore*, 30.
79. Moore, *Salve*, 225–26; for Northcote (1821–1907), see *The Moores of Moore Hall*, 173.
80. *Life of George Moore*, 31.
81. George Moore, "Hugh Monfert," *In Single Strictness* (1922), 47–201.
82. George Moore, *Esther Waters* (1922), 33–35. For an account of the life of Joseph Apply (or Appley), see George Moore, *A Story-Teller's Holiday* (1923), 24–31.
83. Moore, *Confessions of a Young Man* (1972), 51.
84. Ibid., 54.
85. Ibid., 52.
86. Moore, *Vale*, 21.
87. George Moore to Joe [Joseph Apply], 29 July 1869, 39 Alfred Place, Kensington, Becker, 97.
88. Moore, *Confessions of a Young Man* (1972), 52.
89. Moore, *Vale*, 47; *Life of George Moore*, 35.
90. Moore, *Vale*, 25; italics added.
91. George Moore to Joe [Joseph Apply], [September 1869], 39 Alfred Place, Becker, 105.

92. Moore, *Vale*, 26. In a 31 July [1915] letter to W. K. Magee, GM says "Sally" Giles's real name was Amy, and that she lived in Mayfair at 33 South Street before moving to St John's Wood (HRHRC). Catherine Walters, the famous courtesan known as "Skittles," lived at 15 South Street.
93. Moore, *Confessions of a Young Man* (1972), 198; added in the 1889 edition; Moore, *Avowals* (1924), 254; *Life of George Moore*, 45.
94. *Life of George Moore*, 35.
95. Moore, *Vale*, 41.
96. Ibid., 22.
97. Ibid., 27.
98. Ibid., 33; Moore, *Confessions of a Young Man* (1972), 196.
99. Charles Morgan, *Epitaph on George Moore* (Macmillan: New York, 1935), 3.
100. Moore, *Vale*, 40.
101. Robert Ross, "Self Analysis by George Moore," *Times Literary Supplement*, 14 November 1912: 515.
102. Moore, *Memoirs of My Dead Life*, 256. It would be attractive to suggest that Moore learned something from Kant, for instance from Kant's critique of Leibnizian metaphysics which assumes that the human mind can arrive by pure thought at an understanding of God, freedom, or immortality and that entities can never be objects of experience. Moore became inclined toward skepticism, but it would be guesswork to attribute the cast of his thinking to Kant, whose work Moore does not discuss, and whose language he does not echo.
103. Moore, *Confessions of a Young Man* (1972), 53.
104. Ronald Anderson and Anne Koval, *James McNeill Whistler: Beyond the Myth* (John Murray: London, 1994), 174.
105. John H. Ingram, *Oliver Madox Brown: A Biographical Sketch* (Elliot Stock: London, 1883), 31–32; Thomas Wright, *The Life of John Payne* (T. Fisher Unwin: London, 1919).
106. Louise Chandler Moulton, *Arthur*

O'Shaughnessy: His Life and Work with Selections from his Poems (Elkin Mathews and John Lane: London, 1894), 16.

107. Anderson and Koval, *James MacNeill Whistler*, 180.
108. Moore, *Vale*, 34.
109. Ibid., 37.
110. Ibid., 48.
111. Moore, *Confessions of a Young Man* (1972), 49–50, 63.
112. Moore, *Vale*, 62.
113. Barry Duncan, *The St James's Theatre: Its Strange and Complete History, 1835–1957* (Barrie and Rockliff: London, 1964), 160–61; Maurice Moore to Joseph Hone, undated, 5 Sea View Terrace, Dublin, NLI Ms 2648; Moore, *Vale*, 45.
114. Moore, *Vale*, 46.
115. Maurice Moore Papers, NLI Ms 10566(1); Moore, *Confessions of a Young Man* (1972), 235 n.1; *Life of George Moore*, 45; Becker, 110–11.

Chapter 2 Paris, His Oxford and Cambridge

1. William Molony to Joseph Apply, 30 June [1873], Hôtel de Russie, NLI Ms 895; Becker, 115. According to Alick McDonnell, an old fellow around the Moore estate questioned by Maurice Moore in 1912, the "Mullowneys" came from Breaghy to Moore Hall about 1830. Old William Mullowney married Mary McDonnell the cook, and himself served as steward for many years. His son William was first a footman, then came to London with the family as a manservant. After his spell with GM in Paris, he got a place in London as a butler to another family (NLI Ms 10566).
2. *Life of George Moore*, 45.
3. George Moore, *Confessions of a Young Man* (1972), 55.
4. Ibid.
5. John Milner, *The Studios of Paris, the Capital of Art in the Late Nineteenth Century* (Yale University Press: New Haven and London, 1988), 18.

6. Shirley Fox, "An Art Student's Reminiscences of Paris in the Eighties," quoted ibid., 18; Moore, *Confessions of a Young Man* (1972), 197.
7. Documentation of Moore's entry to the Beaux-Arts was discovered by Hilary Laurie ("Chronology", *Esther Waters* [1994]).
8. Milner, *Studios of Paris*, illus. 26, pp. 49–50.
9. W. C. Morrow, "Bohemian Life in Paris Today," quoted in ibid., 22.
10. Moore, *Confessions of a Young Man* (1972), 198; George Moore, *Avowals* (1924), 254.
11. Moore, *Confessions of a Young Man* (1972), 254; George Moore, "Meissonier and the Salon Julian," *Fortnightly Review*, July 1890: 46.
12. Milner, *Studios of Paris*, 12–13.
13. Moore, "Meissonier and the Salon Julian," 187.
14. George Moore, "From the Naked Model," *Hawk*, 24 December 1889: 700.
15. Moore, *Confessions of a Young Man* (1972), 57.
16. Rastignac is a chief character in Balzac's *Comédie humaine*, who over the course of many novels comes to Paris from a family of impoverished provincial nobility, studies law and becomes the lover of a woman of the world who guides his career; he then acquires money, gains political office, becomes a peer, and at last marries the daughter of his mistress. For Julian's history, see the "Centenary Booklet" by Martin Herold, Académie Julian, 31 rue du Dragon, Paris (TCD Ms 7438/32).
17. George Moore, *Impressions and Opinions* (1891), 250–51.
18. Moore, "Meissonier and the Salon Julian," 188.
19. Moore, *Avowals* (1924), 97.
20. Robert Becker, "Artists Look at George Moore," *Irish Arts Review*, 2.4 (Winter 1985).
21. Milner, *Studios of Paris*, illus. 11.
22. *Lady Gregory's Diaries*, 98.
23. Moore, *Avowals* (1924), 97.

24. Moore, "From the Naked Model," *Hawk*: 699–70. In *Confessions of a Young Man* (1972), p. 57, GM says there were eighteen to twenty men of various nationalities, and eight or nine English women.
25. Moore, "From the Naked Model," 699–701.
26. Moore, *Confessions of a Young Man* (1972), 57.
27. George Moore, "Is Education Worth Having?," *St. James's Gazette*, 10 September 1890: 6.
28. The Hôtel de Russie's prices started at 3 francs a day (*New Paris Guide of 1873*, [Calignano: New York and London, 1873], 441).
29. George Moore, *Vale*, 51; *Life of George Moore*, 47.
30. Moore, *Vale*, 51–52.
31. Moore, *Confessions of a Young Man* (1972), 57; *Vale*, 54.
32. Henri Mondor and Lloyd James Austin, eds, *Stéphane Mallarmé: Correspondance*, vol. 8, *1896* (Gallimard: Paris, 1983), 105 n.1; and *Life of George Moore*, 47.
33. Moore, *Confessions of a Young Man* (1972), 59.
34. Moore, *Vale*, 54.
35. K. Baedeker, *Paris and Environs* (Karl Baedeker: Leipzig, 1884), 289, 292.
36. Moore, *Vale*, 57.
37. Ibid., 56.
38. This incident may be a source for "Bernice. To B —," in George Moore, *Flowers of Passion* (65–70), a dramatic monologue by a young man who suffers "famine-smitten nights of impotence, And hungering days yet knowing no desire." He confesses once going for a swim in the nude with Bernice, and when she kissed him, for some unknown reason, he drowned her in the water-lilies. More direct sources are probably to be sought in the verse of Gautier, Baudelaire, and Mendès.
39. Moore, *Vale*, 58.
40. Moore, *Confessions of a Young Man* (1972), 59.
41. Ibid., 72.
42. Ibid., 60.

43. Yann Le Pichon, *The Real World of the Impressionists: Paintings and Photographs 1848–1918*, trans. Dianne Cullinane (Harrison House: New York, 1985), 30–35, 50–51, 53. For an illustration of one of the rooms at the White Horse Inn, see Frédéric Bazille's *Monet after His Accident at the Inn in Chailly* (1866), in ibid., 51.
44. Moore, *Vale*, 59–60.
45. Moore, *Confessions of a Young Man* (1972), 79.
46. The envelope containing this letter is dated in another hand 28 October 1875, months before the season of the masked balls at the opera (prior to Lent, or 25 February in 1874, 16 February in 1875). Hone dates the letter 28 March 1875, by which time it seems that GM was no longer in the Hôtel de Russie (*Life of George Moore*, 49); Noël accepts Hone's dating, and consequently moves the time of GM's meeting with Hawkins forward to early 1875 from the summer of 1873 (Jean C. Noël, *George Moore: l'homme et l'oeuvre* [Marcel Didier: Paris, 1966], 4). Becker plausibly assigns the letter to March 1874, because of the address, the date of the carnival, and the frivolous tone, not to be found in the dutiful correspondence with his mother following his return from London to Paris.
47. Beth Archer Brombert, *Edouard Manet: Rebel in a Frock Coat* (Little, Brown: Boston, New York, Toronto and London, 1996), 338. Manet's *Masked Ball at the Opera* (1873–74) is in the National Gallery of Art, Washington, DC.
48. *Life of George Moore*, 50. Reminiscing in 1922 about Perren's dance hall, GM told Barrett Clark that in his early days in Paris he "met most of the famous cocottes of the day; I danced with them; I was a good dancer then" (Barrett H. Clark, "Portrait of a Writer: Personal Recollections of George Moore", unpublished mss. at the University of Washington Library).
49. Moore, *Vale*, 67.
50. As Becker notes, Moore dwelt on

the terror of the woman-as-serpent and woman-as-Cleopatra in "La Charmeuse" (*Flowers of Passion*), "Bernice," and "The Temptation" (George Moore, *Pagan Poems*). In her hallucinations after being raped, Kitty Hare also envisions a male lover as a serpent in *A Mere Accident* (Becker, 111). It is not a particularly novel image, but it may have its origins in the terrors of his night with *La Belle Hollandaise*.

Walter Sickert may have made his own sardonic comment on Moore's first love with his 1906 painting entitled *La Hollandaise*: it depicts a fat ugly woman sitting up in a common bed with an iron bedstead, her left ham folded over the right thigh. The point of view is from a man's height standing at the foot of the bed. Richard Shone connects the picture to Moore's tale in *Walter Sickert* (Phaidon: Oxford, 1988), 40.

51. Moore, *Avowals* (1924), 257.
52. Moore, *Confessions of a Young Man* (1972), 64; information from Henry Lecomte, *Histoire des théâtres de Paris* cited by Margaret A. Seibert in "George Moore et Paul Alexis: un cas de plagiat," *Les Cahiers-naturalistes*, 62 (1988): 128 n.6.
53. Moore, *Vale*, 79.
54. Moore, *Confessions of a Young Man* (1972), 66.
55. Leigh Hunt, ed., *The Dramatic Works of Wycherley, Congreve, Vanbrugh, and Farquhar* (E. Moxon: London, 1840).
56. Moore, *Confessions of a Young Man* (1972), 200.
57. Moore, *Vale*, 68.
58. Ibid., 79.
59. Moore, *Confessions of a Young Man* (1972), 200. According to other accounts, Molony was sent home by the end of 1873 (six months before GM's return to London) because Paris "went to his head" (*Life of George Moore*, 45), because he "missed his beer and music halls" (George Moore, "Apologia pro scriptis meis," xi), or "because he stood between me and myself," as a reminder of Ireland and

his position as a landlord, when GM wanted to put off the appearance of a gentleman and dress like a French *boulevardier* (Moore, *Vale*, 100).
60. On some occasions, Moore gave the letters of a particularly famous correspondent to an autograph-collecting acquaintance. The subsequent sale of such letters once got him in trouble with Zola. See Moore's letter to the editor of the *Daily Chronicle*, 12 March 1898 (p. 3), in which he expresses his concern that six letters to him from Zola were then for sale at a Holborn bookseller – he claims, without his authorisation. Zola too had been indignant at the sale; GM says, "M. Zola is more careful with his papers than I am with mine, but should he lose or have stolen from him a packet of my letters, and should I afterwards hear of these letters being offered for sale, I should not feel angry or aggrieved."
61. *Life of George Moore*, 74; Clark, *Portrait of a Writer*, 83; and Paul Alexis, *Le Cri du peuple*, 22 August 1885.
62. In *George Moore and the Autogenous Self: The Autobiography and the Fiction* (Syracuse University Press: Syracuse, 1994), Elizabeth Grubgeld has a stimulating and extended discussion of GM's invention of this autobiographical persona "George Moore" (pp. 43–52).
63. Moore, *Vale*, 100.
64. I. A. Williams, *Bibliographies of Modern Authors*, 3, *George Moore* (Leslie Chaundy: London, 1921).
65. Gilcher, 234. Asked for a copy in 1925, GM replied: "I wrote a comedy entitled 'Worldliness' and printed it when I visited London, distributing it in pamphlet form among my friends. All the copies, I believe, have disappeared. I do not keep copies of my books, and I am sure I have not in my possession a single copy of the first edition" (GM to unidentified recipient, 28 August 1925, HRHRC).
66. To judge by Maurice's 28 April and 30 May letters to his sister, he visited GM in Paris in early June; he remembers

returning from Paris to London to read of his having passed the examination in the 13 June 1874 *Gazette*. Maurice Moore to Nina [Moore], 28 April 1874 and 30 May [1874], 39 Alfred Place, NLI Ms 10566(2).

67. George Moore to Joseph [Blake], 15 June [1874], 39 Alfred Place, NLI Ms 4479; Becker, 117. In *Vale* (p. 61), Moore gives many reasons for returning to London: debt, a broken heart, a play to get produced, or, most astonishing of all the reasons subsequently given for his return, the desire for English cooking.

68. In revisions for the 1918 edition of *Confessions of a Young Man*, Moore added the detail about the stage-door keeper advising him to have *Worldliness* "copied and the stage directions inscribed in red ink" (p. 201); in the earlier editions, he says he took the play to a printer, and the correction of proofs "amused me for a while" (p. 67). Page numbers are from the 1972 edition.

69. Barry Duncan, *The St James's Theatre: Its Strange and Complete History, 1835–1957* (Barrie and Rockliff: London, 1964), 163–64. In a hearing about the *opéra bouffe Vert-Vert*, its special new dance, the Riparelle, was described as "like the Can Can, essentially an illustration of the act of . . ." Subsequent to this scandal, the producer of the show, F. C. Fairlie, changed his name to F. C. Philips, and Dick Maitland changed his name to Dick Mansell. See A Journalist [William Mackay], *Bohemian Days in Fleet Street* (John Long: London, 1913), 96–97, and H. G. Hibbert, *Fifty Years of a Londoner's Life* (Grant Richards: London, 1916).

70. Moore, *Vale*, 79.

71. M. Moore to Hone, n.d. [1936?], 5 Seaview Terrace, Dublin, NLI Ms 2648.

72. Wilfrid Meynell, ed., *The Modern School of Art*, vol. 2 (Cassell: London and New York, n.d.), 26.

73. Moore, *Vale*, 37.

74. One of Oliver Madox Brown's sisters married Gosse, and the other married Rossetti; Payne and O'Shaughnessy, as well as being devoted Francophiles, regularly came to the "At Homes" of Ford Madox Brown until the death of his son. See Louise Chandler Moulton, *Arthur O'Shaughnessy, His Life and Work with Selections from his Poems* (Elkin Mathews and John Lane: London, 1894), 15; Thomas Wright, *The Life of John Payne* (T. Fisher Unwin: London, 1919), 51. There is also no evidence that Moore ran into another acquaintance of Oliver Madox Brown, John Butler Yeats, the father of the poet. Through J. B. Yeats, Brown met and fell in love with Isabella Pollexfen, sister of JBY's wife Susan Pollexfen Yeats. See William M. Murphy, *Prodigal Father: The Life of John Butler Yeats (1839–1922)* (Cornell University Press: Ithaca, NY and London, 1978), 85, 561.

75. *Life of George Moore*, 48.

76. For the customs of mashers, see Ralph Nevill and C. E. Jerningham, *Piccadilly to Pall Mall: Manners, Morals, and Man* (Duckworth: London, 1908), 116; and James M. Glover, *Jimmy Glover and his Friends* (Chatto and Windus: London, 1913), 214.

77. Vincent O'Sullivan, *Opinions* (Unicorn Press: London, 1959), 19.

78. George Moore to Joseph [Blake], n.d., NLI Ms 4479; Becker, 118–19. The letter explains that his mother, Mary Blake Moore, is planning to give up her London house at 39 Alfred Place, so it is the right time for his return to Paris. According to Kelly's *Directory*, she remained there into 1876.

79. *Life of George Moore*, 51.

80. Moore, *Vale*, 62.

81. Ibid., 100.

82. Ibid., 65.

83. Ibid., 72. Jean Noël found public records showing that Moore rented both 27 Galerie Feydeau and 61 rue Condorcet in 1875; see Noël, *George Moore*, 680–81.

84. Hone assigns a date of November 1875 to this letter: *Life of George Moore*, 51.

85. George Moore to Joseph [Blake], n.d.,

27 Galerie Montmartre, Passage des Panoramas, NLI Ms 4479; Becker, 124.

86. George Moore to "My dear Mama" [Mary Blake Moore], [26 April 1876, inscribed], Galerie Montmartre, Passage des Panoramas, NLI Ms 4479; Becker, 124–26.

87. Moore, *Vale*, 72.

88. George Moore, *Conversations in Ebury Street* (1930), 106.

89. Moore, *Flowers of Passion*, 107.

90. Noël, *George Moore*, 71; *Life of George Moore*, 60.

91. George Moore and Bernard Lopez, *Martin Luther*, 1. The "poularde financière" is a hen cooked in a sauce of flour, mushrooms, butter, and wine.

92. Ibid., 10–12.

93. In *The Confessions of a Young Man* (1972), Moore says that only when he got into his new rooms in Paris did he begin to "read seriously" (p. 76). That would be in the fall of 1875 by my reckoning, when he took the apartment at 61 rue Condorcet.

94. Moore and Lopez, *Martin Luther*, 26.

95. Ibid., 27.

96. The address of Miss Rose's Paris relatives is taken from the recollections of May Hemphill (May Hemphill to Joseph Hone, Joseph M. Hone Accession, Box 1, Folder 12, Loc. V253d, Washington).

Robert Becker places the whole sequence of letters concerning the pursuit of Miss Rose during the summer in Boulogne in mid-1877, not 1876. However, Moore says that he gave up his Galerie Feydeau apartment upon his return from Boulogne, and that apartment appears in his name in the 1876 *calepin du cadastre* and not in the 1877 (Noël, *George Moore*, 680).

97. George Moore to "My dear Mama" [Mary Blake Moore], n.d., 10 Galerie Feydeau, Passage de Panoramas, NLI Ms 4479; Becker, 156; and George Moore to "My dear Mama," n.d., NLI Ms 4479; Becker, 161.

98. George Moore to "My dear Mama," n.d., 10 Galerie Feydeau, NLI Ms 4479; Becker, 158.

99. Becker, 158; Emile Zola, *Oeuvres complètes*, vol. 10 (F. Bernouard: Paris, 1928), 406; B. H. Bakker, "*Naturalisme pas mort": Lettres inédites de Paul Alexis à Emile Zola, 1871–1900* (University of Toronto Press: Toronto, 1971), 109–11.

100. Of Georgette Coëtlogon, GM writes that "she turned round on me in the gloom of her brougham unexpectedly, and it was as if some sensual spirit had come out of a world of perfume and lace," George Moore, *Memoirs of My Dead Life* (William Heinemann: London, 1906), 63–65; and *Life of George Moore*, 55–56.

101. George Moore to "My dear Mama", NLI Ms 4497; Becker, 161.

102. Moore, *Confessions of a Young Man* (1972), 73, 75, 238 n.1.

103. George Moore to Joseph [Blake], n.d., NLI Ms 4497; Becker, 164.

104. May Hemphill to Hone, Box 1, Folder 12, Loc v253d, Washington.

105. J. A. Chandor, "Augustus M. Moore and 'His Bitterest Enemy,'" *Hawk*, 1.40 (6 June 1893): 12–14. Chandor and Augustus Moore had been feuding for years when he wrote this article, and at the time, Chandor was trying to get A. Moore ("one of the most dangerous individuals [society] has ever permitted to cross its threshold") jailed for rape. So Chandor is not a friendly witness. He says he first met Augustus Moore in 1876 or 1877 when he was staying at the Imperial Hotel: he was approached by "a thin, sickly, cadaverous looking individual, whose head was adorned with long reddish hair. He was accompanied by another person, whom he stated to be his brother . . . when the former mentioned his name as 'George Moore,' I enquired the object of their self-introduction. George Moore, the spokesman, in an humble and abashed tone, explained that the landlord of the hotel had locked their room as they could not settle the bill, and though they had return tickets to London, where their presence was imperative on the following day, they could not

leave without their luggage . . . I handed them two sovereigns," which they promised to repay. "Those two sovereigns were probably lost in the post."

106. Moore, *Flowers of Passion*, 97; George Frederic Lees, "Recollections of an Anglo-Parisian Bibliophile: II – George Moore in Paris," *The Bookman* (September 1932): 296–97.

107. Moore, *Vale*, 75–76.

108. Moore, *Confessions of a Young Man* (1972), 76; Moore and Lopez, *Martin Luther*, 28–29; in "Chez Moi" (*Pagan Poems*, 57–58), GM speaks of his "white Angora cats" and "many-coloured Python." This poem was published before Huysmans's *A Rebours*.

109. Moore, *Vale*, 206.

110. At a public dinner, GM met his father's acquaintance John O'Leary, the Irish Fenian exiled in Paris from 1874 to at least 1879, and introduced him to Lewis Welldon Hawkins; but O'Leary wanted to talk about Ireland, and GM wanted to talk about Cabanel and Ingres (Moore, *Ave*, 102; *Life of George Moore*, 55; Moore, *Vale*, 75).

   For Lizzie Gardner, Mme Bouguereau, see *Life of George Moore*, 71; Moore, *Memoirs of My Dead Life*, 66–71; Moore, *Avowals* (1924), 97. On 22 February 1922, GM told Clark, "Get in touch with Mme. Bouguereau; I write of her in my books as Lizzie Gardiner [*sic*] . . . My mistress nearly fifty years ago. I used to send her everything of mine that was published" (Clark, *Portrait of a Writer*, 27).

111. Mariel Oberthur, *Cafés and Cabarets of Montmartre* (Peregrine Smith Books: Salt Lake City, 1984), 45–46; Seibert, "George Moore et Paul Alexis," 128–29.

112. A. W. Raitt, *Life of Villiers de l'Isle Adam* (Clarendon Press: Oxford, 1981), 168.

113. Ibid., 401 n.5.

114. Moore, *Vale*, 81; *Avowals* (1924), 262. Mallarmé was always polite but also always honest as a critic. One would like to know what he found to say

about the gilt volume when he had time to look it over.

115. Moore, *Vale*, 81.

116. In November 1875, two years before *Flowers* was published, Mallarmé wrote a note for the *Athenaeum* about a new publisher in Paris, Derenne, who was going to bring out *L'Après-midi d'un faune* as well as a magazine, *La République des lettres*, in mid-December. On 28 December 1875, Mallarmé sent the poem to Swinburne. See Jean Noel, "George Moore et Mallarmé," *Revue de littérature comparée* (1958): 363–76.

117. Swinburne's "Une Nocturne" was an Italian sestina done into French, the best of its kind in French, Swinburne reported to friends – a kind, however, with few other examples. See A. C. Swinburne to John Morley, 1 February 1876, Cecil Y. Lang, ed., *The Swinburne Letters*, vol. 3, *1875–1877*, (Yale University Press: New Haven, 1960), 129–31.

118. "Appendix III: Swinburne and Mallarmé: Letter from Mr. George Moore," in Edmund Gosse's *The Life of Algernon Charles Swinburne* (Macmillan: New York, 1917), 327–28.

119. Lang, ed., *The Swinburne Letters*, 132–34. Mallarmé, perhaps after consultation with GM, pressed the issue further by suggesting in addition to Swinburne's three variants of the line a fourth: ". . . du beau pied blessé de l'amour," before apologising for his pedantry (Henri Mondor and Lloyd James Austin, eds, *Stéphane Mallarmé*: *Correspondance*, vol. 2, *1871–1885* [Gallimard: Paris, 1985], 104). My thanks to Professor W. W. Thomas.

120. *Life of George Moore*, 66.

121. Joseph Hone, "Augusta Holmes" [Hone, JM Mss], n.d., HRHRC. In later years, Augusta Holmes was also an acquaintance of Maud Gonne, who arranged for a memorial to Holmes after her death. See Anna MacBride White and A. Norman Jeffares, *The Gonne–Yeats Letters 1893–1938* (Norton: New York and London, 1992), 69, 146.

122. Moore, *Confessions of a Young Man* (1972), 84.
123. Moore, "Le Succube," *Flowers of Passion*, 111; a translation of Catulle Mendès's "La Sérénade," *Poems*, vol. 1, 15. See Noël, *George Moore*, 42–43.
124. In the 1928 edition of *Memoirs of My Dead Life*, GM says Augusta Holmes "instructed" him to call on Nina on her birthday, and Holmes, Mendes, and Villiers are prominent guests in the first account he gives of the party. See Moore, *Memoirs of My Dead Life* (1928), 67; and "Notes and Sensations," *Hawk*, 6: 129 (29 July 1890): 128–30.

Sometimes Nina Villiard (née Marie-Anne Gaillard) called herself Nina de Callais, using the last name of her first husband, Hector de Callais, until he threatened a lawsuit if she continued to associate herself with him in this way. Thereafter, she went as Nina de Villiard, adding an aristocratic prefix. See Bakker, "*Naturalisme pas mort*", 112–13. When Manet used the name "Nina de Callais" in speaking of his portrait, Hector de Callais wrote that, by legal arrangement, the woman was free to "bear any name she chose, except my own"; if she did not, he owed it to his family to take "the most energetic measures"; see T. A. Gronberg, *Manet: A Retrospective* (Park Lane: New York, 1988), 288. GM calls her "the Comtesse Ninon de Calvador" (Moore, *Memoirs of My Dead Life* [1906], 77).
125. Raitt, *Life of Villiers de l'Isle-Adam*, 81–83; Moore, "Notes and Sensations," 129, a passage Moore eliminated when the article was revised for *Memoirs of My Dead Life* (1906), 75–95.
126. Edmond Goncourt, 18 March 1886, Edmond et Jules de Goncourt, *Journal: Mémoires de la vie littéraire, 1879–1890*, vol. 3 (Fasquelle, Flammarion: Paris, 1956), 548.
127. Paul Alexis to Emile Zola, 25 July 1877, Paris, Bakker, "*Naturalisme pas mort*," 109–11. In his *Hawk* article, GM speaks of having come on "a soft

night in June" ("Notes and Sensations," 129).
128. For the textual history of *Memoirs of My Dead Life*, see Gilcher, 71–77.

Nina de Villiard is remembered by Georges Duval in *Le Quartier Pigalle* (Marpon and Flammarion: Paris, 1884); by Catulle Mendès in *La Maison de la vielle* (Chapentier: Paris, 1894); in "Une Soirée chez Nina de Villiard," *Oeuvres complètes*, vol. 4 (Gallimard: Paris) 410–15; by Paul Alexis in *Madame Meuriot, Mœurs parisiennes* (Charpentier: Paris, 1890) On 17 May 1889, Alexis wrote to Zola that, during a recent Paris visit by GM, Alexis had read him the episode from *Madame Meuriot* concerning a bacchanalian night at the house of "Eva de Pommeuse," that is, Nina de Villiard, because Moore had known her in the old days. At the end of the reading, Moore had cried, "It is better than Guy de Maupassant" (Bakker, "*Naturalisme pas mort*," 378–81).

For his book, Moore added to the original article some anecdotes about Verlaine and opinions about Huysmans that in fact belong to a much later period. He clearly used the party scene as a literary device to organise his thoughts about bohemian Paris, his splendid youth, and the passage of time. Jean Noël points out that GM describes Huysmans as the "apologist of Gilles de Rais," but Huysmans did not earn this title until he published *Là-bas* in 1891; he describes Verlaine as having been present, though Verlaine was rarely in Paris in the late 1870s, and was one of the few bohemians not welcome at Nina's house, having once tried to stab Léon Hennique with his penknife; finally, GM has Verlaine recite verses at the party which Verlaine did not write until 1892 (Jean C. Noël, "George Moore at Nina de Villiard's Fête: A Reconsideration of *Memoirs of My Dead Life*, Ch. VII," *Cahiers du Centre d'études irlandaises* [Université de Haute Bretagne, 1984], 31–44).
129. Max Direaux suggests that Moore's dishonorable incivilities to Villiers may

have been inspired by Villiers's own account of the Englishman at Nina's party (Max Direaux, *Villiers de l'Isle Adam: l'homme et l'oeuvre* [Desclée de Brouwer: Paris, 1936], 99–102).

130. Moore, *Memoirs of My Dead Life* (1906), 77–78; "Notes and Sensations," 130.

131. Moore, *Memoirs of My Dead Life* (1906), 89.

132. In the first version of the story of Nina's fête, Catulle Mendès, a "sort of sensual Christ," charms the female guests by improvising naughty verses ("Notes and Sensations," 130); in the book version, Moore takes Mendès's place, and tries his charms on a woman by telling her a story (*Memoirs of My Dead Life*, 1906, 8off.). Emulation proved successful only through a transformation of medium.

133. *La République* took over serialisation after the novel was driven from the pages of *Le Bien public* by angry subscribers. Mallarmé to Zola, 20 November 1875, Mondor and Austin, eds, *Mallarmé: Correspondance*, vol. 2, 83; Robert Baldick, *The Life of J.-K. Huysmans* (Clarendon Press: Oxford, 1955), 136.

134. Moore, *Confessions of a Young Man* (1972), 93–94.

135. Baldick, *Life of J.-K. Huysmans*, 38–39. In his 1922 reminiscences of early Paris for Barrett Clark, Moore thought Hennique might remember him as a very genteel young Englishman, or a stupid young man, or a man who collaborated with Paul Alexis; he was "never very intimate" with Céard; but Alexis he knew very well; Clark, *Portrait of a Writer*," 71.

136. Bernard Lopez to George Moore, February 1877, Paris, Moore and Lopez, *Martin Luther*, 23. The letters are doubtless largely concocted by Moore, but he therefore approved of the date and also allowed the comment to stand, uncorrected by his apparently subsequent enthusiasm for Impressionism and detestation of academicism.

137. The exhibition was then titled "Exposition de peinture par . . . [with names

of the eighteen artists]." It ran from 4 to 30 April in a five-room apartment opposite Durand-Ruel's gallery. Eight thousand visitors attended. See Bernard Denvir, *The Chronicle of Impressionism* (Little, Brown: Boston, New York, Toronto, London, 1993), and Peter Feist, *Impressionist Art, 1860–1920*, ed. Ingo F. Walther, vol. 1 (Benedikt Taschen: Köln, 1993), 199–200.

138. Moore, *Confessions of a Young Man* (1972), 71. GM gives an account of an Impressionist exhibition that includes the mention of Renoir's *Nude in Sunlight* from the Second Impressionist Exhibition (April–May 1876), the two works by Monet from the Third Exhibition (April 1877), and Seurat's *La Grand Jatte* from the Eighth Exhibition (May 1886). In "Monet, Sisley, Pissarro, and the Decadence," he remembers first encountering Monet when he exhibited the *Turkeys*, which GM backdates to 1875 or 1876; in fact, it was first publicly shown on 4 April 1877 (George Moore, *Modern Painting*, 1893, 69).

139. *Life of George Moore*, 66–67.

140. Mondor and Austin, eds, *Mallarmé: Correspondance*, vol. 2, 69–70.

141. In October 1873 Mallarmé had taken John Payne to meet Manet in his studio; in October 1875, Mallarmé had sent copies of his translation of Poe's "The Raven" to Payne and William Michael Rossetti (Manet's drawings seemed to Rossetti "outrageous affairs"). See Roger W. Peattie, ed., *Selected Letters of William Michael Rossetti* (Pennsylvania State University Press: University Park and London, 1990), 328–29.

142. Gordon Millan, *Mallarmé: A Throw of the Dice* (Secker and Warburg: London, 1994), 216.

143. In 1877, Mrs Helen Snee was in prison for attempted suicide. Her letter requesting poison for the purpose of suicide went astray in the mail, and was opened at the Post Office, leading to her arrest and trial. For her fascinating story, see Arthur

O'Shaughnessy, *A Pathetic Episode in a Poet's Life* (No. 18, Clement Shorter, 25 copies printed, BL).

144. Marie Duclaux (Mary F. Robinson), "Souvenirs sur George Moore," *La Revue de Paris*, 40 (1 March 1933): 110–30.

145. Peter Keating, *The Haunted Study: A Social History of the English Novel 1875–1914* (Fontana: London, 1989), 24.

146. George Moore, *A Communication to My Friends*, 20–21. In this last work of Moore, he conflates several encounters with Tinsley, and makes their conversation concern his own manuscript for *A Modern Lover*, not a translation of Zola's *La Curée* (1872). On 1 November 1879, in the second of a four-part article by Paul Alexis in *Le Voltaire*, "Zola à l'étranger: II En Angleterre et en Amérique," a Moore letter is presented as Alexis's interview with that "distinguished poet, the author of *Flowers of Passion*." Moore gives an account of a conversation with an unnamed London editor about *La Curée* about "two years ago," i.e. in 1877.

147. GM's mother, Mary Blake Moore, was now living at Moore Hall. She tried to get George to "stay some time in Ireland" so that he would "get fond of it by degrees." If he made a brief visit to Mayo before his return to Paris, he left no evidence of doing so. See Maurice Moore to My dear Mother, 13 August [1877], The Connaught Rangers, Cape Town, Col. Maurice Moore Papers, NLI 10566(2).

148. Gilcher, A1.

149. Noel, *George Moore*, 44.

150. Ibid., 47–49.

151. Moore, *Flowers of Passion*, 90.

152. Edmund Yates, "A Bestial Bard," *The World*, 7 (20 November 1877): 18.

153. "Sofa Criticism," *Truth*, 2. 49 (6 December 1877): 688.

154. "Minor Notices," *Examiner*, 26 January 1878: 120.

155. *Life of George Moore*, 63.

156. Viola Meynell, *Francis Thompson and Wilfrid Meynell: A Memoir* (Hollis and Carter: London, 1952), 131–32. GM replies to Wilfrid, "I felt the justice of your advice to burn the verses on [re]reading them. I sent them more as an enchantillon . . . of a new form or what I believe to be one."

157. Gertrude Atherton, *Adventures of a Novelist* (Liveright: New York, 1932), 165.

158. Moore, *Avowals* (1924), 259–60. For the date when GM and Lopez actually set to work on *Martin Luther*, see GM's letter to Wilfrid Meynell, written after the reviews of *Flowers of Passion* had come in (i.e. after January 1878): "I am going to write a drama with a Frenchman. He gives me the plan" (Meynell, *Francis Thompson and Wilfrid Meynell*, 131–32).

159. George Moore to "My dear Joseph" [Blake], [February? 1878], NLI Ms 4479; Becker, 168–69.

160. GM to "Fluffie," 11 February 1878, *Book Auction Records, 1921–22*, 19. 1 (Henry Stevens, Son, & Stiles: London, n.d.]; GM to "Jenny," n.d., *Book Auction Records, 1922–23*, 20. 1 (Henry Stevens, Son, & Stiles: London, n.d.]; GM to "Miss Fox," *Book Auction Records, 1923–24*, 21. 1 (Henry Stevens, Son & Stiles: London, n.d.].

161. George Moore to My dear Mama [Mary Blake Moore], [early 1879], 61 rue Condorcet, Paris, NLI Ms 4479; Becker, 185.

162. Paul Alexis to Emile Zola, 9 August [1878], Paris, Bakker, "*Naturalisme pas mort*," 117–18. In a 22 August 1885 article in *Le Cri du peuple*, Alexis said he had known Moore for "seven or eight years, maybe ten," i.e. since 1877 or 1878, or perhaps 1875.

163. A spring 1879 letter from GM to his mother indicates that by that date he was spending half his time at the Café. When he first began to go there is more difficult to establish.

164. Moore and Lopez, *Martin Luther*, 28–36. The letter reprints a "Programme of London Theatres" for 7 December 1878, which dates GM's presence in England.

165. Marston was the brother-in-law of O'Shaughnessy and a friend of Rossetti and the Robinson sisters; earlier, he had been in the group of artists and writers around the young Oliver Madox Brown. See Louise Chandler Moulton, *The Collected Poems of Philip Bourke Marston* (Ward, Lock, Bowden: London, 1892).

166. Moore and Lopez, *Martin Luther*, 32.

167. For Swinburne's residence in, and departure from, London, see Cecily Lang, ed., *The Swinburne Letters*, vol. 4, *1877–82* (Yale University Press: New Haven, 1960), 58, 59. In June 1879, Theodore Watts spirited the poet into a lifetime of seclusion in Putney. See also Ann Thwaite, ed., *Portraits from Life by Edmund Gosse* (Aldershot, Hants: Scolar Press, 1991), 71.

168. George Moore to Edmund Gosse, 2 December 1912, 121 Ebury Street, London, Gosse, *Life of Swinburne*, 329–30.

169. Gosse told T. J. Wise that in his biography he was "carefully concealing . . . the nature of [Swinburne's] peculiar moral aberration" (he liked to be whipped). Together, Gosse and Wise would "try to prevent the world from ever knowing what a pig he sometimes was." Gosse did write an account of the unprintable side of Swinburne's life, which he deposited in the British Museum. See Gosse to Wise, January 1915, quoted in Ann Thwaite, *Edmund Gosse: A Literary Landscape 1848–1928* (Secker and Warburg: London, 1984), 478, and Richard Dellamora, *Masculine Desire: The Sexual Politics of Victorian Aestheticism* (University of North Carolina Press: Chapel Hill and London, 1990), 85.

170. Moore, *Vale*, 80.

171. Lawrence Irving, *Henry Irving: The Actor and his World* (Macmillan: New York, 1952), 57.

172. George Moore to My dearest Mama [early summer? 1879], NLI Ms 4479; Becker, 188. Robert Becker also provides helpful notes on the persons mentioned in the letter. The "princesse" at whose dinner parties GM was such a regular part of the entertainment was the Duchess Marguerite-Jeanne Egle (1840–1913), while the Marquise d'Osmond was the wife of the fifty-two-year-old Ranulphe Marie Eustache, Marquis Osmond. *Memoirs of My Dead Life* suggests that she was a neighbor of Moore's other lady friend, Georgette de Coëtlogon, in the Place des Vosges.

173. Brombert, *Edouard Manet*, 365.

174. Roy McMullen, *Degas: His Life, Times, and Work* (Secker and Warburg: London, 1985), 373. In the late 1880s, Ellen Andrée joined Antoine's Théâtre Libre. When GM first wrote about *L'Absinthe*, he did not exhibit any familiarity with Ellen Andrée; he describes the model as a woman who would wear dirty petticoats and come to the café in loose morning shoes for a breakfast of absinthe: "Heavens! – What a slut!" ("The Grafton Gallery," *The Speaker* 7, 165 [25 February 1893]: 215–17). Andrée was neither slatternly nor stupid: she was outraged at Degas for painting the glass of absinthe in front of her, "We looked like a pair of morons" (Adolphe Tabarant, "Des Peintres et leurs modèles," *Bulletin de la vie artistique*, 1 May 1921: 261–63). It is her body that is sprawled in sexual exhaustion, while her lover "Rolla" puts on his trousers, in the picture by Gervex; but by her insistence the face belongs to another.

175. John Rewald, *The History of Impressionism*, 4th edn (Museum of Modern Art: New York, 1946), 399.

176. Moore, *Confessions of a Young Man* (1972), 102, 161.

177. Ibid., 108.

178. Malcolm Brown, *George Moore: A Reconsideration* (University of Washington Press: Seattle, 1955), xv.

179. Moore, *Confessions of a Young Man* (1972), 104.

180. George Moore, *Hail and Farewell*, 649; Moore, *Vale*, 101–2.

181. Moore, *Vale*, 101; and *Avowals* (1924); 165. The date of Moore's meeting with Manet, and of Manet's portraits of Moore, is a vexed issue, unsettled

by the inquiries of scholars of either Moore or Manet. The first official biography of Moore suggests the meeting occurred before the summer of 1877; the most recent biography of Manet suggests it was 1875 (*Life of George Moore*, 66; Brombert, *Edouard Manet*, 377). Considerable confusion has been created by Moore's suggestion that he met Manet immediately after coming to know Mallarmé, and by the assumption of scholars that the proofs he was correcting at the time of meeting Manet were those for *Flowers of Passion* (1877). In fact, as explained above, Moore met Mallarmé in January 1876, earlier than has often been supposed.

If we take seriously Moore's recollection that he immediately visited Manet and that visit was to the rue d'Amsterdam studio, their meeting comes after 1 April 1879, when Manet took possession of the studio at 77 rue d'Amsterdam. Manet rented the studio in late summer 1878, but did not move in until renovations were completed on 1 April 1879; for the fall and winter, Manet used an interim studio in 70 rue d'Amsterdam, where he painted *In the Conservatory* (Brombert, *Edouard Manet*, 393). As Moore never mentions this interim studio (much less the previous studio at 57 rue de Clichy), one cannot show that he ever visited it. Furthermore, the meeting must have come before 29 April 1879, when Manet introduced Moore to Zola at the Bal d'Assommoir. There is a high probability that the date of Moore's meeting with Manet is early April 1879, and that the proofs Moore was correcting were those of *Martin Luther* (1879). See Noël, *George Moore*, 57; Denvir, *Chronicle of Impressionism*, 112; and Ronald Pickvance, "A Newly Discovered Drawing by Degas of George Moore," *Burlington Magazine*, 105. 723 (June 1963): 276–80.

182. Brombert, *Edouard Manet*, 376, 440; Juliet Wilson-Bareau, *Manet by Himself: Correspondence and Conversation*

(MacDonald: London and Sydney, 1991), 180.

183. Théodore Duret, *Manet and the French Impressionists*, trans. J. E. Crawford Flitch (Grant Richards: London, 1910), 85.

184. Degas's remark on GM from the summer of 1885, quoted by Walter Richard Sickert, *A Free House! or, The Artist as Craftsman*, ed. Osbert Sitwell (Macmillan: London, 1947), 148.

185. Moore, *Modern Painting*, 31; "Handling," *The Speaker*, 6.135 (30 July 1892): 135–36.

186. Denis Rouart and Daniel Wildenstern, *Edouard Manet: Catalogue raisonné, tome II, Pastels, aquarelles et dessins* (La Bibliothèque des Arts: Paris, 1975), illus. 296, p. 234. The painting now belongs to the Metropolitan Museum, New York.

187. John Eglinton, *Irish Literary Portraits* (Macmillan: London, 1935), 127.

188. Edmond Bazire, *Manet* (Paris, 1884), 127; Brombert, *Edouard Manet*, 404.

189. Blanche quoted in Françoise Cachin, *Manet: The Influence of the Modern* (Harry N. Abrams: New York, 1995), 115.

190. Moore, *Conversations in Ebury Street*, 165–66; Jacques-Emile Blanche, *Propos de peintres* 3 sér: Paris, 1919–28), 145. When GM later met Méry Laurent, he says she "sent me messages with her eyes that the intrigue that had revelled years ago in Manet's studio was not forgotten." For further information on Laurent, see Brombert, *Edouard Manet*, 374–75; Millan, *Mallarmé*, 237–38; Moore, *Memoirs of My Dead Life*, 60–62; *Avowals*, 267.

191. *Life of George Moore*, 82.

192. Moore, *Memoirs of My Dead Life* (1906), 61. The pastel was sold with GM's other effects after his sudden decampment from Paris; Countess Albazzi herself bought it at the auction. Years later, she put it back on the market, and GM bought it for his friend, Ernest Beckett, Lord Grimthorpe. See Rouart and Wildenstern, *Edouard Manet*, illus. 35, p. 14.

The Countess Albazzi née Kwia-towska was called Iza; she may be the female figure in several of GM's poems from *Pagan Poems*: "A Parisian Idyll," "La Maîtresse maternelle"; she is mentioned by name in "Chez Moi" and "A Love Letter"; "The Portrait" concerns the Manet pastel portrait of Iza. See Becker, 1117.

193. Moore, *Pagan Poems*, 59–62.

194. Paul Alexis, "Manet," *La Revue moderne et naturaliste* (Paris, 1880): 289–90.

195. Ernest Vizetelly, *Emile Zola: Novelist and Reformer* (John Lane, the Bodley Head: London and New York, 1904), 178; Noël, *George Moore*, 57.

196. George Moore, "My Impressions of Zola," *Impressions and Opinions* (1913), 66; [Paul Alexis], "Les Théâtres," *La Réforme*, 1 April 1880, quoted in Bakker, "*Naturalisme pas mort*," 131.

197. Moore, *Impressions and Opinions* (1913), 66.

198. For the date, see Patrick Waddington, *Ivan Turgenev and Britain* (Berg: Oxford, 1995), 188. For Moore's reminiscences, see "Turgueneff," *Fortnightly Review*, 2680.254 (February 1888): 237–51.

199. Moore, *Confessions of a Young Man* (1927), 94.

200. As long ago as May 1866, when the Salon rejected Manet's submissions (*The Fifer* and *The Artist*), Zola defended him in a series of newspaper articles, stopped because of readers' protests, and then issued complete as a pamphlet; on 1 January 1867, Zola defended *Olympia* as a great painting while others called it a "yellow-bellied odalisque"; Manet praised Zola's 1876 *L'Assommoir*, apparently named his 1877 portrait of a modern prostitute after a character in that novel, and Zola then took Manet's *Nana* as the title and subject of his 1879 novel.

201. Zola's 14–16 June 1879 "Paris Letter" in *Viestnik Europi* is excerpted in T. A. Gronberg, ed., *Manet: A Retrospective* (Park Lane: New York, 1988), 164; Zola's 26 July 1879 article is quoted in Brombert, *Edouard Manet*, 408.

202. Manet to Zola [28 July 1879], Monday, Wilson-Bareau, *Manet by Himself*, 186.

203. Alexis, "Manet," 294–95.

204. *Portrait de George Moore* (1879), Rouart and Wildenstern, *Edouard Manet*, illus. 279, p. 234.

205. Daniel Halévy, *My Friend Degas*, trans. Mina Curtiss (Wesleyan University Press: Middletown, CT, 1964), 41.

206. Moore, *Confessions of a Young Man* (1972), 112.

207. Moore, *Vale*, 102.

208. Ibid., 103–4.

209. Manet's remark recorded by Antonin Proust; reprinted in Wilson-Bareau, *Manet by Himself*, 184.

210. Friedrich Nietzsche, *The Gay Science*, trans. Walter Kaufmann (Random House: New York, 1974), 275. For a discussion of "How one becomes what one is," see Alexander Nehemas's *Nietzsche: Life as Literature* (Cambridge and London: Harvard University Press, 1985), 170–99. For a sample of GM's appreciations of Rousseau, see Moore, *Memoirs of My Dead Life* (Gilcher A29, 2d), 29. Moore advised the young author Leah Rosenbloom: "Now will you do as I tell you? Will you read Rousseau's *Confessions*? The first part is most interesting, but do not read for the interest of the story, read with a view to understanding how it was written" (GM to Rosenbloom, 8 May [1924], Berg 63b1373). In the same year, he tried to get W. K. Magee to translate the first part of the *Confessions* for publication, adding, "The last third I have never read, and I doubt if many people want to read it" (GM to Magee, 30 April 1924, HRHRC).

211. Moore, *Communication to My Friends*, 8–11; for Blake's fear of being shot, see *Avowals* (1924), 269.

212. George Moore to My dear Joseph [August? 1879], NLI Ms 4479; Becker, 196; *Life of George Moore*, 81.

213. This inventory of the contents of GM's apartment is taken from an announcement in the *Moniteur des ventes* announcing an auction at 61 rue Con-

dorcet on 26 March 1881. See Noël, *George Moore*, 682. Why was the sale in March 1881 if GM left Paris in the fall of 1879? Paris apartments were typically leased from July to July, or by quarters. It is possible that GM paid a year's lease in July 1879. Then when Georgette Coëtlogon wrote him in 1881 informing him that, as he would not answer letters, an auction of his belongings had to be held because "three quarters of rent were due," that would be the quarters of July–September, October–December, 1880 and January–March 1881 (Moore, *Confessions of a Young Man* [1972], 118).

George Moore, "Apologia pro scriptis meis," xii; for the final meal with Hawkins, in which GM stole his friend's attention from Hawkins's new mistress, Marie, see *Confessions of a Young Man* (1972), 127–29.

Chapter 3 The Novelist as Absentee Landlord

1. *Life of George Moore*, 87; George Moore, "Love of the Past," *Spectator*, 59.2737 (11 December 1880): 1586; George Moore, "A Modern Poem," *Pagan Poems*, 152–54; George Moore, *Confessions of a Young Man* (1972), 129.
2. Maurice Moore Papers, NLI Ms 10566(1).
3. R. V. Comerford, "The Politics of Distress, 1877–82," in W. E. Vaughan, ed., *A New History of Ireland, VI: Ireland Under the Union, II: 1870–1921* (Clarendon Press: Oxford, 1996), 45.
4. "The Land War in the West," *Freeman's Journal*, 27 July 1880: 2.
5. A copy of *Martin Luther* inscribed "To E. Gosse . . . 1879" is recorded in *Book Auction Records, 1927–28*, 25:1 (Henry Stevens, Son, and Stiles: NY, n.d.). In George Moore, *Avowals* (1924), Moore recalls bringing his "youthful drama" to "a house overlooking a canal, with a screen of poplar

trees between it and the barges," that is to Gosse's house at 19 Delamere Terrace. For Beatty and O'Shaughnessy, see their 1880 letters to Moore in NLI Ms 2648. Thomas Pakenham Beatty published *Three Women of the People and Other Poems* with GM's publisher Newman in 1881; in 1893, he published a second book, *Spretae Carmina Musae, First Series: Songs of Love and Death* (Bell: London, 1893).
6. Heinrich Felbermann, *Memoirs of a Cosmopolitan* (Chapman and Hall: London, 1936), 113.
7. At least in later years, GM affected to look down on his mother's side of the family, and to hold that there was a large divide between the Catholic Blakes and the once-Protestant Moores. So in *A Communication to My Friends* when he tells of coming over to Ireland on the ferry from Holyhead, he says he thought of staying in the Shelbourne Hotel (quite the proper place for a landlord), and out of the Blakes' house of gossip, even if it was on fashionable Merrion Square. But, relenting, he joined the family party, so as not to distress his mother (George Moore, *A Communication to My Friends*, 35). The Blakes of Towerhill and Ballinafad were landed gentry, in the line of descent from Sir Valentine Blake of Galway. They were both wealthy and well-connected.
8. Maurice Moore Papers, NLI Ms 10566(1). Maurice Moore's letter appears in *Freeman's Journal* (26 September 1880).
9. Llewelyn Blake resigned as "receiver" for Arthur O'Connor's estate rather than serve ejectments, as demanded by O'Connor's widow and children (*Freeman's Journal*, 7 August 1880: 2).
10. Moore, *A Communication to My Friends*, 35–42; "Stephen's Green," *Freeman's Journal*, 28 July 1880: 5.
11. Moore, *A Communication to My Friends*, 40–41.
12. Maurice Moore to Joseph Hone, 8 January 1935, 5 Seaview Terrace, Dublin, NLI Ms 2648.
13. For his "inveterate" love of literature

nearly leading him to ruin, see "Apologia pro scriptis meis," xi–xiii.

A spring/summer 1881 letter shows that GM, even after signing the books, still found it difficult to accept a number of items, especially "100 pounds as interest this is impossible that is to say at a legitimate interest" (GM to My dear Joseph, 17 Cecil Street, Strand, NLI Ms 4479; Becker, 212).

14. "The State of the Country," *Freeman's Journal*, 14 August 1880: 3. Reprinted in the *Times* on 16 August 1880.

15. "Ballintubber Demonstration," *Freeman's Journal*, 9 August 1880: 7.

16. Maurice Moore Papers, NLI Ms 10566(1).

17. Lord Oranmore, "The Irish Land Question," *Irish Times*, 25 September 1880: 5; see also Oranmore's letter in the *Irish Times* of 11 October 1880.

18. *Life of George Moore*, 85. My thanks to Gareth Browne.

19. "Terrible Agrarian Outrage: Murder of Lord Montmorres," *Irish Times*, 27 September 1880: 3.

20. Boycott began to work as agent for Lord Erne, and leased 1,000 acres to farm himself, in 1873, after the Moores had settled in London. Before that, he was living near Westport, County Mayo, further from Moore Hall. As he was a "fearless hunter and steeplechase rider," the Moores may have encountered him at hunts and race meetings before his employment with Lord Erne (N. D. Palmer, *Irish Land League Crisis* [Yale University Press: New Haven, 1940] 198).

21. George Moore, *Parnell and His Island*, 124.

22. George Moore to My dear Joseph [September, 1880], The Palace, Elphin, Co. Roscommon, NLI Ms 4479; Becker, 202.

23. The relationship between the Moores and the Ruttledges is through the Blakes (the family of GM's mother): Isidore Blake of Towerhill married Frances, daughter and co-heir of Thomas Ruttledge of Cornfield in

1767 (*Burke's Peerage and Baronetage*, 105th edition, 1970).

24. Moore, *A Communication to My Friends*, 45.

25. "Ejectments," "Process Serving on Mr. Moore's Estate," *Connaught Telegraph*, 25 September 1880: 3, 5. My thanks for these references to Brendan Fleming, St Catherine's College, Oxford.

26. Moore, *Parnell and His Island*, 57.

27. Ibid., 48.

28. Ibid., 73, 113–21. The journalist James Daly of the *Connaught Telegraph* in Castlebar was a leading fomenter of the land agitation, and Father Patrick Lavelle was now an ally of Michael Davitt. See Comerford, "The Politics of Distress," 34.

29. Moore, *Parnell and His Island*, 76.

30. *Mayo Examiner*, 9 October 1880: n.p. My thanks to Brendan Fleming.

31. Viola Meynell, *Francis Thompson and Wilfrid Meynell: A Memoir* (Hollis and Carter: London, 1952), 132.

32. P. Beatty to George Moore, 13 December [1880], 10 Philbeach Gdns, Earls Court, NLI Ms 2648. *Three Women of the People* was published by Newman in 1882.

33. Arthur O'Shaughnessy to My dear Moore, 12 December 1880, Notting Hill, NLI Ms 2648.

34. *Life of George Moore*, 85; Moore, *Communication to My Friends*, 45; Moore, "Apologia pro scriptis meis," xiii.

35. Moore, "Apologia pro scriptis meis," xiii.

36. Dante Gabriel Rossetti to Theodore Watts Dunton, Wednesday [26 January 1881], Oswald Doughty and John Robert Wahl, eds, *Letters of Dante Gabriel Rossetti* (Clarendon Press: Oxford, 1967), 1841.

37. The 19 March 1881 date is from Rossetti's diary; quoted in Roger W. Peattie, ed., *Selected Letters of William Michael Rossetti* (Pennsylvania State University Press: University Park and London, 1990), 401 n. 5.

38. George Moore to Dear Mr. Rossetti, 17 Fleet Street, Strand; Berg; Becker,

205–6. Later in 1881, Newman again got cold feet about a book of poems, withdrawing Mathilde Blind's *The Prophecy of St Oran and Other Poems* on account of its atheistical character; Peattie, ed., *Selected Letters of William Michael Rossetti*, 401.

39. Peattie, *Selected Letters of William Michael Rossetti*, 401 n. 5.

40. George Moore to Dear Mr. Rossetti, 17 Fleet Street, Becker, 209 and 210; Peattie, ed., *Selected Letters of William Michael Rossetti*, 401 n. 5.

41. Henry Pottinger Stephens went to Eton, wrote poetry and light opera libretti, worked on the staff of the *Sporting Times*, spent two years in the USA; served as Paris correspondent of the *Times*, and worked for many years as a *Daily Telegraph* journalist; see J. B. Booth, *Old Pink 'Un Days* (Grant Richards: London, 1924), 183, 249; Guy Deghy, *Paradise in the Strand* (Richards Press: London, 1958); A Journalist [William Mackay], *Bohemian Days in Fleet Street* (John Long: London, 1913), 72.

42. Becker, 210; *Book Auction Records*, 38.1 (Henry Stevens, Son, & Stiles: London, June 1941), 438; *American Book-Prices Current, 1947–48*, ed. Edward Lazare (R. R. Bowker: New York, 1948), 347; *Book Prices Current* (Witherby: London, 1947); George Frederic Lees, "Recollections of an Anglo-Parisian Bibliophile: II – George Moore in Paris," *The Bookman* (September 1932): 296–97.

43. *Spectator*, 60.2749 (5 March 1881): 59.

44. Ibid., 59.2758 (7 May 1881).

45. Ibid., 2791 (24 December 1881): 1653–54.

46. Moore, "Apologia pro scriptis meis," xiv.

47. George Moore, "A Lyrical Argument, Current Literature," *New York Times* (15 June 1884): 2.1; reprinted from the *Temple Bar* (June 1884). The anti-humanitarian principles in this credo are taken from Théophile Gautier: the only morality is the correction of form; and the only immortality for an indi-

vidual is art. For Gautier's influence, see Malcolm Brown, *George Moore: A Reconsideration* (University of Washington Press, Seattle, 1995), 41–46.

48. Moore, "Apologia pro scriptis meis," xiv.

49. George Moore, *Confessions of a Young Man* (1972), 132, 137, 208.

50. Deghy, *Paradise in the Strand*, 24–25, 36.

51. Moore, *Confessions of a Young Man* (1972), 168. For background on the Cecil Street boarding house and its owner Priscilla Harding, see Becker, 212.

52. Moore, *Confessions of a Young Man* (1972), 134.

53. Jean C. Noël, *George Moore: l'homme et l'œuvre* (Marcel Didier: Paris, 1966), 682.

54. George Moore to Cher Monsieur [1 April 1881], 17 Cecil Street, Strand, Bibliothèque Nationale, Paris; Becker, 215–17. Anthony Rota, a bookseller in possession of the fragmentary Moore translation, by a comparison of sample passages shows that the 1884 Vizetelly edition is not based on this Ms. fragment by Moore (Rota to Becker, 8 December 1981). My thanks to Edwin Gilcher.

55. George Moore to Cher Monsieur [12 April 1881], 17 Cecil Street, Becker, 221–22.

56. George Moore, "A Visit to M. Zola," *St. James's Gazette* (26 May 1881): 1979.

57. Ibid.: 1979.

58. Ten pages of Moore's translation of *L'Assommoir* were in the John Quinn collection, listed for sale in *American Book-Prices Current* (1924), 818.

59. Moore, *Confessions of a Young Man* (1972), 153, 211.

60. "Moore Estate, Rental and Schedule, referred to in Declaration of Thomas Ruttledge, subscribed February,1883," Castlebar County Library. My thanks to Padraig Sherlin. It is likely that the tenants won a reduction in their rent. The 16 August 1883 *Spectator* reported that of 61,000 cases appealed

to the Land Court in the previous year, rents were reduced by 18 percent to 23 percent. Moore's tenants are also likely to have had at least a 20 percent reduction (*Spectator*, 2879: 1082). In *Land Owners in Ireland, Return of Owners of Land of One Acre and Upwards . . .* (Dublin, 1876), George Moore is credited with 12,371 acres with a valuation of £3,524, yet tenants did not pay the full "standard valuation" even in better times.

61. Maurice Moore to Mary Blake Moore, 13 October 1881, NLI Ms 10566; quoted in *Confessions of a Young Man* (1972), 251 n. 3.

62. *Sporting Times*, 946 (5 November 1881): 2. GM says that while he did write for James Davis (who owned *Pan* in 1880, partly owned the *Cuckoo* in 1882, and worked for the *Sporting Times* from 1881), he "could not learn to see life paragraphically" (*Confessions of a Young Man* [1972], 185).

63. Lord Westenra Rossmore, *Things I Can Tell* (Eveleigh Nash: London, 1912), 99–104; see also T. W. Moody, F. X. Martin and F. J. Byrne, eds, *A New History of Ireland*, vol. 8: *Chronology of Irish History to 1976* (Clarendon Press: Oxford, 1982), 357.

64. The date of Moore's quarrel is not certain, but Augustus (nicknamed "Burgess") Moore's mention of the "dare-devil deeds of the Pagan" in the 19 November 1881 *Sporting Times* (p. 7) may allude to this event.

65. Moore, *Confessions of a Young Man* (1972), 186. Rossmore's version of the fight is different: "I promptly boxed his ears; he threw something at me; our friends thereupon intervened" (*Things I Can Tell*, 126).

66. Moore, *Confessions of a Young Man* (1972), 189–90, 230–31.

67. Edmund Downey, "An Editor's Reminiscences," *The Irish Book Lover*, ed. John S. Crone; vol. 8, n. 7–8 (February/March 1917): 73–75; Edmund Downey, *Twenty Years Ago: A Book of Anecdote Illustrating Literary Life in London* (Hurst and Blackett: London, 1905).

68. Moore, *Confessions of a Young Man* (1972), 182; Downey confirms that the way to be published at *Tinsley's Magazine* was to get inside its "charmed circle" of authors (*Twenty Years Ago*, 251).

69. George Moore, "Under the Fan," *Tinsley's Magazine*, 30 (February 1882): 135–54.

70. Downey, *Twenty Years Ago*, 88–91; Moore, *Confessions of a Young Man* (1972), 182–83. Hill's first story in *Tinsley's* appears in the November 1881 issue; his novel *The Waters of Marrah* was serialised there from January 1883.

71. George Moore to My dear Mother [inscribed "May 1882"], 17 Cecil Street, Strand, NLI Ms 4479; Becker, 226.

72. *Life of George Moore*, 75. Moore did not work all the time; he attended the "Dramatic Ball" at the Freemasons' Tavern on Ash Wednesday, 1882 (*Sporting Times*, 962 [25 February 1882]: 2–3). In early March 1882, he is also likely to have entertained Manet's friend, Théodore Duret, then in London on wine-trading business (Eugène Manet to Berthe Morisot, 7 March 1882, Bernard Denvir, *The Chronicle of Impressionism* [Little, Brown: Boston, New York, Toronto, London, 1993] 133). GM evidently attended Durand-Ruel's exhibition of French paintings at White's Gallery, 13 King Street, London, which opened 5 May 1882, and ran through July. Degas's *Le Baisser du rideau* from this exhibition is described in *A Mere Accident* as "The Drop Curtain." See George Moore, *A Mere Accident*, 72; Denvir, *Chronicle of Impressionism*, 130; and Ronald Pickvance, "A Newly Discovered Drawing by Degas of George Moore," *Burlington Magazine*, 105. 723 (June 1963): 276–80.

73. Strauss was actually a Ph.D., not an MD, a man in his seventies with an enormous, flowing gray beard, who specialised as an author on two rather different subjects: cookery and poison. See Downey, *Twenty Years Ago*, 97–

101; Deghy, *Paradise in the Strand*, n.p.; William Tinsley, *Random Recollections of an Old Publisher*, vol. 2 (Simpkin, Marshall, Hamilton, Kent: London, 1900), 75.

74. *Sporting Times*, 989 (2 September 1882): 2–3.

75. Ibid., 940 (24 September 1882): 2. The first allusion in this weekly to Augustus Moore's new job as "Literary Advisor" (or theatrical press agent) is in the 24 June 1882 issue.

76. Ibid., 1000 (18 November 1882): 2–3.

77. Augustus M. Moore, ed., *Walnuts and Wine* (Strand: London, [1883]), 18–21. The jealous Russian husband has his Polish wife's friend Vanca arrested. The next morning she is awakened at dawn and taken to the barracks. There Vanca is forced to walk fifty paces between two ranks of soldiers, an executioner with a whip giving him lashes from behind, and another officer in front walking backwards with the point of his sword to Vanca's chest. After ten lashes, Vanca throws himself on the sword.

78. Ibid., 3; Chevalier W. H. Grattan Flood, "George Moore: Poet and Librettist," *Cork Examiner*, 3 March 1928. Swinburne wrote to the 28 December 1883 *Pall Mall Gazette* to complain. He denied knowing either the contributor or the contribution.

79. Dane's Inn was formerly an inn of the Inner Temple. It was opposite from, and east of, Somerset House, and nearly adjacent to the Opéra Comique, destroyed along with Dane's Inn itself in 1900 when Aldwych Crescent was built: A. R. Hope Moncrieff, ed. *Black's Guide to London and Its Environs* (Adam and Charles Black: London, 1913), 23. My thanks to Jim McCord.

80. *Sporting Times*, 1004 (16 December 1882): 2–3. He bragged to his mother in a letter which Becker dates January 1883 that he at last "pretty well know[s] the wires" in London, and will soon ring Fortune's bell (Becker, 228). Moore was credited with having discovered "Melita" of the music-hall

stage, but there is no sign that he made her fortune or his own.

81. *Les Cloches de Corneville*, Folies Dramatiques, Lord Chamberlain's Office, license no. 68, British Library.

82. "An Unknown Work by George Moore," *The Bookman* (April 1923). The original French "Opéra-comique" was by Clairville [pseud. Louis François Nicolaie] and Charles Gabet (1877); the earlier English version, briefly supplanted by the Moores' translation, was by H. B. Farnie and R. Reece, lyrics only (1879).

83. James M. Glover, *Jimmy Glover: His Book* (Methuen: London, 1911), 51–53.

84. In a letter to the *Observer* on 8 April 1923, Glover said their version of the operetta ran for ten days. GM, he recalls, "threw up the sponge" when the translation was only half done, a recollection confirmed by Moore in a 23 March 1923 letter to Ernest Boyd: "I wrote the lyrics of the first two acts, and I think my brother Augustus wrote the lyrics of the third." My thanks to Edwin Gilcher.

85. Moore, "Apologia pro scriptis meis," xv.

86. Moore, *A Communication to My Friends*, 20–21; "Apologia pro scriptis meis," xv; Downey, *Twenty Years Ago*, 10.

87. George Moore to My dear Mama [inscribed 8 April 1883], Dane's Inn, Wych Street, Strand, NLI Ms 4479; Becker, 232–33.

88. Denis Rouart and Daniel Wildenstern, *Edouard Manet: Catalogue raisonné*, tome II, *Pastels, aquarelles et dessins* (La Bibliothèque des Arts: Paris, 1975), "Buste de la femme," illus. 240, p. 198; "Le Clairon," illus. 392.

89. George Moore, *A Modern Lover*, vol. 1, 137–38.

90. Ibid., 147.

91. Ibid., 195.

92. Ibid., vol. 2, 11.

93. Ibid., 28.

94. Ibid., 82.

95. Ibid., vol. 3, 104.

96. For a thorough study of the novel, to

which I am indebted, see John Alden Carstens, "The Anti-Romances of George Moore" (University of Oregon dissertation, December 1973), esp. 78–82.

97. Moore, *A Modern Lover*, vol. 2, 239.

98. After leaving Paris, Moore probably continued to see Hawkins on occasion in London. Hawkins exhibited *By the Wayside* and *Keston Common* at the Suffolk Street gallery in Society of British Artists exhibitions in 1880 and 1881 (E. Benezit, *Dictionnaire critique et documentaire des peintres, sculpteurs, dessinateurs, et graveurs* [Librairie Grund: Paris, 1976]).

99. Georgette de Coëtlogon liked to tell GM about her lovers, just as if he was not one of them himself. See G. de Coëtlogon to George Moore, 28 November [1883], Avenue Bois de Boulogne, NLI Ms 2648.

100. Georg Ebers, *Lorenz Alma-Tadema: His Life and Works*, trans. Mary J. Safford (William S. Gottsberger: New York, 1886); Vern G. Swanson, *The Biography and Catalogue Raisonné of the Paintings of Sir Lawrence Alma-Tadema* (Garton: London, 1990).

101. Gosse published a biographical study of Alma-Tadema in 1882, but it is not the source of the particular details GM used in the novel. [Edmund Gosse], "Lawrence Alma-Tadema," F. G. Damas, ed., *Illustrated Biographies of Modern Artists* (Chapman and Hall: London, 1882), 75–95.

102. "Novels of the Week," *Athenaeum* (London), 7 July 1883: 13–14.

103. "*A Modern Lover* by George Moore," *St. James's Gazette*, 11 July 1883: 7.

104. "New Novels," *Academy*, 24 (14 July 1883): 23.

105. "Books: *A Modern Lover*," *Spectator*, 2,877 (18 August 1883): 1069.

106. Moore, "Apologia pro scriptis meis," xvii. An April 1882 article probably by Tinsley entitled "Is the Novel Moribund?" defends the current system of publication. If novels were sold in cheap one-volume editions, the article warned, there would be fewer books available and authors would make less

money. For authors to make money, he concluded, it was best to build a steady reputation, or, for fleeting success, to "disregard the laws of morality," or, finally, to advertise widely (*Tinsley's Magazine*, 30 [April 1882]: 392–93). Moore tried all three methods.

Months after *A Modern Lover* was published, Tinsley called on GM for his £40 guarantee. GM showed his brother the letter demanding payment, and Augustus told him not to worry: "I know a genial Jew [James Davis] who will just write to him for his accounts and if they are not right he will make it the temperature of a red-hot poker for Mr. Tinsley." Augustus then found out that Tinsley's stock of the novel had been destroyed in a warehouse fire, and insurance had paid Tinsley already for his losses, so GM owed him nothing. GM's depression "vanished like a fog" (*A Communication to My Friends*, 58–59).

107. George Moore, "A New Censorship of Literature," *Pall Mall Gazette*, 40.6163 (10 December 1884): 1–2; *Avowals*, 100.

108. Moore, "A New Censorship of Literature," 1.

Chapter 4 A Ricochet of Zola in London

1. Charles Morgan, "Epitaph on George Moore," *American Mercury*, 36 (1935): 179.

2. George Moore, "Apologia pro scriptis meis," xvii.

3. Ibid.

4. Kate Ede, who has just run off from her husband with a lodger in the house, a manager of a traveling theater company, is unsettled by the actors' bohemian indifference to the morality of property (George Moore, *A Mummer's Wife* (1908), 204).

5. Jimmy Glover to the editor, *Pall Mall Gazette*, 53.8266 (17 September 1891): 3; George Moore to the editor, *Pall Mall Gazette*, 22 September 1891: 2; James M. Glover, *Jimmy Glover: His*

Book (Methuen: London, 1911), 242. Moore's put-down letter suggested that, if Glover's claim was allowed, then a descendant of "the Artful Dodger" in *Oliver Twist* could also make a claim against the estate of Dickens: "It was my father wot stole the 'wipe,' and werry cleverly he did it, too; as for the other bloke, he only 'eard of it, and then 'e goes and writes a book and puts it in."

6. *A Fashionable Beauty* was reworked by Harry Paulton before its 6 April 1885 production at the Avenue Theatre. In a review, the *Bat* reported that "George Moore, I regret to say, originally wrote the piece, but that was a long time ago, and its production must cause him about the same pleasure that a great novelist would feel at seeing his school essays printed as evidence of his capabilities. Afterwards, it was touched up by that melancholy wit, Harry Paulton, and somebody spoiled any idea there might have been in it": *Bat*, 1.3 (14 April 1885): 34.

7. [George] Moore and [Jimmy] Glover, *The Fashionable Beauty: A Comic Opera in Three Scenes and One Act*. Lord Chamberlain's Plays, no. 81 (6 April 1885), 11.

8. Moore, *A Mummer's Wife*. The 1908 edition is an authorised reprint of the 1893 Walter Scott impression of the 1886 Vizetelly second edition. The 1885 Vizetelly first edition is rare; the 1917 Brentano's edition, and all later issues, are so completely revised that they represent a later phase of Moore's style.

9. George Moore, *A Communication to My Friends*, 33.

10. Ibid., 30.

11. Before writing *A Mummer's Wife*, Moore evidently employed his notebook with some industry during a guided tour of the pottery works in High Street, Hanley, and rather directly transferred the notes to Chapter 4 of the novel, where actor Dick Lennox and young landlady Kate Ede take such a tour in the company of three clergymen, and Dick, promptly upon their departure, forces himself on Kate; the couple tumble in a crash of crockery (Moore, *A Mummer's Wife* [1908], 82).

12. Ernest Alfred Vizetelly, *Emile Zola: Novelist and Reformer* (John Lane: London, 1904), 243–48.

13. Moore, *Communication to My Friends*, 25.

14. Vizetelly, *Emile Zola*, 250; George Moore, "A New Censorship of Literature," *Pall Mall Gazette*, 40.6163 (10 December 1884): 2.

15. See GM to Zola [1 April 1881], 17 Cecil Street, Becker, 215–17; Vizetelly, *Emile Zola*, 252.

16. Moore, *Communication to My Friends*, 27–28.

17. *Thérèse Raquin* was published by Vizetelly in March 1886. The translator is not named.

18. George Moore to Cher Monsieur Zola, 17 September 1883, Tillyra, Ardrahan, C. Galway, Becker, 237–39. My paraphrase and translation from Moore's French original.

19. George Moore's mother, Mary Blake, was Maurice Blake's daughter; Maurice Blake's sister Mary had a granddaughter, also Mary (Dolphin), who married Andrew Martyn, the brother of Edward Martyn's father, John. (From the Blake family tree prepared by Philip Deane for Edwin Gilcher.)

20. For the story of Augustus Moore, Edward Martyn, and George, Duke de Stacpoole. attempting to burn down Beaumont School, see Maurice Moore to Joseph Hone, n.d., 5 Seaview Terrace, NLI Ms 2648. For certain dates in Martyn's life, I am indebted to J. C. Nolan, who supplied me with a copy of Martyn's diary, a brief chronicle prepared in his later years, listing travels, births, deaths, and publications.

21. George Moore, *Vale*, 62.

22. Sister Marie Thérèse Courtney says that, upon Martyn's failure, his mother sent him to Paris to live with George Moore, who was expected to take over the conduct of Martyn's

education. Neither Martyn's diary of his travels nor GM's copious memoirs mention such a visit. Sister M. T. Courtney, *Edward Martyn and the Irish Theatre* (Vantage: New York, 1956), 18–19.

23. Timothy d'Arch Smith, *Love in Earnest: Some Notes on the Lives and Writings of English "Uranian" Poets from 1889 to 1930* (Routledge and Kegan Paul: London, 1970), 36. Stenbock and Martyn remained friends up to the time of Stenbock's death in 1895. Yeats recalls a dinner with Stenbock, "scholar, connoisseur, drunkard, poet, pervert, most charming of men," and, previous to GM, Edward's "close friend." See William Butler Yeats, ed., *Oxford Book of Modern Verse, 1892–1935* (Clarendon Press: Oxford, 1936), x; William Butler Yeats, *Memoirs: Autobiography – First Draft, Journal*, ed. Denis Donoghue (Macmillan: London, 1972), 118.

24. John Addington Symonds, *The Letters*, ed. Herbert M. Schueller and Robert L. Peters, vol. 3 (Wayne State University Press: Detroit, 1969), 346.

25. George Moore, *Ave*, 183.

26. Ibid.

27. Ibid., 181. Yeats believed Martyn's homosexuality was "always resisted" (R. F. Foster, *W. B. Yeats: A Life* [Oxford University Press: Oxford, 1997]), 165.

28. George Moore, *Salve*, 94.

29. My thanks to Leo and Aidan Finn for a tour of Tillyra Castle. See also Mark Bence-Jones, *A Guide to Irish Country Houses* (Constable: London, 1988), 276–77.

30. Duke de Stacpoole, *Irish and Other Memories* (A.M. Philpot: London, 1922), 2–4.

31. Information from R. J. Kelly, quoted in Courtney, *Edward Martyn*, 38.

32. Ibid., 39.

33. Denis R. Gwynn, *Edward Martyn and the Irish Revival* (Jonathan Cape: London, 1930), 76.

34. George Barlow, *Selected Poems*, with portrait (Henry J. Glaisher: London,

1921), 128–34. Barlow tried to synthesise aestheticism, cross-gendered eroticism, and Christianity, writing poems, for instance, about the womanly side of Jesus ("God's Motherhood"), about men being saved by the bodily love of women which ultimately comes from God ("Divine Feminine"), and men having within them the astral bodies of women ("The Astral Body").

35. [George Barlow] to My dear Moore, 28 New Cavendish Street, NLI Ms 2648.

36. Becker, 284.

37. GM to My dear Mama, 19 May 1884, 3 Dane's Inn, ibid., 256.

38. George Moore, *Memoirs of My Dead Life* (1906), 64–5.

39. GM to My dear Mama [February 1884], Shelbourne Hotel, Dublin, Becker, 239; *Life of George Moore*, 99.

40. *Land Owners in Ireland, Return of Owners of Land of One Acre and Upwards in the Several Counties, Counties of Cities, and Counties of Towns in Ireland* (Genealogical Publishing Company: Baltimore, 1988; reprinted Dublin, 1976).

41. Maurice Moore to My dear Mother, 25 March [1884], Shalijahanpore, NLI Ms 10566(2). Maurice was astonished to hear that Maud and George were "engaged": "the relationship certainly does seem very close, more than first cousin in fact, but in other ways it would be suitable enough."

42. GM to My dear Mama [February 1884], Shelbourne Hotel, Dublin, Becker, 239.

43. George Moore, *Muslin*, ix.

44. *Life of George Moore*, 99. Aunts were numerous on the Blake side – GM's mother had four sisters. Which one in particular was an ogress is unknown.

45. The possibility of a match may have been rekindled before being snuffed out completely, because on 25 March 1884, Mrs Moore wrote to Maurice, then stationed in India, that GM and Maud were engaged.

46. GM to Mon cher Maître [Zola],

[February 1884], Shelbourne Hotel, Becker, 247.

47. B. H. Bakker, *"Naturalisme pas mort"*: *Lettres inédites de Paul Alexis à Emile Zola 1871–1900* (University of Toronto Press: Toronto, 1971), 266.

48. The unsigned article, "My New Novel by Emile Zola," in the *Pall Mall Gazette* (39.5976 [3 May 1884]: 6), describing an interview with Zola is certainly by Moore (he claims credit for it in a 19 May letter to Zola), and not by William Sharp, a regular contributor of literary articles to London magazines, who also visited Zola in April. See William Sharp to Elizabeth, 10 April 1884, *William Sharp (Fiona Macleod): A Memoir Compiled by His Wife* (William Heinemann: London, 1910), 96.

49. William Rothenstein, *Men and Memories*, vol. 1 (Faber and Faber: London, 1931), 162.

50. George Moore, "Guy de Maupassant," *Illustrated London News*, 2752 (16 January 1892): 82.

51. Michael G. Lerner, *Maupassant* (George Allen and Unwin: London, 1975), 174.

52. Moore, "Guy de Maupassant."

53. GM to My dear Mother, 15 May 1884, 3 Dane's Inn, Becker, 251.

54. Julian Moore's "A Bayswater Barnum" appeared in the June 1884 issue of *Tinsley's Magazine*; it is mentioned by Edmund Downey in "An Editor's Reminiscences," *The Irish Book Lover*, ed. John S. Crone, 8.9–10 (April/May 1917): 9–10.

55. GM to Mon cher ami (Theodore Duret), Friday [15 May 1884], 3 Dane's Inn, Becker, 252.

56. GM to Mon cher maître (Zola), 19 May 1884, 3 Dane's Inn, ibid., 253.

57. Ibid., 256.

58. GM to My dear Sir, 10 August [1884], 3 Dane's Inn, Moore Collection, Bertrand.

59. Henry James to Dear Miss Paget, 21 October [1884], 3 Bolton St W.; Leon Edel, ed., *Henry James: Letters*, vol. 3, *1883–1895* (Harvard University Press: Cambridge, MA, 1980), 49–51.

60. Peter Gunn, *Vernon Lee: Violet Paget, 1856–1935* (Oxford University Press: London, 1964), 101. In fact, it was not Paget's first book, and it would not at all be her last

61. Ibid., 102.

62. George Moore, *Avowals*, 173–74. By the time Moore published *Avowals*, James was dead and GM was eager to assert his equality to, even superiority over, the American novelist.

63. Henry James, "The Art of Fiction," *Longman's Magazine*, 4 (September 1884): 502–21.

64. Moore, *Avowals*, 175.

65. Within a few years, Moore dropped all his hesitations; in *Confessions of a Young Man* (1972), he calls *A Rebours* "a prodigious book, that beautiful mosaic . . . a page of Huysmans is as a dose of opium, a glass of something exquisite and spiritous" (p. 177).

66. George Moore, "A Curious Book," *St. James's Gazette*, 2 September 1884: 6–7.

67. The diary of his journey by Alexis ("Troublot") was published on 7 October 1884, and is reprinted in Bakker, *"Naturalisme pas mort,"* 489–91.

68. Paul Alexis, "Les Filles de Joseph Prudhomme," *Le Matin*, 1 (12 October 1884): 1.

69. Paul Alexis to Mon cher ami (Zola), 15 October 1884; Bakker, *"Naturalisme pas mort,"* 280–82.

70. GM to Cher Maître (Zola), [late October, 1884], 3 Dane's Inn, Becker, 262–63.

71. Emile Zola, *Correspondance*, ed. B. H. Bakker, vol. 5, *1884–86* (Presses de l'Université de Montréal, Editions du Centre National de la Recherche Scientifique: Montreal and Paris, 1978, 1995), 185–86. W. T. Madge, editor of the *People*, told Zola that he had heard of George Moore, but would not take the time to ask Zola for a letter of introduction (*Correspondance*, 181).

72. Bakker, *"Naturalisme pas mort"*, 317 n. 6.

73. *Life of George Moore*, 71.

74. Moore, *A Mummer's Wife* (1908), 45.

75. *A Doctor's Wife* is the same Braddon novel that, in his youth, offered GM an "echo-augury," when the names "Shelley" and "Byron" had thrilling vibrations for him, and led him to read their poetry.

For a study of the relations between Braddon's *A Doctor's Wife*, Flaubert's *Madame Bovary*, and Moore's *A Mummer's Wife*, see Judith Mitchell's "Naturalism in George Moore's *A Mummer's Wife*," in Barbara Leah Harman and Susan Meyer, eds, *The New Nineteenth Century: Feminist Readings of Underread Victorian Fiction* (Garland: New York, 1996), 159–80.

76. Moore, *A Mummer's Wife* (1908), 70.

77. Ibid., 132.

78. George Moore, *A Mummer's Wife* (1886), 115. This famously inflammatory passage was left out of the Walter Scott 1893 edition, and subsequent reissues.

79. A point interestingly underlined by Mitchell, "Naturalism," 170.

80. Moore, *A Mummer's Wife* (1908), 230.

81. Ibid., 253.

82. Ibid., 338.

83. For an account of Zola phobia among the English, see Peter Keating's *The Haunted Study: A Social History of the English Novel 1875–1914* (Fontana: London, 1989), 115–21, 244–53.

84. William Wallace, "New Novels: *A Mummer's Wife*," *Academy*, 26 (29 November 1884): 354. Certain scenes he found "too suggestive," though Wallace went on to say that, as a realist, Moore should not suggest but state things outright.

85. "New Novels," *Graphic*, 30 (29 November 1884): 579.

86. "*A Mummer's Wife*," *Pall Mall Gazette*, 40.6159 (5 December 1884): 4–5.

87 Keating, *Haunted Study*, 116. Zola is not the only French influence on *A Mummer's Wife*; it is also an imitation of Balzac, Goncourt, and especially Flaubert, as Moore recognised himself upon revising the novel in 1917: "the awfullest screed that ever found a printer . . . , written backwards, with imitations of Balzac and plagiarisms from him and Zola and Goncourt." See GM to Dear Magee [John Eglinton/W.K. Magee], 24 March [1917?], 121 Ebury Street, HRHRC.

88. Moore, *A Mummer's Wife* (1908), 160, 253. For further similarities between Zola's theories and Moore's novel, see John Alden Carstens, "The Anti-Romances of George Moore," University of Oregon dissertation (December 1973), 102–20, and Anne Mills King, "Some Aspects of Style in the Fiction of George Moore: Naturalist, Irishman, Melodist," University of Maryland dissertation (1972), 37ff.

89. M. Chaikin, "George Moore's *A Mummer's Wife* and Zola," *Revue de littérature comparée*, 31 (1957): 85–88.

90. My thanks to W. W. Thomas of the Union College French department for discussions about Flaubert.

91. GM to My dear Duret [12 January 1885], Tillyra, Becker, 269.

92. George Moore, "A New Censorship of Literature," *Pall Mall Gazette*, 40, 6163 (10 December 1884): 1–2.

93. Ibid., 2.

94. "Novels of the Week," *Athenaeum*, 2981 (13 December 1884): 767.

95. GM to My dear Duret [12 January 1885], Tillyra, Becker, 269–70.

96. GM to Mon Cher Maître [Zola], 12 January [1885; misdated in original "1884"], Tillyra, ibid., 265–66. Italics added.

97. George Moore, Introduction, *Piping Hot! (Pot-Bouille), A Realistic Novel* (Vizetelly: London, 1885), v–xxviii.

98. GM to Dear Sir [Oscar Adams], [22 December 1884], Tillyra Castle, Becker, 264; Oscar Adams to GM, 6 January 1885, Erie, Pennsylvania, NLI Ms 2648.

Chapter 5 Two Farewells to Ireland

1. J. Fahey, *History and Antiquities of the Diocese of Kilmacduagh* (M. H. Gill: Dublin, 1893), 430. Father Thomas B. Considine first studied at the Irish

College (Rome), then matriculated at Maynooth Seminary in 1862 (*Maynooth Students and Ordinations Index, 1795–1895*, 46). My thanks to Marie Boran, Library of the National University of Ireland at Galway.

2. George Moore, *Ave* (1923), 183.

3. George Moore, *A Drama in Muslin* (1893), 70–72.

4. Ibid., 98–100.

5. GM to Dear Sir [unidentified editor], Tuesday [January 1885], Tillyra Castle, Becker, 274–75.

6. Moore, *A Drama in Muslin* (1893), 100.

7. The editor asked GM for something on censorship and the circulating libraries, the question of the moment in London, but GM expressed irritation with this request, and said he could deal with other questions just as well, such as why England had no dramatic literature. GM's article on that topic came out in the 28 April issue of the *Bat*.

8. For Colonel Dease and Lord Fingall, see Mark Bence-Jones, *Twilight of the Ascendancy* (Constable: London, 1987), 51.

9. Justin McCarthy to My dear George, 18 February 1885, NLI Ms 2648.

10. H. de Burgh to Dear Sir, 25 February [18]85, 18 Fleet Street, Dublin, NLI Ms 2648; Bence-Jones, *Twilight of the Ascendancy*, 67.

11. "Occasional Notes," *Pall Mall Gazette*, 12 February 1885: 3.

12. Moore, *A Drama in Muslin* (1893), 171.

13. Ibid., 181.

14. Becker, 277.

15. Richard Ellmann, *Oscar Wilde* (Viking Penguin: New York, 1987), 273.

16. Ronald Anderson and Anne Koval, *James McNeill Whistler: Beyond the Myth* (John Murray: London, 1994), 265.

17. GM to My dear Duret [12 January 1885], Becker, 269–70; Zola to Mon cher Moore, 25 January 1885, Médan, Emile Zola, *Correspondance*, ed. B. H. Bakker vol. 5, 1884–86 (Université de Montréal: Montréal, Centre National

de la Recherche Scientifique: Paris, 1985), 225–227.

18. GM to Mon cher Maître [Zola], n.d., Moore Hall, Becker, 286–87. Possibly even before letting Zola know, GM also wrote to William Michael Rossetti, his pipeline into the paragraphs of the *Athenaeum*, announcing both Judith Bernard Derosne's translation and Zola's preface (GM to My dear Rossetti, n.d., Moore Hall, Becker, 284).

19. Zola to Mon cher confrère, Paris, Zola, *Correspondance*, vol. 5, 238–39.

20. Huysmans and Céard were research assistants for *Pot-Bouille*; see Ernest Alfred Vizetelly, *Emile Zola: Novelist and Reformer* (John Lane: London, 1904), 207.

21. George Moore, *Confessions of a Young Man* (1972), 165.

22. More prosaically put, 15 April was his planned date of departure for London. See GM to Mon cher Blanche, 7 March [1885], Moore Hall, Berg; Becker, 289–90.

23. George Moore, *Avowals* (1924), 170.

24. "The first novel I began was *very* naturalistic though I did not know it at the time for I had never read a naturalistic novel; indeed, I have read only a few now. I laid it aside because a novel with little sensation is so difficult, & as this sensational story came into my mind I thought I would write it partly by way of practice." F. Mabel Robinson to GM, 7 April [1885], White Cottage, Epsom, NLI Ms 2648.

25. F. Mabel Robinson, *Mr. Butler's Ward*, Vizetelly's One-Volume Novels, vi (Vizetelly: London, 1885).

26. F. Mabel Robinson to GM, 28 March [1885], 20 Earl's Terrace, Kensington, NLI Ms 2648. GM gives the impression in *Avowals* that he could hardly bring himself to linger at Moore Hall through early April, so great was his desire to get to the Robinsons and find out what he could about Pater. In fact he planned only a short stopover in London, before continuing on to Paris for the opening of the Salon in May. He booked a room for 26 April at the

Hôtel Continental (henceforth, his usual haunt for his annual visits to the Paris Salon), and made dates to meet his friends the painter Jacques-Emile Blanche and Georgette de Coëtlogon (G. De Laittayon [Madame de Coëtlogon] to Cher Ami [George Moore], NLI Ms 2648).

27. J. B. Booth, *The Pink Parade* (Thornton Butterworth: London, 1933), 22.

28. *Bat*, 1 (31 March 1885–23 March 1886): Index.

29. James Davis to My dear Pagan, "The Bat," Editorial Offices, 10 Craig's Court, Charing Cross, NLI Ms 2648.

30. "Books to Cut," *Bat*, 1.3 (14 April 1885): 39.

31. Ibid.: 34. Moore's arrival in London was advertised by Davis in the 21 April issue; he reported that Moore was seen at the front of the house for the Opéra-Comique production of *The Guvnor.*

32. Joris-Karl Huysmans, *Certains* (Paris, 1889), 22–27; quoted in John Rewald, *The History of Impressionism* (Museum of Modern Art: New York, 1973), 526. Moore himself associated Degas's attitude in these nudes with the cynicism of the ascetic Middle Ages, its pessimism about life, combined with a modern skepticism about God ("Half a Dozen Enthusiasts," *Bat*, 2.61 [25 May 1886]: 185).

33. *Life of George Moore*, 123. The source of this anecdote is Gerald O'Donovan, who heard it from Martyn. On 26 September 1936, O'Donovan wrote Hone to correct the statement in the biography that Martyn bought a Manet; it was a Monet (Joseph M. Hone Accession, Box 1, Folder 23, V253d, Washington). The date of Edward Martyn's purchases is said by Hone to be January 1886; Martyn himself gives it as 1887. However, a letter Moore wrote to his mother from 3 Dane's Inn describing his Paris fortnight with Edward also mentions a meeting with Maurice Moore, datable to mid-May 1885 (Maurice Moore to Mary Blake Moore, 14 May [1885], 10 Bury Street, St James's, NLI Ms 10566(2); Becker,

295 n). Moore told his mother that at the Salon Zola had been very kind, and their promenade together attracted a good deal of attention (GM to My dear Mother [mid-May 1885], 3 Dane's Inn, Becker, 295).

34. "M. Zola's New Book," *Bat*, 1.33 (10 November 1885): 482.

35. George Moore, *Salve*, 92–93.

36. Marie [Robinson] Duclaux, "Souvenirs sur George Moore," *La Revue de Paris*, 40 (1 March 1933): 110–30.

37. Moore, *Avowals* (1924), 172.

38. Peter Gunn, *Vernon Lee: Violet Paget, 1856–1935* (London: Oxford University Press, 1964), 125.

39. Lawrence Evans, ed., *Letters of Walter Pater* (Oxford: Clarendon Press, 1970), 79.

40. Richard Aldington, *Walter Pater: Selected Works* (New York: Duell, Sloan and Pearce, 1948), 3.

41. See Denis Donoghue, *Walter Pater* (Random House: New York, 1995).

42. Raffalovich's party is reported in the *Court and Society Review* (15 July 1885); see Becker, 296–97; Moore mentions the event in *Avowals*, 200.

43. Moore, *Avowals* (1924), 183.

44. For Tennyson's similar fantasies of homosexual release after death, see Christopher Craft, *Another Kind of Love: Male Homosexual Desire in English Discourse, 1850–1920* (University of California Press: Berkeley, 1994), 170–71, 178–79.

45. GM to My dear Mother [inscribed 5 July 1885], 3 Dane's Inn, Becker, 296–97.

46. Havelock Ellis, *My Life* (William Heinemann: London, 1940), 80.

47. Yaffa Claire Draznin, *"My Other Self": The Letters of Olive Schreiner and Havelock Ellis, 1884–1920* (Peter Lang: New York, 1992), 328.

48. Frank Harris, *Contemporary Portraits: Fourth Series* (New York, 1923), n.p.

49. Draznin, *Letters of Olive Schreiner and Havelock Ellis*, 353.

50. Ibid., 357; GM to My dear Julian [Moore], [June 1885], 3 Dane's Inn, Becker, 351–52; George Moore, *Memoirs of My Dead Life* (1906), 257.

51. Vineta Colby, *The Singular Anomaly: Women Novelists of the Nineteenth Century* (University of London Press: London; New York University Press: New York, 1970), 73.

52. Schreiner to Ellis [30 June 1885], Draznin, *Letters of Olive Schreiner and Havelock Ellis*, 363; for a summary of Hinton's views, see the review of *The Larger Life: Studies in Hinton's Ethics*, by Caroline Haddon; *Academy*, 30. 739 (3 July 1886): 1–3. According to Hinton's gospel, a man's sacred purpose in life was to give pleasure to women (plural), or endure pain for their sake.

53. Schreiner to Ellis [13 July 1885], Draznin, *Letters of Olive Schreiner and Havelock Ellis*, 369.

54. GM to Dear Sir [Frans Netscher], Wednesday [5 August 1885], 3 Dane's Inn, Becker, 302–3.

55. Ellis to Schreiner [5 September 1885], *Letters of Olive Schreiner and Havelock Ellis*, 379; and Schreiner to Ellis, [17 September 1885], ibid., 383.

56. Richard Rive, ed., *Olive Schreiner Letters*, vol. 1: *1871–1899* (Oxford University Press: Oxford, 1988), n.p.

57. GM to Dear Sir [Frans Netscher] 28 October [1885], 3 Dane's Inn, Becker, 320–21. Thanking Netscher for an article in Dutch on GM's work, Moore said he had asked Schreiner to translate it, but it was so complimentary that he was ashamed to make her go through the whole article.

58. Elizabeth Grubgeld, *George Moore and the Autogenous Self: the autobiography and fiction* (Syracuse University Press: Syracuse, NY, 1994), 8–10.

59. Eleanor Marx Aveling to Laura Marx Lafargue, 27 April 1886, quoted in Yvonne Kapp, *Eleanor Marx*, vol. 2 (Virago: London, 1979), 95.

60. Eleanor Marx to Laura Lafargue, 2 Parade Villas, Kingston, *Daughters of Karl Marx: Family Correspondence, 1866–1898*, ed. Olgar Meier, trans. Faith Evans (André Deutsch: London, 1979), 189–90.

61. Gustave Flaubert, *Madame Bovary: Provincial Manners*, trans. Eleanor Marx-Aveling (Vizetelly: London, 1886), xviii.

62. Kapp, *Eleanor Marx*, vol. 2, 103; Michael Holroyd, *Bernard Shaw, The Search For Love*, vol. 1 (Random House: New York, 1988), 199.

63. See the Edward and Eleanor Marx, *The Woman Question* (Swan Sonnenschein: London, 1886), reviewed in the *Court and Society Review*, 3.100 (3 June 1886): 499.

64. George Moore, *Muslin* (1922), ix–xi.

65. George Moore, *Literature at Nurse, or Circulating Morals* (1885), 16–17.

66. To have an adult literature would be better for England, Moore declared, than the "the biggest franchise bill ever planned" (ibid., 22).

67. Richard Dellamora, *Masculine Desire: The Sexual Politics of Victorian Aestheticism* (University of North Carolina Press: Chapel Hill, 1990), 200–2.

68. GM denies the rumor of his authorship of "The Maiden Tribute" in an August letter to Frans Netscher; see Becker, 303.

69. *Bat*, 2.16 (14 July 1885): 219.

70. Ibid.: 215.

71. GM to Mon cher Maître [Emile Zola], 16 August [1885], 3 Dane's Inn, Becker, 305–6.

72. William Alexander Coote, *A Romance of Philanthropy* (National Vigilance Association: London, 1916), 4–8.

73. Ibid., 20–42.

74. Roy Jenkins, *Sir Charles Dilke: A Victorian Tragedy* (Collins: London, 1968), 111–238.

75. *Crawford (v.) Crawford, The Queen's Proctor Intervening: Evidence Taken on the Hearing with Notes* (F. W. J. Henning: London, [1890?]), 22–244.

76. W. T. Stead, *Has Sir Charles Dilke Cleared His Character? An Examination of the Report of the Alleged Commission* (*Review of Reviews* Office, Mowbray House: London, April 1890), 6.

77. GM to J.-E. Blanche, Sunday [4 October 1885], 3 Dane's Inn, Becker, 290–91; J.-E. Blanche, *Portraits of a Lifetime* (Dent: London 1937), 290–91. GM gave Blanche the good news that

the play he had adapted with Alexis
from the scenario of W. S. Gilbert's
Sweethearts – Le Sycomore – had been
accepted by Georges Porel for a
production at the Odéon in Paris. The
play was ultimately put off for production until 20 September 1894 (B. H.
Bakker, *"Naturalisme pas mort": Lettres
inédites de Paul Alexis à Emile Zola,
1871–1900* [University of Toronto
Press: Toronto, 1971], 292–94).

78. GM to My dear Mother [Mary Blake
Moore], 15 October 1885, 3 Dane's
Inn, Becker, 315–16.

79. GM to My dear Mother [Mary Blake
Moore], [14 May 1885], 3 Dane's Inn,
ibid., 295. By October 1886, Moore's
financial situation had improved somewhat; he had made, he wrote his
mother, £400 in the previous year,
"very little when you consider my
reputation," but easily sufficient for a
man of his mode of life (ibid., 385).
Although he stayed in the Hôtel Continental on his annual trips to Paris, in
London GM lived in a shabby apartment, wore common clothes, and often
dined in chophouses. He lived like a
bohemian in the Strand, not like an
absentee Irish landlord with a London
life of fashion.

80. George Moore, *A Mummer's Wife*,
(1886). The new (sixth) edition is
reviewed in the 17 November 1885
issue of the *Bat* (p. 495).

81. GM to Mon cher Maître [Zola],
Tuesday [10 November 1885], 3
Dane's Inn, Becker, 323.

82. Emile Zola, *The Rush for Spoil (La
Curée), A Realistic Novel* (Vizetelly:
London, 1886), vi–vii.

83. "M. Zola's New Book," *Bat*, 1.33 (10
November 1885): 482.

84. GM to Mon cher Maître [Zola],
Sunday [20 December 1885], 3 Dane's
Inn, Becker, 326–27.

85. Sister   Marie-Thérèse   Courtney,
Edward Martyn and the Irish Theatre
(Vantage: New York, 1952), 75.

86. For the revisions in the serial version,
see E. Jay Jernigan, "George Moore's
'Re-tying of Bows': A Critical Study
of the Eight Early Novels and Their

Revisions," Ph.D. diss. (Kansas State
University, 1966), 141–52.

87. GM to My dear Mother [20 October
1884], 3 Dane's Inn, Becker, 261.

88. The plot is not literally taken from the
nursery rhyme, but from the folktale,
"King Cophetua and the Beggar
Maid." In Chapter 1 of *A Drama in
Muslin*, the heroine Alice Barton
writes a little play on this motif for
Prize Day at her convent: all the main
female characters take parts which
strongly foreshadow their destinies
later in the novel. The device is simple
but effective. See Moore, *A Drama in
Muslin* (1893), 1–19.

89. Ibid., 95.

90. Ibid., 264.

91. Ibid., 323.

92. See for instance Grubgeld, *George
Moore and the Autogenous Self*, 14–15.

93. See *Tablet*, 23 January 1886: 137; *Bat*,
26 January 1886: 337–38; and *Court
and Society Review*, 4 February 1886
supplement, 6.

94. William Wallace, "New Novels: A
Drama in Muslin," *Academy*, 30 (17
July 1886): 40.

95. GM to My dear Mother [8 February
1886], 3 Dane's Inn, Becker, 344–45.
Anna Blake Murphy presumably
found details from the lives of her
daughters or herself in Moore's novel.
After Moore was rejected as a suitable
husband for Maud Browne, daughter
of Anna Blake Browne, his resentment
against the tribe of Blakes – already
sparked by Joe Blake's mismanage-
ment of the Moore Hall properties –
was stoked. There is an element of
revenge in the satirical realism of *A
Drama in Muslin*.

96. Moore, *A Drama in Muslin* (1893),
204.

97. Long before Synge's troubles with
Irish nationalists, GM was attacked for
inflammatory treatment of the sexuality of Irish women. An *Athenaeum*
reviewer of GM's *Terre d'Irlande*
(French version of *Parnell and His
Island*) sneered that GM could not be
a nationalist because of his "repeated
allusion to the existence among Irish

women of a state of low morality, the absence of which from their country is the proudest and most justified of all the boasts among the members of the Irish National Party" ("Our Library Table," *Athenaeum*, 3100 [26 March 1887]: 415).

See also John Kelly and Ronald Schuchard, eds, *Collected Letters of W. B. Yeats*, vol. 3, *1901–1904* (Clarendon Press: Oxford, 1994), 49 n.2.

98. At the Impressionists' banquet, Huysmans seconded Pissarro's low opinion of Zola's book. See Camille Pissarro to Lucien Pissarro [March 1886], Paris, John Rewald, ed, *Letters to His Son* (Kegan Paul: London, 1943), 72–74.

99. GM to Dear Sir [Frans Netscher], Thursday [April 1886], 3 Dane's Inn, Becker, 350–51.

100. "The Salon of 1886," *Bat*, 2.59 (11 May 1886): 145.

101. "Paris Salon," *Court and Society Review*, 3.96 (6 May 1886): 389.

102. "Decadence," *Speaker*, 6.140 (3 September 1892): 285–87; Rewald, *History of Impressionism*, 528.

103. "Half-a-Dozen Enthusiasts," *Bat*, 2.61 (25 May 1886): 185.

104. "The Impressionists," *Court and Society Review*, 3.100 (3 June 1886): 488.

105. William Bridger to Dear Sir (Joseph Hone), 3 January 1935, Knightons, Rustington Street; enclosure, copy of GM to William Bridger; Joseph M. Hone Accession, Box 1, Folder 12, Loc V253d, Washington.

106. Moore, *Memoirs of My Dead Life* (1906), 257–62.

107. [Michael Salaman?], "Boycotting on the Bookstalls: A Note on George Moore," *Court and Society Review*, 3.106 (15 July 1886): 632; [James Davis?], "A Realistic Novel," *Bat*, 2.67 (6 July 1886): 325–26.

108. GM to Dear Sir [Netscher], 16 July 1886, 3 Dane's Inn, Becker, 359; the phrase about his novel being "very much misunderstood" is repeated in GM's letter from Southwick to Julian Moore (ibid., 368).

109. GM to Dear Mr Archer, [late July 1886], c/o Mrs Feist, Southwick Green, near Brighton, ibid., 362–64. Moore was angry, however, that Archer questioned the book's morality: "I am as moral as the Bible, Shakespeare, or the newspapers . . . A work of art has nothing to do with morality or immorality, human sympathy or a want of human sympathy; it is neither realistic nor idealistic."

110. *Academy*, 30.741 (3 July 1886): 40; *Athenaeum*, 2996 (24 July 1886): 406; *Saturday Review*, 62 (24 July 1886): 131.

111. "Our Daily Dirt," *Bat*, 2.70 (27 July 1886): 386.

112. For late July–early August letters to Netscher, Duret, and Quilter, see Becker, 360, 366, 374.

113. GM to the editor, 12 August 1886, The Green, Southwick, *Times*: 10, Becker 372–74.

114. See the editorial in the *New York Times*, 13 August 1886: 4.5. "Mr Moore's books are probably stupid as well as indecent . . . though he is probably a poor sort of novelist, [Mr Moore] is an ingenious man. If any device can bring him readers it is the one he has adopted of asserting over his own signature that his books are so filthy that reputable dealers will not handle them."

115. Max O'Rell, *John Bull et son île* (Michel Levy Frères: Paris, 1883). Paul Alexis evidently met both O'Rell/Blouet and Moore on his October 1884 visit to London; he reviewed a book by O'Rell upon his return to Paris, in *Le Matin*. O'Rell had earlier been a master at St Paul's School ("Literary Gossip," *Athenaeum*, 3006 [6 June 1885]: 728). See A. J. Solomon, " '*Parnell and His Island*': A Source for the Title," *Notes and Queries*, 20 (July 1973): 233–34.

116. GM to Monsieur [Charpentier], The Green, Southwick, Becker, 370.

117. Zola to Mon cher ami [GM], 15 August 1886, Médan, Zola, *Correspondance*, vol. 5, 416–17; GM to My dear Duret [August 1886], The Green, Southwick, Becker, 376.

118. GM to Netscher [26 July 1886 and 10 August 1886], The Green, Southwick, Becker, 366–67, 370–71.

119. Moore, *A Drama in Muslin* (1893), 196–97.

120. George Moore, *Parnell and His Island*, 1–3.

121. Ibid., 86–87.

122. People have suspected that Moore's book on Ireland was influenced by Huysmans's *En rade* or Zola's *La Terre* in its treatment of peasants as being animals like the cows and pigs they tend. If there is an influence, chronology requires that it should go in the other direction. For the most aggressive account of Moore's indebtedness to Huysmans, see G. A. Cevasco's "Something Exquisite and Spiritous: J.-K. Huysmans and George Moore," *Research Studies*, 45.3 (September 1977): 147–59. In both *Parnell* (p. 170) and Huysmans's *En Rade*, there is a great snowy owl in a castle, profoundly feared by a fantasising nostalgic city man – an extraordinary coincidence. *En rade* began its serialisation in *Revue indépendante* in November 1886; "Lettres sur l'Irlande" concluded in *Figaro* on 4 September 1886.

123. Susan Mitchell, *George Moore* (Maunsel: Dublin and London, 1916), 68–69.

124. GM to Dear Sir [Netscher], 31 August 1886, The Green, Southwick, Becker, 380–81. For GM's involvement in writing *Dr. Phillips*, see his 14 September [1887] letter to William Archer: Becker, 444.

125. Mrs [Eliza] Aria, *My Sentimental Self* (Chapman and Hall: London, 1922), *passim*.

126. Frank Danby [Julia Davis Frankau], *A Babe in Bohemia* (Spencer Blackett: London, 1889), 34.

127. Ibid., 69.

128. Ibid., 283.

129. Gilbert Frankau, *Self-Portrait: A Novel of his Own Life* (Hutchinson: London, 1940), 100. Gilbert was Julia's son, and, meeting Moore for the first time, he was told by GM, "If your mother had become my mistress when I asked her to, she would write better English." Then he suggested Gilbert's Aunt Eliza had enjoyed that benefit.

130. For her objectivity, Julia Davis Frankau was assaulted in reviews for having no moral sense whatsoever; see "A Maida Vale Idyll," *Court and Society Review*, 4.143 (5 January 1887): 304–5.

131. Frank Danby [Julia Davis Frankau], *Dr. Phillips: A Maida Vale Idyll* (Vizetelly: London, 1887). On 14 September [1887], GM asked William Archer if he had read *Dr. Phillips*; if so, "I suppose you recognised my hand in it" (Becker, 444); in a subsequent letter to Archer, Moore explained, "I wrote none of *Dr. Phillips* – I invented the story and it was written under my direction, that was all" (ibid., 458).

132. "Jewish Society," *Bat*, 3.104 (22 March 1887): 251.

133. Quoted in Frankau, *Self-Portrait*, 23.

134. GM to My dear Mother [October 1886], The Green, Southwick, Becker, 385–86.

135. GM to My dear Duret, October 1886, The Green, Southwick, ibid., 387–88.

136. George Moore, *Spring Days* (1888), 38–43.

137. Ibid., 118.

138. Ibid., 189.

139. GM to My dear Blanche, 7 October 1886, The Green, Southwick, Becker, 384. See also Gordon Millan, *Mallarmé: A Throw of the Dice* (Secker and Warburg: London, 1994), 258.

140. Bakker, *"Naturalisme pas mort"*, 323.

141. GM to Mon cher Maitre, 3 Dane's Inn, Becker, 390–91.

142. *Letters from George Moore to Ed. Dujardin, 1886–1922*, trans. John Eglinton (Crosby Gaige: New York, 1929), 19.

143. GM to Dear Sir [December 1886], 3 Dane's Inn, Becker, 390–91. "Le Sinistre de Tonbridge" was published in *La Revue indépendante* in March 1887; an English version entitled "Two Men: A Railway Story" was published on 20 April 1887 in *Court and Society Review*.

144. GM to My dear Julian [Moore], 3 January 1887, 3 Dane's Inn, Becker, 395.

Chapter 6 Devouring the Father

1. Edouard Dujardin, *Les Hantises* (Léon Vanier: Paris, 1886); Kathleen McKilligan, *Edouard Dujardin: Les Lauriers Sont Coupés and the Interior Monologue*, Occasional Papers in Modern Languages, No. 13 (University of Hull: Hull, 1977), 29–30.

2. GM to Duret [January/February 1887]; GM to My dear Duret, 3 Dane's Inn, Becker, 399–400; GM to Dujardin [inscribed February 1887], 3 Dane's Inn, ibid., 401.

   The Schopenhauer translations are by R. B. Haldane and J. Kemp, *The World as Will and Idea*, 3 vols (Trübner: London 1883–86), J. Bourdeau, *Pensées, maximes, et fragments* (Paris, 1880), and J. A. Cantacuzene, *Aphorismes sur la sagesse dans la vie* (Paris, 1880). For further detailed discussion of Moore's echoes of Schopenhauer's writings, see Patrick Bridgewater, *George Moore and German Pessimism* (University of Durham Press: Durham, 1988).

3. Arthur Schopenhauer, *Essays and Aphorisms*, trans. R. J. Hollingdale (Penguin: London, 1970), 85.

4. Graham Hough asserted, with ridiculous condescension, that Moore was "incapable of what in any ordinary acceptation of the term would be called thought" ("George Moore and the Nineties," in Richard Ellmann, ed., *Edwardians and Late Victorians* [Columbia University Press: New York, 1960], 10). Patrick Bridgewater treats GM's use of Schopenhauer as simply a "fad," "largely a matter of decoration," "period features . . . shock effects . . . talismanic utterances . . . ballast" (Bridgewater, *George Moore and German Pessimism*, 28, 53, 54). On the other hand, Elizabeth Grubgeld takes seriously GM's personal development of his concept of "instinct" from Schopenhauer's notion of "will" (*George Moore and the Autogenous Self* [Syracuse University Press: Syracuse, 1994], *passim*).

5. In August 1887, GM quoted Schopenhauer in making an objection to the representation of incest in the action of Zola's play *Renée*: "As Shopenhauer [*sic*] says – it is the idea of the thing we want, not the thing itself . . . our actions are greater than those of animals because we think" (GM to Duret, Southwick, Becker, 437–38). See Schopenhauer, *Essays and Aphorisms*, 156, 159.

6. "Pessimism à la Mode," *Bat*, 3.94 (11 January 1888): 30.

7. George Moore, *Confessions of a Young Man* (1972), 149.

8. The Schopenhauerian phrase in the *Bat* article echoes one in *A Mere Accident*: "Why precipitate another into the gulf of being?" (George Moore, *A Mere Accident*, 31).

9. Wyzewa obligingly repeated Moore's view of *A Mere Accident* in his review of the novel, "Les Livres," *Revue indépendante*, 4 (September 1887): 274–75.

10. Moore, *A Mere Accident*, 65.

11. Ibid., 66.

12. Ibid., 103.

13. Ibid., 111.

14. Ibid., 147.

15. Linda Dowling, *Hellenism and Homosexuality in Victorian Oxford* (Ithaca, NY, and London: Cornell University Press, 1994), 154.

16. Moore, *A Mere Accident*, 172.

17. Ibid., 282.

18. Ibid., 103.

19. GM to G. B. Shaw [31 December 1887], BL; Becker, 481–82.

20. GM to Edouard Dujardin, 17 May 1887; *Letters to Dujardin*, 20.

21. George Moore, *Avowals* (1924), 196.

22. Emile Zola, *Correspondance*, ed. B. H. Bakker (Presses de Université de Montréal, Editions du Centre National de la Recherche Scientifique: Montreal and Paris, 1978, 1995), vol. 6, 79–80.

23. Ernest Vizetelly, *Emile Zola: Novelist and Reformer* (John Lane: London and New York, 1904), n.p.

24. GM to Dujardin [9 February 1887], Becker, 397.

25. George Moore, *Conversations in Ebury Street* (1930), 179.
26. Jean Ajalbert, *Mémoires en vrac* (Paris, 1938), 163–69; quoted in McKilligan, *Edouard Dujardin*, 5.
27. Elga Liverman Duval, *Teodor de Wyzewa: Critic without a Country* (Librairie Droz: Geneva; Librairie Minard: Paris, 1961), 57–60. Dujardin appears wearing a monocle in Toulouse-Lautrec's color lithograph, *Divan japonais* (1892–93), along with Jane Avril and the torso of the singer Yvette Guilbert (*Paris in the Late Nineteenth Century* [Musée d'Orsay: Paris, 1997], 25, 27).
28. "A Great Poet," *Hawk*, 5.108 (25 February 1890): 223–24.
29. "Francillon," *Hour Glass*, March 1887; reprinted in *Hawk*, 7 August 1888.
30. "Paris Day by Day," *Daily Telegraph*, 14 February 1887; GM to My dear Sir [Paris Correspondent of the *Daily Telegraph*], 3 Dane's Inn, Becker, 402.
31. Morton Norton Cohen, *Rider Haggard: His Life and Works* (Walker: New York, 1960), 124–25.
32. GM to the editor, *Court and Society Review*, 30 March 1887: 305; Becker, 404–7.
33. "Rider Haggard and the 'New School of Romance,'" *Time*, 16 (May 1887): 513–24.
34. Moore, *Confessions of a Young Man*, 138, 160, 172.
35. Darcy Butterworth Kitchen, *Days of My Youth* (Herbert Joseph: London, 1936), 164–69; Walter Sichel, *The Sands of Time: Recollections and Reflections* (Hutchinson: London, 1923), *passim*.
36. Becker provides the text of both Wigram's letters and those of GM on *Parnell*, pp. 411–12.
37. GM to Dear Sir [Swan Sonnenschein, Lowrey, & Co.], The Green, Southwick, Becker, 414. Becker prints additional correspondence from the firm as notes.
38. McKilligan, *Edouard Dujardin: Les Lauriers Sont Coupés*, 40ff.
39. GM to Dujardin, The Green, Southwick, *Letters to Dujardin* 20.
40. GM to Dujardin [inscribed 11 June 1887], The Green, Southwick, Becker, 420.
41. GM to Swinburne, 5 July 1887, The Green, Southwick, ibid., 423.
42. "Mr. George Moore's New Novel," *Pall Mall Gazette*, 19 July 1887: 3; "A Mere Accident," *Athenaeum*, 3118 (30 July 1887): 144; Moore, *Avowals* (1924).
43. Moore, *Avowals* (1924), 197.
44. Lawrence Evans, ed., *The Letters of Walter Pater* (Clarendon Press: Oxford, 1970), 81.
45. Ibid., 75.
46. Moore, *Confessions of a Young Man* (1972), 49.
47. George Moore, *Confessions d'un jeune anglais* (Savine: Paris, 1889), 251–52; Moore, *Confessions of a Young Man* (1972), 255 n. 10. My translation.
48. Thais Morgan (in a borrowing from Eve Sedgwick), "Reimagining Masculinity in Victorian Criticism: Swinburne and Pater," *Victorian Studies*, 36 (1993): 316.
49. Walter Pater, *Studies in the History of the Renaissance*, ed. Donald Hill (1980) 217.
50. Jean C. Noel, George Moore's "Pluridimensional Autobiography," *Cahiers du Centre d'Etudes Irlandaises*, 4 (1979): 49–65.
51. Moore, *Confessions of a Young Man* (1972), 176.
52. "Thoughts in a Strand Lodging," ibid., 167ff.; Noel, "Pluridimensional Autobiography," 55.
53. Brian Reade, *Sexual Heretics: Male Homosexuality in English Literature from 1850 to 1900* (Routledge and Kegan Paul: London, 1970), 199.
54. Moore, *Avowals*, 266; *Vale* (1937), 103–4.
55. GM to Blanche [inscribed Summer 1887], The Green, Southwick, Becker, 432–33.
56. GM to Zola, 23 August [1887], The Green, Southwick, ibid., 439.
57. "Manifeste des Cinq," *Le Figaro*, 18 August 1887, quoted in Frederick Brown, *Zola: A Life* (Farrar Strauss Giroux: New York, 1995), 575–77.

58. Moore, *Confessions of a Young Man* (1972), 110, 115.
59. Moore took even greater pains over the printing of the *Time* serial than over his other books, aware, as he wrote the editor Wigram, that "This book may meet with very searching criticism" ([2 September 1887]). He was especially irritated when the printer ran together the paragraphs of "Synthesis of the Nouvelle Athènes," as if they were all part of one argument, aspects of a single point-of-view (6 September [1887], Becker, 441–43).
60. GM to Wigram [September 1887], The Green, Southwick, ibid., 443–44.
61. GM to Wigram [early October? 1887], ibid., 445–46.
62. Moore, *Confessions of a Young Man* (1972), 179.
63. GM to Wigram [early October? 1887], Tuesday, The Green, Southwick, Becker, 446–47. Moore "toned down" his reflections on religion in the November number of *Time*, cutting out every "abusive epithet," but he insisted on retaining the statement that the message of Christ had been consummated in Socialism, a religion that can therefore do without the person of Christ. (See letters to Wigram in Becker, 447–52; these letters are misdated; the sequence must precede GM's 19 October move to Freshcombe Lodge.) For the date of GM's move, see GM to My dear Sir [J. W. Gleeson White], 19 October [1887], Freshcombe Lodge, Beeding, Sussex, Houghton.
64. Colville's plan for planting furze may have given GM the idea for the scenario of *The Heather Field*, dramatised under GM's direction by Edward Martyn, and performed by the Irish Literary Theatre in May 1899.
65. George Moore, *Ave* (1937), 238–39.
66. GM to My dear Archer, Sunday night, Freshcombe Lodge, Becker, 458–59.
67. It has been said that George Moore was in the party of guests for the housewarming in the rue de la Chaussée d'Antin offices of the *Revue indépendante*, held 26 November 1877

(Mondor, *Vie de Mallarmé*, [Gallimard: Paris, 1950], 520; Robert Baldick, *The Life of J.-K. Huysmans*, Clarendon Press: Oxford, 1955, 114). Mention of a trip to Paris at this time has not been traced.
68. GM to My dear Mother, 22 December [1887], Freshcombe Lodge, Becker, 477.
69. See Gilcher, 63, and *passim* for the publication history of "The Wedding Gown."
70. GM to Blanche, 2 December [1887], Freshcombe Lodge; letter printed in J.-E. Blanche's *Portraits of a Lifetime* (Dent: London; Coward McCann: New York, 1937), 292–93. For Blanche's "Jeune Fille Symbolique" see his *Mes Modèles* (Stock: Paris, 1928), 215.
71. Casanova's memoirs were translated by Jean Laforgue in Paris in 1880.
72. Blanche, *Portraits of a Lifetime*, 293; italics added. Moore also mentions to Blanche the Society of British Artists' exhibition in Suffolk Street. In addition to four new canvases by Monet, GM also saw pictures by Philip Wilson Steer, Walter Sickert, Sidney Starr, and William Stott. From this exhibition one can date Moore's knowledge of, and advocacy for, the group of "British Impressionists" who later formed the heart of the New English Art Club (formed after Whistler was ejected as President of the Society of British Artists). See Kenneth McConkey, *Impressionism in Britain* (Yale University Press, in association with the Barbican Gallery: London, 1995), 42; Kenneth McConkey, *British Impressionism* (Phaidon: Oxford, 1989), 60–61.
73. GM to My dear Mother, 22 December [1887], Freshcombe Lodge, NLI Ms 447–9; Becker, 477–78.
74. Friedrich Nietzsche, *On the Genealogy of Morals*, trans. Walter Kaufmann and R. J. Hollingdale (Vintage Books: New York, 1968), 220.
75. George Moore, "Turgueneff," *Fortnightly Review*, 2680.254 (February 1888): 237–51.

76. The phrase is Pater's, concerning Montaigne, from *Gaston de Latour* (ELT Press: Greensboro, 1995), 114.

77. Brian Greenwood, "George Moore's Fictive Autobiography" (University of Minnesota diss., August 1974), 153.

78. For two accounts of the history of the "gentleman" in nineteenth-century England, see Robin Gilmour, *The Idea of the Gentleman in the Victorian Novel* (George Allen: London, 1981), and Richard Dellamora, *Masculine Desire: The Sexual Politics of Victorian Aestheticism* (University of North Carolina Press: Chapel Hill and London, 1990), esp. 197–98.

79. "Our Library Table: *Confessions of a Young Man*," *Athenaeum*, 3153 (31 March 1888): 402.

80. "*Confessions of a Young Man*, by George Moore," *Academy*, 33.828 (17 March 188): 184–85.

81. Davis's comment in the box was that in his short life he had been granted every experience but death and solvency (Guy Deghy, *Paradise in the Strand* [Richards Press: London, 1958], 178).

82. *Bat*, 3.103 (15 March 1887): 222.

83. "In Pentonville Prison," *Bat*, 3.121 (19 July 1887): 54–56.

84. "Nothing in the Papers," *Bat*, 3.126 (23 August 1887): 156.

85. *Hawk*, 1.2 (14 February 1888): 19.

86. James M. Glover, *Jimmy Glover: His Book* (Methuen: London, 1911), 90.

87. The *Confessions* was possibly at one time contracted by Davis for weekly publication in the *Bat* as a book of "thirty or forty thousand words." When it outgrew this limit, GM was released from his contract and took the growing manuscript to *Time*. (See the preface to the 1889 edition, reprinted in *Confessions of a Young Man* [1972], 35–36.) After *Confessions* was published, the *Hawk* immediately began to develop motifs from *Confessions*, as in the column "Wrinkles," "Being a series of Letters addressed by Sir Affable Hawk to his nephew Tommy Hawk, on commencing Life in London, and showing him Whom To Know, Whom to Avoid, How to Behave Himself, Where To Go, What to Do, and How To Get The Best Value For His Money" (*Hawk*, 1.10 [10 April 1888]: 163). These letters, originally written by Augustus Moore, later by Alec Knowles, address the "young man of the nineteenth century" with the cynical wisdom of *Confessions*, but without GM's literary complexity.

88. William Swan Sonnenschein to GM, 8 February 1888, Becker, 485. GM to Dujardin [12 February 1888], Sunday; Freshcombe Lodge, Becker, 484. GM to My dear Robertson [13 March 1888], Tuesday, ibid., 493.

89. *Letters to Dujardin*, 24–25.

90. Grubgeld, *George Moore and the Autogenous Self*, 52–63, and *passim*. Moore continues to deploy substitutes for himself, including the character Harding, in *Spring Days*, *Mike Fletcher*, and *Vain Fortune*. Indeed, there is periodic backsliding from this moment of recognition for another twenty years.

91. GM to Zola, 17 March 188[8], Freshcombe Lodge, Becker, 496.

92. George Moore, *A Communication to My Friends*, 66–71.

93. The *Bat* complained about the *Pall Mall Gazette* attacks on *La Terre*, coming before "a single copy of the work in question has been issued," and arguing that the novel "contains some of the most pointed and trenchant criticisms on the evils of small holdings ever penned." See "Nothing in the Papers," *Bat*, 5.145 (3 January 1888): 4.

94. Vizetelly, *Emile Zola*, 256–58.

95. "The Salon of '88," *Hawk*, 1.14 (8 May 1888): 257–58.

96. Moore, *Conversations in Ebury Street* (1930), 165–66.

97. Moore, *Avowals*, 48.

98. Moore, *Ave*, 44–46.

99. George Moore, *Memoirs of My Dead Life* (1928), 54–56.

100. Moore, *Confessions of a Young Man* (1972), 113.

101. Edmond et Jules de Goncourt,

Journal: *Mémoires de la vie littéraire,
1879–1890*, vol. 3 (Fasquelle, Flammarion: Paris, 1956), 783. My free
paraphrase.

102. Alexis to Zola, 10 May 1888, B. H.
Bakker, *"Naturalisme pas mort"; Lettres
inédites de Panl Alexis à Emile Zola,
1871–1900* (University of Toronto
Press: Toronto, 1971), 355–56.

103. Moore, *A Communication to My
Friends*, 53–54.

104. Ibid., 54.

105. Moore, *Confessions of a Young Man*
(1972), 39.

106. Charpentier demanded a "yes or no"
from Zola about the Preface on 24
May; on 25 May, Zola wrote that it had
to be "No," though he realised Charpentier would not have accepted the
novel without Zola's promised preface
(Zola, *Correspondance*, vol. 6, 286–87).

107. Moore, *A Communication to My
Friends*, 56.

108. Unsigned paragraph in "On Dits,"
Hawk, 1.15 (15 May 1888): 270.

109. Carl Paul Barbier, ed., *Correspondance
Mallarmé-Whistler: Histoire de la
grande amitié de leurs dernières années*
(A. G. Nizet: Paris, 1964), 298–300.

110. "On Dits," *Hawk*, 2.23 (10 July 1888):
24.

111. "Two French Plays," *Hawk*, 1.18 (5
June 1888): 345–46.

112. Kitchen, *Days of My Youth*, 175.
Quilter was a favorite butt of
Whistler's jokes. Quilter's article on
the May 1888 Salon in the *Universal
Review* is a fair example of his
pompous blind appreciations: Impressionism has "nothing of that quiet
inner voice with which great art
appeals to us" (vol. 1, 328).

113. GM to Dear Quilter, 10 June 1888,
Freshcombe Lodge, Becker, 517; GM
to Dear Quilter [24 June 1888], ibid.,
521.

114. GM to Dujardin, 17 July 1888, Freshcombe Lodge, ibid., 528. GM sent the
pages on 11 August 1888 (*Letters to
Dujardin*, 29–30).

115. Moore *Confessions of a Young Man*
(1972), 218.

116. GM to Blanche [July 1888], Becker, 529.

117. GM to Blanche [9 August 1888],
Thursday, Freshcombe Lodge,
Blanche, *Portraits of a Lifetime*,
295–96; Becker, 531–32.

118. Vizetelly, *Emile Zola*, 268.

119. Daniel Halévy, *J.-E. Blanche–Walter
Sickert à Dieppe 1885–1888* (Exhibi-
tion catalogue, Musée de Dieppe: 16
juillet–20 septembre 1954), 110–11;
Wendy Baron, *Sickert* (Phaidon:
London, 1973), 16.

120. GM to My dear Blanche [19 August
1888], Monday, Freschcombe Lodge,
Box 1 Moore Collection, Beinecke;
Berg; Becker, 533–34.

121. Swan Sonnenschein to GM, 22
August 1888, Becker, 548. It is possible this letter is misdated; Vizetelly
was in prison in August 1889. Whether
he was also being held prior to his trial
is doubtful.

122. According to Vizetelly's son, GM was
one of the only people to stand by the
sixty-eight-year-old publisher in any
way at all.

123. Moore may have advocated a truly literary censorship in order to make
people realise the unliterary and dema-
gogic character of the *de facto* censorship: "I said in my letter that I would
prefer a censorship, but that was
written for the sake of controversy. I
write a great deal that I do not believe
to be true, paradox and ideas that I
sympathize with. . . ."; GM to W. T.
Stead [September 1888], Freshcombe
Lodge, Becker, 538–39.

124. Grant Richards, *Memories of a Mis-
spent Youth 1872–1896* (New York:
Harper and Brothers, 1933), 265. After
the meeting, Richards was told "that
George Moore spoiled his chances of
becoming one of Stead's favorites by
refusing to subscribe to Stead's ideal of
sexual morality."

125. Stead made one small concession,
promising to call off the attack on
Madame Bovary, but it is unclear
whether or not this promise was fulfilled. At the end of his life, GM
recalled that the "hatred" of the Vigilance Society was "stayed," when
"W. T. Stead, an honest heart within

him, declared that if it was their intention to prosecute the Heptameron of the Queen of Navarre written in the 16th century, and Flaubert's *Madame Bovary*, he would be forced to resign from the Council of the Society" (*A Communication to My Friends*, 77).

126. For accounts of the Vizetelly trials, see Vizetelly, *Emile Zola*, 285–91; *Pernicious Literature: Debate in the House of Commons: Trial and Conviction for the Sale of Zola's Novels, With Opinions of the Press* (National Vigilance Association, n.d.).

127. *Times*, 1 November 1888: 3.

Chapter 7 Don Juan Jr. in the Age of the National Vigilance Association

1. "Novels of the Week: *Spring Days*," *Athenaeum* (8 September 1888): 317; [G. Barnett Smith], "New Novels: *Spring Days; A Realistic Novel*," *Academy*, 34 (22 September 1888): 184; "*Spring Days* Again," *Daily Chronicle*, 29 June 1912.

2. George Moore, *Spring Days*, viii. Frank Harris became editor of *Fortnightly* in July 1886.

3. See Robert Holliday, "Complete Moore: An Early Novel that Suggests *Pride and Prejudice*," *New York Times Book Review*, 22 December 1912: 788.

4. Ernest Baker, *History of the English Novel*, vol. 9 (Witherby: London, 1938), 171. For another excellent assessment, see E. Jay Jernigan, "George Moore's 'Re-tying of the Bows': A Critical Study of the Eight Early Novels and Their Revisions," Ph.D. diss. (Kansas State University, 1966), 215–19.

5. Moore, *Spring Days*, 242.

6. For John Harding, GM's more admirable and consistent stand-in, the author saved his worldliness, perceptiveness, and ambition; however, in this novel, Harding's observations are sometimes wide of the mark (*Spring*

Days, 150). When Harding analyses the weakness of Frank Escott, we have Moore creating a Moore to dismantle Moore.

7. *Spring Days, A Realistic Novel* (1888), 129.

8. Ibid., 134.

9. Ibid., 163.

10. GM to——; 28 October [inscribed 1888], Freshcombe Lodge, Becker, 555.

The subplot of Frank's relationship to Lizzie Baker is just one of several engaging motifs in the book. The depictions of county society, of the Strand, of boating on the Thames, are all lively unsentimentalised records of a passing phase not just of Moore's life, but of the life of English society. However, the novel's philosophical detachment – spring days pass, and with no result but another spring to pass away – enforces a plot with no crescendo, no emotional development at all. It is not the worst novel written in twenty-five years, but it is not one of Moore's better books.

11. *Letters to Dujardin*, 30–31.

12. "Mummer Worship," *Universal Review*, 2 (September–December 1888): 105–18.

Regarding the embourgeoisement of the stage simply as a social means to transform the stage into a proper place of employment for middle-class daughters, GM tells the story of three girls from Bayswater who seek careers before the footlights: the first, in order to escape the pressure of other men, takes an older actor as protector and lover; the second marries an actor, then is divorced; the third runs off with a banker who promises to marry her and doesn't. The moral: virtue is not impossible for the actress but it is very difficult. The real problem, he concluded, was not the moral character of the stage, but popular hypocrisy about it. Vice is not something that can be eradicated; in fact, Moore argued, quoting W. E. Lecky, vice is as necessary as virtue; the virtue of wives and daughters depends upon the prostitute.

"Our morality consists in striving to keep them apart."

13. Unidentified article from the file of Edwin Gilcher; the *Standard* (19 September 1888). Publicly, Irving referred to Moore as a "flippant lampooner" in speeches in Edinburgh and in Bolton, the latter fully reported in the *Times*. See Lawrence Irving, *Sir Henry Irving: The Actor and His World* (Macmillan: New York, 1952), 496–97.

14. Becker, 571–73.

15. "The Prurient Prude," *Hawk*, 3.52 (29 January 1889): 110–11.

16. Clara Lanza, "My Friendship with George Moore, Three Thousand Miles Away," *Bookman*, July 1918: 480–86.

17. Swan Sonnenschein to GM, 22 August 1888, Becker, 564 n.4.

18. GM to Clara Lanza, 12 November 1888, Freshcombe Lodge, Becker, 556–58.

19. *Athenaeum*, 12 January 1889: 52–53.

20. To Blanche, Moore explained, "I know how to conduct a polemic and I have drawn attention to the book . . . there is little doubt that I shall take a higher position in public estimation than I have yet done": GM to Blanche, 16 January [1889], 2 Pump Court, Jacques-Emile Blanche, *Portraits of a Lifetime*, trans. Walter Clement (Dent: London, 1937), 296–97; Becker, 571.

21. GM to Dear Madame [Clara Lanza], 17 July 1888, Freshcombe Lodge, Becker, 523–25. Joseph Hone's copies of GM's letters to Lanza are at the University of Washington Library.

22. GM to Clara Lanza, Freshcombe Lodge, Columbia, Becker, 535–56.

23. GM to Clara Lanza, 12 November 1888, Freshcombe Lodge, Becker, 556–58.

24. Clara Lanza, "A Rising Novelist: George Moore, the Author of Several Popular Novels and His Works," *New York Herald*, 29 April 1889: 27; George Moore, "Literature and Art" [article on "the school of Edgar Saltus": Amelie Rives, Clara Lanza, and Gertrude Atherton], *Hawk*, 5.101 (7 January 1890): 14; Clara Lanza, "An Original Temptation," *Hawk*, 5.113 (1 April 1890): 379–80; "One Volume Fiction," review of Lanza's *A Modern Marriage*, *Speaker*, 3.66 (4 April 1891): 413.

25. GM to Clara Lanza, 3 May [1889], 8 King's Bench Walk, HRHRC; Becker, 590–91.

26. GM to *Chère bon maître* [Clara Lanza], Becker, 622.

27. GM to Clara Lanza, 12 November [1889], 8 King's Bench Walk, Washington, Becker, 628–29.

28. Moore was quite conscious of this desire for distance in his relationship. He noted with surprise Lanza's remark that she was "methodical": "I am just the reverse. The time I waste is endless. We get on wonderfully well in this fictitious life of notepaper. I wonder how we should like each other" in real life (GM to Clara Lanza, Saturday [inscribed 25 January 1890], 8 King's Bench Walk, Berg; Becker, 640–42). At other times, he tried to assure himself, and her, that she would like him if they met; after all, he was neither "a vulgar Cockney" nor "a cad" (as if those conditions would suffice to make him attractive to her!) (GM to Clara Lanza, 18 February 1890, 8 King's Bench Walk, HRHRC; Becker, 648–52).

29. GM to Clara Lanza, [25 January 1890] and 18 February 1890, 8 King's Bench Walk, Berg; Becker, 640–42. For recent accounts of the "Cleveland Street Scandal," see Richard Dellamora, *Masculine Desire: The Sexual Politics of Victorian Aestheticism* (University of North Carolina Press: Chapel Hill and London, 1990), 11; and Colin Simpson, *The Cleveland Street Affair* (Weidenfeld and Nicolson: London, 1976).

30. GM to Clara Lanza, 8 December 1906, *The Life of George Moore*, 273; Lanza, "My Friendship with George Moore," 485.

31. Walter Sichel, *The Sands of Time: Recollections and Reflections* (Hutchinson: London, 1923), 233.

32. *Pernicious Literature: Debate in the*

House of Commons: Trial and Conviction for the Sale of Zola's Novels, With Opinions of the Press (National Vigilance Association), 19; for Sonnenschein's letter, see Becker, 560 n.2.

33. George Moore, "M. Zola 'On the Side of the Angels,'" *St. James's Gazette*, 17:2625 (2 November 1888): 3. This review of *Le Rêve* also goes a long way in making up for his insult to Zola of the previous May in Paris, by offering an appreciation of his style at a time when no one else in England would see that Zola was an artist.

34. *Times*, 1 November 1888: 9.

35. Lang replied in the 7 November *St. James's Gazette* by offhandedly sneering at Zola and correcting GM's definition of Romance to the celebration of "what life has *got* for the giving" (p. 3).

36. "On Dits," *Hawk*, 2.46 (18 December 1888): 533. Though the majority favored censorship of all GM's works, a minority found a rule saying that if fifty members requested a book, it should be part of the library. Thus the motion was passed, but not implemented.

37. GM to Blanche [inscribed January 1889], 2 Pump Court, Temple, Blanche, *Portraits of a Lifetime*, 297; Becker, 568.

38. Information about the Temple is taken from Ben Weinreb and Christopher Hibbert, eds, *The London Encyclopaedia* (Macmillan: London, 1983, 1993).

39. George Moore, *Mike Fletcher: A Novel*, 70, 71. For Norton/Martyn's admiration of the Knights Templar ("men who foreswear women"), see p. 74.

40. George Moore, *Memoirs of My Dead Life* (1906), 263–68.

41. GM to Mon cher ami (Dujardin), 2 Pump Court, Beinecke, *Letters to Dujardin*, 23; Becker, 577; Robert Buchanan, "The Modern Young Man as Critic," *Universal Review*, 3 (January–April 1889): 353–72.

42. *Confessions of a Young Man* (1972), 160.

43. The libel action was withdrawn at the last moment, after the jury had been seated; Buchanan paid his own costs ("Bye-Bye, Buchanan," *Hawk*, 4: 94 [19 November 1889]: 550). Moore's attempted reply was rejected by E. T. Cook of the *Pall Mall Gazette* as "dangerous" (GM to Archer [6 June 1889], 8 King's Bench Walk, BL; Becker, 597).

44. Andrew Lang, "Mr. Buchanan's Young Man," *St. James's Gazette*, 18.2760 (10 April 1889): 3.

45. [George Moore], "Is Buchanan Still Possible?," *Truth*, 25: 640 (4 April 1889): 24–26.

46. The "occasional acting-manager and a music conductor" were probably sarcastic allusions to Augustus Moore and Jimmy Glover, sometime admirers of Buchanan's poetry. GM never liked Glover, and he was falling foul of his brother Augustus.

Moore thought that the article had been edited of its sharpest points, and read "a half a note flat" (GM to Archer [6 June 1889], 8 King's Bench Walk, BL, Becker, 597). One wonders what Labouchère was afraid to print. Buchanan fought back with "Imperial Cockneydom" in the *Universal Review*, and Moore kept the game alive with "No! Buchanan is not Still Possible!" in the 6 June issue of *Truth*. In "Our Dramatists" Buchanan was honored as "the most distinguished man of letters the stage can boast of," but still a "minor poet and a tenth-rate novelist" (*Fortnightly Review*, 46.275 [November 1889]: 621). The final kiss-off was Moore's "Bye-Bye Buchanan" in the *Hawk* (19 November 1889), where Buchanan becomes an Aunt Sally, whom one knocks down for fun, only to see pop up again.

47. Gertrude Atherton, *Adventures of a Novelist* (Liveright: New York, 1932), 160.

48. GM to Clara Lanza [June? 1889], *Life of George Moore*, 159. Emily Wortis Leider, *California's Daughter: Gertrude Atherton and Her Times* (Stanford University Press: Stanford, 1991), 101.

49. Leider, *California's Daughter*, 122.

50. Vincent O'Sullivan, *Opinions* (Unicorn Press: London, 1959), 92–94.

51. Lanza sent him news of a rumored affair between Atherton and William Sharp (Fiona Macleod); this surprised and interested GM, who, after his own disappointed approaches, had been assured by American Heron Allen "who knows all about the intimate feeling of women" that "Mrs. Atherton is a very cold woman" (GM to Dear Clara Lanza, 12 October 1889, 8 King's Bench Walk, Washington, Becker, 620).

52. GM to Blanche [inscribed January 1889], 2 Pump Court, Blanche, *Portraits of a Lifetime*, 297–98; Becker, 568–70.

53. Blanche told Hone that Moore was a frequent visitor to Madame Howland's; Degas was also a regular in the late 1880s. See Roy McMullen, *Degas: His Life, Times and Work* (Secker and Warburg: London, 1985), 385.

54. George Moore, "From the Naked Model," *Hawk*, 4.99 (24 December 1889): 699–701.

55. Daniel Halévy, *My Friend Degas*, trans. Mina Curtiss (Wesleyan University Press: Middletown, CT, 1964), 35, 41, 52; McMullen, *Degas*, 400.

56. GM to Blanche, Monday night, Blanche, *Portraits of a Lifetime*, 298; Becker, 659–60.

57. Alexis to Zola, 17 May [18]89, B. H. Bakker, *"Naturalisme pas mort"; Lettres inédites de Paul Alexis à Emile Zola, 1871–1900* (University of Toronto Press: Toronto, 1971), 378–81: "Moore de passage pour huit jours, est venu me voir."

58. Antoine, *Lettres à Pauline*, 297 quoted in Bakker, *"Naturalisme pas mort,"* 372–73.

59. Moore, *Memoirs of My Dead Life* (1906), 42–45. See also the first version of "La Butte," in "Notes and Sensations," *Hawk*, 6.137 (16 September 1890): 323–24.

60. Bakker, *"Naturalisme pas mort"*, 379.

61. Moore, *Memoirs of My Dead Life* (1906), 47. Moore's free use of Alexis's memoir still amounts to plagiarism for Margaret A. Seibert in "George Moore et Paul Alexis: un cas de plagiat," *Les Cahiers-naturalistes*, 62 (1988): 127–40. Since Seibert's arguments rely on somewhat inaccurate scholarship about GM's presence and acquaintance in Paris during the 1870s, the case is not closed on whether Moore ever himself knew Marie or Lucie Pellegrin, if indeed, this particular person as described ever existed to be known by either Moore or Alexis.

62. Moore, *Avowals* (1924), 104.

63. Ernest Alfred Vizetelly, *Emile Zola: Novelist and Reformer* (John Lane: London, 1904), 298.

64. GM to W. T. Stead [*c.* 3 April 1889], 8 King's Bench Walk, Becker, 586. Becker notes that "The Overflow of Mankind" appeared in the 3 April issue of the *Pall Mall Gazette*.

To show his sincerity, GM sent Stead a copy of the new edition of *Confessions*, which develops (rather outlandishly) Moore's dread of the multiplying democratic masses. Stead, returning the compliment, praised GM's sincerity, but wryly admitted he had failed to gather that the main idea of *Confessions* was the population question. See GM to W. T. Stead [May? 1889], 8 King's Bench Walk, Becker, 594.

65. GM to W. T. Stead [June 1889], 8 King's Bench Walk, Becker, 599–600.

66. The *Pall Mall Gazette* reported on 26 June 1889 that Moore gave the petition to the Home Secretary (Becker, 600). Moore's "A New Censorship of Literature," published by the *New York Herald* on 28 July 1889, expressed surprise that the *Pall Mall Gazette*, "the most honest paper in England," supported the hypocritical prosecution of Vizetelly.

67. Edmund Downey, *Twenty Years Ago: A Book of Anecdote Illustrating Literary Life in London* (Hurst and Blackett: London, 1905), 113. On 24 August 1890, when the manuscript was in proof, GM sold a number of Downey's

sheets to Belford, Clarke, a Canadian-based company notorious for pirating foreign authors. Belford, Clarke went bankrupt before *Mike Fletcher* had seen the light of North American day. Moore prevailed upon Clara Lanza to shop his novel around Manhattan; she could persuade no one but Minerva Publishing to take it (GM to Clara Lanza, 24 August 1889, 8 King's Bench Walk, Becker, 601).

68. George Moore, "Some of Balzac's Minor Pieces," *Fortnightly Review*, 46.274 (July–December 1889): 491–504.

69. Walkley and Scott are quoted in Karl Beckson's *London in the 1890s: A Cultural History* (W. W. Norton: New York, 1992), 160.

70. Peter Whitebrook, *William Archer: A Biography* (Methuen: London, 1993), 98.

71. "On Dit," *Hawk*, 4.77 (23 July 1889): 89.

72. GM to Archer [September 1889], 8 King's Bench Walk, BL; Becker, 608–9.

73. "New Plays: 'A Man's Shadow,' At the Haymarket," *Hawk*, 4.85 (17 September 1889): 299–300. Moore's letter to Archer (Becker, 608) indicates his authorship of this piece: "I must have it out with Tree. It is difficult to believe but A Man's Shadow produced in me such dreadful depression of spirits that I had to go to Brighton."

74. GM to Dear Hopkins [Fall 1889], 8 King's Bench Walk, Becker, 605–6. Becker notes that GM's letter was quoted in Hopkins's article, "Anonymity," *New Review*, November 1889.

75. Gilbert Frankau, *Self-Portrait: A Novel of His Own Life* (Hutchinson: London [1940]), 100.

76. George Moore, "Our Dramatists and Their Literature," *Fortnightly Review*, 46.275 (November 1889): 620–32.

77. GM to Clara Lanza, 12 October 1889, 8 King's Bench Walk, Becker, 620–21.

78. Moore, "Our Dramatists," 626. Earlier, Moore had asked Jones to collaborate on a play about "a very rare and lovely creature married to a man who did not in the least understand her; she meets her soul-mate, also a rare and beautiful creature, and after prolonged moral struggles they elope." Jones thought the story more suitable to GM's talent than his own. See Doris Arthur Jones, *The Life and Letters of Henry Arthur Jones* (Victor Gollancz: London, 1930), 103.

79. GM to Clara Lanza [26 October 1889], 8 King's Bench Walk, HRHRC; Becker, 623–24.

80. Augustus Moore, "On Dits," *Hawk*, 4.92 (5 November 1889): 488.

81. George Moore, "My Article and My Critics," *Hawk*, 4.93 (12 November 1889): 519–20.

82. GM to Dear Downey [after 12 November 1889], office stationery, Ward and Downey, 12 York Street, Covent Garden; NLI Ms 10060(4).

83. GM to Clara Lanza [13 November 1889], 8 King's Bench Walk, Becker, 634–36.

84. GM to Clara Lanza, Saturday, 8 King's Bench Walk, Beinecke; Becker, 615–16.

85. William Wallace, "New Novels," *Academy*, 35 (28 December 1889): 417.

86. "Novels of the Week," *Athenaeum*, 3243 (21 December 1889): 851.

87. Ward and Downey "tell me that Mike Fletcher although badly reviewed is not a commercial failure" (GM to Clara Lanza, 14 February 1890, 8 King's Bench Walk, Columbia; Becker, 646).

88. A. M. M., "A Woman's Man," *Hawk*, 4.98 (17 December 1889): 673–74.

89. James M. Glover, *Jimmy Glover: His Book* (Methuen: London, 1911), 91.

90. J. A. Chandor, "Chronological Epitome of Moore's Career," *Hawk*, 1.40 (6 June 1893): 14.

91. "Notice," *Hawk*, 2.36 (9 October 1888): 309; "Notice," *Hawk* 2.47 (25 December 1888): 551. Glover, *Jimmy Glover: His Book*, 91.

92. Augustus, returning from a weekend at Harris's country house in October 1889, denied press reports that Frank Harris had bought the *Hawk* (*Hawk*,

4.90 [22 October 1889]: 419). For brief accounts of the blackmail attempt, see Glover, *Jimmy Glover: His Book*, 91, and Vincent Brome, *Frank Harris: The Life and Loves of a Scoundrel* (Thomas Yoseloff: New York and London: 1959), 70. A search revealed no evidence that Buckle was libeled in the *Hawk*.

93. Augustus was a witty man. In a bar one day, an acquaintance, quite ruffled, said: "Look here, X— called me a bounder – what is a bounder?" "I don't know," Moore said, "you're the only one I have ever seen" (Glover, *Jimmy Glover: His Book*, 230).

94. Moore, *Mike Fletcher*, 20.

95. Ibid., 64.

96. Ibid., 67.

97. Ibid., 85.

98. Ibid., 234, 261.

Chapter 8 Three Reformations: Of the Stage, Modern Painting, and George Moore

1. Frank Harris, *Oscar Wilde: His Life and Confessions* (The Author: New York, 1916), vol. 2, 475.

2. GM to Clara Lanza, Saturday, 8 King's Bench Walk, Beinecke; Becker, 615.

3. "Part of a sixth": only a few stories in *The Untilled Field* derive from his periodical writings of the early 1890s; see Gilcher, 63.

4. Charles Morgan, *Epitaph on George Moore* (Macmillan: New York, 1935), 16.

5. Henley to Charles Whibley [December 1890], John Connell, *W. E. Henley* (Constable: London, 1949), 205, 225.

6. George Moore, "There are Many Roads to Rome," *Hawk*, 4.96 (3 December 1889): 611–12.

7. Strangely, Moore did not comment directly on the O'Shea divorce suit naming Parnell as co-respondent (November 1890), or about the split in the Irish party that occurred when the Liberals turned against Parnell.

8. *Hawk*, 4.96 (3 December 1889): 611–12.

9. Ibid.

10. He carried his line of thought about the two religions a step further in his 31 December review of books by William Morris and Walter Pater. Moore had no time for Morris's *At the Roots of the Mountains*: "Wall-paper is Mr. Morris; whether he is designing it, whether he is writing verse, whether he is preaching socialism; he sees all things, even the emotions, decoratively." Moore liked better what Pater had to give him, not optimism beautifully decorated, but pessimism in which beauty has been discovered, and an aesthetic appreciation of church ritual and pietistic forms that stopped just short of faith. Pater, Wordsworth, Buddha – they all denied the self, and immersed themselves in nature, "our implacable mother, against whose laws there is no appeal." Like the great poets, they sing "only of the web in which man is entangled, the woof of which was spun centuries before his birth." Catholicism still has traces of that magnificent and pessimistic wisdom of the East; but Protestantism is entirely a Western religion, "given over to an optimism as repellent as it is silly, silly as it is prosaic." See George Moore, "Three Books," *Hawk*, 4.100 (31 December 1889): 734–35.

11. GM to W. Kineton Parkes [inscribed 3 February 1890; possibly inaccurate], 8 King's Bench Walk, NYU; Becker, 643. George Moore, *Pagan Poems*, 16–19; George Moore, *Mike Fletcher*, 252–53. The poem was published as "A Une Poitrinaire" in *Pagan Poems*, as "To a Consumptive Girl" in *Belford's Magazine* (October 1889, Toronto), and as "A une Poetrenaire" [sic] in *Vain Fortune*. Its prose version was variously titled "Notes and Sensations" in the *Hawk* (11 February 1890); "Moods and Memories" in *Dana* (June 1904) and *Lippincott's Magazine* (July 1904), and "A Waitress" in *Memoirs of My Dead Life*.

12. By "Mlle. D'Avray," GM may have wished to reveal to the initiated, and conceal from others, the identity of Madame Valtesse de la Bigne, a courtesan capable of reciting Baudelaire at the opportune moment, or quoting Nietzsche. Zola described her golden bed in *Nana* (1880). This beautiful bluestocking was Gervex's lover for a number of years. For her portrait, see Jane Kinsman, ed., *Paris in the Late Nineteenth Century* (National Gallery of Australia: Canberra, 1997), 159.

13. GM to Clara Lanza, Saturday, 8 King's Bench Walk, Beinecke; Becker, 615.

14. Moore, *Pagan Poems*, 14.

15. George Moore, *Parnell and His Island*, 234.

16. Arthur Schopenhauer, *Essays and Aphorisms*, selected and trans. by R. J. Hollingdale (Penguin: London, 1970), 139.

17. George Moore, "Pruriency," *Hawk*, 5.112 (25 March 1890): 348 (quoted from Théophile Gautier).

18. Moore, *Pagan Poems*, 58.

19. "In Blue Silk and Brass," *Hawk*, 5.116 (22 April 1890): 463–64.

20. "Notes and Sensations," *Hawk*, 5.107 (18 February 1890): 195–96.

21. "Le Revers d'un grand homme," *Hawk*, 5.104 (28 January 1890): 104–5.

22. This quality of being aware of a supplementary significance beyond telling, a plenitude of beauty in ordinary life to which art merely points, is especially present in "London in April" (later titled "Spring in London" in *Memoirs of My Dead Life*). On a Sunday morning, GM walks meditatively from King's Bench Walk to Regent's Park, then up Primrose Hill, cabs it back to Marble Arch by Bayswater Road, then visits Hyde Park, all the time Hamletising on the beautiful enigma of London crowds, a London he loves so much. He sees in female passersby their "womanhood bursting upon them," and hears in the different gaits of horses, omnibus, and coach, the varied gaits of desire in the humans they bear forward on errands of desire, and he sees in the varied districts of London the separate periods of his past life there. It is a triumphant piece of writing, a recognition of the great dance of the species-being (*Hawk*, 5.114 [8 April 1890]: 403–4).

23. Max Beerbohm, "George Moore," Beinecke. For a published version see *Atlantic Monthly*, 186 (December 1950): 34–39.

24. George Moore, "Baboonacy," *Hawk*, 5.103 (21 January 1890): 75–76. Like a dog after rats, Haggard enjoys the killing; GM quipped that if the dog could write, his books would read like Haggard's.

25. GM to David Croal Thomson, [18 November 1889], 8 King's Bench Walk, Berg; Becker, 633. The show exhibited paintings by ten artists: Starr, James, Thomson, Bernard Sickert, Walter Sickert, Wilson Steer, Fred Brown, Paul Maitland, Theodore Roussel, and Francis Bate. See Anna Greutzner Robins's essay, "The London Impressionists at the Goupil Gallery," in Kenneth McConkey, *Impressionism in Britain* (Yale University Press: London, 1995), 87–96.

26. While living in King's Bench Walk, Moore used to dine for three shillings at the Cock Tavern among Henley's set, at the Cheshire Cheese with some of the poets of the Rhymers' Club, or the Rainbow Tavern with a theater crowd: George Moore, *Conversations in Ebury Street*, 130; George Moore, *Lewis Seymour and Some Women* (1922), xi.; Francis Gribble, *Seen in Passing: A Volume of Personal Reminiscences* (Ernest Benn: London, 1929), 224.

27. D. S. MacColl, *Life, Work, and Setting of Philip Wilson Steer* (Faber and Faber: London, 1945), 68, 193.

28. Ysanne Holt, *Philip Wilson Steer* (Seren: Mid-Glamorgan, 1992), *passim*.

29. "Impressionism," *Hawk*, 4.98 (17 December 1889): 670–71.

30. Moore thought Leighton produced pictures "rubbed all over with . . . a

coat of strawberry ice" ("The Royal Academy," *Hawk*, 5.118 [6 May 1890]: 523–24). In a picture like Alma-Tadema's *Sappho*, Moore complained that archaeological curiosity took the place of art: "We look at it and we say: 'How curious! how very curious! and that was how the Greeks washed and dressed themselves!'" ("Curiosity in Art," *Speaker*, 4.99 [21 November 1891]: 616–18).

31. See, for instance, "Handling," *Speaker*, 6.135 (30 July 1892): 135–36. There are excellent examples of Moore's brilliant descriptions of the painterly achievements of the French and British Impressionists in McConkey's *Impressionism, passim*.

32. Walter Richard Sickert, *A Free House! or The Artist As Craftsman*, ed. Osbert Sitwell (Macmillan: London, 1947), 184.

33. Elie Halévy to Louise Halévy, 9 November 1890, quoted in Henri Loyrette, *Degas* (Fayard: Paris, 1991), 609; 794 n. 377.

34. For Steer's *Knucklebones*, see McConkey's *Impressionism*, 84, pl. 79.

35. "Pictures," *Hawk*, 5.102 (14 January 1890): 47–48.

36. "Sport in Art," *Hawk*, 5.105 (4 February 1890): 134.

37. George Moore, "Degas," *Impressions and Opinions* (1913), 226.

38. "The Grosvenor Gallery," *Hawk* (13 May 1890): 553–54; for an illustration of Clausen's *The Mowers*, see McConkey, *Impressionism*, 66, pl. 30.

39. "Meissonier and the Salon Julian," *Fortnightly Review*, 283 (July 1890): 45–55; "Is Education Worth Having?," *St. James's Gazette*, 21.3200 (10 September 1890): 6. Julian's Academy was attacked by Moore again in "The Paris Salon," *Speaker*, 3.73 (23 May 1891): 609.

40. "A Great Artist," *Speaker*, 3.66 (4 April 1891): 396–97.

41. "The Louvre Revisited – II," *Speaker*, 3.76 (13 June 1891): 700–1.

42. The topic of Nationalism's relation to Impressionism has not, however, been overlooked by Anna Greutzner Robins. See "Two Reactions to French Painting in Great Britain," *Post-Impressionism* (Royal Academy of Arts exhib. cat.: London, 1979–80), 179–80.

43. MacColl, *Life, Work and Setting of Philip Wilson Steer*, 177; Holt, *Philip Wilson Steer*, 50–52; Robins, "The London Impressionists," 89.

44. "The New Gallery," *Speaker*, 3.71 (9 May 1891): 548–49. In *Classic Landscape, Richmond* (1893), Steer began not only to paint distinctively English sites but to render them in ways reminiscent of classic English painters: he began to aim for qualities of majesty, even nationalistic majesty, not apparent in the landscape work of Monet, Pissarro, or Van Gogh. See Kenneth McConkey's excellent *Impressionism in Britain*, 57.

45. Wendy Baron, *Sickert* (Phaidon: London, 1973), 37; George Moore, "A Book About Bastien-Lepage," *Speaker*, 5.112 (20 February 1892): 227.

46. MacColl, *Life, Work, and Setting of Philip Wilson Steer*, 2.

47. "Sex in Art – II," *Speaker*, 5.130 (25 June 1892): 766–68.

48. Moore, *Impressions and Opinions* (1913), 221.

49. Ibid., 232.

50. Ibid., 230.

51. Loyrette, *Degas*, 425; Roy McMullen, *Degas: His Life, Times, and Work* (Secker and Warburg: London, 1985), 242–43.

52. "Letters from the Whistler Collection," ed. Margaret MacDonald and Joy Newton, *Gazette des Beaux-Arts* (December 1986): 209. *Selected Letters of Stéphane Mallarmé*, trans. Rosemary Lloyd (University of Chicago Press: Chicago and London, 1988), 171; Carl Paul Barbier, ed., *Correspondance Mallarmé-Whistler: Histoire de la grande amitié de leurs dernières années* (A. G. Nizet: Paris, 1964), 71.

53. Diary of Daniel Halévy, 17 May 1891, Daniel Halévy, *My Friend Degas*, trans. Mina Curtiss (Wesleyan University Press: Middletown, CT, 1964), 59.

54. "Degas in Bond Street," *Speaker*, 5.105 (2 January 1892): 19–20; see also "Art Patrons," *Speaker*, 3.78 (27 June 1891): 757–59.

55. By choosing to identify true "Impressionism" with Manet and Degas, rather than with Monet or Cézanne (for instance), Moore was in line with the positions of the two other major advanced London art critics of the 1890s, D. S. MacColl and R. M. Stevenson. See McConkey, *Impressionism*, 62, 80–81.

56. George Moore, *Ave* (1937), 47, Vincent O'Sullivan, *Opinions* (Unicorn Press: London, 1959), 49.

57. *Les Revenants* was played at the Théâtre Libre on 20 May 1890. See N. Schoonderwoerd, *J. T. Grein: Ambassador of the Theatre, 1862–1935* (Van Gorcum: Assen, 1963), and Karl Beckson, *London in the 1890s: A Cultural History* (W. W. Norton: New York, 1992), 162.

58. The scene impressed Moore so much that it had an impact upon the final mother and son scene in *Esther Waters*.

59. George Moore, "The New Théâtre Libre," *Hawk*, 6.127 (8 July 1890): 46.

60. George Moore, "A London 'Théâtre Libre,'" *St. James's Gazette*, 21.3144 (19 July 1890): 3.

61. J. T. Grein, "A London Théâtre Libre," *St. James's Gazette*, 21.3156 (21 July 1890): 5–6.

62. For a study of the anti-populist element in the Irish theater, see Adrian Frazier, *Behind the Scenes: Yeats, Horniman, and the Struggle for the Abbey Theatre* (University of California Press: Berkeley, 1990), *passim*.

63. GM to Clara Lanza, Saturday [14? June 1890], 8 King's Bench Walk, Washington; Becker, 658–59. In "The New Théâtre Libre," GM claimed precedence in the discussion of theater reform (*Hawk*, 5.125 [24 June 1890]: 726).

64. "On Dits," *Hawk*, 6.128 (15 July 1890): 68.

65. "On Dits," *Hawk*, 5.102 (14 January 1890): 39.

66. "On Dits," *Hawk*, 6.127 (8 July 1890): 40. For a description of the very rich, and somewhat literary American, Mrs Bloomfield Moore, see "American Ladies at Home: Mrs Bloomfield Moore," *Lady's Pictorial*, 22.551 (19 September 1891): 472–73.

67. "On Dits," *Hawk*, 6.128 (15 July 1890): 69; J. M. Glover, *Jimmy Glover and His Friends* (Chatto and Windus: London, 1913), 2–5.

68. Whistler's grievance against Augustus Moore remains a mystery. Augustus reported that a mutual friend told him Whistler was angry about something Augustus had written about E. W. Godwin's involvement in the production of a Greek play. E. W. Godwin had been before his death Whistler's current wife's husband. Augustus justly pointed out that it was like a French farce for a man to be so worked up about the honor of his wife's first husband (*Hawk*, 6.136 [9 September 1890]: 290). The "mutual friend" was H. G. Hibbert who heard this explanation from Whistler immediately after the event (H. G. Hibbert, *Fifty Years of a Londoner's Life* [Grant Richards: London, 1916], 174). Ronald Anderson and Anne Koval in *Whistler: Beyond the Myth* (John Murray: London, 1994) believe that the real cause of Whistler's wrath was an article in the 22 January 1889 *Hawk* in which it was explained that Stott of Oldham, a painter, had fought with Whistler in the Hogarth Club, because Maud Franklin had been ditched by her lover Whistler after many years of cohabitation, and she had since taken up with Stott. That seems a better reason for Whistler's anger, but why did he wait twenty-one months to chastise Augustus?

69. Alice Lingard (1847–97) was the actress who played "Jenny" in W. S. Gilbert's *Sweethearts* (Becker, 345), and later became an actor-producer who owned a traveling company. She was something of a fashion-plate and wore a distinctively elaborate hat to which was given her name – a wide

green hat trimmed in otter (*Court and Society Review*, 2.79 [7 January 1886]: 559). In November 1885 she had hired Augustus as her acting manager (*Bat*, 1.35 [24 November 1885]: 517). Among the performances on the tour was Clement Scott and Wilson Barrett's *Sister Mary* (performed in Brighton in March 1886), about a Red Cross nurse who nearly marries an adulterer, then goes off to Africa for the Zulu and Boer Wars. Clement Scott later sought to have Augustus dismissed from Lingard's employment, by saying he would not review her plays if Augustus remained, and Scott was the bellwether of London theater critics. Augustus sued Scott, and received an out-of-court settlement of £150, which enabled him to buy the *Hawk* (*Hawk*, 2.46 [18 December 1888]: 537). Her husband the actor Horace Lingard may have taken offense because in the 3 June 1890 *Hawk* Augustus had written that provincial acting-managers were thieves; he knows, because he had been in the business for a while, though he doesn't name Alice Lingard as his employer at the time.

70. Whistler to Mallarmé [8 September 1890], 21 Cheyne Walk, Barbier, *Correspondance Mallarmé–Whistler*, 64.

71. Augustus Moore, "The Gentle Art of Making a Goose of Oneself," *Hawk*, 6.136 (9 September 1890): 290.

72. The wittiest account was a limerick in the *Globe*, entitled "Knock-turn in Black and White":

Only a word in the foyer,
Only a form on the floor –
A popular painter
Went home feeling fainter,
And the stalls held one less and one Moore!

Quoted in "Exit Whistler," *Hawk*, 6.137 (16 September 1890): 321.

73. After Augustus married Justina Monckton in early 1891, he wanted to take his wife on a honeymoon to Moore Hall. GM told his mother it was an "odd arrangement if we are not

friends . . . To edit the *Hawk* from Moore Hall is a thing I most distinctly object to. When I say the *Hawk* I mean the paper he has been bringing out for the last two years. The paper may improve. I hope it will" (Becker, 691). On 1 March 1892 GM explained to Maurice Moore that "reconciliation between Augustus and me is impossible. I cannot forget or forgive the shocking manner in which he has spoken of me in his journal. I went to him and warned him that if he called the finances of the independent theatre into question, I would never speak to him again. I told him that to do so was equivalent to calling me a thief. He refused to take warning; now let him take the consequences" (GM to Maurice Moore, 1 March 1892, NLI Ms 2646–47; Becker 747–48).

On 21 December 1910, GM explained to Maurice that, after receiving a desperate letter from the dying Augustus, he would send him all the money he could afford to pay for an operation, but he would not go to the deathbed (*George Moore on Parnassus*, 188).

74. Quoted in Barbier, *Correspondance Mallarmé–Whistler*.

75. Mallarmé to Whistler, 25 October 1890, *Selected Letters of Stéphane Mallarmé*, trans. Lloyd, 171.

76. "All My I," *Pelican: A Journal of To-Day*, 10.263 (3 September 1892): 745.

77. For the two women's relationship to Ruskin and Symons, see the "Michael Field Correspondence," presented to the British Museum by T. Sturge Moore, Ms 46,867; and Emma Donoghue, *We Are Michael Field* (Absolute Press: Bath, 1998), 57.

78. GM to Michael Field, Monday night, 8 King's Bench Walk, BL; Becker, 671–72; Michael Field, *Works and Days*, ed. T. and D. C. Sturge Moore (John Murray: London, 1933), 134–35.

79. "Michael Field and the *Tragic Mary*," *St. James's Gazette*, 21.3180 (18 August 1890): 6.

80. George Meredith's conversation, they

thought, was "of value and of range beyond that of any man I have ever met – except G.M. at his very best" [March?] 1892, Field, *Works and Days*, n.p.

81. Edith Cooper diary for [1? August 1890], ibid., 198–200.

82. Ibid., 199.

83. GM to Clara Lanza [March 1890], 8 King's Bench Walk, Washington; Becker, 653–54.

84. GM to Archer, 1 April [1891], 8 King's Bench Walk, BL; Becker, 698.

85. In a letter to Archer about *Strike at Arlingford*, GM repeated this fear: "in a conversation with Arthur Symons, [I said] I shall succeed everywhere except in the dialogue – there is something which I feel I shall not get . . . the play is wanting in mystery . . . it is a world without air" (Wednesday night [17 July 1893], BL; Becker, 822–26).

86. Quoted in Peter Whitebrook's *William Archer: A Biography* (Methuen: London, 1993), 112.

87. George Moore, "Our Dramatic Critics," *Pall Mall Gazette*, 53.8259 (9 September 1891): 1.

88. William Archer, "The Free Stage and the New Drama," *Fortnightly Review*, 56 (November 1891): 663–72.

89. Shaw to William Archer, 7 November 1891, 29 Fitzroy Square W., Dan H. Lawrence, ed., *Bernard Shaw: Collected Letters 1874–1897* (Max Reinhardt: London, 1965), 320–23; see also page 323, where Shaw says it was wrong of Archer to "flatly contradict . . . George Moore"; and pages 324–25, where Shaw says that GM has put Archer "in the wrong at every step of the argument."

90. The episode is nicely summarised by Whitebrook, *William Archer*, 137–39.

91. "George Moore Accepts Dagonet's Challenge," *Pelican*, 10.237 (5 March 1892): 333.

92. GM to Clara Lanza, 24 April [1891], 8 King's Bench Walk, Berg; Becker, 702–4. The book was originally commissioned by Alfred Gibbons, editor of *Lady's Pictorial*, as a collaboration

with Ella Hepworth Dixon. She withdrew on account of poor health. My thanks to Edwin Gilcher.

93. "Meissonier and the Salon Julian," *Fortnightly Review*, 283 (1 July 1890): 45.

94. GM to Maurice Moore, 1 August 1890, 8 King's Bench Walk, NLI Ms 2646–47; Becker, 675.

95. "Vain Fortune," Chapter 7; *Lady's Pictorial*, 22: 45 (8 August 1891): 253.

96. In negotiations with Lemuel W. Bangs, the Scribner editor, GM begged to be allowed a few pounds extra – over the £20 offered for the US rights, a derisory sum – to rewrite the first one hundred pages of the novel, putting Emily Watson more in the center of the picture. He was allowed another £5, and then in ten days rewrote the opening of the book. How he imagined he could do good work in such a short time is a mystery. See GM's letters to Scribner's of 12, 19, 29 December and 9 and 28 January, 732–41.

97. Mrs [Eliza] Aria, *My Sentimental Self* (Chapman and Hall: London, 1922), 58.

98. Violet Wyndham, *The Sphinx and Her Circle: A Biographical Sketch of Ada Leverson, 1862–1933* (Vanguard Press: New York, 1963), 1–21.

99. Ibid., 22–23.

100. Julie Speedie, *Wonderful Sphinx: The Biography of Ada Leverson* (Virago: London, 1993), 23–31. My thanks to Julie Speedie for help with understanding this relationship.

101. Charles Burkhart, *Ada Leverson* (Twayne Publishers: New York, 1973), 21.

102. Oswald Crawfurd published Leverson's first story, "New Year's Gifts," in *Black and White* on 30 January 1892; she did not meet Wilde, it seems, until a month later (Speedie, *Wonderful Sphinx*, 53). On 17 November 1920, thanking Leverson for the gift of a book, Moore praised it as an expression of "the essential Ada, whom I had the honour of introducing into literature" (*George Moore on Parnassus*, 485).

103. GM to Downey, n.d., 8 King's Bench

Walk, NLI Ms 19060(4). Moore included in his prospectus two articles never written, "The Philosophy of Suicide" and "The Great Moral Question." GM to Lanza, 5 November 1890, 8 King's Bench Walk, Becker, 684–85. Nutt was a bookseller, publisher, folklorist, and acquaintance of W. B. Yeats.

104. "Mr. George Moore's Essays," *Speaker*, 3 (21 March 1891): 352–53.

105. Arthur Symons, "Literature: *Impressions and Opinions*," *Academy*, 34 (21 March 1891): 274–75.

106. GM to Mary Blake Moore, 8 King's Bench Walk, NLI Ms 4479; Becker, 708.

107. "Literature," *Athenaeum*, 3326 (25 July 1891): 117.

108. GM to Clara Lanza, 24 April [1891], 8 King's Bench Walk, Berg; Becker, 702–4.

109. GM to Clara Lanza, 5 November 1890, 8 King's Bench Walk, Becker, 684. Tree offered GM £100 if he would introduce his characters into a plot constructed by Montague Williams.

110. GM to Archer, Monday night [12 December 1892], Hogarth Club, BL; Becker, 771. For a complaint about GM's slow progress in fulfilling the terms of the Sims bet, see "All My I," *Pelican*, 10.265 (17 September 1892): 776.

111. GM to Miss Robins, Tuesday night [10 January 1893], 8 King's Bench Walk, NYU; Becker, 772.

112. GM to Miss Robins, n.d., 8 King's Bench Walk, NYU; Becker, 775.

113. GM to Miss Robins; 17 January [1893], 8 King's Bench Walk, NYU; Becker, 777.

114. "Miss Robins and the Master Builder: A Conversation Reported," *Speaker*, 7. 164 (18 February 1893): 187.

115. GM to Miss Robins [22 January 1893], 8 King's Bench Walk, NYU; Becker, 780.

116. GM to Miss Milman, Thursday night [26 January 1893], 8 King's Bench Walk, Becker, 781.

117. Whitebrook, *William Archer*, 152; William Archer, "The Strike at Arlingford," *The Theatrical World for 1893* (Walter Scott: London, 1894), 70–73.

118. GBS to William Archer, 29 Fitzroy Square, Lawrence, ed., *Bernard Shaw: Collected Letters 1874–1897*, 383.

119. The *Stage* said *Strike* was conventional, unoriginal, and feeble; *Era* agreed that it was "conventional"; according to *Theatre*, it was "tame." See Langenfeld, 42–44.

120. George Moore, *The Strike at Arlingford*, 95–96.

121. GM to Archer, Wednesday night [17 July 1893], BL; Becker, 822–26.

122. GM to William Morris Colles [inscribed March 1893], 8 King's Bench Walk, Berg; Becker, 789.

123. GM to Will H. Dircks [May? 1893], private collection. Dircks was an editor at Walter Scott, publisher of *The Strike at Arlingford*.

124. GM to Lena Milman, Monday [12? June 1893], 8 King's Bench Walk, Kansas; Becker, 811; GM to Dujardin, 13 June 1893, *Letters to Dujardin*, 33–34.

125. GM to Lena Milman, Wednesday [5 July 1893], Becker, 819.

126. GM to Lena Milman, 20 August [1893], 8 King's Bench Walk, Becker, 833–34.

127. George Moore, *Works* [*Esther Waters*: Chapter 25]; Ams/inc with A revisions [36pp]; HRHRC.

128. GM to D. S. MacColl, 12 August 1893, 8 King's Bench Walk, Becker, 832–33; "Pages from the Life of a Workgirl" were published in the *Pall Mall Gazette* from 2 to 14 October.

129. GM to Maurice Moore [31? July 1893], 8 King's Bench Walk, NLI; Becker, 828–29. On 11 September, GM explained to Maurice that *Esther Waters* was not the deep critique of the Saxon; that would be another book. However, it seems to me that his future intention transpired within the text he was currently writing.

130. In an earlier draft, GM insinuated a character much like himself or

Harding from the earlier books, a literary, well-traveled gentleman living at "Norman's Inn" (King's Bench Walk) named Mr Bryant, who is a friend of Esther's employer, Miss Rice (based on GM's friend Lena Milman). Esther has a crush on Mr Bryant. Later, GM wisely suppressed this narcissistic stand-in for himself. The deleted section, however, illuminates GM's relationship with Milman. Bryant comes once a week to see Miss Rice (a sweet literary spinster like Milman), and yet she never seems to want more from him than conversation; Esther reflects that she herself would "do more than that with her young man," as doubtless GM wished Milman would do with him. See Moore, *Works* [*Esther Waters*: Chapter 20]; Ams/inc with A revisions [55 folio pages]; HRHRC.

131. Sir [Montgomerie William Nevill] Geary, 5th Bart [Untitled memoir on George Moore]. TmsS with A revisions. 14pp. nd. HRHRC.

132. GM to Lena Milman [April 1889], 8 King's Bench Walk, Becker, 584.

133. GM to Lena Milman, 1 October 1891, 29 March 1892 [26 January 1893], 8 King's Bench Walk, Becker, 721, 757–58, 781. Both Henniker and Milman later toyed with the affections of Thomas Hardy, but Henniker was willing to go to greater lengths of dalliance than Milman.

134. William Geary to Joseph Hone, 10 October 1936 Accession, Joseph M. Hone, Box 1, Folder 17, V253d, Washington.

135. GM to Milman, Sunday [March? 1893], 8 King's Bench Walk, Becker, 788.

136. GM to Milman, Monday [March? 1893], 8 King's Bench Walk, 789.

137. GM to Lena Milman, Thursday [11 May 1893], 8 King's Bench Walk; Becker, 800.

138. GM to Lena Milman, 17 May [1893], 8 King's Bench Walk, Becker, 801. "Sex in Art" first appeared in the *Speaker*, 5.129–30 (18 and 25 June 1893): 737–38; 766–68. It was

reprinted in *Modern Painting* (1893). GM baited the New Woman novelists by saying that memoirs by women are ordinarily "a tissue of lies, suppressions, and half-truths"; a serious drawback, he claimed, "for all art that lives is full of sex . . . *Jane Eyre* and *Aurora Leigh* are full of sex; *Daniel Deronda* and *Romola* are not."

139. GM to Lena Milman, Sunday [28 May 1893], 8 King's Bench Walk, Becker, 807. Martin Seymour-Smith, *Hardy* (Bloomsbury: London, 1994), 471.

140. George Moore, "Half a Dozen Pictures in the Academy," *Speaker*, 8.186 (23 July 1893): 73–74.

141. GM to Lena Milman, 14 December [1893], 8 King's Bench Walk, Becker, 878.

142. GM to Lena Milman [July 1893], Becker, 820.

143. GM to Lena Milman, Thursday night [July 1893], 8 King's Bench Walk, Becker, 821.

144. GM to Lena Milman, 20 August [1893], 8 King's Bench Walk, Becker, 833–34.

145. GM to Maurice Moore, 21 September [1893], 8 King's Bench Walk, NLI Ms 2646–47; Becker, 844–48.

146. Seymour-Smith, *Hardy*, 474.

147. GM to Lena Milman [September/October, 1893], 8 King's Bench Walk, Becker, 848–49.

148. On 5 September 1893, GM suggested that for Walter Scott Ltd, Milman might "like to translate Turgueneff – to translate Turgueneff from the Russian would be very swell and would bring you in some money. What do you say?" (Becker, 839). He then shopped around her translation of *Poor Folk* to various publishers, including Fisher Unwin and Heinemann, before getting an agreement from John Lane at Bodley Head.

149. GM to Lena Milman, Wednesday [20 December 1893], 8 King's Bench Walk, Becker, 881. Becker notes that the contract for Milman's translation of *Poor Folk*, with the requirement for GM's contribution, is in the Bodley Head archives.

150. John Oliver Hobbes, *Some Emotions and a Moral* (T. Fisher Unwin: London, 1891) published in the Pseudonym Library series, is a novelette in a brisk, flip, sententious style, decorated with arch speeches like the following from Godfrey: "There are some men I know who can analyze their first love and wonder with Hume if their passion is the appetite for generation sandwiched between appreciation for beauty and a generous kindness. They can reduce their God to a diagram and their emotions to a system. If that is philosophy, I have not the first makings of a philosopher. But I know this: I cannot be happy merely because I am unhappy." He has the misfortune to become fascinated with Cynthia, who in men likes titles and riches very much, but celebrity still more; what she doesn't like is sex: "Don't touch me please," she says to her fiancée, "We are not Hodge and Betsy. And let me warn you, if you want to make me angry – so angry that I will never speak to you again – try to kiss me, or something unpleasant of that sort" (*Tales of John Oliver Hobbes* [T. Fisher Unwin: London, 1894], 69). GM might well have taken warning.

151. John Morgan Richards, *The Life of John Oliver Hobbes, Told in Her Correspondence with Numerous Friends* (John Murray: London, 1911; second impression), 86; Moore, *Memoirs of My Dead Life* (1960), 24. In "Lui Et Elles," "Agate" is "Pearl" Craigie. Craigie's first extant letter to GM, 4 January 1894, mentions a meeting the two had before GM "went away," presumably on his Christmas visit to Paris (Mrs Craigie, Letters to George Moore, NLI Ms 2135; Richards, *Life of John Oliver Hobbes*, 78).

152. Moore, *Memoirs of My Dead Life* (1960), 26.

153. O'Sullivan, *Opinions*, 144.

154. Moore, *Memoirs of My Dead Life* (1960), 27.

155. Vineta Colby, *The Singular Anomaly: Women Novelists of the Nineteenth Century* (University of London Press: London; New York University Press, New York: 1970), 185.

156. Stanley Weintraub, *The London Yankees: Portraits of American Writers and Artists in England, 1894–1914* (W. H. Allen: London, 1879), 61, 65.

157. Colby, *Singular Anomaly*, 187.

158. David Cecil, *Max: A Biography* (Constable: London, 1964), 367. Regarding Craigie's belief that she was a new George Eliot, Lewis Hind remarked: "George Eliot was a recluse, John Oliver Hobbes was a mondaine: George Eliot never thought that she was a mondaine; John Oliver Hobbes sometimes thought she was a recluse" (*Authors and I* [John Lane: London, 1921], 149).

159. Craigie to GM, 25 February, Hôtel Continental, Paris, NLI Ms 2135.

160. "A Literary Causerie, the Reverend J. E. C. Welldon on M. Zola," *Speaker*, 8.198 (14 October 1893): 411.

161. Pearl Craigie to GM, 11 January 1894, Richards, *Life of John Oliver Hobbes*, 78.

162. *Modern Painting* got good reviews. The *Saturday Review*, for instance, said, "It is impossible to give an idea of its clever humour, its slashing satire, its brilliant style, and the great interest of those parts in which Mr. Moore is speaking of what he feels and understands ... We can only say that *Modern Painting* is never dull; and that, whether he makes you angry, dissentient, amused, or interested, Mr. Moore never makes you wish to lay his book down" ("Two Books on Art," *Saturday Review* [7 October 1893]: 422). Pater gave the imprimatur of measured praise in the *Daily Chronicle* (10 June 1893: 3).

163. Craigie to GM, 24 January 1894; the phrase appears in the National Library of Ireland copies of the letters, made by Clement Shorter when he helped John Morgan Richards write Pearl's biography; Richards deleted the phrase, along with all other intimacies, from his published versions of the letters (Richards, *Life of John Oliver Hobbes*, 80).

164. GM, "The Grafton Gallery," *Speaker*, 9.213 (27 January 1894): 109–10.

165. Moore, *Memoirs of My Dead Life* (1960), 29.

166. GM to Lena Milman [late January/early February], Becker, 899.

167. Craigie to GM, 28 January 1894, NLI Ms 2135.

168. The Dolmetsch concert was held on 30 January 1894: see GM to Dolmetsch, Saturday [Fall, 1894], 8 King's Bench Walk, Becker, 941; Craigie to Moore, 30 January 1894, NLI Ms 2135; Carl Dolmetsch, Becker, 941; Sara Ruth Watson, "George Moore and the Dolmetsches," *English Literature in Transition*, 6 (1963): 65–75; and Margaret Campbell, *Dolmetsch: The Man and His Work* (Hamish Hamilton: London, 1975), 64–66.

169. Moore, *Ave*, 34. Craigie could not get tickets for *The Comedy of Sighs* ("Pearl" to "My dear George," Thursday night, NLI Ms 2135), but Shaw had GM sent complimentary passes for *Arms and the Man*, which was also double-billed with *Land of the Heart's Desire* (Lawrence, ed., *Bernard Shaw: Collected Letters 1874–1897*, 424–25). Craigie wrote to say she would accompany GM to the Saturday production on 24 April 1894 (NLI Ms 2135).

170. Pearl to Dearest [George Moore], Wednesday [4? April 1894], 56 Lancaster Gate, NLI Ms 2135: "Do you know anything about the Yellow Book dinner? It sounds reckless! May I go?" After going, she told him she was, "on the whole," "amused" (Pearl to Dearest, 17 April 1894). Craigie was later distressed by the scandal of Symons's contribution and Beardsley's illustrations for the *Yellow Book*. Harland blamed GM for a satirical review of the first number in the *Speaker* (Karl Beckson, *Henry Harland: His Life and Work* (Eighteen Nineties Society: London, 1978), 71, 147 n. 35); but Craigie thought "'The Speaker' on the Y. B. is only too just . . . I have never seen such a vulgar

production . . . Reserve is a gift: I have always prayed for it" (28 April 1894). She was here speaking in the prudish voice Moore had been resisting for over ten years, the voice that had been raised against him over and over; and Symons was his close friend. It is to be doubted that Moore turned hypocrite for love and wrote the *Speaker* review, but he may have kept his opinions to himself. For two of many accounts of the dinner, see Stanley Weintraub, *Aubrey Beardsley: Imp of the Perverse* (Pennsylvania State University Press: University Park, 1976), 104; and Beckson, *Henry Harland*, 68–69.

171. Quite desperate, she wrote to him in an undated letter, "I never wanted to talk to you as I do today. The silence of my life overwhelmed me . . . I have seen visitors today – but the silence – the silence of it all. I have written Lady Jeune that I cannot attend her party this evening. I cannot face the loneliness of a crowded drawing-room . . . I try to forget myself in other people; I try to think only of others and never of myself: I choke my soul with work and yet – and yet – !" (NLI Ms 2135).

172. Richards, *Life of John Oliver Hobbes*, 86.

173. As Moore bitterly put it in 1922, "She took the script and added some pretty little epigrams and speeches – I always called them her little liver pills" (Barrett Clark, Notes on George Moore [1923], 101; Berg).

174. "Mr. George Moore's Success," *Daily Chronicle* (28 March 1894): 3. Though GM thanked Johnson for the praise, he was miffed by Johnson's insistence on the Zolaesque elements in the novel: "Nobody who knows anything," Moore complained to Vincent O'Sullivan, "would say such a thing. They would know that if I have a master, it is Flaubert. Open *Esther Waters* and read that scene where she meets her son after a long separation. What an embrace! That, my dear friend, is pure Flaubert" (Vincent O'Sullivan,

Memoirs [Unicorn Press: London, 1959], 46–47).

175. Arthur T. Quiller-Conch, "Esther Waters," *Speaker*, 9.222 (31 March 1894): 366–67. GM buttered Quiller-Couch up in a 4 November 1893 letter about the book (Becker, 860–62).

176. *New York Times*, 1 April 1894: 1.

177. *Sketch*, 5.64 (18 April 1894): 630.

178. *Athenaeum*, 3470 (28 April 1894): 537–38.

179. Malcolm MacColl, "The Clergy and Fiction," *Speaker*, 9.227 (5 May 1894): 486.

180. See note 130 for "Mr Bryant."

181. *Daily Chronicle*, 3 May 1894: 3; Becker, 924–26.

182. George Moore, *A Communication to My Friends*, 74–75; Moore, *Lewis Seymour and Some Women* xxi.

183. Clark, Notes on George Moore, 98–100.

184. In the proof of "Lui et Elles," GM at first said that in the dark coach, sex "sometimes seemed to descend from [Pearl's] brain," though he "was not sure that our relations would become less and less restrained." In a slight revision, he added that sex "seemed about to descend from her brain"; apparently, it never did. See "Proof Sheets with Autograph Corrections" of *Memoirs of My Dead Life* (1921), 19, HRHRC.

185. Ibid., 18.

186. Craigie to GM, 5 May 1894; Craigie to Ellen Terry, 7 May 1894, NLI Ms 2135.

187. *Memoirs of My Dead Life* (1960), 29–32; Clark, Notes on George Moore, 99–100.

188. GM based his impression of her reaction on her reply to his letter of sympathy at her divorce trial (3 July 1895). It should be noted that she also takes responsibility for her capriciousness: "Thank you. I thought I could not have been mistaken in you: I had a higher opinion of you, and I am more glad than I can say that it may remain unshaken. I only remember that you were very kind to me, and that we were great friends, that there was on my side at least a sincere if bewildering affection. I know my faults, my peculiarities, my inconsistencies. I am always surprised any one expresses either sympathy or regard for me — trouble, bodily pain, and overwork have done their bravest. The boy is waiting. Again, thank you"; Craigie to George Moore, Monday, 56 Lancaster Gate, NLI Ms 2135.

Vincent O'Sullivan suggested to Joseph Hone other possible causes for Moore being jilted, such as the disapproval of Craigie's parents. John Morgan Richards was a Massachusetts Protestant with contempt for Irish Catholics, and the plain Mrs Richards found English society baffling and so "clung on to a title, when one appeared, as to a life-buoy in the sea of her bewilderment" (27 Jan [1935], Joseph M. Hone, Accession Box 1, Folder 24, V253d, Washington). Craigie herself often first demanded then suffocated from attentiveness: "O how I hate having any one person forever down my throat" (Pearl to My dearest Papa, Grand Hotel, Italy, Berg).

189. William Geary to Hone, Joseph M. Hone Accession, Washington. In his quotation from Geary's letter, Hone changes "lordling" to "worldling."

190. Moore, *Memoirs of My Dead Life* (1920), 32. Moore felt guilty for the use to which he put this unnamed woman, guilty for not loving her for herself, but, he recalled, once a distraught woman had taken him from the street, and for that night, he was the anodyne for her sorrow.

Chapter 9 From Celibate Lives to the "One Great Love"

1. GM to Dear Miss Terry, 12 May [1894], 8 King's Bench Walk, Becker, 931.

2. GM to [Lena Milman], [3 May 1894], Becker, 924; George Moore, *Memoirs*

of My Dead Life (1960), 31 (where GM says he met "unexpectedly among the crowds of a great cosmopolitan hotel" "the woman whom I met with Agate [Pearl] in the picture gallery."

3. GM to Dujardin, 13 May 1894, Hôtel Continental, trans., *Letters to Dujardin*, 34.

4. GM to My dear Lady Eden, 12 June 1894, 8 King's Bench Walk, Bertrand. Moore, *Memoirs of My Dead Life* (1960), 33.

5. Moore, *Memoirs of My Dead Life* (1960), 33–34; *Vale* (1937), 203; George Moore, *Celibates*, 81; GM to Lady Cunard, Monday [23 November? 1925], Hôtel Continental, Hart-Davis, 140.

6. Moore, *Memoirs of My Dead Life* (1906), 154. Maybe the Maud of that earlier meeting is depicted as the young American flirt "Mildred" in the story "In the Luxembourg Gardens": both the fictive and the real woman play music, have sex often and early in life, talk frankly about sex, have a "deflected" line to their chins, and travel widely with a complaisant mother. The narrator of the story, very much GM, took Mildred on an outing from the hotel where they both were guests. They went to a museum, and she interrupted his aestheticising with her confessions about a tall young man with hairy legs, "Lovely! Last night we stood side by side before the glass without a stitch on. I did look a little tot beside him, and it is jolly to put one's hand into a shaggy chest." The narrator admires her as one who had "the courage of her instincts." See "In the Luxembourg Gardens," *Memoirs of My Dead Life* (1906), 225–55.

7. From *Memoirs of My Dead Life* (Tauchnitz: Leipzig, 1906), quoted in Hart-Davis, 13.

8. Nancy Cunard, *GM: Memories of George Moore* (Hart-Davis: London, 1956), 114; John Eglinton, *Irish Literary Portraits* (Macmillan: London, 1935), 100.

9. Robert Becker discovered in R. Burnham Moffat's *The Barclays of New York: Who They Are and What They Did* (R. G. Cooke: New York, 1904) a date of birth for Maud of 31 August 1876; Rupert Hart-Davis notes that the year given on her marriage certificate is 1872 (Hart-Davis, 9).

10. Robert Becker did a thorough job of assembling information about Maud Alice Burke Cunard from the San Francisco *Examiner*, the San Francisco *Chronicle*, the *Social Register*, the New York *Tribune*, and other sources. I am indebted to the results of his research on this as on other occasions (Becker, 954–59).

11. Moore was crestfallen at her refusal to cooperate with Morgan; see GM to Lady Cunard [p.m. 14 May 1931], 121 Ebury Street, Hart-Davis, 189; see also Charles Morgan, "George Moore: A Centenary Appreciation," *Listener*, 47 (28 February 1952): 349–51.

12. Shane Leslie, who had heard Cunard read some of the letters during the war, is certain that she destroyed most of them before her death; see "George Moore in Love," *Time and Tide*, 38 (26 September 1957): 1198–99. Hone was surprised that any of GM's letters to Cunard survived to be published by Hart-Davis: Hone to Nancy Cunard, 28 February 1956, HRHRC. In "Private Moore, Public Moore," Robert Becker suggests that the bulk of the letters may have been deposited in a US bank during the war (*George Moore in Perspective*, ed. Janet Egleson Dunleavy [Malton Press: Nass, Co. Kildare; Colin Smythe: Gerrards Cross, Bucks; and Barnes and Noble: Totowa, NJ, 1983], 83). If a hoard of unpublished letters remains, Sir Noel Guinness, named in Cunard's will as her trustee, would have legal authority over them.

13. William Archer, *The Theatrical "World" for 1894* (Walter Scott: London, 1895), 170–74.

14. GM to Dear Mrs. Leverson [late June? 1894], Adur Lodge, Old Shoreham, University of British Columbia; Becker, 911–13. Becker places the letter between 11 and 21 March; I

think it may be later. GM is replying to Leverson's letter of thanks for *Esther Waters*, and he apologises that it has taken him so long to answer; he has been for some time in Sussex. *Esther Waters* was published on 21 March. No mention is made in the almost daily correspondence of Craigie to Moore in March or April of a trip to Sussex. Moore was in Paris from 12 May, probably for less than a fortnight, before his return to London, where he evidently remained at least until his 12 June letter to Sybil Eden. It can be surmised that Moore spent the final weeks of June at Adur Lodge.

15. Moore's story "A Faithful Heart" – centering on Colville Bridger's secret wife in Brighton – contains a vivid depiction of the sharpness of the two Bridger sisters' treatment of Colville (*Speaker*, 5.120–21 [16 & 23 April 1892]: 469–71).

16. Moore kept his role in the authorship of *The Heather Field* a secret until a quarrel broke out with Martyn over *The Bending of the Bough*; then he told Yeats that he had written "most of 'The Heather Field'" (27 January 1900, *Lady Gregory's Diaries*.)

17. See ibid., 27 January 1900: "Then [Yeats] declares that Moore wrote most of 'The Heather Field' & a great part of 'Maeve' – (a new story) – says Moore told him so & he believes him"; on 28 September 1900, Martyn wrote to GM: "As regards the help you gave me on 'The Heather Field,' much of it was valuable & I am sure I always told you how much obliged I was" quoted in *Lady Gregory's Diaries*, 281 n.236; see also W. B. Yeats, *Memoirs*, ed. Denis Donoghue (Macmillan: London, 1972), 122; W. B. Yeats, *Autobiography* (Collier: New York, 1965), 426. Becker (pp. 1059–63) assembles a case that the play was drafted by Martyn in the early 1890s from a plot synopsis prepared by GM, and then offered to George Alexander just before the producer put on the hit play of the year, *The Second Mrs. Tanqueray*. There is insufficient evidence

to be certain about the date of composition of the play, but the evidence of Moore's collaboration in it is strong.

18. Coincidentally, it seems also to have been in July that Moore, along with Martyn and Milman, dined with Lady Gregory at Nevill Geary's, and a few days later she met "Yates, looking every inch a poet." Yet all these future directors of the Irish Literary Theatre had not yet begun to make common cause (*Lady Gregory's Diaries*, 29–30, 32).

19. George Moore, *Ave* (1937), 34–36.

20. Clement Shorter, ed., *A Pathetic Love Episode in a Poet's Life: Being Letters to Arthur W.E. O'Shanghnessy* (London, 1916); Thomas Wright, *The Life of John Payne* (T. Fisher Unwin: London, 1919), 43.

21. Susan L. Mitchell, *George Moore* (Maunsel: Dublin, 1916), 43.

22. GM to Dear Miss Terry, 11 July 1894, 8 King's Bench Walk, Ellen Terry Memorial Museum; Becker, 933–34.

23. GM to Dear Miss Terry, 18 July 1894, 8 King's Bench Walk, Ellen Terry Memorial Museum; Becker, 933–34.

24. GM to Fisher Unwin, 31 January 1905, 4 Upper Ely Place, *George Moore in Transition*, 292.

25. Many years later, after Craigie sent *Journeys End* to Fisher Unwin for publication as her own unassisted work in *Tales about Temperaments*, Moore raised hell with Unwin. To prove her authorship, Craigie sent the publisher a copy in her own hand of a letter, or part of a letter, written on 25 July, perhaps in 1894, perhaps in 1904: "I am sorry to trouble you, but I should like to know if you are agreeable to the proposal contained in my last letter? – that *you* sign Journeys End, that I *withdraw* my name. (Signed) George Moore" (Berg; Becker, 935–36). The date of the Moore letter is difficult to determine. Moore's explanation to Unwin was that Craigie furnished only a part of a letter written in 1904: "The proposal referred to was that I should relinquish my claim to *Journeys End* on consideration that I should

sign, alone, the play we wrote last year"; i.e. "The Peacock's Feathers" (later *Elizabeth Cooper*, later still *The Coming of Gabrielle*). Moore says she never responded to his proposal. See GM to Fisher Unwin, 6 February 1905, 4 Upper Ely Place, *George Moore in Transition*, 293.

26. Robert Hartford, ed., *Bayreuth: The Early Years* (Cambridge University Press: Cambridge, 1980), 164–68.

27. George Moore, "The Nineness in the Oneness," *Century Magazine* (November 1919); Edouard Dujardin, *Rencontres avec Houston Stewart Chamberlain* (Bernard Grasset: Paris, 1943). The Wagner concerts at Drury Lane are reviewed in the *Times* for 1 July 1892 (15c3). Moore's recollection of the concerts "three years ago" appears in the 20 July 1895 *Speaker* (73–74).

28. GM, "A Reaction," *Speaker* (13 July 1895): 42; Mark Twain, "At the Shrine of Wagner," Hartford, ed., *Bayreuth: The Early Years*, 151. Moore seems to have left the planned tour at Dresden before Martyn's last visit to the Cöln Choir, Martyn's favorite boys' choir (Edward Martyn's Diary, 1859–1921; my thanks to Gerald Nolan); see also Moore, *Ave*, 179.

29. Yeats, *Autobiography*, 426.

30. GM advised Martyn "to do the second act with the theme of the wife trying to shut her husband up in a madhouse," and Martyn added, "critics would probably say I was cribbing from Strindberg's 'Father,'" a play Martyn had not read (Martyn to GM, 28 September 1900, Tillyra Castle, Berg).

31. David B. Eakin and Michael Case, eds, *Selected Plays of George Moore and Edward Martyn* (Catholic University Press: Washington, DC; Colin Smythe: Gerrards Cross, Bucks, 1955), 268.

32. GM to My dear Shorter, 29 August 1894, Hôtel Belle Vue, München, BL; Becker, 936–37.

33. Vincent O'Sullivan, *Opinions* (Unicorn Press: London, 1959), 51.

34. GM to Lena Milman [late September 1894], Hôtel Belle Vue, München, Becker, 937–38.

35. GM to Cunard, September 1928, Hart-Davis, 168.

36. George Moore, *Vale* (1937), 204. The episode is also reflected in *Evelyn Innes*: Owen and Evelyn recall "a lake where they had spent a season five years ago. She saw again the reedy reaches and the steep mountain shores. They had been there in the month of September, and the leaves of the vine were drooping, and the grapes ready for gathering. They had been sweethearts only a little while, and the drive about the lake was one of his happiest memories" (p. 361). Moore revised the page between the first and second editions, both printed in 1898 (my thanks to Edwin Gilcher).

37. The rejected chapter – sometimes incorrectly called the "suppressed chapter" – is an incomplete draft of new material added to the 1906 Tauchnitz edition, which Moore said had been stolen and sold by one of his secretaries (Gilcher, 118). See Moore, *Memoirs of My Dead Life* (Tauchnitz: Leipzig, 1906), 16–20; James Joyce's copy from his Trieste library is at HRHRC.

38. GM to My Dear, 9 January 1906, 4 Upper Ely Place, Hart-Davis, 47–48.

GM stayed into a second week at Aix-les-Bains. Alexis came to visit in order to talk about the forthcoming 20 September Paris production of *Le Sycomore*, ten years after the two had made this French version of Gilbert's *Sweethearts*. GM did not wish to have his name mentioned on the programme; Gilbert's name, Moore advised, should take the place of his own because "the literary situation in England" made it inadvisable for him to be linked in the public mind with the naturalists, but he welcomed his old friend's company. See Alexis to Zola, 17 [September 1894], Monday, Paris, B. H. Bakker, "*Naturalisme pas mort*"; *Lettres inédites de Paul Alexis à*

Emile Zola 1871–1900 (University of Toronto Press: Toronto, 1971), 419.

39. GM to "My dear" [Maud Cunard], 9 January 1906, 4 Upper Ely Place, Hart-Davis, 47–48; W. R. Rodgers, *Irish Literary Portraits* (BBC: London, 1972), 75–93; Oliver St John Gogarty, *Sackville Street* (Abacus/Sphere Books: London, 1988), 74. Jean Noel makes a careful argument that "Orelay" is Aix-les-Bains, not Avignon, in "George Moore and the Dryad: A Reconsideration of 'Lovers of Orelay,'" *Cahiers irlandais*, No. 8 (1983), 37–40, 67 n.8. The scenes of courtship in *Mildred Lawson* and Moore's poem to Cunard entitled "Barbazon" (see p. 247 below) suggest that a romantic visit to Barbizon occurred before January 1895, perhaps even in time for the *fête de Marlotte* given by painters for the poor; Dujardin was involved in the festivities. There is insufficient evidence to be certain where the lovers went after leaving Aix-les-Bains.

40. *Memoirs of My Dead Life* (Tauchnitz: Leipzig, 1906), 203.

41. Ibid., 95.

42. George Moore to My dear Hilda [Hawthorne], 14 September [1907], 4 Upper Ely Place, Berg 52B2494; *George Moore on Parnassus* 139; GM to My dear Hilda, 16 November 1907, 4 Upper Ely Place, Berg, 143. Marcel Prévost's *Les Demi-vierges* was published in Paris in 1894; GM recommended Prévost's books to Ada Leverson and Lena Milman, and Milman scolded him for his taste (Becker, 911–13).

43. For the *fête de Marlotte*, see Stéphane Mallarmé, *Correspondance*, vol. 7, 1894–95, ed. Henri Mondor and Lloyd James Austin (Gallimard: Paris, 1982), 47–48, 48 n.4. GM seems to have drawn upon the scenes and stories of Marlotte for Chapters 14–16 of *Mildred Lawson*; the visit is also commemorated in "Barbazon," his poem addressed to Maud Burke (Becker, 954).

44. GM is unlikely to have read *The Gay Science* at this time (it was not translated into French or into English until 1901), but he could have been given the passage from Section 279 by either Dujardin or Daniel Halévy, both prominent French Nietzscheans. See Patrick Bridgewater, *George Moore and German Pessimism* (University of Durham Press: Durham, 1988), 60.

45. Becker, 954.

46. *Memoirs of My Dead Life* (Tauchnitz: Leipzig, 1906), 23.

47. Margaret Campbell, *Dolmetsch: The Man and His Work* (Hamish Hamilton: London, 1975), 64–65; George Moore, *Evelyn Innes* (1898), Chapter 2; Moore to Dolmetsch [Fall 1894], Saturday, 8 King's Bench Walk, Becker, 941; Craigie to Mr Moore, 30 January 1894, 56 Lancaster Gate, NLI Ms 2135; Sarah Ruth Watson, "George Moore and the Dolmetsches," *English Literature in Transition*, 6 (1963): 65–75.

48. Mabel Dolmetsch, *Personal Recollections of Arnold Dolmetsch* (Routledge and Kegan Paul: London, 1958), *passim*.

49. GM to Gosse [inscribed 30 January 1894], 8 King's Bench Walk, Brotherton; Becker, 902.

50. [Pearl Craigie to GM], [n.d.], 56 Lancaster Gate, NLI Ms 2135; Bishop Welldon, introduction, John Morgan Richards, *The Life of John Oliver Hobbes Told in Her Correspondence with Numerous Friends* (John Murray: London, 1911, second impression), xvii.

51. During the spring of 1895, GM went to hear Benedictine nuns sing plainsong with Huysmans [GM to Maud Cunard, May 1894] Hôtel Continental, Becker, 978. George Frederic Lees told Huysmans that Moore was planning a new novel about "a prima donna who has scruples about the life she is leading and escapes to a convent. Half the book is on the stage, half in the convent." Huysmans did not think that any English convent could supply the writer "with that curious and out-

of-the-way information which was necessary if the reader's interest were to be kept at high tension" (George Frederic Lees, "Recollections of an Anglo-Parisian Bibliophile," *Bookman*, 82 [September 1932], 296–97). For an account of the relations between *Evelyn Innes* and Huysmans's novels that is hostile to Moore, see G. A. Cevasco, "Something Exquisite and Spiritous: J.-K. Huysmans and George Moore," *Research Studies*, 45 (1977): 156–58.

52. "Mr. George Moore on Music and Literature," *Musician*, 1.21 (29 September 1897): 392–94.

53. GM to Stead, 10 October [1894], 8 King's Bench Walk, Becker, 942.

54. W. T. Stead, *Has Sir Charles Dilke Cleared His Character? An Examination of the Report of the Alleged Commission* (*Review of Reviews* Office: London, April 1890); Roy Jenkins, *Sir Charles Dilke: A Victorian Tragedy* (Collins: London, 1968), *passim*. Works by Crawford include *Saint Clothilde*, 1898; *Studies in Foreign Literature*, 1899; *Fra Angelico* (for the Catholic Truth Society), 1900; *Studies in Saintship*, 1903; *Legends of the Saints*, 1907; and *Ideals of Charity*, 1908.

55. GM to My dear friend [Sybil Eden], 4 Ely Place, Bertrand. For the date, see GM to Unwin, 14 March 1896, 92 Victoria Street, *George Moore in Transition*, 124. Virginia Crawford informed Hone that she had first met GM in spring 1897 (Crawford to Hone, 14 February 1935, 35 Campden Street, NLI Ms 2648). It is likely her memory was at fault.

56. GM proposed such a meeting at the time of a planned visit to Monet at Giverny, and Crawford seems to have been willing; see GM to Virginia Crawford [28 March 1900], [inscribed 14 April 1900] and 26 [April 1900], 92 Victoria Street, NLI Ms 2645; Becker, 1276, 1279, 1287. Moore told Barrett Clark that Crawford at first hesitated to have an affair because of the admonitions of her priest; at Rouen, she seemed willing but nothing hap-

pened (Barrett Clark, Notes on George Moore [1923], 86; Berg). It is difficult to conclude from the spring 1900 letters that the two ever made it to Rouen together; Moore seems to have chosen to remain faithful to his writing desk and the revisions of *Evelyn Innes* rather than pursuing the consummation of an affair with his model. In June 1903, "Nia" Crawford went into a convent and, while she did not stay there forever, the temper of their letters afterwards is less intense than during spring 1900 (*Letters to Dujardin*, 47).

57. GM to My dear Lady Eden [late December 1894], 8 King's Bench Walk, Bertrand. The story GM outlines in the letter was not included in the collection.

58. GM to My dear Lady Eden, 7 February [1895], 8 King's Bench Walk, Bertrand.

59. GM to Milman, Wednesday [13/20? February 1895], 8 King's Bench Walk, 965; GM to My dear [Will H.] Dircks, 21 February 1895, private collection; my thanks to Edwin Gilcher; [GM to Milman, late February/early March], Becker, 965, 966. GM added that Symons, Harris, and Martyn all liked the story.

60 George Moore, "Mildred Lawson," galley proofs, pp. 6–7, HRHRC.

61. George Moore, *Celibates*, 6–7.

62. Ibid., 95.

63. Olga Meir, ed., *Daughters of Karl Marx* (André Deutsch: London, 1982), 120–23.

64. Richard Ellmann, *James Joyce*, new and revised edition (Oxford University Press: Oxford, 1982), 187–88.

65. "George Moore at His Worst," *New York Times*, 2 June 1895, n.p.

66. "Celibates," *Bookman*, 8 (April–September 1895): 114.

67. GM to My dear Lady Eden [late December 1894], 8 King's Bench Walk, Bertrand.

68. "Literary Chat," *Munsey's Magazine* (August 1895); my thanks to Edwin Gilcher.

69. Timothy Eden, *The Tribulations of a*

Baronet (Macmillan: London, 1933), 54.

70. [George Moore], "Some Amateur Water-colours," *Saturday Review*, 78.2043 (22 December 1894): 679.

71. GM to Lena Milman, Sunday [31 December 1893], 4 rue de Presbourg, Paris; Becker, 883.

72. Walter Sickert had tried to act as a peacemaker between Whistler and Moore. "Look here," Sickert told "the Butterfly," "Moore is calling you the Champion of Contemporary Art." "The Champion, eh!" Whistler responded. "But he writes about other people too." Whistler was not content to be first above all; he wanted to be the only painter.

73. Ronald Anderson and Anne Koval, *Whistler: Beyond the Myth* (John Murray: London, 1994), 373; see also, Lyall Wilkes, *The Aesthetic Obsession: A Portrait of Sir William Eden, Bt* (Oriel Press: London, Boston, Henley, 1985).

74. Whistler to Mallarmé [15 February 1895], Long's Hotel, New Bond Street, London, Carl Paul Barbier, ed., *Correspondance Mallarmé–Whistler: Histoire de la grande amitié de leurs dernières années* (A. G. Nizet: Paris, n.d.), 240.

75. The English art critic John Ruskin wrote a caustic article about Whistler's 1877 exhibition of "nocturnes," and Whistler, charging slander, sued Ruskin for damages. He won the celebrated case but only insignificant damages, and the expense of the trial forced him into bankruptcy. Selling the contents of his studio, Whistler left England to spend 1879–80 in Venice.

76. "Central Criminal Court, June 2," *Times*, 3 June 1893: 9c5.

77. Harold Frederic, untitled, *New York Times*, 28 May 1893: 2:1; *Hawk*, 1.39 (30 May 1893): 5, 11.

78. GM to Duret, 23 May 1893, 8 King's Bench Walk, Berg; Becker, 803–4. Vincent O'Sullivan claims to have seen GM at Boodle's on the night the trial was concluded, and says that GM was "ravaged" with distress, not for his brother, however, but for himself. There are reasons to doubt this story: elsewhere, O'Sullivan says he had not met GM till the fall of 1894, more than a year later; and there is no evidence that GM was a member of Boodle's in May 1893 (O'Sullivan, *Opinions*, 36–37).

79. GM to Dujardin [inscribed 5 March 1895 and 7 March], Hôtel Continental, Beinecke; Becker, 967.

80. *Pall Mall Gazette*, 29 March 1895: 3; "The Three Mr. Whistlers," *Speaker*, 11.274 (30 March 1895): 349–50. For the character of Vielé-Griffin, a French-American poet, see Vincent O'Sullivan's memoir in the *Dublin Magazine* (January–March 1938): 47–50.

81. Quoted in Anderson and Koval, *Whistler*, 387.

82. Afterwards, GM went back to praising Whistler's pictures ("The New Gallery," *Speaker* [19 October 1895]: 415–16), and Whistler went back to putting an embargo on friends who befriended Moore. He warned W. H. Heinemann not to publish GM, and in October 1896 he cut Sickert for walking in the street with Eden and Moore (American Art Association sale catalogue, 13 January 1922 [Becker, 971]; Anderson and Koval, *Whistler*, 403).

83. GM to Mary Blake Moore, Wednesday [January/February 1895], NLI Ms 4479; Becker, 859.

84. GM to Lena Milman, 23 May [1895], 8 King's Bench Walk, Becker, 982; *Memoirs of My Dead Life* (1906), 297ff.; the story was first published as "My Own Funeral" in the November 1901 *Lippincott's Magazine*.

85. [GM to Sybil Eden], [early June, 1895], Westport, Bertrand. There is evidence to support his despair prior to the funeral, and probably resulting from the loss of Cunard; from Paris, he wrote to Ella Hepworth Dixon: "Notwithstanding very good health, life is not very tenacious in me. I should be rather glad if someone came and blew out my brains": GM to My

dear Miss Dixon [mid-May 1895], 22 Avenue Montaigne, Paris, Becker, 980.

86. Either this Michael Melia (or, as it is sometimes spelt, Malia) or an older one is listed in the 1857 *General Valuation* as holding a lease from G. H. Moore to a tiny plot of 32 perches (not an acre), on which he had a house and garden, and for which he paid 8 shillings a year in rent.

87. *Memoirs of My Dead Life* (Tauchnitz: Leipzig, 1906), 335.

88. The passage on eternal recurrence resembles *The Gay Science* (section 341) and *Thus Spake Zarathustra* (section 57).

When Moore read Nietzsche, and what he read, are difficult to determine; most likely, he read the essays of, or talked with, people who themselves had read Nietzsche, more than he ever consulted French or English translations of the German philosopher: people such as Dujardin, Wyzewa, and Daniel Halévy. His passing acquaintance with the philosophy may date to as early as 1886. Certainly, when Havelock Ellis published a three-part article in the *Savoy* on Nietzsche in April, July, and September of 1896, Moore must have seen it. Unwin's *Cosmopolis* published Stanislaus Rzewuski's "La Philosophie de Nietzsche" in October 1898 (pp. 134–46), and GM wrote for and was reviewed in this journal operated by his publisher. He worked into *Evelyn Innes* Nietzsche's notion of "stellar friendship" (*Evelyn Innes* [1898], 416). In *Ave* GM credits Dujardin with talking to him about Nietzsche (p. 49). Nietzschean conceptions of friendship, the aesthetic life, moral relativism, and eternal return appealed to Moore, but he may only have looked into *Ainsi parlait Zarathoustra* (trans. Henri Albert, 1898), which John Quinn saw on Moore's library table at 6 Upper Ely Place in 1902, and consequently alerted WBY to try to catch up with his then competitor and put Nietzscheanism into his plot for *Where There Is Nothing* (*Letters to W. B.*

Yeats, ed. Richard J. Finneran, George Mills Harper, and William M. Murphy, vol. 1, 106). See Bridgewater, *George Moore and German Pessimism*, 57–77, for the full story.

89. [GM to Sybil Eden], early June 1895], Westport, Bucknell.

90. Maurice and George Moore, NLI Ms 4894.

91. There is no evidence that it was kept a secret from Maurice that GM and Ruttledge planned to break the entail; indeed, GM probably did more than hint that he planned to leave the place to Maurice or his sons. On 15 June 1895, GM wrote Maurice that he had stopped in Dublin [3 June] to see a man at the office of the Moore solicitors, Edward and George Stapleton, "and told him everything." He invited Maurice to join him in London before the end of the "season" (GM to Maurice Moore, 15 June 1895, 8 King's Bench Walk, NLI Ms 2646; Becker 985).

92. GM to Lady Cunard [14 May 1895], Hôtel Continental, Hart-Davis, 21.

93. *Memoirs of My Dead Life* (Tauchnitz: Leipzig, 1906), 26–28.

94. Eden, *Tribulations of a Baronet*, 86.

95. GM to Mary Hunter, 21 July [1895], 8 King's Bench Walk, Washington; Becker, 988; GM to Sybil Eden [7 August 1895], Bertrand; Becker, 966; and a very flirtatious letter not in Becker, GM to [Sybil Eden], [Fall? 1895], Boodle's; club stationery, Bertrand: "we are intimate friends now, we see each other often, but the day will come when we shall no longer be intimate friends, when we shall see each other rarely if ever . . . Then I shall look back upon the present time with the same sad and regretful eyes with which I now look back on the time long ago in Paris. I think I should like to read this reverie to you some day after dinner when you are lying on the sofa."

96. GM to Maurice Moore, Wednesday night [inscribed 14 August 1895], NLI Ms 2646; Becker, 998.

97. GM to Maurice Moore [n.d.],

[Windlestone], NLI Ms 2646; Becker, 1001.

98. Note by Nancy Cunard on a letter from GM's nurse Mrs May Cooper; see Anne Chisolm, *Nancy Cunard: A Biography* (Knopf: New York, 1979), 303; Scrapbook: Reviews of *G. M.*, Ms. Cunard, HRHRC. Nancy wished to remove the question from *GM: Memories of George Moore*. She wrote to the publisher Rupert Hart-Davis on 4 November 1955: "I can't put in that moment about paternity; no. Really, I have thought about this, and – no! That would be friser le bad taste, I think; something for a number of years later, if such were the point. Do you see this?" (HRHRC). In 1922, Barrett Clark wrote that Blanche had been told by GM that Nancy was his daughter (Clark, George Moore and His Friends; Berg, Becker, 958).

99. Book of Gosse, Brotherton.

100. Symons to Herbert Horne [4 September 1895], 2 rue de l'Oranger, Dieppe, Karl Beckson and John M. Munro, *Arthur Symons: Selected Letters, 1880–1935* (University of Iowa Press: Iowa City, 1989), 111.

101. Listed in *Book Auction Records, 1922–1923* [20.1] (Henry Stevens, Son, and Stiles: n.p., n.d.]).

102. R. F. Foster, *W. B. Yeats: A Life; I: The Apprentice Mage 1865–1914* (Oxford University Press: Oxford, 1997), 154, 156. Yeats had moved to Fountain Court by 26 September 1895. See also LWBY1, 475 n.1.

103. Moore, *Ave* (1937), 41. On 23 November 1895, Yeats wrote Gosse that he had been "busy of late working against time at a wretched story which has in the end refused to achieve itself ... " The "wretched story" was not *The Speckled Bird*, the novel he had so much trouble finishing, but did not begin until late February 1896 after he had moved out of Fountain Court, but perhaps a story that if successful would have been added to *The Secret Rose* (pub. April 1897) or one that actually became "Rosa Alchemica" (*Savoy*, April 1896). See LWBY1,

476, 476 n.2; LWBY2, xv, 35 n.2, 36 n.1.

104. Moore, *Ave* (1937), 43–47.

105. GM, "A Reaction," *Speaker*, 12.289 (13 July 1895): 42–43; reprinted as "After Parsifal" as a supplement to the 30 November 1895 *Speaker*.

106. *Oeuvres complètes de Charles Baudelaire*, vol. 1 (Louis Conard: Paris, 1925), 204–9; *Oeuvres complètes de J.-K. Huysmans*, vol. 8 (Slatkine Reprints: Geneva, 1972), 168.

107. *Lady Gregory's Diaries*, 82, 84, 78, 90. Unable to reach a settlement, the conservative Edward was preparing to clear the land and stock it with cattle: Edward's exasperation with his tenants fed into Carden Tyrell in *The Heather Field*.

108. George Moore, Introduction, in Edward Martyn, *The Heather Field and Maeve* (Duckworth: London, 1899), xi–xii. *The Second Mrs Tanqueray* was a success in 1893, before *The Heather Field* seems to have been completed.

109. GM to Archer, Wednesday [January 1895], Boodle's, BL; Becker, 1012.

110. Archer, "Mr. George Moore as a Dramatic Critic," *Daily Chronicle*, 20 January 1890: 3, cc–d.

111. Robert Hichens, *Yesterday* (Cassell: London, 1947), 93.

112. Moore, Introduction, in Martyn, *The Heather Field and Maeve*, xii–xix; GM to the editor, *Daily Chronicle*, 20 January 1899; 25 January 1899: 3, cf–g.

113. GM to Maurice Moore, Friday night [27 September 1895], Boodle's, NLI Ms 2646–2647; Becker, 1002. The reason for the precision of Becker's dating here is not clear.

114. Moore, *Ave* (1937), 67.

115. Moore made the move to Victoria Street between 20 February and 3 March. GM to Maurice Moore, Wednesday [inscribed 6 May 1896], 92 Victoria Street; NLI; Becker, 1026.

116. From an 1890s guidebook, quoted in Ben Weinreb and Christopher Hibbert, eds, *The London Encyclopedia* (Macmillan: London, 1983, 1993), 942.

117. Passing Turgenev's *Smoke* to Mary

Hunter, he lectured her against speed reading: "Of all the vain things quick reading is the vainest. To be able to sit up all night reading is the certain sign of a shallow mind; and it is more profitable to think than to read" (GM to Mrs. Hunter [early 1897], 92 Victoria Street, HRHRC). In an interview published in the *Musician*, he explained, "I do not read for distraction, I read to learn, I read as an expert ..." See "Mr. George Moore on Music and Literature," *Musician*, 1.21 (29 September 1897): 392–94. Later, he did not even read for information; he hired Virginia Crawford to read in the library for him, sent his secretary, or called upon a knowledgeable authority.

118. C. Lewis Hind, *Authors and I* (John Lane: London, 1921), 230–31; C. Lewis Hind, *Napthali* (John Lane: London, 1926), 106.

119. Max Beerbohm, "George Moore," *Listener*, 2 November 1950: 465–67.

120. T. A. McCullogh to [Joseph Hone], 11 Market Place, Bishop Auckland, Washington; GM to Lena Milman, 3 January [1897], Windlestone, *George Moore in Transition*, 136; GM to May [?], 3 January [1897], Windlestone, Becker, 1051; GM to Gosse, Saturday, 92 Victoria Street, Brotherton; Becker, 1058; GM to Mrs Charles Hunter [late December, 1896], Windlestone, HRHRC.

121. Beerbohm, "George Moore"; Eglinton, *Irish Literary Portraits*, 118.

122. Book of Gosse, Brotherton; LWBY2, 36, 36 n.1.

123. GM to Maurice Moore [inscribed 8 July 1896], 92 Victoria Street, NLI; Becker, 1029–30. Becker believes Moore visited Tillyra while on a trip to Moore Hall to deal with his brother Julian's property settlements, but it would seem that if GM had been at Tillyra, the fact would have been mentioned in the autobiographies, diaries, articles, and letters written by Moore, Symons, Yeats, and Lady Gregory. Furthermore, one of the attractions to the area was the French novelist Paul Bourget, who was staying at the Count de Basterot's in Duras; yet Bourget was no attraction for GM, who, when asked his opinion of the French novelist, replied to O'Sullivan, "Bourget is a shit" (*Opinions*, 22); to Gosse Bourget is "a great ass." He added the following scatological poem:

Je haïs les Couilles de Paul Bourget
Un âme énorme que pisse à songre,
Le pauvre Ortmans toche de la légende,
Jaune et verte et horriblement foetide,
S'efface sous les pieds de l'animal
Dont l'urine coule à flots en Pall Mall.
Et le high life de tous les pays du monde
Arrive en dog cart pour boire à cette onde.

GM to Gosse [late November 1896], Wednesday night, 92 Victoria Street, Brotherton.

124. See Pethica's summary, *Lady Gregory's Diaries*, xxv–xxvi.

125. GM to Lady Gregory, 9 March [1897], 92 Victoria Street, Berg; *Lady Gregory's Diaries*, 28 March 1897. Yeats missed the 28 March dinner because of an engagement with Robert Bridges, and Moore was not a successful substitute: "rather paradoxical – & evidently pleased with himself," according to Lady Layard.

126. George Moore, "Mr. Yeats's New Book," *Daily Chronicle*, 24 April 1897: 3.

127. If one takes seriously the hints in *Memoirs of My Dead Life* (Tauchnitz: Leipzig, 1906), GM was separated from Maud for two years after the birth of Nancy, until he ran into Maud while they were driving opposite ways in hansoms on Victoria Street, and later she invited him to visit her in the country. Riding together on a train in the summer of 1897, she allowed him to place his hand on her knee, and sighed, "Well, you've got me again" (p. 113). A 10 September [1897] letter to Cunard written after his return from Bayreuth longs for further meetings:

"All this writing is vain if I am not to see you" (Hart-Davis, 23–24; Becker, 1082).

128. See GM's answer to Martyn, 14 July 1897, 92 Victoria Street, NLI Ms 18275; Becker, 1076; LWBY2, 123.

129. WBY to T. Fisher Unwin, 24 October [1898], Sligo; LWBY2, 2, 279.

130. *Lady Gregory's Diaries*, 149; GM to Lena Milman [late July 1897], 3 Karl Strasse, Berg; Becker, 1079; Havelock Ellis, *My Life* (Heinemann: London, 1940); Symons, "Notes on Wagner and Bayreuth," Papers of A. Symons, Bodleian Ms Walpole, d17.

131. LWBY2, 285 n.6; GM to Martyn, 14 July 1897, 92 Victoria Street, NLI Ms 18275; Becker, 1076.

132. O'Sullivan, *Opinions*, 52.

133. Houston Stewart Chamberlain, *Wagner in Excelsis*, trans. G. Ainslie Hight (Dent: London, 1897).

134. Chamberlain to Dujardin, 21 November 1898, Dujardin, *Rencontres avec Houston Stewart Chamberlain*, 106.

135. Moore, *Vale* (1937), 25.

136. GM to Martyn, Monday [22 November? 1897], Columbia; Becker, 1059–63.

137. Book of Gosse, Brotherton. Symons, Will Rothenstein, and Bertha Newcombe were the others who dined with Gosse on 9 January 1898.

138. Moore, *Ave* (1937), 30–31.

139. Yeats, a poet to beat all patrons, was self-consciously astute in his handling of the wealthy landlord from the West of Ireland. He tried to arrange for Martyn to be installed as chairman at a London Irish Literary Society meeting on 4 December 1897 because it would mean so much "to a man who is not very young & not at all successful . . . Get men so much attention that they will feal [*sic*] that their words are effective & they will go in the path that you have shown them." O cunning rook! See W. B. Yeats to William Sharp, 20 November [1897], 27 South Frederick Street, Dublin, LWBY2, 149. To do him credit, Martyn himself later judged his investment in the ILT the most significant act of his life.

140. Moore, *Ave* (1937), 85.

141. *Lady Gregory's Diaries*, 1 March 1898, 173–74.

142. Yeats, *Autobiography*, 431, 403.

143. *The Bookman*, July 1898, 103–4.

144. George Moore, *Evelyn Innes* (1898), 338.

145. Ibid. 253, 263–64.

146. Yeats, *Autobiography*, 431.

147. GM to Maurice Moore, 18 April [1898], 92 Victoria Street, NLI Ms 2646–2647; Becker, 1132.

148. My guess is that GM met with Symons and Yeats to give them presentation copies of the book on Thursday, 7 June 1898, during WBY's one-week stopover in London betweeen Paris and Dublin; at the earlier possible date, 23 March, the book was not bound; it was not even completely printed until Easter weekend, when it lay in the Unwin office. On 13 June 1898, GM was suddenly discouraged about the novel, telling Unwin, when 7,000 copies were sold, that he wished to alter the text for a second edition (GM to Unwin [13 June 1898], Monday night, 92 Victoria Street, Berg; Becker, 1148). Moore was further disappointed when most reviewers saw the novel as simply the story of a girl with a beautiful voice who elopes with a baronet, gets bitten by religion, and repents. For him it was the story of the helplessness of humans to violate the instinctive grain of their natures: "we do not become mad, we are born mad, and Evelyn was born what she is" (GM to Gosse, Monday [20 June 1898], BL; Becker, 1151).

149. GM to Unwin, Wednesday [20 July 1898], Hôtel Continental, Paris, Berg; Becker, 1165.

150. For the Unwin correspondence, see *George Moore in Transition*, 150–73. GM prevailed upon Yeats to write a farewell letter to Evelyn in the person of Ulick Dean; see LWBY2, 308–10, and notes. Rather than ventriloquise, Moore would often in later years get

the models for characters to write their own parts (Virginia Crawford wrote the letters of Rose in *The Lake*).

151. J. B. Yeats to Lady Gregory, *Letters from Bedford Park: A Selection from the Correspondence (1890–1901) of John Butler Yeats*, ed. William M. Murphy (Cuala Press: Dublin, 1972), 42.

152. GM to WBY, 13 October 1898, 92 Victoria Street, NLI; Becker, 1187.

153. *Daily Chronicle*, 20 January 1899: 3, cc–d.

154. Oscar Wilde to Reggie [Turner], Hôtel des Bains, Napoule, Rupert Hart-Davis, ed., *Letters of Oscar Wilde* (Hart-Davis: London, 1962), 778.

155. "Mr. George Moore Replies," *Daily Chronicle*, 25 January 1899: 3, cf–g. WBY's answer, "Mr. Moore, Mr. Archer, and the Literary Theatre," was published in the 30 January 1899 *Daily Chronicle*.

156. "Mr. Archer, Mr. Moore, and the Stage," *Daily Chronicle*, 26 January 1899: 3, cd.

157. Max Beerbohm to W[illiam] A[rcher], 14 May 1902, 48 Upper Berkeley Street, BL Add. Ms 45290.

158. Clifford Bax, *Florence Farr, Bernard Shaw, W. B. Yeats: Letters* (Dodd, Mead: New York, 1942), 21–22.

159. LWBY2, 356; *Lady Gregory's Diaries*, 210.

160. Moore, *Ave* (1937), 70.

161. *Beltaine* (May 1899): 6–9; Robert Hogan and Michael J. O'Neill, eds, *Joseph Holloway's Abbey Theatre* (SIU Press: Carbondale, 1967), 7.

162. *Lady Gregory's Diaries*, 214.

163. Margaret Webster, *The Same Only Different: Five Generations of a Great Theater Family* (Knopf: New York, 1969), 206.

164. Gerald O'Donovan to Joseph Hone, 26 September 1936, 8 Westbourne Gardens, London, Washington.

165. A reconstruction of the euphemistically reported comment in *Lady Gregory's Diaries*, 220.

166. See the excellent summary of sources in LWBY2 377–84, and notes. The editors propose the identification of Father Cyril Ryan as the censor.

167. Yeats to Gregory, Sunday [9 April 1899], 18 Woburn Buildings, ibid., 390–91.

168. Martyn to GM, 28 September 1900, Tillyra Castle, Berg, quoted in *Lady Gregory's Diaries*, 281 n. 236.

169. Moore, *Ave* (1937), 70; Yeats, *Autobiography*, 415.

170. Edward Martyn to George Moore, 28 September 1900, Tillyra Castle, Berg.

171. Moore, *Ave*, 80.

172. See for instance the review from the 9 May 1899 *Irish Times*, reprinted in Norman Jeffares, ed., *W. B. Yeats: The Critical Heritage* (Routledge and Kegan Paul: London, 1977), 114 ("offends against the tenor of Irish history").

173. "The Irish Literary Theatre," *Freeman's Journal*, 10 May 1899: 5, quoted in Robert Hogan and James Kilroy, *The Irish Literary Theatre 1899–1901* (Dolman Press: Dublin; Humanities Press: Atlantic Highlands, NJ: 1975), 46.

Chapter 10 The Irish Literary Theatre

1. George Moore, *Ave* (1937), 281.

2. George Moore, *Vale* (1937), 179.

3. Moore, *Ave* (1937), 111–17. Tyrrell is identified by Yeats in WBY to Augusta Gregory, 24 January 1910, Allan Wade, ed., *The Letters of W. B. Yeats* (Macmillan: New York, 1955), 547.

4. Moore, *Ave* (1937), 104.

5. Beerbohm said Moore "simply evaporated" in public "George Moore," *Listener*, 64 (2 November 1950), 465–67; Robert Hogan and Kilroy, *The Irish Literary Theatre, 1899–1901* (Dolman Press: Dublin; Humanities Press: Atlantic Highlands, NJ, 1975), 48.

6. W. R. Rodgers, ed., *Irish Literary Portraits* (BBC: London, 1972), 79; James H. and Margaret E. Cousins, *We Two Together* (Ganesh: Madras, 1950), 56.

7. Beerbohm, "George Moore," *Listener*, 465–7.

8. "The Irish Literary Theatre, Dinner at Shelbourne Hotel, Interesting Speeches," *Daily Express*, 12 May 1899.

9. Yeats, however, had read the dawn of a literary revival in just this way a few months before GM's speech: see "The Academic Class and the Agrarian Revolution", *Daily Express*, 11 March 1899, possibly an influence on GM's speech.

10. *Lady Gregory's Diaries*, 247. For the strategic melding of interests in cultural nationalism between republicans, Home Rulers, and constructive Unionists, see Andrew Gailey, *Ireland and the Death of Kindness: The Experience of Constructive Unionism 1890–1905* (Cork University Press: Cork, 1987), esp. 25–69, 136–60. My thanks to Lionel Pilkington for explaining to me the implications of this study for Irish theater.

11. Moore, *Ave* (1937), 117. Judging Yeats to be far greater than Kipling looked absurd to many in 1899; it does not look that way now.

12. GM to Gosse, 11 April [1899], 92 Victoria Street, Beinecke; Becker, 1227.

13. W. L. Alden, "Literary Letter," *New York Times*, 17 June 1899: 388.1; GM to Gosse, 11 April [1899].

14. Gerald O'Donovan to Joseph Hone, 18 July 1935, Washington.

15. GM to Martyn, Friday [28 July 1899], 92 Victoria Street, NLI; Becker, 1238.

16. Vineta Colby, *The Singular Anomaly: Women Novelists of the Nineteenth Century* (New York University Press: New York, 1970), 217; Craigie to Dear Papa, 14 August 1899, 21 Richard Wagner Strasse, Berg; Roger Lhombreaud, *Arthur Symons: A Critical Biography* (Dufour: Philadelphia, 1963), 163; Karl Beckson, *Arthur Symons: A Life* (Clarendon Press: Oxford, 1987); Moore, *Ave* (1937), 166.

17. Gerald O'Donovan to Hone, 18 July 1935, Washington, Hone Accession, Box 1, Folder 23, V253d.

18. Moore, *Ave* (1937), 131.

19. GM to Maud Cunard, 10 February 1899, 92 Victoria Street, Becker, 1115.

20. GM to Maud Cunard, 14 February 1899, 92 Victoria Street, Becker, 1116.

21. George Moore, *Memoirs of My Dead Life* (Tauchnitz: Leipzig, 1906), 32.

22. George Moore, *Sister Teresa* (T. Fisher Unwin: London, 1901), 36.

23. George Moore, *Sister Teresa* (1929), 38; GM to Maud Cunard, Saturday [17 September? 1898], Airlie Castle, Alyth, Becker, 1179; GM to Maud Cunard, 12 October [1898], 92 Victoria Street, Hart-Davis, 28–30.

24. There is a vague allusion to the most painful week of his life, when at Windlestone a woman made him miserable, in GM to Tonks, 28 December 1917, 121 Ebury Street, J. M. Hone, "George Moore and Some Correspondents," *Dublin Magazine*, 22.1 (January–March 1937): 13–14. Moore, *Memoirs of My Dead Life* (Tauchnitz: Leipzig, 1906) also laments that there were "always younger men" (p. 35).

25. GM to Maud Cunard [18 September 1900] Tuesday, Shelbourne Hotel, Hart-Davis, 30–31; Theo Snoddy, *Dictionary of Irish Artists, 20th Century* (Wolfhound: Dublin, 1996).

26. NLI, Genealogical Office, Ms 182. Moore stopped on his way to Holyhead and the Dublin boat to visit Christian at Llanfairfechan, Wales, in July 1900; see Becker, 1304.

27. Moore, *Ave* (1937), 193.

28. Mary Anne Stevens, ed., *The Edwardians and After: The Royal Academy 1900–1950* (Royal Academy: London, 1988).

29. Moore, *Ave* (1937), 178–80.

30. Ibid., 180.

31. Edward Martyn's Diary 1859–1921 (my thanks to Gerald Nolan); George Moore, "Vers," dated "The Hague, 1899," *Daily Express*, 30 September 1899. The poem concerns the portrait of Hélène Froment by Rubens.

32. Moore, *Ave* (1937), 185.

33. Ibid., 216.

34. Ibid., 219.

35. LWBY2, 460.

36. *Lady Gregory's Diaries*, 31 December 1899, p. 223.
37. George Russell, Letters to I. A. P., Lady Gregory [p.m. 12 October 1899], 22 Lincoln Place; and 1 November 1899, Berg 65B1672–73.
38. Douglas Hyde to Augusta Gregory, 19 October 1899, Dublin College Historical Society, Berg 63B0679. Tomas Ua Concheanainn had begun work as the first fulltime Gaelic League organiser in Connaught in August 1899 (*An Claidheamh Solais* [5 August 1899]: 333). This scheme is the mustard seed from which grew *The Untilled Field*, GM's 1903 short story collection first partially published in Irish.
39. LWBY2, 461.
40. Moore, *Ave* (1937), 207.
41. Yeats to My dear Russell, November [1899], Coole Park, Wade, *Letters of W. B. Yeats*, 327.
42. GM to Augusta Gregory [inscribed 6 November 1899], Monday night, Shelbourne Hotel, Berg; Becker, 1245–46.
43. GM to WBY [inscribed 2 November 1899], Shelbourne Hotel, Berg; Becker, 1243.
44. Moore, *Ave* (1937), 222; George Moore, *Salve*, 69; *Lady Gregory's Diaries*, 31 December 1899 and 22 February 1900. Gill was a great help to Moore in illustrating the play's theme that current Irish leaders were all for sale. Gill was angling to get a high-paying secretaryship in the new Irish Agricultural Organisation Society from the Unionist Balfour government, partly by writing private letters about his political stance to Betty Balfour that give an impression that he is a safe man (T.P. Gill to Dear Lady Betty, 4 October 1899, 11 Clare Street, T. P. Gill Papers, NLI Ms 13481[7], and Lady Betty to Gill, 26 November 1899). Moore listened with amusement to Gill, a former nationalist, rationalising his decision to work for the Unionist Plunkett under a Conservative government. Gill read GM his letter to Arthur Balfour, and GM then, tongue in cheek, gave him the push he

wanted: "But you leave it to Balfour to decide whether you should accept . . . Remember your wife and children" (*Salve*, 68–69). On 3 January 1900, Martyn wrote to congratulate Gill, for his children's sake, on getting the appointment (NLI Ms 13482 [1]).
45. These identifications are largely the work of Gould, Kelly, and Toomey, in LWBY2, 497 n.3.
46. GM to Edward Martyn, n.d., Shelbourne Hotel, NLI Ms 18275, property of J. J. Horgan. This considerate touch did not indicate that GM intended to show any mercy to what remained of Edward's part in *The Tale of a Town*. Once back in London on 23 November 1899, GM negotiated terms according to which T. Fisher Unwin would be permitted to bring out an edition of the play (proofs within a fortnight; issue date of 19 February 1900; 15 percent royalty; UK rights only; no copies under list price), just as if it was his own absolute property. See GM to Unwin, Thursday night [23 November 1899] and [4 December], 92 Victoria Street, Berg; Becker, 1248, 1250. The terms are far more to the author's advantage than was normal then or now.
47. GM to Yeats, Friday, 92 Victoria Street, NLI; Becker, 1241.
48. James Joyce, *A Portrait of the Artist as a Young Man*, ed. Hans W. Gabler with Watton Hettche (Garland: New York and London, 1993), 281.
49. LWBY2, 537; W. B. Yeats, *Autobiography* (Collier, New York, 1965), 431.
50. Ibid., 479.
51. Edward Martyn to T. P. Gill, 3 January 1900, Reform Club, London, NLI Ms 13482 (1).
52. WBY to Augusta Gregory, 4 January [1900], 3 Blenheim Road, Bedford Park, LWBY2, 485–86.
53. For the date of GM signing and retitling the play, see *Lady Gregory's Diaries*, 24 January 1900 (p. 227). WBY to Augusta Gregory [18 January 1900], 18 Woburn Buildings, LWBY2 489–90. Moore met Martyn at the Reform Club and told him, Martyn

recalled, that GM "had changed it all, that it was no longer my play, that it was no longer my play except the subject, & that it would not be fair to ask me to sign" (Martyn to GM, 28 September 1900, Tillyra, Berg).

54. Lady Gregory, *Seventy Years: Being the Autobiography of Lady Gregory*, ed. Colin Smythe (Colin Smythe: Gerrards Cross, Bucks: 1974), 353.

55. *Lady Gregory's Diaries*, n.d., 259.

56. Ibid., 24 January 1900; 26 January. Moore had known Herman de Lange since 1883; de Lange was one of his informants about theatrical life during the composition of *A Mummer's Wife* (see above, Chapter 4).

57. *Lady Gregory's Diaries*, 28 January 1900 (p. 231).

58. LWBY2, 492–93.

59. *Lady Gregory's Diaries*, 19 March 1900 (p. 260).

60. Moore, *Salve* (1937), 92. Gregory was, for Martyn, "the old proselytizer" because her mother, Mrs Dudley Persse, had been "of the extreme Irish evangelical school," and believed that the "way to gain credit with the Almighty was to try & convert R. Catholics – or at least turn them against their own religion." Augusta Gregory did not approve of her mother's proselytising (*Lady Gregory's Diaries*, 111).

61. GM signed the Nevill Holt visitors' book on 2 February 1900 (Ms Nancy Cunard, Misc. Notes for GM, HRHRC).

62. *Lady Gregory's Diaries*, 4 February 1900 (p. 236).

63. *Three Men in a Boat* is a popular comic novel by Jerome K. Jerome. In "An Unreported Rehearsal," "Imaal" burlesques *Shadowy Waters* in a similar way. When the director [Yeats], after putting the actors in barrels to focus attention on voice-production, next demands that they "celticize" the acting, the lead actor speaks his part in Irish, throwing the rehearsal into confusion (*Leader*, 5.15 [6 December 1902]: 242–43).

64. Moran crowed about the conversion of Moore in "The Battle of Two Civilisations," *New Ireland Review* 13.6 (March 1900): 330.

65. ". . . but not drink Irish": the language movement was linked up with the anti-drink movement: Father O'Donovan's Loughrea chapter of the Gaelic League, for instance, met on off-nights in the rooms he had established for his chapter of the Total Abstinence Association.

66. Hyde to Augusta Gregory, 12 October 1899, Ratra, Co. Roscommon, Berg 63B0678.

67. Hyde to Augusta Gregory [p.m. 14 November 1899], Berg 65B0681; in an undated letter from the Shelbourne Hotel (possibly November 1899, late February 1900, or still later), GM thanked MacNeill for his "admirable letter" and proposed a £5 literary prize for Irish schoolchildren, and a lecture tour in Ireland (NLI Ms 10882); George Roberts, "Memoirs of George Roberts: George Moore in Dublin," *Irish Times*, 19 July 1955: 5. My thanks to Roy Foster.

68. The facts of the Boer War are widely available, for instance in R. C. K. Ensor's *England, 1870–1914* (Oxford University Press: Oxford and New York, 1936, 1992).

69. LWBY2, 461 nn.7, 9.

70. When in Mooltan in the late 1880s, Maurice found it hard to live on his income as a sub-adjutant, one rank below captain (undated letter to his mother). On 1 March 1890 he was trying to get an Australian appointment in the army (£100 a year for five years), but was disappointed; Maurice Moore to dear Mother, Connaught Rangers, Dinapore, India, NLI Ms 10566(2). GM tried to cultivate relations with Asquith, Balfour, George Wyndham, and Harry Cust ("the Souls"), in order to get Maurice Moore an appointment; he failed. See GM to Maurice Moore, 29 July 1895, Boodle's, NLI Ms 2646–2647; Becker, 990.

71. Becker, 1245.

72. D. S. MacColl, *The Life, Work, and Setting of Philip Wilson Steer* (Faber

and Faber: London, 1945), 66; Moore, *Ave* (1937), 84, 226; GM to Unwin, Thursday night [inscribed 23 November 1899], 92 Victoria Street, Berg; Becker, 1248.

73. William Rothenstein, *Men and Memories: Recollections of William Rothenstein, 1872–1900* (Faber and Faber: London, 1931), 170.

74. *Lady Gregory's Diaries*, 15 February 1899 (p. 233).

75. Arthur Machen, "Mr. George Moore and His Friends," *Evening News*, 11 March 1914: 6cd.

76. *Lady Gregory's Diaries*, 28 January 1900 (p. 241).

77. A compliment deleted from her diaries when she printed *Seventy Years* (p. 358). See also Moore, *Ave*, 250.

78. Holloway, Diaries [17 February 1900], NLI Mss 1798–1808.

79. Ibid. [19 February 1900].

80. David B. Eakin and Michael Case, *Selected Plays of George Moore and Edward Martyn* (Catholic University Press: Washington, DC; Colin Smythe: Gerrards Cross, Bucks, 1995), 296, 289–91.

81. Hogan and Kilroy, *Irish Literary Theatre*, 74–76.

82. *Lady Gregory's Diaries*, 22 February 1900 (p. 244); the praise was repeated by Hyde in his Gresham luncheon speech, *Freeman's Journal*, 23 February 1900: 6. "Poor Edward" came to see Augusta Gregory, and, though sad, honorably pointed out it was good luck *Bending* went so well, because it would "save the venture" in which they were all engaged. "There his real goodness comes out," she noted in her diary for 20 February. She performed another human service by asking Moore to thank Edward for his large contribution to the play in a letter to the press, and GM said he would. Both good deeds came to nothing: four days later Martyn denounced *The Bending of the Bough* and swore he would in future pay only for his own plays. *Lady Gregory's Diaries*, 20 February 1900 (pp. 243, 245).

83. Moore, *Ave*, 215.

84. In Rodgers, *Irish Literary Portraits* (p. 86), Magee says that Augusta Gregory introduced him to Moore at "a picture-show in Dublin about the year 1898." GM did not come to Dublin in that year, and Gregory herself did not meet Magee until December 1898, but Magee was recorded by Gregory as attending Jack Yeats's "picture-show" on 24 February 1990, along with many others, including, it is likely, George Moore (*Lady Gregory's Diaries*, 246). In Moore's arrangement of his experience in *Ave*, he places the meeting with Magee in May 1899, after the performance of a play – not *The Bending of the Bough* but *The Heather Field*.

85. Reverend Hamilton Magee, DD, *Fifty Years in "The Irish Mission"* (Religious Tract and Book Depot: Belfast, 1905), 10. Magee won the Vice-Chancellor's Prize for verse in 1889 and 1890, and for English prose in 1892 and 1893, but he did not take his degree with honors (see the *Dublin University Calendar* [Hodges, Figgis: Dublin] for those years).

86. Moore, *Ave* (1937), 125.

87. Rodgers, *Irish Literary Portraits*, 86.

88. LWBY2, 495 n.3.

89. As a Gaelic Leaguer, Moore was like a new convert to Christianity who thinks he is called upon to quit work (neither toil nor spin), avoid funerals (let the dead bury their dead), and give away the family money; some Christian would have to take the credulous believer aside to explain that it was not necessary actually to *do* anything. Literalistic Christianity, *à la The Idiot*, is the *donnée* of *Where There Is Nothing* (1902), a play that Yeats wrote with Augusta Gregory, John Quinn, and Hyde, after breaking off a collaboration on it with GM.

90. Declan Kiberd, "George Moore's Gaelic Lawn Party," in Robert Welch, ed., *The Way Back: George Moore's The Untilled Field and The Lake* (Wolfhound Press: Dublin, 1982), 15.

91. In the *New York Times*, Arthur Ditmar thought GM's Irish enthusiasms, in

the preface to *Bending*, "grave foolery," "his paradoxes outdo Bernard Shaw's," yet "some folks suspect Moore takes himself seriously" ("At the Play with the Players," 1 April 1990: 18).

92. GM to Maurice Moore, [23 February 1900], Shelbourne Hotel, NLI Ms 2646–47; Becker, 1259–60.

93. GM to Douglas Hyde, Tuesday night [19? June 1900], 92 Victoria Street, Becker, 1292–93. Such was Maurice Moore's enthusiasm for Irish that by April 1903 Hyde would lobby for his election to the leadership of the Gaelic League, the Coisde Gnótha, and project him as its future Vice-President (Hyde to Eoin MacNeill, 26 April 1903, quoted in Michael Tierney, *Eoin MacNeill* [Clarendon Press: Oxford, 1980], 75).

94. LWBY2, 499–500; GM's letter was published in the *Times* and *Freeman's Journal* on 14 March 1900; in other Irish papers on 17 March.

95. *Diaries of Lady Gregory*, 255.

96. WBY to editor, *Freeman's Journal*, 20 March 1900, LWBY2, 502–4.

97. *Diaries of Lady Gregory*, 8 April 1900 (p. 265).

98. WBY to Augusta Gregory, 29 March [1900], Wade, *Letters of W. B. Yeats*, 337.

99. GM to Ellen Gosse, n.d., 92 Victoria Street, Cambridge; Becker, 1278.

100. W. B. Yeats, "Noble and Ignoble Loyalties," *United Irishman*, 21 April 1900.

101. GM to the editor, *Freeman's Journal*, 16 April 1900: 6.

102. GM to James Burton Pond, 2 June 1900, 92 Victoria Street, Becker, 1294. GM was drunk on a new idea. "I have completely changed since you last saw me," he wrote to Maurice Moore, who was giving him bitter accounts of the English tactics against Boers: "what once seemed wrong now seems right and what once seemed right now seems wrong." GM offered to pay all costs of the children's education if Maurice would let Rory and Toby Moore be brought up as Irish-speakers. When Maurice left the army,

GM proposed that they could all live together "in Dublin or in Moore Hall." See GM to Maurice Moore [late April 1900], NLI Ms 2646–2647; Becker, 1286.

103. GM to Maurice Moore, Saturday, 92 Victoria Street; NLI; Becker, 1290.

104. Douglas Hyde to Augusta Gregory, Ratra, Co. Roscommon, Berg 65B0693; GM to Douglas Hyde, Tuesday [5 June 1900], 92 Victoria Street, NLI; Becker, 1296.

105. Russell to Augusta Gregory, 24 May 1900, 25 Coulson Avenue, Dublin, Berg 65B1676.

106. Yeats to Augusta Gregory [2 June 1900], 18 Woburn Buildings, Wade, *Letters of W. B. Yeats*, 344–45.

107. Yeats to Augusta Gregory [5 June 1900], LWBY2, 532–534.

108. GM to Virginia Crawford, 5 July 1900, Queen's Hotel, Llanfairfechan, NLI; Becker, 1305; GM, letter to editor, *An Claidheamh Solais*, 14 July 1900.

109. The prizes and the Irish play are mentioned in GM to Augusta Gregory, 11 August 1900, 92 Victoria Street, Berg; Becker, 1321.

110. GM to Augusta Gregory, 16 August 1900, 92 Victoria Street, Berg 65B2341.

111. GM to Evelyn Moore, 14 July [1900], 92 Victoria Street, NLI; Becker, 1309.

112. William L. Alden, "London Letter," *New York Times*, 12 April 1902.

113. Edmund Gosse, letter to editor, *Times*, 19 July 1900: 11.

114. Moore, *Ave* (1937), 262.

115. The visionary painting expeditions of Yeats and Russell were giving Robert Gregory nightmares of deracination. He dreamt that painting fairies would spoil his eyesight, so that he would lose the power to play cricket (*Lady Gregory's Diaries*, 23 July 1900, p. 275).

116. GM to Fisher Unwin, 1 March 1900, 92 Victoria Street, Berg; Becker, 1265.

117. GM to Virginia Crawford, Wednesday [28 March 1900], Saturday [inscribed 14 April 1900], Thursday 26 [April 1900], and Tuesday night [inscribed 8

May 1900], all from 92 Victoria Street, NLI Ms 2645; Becker, 1276, 1279, 1287, 1289.

118. She is ennobled by her dedication to "the intense yet involuntary life of the soul – that intricate and unceasing life, incomprehensible as an ant heap, and so personal though it is involuntary" (Moore, *Sister Teresa* [1900], 207).

119. GM to Augusta Gregory, 16 August 1900, 92 Victoria Street, Berg 65B2341.

120. GM to Lady Cunard, Tuesday [18 September 1900], Shelbourne Hotel, Hart-Davis, 30–31; George Russell to Augusta Gregory, 8 August 1900, 22 Lincoln Place, Berg 65B1630.

121. Russell to Augusta Gregory, 23 August 1900, Berg 65B1682; Russell to Augusta Gregory, 24 August 1900, 25 Coulson Avenue, Rathgar, Berg 65B1683.

122. John Eglinton, *Irish Literary Portraits* (Macmillan: London, 1935), 52.

123. John Eglinton, *A Memoir of AE: George William Russell* (Macmillan: London, 1937), 34, 37–38.

124. Henry Summerfield, *That Myriad-Minded Man: A Biography of George William Russell, "A.E."* (Rowan and Littlefield: Totowa, NJ, 1975; Colin Smythe: Gerrards Cross, Bucks, 1975), 106.

125. Moore, *Salve* (1937), 58. Moore used to nettle Russell by saying, "'What your pictures lack is . . . quality' – a word which always puzzled . . . Russell" (Eglinton, *Memoir of AE*, 56).

126. Moore, *Salve* (1937), 29; Yeats to Fisher Unwin, Monday [7 January 1901], 92 Victoria Street, Berg; Becker, 1343.

127. Eglinton, *Memoir of AE*, 69.

128. GM to WBY, 30 July 1900, Berg; Becker, 1318; GM to Augusta Gregory, 11 August 1900, 92 Victoria Street, Berg; Becker, 1321.

129. Hyde appreciated this and GM's other efforts for the Irish language: "George Moore is really a brick to have worked so hard for us," he wrote Augusta Gregory on 23 September 1900 (Berg 650700).

130. *Lady Gregory's Diaries*, 21 September 1900, p. 279.

131. Moore, *Salve* (1937), 263–67.

132. *Lady Gregory's Diaries*, 2 October 1900, p. 280.

133. Moore put his irritation with Yeats about style directly into *Sister Teresa*, where Harding says he knew Hugo and Turgenev, and they never spoke of "style": "the gods do not talk theology"; that's left to the lesser clergy (p. 17).

134. Gould, Kelly, and Toomey note that GM's telegram on 22 September – "picturesque description of the times turbulent fianna" – was an inflammatory warning that Yeats had violated his own prohibition against the picturesque (LWBY2, 570 n.1).

135. *Lady Gregory's Diaries*, 280 n.232; LWBY2, 580.

136. Russell to Augusta Gregory, 26 September 1900, 22 Lincoln Place, Berg 65B1686.

137. WBY was not the only censor of style; on 13 October, Lady Gregory went over the play "altering Moore's words" (*Lady Gregory's Diaries*, 281).

138. Yeats to Augusta Gregory, Friday [26 October 1900], 18 Woburn Buildings, LWBY2, 580–81.

139. *Diaries of Lady Gregory*, 288.

140. LWBY2, 585, 587–88.

141. W. B. Yeats, *The Variorum Edition of the Plays of W. B. Yeats*, ed. Russell K. Alspach (Macmillan: London and New York, 1966), 1176. In the Texas manuscripts, Grania's line – "Oh, that another should clasp this delicate body, and that these breasts should belong to another" – is deleted, and WBY has written in: "that these breasts should belong to another, and the sacred usage of this body" (William Butler Yeats, Diarmid [*sic*] and Grania. A play in three acts. Typed carbon copy, HRHRC; see also Yeats and Moore, Diarmid and Grania; HRHRC). Moore was evidently satisfied with how Symons played his part as mediator: on 6 January 1901 he sent Symons two Degas lithographs as a

wedding present (Beckson, *Arthur Symons*, 214).

142. LWBY2, 597–98.

143. Vincent O'Sullivan, *Opinions* (Unicorn Press: London, 1959), 49.

144. Ensor, *England, 1870–1914*, 345.

145. GM to Nia Crawford [inscribed 18 October 1900], 92 Victoria St, NLI Ms 2645; Becker, 1332.

146. GM to W. T. Stead, Saturday [3 November 1900], 92 Victoria Street; Becker, 1334; *Lady Gregory's Diaries*, 18 November 1900, p. 289. Stead also used information from Maurice Moore in *How Not To Make Peace: Evidence as to Homestead Burning, Collected and Examined by W. T. Stead* (London, December 1900). See Joseph Baylen, "George Moore, W. T. Stead, and the Boer War," *University of Mississippi Studies in English*, 3 (1962): 49–60. Moore's account in *Ave* (pp. 280–82) and repeated by Hone (*List of George Moore*, p. 225) puts the event out of chronological sequence, changes the place of publication to the *Freeman's Journal*, and suppresses Maurice's authorship (one function of all these divagations from the facts).

147. Baylen, "George Moore," 57.

148. Though G. S. Street, William Archer, and Dr Barry thought *Sister Teresa* a great novel, comparable with Huysmans, Flaubert, or Tolstoy, and the *Freeman's Journal* approved of its treatment of Catholicism, the book was still banned by W. H. Smith. Admittedly, the book contains a heated if vague description of Evelyn masturbating and descriptions of her difficulties in doing without sex, but the ban was probably again part of Moore's old quarrel with the circulating libraries. See "News of the Week," *New York Times* (31 August 1901), and "Literary Letter," *New York Times* (7 September 1901): 635. For the scene with Gosse, see George Moore, *Communication to My Friends*, 81.

149. In his review of *Parnell and His Island*, Barry O'Brien referred to GM as a "night-soil novelist" (*Truth*, 11 August 1887: 246).

150. LWBY2, 609–10, 615–20; LWBY3, 49–50. See also the *Dublin Daily Express* (19 January 1900). Hyde was not so exercised over the rejection of Moore: the Irish Literary Society, he observed, is "not like a . . . French Academy," "more a social than a literary club" (Hyde to Augusta Gregory, 31 December 1900, Berg 650715).

151. Yeats resigned in March 1901, and was then reinstated as an honorary member (LWBY1, 496).

152. R. F. Foster, *W. B. Yeats: A Life, I: The Apprentice Mage 1865–1914* (Oxford University Press: Oxford, 1997), 236–37; LWBY2, 622.

153. LWBY3, 3–4.

154. Moore, *Salve* (1937), 11; Hyde to Augusta Gregory [p.m. 14 January 1900], Berg 650717.

155. Hyde to Augusta Gregory [p.m. 29 January 1901], Berg 657019.

156. 14 January 1901, A Dublin Playgoer's Impressions, NLI Mss 1798–1808.

157. *Lady Gregory's Diaries*, 14 January 1901, p. 296.

158. Ibid., 20 January 1901, p. 297; Moore, *Vale* (1937), 168; Moore, *Ave* (1937), 281–82.

159. In a 22 December 1900 review of T. W. Rolleston's *A Treasury of Irish Poetry in the English Tongue*, Moran said there was no such poetry; it was English poetry if it was in the English tongue; what is more, "Celtic symbolists" like Yeats could never touch the heart of the true Catholic Irish people. See LWBY3, 6 n.1; Hyde to Augusta Gregory [p.m. 7 January 1901], and [p.m. 14 January 1901], Berg 650716.

160. "Literary Expression," *Leader*, 19 January 1901, quoted in LWBY3, 19–20, n.5. The *Leader* especially hated Yeats's hound with one red ear in "The Wanderings of Ossian" (7 September 1901, p. 27).

Yeats thought Moran was just a puzzled, self-taught man; such men "value nothing but the obviously useful, the obviously interesting, the obviously forcible" (LWBY3, 18–20). Moran kept up the abuse, writing about Yeats six months later: "he sometimes writes poetry which no Irishman understands; or rather which no Irishman troubles his head to read; he thinks Catholics are superstitious and he believes in spooks himself; he thinks they are priest-ridden and he would like to go back to Paganism; he is a bigot who thinks he is broad-minded; a prig who thinks he is cultured; he does not understand Ireland – a fact which would not be of much import if he did not firmly believe that he is a philosopher." See "Protestants and the Irish Nation," *Leader*, 2.22 (27 July 1901): 342.

161. John Hughes to Sarah Purser; Sunday [20 Jan? 1901; possibly April/May], 28 Lennox St, Alan Denson, *John Hughes: Sculptor, 1865–1941* (Alan Denson: Kendal, 1969), 140. St Brendan's Cathedral was to be a completely neo-Celtic building, largely funded by Edward Martyn and his cousins, the Smyths of Masonbrook. The making of the stained-glass windows was overseen by Sarah Purser; the banners were by the Yeats sisters; the whole project was managed by Father Gerald O'Donovan.

162. Oliver St John Gogarty, "Next Door to George Moore," *Saturday Review* (18 July 1936): 3.

163. GM to Virginia Crawford, 29 April [1901], 4 Upper Ely Place, NLI Ms 2645; *George Moore on Parnassus*, 93.

164. Russell to Augusta Gregory, 6 May 1901, Berg 65B1692.

165. Hyde to Augusta Gregory, 20 April 1901, Berg 650725.

166. F. C. Moore, "George and Mr. Moore," *John O'London's Weekly* (28 April 1950): 268.

167. Yeats, *Autobiography*, 445.

168. GM to Virginia Crawford, 14 May 1901, 4 Ely Place, NLI Ms 2645; *George Moore on Parnassus*, 95. Yeats to Augusta Gregory, Tuesday [21 May 1901], LWBY3, 72; Susan Mitchell, *George Moore* (Maunsel: Dublin, 1916), 109; Yeats, *Autobiography*, 444.

169. Mark Bence-Jones, *Twilight of the Ascendancy* (Constable: London, 1987), 59.

170. *Lady Gregory's Diaries*, 29 May 1901, p. 307.

171. *Thom's Official Directory* (Alex. Thom: Dublin, 1902), 1422. Stephen Cunningham was the former owner of the Ship Hotel in Lower Abbey Street, a caustic wit with a thorough knowledge of Dublin civic life; he had written a weekly column about Dublin life (*Irish Times*, 23 April 1908: 9).

172. [T. P. O'Connor], "George Moore in Dublin," *M. A. P.* (12 October 1901): 355–56; Ella Young, *Flowering Dusk: Things Remembered* (Longmans, Green: 1945), 93.

173. Russell to Augusta Gregory, Friday [5 July 1901], Berg 65B1693.

174. GM, "The Culture Hero in Dublin Myths," *Leader*, 2.21 (20 July 1901): 329–31.

175. Moore *Salve* (1937), 118; Douglas Hyde to Augusta Gregory, 21 July 1901, Berg 650734; Maurice Moore to Hone, 8 January 1935, 5 Sea View Terrace, Dublin, NLI Ms 2648.

176. Yeats to Augusta Gregory [5 June 1900], LWBY1, 532–34.

177. GM to Virginia Crawford, 14 May 1901, 4 Ely Place, *George Moore on Parnassus*, 95–96.

178. LWBY3, 70–72.

179. Moore, *Salve* (1937), 81.

180. The League feared that the priests who were its chief support would not approve of actresses traveling about the country "unprotected." (Moore claims to have replied, "girls are seducing young men . . . and old men, too, for that matter, all over the world, and every hour of night and day"; why should this hold up the important object, the revival of the language?)

181. LWBY3, 74–75. Yeats, however, was canny enough to tell Frank Fay, "I wish very much that my work were for the Irish language" (pp. 97–99).

182. Huneker thought GM looked like "a golden crested bird, with a chin as diffident as a poached egg, and with melancholy pale blue eyes, and an undecided gait" ("The Seven Arts by James Huneker," *Puck*, 75.1938 [25 April 1914]: 17).

183. GM to Yeats, Tuesday [3 September? 1901], Hôtel Continental; Charles Joseph Burkhart, ed., "Letters of George Moore to Edmund Gosse, W. B. Yeats, R. I. Best, Miss Nancy Cunard, and Mrs. Mary Hutchinson", diss. (University of Maryland, 1958), 273; Moore, *Salve* (1937), 77.

184. "The Irish Literary Theatre," *Freeman's Journal* (13 September 1901): 5.

185. GM to Douglas Hyde, 17 September 1901, Hogan and Kilroy, *Irish Literary Theatre*, 93–94.

    Moore evidently did not know everything about the training of dogs.

    After taking Moran for a walk up Grafton Street, where GM demanded goods of Irish manufacture in the fashionable shops, Moran wrote an article approving of GM's choice of Elgar as composer ("The Irritation of Mr. George Moore," *Leader*, 3.5 [28 September 1901]: 79–80).

186. Hyde to Augusta Gregory, 22 September 1901, Berg 650740.

187. Moore, *Salve*, 79; GM to Fisher Unwin, 27 September 1901, *George Moore in Transition*, 220; Hyde to Augusta Gregory [p.m. 2 October 1901], Berg 650743.

188. W. G. Fay and Catherine Carswell, *The Fays of the Abbey Theatre* (Rich and Cowan: London, 1935), 114–15; GM to Augusta Gregory, 10 October 1901, Berg 65B2341. Even after Fay was hired, rehearsals were not held when GM could not be present; see Hyde to Augusta Gregory [p.m. 12 October 1901], Berg 65B0745.

189. J. C. Trewin, *Benson and Bensonians* (Barrie and Rockcliff: London, 1960), 130–31. On 16 October 1901, Yeats vented his disgust not at the actors but at the audience: "Here we are, a lot of intelligent people . . . going through all sorts of trouble & annoyance for . . . ignoramuses who prefer Boucicault, an audience, a mob that prefers . . . the *Freeman's Journal* to [Ruskin?], a mob that knows neither literature nor art. I might have been away in the country, in Italy perhaps, writing poems for my

equals & my betters" (LWBY 3, 117). In fact, Yeats stayed with Ireland and its theater well past the time of Moore's departure for Dublin.

190. Yeats abused the English actors at the curtain call, until Mrs Benson, herself three parts Irish, pulled him by the coattails backstage and told him off. See F. R. Benson, *My Memoirs* (1930), 311.

191. Joseph Holloway, Diaries, 21 October 1901, NLI. Holloway fantasised: "I have always been told that Irish is a splendid language to make love in, or abuse, & having heard Dr. Hyde, I can well believe it."

192. Quoted in Hogan and Kilroy, *Irish Literary Theatre*, 105.

193. "By the Way," *Freeman's Journal* (24 October 1901). See also the *Leader*'s 2 November assault on the "heartless vandalism" of the legend (pp. 155–58). GM vigorously counterattacked in "On the Thoughtlessness of Critics," *Leader*, 3.11 (9 November 1901): 174–76, in which he showed that at bottom the plot of Hyde's play was the same as the plot of *Diarmuid and Grania*, and sadly ridiculed Moran for attempting to be "the most perfectly virtuous man in Ireland."

194. Quoted in *Life of George Moore*, 239.

195. Gifford Lewis, ed., *Selected Letters of Somerville and Ross* (Faber and Faber: London, 1989), 154.

196. In spite of this epitaph, the ILT Committee discussed a fourth year throughout November (Daniel Murphy, ed., *Lady Gregory's Journals*, vol. 2 [Oxford University: Oxford and New York, 1987], 528).

197. *Freeman's Journal* (8 November 1901): 4.

198. *Freeman's Journal* (13 November 1901): 5–6; GM repeated his support for censorship by the Archbishop the following day in the same paper (p. 4).

199. Yeats, *Autobiography*, 299.

200. "The Dublin Stage: Letter from His Grace, the Archbishop," *Freeman's Journal* (19 October 1901): 5, cf. reprint of shorthand report of speech

given on 26 November 1900 at St Margaret's Church.

201. In his review of "A Year's Work for 'The *Leader*,'" Martyn said he "cannot but deplore" the "denunciation of symbols" but that was forgivable because "a less truculent paper" would not have served Ireland so well (*Leader*, 3.1 [31 August 1901]: 12). One can picture Martyn chuckling as Moran made it hot for the Protestant Yeats.

202. Edward Martyn, "Dublin At Last the Capital of Ireland," *Leader*, 3.15 (7 December 1901): 238–39.

203. LWBY3, 120 nn. 1–2.

204. Ibid., 119–21.

205. Richard Ellmann, *James Joyce*, new and revised edition (Oxford University Press: Oxford, 1982), 147.

206. Moore, *Salve* (1937), 118, 121; *Letters to Dujardin*, 14.

207. GM to Fisher Unwin, 3 October 1901, 4 Upper Ely Place, *George Moore in Transition*, 220. Later Taidgh O'Donoghue and Padraig O Suilleabain took over the translation.

208. *New Ireland Review*, 13.2 (April 1901): 65–72; Moore, *Salve* (1937), 114–18.

209. P. Finlay, SJ, "Religion and Civil Life," *New Ireland Review*, 14.6 (February 1900): 321–33.

210. Moore, *Salve* (1937), 110.

211. Like "The Wedding Gown," "Almsgiving" and "The Clerk's Quest" are stories from *The Untilled Field* long previously published in English magazines, and they are the only ones Father Finlay published; see Gilcher, 63.

212. This naturalistic analysis of fairy folklore anticipates Hubert Butler's great essay, "The Eggman and the Fairies," in R. F. Foster, ed., *The Sub-Prefect Should Have Held his Tongue and Other Essays* (Penguin: London, 1990), 102–12.

213. O'Donovan told Hone that after the spring 1901 work began on statuary and stained glass for St Brendan's, he saw Moore "at least once a week, sometimes twice or more, at Ely Place," always between Tuesday and

Friday (Washington). O'Donovan defended Yeats and Moore in the *Leader* on 7 December 1901 (249), the period when the *Untilled Field* was being written. See also John F. Ryan, "Gerald O'Donovan, Priest, Novelist, and Intellectual: A Forgotten *Leader* of the Irish Revival," MA thesis (University College Galway, 1983).

214. Lawrence J. Taylor, *Occasions of Faith: An Anthropology of Irish Catholics* (Lilliput Press: Dublin, 1997), 64.

215. Emmet Larkin, *The Historical Dimensions of Irish Catholicism* (Catholic University of America Press: Washington, DC; Four Courts Press: Dublin, 1997), 27, 78, 83.

216. Thomas P. Kennedy, "Church Building," *The Church since Emancipation* (Gill and Macmillan: Dublin, 1970), 8; Larkin, *Historical Dimensions*, 35.

217. Moore, *Salve* (1912), 331.

218. Denson, *John Hughes*, 424–25; Beatrice Lady Glenavy, "*Today We Will Only Gossip*" (Constable: London, 1964), 26–27.

219. GM to Virginia Crawford, 19 August 1902, 4 Upper Ely Place, *George Moore on Parnassus*, 105. He expanded this critique while revising proofs for *The Untilled Field* on 16 December 1902: "I am tired of priests, the religious orders absorb the country, all is trade . . . My book is a plea for the harmless and necessary laity. After all, celibates cannot continue a country" (ibid., 107).

220. Cousins and Cousins, *We Two Together*, 69–70.

221. Welch, ed., *The Way Back*, 21; GM to Maurice Moore, n.d., *Life of George Moore*, 240.

222. Letter from Moore to Hyde enclosed in Hyde to Augusta Gregory, 13 February 1902, Berg 65B0755–56.

223. Robert Hogan and James Kilroy, *Laying the Foundations, 1902–1904; The Modern Irish Drama, a Documentary History II* (Dolmen Press: Dublin; Humanities Press, Atlantic Highlands, NJ, 1976), 20–24; Janet Egleson Dunleavy and Gareth W. Dunleavy, *Douglas Hyde* (University of

California Press: Berkeley and Los Angeles, 1991), 221–22.

224. GM to Hyde, 28 March 1902, Hogan and Kilroy, *Laying the Foundations*, 25; "I thought Moore a great big child," Hyde later reflected, "but when he came to Dublin he certainly set us all an example of hard work" (*Life of George Moore*, 224).

225. GM to Hyde, 29 March 1902, Hogan and Kilroy, *Laying the Foundations*, 26.

226. The little bit of gall in his cup of pleasure was the protest by the London delegates to the Oireachtas against having anything to do with George Moore, and Hyde conceded to their request that a statement be printed in *An Claidheamh Soluis* saying that the League Committee had nothing to do with the lawn party. See Hyde to Augusta Gregory, 13 May 1902, Berg 65B0766.

227. After the performance, Sinead ni Fhlanagain (1878–1975) asked Moore if he thought she had a career on stage; he replied, "Height, five feet four; hair, red; name, Flanagan. No, my dear" (quoted in LWBY3, 186 n.10).

228. GM to Mark Fisher [20? May 1902], 4 Upper Ely Place, NLI; *George Moore on Parnassus*, 101–2 (misdated there); *Life of George Moore*, 240; J. B. Yeats to WBY [22 May 1902] quoted in LWBY3, 186 n.10.

229. LWBY3, 166–69.

230. Ibid., 169.

Chapter 11 George Moore in Dublin

1. LWBY3, 200–2; Adrian Frazier, *Behind the Scenes: Yeats, Horniman, and the Struggle for the Abbey Theatre* (University of California Press: Berkeley and Los Angeles, 1990), 54–59.

2. George Moore, *Salve* (1937), 169.

3. GM to Kuno Meyer, 27 May [1902], 4 Upper Ely Place, quoted in Séan O Lúing, *Kuno Meyer, 1858–1919: A Biography* (Geography Publications: Dublin, 1991), 19. Meyer had been

appointed the outside assessor; the Board would not trust a Gaelic Leaguer. Meyer edited and translated *Liadan and Curithir* in 1902 and published the work with David Nutt in London; it was reviewed in the *New Ireland Review*, 19.3 (May 1903): 190.

4. Hyde, Moore, and Yeats, to the editor, *Times* (London), 27 June 1902: 11; reprinted in LWBY3, 212–14. See also John Eglinton's recollection of this journey in *Irish Literary Portraits* (Macmillan: London, 1935), 53.

5. "In the Seven Woods," dated August 1902, Yeats, *In the Seven Woods* (Dun Emer Press: Dundrum, 1903), 1.

6. LWBY3, 209.

7. Moore, *Salve* (1937), 97–98. Yeats sent these two one-acts, the first a miracle play, the second a folk play, to Fay on 24 July 1901, after completing them at Coole with Augusta Gregory (LWBY3, 99–102).

8. AE, *The Living Torch* (Macmillan: London, 1937), 155.

9. "Could only find god . . . ," from James Cousins, reported in Holloway, Diaries, 8 January 1903 (NLI); AE to Augusta Gregory, 29 April 1902, 22 Lincoln Place, Berg 65B1698; AE, "The Sunset of Fantasy," *Dublin Magazine* (January–March, 1938): 8.

10. Charles Burkhart, Letters of George Moore to Edmund Gosse, W. B. Yeats, R. I. Best, Miss Nancy Cunard, and Mrs. Mary Hutchinson (University of Maryland dissertation, 1958), 265.

11. AE to Augusta Gregory [August? 1902], 25 Coulson Avenue, Berg 65B1709.

12. Eglinton, *Irish Literary Portraits*, 131, 137.

13. James Joyce, *Ulysses* (Random House: New York, 1961), 192, 195.

14. Oliver St John Gogarty, "Next Door to George Moore," n.p., Joseph Hone, ed., *J. B. Yeats: Letters to his Son W. B. Yeats and Others* (London, 1944), n.p. GM developed the idea much later into a successful play, *The Making of an Immortal* (1927).

15. W. R. Rodgers, ed., *Irish Literary Por-*

traits (BBC: London, 1972), 90–93. When GM heard Kelly was being paid only 10 shillings a week by her employment agency, he raised her wages to £2 a week (p. 84).

16. Gogarty, "Next Door to George Moore," 16, gives "dogs" as the pet in question; Israel Shenker, "For Colum at 90, Tributes and Memories of Ireland," *New York Times* (8 December 1971); W. B. Yeats, *Autobiography* (Collier: New York, 1965), 445.

17. Walter Osborne to My dear Stoker, Saturday [19 July 1902], Hill Cottage, HRHRC.

18. AE to Sarah Purser, 15 August 1902, 22 Lincoln Place, Irish Homestead, NLI Ms 81149.

19. Richard Ellmann, *James Joyce*, new and revised edition (Oxford University Press: Oxford, 1982), 89.

20. AE to Yeats, Monday [?11 August 1902], 22 Lincoln Place, Alan Denson, ed., *Letters from AE* (Abelard-Shuman: London, New York, Toronto, 1961), 43. James Joyce, *The Critical Writings*, ed. Ellsworth Mason and Richard Ellmann (Cornell University Press: Ithaca, NY, 1989), 71. Joyce soon showed Moore greater respect than in "The Day of the Rabblement"; in "Ireland, Island of Saints and Sages," he called Moore "an intellectual oasis in the Sahara of false spiritualistic, Messianic, and detective writings whose name is legion in England" (p. 171).

21. A. J. Solomon, "A Moore in Ulysses," *James Joyce Quarterly*, 10 (1973): 217.

22. Ellmann, *James Joyce*, 135.

23. [James Sullivan Starkey, 1879–1958], George Moore [notes], HRHRC.

24. E. H. Mikhail, *The Abbey Theatre: Interviews and Recollections* (Barnes and Noble: Totowa, NJ, 1988), 23.

25. Not only Joyce, but James Starkey, James Stephens, and W. K. Magee (John Eglinton) made pilgrimages to Paris, and there sought out the haunts of Verlaine. See W. K. Magee to James Starkey [p.m. 1908], postcard of Verlaine, HRHRC. The "French letters"

pun comes from Malachi Mulligan in *Ulysses* (pp. 214–15).

26. Moore, *Salve* (1937), 273; Col. Maurice Moore, "George Moore," copybook 2, p. 22, NLI Ms 10565.

27. *Galway Observer*, 23 August 1902; George Moore, *Memoirs of My Dead Life* (1906), 75. It is unknown if this Father Considine was the parish priest of Ardrahan mocked by Moore in *A Drama in Muslin* (1893) (see Chapter 5, p. 117). There were five Father Considines in the Irish clergy at the time.

28. Yeats, *Autobiography*, 404; LWBY3, 456 n.3.

29. One account of the complications may be found in LWBY3, 228.

30. AE to Augusta Gregory [early September 1902], 25 Coulson Avenue, Berg 65B1711. About the human tendency to "play act," GM made the following epigram: "We are never altogether natural; the educated cannot be. Even dogs are actors; only cats are themselves and nothing but themselves" (George Moore, *Conversations in Ebury Street* [1930], 129).

31. WBY to Augusta Gregory, 19 September 1902; dedicatory letter, *Where There Is Nothing* (John Lane: New York, 1902); LWBY3, 232.

32. WBY to Augusta Gregory [6 October 1902], Nassau Hotel, Dublin, LWBY3, 233–34.

33. WBY to Quinn, 22 October [1902], Coole Park, LWBY3, 238; see also 243–44; and esp. R. F. Foster, *W. B. Yeats: A Life, I: The Apprentice Mage, 1865–1914* (Oxford University Press: Oxford, 1997), 272.

34. Hyde to Augusta Gregory [pm 14 October 1902] and 23 October 1902, 35 Harcourt Street, Berg 65B0780 and 81. Lane was seeking a contribution from Moore for the Loan Exhibition at the Royal Hibernian Academy (8 January 1903); Moore lent *Portrait of Rachel* by Thomas Couture (1815–79). See Holloway, Diaries (NLI), 8 January 1903.

35. LWBY3, 241.

36. AE to Augusta Gregory [25 November 1902], 25 Coulson Avenue, Berg 65B1710.

37. Foster, *The Apprentice Mage*, 267.

38. WBY and Augusta Gregory to John Quinn, 8 November [1902], Nassau Hotel, LWBY3, 243–44.

39. WBY to Sydney Cockerell, 17 October [1902], Coole Park, LWBY3, 236; Yeats, *Autobiography*, 454.

40. GM to Archer, 4 November 1902, 4 Upper Ely Place, BL, Add. Ms 45293. Not liking Archer's translation, Moore repeated the request to Virginia Crawford on 11 December 1902 (*George Moore on Parnassus*, 106, 107); Nietzsche quotation is from that letter, probably Archer's text amended by GM.

41. Testifying to a Committee of Inquiry into art education in Ireland, GM was asked about the Royal Hibernian Academy's traveling scholarships. He replied: "Yes, Hughes got two scholarships and went to Paris. That was an excellent thing for Hughes; but what benefit it is to the nation that Hughes should reside in Paris I am a little at a loss to see. Hughes is a great friend of mine, and I think he merited his scholarships." Maybe he would return? Moore was asked. "People who want to paint pictures go to Paris. People who want to become priests come to Ireland: why people should come to Ireland to paint pictures I can't understand." See "Report of the Committee of Inquiry into the Work Carried on by the Royal Hibernian Academy and the Metropolitan School of Art, Dublin," Parliamentary Papers. xxxi. Cd. 3256 (1906), 27–29.

42. AE to Joyce [mid-November 1902], 22 Lincoln Place, Denson, ed., *Letters from AE*, 44; John Hughes to Sarah Purser, Alan Denson, ed., *John Hughes: Sculptor, 1865–1941* (Alan Denson: Kendal, 1969), 143.

43. GM to Mark Fisher, 31 December 1902, 4 Upper Ely Place, *George Moore on Parnassus*, 108–9.

44. GM to Virginia Crawford [11 Febuary 1903], Hôtel Continental, Paris, ibid., 110.

45. GM to Dujardin, 5 May 1903, *Letters to Dujardin*, 46.

46. Sickert to Steer, n.d., Robert Emmons, *Life and Opinions of Walter Richard Sickert* (Lund Humphries: London, 1941), 89–90.

47. GM to Tonks, 26 March 1902, 4 Upper Ely Place, Joseph Hone, "George Moore and Some Correspondents," *Dublin Magazine*, new series 22 (1947), 10.

48. O'Donovan to Hone, 9 August 1935, Washington.

49. AE to John Quinn, 13 February 1911, Denson, ed., *Letters from AE*, 72.

50. O'Donovan to Hone, 9 August 1935, Washington: O'Donovan says he saw Moore "at least once a week, sometimes twice or more," "except for winters in London after 1904," until October 1909 when O'Donovan moved to London permanently. J. O'Donovan, "Priests as Nation-Builders," *Record of the Maynooth Union 1900–1901* (Dublin), 45–55; quoted in John F. Ryan, "Gerald O'Donovan: Priest, Novelist, and Irish Revivalist," *Journal of the Galway Archaeological and Historical Society*, 48 (1996): 30. Apparently the lecture Joseph Holloway heard O'Donovan give to the National Literary Society on 25 March 1901 was nearly identical to the Maynooth Union talk (Holloway Diaries, NLI). John O'Grady, *Life and Work of Sarah Purser* (Four Courts: Dublin, 1996), 95.

51. Ryan, "Gerald O'Donovan," 4, 34–35.

52. Horace Plunkett Diary, 30 October 1904, Plunkett House, Oxford, quoted in John F. Ryan, Preface, in Gerald O'Donovan, *Father Ralph* (Brandon: Dingle, Co. Kerry, 1993), ix; GM to Unwin, 1 November 1904, *George Moore in Transition*, 289; O'Donovan's essay "The Churches and the Child" was subsequently published in Unwin's monthly, *Independent Review* (February 1905), as noted by Ryan, "Gerald O'Donovan," 37.

53. John Hughes to Sarah Purser [April? 1901], 28 Lennox Street, Denson, ed., *John Hughes: Sculptor*, 140–41, 143.

54. Beatrice, Lady Glenavy, *"Today We Will Only Gossip"* (Constable: London, 1964), 26–27.

55. Eglinton, *Irish Literary Portraits*, 96.
56. Moore, *Salve* (1937), 121; GM to Magee, 7 February 1928, HRHRC; the relevant passage, a sketch by Moore for Eglinton's essay on Moore, is deleted from Eglinton's edition of Moore's letters (Eglinton, p. 79).
57. Eglinton, 4.
58. Eglinton, *Irish Literary Portraits*, 92.
59. Lady Glenavy, "*Today We Will Only Gossip*", 41–42. An Tur Gloine opened January 1903. Moore liked to ask Sarah Purser how it could be that so stupid a woman as Sarah Cecilia Harrison should paint so well and so clever a person as Miss Purser herself should paint so badly (JBY to Rosa Butt, 10 October 1908, Bodleian Ms. Eng. Litt. Fol. e87); for the identification of Purser as author of this oft-cited quip, see F. S. L. Lyons, "George Moore and Edward Martyn," *Hermathena*, 98 (1964): 13.
60. George Moore, *Vale* (1937), 332; Jeanne Sheehy, *Walter Osborne, 1859–1903* (Town House: Dublin, 1991) and *Walter Osborne* (Gifford and Craven: Cork, 1974), 58.
61. GM to Mark Fisher, 24 April 1903, *George Moore on Parnassus*, 110.
62. JBY to Charles Fitzgerald, 30 January 1905, 7 St Stephen's Green, Joseph Hone, ed., *J. B. Yeats: Letters to His Son W. B. Yeats and Others* (Faber and Faber: London, 1944), 81–82. JBY was already a friend of Moore's by 23 March 1902 when he wrote WBY about reading his short story to Moore and gaining his commendation (Hone, ed., *J. B. Yeats* 70). JBY painted GM's portrait from September 1905 to January 1906. See William M. Murphy, *Prodigal Father: The Life of John Butler Yeats (1839–1922)* (Cornell University Press: Ithaca, New York, 1978), 286.
63. R. I. Best to Kuno Meyer, [17 April 1914], R. I. Best Papers, NLI Ms 11002 (61).
64. Orpen came to visit Moore at Ely Place and came away "glowing with Manet from head to foot": Orpen to My dearest wife, Monday [July?

1903], Oriel, Blackrock, Orpen Archive, NGI.
65. Orpen to his wife [*c.* 27 January 1907], ibid.
66. GM to Virginia Crawford, Sunday [25 May 1902], 4 Upper Ely Place, *George Moore on Parnassus*, 112. See also GM to Sybil Eden, 9 June [1903], Bertrand. Fisher may have lodged not with Moore, but near Christian's Tymon Lodge in Tallaght (*George Moore on Parnassus*, 111). One clear day in County Dublin, Moore was curious to see what Fisher, who loved a dappled sky, would do with his picture. Fisher worked with industry and skill for an hour, but then a cloud came into the sky, and at once Fisher became interested; Moore could not help smiling when he said, "I think this picture will come out rather nicely, don't you?" (J. M. Hone, interview with George Moore, *c.* 1912, HRHRC).
67. GM to Virginia Crawford, Sunday [11 May 1902], 4 Upper Ely Place, *George Moore on Parnassus*, 111. Later in the year, Moore wrote a very positive review of Filson Young's anti-Catholic *Ireland at the Crossroads: The Tragedy of a Nation* (*Daily Mail* [24 November 1903]: 4cd).
68. Robert Welch, ed., *The Way Back: George Moore's* The Untilled Field *and* The Lake (Wolfhound Press: Dublin, 1982), 25; Lyons, "George Moore and Edward Martyn," 23; the review of *The Untilled Field* in *New Ireland Forum* is untraced.
69. *Letters to Dujardin*, 46–47.
70. Mikhail, *The Abbey Theatre*, 344–45; Holloway, Diaries, 22 June 1903 (NLI).
71. Moore, *Conversations in Ebury Street* (1930), 156.
72. Pádraig Colum, "Early Days of the Irish Theatre," *Dublin Magazine*, 24 (October 1949): 11–17; Mikhail, *The Abbey Theatre*, 60.
73. See Ben Levitas, "Irish Theatre and Cultural Nationalism 1890–1916," Ph.D. diss. (Oxford University, 1997).
74. Bruce Arnold, *Orpen: Mirror to an Age* (Jonathan Cape: London, 1981), 130.

75. GM to Sybil Eden, 6 July [1903], 4 Upper Ely Place, Bertrand.

76. GM to Mark Fisher, 18 August 1903, *George Moore on Parnassus*, 112.

77. Moore, *Salve* (1937), 205.

78. *The Moores of Moore Hall*, 219.

79. Maurice Moore, "George Moore," NLI Ms 10565.

80. GM to Dujardin, 10 July 1903, *Letters to Dujardin*, 47–48.

81. Moore, *Salve* (1937), 266; *Life of George Moore*, 249; *Thom's Official Directory* (Alex Thom & Co.: Dublin, 1902), 1422.

82. Susan L. Mitchell, *George Moore* (Maunsel: Dublin and London; Dodd, Mead: New York, 1916), 117.

83. *Irish Times*, 24 September 1903: 5; reprinted in George Moore, *Hail and Farewell*, 669–70; Moore, *Salve* (1937), 274–77.

84. *New York Times*, 17 October 1903: 742; Kate Carew, Interview with W. B. Yeats, *New York World*, magazine section, 3.

85. "George Moore and Roman Catholicism," *Irish Times*, 25 September 1903: 5.

86. See Frazier, *Behind the Scenes*, 64–108. Synge's play was performed with Yeats's *The King's Threshold*, a fable demanding the submission of politics (the King) to literature (the Bard Seanchan) by ancient Irish right. Moore deprecated Yeats's stagecraft to Padraic Colum: "W. B. Yeats saw 'Everyman' where one does something or wants to do something & a lot of people come & try to prevent him doing it; & then he went off and wrote 'The Hour-Glass' . . . & now 'On the King's Threshold' follows the same lines, & yet some think Yeats a dramatist" (Holloway, Diaries, 14 October 1903, NLI).

87. The precise date of the Countess's first letter is unknown; GM dated a copy of *The Untilled Field* inscribed to her "November 1903."

88. The whole correspondence may be read in an excellent edition by David Eakin and Robert Langenfeld, *George Moore's Correspondence with the Mysterious Countess* (English Literary Studies: University of Victoria, 1984).

89. GM to Dujardin, 5 April 1904, *Letters to Dujardin*, 50.

90. George Moore, Elizabeth Cooper, page proofs with A corrections, 2–3 December 1904, HRHRC.

91. Moore, *Vale* (1937), 202.

92. Oliver St John Gogarty, *As I was Going Down Sackville Street: A Phantasy in Fact* (Rich and Cowan: London, 1937), 125; Richard Allen Cave, "George Moore's 'Stella'," *Review of English Studies*, 28 (1977): 181–88.

93. Nevill Holt visitors' book, MS Nancy Cunard, HRHRC; Hart-Davis, 36–37.

94. Hart-Davis, 31–33; Seymour Leslie, *The Jerome Connection* (John Murray: London, 1964), 93; Gogarty to G. K. A. Bell [27 August 1904], the Tower, Sandycove, O. Gogarty, *Many Lines to Thee: Letters to G. K. A. Bell* (Dolmen: Dublin, 1971), 32.

95. Frank Fay to Mary Garvey (NLI Ms 8320).

96. WBY to Augusta Gregory, 3 August 1904, Nassau Hotel, LWBY3, 630.

97. WBY to Archer, 23 August [1904], Coole Park, ibid., Gogarty, 639; *Many Lines to Thee*, 32.

98. For Beerbohm's comparison of the Abbey players with the exotic Negroes playing "In Dahomey," see Foster, *The Apprentice Mage*, 318–19.

99. "Paul Ruttledge," "Stage Management at the National Theatre," *Dana*, 5 (September 1904): 152; Holloway, Diaries, 27 October 1908, NLI.

100. Frazier, *Behind the Scenes*, 175–79.

101. GM to Gogarty, 2 September [1904?], 4 Upper Ely Place, Gogarty Collection, 795, Bertrand.

102. GM to Virginia Crawford, 7 September [1904], Steephill Castle, Ventnor, Isle of Wight, George Moore on Parnassas, 117.

103. GM to Dujardin, *Letters to Dujardin*, 52–54.

104. GM to Dujardin, 4 February 1905, ibid., 55–56.

105. *Life of George Moore*, 254–55; Stanley Weintraub, *The London Yankees: Portraits of American Writers and Artists in*

England, 1894–1915 (London: W. H. Allen, 1989), 70–71.

106. Pearl Craigie to John Morgan Richards, 30 July 1904, 56 Lancaster Gate, Folder 24, Berg 65B3402.

107. Gerald O'Donovan to Hone, 26 September 1936, Washington.

108. Virginia Crawford to Hone, 14 February 1935, 35 Campden Street, NLI Ms 2648; for the offensiveness of GM's conversation at Ventnor, see Craigie to Unwin, 1 February 1905, quoted in Vineta Colby, *Singular Anomaly: Women Novelists of the Nineteenth Century* (New York University Press: New York, 1970), 218) – "My sister-in-law and my cousin (young married women) were terrified by his conversation. The Vicar-General of Southwark was also much disgusted."

109. *Freeman's Journal*, 13 December 1904: 4.

110. *Observer*, 7 January 1917: 10.

111. Moore, *Hail and Farewell*, 529.

112. Lyons, "George Moore and Edward Martyn," 21.

113. Holloway, Diaries, 9 December 1904, NLI.

114. *Daily Express*, 9 December 1904: 5.

115. Robert Hogan and Michael J. O'Neill, eds, *Joseph Holloway's Abbey Theatre: A Selection from his Unpublished Journal "Impressions of a Dublin Playgoer"* (Southern Illinois University Press: Carbondale and Edwardsville, 1967), 48.

116. Pearl Craigie informed her father that she "had reduced Moore to order & Bourchier is delighted. All the same, Moore has behaved disgracefully & B. will *not* have him in the theatre" (Pearl Craigie to John Morgan Richards, 4 December 1904, 56 Lancaster Gate, Berg 65B3402).

117. *George Moore in Transition*, 289–90, and *passim*.

118. LWBY3, 679. There is a set of these page proofs, with author alterations, and dated 2–3 December 1904, at HRHRC. Moore had James Starkey print his copy of the mss at Ballantyne Press (see Gilcher, 88). This December 1904 period of reconciliation is a

likely date for Starkey's anecdote about a visit of WBY to GM's Saturday "At Home," when Moore turned the company's attention to the Golden Treasury of Dublin Limericks he wished to assemble. Was the final line of "There was a young man of St. John's, Who used to roger the swans, O no said the porter, Oblige with daughter, But the swans are reserved for the dons," really supposed to be "The birds are reserved for the dons"? "With a wicked gleam in his pale blue eyes, [Moore] turned to the poet and asked him to give a judgement on the respective merits of the two versions." With "one long delicately fashioned hand raised in the air as he chanted softly, *Swans are reserved, Birds are reserved,*" Yeats made a "slow and deliberate decision, 'Birds, Moore, birds.'" James Sullivan Starkey, George Moore, HRHRC. Gogarty's 12 December 1904 letter to Bell mentions a visit by Yeats to GM's "the other Saturday," when Yeats recited parts of "Deirdre" (*Many Lines to Thee*, 54).

119. Moore came through with a 5 December 1904 *Daily Express* letter attacking the Royal Hibernian Academy for not keeping the Loan Exhibition on display into January; Yeats followed up with a letter supporting GM on 6 December.

120. Friedrich Nietzsche, *The Gay Science*, trans. Walter Kaufmann (Random House: New York, 1974), 275.

121. Moore, *Vale* (1937), 111.

122. Moore, *Hail and Farewell*, 651.

123. But JBY thought GM belonged in Paris or London; for Ireland "he is too surprising." See J. B. Yeats to Rosa Butt, n.d., Letters 56 and 57; Bodleian, Ms Eng. Litt. Fol. e87.

124. *Observer*, 8 December 1917: 10.

125. See Moore's campaign against the bad taste of Henry Tate in the February/March 1892 issues of the *Speaker*, 5, nos 111, 113, 115.

126. Not long after Moore's lecture, Augusta Gregory provided some damage control on this point in a *Freeman's Journal* article, which

assured readers that the Hugh Lane Municipal Gallery would not be a Tate or Chantry "over again," since only the best pictures from the collection would be kept, and they would set a standard for others to be added, a "criterion," as GM called it in his lecture ("A Stone for the Building," *Freeman's Journal*, 13 December 1904: 5).

127. Augusta Gregory had compared the Modern Art Gallery to the Irish Literary Theatre, the Gaelic League, and the School of Irish Learning ("A Stone for the Building").

128. "Sunset at Malahide": a crack by Moore about Nathaniel Hone, dean of Irish painters (1831–1917), who worked in France for seventeen years with Corot and Millet, then settled at Malahide and painted beach scenes for the next forty years. See, for instance, *Gathering Seaweed on the Strand at Malahide* (NGI).

129. Moore, *Hail and Farewell*, 662.

130. Ibid., 652–53, 663. Alongside the *Freeman's Journal* report of GM's speech appeared a report about another speech, this one by the Protestant Archbishop Gaffney asking Catholics not to apply for the empty position of nurse at the Mullingar Lunatic Asylum, so that the Protestant mad (though a minority, he pointed out) could be looked after by a Protestant keeper (*Freeman's Journal*, 9 December 1904: 5).

131. GM to Augusta Gregory, 2 January 1905, Berg; the letter, signed by WBY, Augusta Gregory, AE, Martin Ross, Edith Somerville, and others, was printed in the 5 January 1905 London *Times* and *Irish Times*.

132. Oliver St John Gogarty, *Rolling Down the Lea*; reprinted in *Sackville Street*, 74.

133. "Broken Dreams," in Richard Finneran, ed., *Collected Poems of W. B. Yeats* (Macmillan: New York, 1989), 153.

134. Eglinton, *Irish Literary Portraits*, 135.

135. Stanislaus Joyce's journal for 2 February 1904; quoted in Ellmann, *James Joyce*, 147.

136. GM to Dujardin, 17 March 1904, 23 Maddox Street, Hanover Square, London, *Letters to Dujardin*, 49–50.

137. George Moore to editor of the *Daily Chronicle*, *Dana* Publishing Offices, 26 Dawson Chambers, Dublin, NLI Ms 24998. A similar letter to the editor of the *Academy* is at HRHRC; a third asking for free advertisement was sent to Fisher Unwin on 27 February 1904 (*George Moore in Transition*, 285).

138. Moore, *Memoirs of My Dead Life* (1906), 75.

139. GM to Maud Cunard, 27 October [1904], 4 Upper Ely Place, Hart-Davis, 46.

140. GM to Maud Cunard, 9 January 1906, 4 Upper Ely Place, ibid., 47–48.

141. Moore, *Memoirs of My Dead Life* (1906), 201.

142. Michel Foucault, *Ethics, Subjectivity, and Truth*, ed. Paul Rabinow, *Essential Works of Foucault 1954–1984*, vol. 1 (New Press: New York, 1997), 150.

143. My thanks to Cliodhna Carney of the National University of Ireland, Galway.

144. Moore may have stolen the name of his hero from Oliver St John Gogarty as revenge for Gogarty's refusal to give his name to "Stage Management at the Irish National Theatre." When Gogarty's mother took umbrage, however, Moore gave a different rationale: "But, Madam, if you can supply a name with two such joyous double dactyls, I will change it" (Gogarty, *Sackville Street*, 306). Joyce would have been able to supply him with those dactyls – "Malachi Mulligan," the name of Gogarty in *Ulysses*.

145. Moore was writing the final section of *The Lake* just as O'Donovan was throwing up his parish duties in Loughrea and seeking advice on how to support himself by his pen (GM to Dujardin, 13 September 1904, *Letters to Dujardin*, 52), yet only the general theme of the book, the probing, troubled thoughtfulness of its hero, and the particular sort of new vocation he envisions seem to have been based on O'Donovan's life. The final inci-

dent of the priest's swim across the lake was taken from a real incident in the life of an Irish Catholic priest, one Father Connell, whose published account of it Moore had read (O'Donovan to Hone, 26 September 1936, Washington). O'Donovan did not apparently denounce a lovely music teacher from his Loughrea altar, nor did he minister to a handful of the faithful in a small County Mayo village. The Loughrea Cathedral was a considerable place of worship in a busy County Galway market town, and the scope of O'Donovan's activist ministry was international. However, like Father Gogarty he did dream of becoming a writer, and once O'Donovan left Loughrea in September 1904, Moore aided him in this ambition. GM had Pearl Craigie call on O'Donovan in late 1904 after the priest took rooms at 24 Palace St, Buckingham Gate, London. Moore also asked Fisher Unwin to give O'Donovan some work as a publisher's reader (GM to Unwin, 1 November 1904, 4 Upper Ely Place, *George Moore in Transition*, 289). O'Donovan did not find the free secular life an easy one; he nearly starved in 1909, eking out a marginal life between Dublin and London as Horace Plunkett's part-time secretary before getting his career as a novelist launched with *Father Ralph* (1913), his own story of the unmaking of an Irish priest. See John Ryan, "Gerald O'Donovan," MA thesis (University College Galway, 1983).

146. Anne Coffin Hanson, *Manet and the Modern Tradition* (New Haven and London: Yale University Press, 1977): 167.

147. Tamara Garb, "Gender and Representation," *Modernity and Modernism: French Painting in the Nineteenth Century*, ed. Francis Frascina (New Haven and London: Yale University Press, 1993), 273.

148. Morisot wrote to her sister Edma: "Manet sermonizes me and proposes that tiresome Mlle Gonzales as an example; she has self-discipline, perse-

verance, she knows how to see a thing through to the end, whereas I am capable of nothing. In the meantime, he has done her portrait over for the twenty-fifth time . . ." (quoted in Beth Archer Brombert, *Edouard Manet: Rebel in a Frock Coat* [New York: Little, Brown, 1996], 249).

149. GM to Cunard, 9 January 1906, Hart-Davis, 48.

150. As High Sheriff, Moore was required to carry a sword and go into court with the judge; to host a dinner for the judges; and, he joked, should the executioner fail to appear, to cut off the criminal's head: GM to Cunard, 13 July 1905, Imperial Hotel, Castlebar, Hart-Davis, 40–43; *Life of George Moore*, 258; GM to Dujardin, 4 February 1905, *Letters to Dujardin*, 56; Susan Mitchell, "George Moore – A Ballad History: Becomes High Sheriff of Mayo," *Aids to the Immortality of Certain Persons in Ireland* (Maunsel: Dublin, 1908).

151. "Chats on Art with George Moore," *Evening Mail*, 3 August 1905: 2cf. Arnold, *Orpen*, 148. The name of the Prince of Wales was transferred to another picture, one of undisputed authenticity, a few days later ("Modern Art Gallery," *Freeman's Journal*, 9 August 1905: 5).

152. "Mr. Moore's Mistake," *Evening Mail*, 5 August 1905: 4ce–f.

153. See the description of Moore's paintings in J. M. Hone, "An Interview with George Moore, *circa* 1912," HRHRC.

154. Arnold, *Orpen*, 161; "Report of the Committee of Inquiry into the Work Carried on by the Royal Hibernian Academy and the Metropolitan School of Art, Dublin," Parliamentary Papers xxxi. Cd. 3256 (1906), 512–13.

155. *Freeman's Journal*, 23 December 1904.

156. See, for instance, "Can the Nineteenth Century Produce a Dramatic Literature?" *Bat* 1.5 (28 April 1885): 64.

157. "Mr. George Moore on Dublin," Dublin *Evening Mail* (6 December 1905): 3. The opinion was not a one-off crack; Moore wrote Dujardin in January 1908 that the Celtic Renais-

sance "does not exist, it is a myth, like a good many other things" (*Letters to Dujardin*, 64).

158. GM to Synge, 6 March 1907, TCD Ms 4424–5/17 (GM here suggests a silly revision of the play's conclusion: old Mahon should, he said, push Christy into marrying Pegeen on account of her fortune): Moore, *Vale* (1937), 136–39; Foster, *The Apprentice Mage*, 403.

159. Just that October of 1905, GM bought a sketch by Jack B. Yeats, *Micky Mack and John Devine*, at a Leinster House exhibition (Hilary Pyle, *Jack B. Yeats: His Watercolours, Drawings, and Pastels* [Irish Academic Press: Dublin, 1993]: 142). While in Dublin, GM had his portrait painted by J. B. Yeats, Sarah Cecilia Harrison, William Orpen, and AE.

160. William Orpen to "My dear Petticoat" [Lane], 10 January 1906, Paultons, Romsey, Hampshire, Orpen Archive, National Gallery of Ireland. My thanks to Bruce Arnold, who deposited these papers at the NGI.

161. Arnold, *Orpen*, 228–29.

162. GM to AE, Sunday Evening [13 May] 1906, Hôtel Continental, *George Moore in Transition*, 315.

163. *Letters of George Moore*, 15.

164. The chronological sequence of *Hail and Farewell* is governed by the needs of the narrative, rather than by accurate dating. In the completed trilogy, events principally come from, but are not limited to, the period 1897 to 1906; for instance, the "Playboy riots" appear (26 January 1907, *Vale* [1937], 136); so does the departure of the Fays from the Abbey (January 1908, *Vale* [1937], 139); and GM's spell of performance anxiety with a young woman is datable to 1907–8 (*Vale* [1937], 208).

165. GM to Cunard, 9 January 1906, Hart-Davis, 48; GM to AE (1937) [13? May 1906], Hôtel Continental, *George Moore in Transition*, 315; GM to Hilda Hawthorne, 19 March 1907, 4 Upper Ely Place, *George Moore on Parnassus*, 132–33.

166. George Moore, "The Garret," *Saturday Review*, 23 June 1906, n.p.

167. To Hilda Hawthorne, Moore explained that *Hail and Farewell* was "a messianic work which like most messianic works will be popular, though probably the Gospels will always keep the lead" (May 1909?, *George Moore on Parnassus*, 161).

168. Moore, *Vale* (1937), 208–9.

169. GM to Hilda Hawthorne, 14 August [1907], 4 Upper Ely Place, *George Moore on Parnassus*, 137. This letter mentions the Americans at the Shelbourne. Viola Rodgers to J. Hone, 6 March 1935, Washington.

170. Viola Rodgers, "Next Stop – Park Row," Bancroft.

171. Quoted in *Life of George Moore*, 281.

172. GM to Honor Woulfe, 19 December [1911], HRHRC.

173. GM to Honor Woulfe, 2 March [1908], Travellers' Club, Paris, ibid. The letter offers GM's consolations on the death of Woulfe's mother; Margaret Woulfe died 23 January 1908, thus determining the date of this letter (Fall and Puckett Funeral Records, 1892–1931, Texas Genealogical Society, 1974).

174. GM to Honor Woulfe, 2 June 1917, Shelbourne Hotel, HRHRC. Never a man to be jealous, Moore ended by asking Woulfe to tell him "about your work or your lover or your lovers if you are fortunately in love or have been."

175. "Euphorion in Texas" was first published in the July 1914 *English Review*, then added to the 1915 Heinemann edition of *Memoirs of My Dead Life*.

176. "La Fin d'un art de vivre: un grand restaurant français à Dublin (1900–1967)," *Contacts*, Alliance Française d'Irlande (Spring 1980): 13–15; O Lúing, *Kuno Meyer*, 45.

177. Honor Woulfe, "George Moore and the Amenities," *English Literature in Transition*, 35.4 (1992): 447–61.

178. GM to Hilda Hawthorne, 29 January 1907, Hôtel Continental, Berg 52B2891.

179. GM to Hilda Hawthorne, 14 September [1907], *George Moore on Parnassus*, 139.
180. GM to Hilda Hawthorne, 16 November 1907, 4 Upper Ely Place, Berg, 52B2495 142–43.
181. GM to Hilda Hawthorne [7 August 1913], 121 Ebury Street, *George Moore on Parnassus*, 278–79; GM to Cunard, 23 August [1913], Hart-Davis, 82–84; GM to Hilda Hawthorne, 25 August [1914], *George Moore on Parnassus*, 292.
182. Craigie gave Unwin a copy of a letter from Moore dated 25 July, but with no year indicated: "I am sorry to trouble you, but I should like to know if you are agreeable to the proposal contained in my last letter? – that *you* sign Journeys End, that I *withdraw* my name" (Becker, 935). She claimed the year of the letter was 1894, and that it gave her complete rights over the play; Moore asserted that the letter was written in 1904, and that it referred to a compromise that "I should relinquish my claim to 'Journeys End' on consideration that I should sign, alone, the play that we wrote last year. As Mrs. Craigie did not agree to the proposal the matter stands exactly as it was" (GM to Unwin, 6 February 1905, *George Moore in Transition*, 294).
183. Craigie to Unwin, 1 February 1905, Berg; Colby, *Singular Anomaly*, 218.
184. GM to Unwin, 17 February 1905, *George Moore in Transition*, 294–95; see the further correspondence from Moore to Unwin, from 26 January to 6 October 1905 in ibid., pp. 291–301.
185. Weintraub, *London Yankees*, 82–83. Moore told Barrett Clark: "One night she went to bed and was found dead in the morning. She had taken a dose of something. Probably suicide. Some time after that, her mother was on the point of telling me when the father interrupted" (Clark to Joseph Hone, HRHRC). In fact, while Craigie was suicidal, she was also born with an "interatrial septal defect" (ibid., 83n.), and death most probably came from natural causes.
186. GM to Maurice Moore [late August, 1906], 4 Upper Ely Place, *George Moore on Parnassus*, 129.
187. GM to Emily Lorenz Meyer, 1 October 1908, *George Moore on Parnassus*, 150.
188. GM to John Morgan Richards, Friday [19? February 1909] and 24 February 1909, Rochester; GM to Dujardin [3 March 1909], Beinecke. Moore gave copies of Craigie's love letters to Richards (and promised to destroy the originals), and Richards gave them to Shorter but with instructions to use only particular ones, and only parts of those: "I am *certain* that not another one of them should be published" (Richards to Shorter, 19 August 1909, Brotherton). The father did not wish it to be known that his daughter had actually been in love with Moore. With a free hand, Shorter thought he could have made the book "a much more interesting biography" (Shorter to William Robertson Nicoll, 27 March 1911, ibid.); Shorter later proposed to Richards that more letters be added if there were a second edition (Shorter to Richards, Good Friday, 1911, Berg 62B9636). Shorter apparently had the Craigie–Moore letters bound in leather, and the volume is in the National Library of Ireland, Ms 2135.

GM sent a letter about his collaboration with Craigie on *Journeys End* for publication in the biography, then threatened to complain in "the Public Press" if Richards continued to refuse to publish it (Richards to Shorter, 10 June 1911, Brotherton). In late 1915, Richards heard a rumor that Moore had not destroyed the originals of Craigie's love letters and planned to publish them himself with an account of the affair, so Richards threatened Moore by referring to their 1909 agreement (GM to Richards, 2 December 1915, Berg 62B9635).

As for the authorship of the biography, Richards asked Shorter on 19 August 1909 if he could "not get hold of an *expert* at arranging and 'lining up' letters with narrative, dividing into chapters, 'headings' for chapters, and finally the index," in other words, if Shorter could not find someone to write the biography. Shorter decided he himself was the expert required.

189. GM to Dujardin, 8 March 1909, *Letters to Dujardin*, 75.

190. "The Stage Society – 'Elizabeth Cooper,'" *Times*, 24 June 1913; William Archer described *The Coming of Gabrielle* to Granville-Barker as "the most inept, childish twaddle imaginable" (19 July 1923, BL).

191. GM to Hilda Hawthorne, 29 September [1910], 4 Upper Ely Place, *George Moore on Parnassus*, 186.

192. GM to Maurice Moore 29 September 1910, 4 Upper Ely Place, NLI; ibid., 186.

193. *Elizabeth Cooper*, page proofs, 1904, 2–3 December, HRHRC, p. 9.

194. GM to Archer, 9 January 1906, 4 Upper Ely Place, BL.

195. GM to Dujardin, 13 June 1906, *Letters to Dujardin*, 58; GM to Julian Hawthorne, 16 January [1907], 4 Upper Ely Place, *George Moore on Parnassus*, 131.

196. William Patrick Ryan, *The Plough and the Cross: A Story of New Ireland* (Point Loma, Cal.: Aryan Theosophical Press, 1910; London: Theosophical Book Co., 1910), 19–23.

197. "SUPPRESSED???," *The Irish Peasant*, 29 December 1906: 1.

198. *The Moores of Moore Hall*, 220.

199. Moore, *Salve* (1912), 333–38; George Moore, *A Story-Teller's Holiday* (1923), 31–42; for the newspaper reports on the suicide of Stephen Cunningham, see *Irish Times*, 23 April 1908: 9; *Freeman's Journal*, 23 and 24 April 1908. For the Church's aggressive pursuit of legacies, see Emmet Larkin, *Historical Dimensions of Irish Catholicism* (Catholic University of America Press: Washington, DC; Four Courts Press: Dublin, 1997), 28–31.

200. GM to Lady Cunard, 13 July 1905, Imperial Hotel, Castlebar, Hart-Davis, 40–43; GM to Maurice Moore [January 1910], 4 Upper Ely Place, *George Moore on Parnassus*, 176.

201. James Jones & Sons to Maurice Moore, 3 September 1906, NLI 10566 (3).

202. Alfred Kearney to George Moore, Esq., 5 July 1909, National Bank Ltd, Dublin, NLI Ms 2648.

203. GM to My dear Edward [Martyn], [July? 1909], 4 Upper Ely Place, NLI Ms 18275.

204. *George Moore on Parnassus*, 143, 144, 165–70; *Moores of Moore Hall*, 224; GM to Maurice Moore, [March/April? 1909], 4 Upper Ely Place, NLI Ms 10565. Newbrook House, near Claremorris, was burnt in 1837 and never rebuilt.

205. Moore and Davitt were among the leaders of the 1904 Pan-Celtic Congress (*Evening Mail*, 24 August 1904: 6c3). Afterwards, and before Davitt's death in 1907, they planned to start an anti-clerical journal together (Moore, *Vale*, 210; *Life of George Moore*, 271).

206. Letter quoted in Thomas Ruttledge [Jr.] to Hone, 3 November 1935, Washington. Maurice Moore told Tom Ruttledge (Senior) that he had GM's authority for charging the school fees to the estate accounts; GM vigorously denied this (GM to Thomas Ruttledge, 18 November 1914, 121 Ebury Street, NLI Ms 4894).

207. *Life of George Moore*, 291.

208. GM to the editor, *Irish Times*, 30 December 1910.

209. GM to Maurice Moore [January 1910], 4 Upper Ely Place, *George Moore on Parnassus*, 176.

210. *The Moores of Moore Hall*, 228.

211. Moore, *Vale* (1937), 234.

212. Ibid., 253.

213. GM to Dujardin, 4 February 1911, 4 Upper Ely Place, Beinecke.

214. Russell to Quinn, 13 February 1911, Denson, ed., *Letters from AE*, 72.

215. GM to Dujardin, 3 April 1911, 121 Ebury Street, *Letters to Dujardin*, 88.

216. Yeats to AG, 28 October 1911, Nassau Hotel, Alan Wade, ed., *The Letters of W. B. Yeats* (Macmillan: New York, 1955), 564.

217. GM to Filson Young, 2 October 1905, 4 Upper Ely Place, HRHRC, *George Moore on Parnassus*, 123–24.

218. *Life of George Moore*, 310.

219. Moore, *Ave* (1937), 94–97, 106–7.

220. John Eglinton, "Life and Letters," *Irish Statesman*, 8 November 1919.

221. Not all characters appear under their own names. The women with whom Moore was sexually involved – Clara Christian and Maud Cunard – are awarded pseudonyms ("Stella" and "Elizabeth," respectively), and Oliver St John Gogarty, whose name had been poached for the priest-hero of *The Lake*, was consoled with a fictive name ("Conan") in *Hail and Farewell*.

222. GM to Julian Hawthorne, 16 January [1907], *George Moore on Parnassus*, 131.

223. Eglinton, *Irish Literary Portraits*, 90.

224. Starkey, "George Moore" [notes], W. R. Rodgers Misc., HRHRC. The Yarrow poems of Wordsworth moved Moore to tears when he read them in Dublin (Eglinton, *Irish Literary Portraits*, 89).

225. *Life of George Moore*, 309.

226. Maud Gonne to John Quinn [3 November 1911], Nassau Hotel; my thanks to Richard and Janis Londraville. See also Anna MacBride White and A. Norman Jeffaries, eds, *Gonne–Yeats Letters 1893–1938* (Norton: New York, London, 1992), 255. Evidence in the MacBride divorce case, tried in Paris, was given in August 1905 (*Evening Mail* [Dublin], 10 August 1905: 3cc).

227. Moore, *Vale* (1914), 167–68.

228. AE [George Russell] to John Quinn, 1 October 1908, Denson, ed., *Letters from AE*, 63.

229. John Eglinton, *A Memoir of AE* (Macmillan: London, 1937), 70. See Peter Kuch, *Yeats and AE: The Antagonism that Unites Dear Friends* (Colin Smythe: Gerrards Cross, Bucks, 1986), 225–38.

230. Eglinton, *A Memoir of AE*, 74–75.

231. Holloway, Diaries, 10 November 1908, quoted in Robert Hogan and James Kilroy, *The Abbey Theatre: the Years of*

Synge 1905–1909 (Dolman Press: Dublin; Humanities Press: Atlantic Highlands, NJ, 1978), 231. The poem is reprinted in Susan Mitchell's *Aids to the Immortality of Certain Persons, Charitably Administered* (New Nation Press: Dublin, 1908).

232. AE to Quinn, 27 April 1909, 17 Rathgar Avenue, Denson, ed., *Letters from AE*, 66.

233. AE to Quinn, 7 February 1913, ibid., 82.

234. Moore, *Vale* (1937), 172, 176; this part of *Vale* was probably written in October 1913; see *Letters of George Moore*, 19–20.

235. GM to Longworth, 17 November 1913, excerpt in *Life of George Moore*, 309.

236. JBY to Rosa Butt, Friday [20 December 1907], Bodleian Ms Eng. Litt. e88 (Fol. 85). My thanks to William M. Murphy. In a recent biography of Mitchell, Hilary Pyle argues that her "intimacy with Russell" was "innocent." There is presently no evidence by which one could conclude that the two did, or did not, engage in sexual relations; there is evidence in Pyle's book that Russell wrote her flirtatious letters, worried over her health, inspired her to write poems much like his own, decorated her writings with his erotico-mystical paintings, and maintained a devotion to her for many years. It may have been because of her relation to Russell that Mitchell (in the words of J. B. Yeats) "remained unmarried, to her own loss & to everybody's loss." In *Vale*, Moore was bringing up the subject of their intimacy, and implying that Russell's marriage suffered. See Hilary Pyle, *Red-Headed Rebel: Susan L. Mitchell, Poet and Mystic of the Irish Cultural Renaissance* (Woodfield Press: Dublin, 1998), 120–21, 146.

237. GM to Edward Martyn, Saturday [Summer 1909?], 4 Upper Ely Place, NLI Ms 18275.

238. Moore, *Salve* (1937), 129.

239. *Life of George Moore*, 122; Rupert Hart-Davis, ed., *Letters of Max Beer-*

bohm, 1892–1956 (Norton: New York, 1988), 81.

240. Yeats, *Autobiography*, 259.

241. Gregory to Sydney Pawling, 5 January 1914, Lindsay House, Cheyne Walk, Berg 65B3320. Her letter also indicates she suspects GM got the proselytiser story from her Galway neighbor Edward Martyn, who got it from a servant formerly of Coole Park and later on the staff at Tillyra. In fact, while AG's mother was a notorious anti-papist evangeliser, and so were AG's sisters, she herself had disapproved even early in life of corrupting people's faith in their native religion.

242. My thanks to Ciaran McGonigail for passing along Harry Clarke's story about Lane and the Spanish costume, and to Lucy McDiarmid for telling me about the photographs of Lane in various costumes held in the Dublin Municipal Gallery of Modern Art archives.

243. Hugh Lane to Augusta Gregory, 4 October 1913, Berg. My thanks to Roy Foster.

244. Hugh Lane to Augusta Gregory, 8 April [1914], ibid. My thanks to Roy Foster.

245. Orpen to Hugh Lane [?March 1906?], Orpen Archive, NGI.

246. Robert Ross, "*Salve*," *Times*, 14 November 1912: 515.

247. Violet Martin to Augusta Gregory, 1 January 1912, Berg. My thanks to Roy Foster.

248. GM to Filson Young, 2 October 1905, 4 Upper Ely Place, HRHRC; *George Moore on Parnassus*, 123–24.

249. GM to Gosse, 15 November 1907, 4 Upper Ely Place, Brotherton. Italics added.

GM was the decisive influence in pushing Gosse to give up turning out his *Critical Kit-Kats* for a time and write *Father and Son*, the one book for which he will be remembered. Moore told Gosse, you "cannot write a novel, but you can paint marvellous portraits . . . Man [is] the subject; literature the background." Gosse's "required

subject," GM judged, should be "your biography of your father . . . you will not find a better if you search the world over . . . nothing can stop you if your courage does not fail you." Gosse gave due thanks to Moore after publication of *Father and Son*; Moore replied handsomely, "All I did was egg you on to write a subject you related to me: you'll say that is a good deal – well, if you like it was a good deal, and it is pleasanter that you should think it a good deal than that you should think it nothing at all" (GM to Gosse, 17 October 1907, Burkhart, *Letters of George Moore to . . .*, 63). See also GM to Gosse, 1 April 1896 [27 November 1896], [1-31 December 1900], 22 February 1906, 17 October 1907, Brotherton; and Evan Charteris, *Life and Letters of Sir Edmund Gosse* (Heinemann: London, 1931), 308–9.

250. Nancy Cunard, *GM: Memories of George Moore* (Hart-Davis: London, 1956), 17.

251. Nancy Cunard [Diaries], HRHRC.

252. Cunard, *GM: Memories of George Moore*, 17.

253. GM to Maud Cunard, Thursday [26 January 1905], 4 Upper Ely Place, Hart-Davis, 37–38; GM to Maud Cunard, 22 October [1904], 4 Upper Ely Place, ibid., 35–36; GM to Maud Cunard, 9 January 1906, 4 Upper Ely Place, ibid., 47–48.

254. GM to Maud Cunard, 13 July 1905, Imperial Hotel, Castlebar, Co. Mayo, ibid., 40–43.

255. GM to Maud Cunard, Sunday [August 1905], Val Changis, Fontainebleau, ibid., 44–46.

256. George Moore, *Sister Teresa* (1929), 89, 108, 273, 279.

257. Ibid., 109. See also GM's expression of regret that he did not marry "Doris" (Maud Cunard) in *Vale*, 254.

258. Cunard, *GM: Memories of George Moore*, 28.

259. Ibid., 31.

260. Ibid., 29.

261. Ibid., 101.

262. Ibid., 35.

263. GM to Nancy Cunard [August 1909], 4 Upper Ely Place, NLI Ms 2648.
264. GM to Maud Cunard, Monday [Summer 1911], 121 Ebury Street, Hart-Davis, 80–81.

Chapter 12 Jesus of Nazareth and the Sage of Ebury Street

1. George Moore, *Conversations in Ebury Street* (1924), 207.
2. Chamberlain, later Hitler's favorite race-theorist, had written a book trying to prove that Jesus was not a Jew, about which he corresponded with Dujardin in 1904 (Edouard Dujardin, *Rencontres avec Houston Stewart Chamberlain* [Bernard Grasset: Paris, 1943], 141–42). A German-loving Englishman, Chamberlain's concoction of Gobineau, Darwin, Nietzsche, and historical criticism of the Bible made him one of the great thought-criminals of the century. Dujardin remained his friend until Chamberlain's death, and a Nazi fellow-traveler through World War II. There is no evidence of meetings of Moore with Chamberlain, or readings by Moore of Chamberlain's works. For Moore, all races were alike, "all muck," and nations were by him seen as elective styles of identity.
3. Kathleen M. McKilligan, *Edouard Dujardin: "Les Lauriers sont coupés" and the Interior Monologue* (University of Hull Press: Hull, 1977), 12.
4. Edouard Dujardin, *The Source of the Christian Tradition*, trans. Joseph McCabe (Watts: London, 1911), 53.
5. Ibid., 259, 260, 262.
6. GM to Dujardin, 21 September 1907, *Letters to Dujardin*, 62. Hone suggests that in 1908 Moore was reading Edward Berwick's translation of Philostratus' life of Apollonius as part of his own investigation of the historical sources on early Christianity ("George Moore and Vicar of Leixlip," *Dublin Magazine*, 18. 4 [October–December, 1943]: 47–52).

For Moore's opinions about Acts, see *Conversations in Ebury Street* (1930), 207.
7. John Eglinton, *Irish Literary Portraits* (Macmillan: London, 1935), 109; George Moore, "Prefatory Letter," *The Apostle*, 33; GM to Magee, 19 December 1927, HRHRC. In this letter, GM recalls that when the inspiration for *The Brook Kerith* came to him, he and Magee were standing face to face: "you had just told me a story about the death or stupor caused by the pain of being tied on the cross. You have always denied that I remember correctly what you said – some physiological details you had just read in a German book?"
8. GM to Dujardin [13 June 1908], 4 Upper Ely Place, Beinecke.
9. GM to Dujardin, 8 August 1910, *Letters to Dujardin*, 82–83; "George Moore Has Made a Play Out of His Popular Novel," *New York Times*, 23 October 1910, 3:3; Lennox Robinson, *Curtain-Up* (Michael Joseph: London, 1942), 28–33. Moore encouraged the "Cork Realists" – Lennox Robinson and T. C. Murray – as the tide turned in Yeats's war against Ibsenism in the Abbey Theatre; see Robert Hogan and Michael J. O'Neill, eds, *Joseph Holloway's Abbey Theatre: A Selection from his Unpublished Journal, "Impressions of a Dublin Playgoer"* (Southern Illinois University Press: Carbondale and Edwardsville, 1967), 145, describing a night at the Abbey (28 October 1910), in which Murray talks against Lady Gregory and Yeats, and Lady Gregory against Murray, while Moore comes up to tell Murray "not to alter a word" of his play *Birthright*. Moore proclaimed victory in a 23 September 1911 article in the *Boston Evening Transcript*: "Yeats's original idea of theatre was a little mist, some fairies and psaltery, and his achievements are realistic plays and an admirable company of actors and actresses."
10. GM to Dujardin, 25 August 1910, *Letters to Dujardin*, 84.

11. Earlier, Moore had tried to sell Dujardin on using as the basis for a great opera the scenario of Gautier's *Une Nuit de Cléopâtre*, AE's *Deirdre*, or Synge's *Well of the Saints* (*Letters to Dujardin*, 67, 68–69, 70–72).

12. GM to Dujardin, 10 October 1910, 4 Upper Ely Place, Beinecke.

13. Report of village folklore in Anne Chisolm, *Nancy Cunard: A Biography* (Knopf: New York, 1979), 23.

14. Nancy Cunard [Diaries], HRHRC. Evidently on the same day, 23 July 1910, fresh from a recent visit, Moore wrote Cunard a love letter in purple prose from Hill Hall. So at this stage, her relations with Beecham did not involve any sort of rupture with Moore (Hart-Davis, 77).

15. Chisolm, *Nancy Cunard*, 31.

16. A 1908 photograph of Beecham appears in Alan Blackwood's *Sir Thomas Beecham: The Man and the Music* (Ebury Press: London, 1994).

17. Ibid., 55. For the Beecham family history, see Anne Francis, *A Guinea a Box: A Biography* (Hale: London, 1968).

18. Seymour Leslie, *The Jerome Connection* (John Murray: London, 1964), 92. Stanley Owen Buckmaster (1861–1934) was Lord Chancellor from 1915 to 1916.

19. GM to Dujardin, 2 September 1910, Grand Hotel, Munich, Beinecke; *Letters to Dujardin*, 84.

20. *Irish Times*, 6 September 1910, *Continental Daily Mail*, 6 September 1910; Hart-Davis, 78–80.

21. GM to Maurice Moore, 29 September 1910, *George Moore on Parnassus*, 186.

22. Hart-Davis, 80–81.

23. Rupert Hart-Davis, ed., *The Lyttelton Hart-Davis Letters* (John Murray: London, 1988), 207; Hart-Davis to Nancy Cunard, 7 November 1956 (Ms Cunard, HRHRC).

24. 23 March 1911, Book of Gosse (Brotherton); 15 May 1911, *Journal of Arnold Bennett* (Viking: New York, 1933), 409; GM to Dujardin, 15 May 1911, Beinecke; Denys Sutton, *Walter Sickert: A Biography* (Michael Joseph:

London, 1976), 162–64; Timothy Eden, *The Tribulations of a Baronet* (Macmillan: London, 1933), 86ff.; GM to Dujardin, 27 July 1911, Beinecke.

25. Leon Edel, *Henry James: The Master, 1901–1916* (Rupert Hart-Davis: London, 1916), 462.

26. "Mr. George Moore on America," *Observer*, 17 December 1916: 5c.

27. Shaw to GM [October 1911], Dan. H. Lawrence, ed., *Bernard Shaw: Collected Letters 1911–1925* (Max Reinhardt: London 1985), 52–53; GM to Dujardin, 20 November 1911, Beinecke.

28. GM to Revd J. O. Hannay [George Birmingham], 27 October 1911, NLI Ms 8271.

29. See Langenfeld for excerpts from the reviews of *Ave*.

30. GM to T. Werner Laurie, 14 December 1910, *George Moore on Parnassus*, 188.

31. A. M., "Mr. George Moore," *Evening News*, 19 June 1912: 4.

32. GM to Dujardin, 9 September 1912, Beinecke.

33. GM to Magee, 12 August 1912, *Letters of George Moore*, 19.

34. Russell to John Quinn, 7 February 1913, Alan Denson, ed., *Letters from AE* (Abelard-Schuman: London, New York, Toronto, 1961), 82.

35. Ruttledge to Maurice Moore, 12 February 1913, Estate Office, Westport, NLI Ms 4894.

36. Becker, 395, 403, 498–501, 675, 691; and letters in NLI Ms 2648.

37. GM to Mary Blake Moore [March 1891], Becker, 691; and 15 July [1891], Becker, 708. Julian Moore published a story in *Tinsley's Magazine* ("A Bayswater Barnum," June 1884) when he was just a young man; for identification, see Edmund Downey, "An Editor's Reminiscences," *Irish Book Lover*, 8. 91–10 (April–May 1917): 100.

38. GM to Maurice Moore, 23 October [1893], Becker, 854–56.

39. See the biographical note in Becker, 1008. Julian Moore wrote a letter of advice about the design of a

monument to Queen Victoria in the 10 April 1910 *Freeman's Journal*.

40. GM to Maurice Moore [inscribed 6 May 1896], Becker 1026; and [15 June 1896], Becker 1027.

41. C. D. Medley to Joseph Hone, 21 February 1936, HRHRC. The regular payments to Julian Moore had begun by 1913.

42. For date of composition, see GM to Viola Rodgers, 10 May [1921], 121 Ebury Street, Bancroft; George Moore, *Celibate Lives* (1937), 25.

43. GM to Maurice Moore, 3 June 1912, NLI Ms 4894.

44. Ibid.

45. GM to Maurice Moore, 14 June 1912, ibid.

46. At a dinner hosted by Thornley Stoker (probably in spring 1910) in company with Gogarty and Birrell, Moore pretended never to have read *Obiter Dicta*, or to know Birrell had written it. This was the dinner at which, according to Gogarty, Lady Stoker suddenly arrived in mid-course, nude, with the cry, "I like a little intelligent conversation." After hustling her out of the room, Stoker sternly instructed his guests to keep under the table their knowledge of his wife's erratic behavior. "But it was charming," Moore replied, "I demand an encore." Stoker ejected him from the house. (Oliver St John Gogarty, *Sackville Street and Other Stories* (Sphere: London, 1988), 301).

47. *The Moores of Moore Hall*, 213.

48. GM to Maurice Moore, 7 October 1912, NLI Ms 4894.

49. George Moore, *Salve* (1912), 155–56; Max Beerbohm, *The Incomparable Max* (Dodd, Mead: New York, 1962), 94. For a discussion of Moore and caricature, see Elizabeth Grubgeld, *George Moore and the Autogenous Self: The Autobiography and the Fiction* (Syracuse University Press: Syracuse, NY, 1994), 104, 120–21.

50. Reconstruction of events by Maurice Moore, NLI Ms 4894.

51. Maurice Moore to GM, 24 October 1912, ibid.

52. Arthur Machen, "Some Novels of the Moment," *Evening News*, 29 October 1913: 3c.

53. Robert Lynd, "Mr. George Moore's Caricature," *Bookman* (London) 41 (January 1912): 214; and Lynd, "Hail and Farewell, II. Salve," *Bookman* (London) 43 (Christmas supplement, 1912): 120–22.

54. Robert Ross, "*Salve*," *Times Literary Supplement*, 14 November 1912: 515.

55. "The Burden of Humor," *Smart Set*, 39 (February 1913): 156–57.

56. T. Werner Laurie to GM, Clifford's Inn, Fleet Street, NLI Ms 4894.

57. GM to Maurice Moore, 24 April [1913], *George Moore on Parnassus*, 263.

58. GM to Maurice Moore, 26 April [1913], ibid., 264.

59. GM to Maurice Moore, 1 May 1913, ibid., 267.

60. GM to Gosse [inscribed 11 April 1913], c/o Thomas Ruttledge, Westport, Brotherton.

61. Ruth Gordon, *Myself and Others* (Athenaeum: New York, 1971), n.p. Due to a delay caused by recasting *Sebastian*, the performance was delayed until 23 June 1913.

62. *George Moore on Parnassus*, 267–69.

63. *An Irish Gentleman*, xviii.

64. "George Moore – Preface, *An Irish Gentleman*, Galley," NLI Ms 10570.

65. GM to Maurice Moore, Monday [26 May 1913], Hotel Brighton, *George Moore on Parnassus*, 273.

66. GM to Maurice Moore, Tuesday [27 May 1913], ibid., 274.

67. GM to Dujardin, 26 March 1913, Beinecke. Paul Abraham Dukas (1865–1935), composer of *The Sorcerer's Apprentice* (1897) and the opera *Ariane et Barbe-bleue* (1907), was a friend and favorite of Dujardin.

68. Carl Van Vechten to Fania Marinoff [2 June 1913], Bruce Kellner, ed., *Letters of Carl Van Vechten* (Yale University Press: New Haven and London, 1987), 5–6. Carl Van Vechten (1880–1964), writer, literary organiser, and photographer, later advertised, and partly inspired, the Harlem Renaissance.

On 11 June 1913 Yeats told Edward Marsh a similar story of "George Moore making friends with a woman and saying, 'How I regret, for your sake, that I'm impotent'" (Christopher Hassall, *Biography of Edward Marsh* [Harcourt Brace: New York, 1959], 228).

69. Hone telescopes these events in *Moores of Moore Hall*, 237–39; see GM to Maurice Moore, 17 July 1913, *George Moore on Parnassus*, 278.

70. Gogarty's overwritten account of a conversation with the Colonel has GM still living at Ely Place and other dubious material (the super-pious character given Maurice is unconvincing), but it correctly indicates the indignation of Maurice about GM's preface ("Next Door to George Moore," *Saturday Review of Literature*, 18 July 1936: 3–4, 15). Maurice's 18 July 1913 letter to Laurie includes the scored-out sentence about the slip: "all the relations want it made clear & I have the right to express my view", NLI Ms 4894. See also Maurice's 19 July 1913 letter to GM.

71. Maurice Moore to GM, 18 July 1913 [draft of letter sent?], NLI Ms 4894.

72. Maurice Moore to GM, "July? 1913", draft, ibid.

73. *Moores of Moore Hall*, 240–41.

74. GM to Magee, 17 October 1913, Eglinton, 19–20.

75. GM to Nora Robertson [November? 1913], 121 Ebury Street, NLI Ms 10751(2).

76. Mrs Murray Robertson to Joseph Hone, 6 May [1935?], Dooagh, Achill, Co. Mayo, Washington.

77. GM to Mrs Gosse, 25 December [1913], Chirk Castle, Denbighshire, Brotherton. See also GM to Cunard, 28 December [1913], Hart-Davis, 85.

78. GM to Cunard, 28 January [1913], Chirk Castle, and GM to Cunard [early January 1914], 121 Ebury Street, ibid., 84–86, italics added.

79. GM to Longworth, 17 November 1913 and 14 January 1914, *Life of George Moore*, 309.

80. Moore detested Gregory's account of the Irish Literary Theatre: "That lady seems to produce books as easily as a mouse produces mice," he complained to Hilda Hawthorne, "she babbles just like an old retainer" (GM to Hawthorne, 19 December 1913, *George Moore on Parnassus*, 282–83).

81. *Lady Gregory's Diaries*, 119.

82. Gregory to Pawling, 5 January 1914, Lindsay House, Cheyne Walk, Berg 65b3320.

83. GM to Gregory, 9 January 1914, Berg 65b2342.

84. GM to Gregory, 15 January 1914, ibid.

85. GM to Magee, 19 January 1914, HRHRC.

86. Eliza Aria, *My Sentimental Self* (Chapman and Hall: London, 1922), 195; GM to Eliza Aria, 17 March [1914], NLI Ms 2648; George Moore, "Apologia pro scriptis meis," xxiv.

87. *Life of George Moore*, 311; O'Donovan to Hone, 26 September 1936, Washington; George Moore, *Vale* (1937), 258.

88. GM to Cunard, 20 February 1914, SS Macedonia, Hart-Davis, 87.

89. George Moore, *Avowals* (1924), 21; GM to Gosse, 21 February [1914], Berg 242919b. O'Donovan contradicts Moore's claim in *Avowals* that this was his first reading of Sterne; "He bored Edward and myself at Tillyra by reading aloud with great gusto the obstetrical opening chapters of *Tristram Shandy*, and later, he frequently discussed *The Sentimental Journey* with me – long before *Hail and Farewell*" (O'Donovan to Hone, 26 February 1936, Washington).

90. GM to Gosse, 21 February [1914], Berg 242919b.

91. GM to Cunard, 26 February 1914, Grand New Hotel, Jerusalem; Hart-Davis, 88–90.

92. Aria, *My Sentimental Self*, 195.

93. George Moore, *The Brook Kerith: A Syrian Story*, 66.

94. GM to Eliza Aria, 17 March [1914], NLI Ms 2648; Aria, *My Sentimental Self*, 195.

95. Flavius Josephus wrote about the Essenes in *The Jewish War* and *Jewish Antiquities*, Philo of Alexandria in *Apologia pro Judais* and *Quod omnis probus Fiber sit*, and Pliny the Elder in *Natural History*. Excerpts from their works, as well as selections from the scrolls, may be found in *The Essene Writings from Qumran* (World Publishing Company: New York, 1962).

96. Moore, *Brook Kerith*, 81.

97. Moore stayed over in Paris because Dujardin was producing his version of *Elizabeth Cooper*, entitled *Clara Florise*, at the Comédie Royale, with Dujardin's mistress, a dancer, in a key role. In a fury at the Grand New Hotel, Jerusalem, Moore complained, "My friend, it is not right" (*Letters to Dujardin*, 102). As the play was not doing well, Moore tried to rewrite scenes in his own French at the Hôtel Brighton at the end of the month, but the production came to a close before the new scenes could be rehearsed (GM to Dujardin [31 March 1914] and 1 April, Hôtel Brighton, and 5 April, 121 Ebury Street, Beinecke). See also the preface to Moore's *Coming of Gabrielle* (privately printed, 1920).

98. GM to Magee, 2 May 1914, HRHRC. Moore chose to identify Arimathea with Ramah, birthplace of Samuel (1 Samuel 1:19), called "Armathaim" in the Septuagint, and "Armatha" by Josephus. See GM to Magee, 7 May 1914, ibid.

99. For Moore's critique of Jesus's teachings on family and property, see Moore, *Brook Kerith*, 133, 181, 184, 281.

100. GM to Phyllis Williamson [p.m. 29 May 1915], HRHRC; GM to Magee [22? March 1916], ibid.

101. GM to Honor Woulfe, 24 January 1913, ibid.; Honor Woulfe, "George Moore and the Amenities," *English Literature in Transition*, 33.4 (1992): 12. For a fuller story of Woulfe's relation to Moore, see Adrian Frazier, "George Moore and Some Women," in the same issue of *ELT*: 422–46.

102. Carl Van Vechten, *Sacred and Profane Memories* (Knopf: New York, 1932), 62.

103. GM to Gosse, 22 February [1914], Berg 242919b; Van Vechten, *Sacred and Profane Memories*, 62. Anthony Comstock (1844–1915), secretary of the Society for the Suppression of Vice in New York, lobbied Congress to pass anti-obscenity laws – "Comstock laws" – in 1873.

104. Moore, however, did not send her a copy of the July *English Review* until October 1914: GM to Woulfe, 21 October [p.m. 1914], HRHRC.

105. Honor Woulfe to Joseph Hone, 24 February 1936, ibid.; Woulfe, "George Moore and the Amenities," 447.

106. Ernest Boyd, "Mainly about Moore," *Saturday Review of Literature*, 7 December 1935: n.p.

107. GM to Whitall, 5 March 1915, Virginia. For Whitall's account and some Moore letters, see James Whitall, *English Years* (Harcourt, Brace: New York, 1935), 85ff.; and James Whitall, "George Moore," *Bookman*, 76. 3 (March 1933): 209. Whitall's manuscript of "How Literature Came to Texas" is at Virginia.

108. Frazier, "George Moore and Some Women," 437.

109. See Langenfeld for a full selection of comments (pp. 100–3).

110. Hassall, *Biography of Edward Marsh*, 228.

111. Boyd to Starkey, 25 March 1914, TCD Mss 4630–4649/268.

112. Edward Martyn, *The Dream Physician* (Dublin: Talbot Press; T. Fisher Unwin: London, [1918]), 47, 56.

113. Joseph Holloway, however, judged *The Dream Physician* to be "crude and preposterous piffle . . . unconvincing as drama" (Hogan and O'Neill, eds, *Joseph Holloway's Abbey Theatre*, 168).

114. GM to Magee, 17 February, 22 February, and 12 March 1916, HRHRC. Martyn evidently communicated with Moore at least once, probably either during Moore's June 1917 or his August 1918 visit to Dublin. GM told

Martyn that Ernest Boyd was to do the "official life," and Martyn twitted his friend: "Miss Mitchell's will always be the real one accepted, she took the only possible way of dealing with you, treating you as 'Mon ami Moore'" (Martyn's nickname for GM) (Daniel Murphy, ed., *Lady Gregory's Journals*, vol. 1 [Oxford University Press: Oxford and New York, 1978], 295).

115. Susan Mitchell to Starkey, Monday [late May? 1915], TCD Ms 4646/-3836.

116. Susan L. Mitchell, "Elizabeth Cooper," *Irish Review*, October 1913: 440.

117. Russell to Quinn, 14 March [1914], Denson, ed., *Letters from AE*, 96.

118. GM to Susan Mitchell, 10 June [1916], UCD.

119. *The Moores of Moore Hall*, 255; Maurice Moore, "History of the Irish Volunteers," *Irish Press*, January–March 1938; Michael Tierney, *Eoin MacNeill: Scholar and Man of Action 1867–1945*, ed. F. X. Martin (Clarendon Press: Oxford, New York, 1980), 124, 129–30, 134–39, 230.

120. Susan Mitchell to J. B. Yeats [October 1915], Hilary Pyle, *Red-Headed Rebel: Susan L. Mitchell, Poet and Mystic of the Irish Cultural Renaissance* (Woodfield Press: Dublin, 1998), 164. After the book was published, Maurice Moore called on Mitchell to express his delight with it (ibid., 171).

121. Susan L. Mitchell, *George Moore* (Maunsel: Dublin, 1916), 47.

122. Ibid., 9.

123. GM to Magee, 30 March 1920, HRHRC. On summer vacations in Donegal, Russell painted landscapes with fairies, and painted them badly according to GM's taste; thus Russell became "DD," the "Donegal Dauber."

124. When the charge that all his love affairs were invented reappeared in the proofs of John Abthorne, *The Opinions of John Abthorne on the Arts and Living* (Heinemann: London, 1920), Moore demanded that the "libel" be removed: "I am prepared to go into a Law Court and to swear that these love affairs are facts not fictions, and that I believe the statement that they are fictions depreciates the value of [my] books" (GM to Sydney Pawling, 9 April 1919, TCD Mss 4630–49/477).

125. GM to Ernest Boyd, 14 October 1916, *George Moore on Parnassus*, 336.

126. GM to Eglinton, 8 November [1918], 121 Ebury Street; GM to Eglinton, 24 November 1918, 121 Ebury Street, HRHRC.

127. Joseph Hone, *Life of Henry Tonks* (Heinemann: London, 1939), 110.

128. Peter Moore to Hone, 20 September 1935, Washington.

129. "A German Professor on Ireland," *Irish Times*, 27 November 1914.

130. "Dr. Kuno Meyer's Honour: Seditious Address to the Clan-na-Gael," *Irish Times*, 24 December 1914.

131. "Mr. George Moore and Professor Kuno Meyer," *Daily Telegraph* [2 January 1915?], reprinted *Manchester Guardian*, 4 January 1915.

132. "Dusk of the Gods," *Atlantic Monthly*, August 1916. The interview was conducted in April 1916 (*George Moore on Parnassus*, 314).

133. GM to Viola Rodgers, 23 August 1916, Bancroft.

134. GM to Viola Rodgers, 9 November 1916, ibid.

135. Hassall, *Biography of Edward Marsh*, 395.

136. GM to Magee [early October? 1914], HRHRC.

137. GM to Dujardin, 30 April 1914, *Letters to Dujardin*, 104.

138. GM to Magee, 11 July 1914, Eglinton, 23.

139. GM to Magee, 27 July 1914, ibid., 24.

140. GM to Magee, 30 July 1914, ibid., 25.

141. GM to Magee, 16 October 1914, ibid., 25.

142. GM to Magee [15 November 1915], HRHRC.

143. GM to Magee, 18 December 1915, ibid. Moore's language here matches

that of pp. 356–58 of *The Brook Kerith: A Syrian Story*.

144. See Michael Brooks, "George Moore, Schopenhauer, and the Origins of *The Brook Kerith*," *English Literature in Transition*, 12 (1969): 21–31. Schopenhauer also took his post-Christian philosophy in the direction of Buddhist relinquishment. For Moore's own comments on Jesus and Buddha, see GM to Magee, 10 May 1916, HRHRC.

145. GM to Magee, 21 March 1916, ibid.; Moore, *The Brook Kerith: A Syrian Story*, 379.

146. *The Brook Kerith: A Syrian Story*, 429.

147. Ibid.

148. Ibid., 434.

149. Ibid., 358.

150. Ibid., 465.

151. Lily Yeats to J. B. Yeats, 5 June 1916; my thanks to William Murphy. The articles published by the *Evening News* are "Whistle, Whistle, Whistle" (25 May); "Dublin Revisited" (5 June); and "A June Trip Through Ireland" (29 June).

152. GM to Stephens [early June, 1916] and 2 June [1916], Shelbourne Hotel, Berg 243015b.

153. GM to Miss Palmer, 1 June [1917], Shelbourne Hotel, *George Moore on Parnassus*, 351.

154. George Moore, "James Stephens as Poet," *Observer*, 9 June 1918: 4.

155. James Stephens, "A Conversation with George Moore," *Listener*, 14 January 1947.

156. For a detailed record of the many reviews and large correspondence about *The Brook Kerith*, see Langenfeld, 105–117; and *George Moore on Parnassus*, 333–35.

157. "Brook Kerith. Process for Blasphemy Denied," *Times*, 7 September 1916.

158. GM to Ross [September 1916], Margery Ross, *Robert Ross: Friend of Friends* (Jonathan Cape: London, 1952), 277. Following in his father's footsteps, Lord Alfred Douglas had publicly called Ross a "notorious Sodomite" in January 1914, and in a trial on 19 November 1914, Ross, following in the footsteps of Wilde, failed

to prove that this allegation was untrue, and stopped further damaging testimony from witnesses by paying Douglas's costs. The trial ruined the reputation and career of Ross.

159. The best review of *The Brook Kerith* is by I. A. Richards, written many years later when the book was reissued. In the *New York Review of Books* (3 December 1970), Richards gave an appreciative account of the risks undertaken by such a narrative, and the subtle manner in which they were overcome. The minor characters all had minds whose idiosyncratic differences were "realized, displayed, allowed for." Joseph, Jesus, and Paul he judged to be surprisingly satisfying. "Fewer come nearer to their own thoughts than Moore's chief characters. It may be the roominess and richness of their awarenesses of their own thinking that allows the book to retell such a story with impunity."

160. *New Republic*, 8 (23 September 1916): 196; *Dial*, 61 (21 September 1916): 191–93; *Life*, 68 (12 October 1916): 643.

161. GM to Magee, 25 September 1916, HRHRC.

162. GM to Gerald Kelly, 17 August, ibid. In March 1917, an actor named "Louis N. Seymour" charged Moore and his publisher with libel for having used his name in a book about a man of no character. The case actually went to trial. The defense by Moore's counsel was that if Seymour got a verdict, he could change his name to Tom Jones, or John Falstaff, and win awards from other publishers. See "A Novel by Mr. George Moore: Libel Action," *Times*, 23 November 1917: 4a; and George Moore, *Lewis Seymour and Some Women*, xxvii.

163. GM to Gosse [26 March 1917], Brotherton.

164. GM to Viola Rodgers, 9 December [1917], Bancroft.

165. GM to Robert Ross, Monday [1917], Ross, *Robert Ross*, 313.

166. Moore's fears about the success of improbable prosecutions were well

founded. Less than a year later, Justice Darling lost control of a libel case instigated by Noel Pemberton Billing, MP. Billing's newspaper, the *Imperialist*, charged dancer Maud Allan and J. T. Grein with creating "A Cult of the Clitoris" by means of their production of Wilde's *Salomé*. Billing won his case by turning the courtroom into a carnival of abuse of those he claimed threatened England and the war effort: homosexuals, Jews, and aristocrats of German education or ancestry. See Philip Hoare, *Wilde's Last Stand: Decadence, Conspiracy, and the First World War* (Duckworth: London, 1997).

167. George Moore, *A Story-Teller's Holiday* (1918), v.

168. GM to Magee, 29 August 1916, HRHRC.

169. Moore, *Brook Kerith: A Syrian Story*, 360. The Adam and Eve story appears in *Story-Teller's Holiday* (1923), 210–59.

170. GM to Best, 21 March 1917, HRHRC.

171. GM to Best, 9 April 1917, ibid.

172. GM to Viola Rodgers [p.m. 18 May 1917], Bancroft; GM to Magee, 14 January 1918, HRHRC.

173. *Journal of Arnold Bennett*, 666.

174. GM to Heinemann, 4 August [1917], HRHRC; GM to Gosse, 14 August 1917, Brotherton; GM to Magee, 14 August 1917, HRHRC; GM to Magee, 22 September 1917, Eglinton, 38.

175. GM to Magee, 22 September 1917, HRHRC; GM to Phyllis Williamson [p.m. 15 October 1917], ibid.; GM to Magee, 20 November 1917, ibid.

176. GM to Magee [19?] April 1918, Eglinton, 44; Steer to Lady Howard de Walden [May? 1918], D. S. MacColl, *Life, Work and Setting of Philip Wilson Steer* (Faber and Faber: London, [1945]), 91 ("I feel doubtful as to whether I am sufficiently grown up to read this kind of literature").

177. GM to Edward Marsh, 3 August 1916, Berg 63b1773; Richard Ellmann, *James Joyce*, new and revised edn (Oxford University Press, Oxford, 1982), 405–6. Nancy Cunard recalls

Moore in her mother's drawing room at Cavendish Square, listening to Ezra Pound stress the need to help Joyce (*GM: Memories of George Moore* [Hart-Davis: London, 1956], 103). In his eventual letter of support for a pension, Moore sandwiches a long diatribe about Sinn Fein with comments that "The Dead": "seemed to me perfection . . . I regretted I was not the author of it" and that "I am sure from a literary point of view Joyce is deserving of help."

178. For a summary of Moore's direct influences on Lawrence, see Richard Allen Cave, *A Study of the Novels of George Moore* (Colin Smythe: Gerrards Cross, Bucks, 1978), 235–36.

179. GM to Magee, 22 September 1917, HRHRC.

180. Lawrence to Hone, 12 January 1918, ibid.

181. GM to Magee, 22 December 1917, ibid. Lawrence must have been misinformed when he wrote the agent J. B. Pinker on 18 December 1917 that he had heard "indirectly that George Moore had read the MS . . . and praised it highly" (James Boulton, ed., *Letters of D. H. Lawrence*, vol. 1 [Cambridge University Press: Cambridge, 1979], 534).

182. Berenice C. Skidelsky, "Tea and Talk with George Moore," *The World*, 15 February 1925.

183. GM to Magee, 22 January 1918, HRHRC.

184. GM to Lawrence, 22 January 1918, ibid.

185. Two years later, Moore came up with an astonishing plan to help Lawrence, by appointing him GM's biographer. See Moore to Laurie, 16 April [1920], *George Moore on Parnassus*, 461.

186. Cunard, *GM: Memories of George Moore*, 28.

187. Murphy, ed., *Lady Gregory's Journals*, vol. 1, 255.

188. GM to Maud Cunard, 7 December [1920], Hart-Davis, 106, 107.

189. David Cannadine, *The Decline and Fall of the British Aristocracy* (Yale

University Press: New Haven and London, 1990), 501–57.

190. GM to Werner Laurie, 28 May [1919], *George Moore on Parnasus*, 419.

191. GM to Mary Hunter [August 1918], HRHRC.

192. GM to Mary Hunter [August 1918], ibid.

193. GM to Magee, 9 November 1916, ibid. When newspapers were praising the author of *The Brook Kerith* as "the best since Thackeray," Moore wondered "how people can be reading my writings when such as Landor's are within reach of everybody." Moore was still reading Landor "every evening" on 5 March 1917 (Ross, *Robert Ross*, 298).

194. John Lloyd Balderston, "The Dusk of the Gods: A Conversation with George Moore," *Atlantic Monthly*, August 1916; John Lloyd Balderston, "Freedom of the Pen: A Conversation with George Moore," *Fortnightly Review*, October 1917.

195. Evan Charteris, *Life and Letters of Sir Edmund Gosse* (Harper: New York; Heinemann: London, 1931), 425.

196. Gosse to Moore, 22 March 1918, ibid., 426.

197. The *Fortnightly Review* printed the "Imaginary Conversations" in four installments (October 1918–February 1919) (Moore to Dujardin, 17 January 1920, Beinecke).

198. George Moore, *Avowals* (1924), 52–54. To Mallarmé's story, Moore added extra French verses for the choir to sing to "le beau Coq" (GM to Dujardin, 17 January 1920, Beinecke).

199. "Winged Phrases," *Times Literary Supplement*, 30 October 1919.

200. Conrad Aiken, "The Moorish Arabesque," *Chicago News*, 22 October 1919; reprinted in Conrad Aiken, *A Reviewer's ABC: Collected Criticism from 1916 to the Present* (Meridian Books: New York, 1958), 303–6. My thanks to Harry Marten.

201. GM to Magee, 19 July 1918, HRHRC.

202. GM to Phyllis Williamson [21 Oct. 1918], ibid.; GM to Magee, 2 November [1918], ibid.

203. GM to Rothenstein, 15 May [1919], Houghton BMS ENG 1148 (1037).

204. O'Donovan to Hone, 9 August 1935, Eglinton, 53. Whittaker (1856–1935) was the director of the Rationalist Press Association and author of books on philosophy.

205. GM to Rodgers, 14 December [1918], Bancroft; GM to Dujardin, 17 January 1920, *Letters to Dujardin*, 104–5.

206. GM to Crawford, 23 July [1919], *George Moore on Parnassus*, 422.

207. Moore said he would wish her luck "... if you were not standing in the labour interest. Rocketting rates, etc. But of course mine is the selfish point of view" (GM to Crawford [3 November 1919], *George Moore on Parnassus*, 437). Crawford was elected and served twelve years.

208. Ibid., 425, 431, 438.

209. GM to Magee, 26 January [1919], HRHRC. Viola Rodgers had called off her visit with Moore at Ebury Street that was planned to occur about this time (GM to Rodgers, 14 December [ah 1918], Bancroft). Hilda Hawthorne had returned to New York from France by 15 January 1919 (*George Moore on Parnassus*, 409). There is no sign of a visit to London by Honor Woulfe at this date. The name of Moore's visitor on this occasion remains undetected.

210. Hone, *Life of Henry Tonks*, 96. Before joining Tonks at the Hutchinsons' house, GM sent the following telegram: "WHAT IS THE WATER CLOSET LIKE MOORE" (HRHRC).

211. Cunard, *GM: Memories of George Moore*, 125.

212. Arlen's "Confessions of a Naturalised Englishman" (1929) is quoted by Chisolm, *Nancy Cunard*, 70–71.

213. Cunard, *GM: Memories of George Moore*, 126.

214. GM to Phyllis Williamson [autumn 1919?], HRHRC.

215. "*Heloise and Abelard* – A ms/accounts in unid hand. 4 June 1921–5 November 1921," HRHRC.

216. GM to Magee, 7 September 1920, ibid.

217. GM to Magee, 9 October 1920, ibid.
218. Moore publicised the value of handset print by means of a controversy in the *Daily Mail* on 24 February, 4, 7, 8, and 10 March 1921; and in the 17 March 1921 *Times Literary Supplement*.
219. "The Happy Author. Mr. George Moore Interviews Himself," *Observer*, 25 January 1920: 13.
220. Moore dined in company with T. J. Wise at Gosse's on 6 August 1916 (Book of Gosse, Brotherton).
221. J. S. Stooke Vaughan to Laurie, 11 February 1920, Laurie to Moore, 12 February 1920, HRHRC.
222. GM to Cunard [April? 1918], Hart-Davis, 96.
223. GM to Cunard, Wednesday night [September 1919], ibid., 102.
224. Ibid., 104.
225. GM to Cunard, 22 December [p.m. 1920], ibid., 107–8.
226. GM to Cunard, 26 December [1920], ibid., 108.
227. W. B. Yeats, *Autobiography* (Collier: New York, 1965), 406.
228. Chapter 22, *Héloïse and Abélard*; the relevant pages are reprinted by Hart-Davis, 196–200.
229. Hart-Davis, 114. Moore misspells the name "Gauslin," a strange mistake, since the correct form "Gaucelm" of the name appears to be a partial anagram of GM and Lady CUnArd.
230. George Moore, "Proof Sheets with Autograph Corrections," *Memoirs of My Dead Life* (1921), 273. Dated by GM "July 1921", HRHRC.

Chapter 13 Hardy, James, Conrad, and Moore

1. GM to Elizabeth Aria, 7 March [1920], Berg 63B1394.
2. *George Moore on Parnassus*, 301–2, 314–15; Tom Dardis, *Firebrand: The Life of Horace Liveright* (Random House: New York, 1995), 132.
3. Dardis, *Horace Liveright*, 130.
4. George Moore, "Apologia pro scriptis meis," xxiv.

5. GM to Barrett Clark, 26 January 1921, *George Moore on Parnassus*, 495; GM to Richard Clay & Sons, Ltd, 27 January 1921, ibid., 496.
6. Speaking of Liveright and the "Carra Edition," Moore wrote Viola Rodgers on 2 June 1921, "I have no agreement with him fortunately . . . I have taken the necessary steps to protect myself in case ardour should take the place over yonder of judgement" (Bancroft).
7. GM to Phyllis Williamson, 20 January [1921], HRHRC.
8. GM to Laurie, 11 March 1920 and 15 March 1920, *George Moore on Parnassus*, 453–54, 456; GM to Symons, 9 April 1920, Karl Beckson, *Arthur Symons: A Life* (Clarendon Press: Oxford, 1987), n.p. A meeting between Moore and Symons on the subject of this biography may have led to a quarrel: "'I said to him,'" Moore told Vincent O'Sullivan in Paris, "'There is a right side of a question and a wrong side . . . When you have come to your senses, you can come to see me again. He went away in a great rage . . . The man who maintains to my face what he maintained must be either stupid or mad'" (Vincent O'Sullivan, *Opinions* [Unicorn Press: London, 1959], 49).
9. Max Beerbohm, "George Moore," *Listener*, 64 (2 November 1950).
10. Moore to Gosse, Wednesday [April 1920], Charles Burkhart, *The Letters of George Moore to Edmund Gosse, W. B. Yeats, R. I. Best, Miss Nancy Cunard, and Mrs. Mary Hutchinson* (University of Maryland diss., 1958), 175–76.
11. *George Moore on Parnassus*, 456.
12. GM to Laurie, 16 April 1920, ibid., 461.
13. GM to Laurie, 18 May 1920, ibid., 466.
14. Eglinton, 14.
15. GM to John Freeman, 9 July 1920, *George Moore on Parnassus*, 470.
16. Ibid., 58–61; Janet Irvin, "John Freeman: An Annotated Bibliography of Writings About Him," *English Literature in Transition* 19.1 (1976): 35–47.

17. GM to Nancy Cunard, 12 December 1916, HRHRC.

18. Nancy Cunard, *GM: Memories of George Moore* (Hart-Davis: London, 1956), 116, 123.

19. David Garnett, *Great Friends: Portraits of Seventeen Writers* (Athenaeum: New York, 1980), 169–70.

20. GM to Nancy Cunard, 21 January 1921, HRHRC.

21. GM to Lady Cunard, 27 March [1921], Hart-Davis, 121.

22. GM to Nancy Cunard, 13 August 1921, Cunard, *GM: Memories of George Moore*, 128.

23. GM to Viola Rodgers, Saturday [16? April 1921], Bancroft.

24. GM to Viola Rodgers, Friday [22? April 1921], ibid.

25. GM to Viola Rodgers, Saturday [30? April 1921] and 10 May [1921], ibid.

26. GM to Mrs A. Harter, 25 May 1921, Berg 63b1383; GM to Gosse, 20 January [1921], HRHRC.

27. GM to Viola Rodgers, 17 August [1921], Bancroft.

28. GM to Viola Rodgers, Saturday [2 May 1921], Val Changis, ibid.; GM to Magee [8 May 1921], 121 Ebury Street, HRHRC.

29. *Journal of Arnold Bennett* (Viking: New York, 1933), 731.

30. GM to Magee, Wednesday [8 June 1921], HRHRC.

31. Ford Madox Ford, "A Haughty and Proud Generation," *Yale Review*, 11 (July 1922): 703; quoted in Langenfeld, 151.

32. GM to Freeman, 28 July 1921, *George Moore on Parnassus*, 532; GM to Rodgers, 31 August [1921], Beinecke.

33. Malcolm Easton, *Aubrey and the Dying Lady: A Beardsley Riddle* (Secker and Warburg: London, 1972), 62–63, 231, 246.

34. George H. Doran, *Chronicles of Barabbas 1884–1935* (Harcourt, Brace: New York, 1935), 269–70.

35. GM to Gosse; quoted in Gilcher, 115.

36. GM to Gosse, 4 May [1922], Hôtel Foyot, Paris, Brotherton; George Moore, *In Single Strictness* (Boni and Liveright: New York, 1922), 197.

37. Arthur Clutton,-Brock [*sic*], "Mr. George Moore," *Times Literary Supplement*, 5 October 1922: 621; Stewart March Ellis, "Current Literature," *Fortnightly Review*, 118.112 (2 October 1922): 700–3.

38. George Moore, *In Single Strictness* (1923), 274–75.

39. Conrad Aiken, *A Reviewer's ABC: Collected Criticism from 1916 to the Present* (Meridian Books: New York, 1958), 307–8.

40. In 1915, John Morgan Richards heard a rumor that GM was going to publish Craigie's love letters to Moore, along with other letters by Craigie and to her. He warned Moore that the copyright for Craigie's letters belonged to her family. Moore denounced the rumor, and deplored the fact that in Richards's biography of his daughter, the "libel" had been repeated that GM had merely suggested the situation for their co-authored play, *Journeys End in Lovers' Meeting* (GM to Richards, 2 December 1915, Berg 62b9635). The motif of telltale letters as well as the idea of writing the last end of Pearl Craigie nevertheless stayed with Moore, even if disguised as fiction.

41. GM to Rodgers, Saturday [9 July 1921], Bancroft.

42. Cunard, *GM: Memories of George Moore*, 131.

43. GM to Mrs Harter, 2 September [1920], Berg 63b1382.

44. GM to Mrs Harter, 10 October 1920, ibid.

45. GM to Mrs Harter, 3 February 1921, ibid.

46. GM to Mrs Harter, 16 June 1921, ibid.

47. GM to Laurie, 14 October 1921, *George Moore on Parnassus*, 546–47.

48. GM to Laurie, 11 October 1921 and 1 November, ibid., 546, 549.

49. GM to Mrs Harter, 12 February [1922], Berg 63b1382.

50. Gilcher, 92.

51. The copy of the 1916 Werner Laurie

edition of *The Brook Kerith* evidently passed from GM to F. M. Atkinson to Victor Gollancz, and finally to the HRHRC. The change in Jesus's final recantation comes at pp. 437–38 of this edition.

52. GM to Cunard, 9 December [1921], Hart-Davis, 118.

53. Shaw replied that Harris was not unmasking his subjects, but applying "maquillage" to them. See Harris to G. B. Shaw, 14 September 1920, and G. B. Shaw to Harris, 15 September 1920, Stanley Weintraub, ed., *The Playwright and the Pirate* (Colin Smythe: Gerrards Cross, Bucks, 1982), 154, 159. See also Frank Harris, "George Moore and Jesus," *Contemporary Portraits* (Frank Harris: New York, 1919), 107–40.

54. Weintraub, ed., *The Playwright and the Pirate*, 20–22.

55. Harris called *The Brook Kerith* "a nightmare of ignorance and profanity"; according to Shaw it was "preposterously dull" (Weintraub, ed., *The Playwright and the Pirate*, 48–49, 61); Graves was irritated with the book's anachronisms – mules, sherbet, and the Talmud turning up in 33 BCE Palestine (*New Republic*, 15 October 1956: 25–26).

56. Shaw to Harris, 21 April 1931, *Bernard Shaw: Collected Letters 1926–50*, vol. 4, ed. Dan H. Lawrence (Viking: New York, 1987), 235–36.

57. Nor does Moore mention having seen *Moore versus Harris: An Intimate Correspondence* (Privately printed: Detroit, 1921). The introduction claims that the pamphlet proves that GM is "a self-centered, conceited egotist, vain, ignorant, and totally unappreciative of other men's genius," i.e. the genius of Frank Harris. Moore was not pleased when his letters were sold and published without his consent.

58. Weintraub, ed., *The Playwright and the Pirate*, 154. Moore wrote Harris, "You have, in yourself, a subject that will carry your name down the ages, if you write it with the necessary sincerity,

that of Jean-Jacques [Rousseau]" (Vincent Brome, *Frank Harris: The Life and Loves of a Scoundrel* [Thomas Yoseloff: New York and London, 1959], 189).

59. GM to Frank Harris, 15 August 1921, HRHRC.

60. GM to Viola Rodgers, 8 February [1922], Bancroft; GM to Cunard, 14 February [1922], Hart-Davis, 121; GM to Cunard, 14 February [1922], ibid., 121.

61. Cunard, *GM: Memories of George Moore*, 135.

62. GM to Nancy Cunard, July 1922, ibid., 137.

63. T. S. Eliot was outraged that the *Dial* offered him $150 for "The Waste Land" while it paid Moore £100 for a short story, "Peronnik the Fool" (pub. November 1921): "these people should learn to recognise Merit instead of senility" (Eliot to Pound, 12 March 1922, *Letters of T. S. Eliot*, vol. 1, ed. Valerie Eliot [Harcourt Brace Jovanovich: San Diego, New York, London, 1988], 506–8).

   Moore was asked by Horace Liveright to review *Ulysses* for the *New York Times*: "send me a cable Yes Joyce or No Joyce." The answer was evidently "No Joyce" (*George Moore on Parnassus*, 579).

64. GM to Gosse [25? February 1922], Hôtel Brighton, Brotherton. Evidently, the seventy-year-old author and eighty-one-year-old painter got on well together. On 24 March 1922, Moore proposed buying a house with Viola Rodgers in France "near my old friend Monet" (Bancroft).

65. GM to Leon Lion, 21 April 1922, Rochester.

66. GM to Leon Lion, 30 June 1922, ibid. [Apropos *Esther Waters*.]

67. GM to Viola Rodgers [p.m. 25 April 1922]; Mary Duclaux to Edmund Gosse, 5 May [1922?], Brotherton.

68. GM to Mona Kingdon, 26 April [1922], and GM to Clark, 29 April [1922], *George Moore on Parnassus*, 579, 582.

69. Notes from Clark's diary in letter from Clark to Hone, 1 February 1935, HRHRC.

70. GM to Dujardin, 11 April 1922, *Letters to Dujardin*, 111–12.

71. GM to Duchess of Sutherland, [n.d.], Hôtel Brighton, Berg.

72. GM to Duchess of Sutherland, 11 May [1922], Val Changis, ibid.

73. Notes from Clark's diary in letter from Clark to Hone, 1 February 1935, HRHRC.

74. Dujardin and Marie M. Chenou were married on 26 June 1924. See Kathleen McKilligan, *Edouard Dujardin: "Les Lauriers sont coupés' and the Interior Monologue* (University of Hull Publications: Hull, 1977), 14; Marie Dujardin, "Souvenir d'Edouard Dujardin," *Synthèses* (May 1959): 93.

75. Notes from Clark's diary in letter from Clark to Hone, 1 February 1935, HRHRC.

76. GM to Dujardin, 26 June 1922, *Letters to Dujardin*, 112–13. For an explanation of the letter, see GM to Magee, 17 January 1928, Eglinton, 78.

77. The Odéon story was first told in the *Bat*, 2.61 (25 May 1886): 180.

78. Barrett Clark, "George Moore and His Friends," 1922.

79. GM to Lady Cunard, Tuesday night [? November 1921], Hart-Davis, 116.

80. Beerbohm praised Moore for his courage in saying nothing in a drawing room when he had nothing to say – "I used to rate Moore's silences as his fin[est] triumph. They were so long, so unutterably blank." "George Moore," *Listener*, 2 November 1950: 465.

81. GM to Lady Cunard, 18 August [1922] and [19 or 20 August 1922], Hart-Davis, 123–24.

82. GM to Dearest Elizabeth [Countess Russell], Friday [July? 1923], Huntington.

83. Diary of Mary Annette (Beauchamp) Russell, Countess Russell, ibid. Immediately following three of the diary entries for these dates, she writes, "Yes," in what may be no more than an arcane indication that a meeting that was planned actually occurred:

> December 9. Dorothy Silk Concert, Steinway Hall, 3:15. Tea afterwards with George Moore. Yes.

84. GM to Countess Russell, Sunday night [3? June 1923], Huntington. "I have just been through two miserable days of nervous apprehensions and foreboding in which there were hours I thought I could not outlive, but some how I did . . . I became reconciled to the inevitable decay of my body and mind."

85. GM to Lion, 21 April 1922, Rochester.

86. GM to Lion, 30 June 1923, ibid.

87. Lion to Moore, 13 July 1923, ibid.

88. Leon Lion, *The Surprise of My Life: The Lesser Half of an Autobiography* (Hutchinson: London, n.d.), 138.

89. Ibid., 133.

90. Lion to Moore, 13 July and 17 July, 1923, Rochester.

91. *Letters of T. S. Eliot*, vol. 1, ed. Eliot, 367, 369–70.

92. GM to Lion, 18 July 1923, Rochester; Gosse to GM, 18 July 1923, Evan Charteris, *Life and Letters of Sir Edmund Gosse* (Heinemann: London, 1931), 474–75.

93. "A Theatrical Manager," "Why Novelists Are Bad Dramatists," *Daily Mail*, 24 July 1923: 6; Langenfeld, 163.

94. On 19 July 1923, William Archer wrote to Harley Granville Barker about *The Coming of Gabrielle* ("the most inept, childish twaddle imaginable"), "in his way Moore is an authentic man of genius. He & his kind seem to be afflicted with a sort of paralysis of the intelligence the moment they approach the theatre. Witness Conrad!" (BL, Add. Ms 45290). Archer probably refers to Conrad's dramatisation of *The Secret Agent*, withdrawn after nine days at the Ambassador Theatre in November 1922. A better witness still is Henry James, and the total débâcle of his *Guy Domville*. My thanks to Susan Jones.

95. GM to Countess Russell, 21 July [1923], Huntington.

96. GM to Countess Russell [early August 1923], Woodgreen, Braemore, Hants, ibid. Countess Russell expresses her opinions of the body in a diary comment on the novels of Ann Thackeray Ritchie: "From her writing one would suppose that she had never been aware that there was such a thing as a real naked body . . . Christ, the gentility of the genteel Victorians!" (20 September 1924).

97. GM to Viola Rodgers [p.m. 24 March 1922], Bancroft; GM to Countess Russell [1 August? 1923], Huntington.

98. For the complicated periodical history of the contents of *Conversations in Ebury Street*, see Gilcher, 118–19.

99. GM to Countess Russell [3? August 1923], Huntington.

100. GM to Countess Russell, 13 August [1923], ibid.

101. GM to Magee, 10 January [1925], HRHRC.

102. GM to Countess Russell, 29 September [1929], Huntington.

103. George Moore, *Conversations in Ebury Street* (1924), 288.

104. James Reilly to Maurice Moore, 25 September 1935, Moore Hall, Ballyglass, Co. Mayo, NLI Ms 2648; interview with Jimmy O'Reilly and others in Carnacun, 8 July 1996.

105. GM to Sybil Eden, 10 February [1920], *George Moore on Parnassus*, 446.

106. It was "professionally burnt," as Jimmy O'Reilly, James Reilly's descendant, said in an interview. O'Reilly now runs the boat-hire business on Lough Carra.

107. Interview with Art O'Sullivan, Carnacun, 8 July 1996. O'Sullivan, formerly the local schoolteacher, is the driving force behind the current restoration of Moore Hall.

108. Interview with Sean Murphy, Carnacun, 9 July 1996.

109. In 1910, Mary Reilly, GM's Ely Place servant, proposed that her brother, James Reilly, wished to come up from County Longford to work at Moore Hall as a gardener, and Reilly's employment began there in 1911 (GM to Maurice Moore, 29 September 1910, *George Moore on Parnassus*, 186; interview with Jimmy O'Reilly, 8 July 1996; *The Moores of Moore Hall*, 255).

110. Interview with Jimmy O'Reilly, Castlebar, 8 July 1996. There is local disagreement about whether Moore Hall was used by Free State soldiers, or Irregulars, or both. Later, when de Valera was elected to government in 1932, he made Maurice Moore a senator, and reportedly told him that he regretted having given the order to burn Moore Hall.

111. One of the descendants of the steward James Reilly believes Moore Hall was burned for a complex of reasons in addition to its having been used as a barracks; it was burned "for the Land, for what was in it, and for the politics of Senator Maurice Moore" (Interview with Jimmy O'Reilly, Carra Boat Hire, 7 July 1996).

112. "The Burning of Moore Hall," *Observer*, 11 February 1923: 15.

113. GM to Best, 17 October 1923, HRHRC.

114. Moore, *Conversations in Ebury Street* (1924), 289.

115. Ibid.

116. Cunard, *GM: Memories of George Moore*, 148–50.

117. Ibid., 151,

118. Nancy Cunard dates the incident in the spring or summer of 1925. It certainly preceded the completion of *Ulick and Soracha* (1926).

119. Charles Duff to Nancy Cunard, 30 August 1955, HRHRC. Having seen the passage only after the book was published, Hart-Davis wrote Nancy: "I absolutely loved the weasel episode, and if you had shown it to me before I should have *begged* you to include it . . . I wonder whether GM was thinking of Hamlet and the cloud 'that was backed like a weasel'?" Hart-Davis to N. Cunard, 7 December 1956, ibid.

120. Nancy Cunard to Rupert Hart-Davis,

23 October 1955, Lamothe Fenelon, Lot, France, ibid.

121. Nancy Cunard, "The Back like a Weasel," 28 July 1955, ibid.

122. The surgeries were curettage, appendectomy, and hysterectomy (Anne Chisolm, *Nancy Cunard* [Knopf: New York, 1979], 68).

123. George Moore, *Ulick and Soracha*; no. 887 of 1250. The volume inscribed to Nancy Cunard is at HRHRC.

124. GM to Marion Balderston [p.m. 14 January 1924], Huntington.

125. Marion Balderston (Rusincam), [George Moore], ibid.

126. *George Moore on Parnassus*, 733.

127. Marion Balderston (Rusincam), [George Moore], Huntington.

128. Henry James, "In the Cage," *Complete Stories, 1892–1898* (Library of America: New York, 1984), 844.

129. Hardy to Quiller Couch, 22 October 1916, Richard Little Purdy and Michael Millgate, eds, *Collected Letters of Thomas Hardy* (Clarendon Press: Oxford, 1985), vol. 5, 183.

130. GM to Phyllis Williamson [21 October 1918], 121 Ebury Street, HRHRC; GM to Mary Hunter, [December? 1916] and 15 January [1918?], ibid.

131. Moore, *Conversations in Ebury Street* (1924), 112–20.

132. Seymour Leslie, *The Jerome Connection* (John Murray: London, 1964), 94–95.

133. Michael Millgate, *Thomas Hardy: A Biography* (Oxford University Press: Oxford, 1982), 533.

134. Hardy to Middleton Murry, 28 March 1924, Purdy and Millgate, eds, *Collected Letters of Thomas Hardy*, vol. 6, 242–43.

135. Millgate, *Thomas Hardy*, 571.

136. George Moore, ed., *An Anthology of Pure Poetry* (Boni and Liveright: New York, 1924), 25.

137. John Eglinton, "Mr. George Moore as Shanachie," *Dial*, November 1926: 432.

138. GM to Magee, 11 February 1924, HRHRC; GM to David Garnett, 15 February 1924, ibid.

139. GM to Gogarty [p.m. 29 October 1923], Bucknell.

140. GM to Mr Johnstone, 25 January [1924], ibid. Another educated person who assisted Moore was Mary Somerville (1897–1963), Oxford BA 1925, writer and broadcaster. See GM to Mary Somerville, 31 August [1924], *George Moore on Parnassus*, 683.

141. GM to Magee, 6 April 1924 and [18? April 1924], HRHRC. GM paid Magee £30 for his help (GM to Magee, 12 May 1924, ibid.).

142. GM to Viola Rodgers, 2 April [1924], Bancroft; GM to Magee, 11 April 1924, HRHRC.

143. GM to Magee, 15 April 1924, HRHRC.

144. GM to Magee, 19 April 1924, ibid.

145. GM to Mary Hutchinson [p.m. 19 April 1924], ibid.

146. J. Spencer Northcote to G. H. Moore, 20 September 1866, NLI Mss 889–899; Becker, 1366.

147. Leah Rosenbloom to GM, 16 May 1924 and 30 May 1924, HRHRC.

148. GM to Leah Rosenbloom [p.m. 24 January 1924], Berg 63b1373.

149. GM to Leah Rosenbloom, 8 May [1924], ibid.

150. Leah Rosenbloom to GM, 6 June 1924, HRHRC.

151. Leah Rosenbloom to GM, 14 June 1924, ibid.

152. For instance, Moore sent £6 for an August visit to London (Leah Rosenbloom to GM, 18 July 1924, ibid.). After that visit, he wrote her a letter of recommendation to David Garnett (GM to Garnett, 8 September 1924, ibid.).

153. Leah Rosenbloom, 2 December 1924, ibid.

154. Ilka Chase, *Past Imperfect* (R. Hale: London, 1943), 37.

155. Mary Somerville to Hone, n.d., Washington.

156. K. A. Tolhearst to Joseph Hone, 2 November 1934, 15 Comapyne Gardens, Hampstead, HRHRC. No books were published under the name K. A. Tolhearst. Oliver St John

Gogarty tells of bringing a young American novelist to Ebury Street, where Moore gave her a rough time (Oliver St John Gogarty, *Sackville Street and Other Stories* [Sphere: London, 1988], 255–57).

157. "Lorine Pruette," "Leda and the Lion," *Story* (New York), 5 (July 1934): 3–13. "Pruette" is described in a note on the author as having studied at Clark University, graduated from the University of Chattanooga, and worked at Smith College, University of Virginia, and New York University. When Edwin Gilcher met her in the 1930s, she was teaching at NYU (my thanks to Edwin Gilcher). Nelson Crawford, a psychologist at Kansas State, sent the story to Joseph Hone.

158. Magee won prizes for verse composition in 1889 and 1890, for prose in 1892 and 1893 (*Dublin University Calendar* [Hodges, Figgis: Dublin; Longmans, Green: London, 1901]). For Magee's rivalry with Yeats, see John Eglinton, *Confidential, or, Take It or Leave It* (Fortune Press: London, 1951), 5–8.

159. Magee to James Starkey, 21 February 1924, TCD Mss 4630–4649.

160. Moore to Magee, 5 December 1912, HRHRC.

161. Moore to Magee [mid-November 1919], ibid.

162. John Eglinton, "Life and Letters," *Irish Statesman*, 8 November 1919.

163. GM to Magee, 4 April 1922, Eglinton, 60.

164. GM to Magee, 16 August 1923, ibid., 61–63.

165. Ibid., 61.

166. GM to Magee, 16 August 1923, ibid., 61–63.

167. GM to Magee, 28 November 1923, HRHRC.

168. GM to Magee, 14 November 1927, ibid.

169. GM to Magee, 14 December 1927, ibid.

170. Magee got £300 for the translation of GM's letters to Dujardin

(GM to Magee, 31 August 1927, ibid.).

171. GM to Magee, Wednesday [6? July 1927], [1? August 1927], ibid.

172. Ernest Boyd, *Ireland's Literary Renaissance* (Knopf: New York, 1916), 239.

173. George Moore, *Vale* (1937), 177.

174. Future visits planned, or recent visits mentioned, in GM to Magee, 2 April 1925, 1 April 1926, 17 June 1927, 13 September 1927, HRHRC.

175. John Eglinton, *Irish Literary Portraits* (Macmillan: London, 1935), 122.

176. Ibid., 127.

177. Ibid., 86.

178. GM to Cunard, 1 March 1928, Hart-Davis, 161–62; GM to Magee, 4 April 1929, Eglinton, 82; GM to Magee, 12 May 1929, HRHRC.

179. Edmund Curtis (1881–1943), author of *A History of Medieval Ireland* (1923), visited Moore, for instance on 26–27 March 1925 (GM to Magee, 26 March 1925, HRHRC). After completing *Ulick and Soracha*, Moore contemplated collaborating with Curtis on "the story of the Bruces in Ireland" (GM to Best, 29 August [1926], ibid.).

180. GM to Magee, 28 July 1926, ibid. Moore thought Clarke was a mixture of "George Meredith and John Synge," with the mental obscurity of the first and the deliberate Irishness of the second.

181. Austin Clarke, "Speaking of Books: A Visit with George Moore," *New York Times Book Review*, 29 November 1966: 2, 88–89.

182. For Moore's opinions on overpopulation, urbanisation, and the machine age, see Henry Albert Phillips, "George Moore on Art, Whirling Mechanism of Modern Life," *Sunday Express*, 28 March 1926: 8; and "Overgrown London, Mr. George Moore Sees Danger," *Observer*, 19 March 1927: 19.

183. Austin Clarke to [T. Fisher Unwin, Publishers], Monday [p.m. 5 April 1927], Reading University Library. My thanks to Dillon Johnston.

184. Yeats's antipathy to Clarke climaxed when he excluded Clarke's poems from the *Oxford Book of Modern Verse* (1936), while including many by Gogarty, F. R. Higgins, and other Irish poets.

185. Kenneth McConkey, *Sir John Lavery* (Canongate: Edinburgh, 1993), 169–74.

186. For the somewhat competitive friendship of Lady Cunard and Lady Lavery, see Sinéad McCoole's *Hazel: A Life of Lady Lavery* (Lilliput Press: Dublin, 1996), 51, 102, 110, 116, 180.

187. Hart-Davis, 131 (evidently placed too early in the sequence of letters), 134, 140.

188. GM to Mona Kingdon [p.m. 4 November 1925], Hôtel Continental, Paris, *George Moore on Parnassus*, 706.

189. GM to Lady Cunard [6? November 1925], Hart-Davis, 139.

190. "News in Brief," *Times*, 10 November 1925: 11.

191. GM to Lady Cunard, 9 December [1925], Hart-Davis, 140.

192. *The Journal of Arnold Bennett* (4 September 1926), 896.

193. James Stephens to George Moore, 1 April 1926, Mentor, Kentucky, Brotherton.

194. Sir Shane Leslie, "George Moore in Love," *Time and Tide*, 28 September 1957: 1198–99.

195. It is puzzling, however, that Gosse published a review of *Conversations in Ebury Street* that registered no outrage at the pages about Hardy; indeed, he makes the case that Moore at least makes his victims live, while other critics cannot do that even for those they praise. See Edmund Gosse, "The Carpet and the Clock," *Sunday Times*, 3 February 1924: 6. Other reasons may be that Gosse felt that GM did not have a proper reverence for this honor, that he was not worthy of it, or that he did not merit an honor so far beyond what Gosse himself had received.

196. GM to Lady Cunard, 7 January 1926, Hart-Davis, 143.

197. GM to Gosse, 31 January 1928, Brotherton.

198. GM to Lady Cunard, Thursday [April? 1928], Hart-Davis, 162.

199. Mrs May Cooper to Nancy Cunard, 1958; Johannesburg, HRHRC.

200. "Arts Theatre Club, Mr. George Moore's New Play," *Times*, 2 April 1928: 12.

201. GM to Gosse, 29 February 1928, 7 Portland Place, Brotherton.

202. GM to Magee, 13 September [1927], HRHRC.

203. Virginia Woolf to Vita Sackville-West, 16 March 1926, *Letters of Virginia Woolf*, vol. 3 (Harcourt Brace Jovanovich: New York and London, 1977), 249.

204. GM to Tonks, 18 March [1927], HRHRC; GM to Cunard, 20 March [1927], Hart-Davis, 153.

205. GM to Lady Cunard [p.m. 5 November 1927], Hart-Davis, 157.

206. GM to Gosse, 31 January 1928, Brotherton.

207. GM to Tonks, Saturday [18 February 1928], HRHRC.

208. "Condition of Invalids," *Times*, 20 February 1928: 12.

209. GM to Magee, 23 February 1928, HRHRC. It is possible the numbers are measures of creatinine or of urea. My thanks to Dr Frances Knott. In 1998 Dr Knott consulted a Dublin specialist on the significance of Moore's tests; the specialist, with a look of alarm, said, "Bring Mr. Moore to the surgery immediately! He's going to die!"

210. GM to Countess Russell, 26 February [1928], Huntington.

211. GM to Duchess of Marlborough, 10 December [1928], NLI Ms 24898.

212. Richard Ellmann, ed., *Letters of James Joyce*, vol. 3 (Viking: New York, 1966), 193–94.

213. Gogarty, *Sackville Street*, 74; "Lorine Purette," "Leda and the Lion."

214. GM to Lady Cunard, 1 March 1928, 7 Portland Place, Hart-Davis, 161–62.

215. May Cooper to Lady Cunard [sent to Nancy Cunard], 6 November 1956, HRHRC.

216. Chisolm, *Nancy Cunard*, 303. Hart-Davis urged Nancy to include this

story in her book on Moore, but Nancy refused: "I can't put in the moment about paternity; no. Really, I have thought about this, and – no! That would be *friser le* bad taste, I think; something for a number of years later, if such were the point. Do you see this?" (Nancy Cunard to Rupert Hart-Davis, 4 November 1955, Toulouse, France, HRHRC).

There is some uncertainty about the date of this episode. The "question" may be the one Nancy refuses to repeat on page 191 of *GM: Memories of George Moore*, and which she dates December 1930. In that case Nurse Cooper would have heard it from Moore on his second visit to the nursing home in 13 May 1930, or his third in late January 1931.

217. May Cooper to [Nancy Cunard], 29 December 1958, HRHRC.

218. May Cooper to Nancy Cunard, [n.d.], ibid.

219. "Mr. George Moore's Lamentations," *Daily Chronicle*, 3 April 1928; GM to Lady Cunard, 20 April 1928, Hart-Davis, 163–64.

220. "Condition of Invalids," *Times*, 23 April 1928: 14; GM to Viola Rodgers, 11 July 1928, Bancroft.

221. GM to Magee, 11 August 1928, HRHRC; GM to Lady Cunard, 1 September 1928, Hart-Davis, 167.

222. GM to Magee, Sunday [17 March 1929], HRHRC.

223. GM to Magee, 22 March 1929, ibid.

224. Once in Bournemouth, Moore sent for a copy from St John Hutchinson; see GM to St John Hutchinson, 15 April [1929], East Cliff Mansions, Bournemouth, HRHRC. For a fuller account, see Adrian Frazier, "'Rapprochement with a Very Old Man': James Joyce's London Meetings with George Moore," *James Joyce Annual* (1992).

225. John Eglinton, "Dublin Letter," *Dial*, May 1929: 419.

226. AE, *The Living Torch* (Macmillan: London, 1937), 9.

227. George Russell to James Stephens, 8 May 1928, Richard Finneran and Mary M. Fitzgerald, eds, *Some*

Unpublished Letters from AE to James Stephens (Cuala Press: Dalkey, 1979), 38.

228. Stuart Gilbert, ed., *Letters of James Joyce*, vol. 1 (Viking: New York, 1957), 286.

229. James Joyce, "Gas from a Burner," *Critical Writings* (Viking: New York, 1959), 243.

230. Joyce's Trieste Library is at HRHRC.

231. Ellmann, ed., *Letters of James Joyce*, vol. 3, 192 n.

232. A second meeting occurred on Saturday, 14 September, when Joyce dined alone with GM at 121 Ebury Street (GM to Magee, 14 September 1929, HRHRC); the third meeting was on 20 September 1931 (GM to Magee, 20 September [1931], ibid.).

233. Louis Gillet, *Claybook for James Joyce* (Abelard-Schuman: London and New York, 1958), 33.

234. The satirical edge to Moore's reading-desk anecdote is sharpened in his retelling of it to a *Sunday Times* interviewer ("George Moore's Last Book," *Sunday Times*, 15 September 1929).

235. Gillet, *Claybook*, 42–43.

236. GM to Magee, 4 October 1929, HRHRC.

237. GM to Joyce, 11 October 1929, Ellmann, ed., *Letters of James Joyce*, vol. 3.

238. James Joyce, *Ulysses* (Random House: New York, 1961), 192. In *Anglo-Irish Essays* (Talbot Press: Dublin; Unwin: London, 1917), Eglinton suggests that *Hail and Farewell* may be a candidate for Ireland's national epic (87–89).

239. "I am returning to London to write a Greek story," GM to Phyllis Williamson [p.m. 9 May 1927], HRHRC; "Today is my day of days, [Aphrodite] is going to the printer," GM to Duchess of Marlborough, 1 November 1929, NLI Ms 24898.

240. "Aphrodite in Aulis," *Times Literary Supplement*, 3 September 1931: 661.

241. Joyce, *Ulysses*, 176.

242. GM to Joyce, 10 May 1930, Ellmann, ed., *Letters of James Joyce*, vol. 3, 197. See Charles Morgan's *Epitaph on George Moore* (Macmillan: London

and New York, 1935) for an appreciation of GM's method by one who prefers it to that of Joyce and Faulkner.

243. Joyce to Beach, 10 May 1931, Gilbert, ed., *Letters of James Joyce*, vol. 1, 304.

244. GM to Mary Hutchinson [20 January 1930], HRHRC.

245. GM to Tonks, 4 September 1930, Hone, "George Moore and Some Correspondents," *Dublin Magazine*, 22.1 (January–March 1947): 18–19.

246. GM to Tonks, 9 November [1930], HRHRC.

247. GM to Tonks, 6 December 1932, ibid.

248. Tonks to Emily Sargent [February? 1933], Hone, *Life of Henry Tonks* (Heinemann: London, 1939), 246.

249. Moore was introduced to Charles Morgan by Elizabeth Aria, apparently in December 1927 (GM to Elizabeth Aria, 6 December 1927, Berg 63b1394–95). By December 1929, Moore had settled on Morgan as his biographer, and was trying to arrange an introduction with Lady Cunard (Hart-Davis, 178).

250. Charles Morgan, "George Moore: A Centenary Appreciation," *Listener*, 28 February 1952: 349.

251. Charles Morgan to C. D. Medley, 28 February 1933, Eiluned Lewis, ed., *Selected Letters of Charles Morgan* (Macmillan: London, 1967), 107.

252. Lady Cunard evidently lost or destroyed most of Moore's letters; she left the remainder to Sacheverell Sitwell, and these are the ones published by Rupert Hart-Davis.

253. Charles Morgan to Tonks, 19 November 1930, HRHRC.

254. Morgan to Tonks, 29 October 1930, ibid.

255. See, for instance, GM's letter to Lady Cunard of early 1926, in which he describes a conversation with Nancy in Hyde Park, during which they talked about her prose story, and GM showed her his dedication to Lady Cunard written for *Ulick and Soracha*, which she "appeared to like" (Hart-Davis, 142). He also forwarded to Lady Cunard some of Nancy's letters to him

(ibid., 154). Moore's efforts to heal the rift may be one factor in the *rapprochement* between GM and Lady Cunard in 1925.

256. Nancy Cunard to GM, 24 January 1931, HRHRC; Chisolm, *Nancy Cunard*, 162. Moore said that, oddly, he had never himself known any person of color – of any color (Cunard, *GM: Memories of George Moore*, 190).

257. Nancy Cunard, *Black Man and White Ladyship: An Anniversary* (privately printed, 1931), 1.

258. Thomas Beecham to Nancy Cunard [p.m. 23 December 1930], addressed to Hôtel Crystal, rue Saints Pères, Paris, telegram, HRHRC.

259. Cunard, *Black Man and White Ladyship*, 2.

260. Nancy Cunard to GM, 24 January 1931, HRHRC; Chisolm, *Nancy Cunard*, 162. The crisis was already in full bloom: Lady Cunard was making "loud threats at the luncheon table" (Harold Acton to Nancy Cunard, 20 February 1931, HRHRC).

261. Harold Acton to Nancy Cunard, 20 February 1931, HRHRC.

262. Chisolm, *Nancy Cunard*, 167.

263. Moore's last trip to France occurred in September 1930, when he visited Viola Rodgers at Le Coine-sur-Juine, Lardy (Seine-et-Oise). Consequently, he was there during the successful Arts Theatre Club production of *Passing of the Esssenes*, his final version of a play based on *The Brook Kerith*. J. T. Grein gave the play a glowing review in the *Illustrated London News* on 18 October 1930, though Moore himself – after attending a performance on his return from France – thought the production "odious" (GM to Viola Rodgers, 29 October 1930, Bancroft). Ian Fleming as Jesus was "the image and likeness of a monthly nurse" (GM to Magee, 30 October 1930, Eglinton, 87).

264. Beecham to Nancy Cunard, 11 June 1931, HRHRC. Prior to the fateful Christmas of 1930, Nancy had been happily corresponding with GM about a little story – just the text of a dream

– which he had told Nancy and she had asked him to write. He gave it to her to be handset on the Houris Press (Nancy had followed GM into love of limited editions of well-made books). In mid-December they had exchanged letters about possible titles for what was finally called *The Talking Pine*. In 1931, however, GM became reluctant to sign the title pages, because, as he argued, he could not "resign [him]self to making money out of such a trivial scrap of literature – about ten or twelve lines." Yet certainly the charm of the book was the combination of a very little text from the author and a very large effort from the printer and publisher. The point was to make a public declaration of mutual admiration. When GM refused to do his part, Nancy immediately suspected her mother had "gotten to" him. The suspicion is plausible.

265. Hone to Nancy Cunard [1956], HRHRC. When Hone was doing his research, he asked Lady Cunard for her memories of George Moore; she sent him the following freezing note: "I am sorry not to be able to see you now. My relations with George Moore were very personal as I knew none of his relations or friends & I really only knew him at my own house with *my* friends who were *not* his. So it makes it difficult to help anyone for I was quite outside his life" (NLI Ms 2648).

266. GM to Lady Cunard [p.m. 14 May 1931], Hart-Davis, 189–90.

267. Marie Belloc Lowndes to Joseph Hone, 23 August 1935, Washington.

268. *George Moore on Parnassus*, 800–4, 816–23.

269. GM to Virginia Crawford, 9 June [1931], NLI; *George Moore on Parnassus*, 821.

270. Hilda Neal to Joseph Hone, 30 January 1936, HRHRC.

271. GM to Magee, 2 January 1933, ibid.

272. Manuel Komroff, "Telling Tales – II." Source untraced; my thanks to Edwin Gilcher for a copy.

273. David Garnett, *Great Friends: Portraits of Seventeen Writers* (Athenaeum: New York, 1980), 171.

274. D. S. MacColl, *Life, Work, and Setting of Philip Wilson Steer* (Faber and Faber: London, [1945]).

275. Joyce to Magee, 6 February 1933, Gilbert, ed., *Letters of James Joyce*, vol. 1, 335.

276. *Life of George Moore*, 453. "My Own Funeral" (*Lippincott's Magazine*, November 1901) was revised as "Resurgam," the final chapter of *Memoirs of My Dead Life*.

277. Interview with Jimmy O'Reilly, Castlebar, 8 July 1933.

278. Gogarty's claim to have been the oarsman is disputed by the son of the Moore Hall coachman, who says his father rowed Gogarty and Nina Moore Kilkelly out to Castle Island.

279. Alan Denson, ed., *Letters from AE* (Abelard-Schuman: London, New York, Toronto, 1961), 202–3.

280. Una Jeffers, typescript, NLI Ms 2648.

281. Lionel Fleming, *Head or Hare* (Barrie and Rockcliff: London, 1965), 175. Fleming covered the event for the *Irish Times*. My thanks to Elizabeth Grubgeld for this reference.

282. When the wooden sign erected the day of his interment was replaced by a stone carving, the word "deserted" was softened to "forsook." In 1937, James Reilly, the former steward of Moore Hall, rowed Una Jeffers out to Castle Island, and he complained to her that it was a spiteful inscription: "[George Moore] never deserted his friends . . . Moore had a violent temper but he helped his family and friends constantly" (Una Jeffers, typescript, NLI Ms 2648).

283. Langenfeld, 230–46.

284. Ford Madox Ford, "Contrasts: Memories of John Galsworthy and George Moore," *Atlantic Monthly*, May 1933: 559–62.

285. Morgan, "Epitaph on George Moore," *American Mercury*, 36 (October 1935): 179.

286. Max Beerbohm, "George Moore," *Atlantic Monthly*, 186 (December 1950): 39.

Index

Page numbers in italic refer to illustrations.